W. H. Freeman and Company
New York

The Basic Practice of Statistics

Fourth Edition

David S. Moore

Purdue University

Publisher: **Craig Bleyer**
Executive Editor: **Ruth Baruth**
Associate Acquisitions Editor: **Laura Hanrahan**
Marketing Manager: **Victoria Anderson**
Editorial Assistant: **Laura Capuano**
Photo Editor: **Bianca Moscatelli**
Photo Researcher: **Brian Donnelly**
Cover and Text Designer: **Vicki Tomaselli**
Cover and Interior Illustrations: **Mark Chickinelli**
Senior Project Editor: **Mary Louise Byrd**
Illustration Coordinator: **Bill Page**
Illustrations: **Techbooks**
Production Manager: **Julia DeRosa**
Composition: **Techbooks**
Printing and Binding: **Quebecor World**

Library of Congress Control Number: 2006926755

ISBN-13: 978-0-7167-7478-5 (Hardcover)
ISBN-10: 0-7167-7478-X (Hardcover)

ISBN-13: 978-0-7167-74631 (Softcover)
ISBN-10: 0-7167-7463-1 (Softcover)

Third printing

W. H. Freeman and Company
41 Madison Avenue
New York, NY 10010
Houndmills, Basingstoke RG21 6XS, England
www.whfreeman.com

Analyzing Data for One Variable

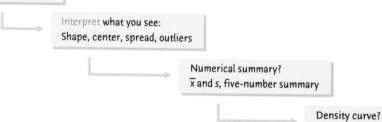

Plot your data:
Stemplot, histogram

→ Interpret what you see:
Shape, center, spread, outliers

→ Numerical summary?
$\bar{x}$ and s, five-number summary

→ Density curve?
Normal distribution?

Analyzing Data for Two Variables

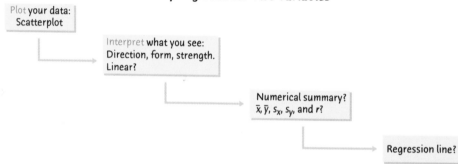

Plot your data:
Scatterplot

→ Interpret what you see:
Direction, form, strength.
Linear?

→ Numerical summary?
$\bar{x}$, $\bar{y}$, s_x, s_y, and r?

→ Regression line?

Overview of basic inference methods

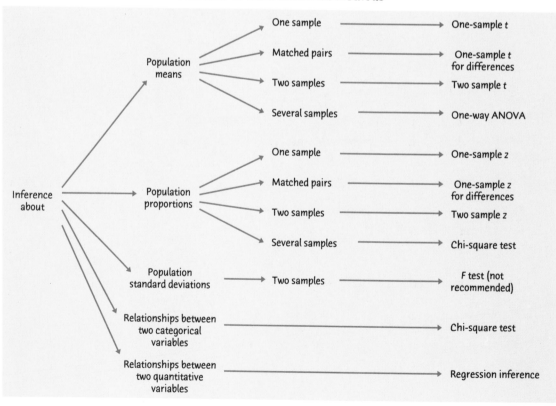

Inference about

- Population means
  - One sample → One-sample t
  - Matched pairs → One-sample t for differences
  - Two samples → Two sample t
  - Several samples → One-way ANOVA
- Population proportions
  - One sample → One-sample z
  - Matched pairs → One-sample z for differences
  - Two samples → Two sample z
  - Several samples → Chi-square test
- Population standard deviations
  - Two samples → F test (not recommended)
- Relationships between two categorical variables → Chi-square test
- Relationships between two quantitative variables → Regression inference

ORGANIZING A STATISTICAL PROBLEM: A FOUR-STEP PROCESS

STATE: What is the practical question, in the context of the real-world setting?

FORMULATE: What specific statistical operations does this problem call for?

SOLVE: Make the graphs and carry out the calculations needed for this problem.

CONCLUDE: Give your practical conclusion in the setting of the real-world problem.

CONFIDENCE INTERVALS: THE FOUR-STEP PROCESS

STATE: What is the practical question that requires estimating a parameter?

FORMULATE: Identify the parameter and choose a level of confidence.

SOLVE: Carry out the work in two phases:

(a) Check the conditions for the interval you plan to use.
(b) Calculate the confidence interval.

CONCLUDE: Return to the practical question to describe your results in this setting.

TESTS OF SIGNIFICANCE: THE FOUR-STEP PROCESS

STATE: What is the practical question that requires a statistical test?

FORMULATE: Identify the parameter and state null and alternative hypotheses.

SOLVE: Carry out the test in three phases:

(a) Check the conditions for the test you plan to use.
(b) Calculate the test statistic.
(c) Find the P-value.

CONCLUDE: Return to the practical question to describe your results in this setting.

Brief Contents

*Starred material is optional.

Contents

*Starred material is optional.

![icon] PART V
Optional Companion Chapters
(on the *BPS* CD and online)

To The Instructor: About This Book

The Basic Practice of Statistics (BPS) is an introduction to statistics for college and university students that emphasizes balanced content, working with real data, and statistical ideas. It is designed to be accessible to students with limited quantitative background—just "algebra" in the sense of being able to read and use simple equations. The book is usable with almost any level of technology for calculating and graphing—from a $15 "two-variable statistics" calculator through a graphing calculator or spreadsheet program through full statistical software. BPS was the pioneer in presenting a modern approach to statistics in a genuinely elementary text. In the following I describe for instructors the nature and features of the book and the changes in this fourth edition.

Guiding principles

BPS is based on three principles: balanced content, experience with data, and the importance of ideas.

Balanced content. Once upon a time, basic statistics courses taught probability and inference almost exclusively, often preceded by just a week of histograms, means, and medians. Such unbalanced content does not match the actual practice of statistics, where data analysis and design of data production join with probability-based inference to form a coherent science of data. There are also good pedagogical reasons for beginning with data analysis (Chapters 1 to 7), then moving to data production (Chapters 8 and 9), and then to probability (Chapters 10 to 13) and inference (Chapters 14 to 29). In studying data analysis, students learn useful skills immediately and get over some of their fear of statistics. Data analysis is a necessary preliminary to inference in practice, because inference requires clean data. Designed data production is the surest foundation for inference, and the deliberate use of chance in random sampling and randomized comparative experiments motivates the study of probability in a course that emphasizes data-oriented statistics. BPS gives a full presentation of basic probability and inference (20 of the 29 chapters) but places it in the context of statistics as a whole.

Experience with data. The study of statistics is supposed to help students work with data in their varied academic disciplines and in their unpredictable later employment. Students learn to work with data by working with data. BPS is full of data from many fields of study and from everyday life. Data are more than mere numbers—they are numbers with a context that should play a role in making sense of the numbers and in stating conclusions. Examples and exercises in BPS, though intended for beginners, use real data and give enough background to allow students to consider the meaning of their calculations. Even the first examples carry a message: a look at Arbitron data on radio station formats (page 7) and on use of portable music players in several age groups (page 8) shows that the Arbitron data don't help plan advertising for a music-downloading Web site. Exercises often ask for conclusions that are more than a number (or "reject H_0"). Some exercises require judgment in addition to right-or-wrong calculations and conclusions. Statistics, more than mathematics, depends on judgment for effective use. *BPS* begins to develop students' judgment about statistical studies.

The importance of ideas. A first course in statistics introduces many skills, from making a stemplot and calculating a correlation to choosing and carrying out a significance test. In practice (even if not always in the course), calculations and graphs are automated. Moreover, anyone who makes serious use of statistics will need some specific procedures not taught in her college stat course. *BPS* therefore tries to make clear the larger patterns and big ideas of statistics, not in the abstract, but in the context of learning specific skills and working with specific data. Many of the big ideas are summarized in graphical outlines. Three of the most useful appear inside the front cover. Formulas without guiding principles do students little good once the final exam is past, so it is worth the time to slow down a bit and explain the ideas.

These three principles are widely accepted by statisticians concerned about teaching. In fact, statisticians have reached a broad consensus that first courses should reflect how statistics is actually used. As Richard Scheaffer says in discussing a survey paper of mine, "With regard to the content of an introductory statistics course, statisticians are in closer agreement today than at any previous time in my career."[1]* Figure 1 is an outline of the consensus as summarized by the Joint Curriculum Committee of the American Statistical Association and the Mathematical Association of America.[2] I was a member of the ASA/MAA committee, and I agree with their conclusions. More recently, the College Report of the Guidelines for Assessment and Instruction in Statistics Education (GAISE) Project has emphasized exactly the same themes.[3] Fostering active learning is the business of the teacher, though an emphasis on working with data helps. *BPS* is guided by the content emphases of the modern consensus. In the language of the GAISE recommendations, these are: develop statistical thinking, use real data, stress conceptual understanding.

Accessibility

The intent of *BPS* is to be modern *and* accessible. The exposition is straightforward and concentrates on major ideas and skills. One principle of writing for beginners is not to try to tell them everything. Another principle is to offer frequent stopping points. *BPS* presents its content in relatively short chapters, each ending with a summary and two levels of exercises. Within chapters, a few "Apply Your Knowledge" exercises follow each new idea or skill for a quick check of basic

APPLY YOUR KNOWLEDGE ————

---

* All notes are collected in the Notes and Data Sources section at the end of the book.

1. **Emphasize the elements of statistical thinking:**

   (a) the need for data;
   (b) the importance of data production;
   (c) the omnipresence of variability;
   (d) the measuring and modeling of variability.

2. **Incorporate more data and concepts, fewer recipes and derivations. Wherever possible, automate computations and graphics.** An introductory course should:

   (a) rely heavily on *real* (not merely realistic) data;
   (b) emphasize *statistical* concepts, e.g., causation vs. association, experimental vs. observational, and longitudinal vs. cross-sectional studies;
   (c) rely on computers rather than computational recipes;
   (d) treat formal derivations as secondary in importance.

3. **Foster active learning,** through the following alternatives to lecturing:

   (a) group problem solving and discussion;
   (b) laboratory exercises;
   (c) demonstrations based on class-generated data;
   (d) written and oral presentations;
   (e) projects, either group or individual.

FIGURE 1 Recommendations of the ASA/MAA Joint Curriculum Committee.

mastery—and also to mark off digestible bites of material. Each of the first three parts of the book ends with a review chapter that includes a point-by-point outline of skills learned and many review exercises. (Instructors can choose to cover any or none of the chapters in Parts IV and V, so each of these chapters includes a skills outline.) The review chapters present many additional exercises without the "I just studied that" context, thus asking for another level of learning. I think it is helpful to assign some review exercises. Look at the first five exercises of Chapter 22 (the Part III review) to see the advantage of the part reviews. Many instructors will find that the review chapters appear at the right points for pre-examination review.

Technology

Automating calculations increases students' ability to complete problems, reduces their frustration, and helps them concentrate on ideas and problem recognition rather than mechanics. *All students should have at least a "two-variable statistics" calculator* with functions for correlation and the least-squares regression line as well as for the mean and standard deviation. Because students have calculators, the text doesn't discuss out-of-date "computing formulas" for the sample standard deviation or the least-squares regression line.

Many instructors will take advantage of more elaborate technology, as ASA/MAA and GAISE recommend. And many students who don't use technology in their college statistics course will find themselves using (for example)

Excel on the job. *BPS* does not assume or require use of software except in Chapters 24 and 25, where the work is otherwise too tedious. It does accommodate software use and tries to convince students that they are gaining knowledge that will enable them to read and use output from almost any source. There are regular "Using Technology" sections throughout the text. Each of these displays and comments on output from the same four technologies, representing graphing calculators (the Texas Instruments TI-83 or TI-84), spreadsheets (Microsoft Excel), and statistical software (CrunchIt! and Minitab). The output always concerns one of the main teaching examples, so that students can compare text and output.

Using technology

A quite different use of technology appears in the interactive applets created to my specifications and available online and on the text CD. These are designed primarily to help in learning statistics rather than in doing statistics. An icon calls attention to comments and exercises based on the applets. I suggest using selected applets for classroom demonstrations even if you do not ask students to work with them. The *Correlation and Regression, Confidence Interval,* and new *P-value* applets, for example, convey core ideas more clearly than any amount of chalk and talk.

What's new?

BPS has been very successful. There are no major changes in the statistical content of this new edition, but longtime users will notice the following:

- **Many new examples and exercises.**
- **Careful rewriting** with an eye to yet greater clarity. Some sections, for example, Normal calculations in Chapter 3 and power in Chapter 16, have been completely rewritten.
- **A new commentary on Data Ethics** following Chapter 9. Students are increasingly aware that science often poses ethical issues. Instruction in science should therefore not ignore ethics. Statistical studies raise questions about privacy and protection of human subjects, for example. The commentary describes such issues, outlines accepted ethical standards, and presents striking examples for discussion.

In preparing this edition, I have concentrated on pedagogical enhancements designed to make it easier for students to learn.

- **A handy "Caution" icon** in the margin calls attention to common confusions or pitfalls in basic statistics.

- **Many small marginal photos** are chosen to enhance examples and exercises. Students see, for example, a water-monitoring station in the Everglades (page 22) or a *Heliconia* flower (page 54) when they work with data from these settings.

Check Your Skills ———

- A set of "Check Your Skills" multiple-choice items opens each set of chapter exercises. These are deliberately straightforward, and answers to all appear in the back of the book. Have your students use them to assess their grasp of basic ideas and skills, or employ them in a "clicker" classroom response system for class review.

4 STEP

- A new four-step process (State, Formulate, Solve, Conclude) guides student work on realistic statistical problems. See the inside front cover for an overview. I outline and illustrate the process early in the text (see page 53), but its full usefulness becomes clear only as we accumulate the tools needed for realistic problems. In later chapters this process organizes most examples and many exercises. The process emphasizes a major theme in *BPS*: statistical problems originate in a real-world setting ("State") and require conclusions in the language of that setting ("Conclude"). Translating the problem into the formal language of statistics ("Formulate") is a key to success. The graphs and computations needed ("Solve") are essential but not the whole story. A marginal icon helps students see the four-step process as a thread through the text. I have been careful not to let this outline stand in the way of clear exposition. Most examples and exercises, especially in earlier chapters, intend to teach specific ideas and skills for which the full process is not appropriate. It is absent from some entire chapters (for example, those on probability) where it is not relevant. Nonetheless, the cumulative effect of this overall strategy for problem solving should be substantial.

CrunchIt!

- CrunchIt! statistical software is available online with new copies of *BPS*. Developed by Webster West of Texas A&M University, CrunchIt! offers capabilities well beyond those needed for a first course. It implements modern procedures presented in *BPS*, including the "plus four" confidence intervals for proportions. More important, I find it the easiest true statistical software for student use. Check out, for example, CrunchIt!'s flexible and straightforward process for entering data, often a real barrier to software use. I encourage teachers who have avoided software in the past for reasons of availability, cost, or complexity to consider CrunchIt!.

Why did you do that?

There is no single best way to organize our presentation of statistics to beginners. That said, my choices reflect thinking about both content and pedagogy. Here are comments on several "frequently asked questions" about the order and selection of material in *BPS*.

Why does the distinction between population and sample not appear in Part I? This is a sign that there is more to statistics than inference. In fact, statistical inference is appropriate only in rather special circumstances. The chapters in Part I present tools and tactics for describing data—any data. These tools and tactics do not depend on the idea of inference from sample to population. Many data sets in these chapters (for example, the several sets of data about the 50 states) do not lend themselves to inference because they represent an entire population. John Tukey of Bell Labs and Princeton, the philosopher of modern data analysis, insisted that the population-sample distinction be avoided when it is not relevant. He used the word "batch" for data sets in general. I see no need for a special word, but I think Tukey is right.

Why not begin with data production? It is certainly reasonable to do so—the natural flow of a planned study is from design to data analysis to inference. But in their future employment most students will use statistics mainly in settings other than planned research studies. I place the design of data production (Chapters 8 and 9) after data analysis to emphasize that data-analytic techniques apply to any data. One of the primary purposes of statistical designs for producing data is to make inference possible, so the discussion in Chapters 8 and 9 opens Part II and motivates the study of probability.

Why do Normal distributions appear in Part I? Density curves such as the Normal curves are just another tool to describe the distribution of a quantitative variable, along with stemplots, histograms, and boxplots. Professional statistical software offers to make density curves from data just as it offers histograms. I prefer not to suggest that this material is essentially tied to probability, as the traditional order does. And I find it very helpful to break up the indigestible lump of probability that troubles students so much. Meeting Normal distributions early does this and strengthens the "probability distributions are like data distributions" way of approaching probability.

Why not delay correlation and regression until late in the course, as is traditional? *BPS* begins by offering experience working with data and gives a conceptual structure for this nonmathematical but essential part of statistics. Students profit from more experience with data and from seeing the conceptual structure worked out in relations among variables as well as in describing single-variable data. Correlation and least-squares regression are very important descriptive tools and are often used in settings where there is no population-sample distinction, such as studies of all a firm's employees. Perhaps most important, the *BPS* approach asks students to think about what kind of relationship lies behind the data (confounding, lurking variables, association doesn't imply causation, and so on), without overwhelming them with the demands of formal inference methods. Inference in the correlation and regression setting is a bit complex, demands software, and often comes right at the end of the course. I find that delaying all mention of correlation and regression to that point means that students often don't master the basic uses and properties of these methods. I consider Chapters 4 and 5 (correlation and regression) essential and Chapter 24 (regression inference) optional.

What about probability? Much of the usual formal probability appears in the *optional* Chapters 12 and 13. Chapters 10 and 11 present in a less formal way the ideas of probability and sampling distributions that are needed to understand inference. These two chapters follow a straight line from the idea of probability as long-term regularity, through concrete ways of assigning probabilities, to the central idea of the sampling distribution of a statistic. The law of large numbers and the central limit theorem appear in the context of discussing the sampling distribution of a sample mean. What is left to Chapters 12 and 13 is mostly "general probability rules" (including conditional probability) and the binomial distributions.

I suggest that you omit Chapters 12 and 13 unless you are constrained by external forces. Experienced teachers recognize that students find probability difficult. Research on learning confirms our experience. Even students who can do formally posed probability problems often have a very fragile conceptual grasp of probability ideas. Attempting to present a substantial introduction to probability in a data-oriented statistics course for students who are not mathematically trained is in my opinion unwise. Formal probability does not help these students master the ideas of inference (at least not as much as we teachers often imagine), and it depletes reserves of mental energy that might better be applied to essentially statistical ideas.

Why use the z procedures for a population mean to introduce the reasoning of inference? This is a pedagogical issue, not a question of statistics in practice. Sometime in the golden future we will start with resampling methods. I think that permutation tests make the reasoning of tests clearer than any traditional approach. For now the main choices are z for a mean and z for a proportion.

I find z for means quite a bit more accessible to students. Positively, we can say up front that we are going to explore the reasoning of inference in an overly simple setting. Remember, exactly Normal population and true simple random sample are as unrealistic as known σ. All the issues of practice—robustness against lack of Normality and application when the data aren't an SRS as well as the need to estimate σ—are put off until, with the reasoning in hand, we discuss the practically useful t procedures. This separation of initial reasoning from messier practice works well.

Negatively, starting with inference for p introduces many side issues: no exactly Normal sampling distribution, but a Normal approximation to a discrete distribution; use of $\hat{p}$ in both the numerator and the denominator of the test statistic to estimate both the parameter p and $\hat{p}$'s own standard deviation; loss of the direct link between test and confidence interval. Once upon a time we had at least the compensation of developing practically useful procedures. Now the often gross inaccuracy of the traditional z confidence interval for p is better understood. See the following explanation.

Why does the presentation of inference for proportions go beyond the traditional methods? Recent computational and theoretical work has demonstrated convincingly that the standard confidence intervals for proportions can be trusted only for very large sample sizes. It is hard to abandon old friends, but I think that a look at the graphs in Section 2 of the paper by Brown, Cai, and DasGupta in the May 2001 issue of *Statistical Science* is both distressing and persuasive.[4] The standard intervals often have a true confidence level much less than what was requested, and requiring larger samples encounters a maze of "lucky" and "unlucky" sample sizes until very large samples are reached. Fortunately, there is a simple cure: just add two successes and two failures to your data. I present these "plus four intervals" in Chapters 20 and 21, along with guidelines for use.

Why didn't you cover Topic X? Introductory texts ought not to be encyclopedic. Including each reader's favorite special topic results in a text that is formidable in size and intimidating to students. I chose topics on two grounds: they are the most commonly used in practice, and they are suitable vehicles for learning broader statistical ideas. Students who have completed the core of *BPS*, Chapters 1 to 11 and 14 to 22, will have little difficulty moving on to more elaborate methods. There are of course seven additional chapters in *BPS*, three in this volume and four available on CD and/or online, to guide the next stages of learning.

I am grateful to the many colleagues from two-year and four-year colleges and universities who commented on successive drafts of the manuscript. Special thanks are due to Patti Collings (Brigham Young University), Brad Hartlaub (Kenyon College), and Dr. Jackie Miller (The Ohio State University), who read the manuscript line by line and offered detailed advice. Others who offered comments are:

Holly Ashton,
   Pikes Peak Community College
Sanjib Basu,
   Northern Illinois University
Diane L. Benner,
   Harrisburg Area Community College
Jennifer Bergamo,
   Cicero-North Syracuse High School
David Bernklau,
   Long Island University,
   Brooklyn Campus
Grace C. Cascio-Houston, Ph.D.,
   Louisiana State University at Eunice
Dr. Smiley Cheng,
   University of Manitoba
James C. Curl,
   Modesto Junior College
Nasser Dastrange,
   Buena Vista University
Mary Ellen Davis,
   Georgia Perimeter College
Dipak Dey,
   University of Connecticut
Jim Dobbin,
   Purdue University

Mark D. Ecker,
   University of Northern Iowa
Chris Edwards,
   University of Wisconsin, Oshkosh
Teklay Fessahaye,
   University of Florida
Amy Fisher,
   Miami University, Middletown
Michael R. Frey,
   Bucknell University
Mark A. Gebert, Ph.D.,
   Eastern Kentucky University
Jonathan M. Graham,
   University of Montana
Betsy S. Greenberg,
   University of Texas, Austin
Ryan Hafen,
   University of Utah
Donnie Hallstone,
   Green River Community
   College
James Higgins,
   Kansas State University
Lajos Horvath,
   University of Utah

Patricia B. Humphrey,
  University of Alaska
Lloyd Jaisingh,
  Morehead State University
A. Bathi Kasturiarachi,
  Kent State University, Stark Campus
Mohammed Kazemi,
  University of North Carolina, Charlotte
Justin Kubatko,
  The Ohio State University
Linda Kurz,
  State University of New York, Delhi
Michael Lichter,
  University of Buffalo
Robin H. Lock,
  St. Lawrence University
Scott MacDonald,
  Tacoma Community College
Brian D. Macpherson,
  University of Manitoba
Steve Marsden,
  Glendale Community College
Kim McHale,
  Heartland Community College
Kate McLaughlin,
  University of Connecticut
Nancy Role Mendell,
  State University of New York, Stonybrook
Henry Mesa,
  Portland Community College
Dr. Panagis Moschopoulos,
  The University of Texas, El Paso

Kathy Mowers,
  Owensboro Community and Technical College
Perpetua Lynne Nielsen,
  Brigham Young University
Helen Noble,
  San Diego State University
Erik Packard,
  Mesa State College
Christopher Parrett,
  Winona State University
Eric Rayburn,
  Danville Area Community College
Dr. Therese Shelton,
  Southwestern University
Thomas H. Short,
  Indiana University of Pennsylvania
Dr. Eugenia A. Skirta,
  East Stroudsburg University
Jeffrey Stuart,
  Pacific Lutheran University
Chris Swanson,
  Ashland University
Mike Turegun,
  Oklahoma City Community College
Ramin Vakilian,
  California State University, Northridge
Kate Vance,
  Hope College
Dr. Rocky Von Eye,
  Dakota Wesleyan University
Joseph J. Walker,
  Georgia State University

I am particularly grateful to Craig Bleyer, Laura Hanrahan, Ruth Baruth, Mary Louise Byrd, Vicki Tomaselli, Pam Bruton, and the other editorial and design professionals who have contributed greatly to the attractiveness of this book.

Finally, I am indebted to the many statistics teachers with whom I have discussed the teaching of our subject over many years; to people from diverse fields with whom I have worked to understand data; and especially to students whose compliments and complaints have changed and improved my teaching. Working with teachers, colleagues in other disciplines, and students constantly reminds me of the importance of hands-on experience with data and of statistical thinking in an era when computer routines quickly handle statistical details.

David S. Moore

Media and Supplements

For students

A full range of media and supplements is available to help students get the most out of *BPS*. Please contact your W. H. Freeman representative for ISBNs and value packages.

NEW!

STATS P◯RTAL

One click. One place. For all the statistical tools you need.

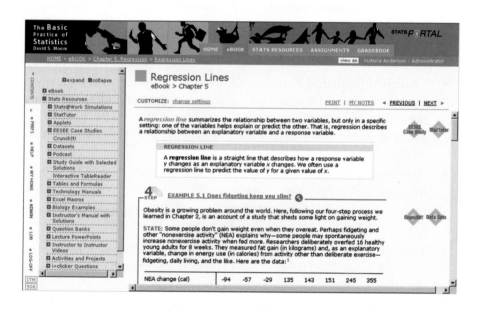

www.whfreeman.com/statsportal (Access code required. Available packaged with *The Basic Practice of Statistics 4th Edition* or for purchase online.)

StatsPortal is the digital gateway to *BPS 4e*, designed to enrich your course and enhance your students' study skills through a collection of Web-based tools. StatsPortal integrates a rich suite of diagnostic, assessment, tutorial, and enrichment features, enabling students to master statistics at their own pace. Organized around three main teaching and learning components:

*   **Interactive eBook** offers a complete online version of the text, fully integrated with all of the media resources available with *BPS 4e*.

- **StatsResource Center** organizes all of the resources for *BPS 4e* into one location for the student's ease of use. Includes:
  - **Stats@Work Simulations** put the student in the role of the statistical consultant, helping them better understand statistics interactively within the context of real-life scenarios. Students will be asked to interpret and analyze data presented to them in report form, as well as to interpret current event news stories. All tutorials are graded and offer helpful hints and feedback.
  - **StatTutor Tutorials** offer 84 audio-embedded tutorials tied directly to the textbook, containing videos, applets, and animations.
  - **Statistical Applets** these sixteen interactive applets help students master statistics interactively.
  - **EESEE Case Studies** developed by The Ohio State University Statistics Department provide students with a wide variety of timely, real examples with real data. Each case study is built around several thought-provoking questions that make students think carefully about the statistical issues raised by the stories.
  - **Podcast Chapter Summary** provides students with an audio version of chapter summaries so they can download and review on their mp3 player!
  - **CrunchIt! Statistical Software** allows users to analyze data from any Internet location. Designed with the novice user in mind, the software is not only easily accessible but also easy to use. Offers all the basic statistical routines covered in the introductory statistics courses and more!
  - **Datasets** are offered in ASCII, Excel, JMP, Minitab, TI, SPSS, S-Plus, Minitab, ASCII, and Excel format.
  - **Online Tutoring with SmarThinking** is available for homework help from specially trained, professional educators.
  - **Student Study Guide with Selected Solutions** includes explanations of crucial concepts and detailed solutions to key text problems with step-through models of important statistical techniques.
  - **Statistical Software Manuals** for TI-83, Minitab, Excel, and SPSS provide chapter-to-chapter applications and exercises using specific statistical software packages with *BPS 4e*.
  - **Interactive Table Reader** allows students to use statistical tables interactively to seek the information they need.
  - **Tables and Formulas** provide each table and formulas from the chapter.
  - **Excel Macros.**

StatsResources (instructor-only)

- **Instructor's Manual with Full Solutions** includes worked-out solutions to all exercises, teaching suggestions, and chapter comments.

- **Test Bank** contains complete solutions for textbook exercises.
- **Lecture PowerPoint Slides** gives instructors detailed slides to use in lectures.
- **Activities and Projects** offers ideas for projects for Web-based exploration asking students to write critically about statistics.
- **i>clicker Questions** these conceptually-based questions help instructors to query students using i>clicker's personal response units in class lectures.
- **Instructor-to-Instructor Videos** provide instructors with guidance on how to use these interactive examples in the classroom.
- **Biology Examples** identify areas of *BPS 4e* that relate to the field of biology.
- **Assignment Center** organizes assignments and guides instructors through an easy-to-create assignment process providing access to questions from the Test Bank, Check Your Skills, Apply Your Knowledge, Web Quizzes, and Exercises from *BPS 4e*. Enables instructors to create their own assignments from a variety of question-types for self-graded assignments. This powerful assignment manager allows instructors to select their preferred policies in regard to scheduling, maximum attempts, time limitations, feedback, and more!

New! Online Study Center: www.whfreeman.com/bps4e/osc (Access code required. Available for purchase online.) In addition to all the offerings available on the Companion Web site, the OSC offers:

- **StatTutor Tutorials**
- **CrunchIt! Statistical Software**
- **Stats@Work Simulations**
- **Study Guide**
- **Statistical Software Manuals**

The Companion Web Site: www.whfreeman.com/bps. Seamlessly integrates topics from the text. On this open-access Web site, students can find:

- **Interactive statistical applets** that allow students to manipulate data and see the corresponding results graphically.
- **Datasets** in ASCII, Excel, JMP, Minitab, TI, SPSS, and S-Plus formats.
- **Interactive exercises and self-quizzes** to help students prepare for tests.
- **Key tables and formulas** summary sheet.
- **All tables** from the text in .pdf format for quick, easy reference.

- **Additional exercises** for every chapter written by David Moore, giving students more opportunities to make sure they understand key concepts. Solutions to odd-numbered additional exercises are also included.
- **Optional Companion Chapters 26, 27, 28, and 29,** covering nonparametric tests, statistical process control, multiple regression, and two-way analysis of variance, respectively.
- **CrunchIt!** statistical software is available via an access-code-protected Web site. Access codes are available in every new text or can be purchased online for $5.
- **EESEE** case studies are available via an access-code-protected Web site. Access codes are available in every new text or can be purchased online.

Interactive Student CD-ROM: Included with every new copy of *BPS*, the CD contains access to most of the content available on the Web site. CrunchIt! statistical software and EESEE case studies are available via an access-code-protected Web site. (Access code is included with every new text.)

Special Software Packages: Student versions of JMP, Minitab, S-PLUS, and SPSS are available on a CD-ROM packaged with the textbook. This software is not sold separately and must be packaged with a text or a manual. Contact your W. H. Freeman representative for information or visit **www.whfreeman.com**.

NEW! SMARTHINKING Online Tutoring: (Access code required) W. H. Freeman and Company is partnering with SMARTHINKING to provide students with free online tutoring and homework help from specially trained, professional educators. Twelve-month subscriptions are available to be packaged with BPS.

The following supplements are available in print:

- **Student Study Guide** with Selected Solutions.
- **Activities and Projects Book.**

For instructors

The **Instructor's Web site** requires user registration as an instructor and features all of the student Web material plus:

- Instructor version of **EESEE** (Electronic Encyclopedia of Statistical Examples and Exercises), with solutions to the exercises in the student version.
- The **Instructor's Guide**, including full solutions to all exercises in .pdf format.
- **Text art images** in jpg format.

- **PowerPoint slides** containing textbook art embedded into each slide.
- **Lecture PowerPoint slides** offering a detailed lecture presentation of statistical concepts covered in each chapter of *BPS*.
- **Class Teaching Examples**, one or more new examples for each chapter of *BPS* with suggestions for classroom use by David Moore. Tables and graphs are in a form suitable for making transparencies.
- **Full solutions** to the more than 400 extra exercises in the **Additional Exercises** supplement on the student Web site.

Enhanced Instructor's Resource CD-ROM: Designed to help instructors create lecture presentations, Web sites, and other resources, this CD allows instructors to **search** and **export** all the resources contained below by key term or chapter:

- All text images
- Statistical applets, datasets, and more
- Instructor's Manual with full solutions
- PowerPoint files and lecture slides
- Test bank files

Annotated Instructor's Edition

Printed Instructor's Guide with Full Solutions

Test Bank: Printed or computerized (Windows and Mac on one CD-ROM).

Course Management Systems: W. H. Freeman and Company provides courses for Blackboard, WebCT (Campus Edition and Vista), and Angel course management systems. These are completely integrated solutions that you can easily customize and adapt to meet your teaching goals and course objectives. Upon request, we also provide courses for users of Desire2Learn and Moodle. Visit **www.bfwpub.com/lms** for more information.

NEW! i-clicker Radio Frequency Classroom Response System: Offered by W. H. Freeman and Company, in partnership with i-clicker, and created by educators for educators, i-clicker's system is the hassle-free way to make class time more interactive. Visit **www.iclicker.com** for more information.

i-clicker

Applications

The Basic Practice of Statistics presents a wide variety of applications from diverse disciplines. The list below indicates the number of examples and exercises which relate to different fields:

Examples

Agriculture: 8
Biological and environmental sciences: 25
Business and economics: 10
Education: 29
Entertainment: 5
People and places: 20
Physical sciences: 5
Political Science and public policy: 3
Psychology and behavioral sciences: 6
Public health and medicine: 33
Sports: 7
Technology: 16
Transportation and automobiles: 14

Exercises

Agriculture: 56
Biological and environmental sciences: 128
Business and economics: 145
Education: 162
Entertainment: 33
People and places: 168
Physical sciences: 23
Political Science and public policy: 37
Psychology and behavioral sciences: 22
Public health and medicine: 189
Sports: 36
Technology: 37
Transportation and automobiles: 65

For a complete index of applications of examples and exercises, please see the Annotated Instructor's Edition or the Web site: **www.whfreeman.com/bps**.

Statistics is about data. Data are numbers, but they are not "just numbers." **Data are numbers with a context.** The number 10.5, for example, carries no information by itself. But if we hear that a friend's new baby weighed 10.5 pounds at birth, we congratulate her on the healthy size of the child. The context engages our background knowledge and allows us to make judgments. We know that a baby weighing 10.5 pounds is quite large, and that a human baby is unlikely to weigh 10.5 ounces or 10.5 kilograms. The context makes the number informative.

Statistics is the science of data. To gain insight from data, we make graphs and do calculations. But graphs and calculations are guided by ways of thinking that amount to educated common sense. Let's begin our study of statistics with an informal look at some principles of statistical thinking.

Stockbyte/PictureQuest

DATA BEAT ANECDOTES

An anecdote is a striking story that sticks in our minds exactly because it is striking. Anecdotes humanize an issue, but they can be misleading.

Does living near power lines cause leukemia in children? The National Cancer Institute spent 5 years and $5 million gathering data on this question. The researchers compared 638 children who had leukemia with 620 who did not. They went into the homes and measured the magnetic fields in the children's bedrooms, in other rooms, and at the front door. They recorded facts about power lines near the family home and also near the mother's residence when she was pregnant. Result: no connection between leukemia and exposure to magnetic fields of the kind produced by power lines. The editorial that accompanied the study report in the *New England Journal of Medicine* thundered, "It is time to stop wasting our research resources" on the question.[1]

Now compare the effectiveness of a television news report of a 5-year, $5 million investigation against a televised interview with an articulate mother whose child has leukemia and who happens to live near a power line. In the public mind, the anecdote wins every time. A statistically literate person knows better. **Data are more reliable than anecdotes because they systematically describe an overall picture rather than focus on a few incidents.**

ALWAYS LOOK AT THE DATA

Yogi Berra said it: "You can observe a lot by just watching." That's a motto for learning from data. **A few carefully chosen graphs are often more instructive than great piles of numbers.** Consider the outcome of the 2000 presidential election in Florida.

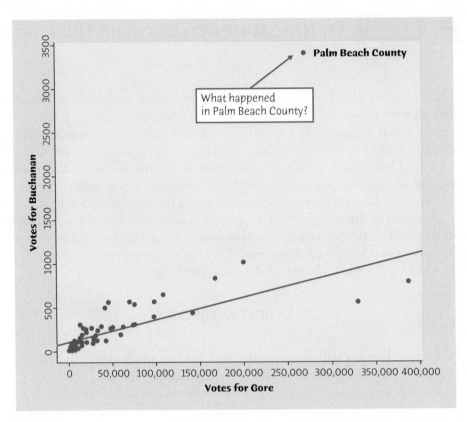

FIGURE 1 Votes in the 2000 presidential election for Al Gore and Patrick Buchanan in Florida's 67 counties. What happened in Palm Beach County?

Elections don't come much closer: after much recounting, state officials declared that George Bush had carried Florida by 537 votes out of almost 6 million votes cast. Florida's vote decided the election and made George Bush, rather than Al Gore, president. Let's look at some data. Figure 1 displays a graph that plots votes for the third-party candidate Pat Buchanan against votes for the Democratic candidate Al Gore in Florida's 67 counties.

What happened in Palm Beach County? The question leaps out from the graph. In this large and heavily Democratic county, a conservative third-party candidate did far better relative to the Democratic candidate than in any other county. The points for the other 66 counties show votes for both candidates increasing together in a roughly straight-line pattern. Both counts go up as county population goes up. Based on this pattern, we would expect Buchanan to receive around 800 votes in Palm Beach County. He actually received more than 3400 votes. That difference determined the election result in Florida and in the nation.

The graph demands an explanation. It turns out that Palm Beach County used a confusing "butterfly" ballot, in which candidate names on both left and right pages led to a voting column in the center. It would be easy for a voter who intended to vote for Gore to in fact cast a vote for Buchanan. The graph is convincing evidence that this in fact happened, more convincing than the complaints of voters who (later) were unsure where their votes ended up.

BEWARE THE LURKING VARIABLE

The Kalamazoo (Michigan) Symphony once advertised a "Mozart for Minors" program with this statement: "Question: Which students scored 51 points higher in verbal skills and 39 points higher in math? Answer: Students who had experience in music."[2] *Who would dispute that early experience with music builds brain-power?* The skeptical statistician, that's who. Children who take music lessons and attend concerts tend to have prosperous and well-educated parents. These same children are also likely to attend good schools, get good health care, and be encouraged to study hard. No wonder they score well on tests.

Brendan Byrne/Agefotostock

We call family background a *lurking variable* when we talk about the relationship between music and test scores. It is lurking behind the scenes, unmentioned in the symphony's publicity. Yet family background, more than anything else we can measure, influences children's academic performance. Perhaps the Kalamazoo Youth Soccer League should advertise that students who play soccer score higher on tests. After all, children who play soccer, like those who have experience in music, tend to have educated and prosperous parents. **Almost all relationships between two variables are influenced by other variables lurking in the background.**

WHERE THE DATA COME FROM IS IMPORTANT

The advice columnist Ann Landers once asked her readers, "If you had it to do over again, would you have children?" A few weeks later, her column was headlined "70% OF PARENTS SAY KIDS NOT WORTH IT." Indeed, 70% of the nearly 10,000 parents who wrote in said they would not have children if they could make the choice again. *Do you believe that 70% of all parents regret having children?*

You shouldn't. The people who took the trouble to write Ann Landers are not representative of all parents. Their letters showed that many of them were angry at their children. All we know from these data is that there are some unhappy parents out there. A statistically designed poll, unlike Ann Landers's appeal, targets specific people chosen in a way that gives all parents the same chance to be asked. Such a poll showed that 91% of parents *would* have children again. Where data come from matters a lot. If you are careless about how you get your data, you may announce 70% "No" when the truth is close to 90% "Yes."

Here's another question: *should women take hormones such as estrogen after menopause, when natural production of these hormones ends?* In 1992, several major medical organizations said "Yes." In particular, women who took hormones seemed to reduce their risk of a heart attack by 35% to 50%. The risks of taking hormones appeared small compared with the benefits.

The evidence in favor of hormone replacement came from a number of studies that compared women who were taking hormones with others who were not. Beware the lurking variable: women who choose to take hormones are richer and better educated and see doctors more often than women who do not. These women do many things to maintain their health. It isn't surprising that they have fewer heart attacks.

To get convincing data on the link between hormone replacement and heart attacks, do an *experiment*. Experiments don't let women decide what to do. They assign women to either hormone replacement or to dummy pills that look and taste the same as the hormone pills. The assignment is done by a coin toss, so that all kinds of women are equally likely to get either treatment. By 2002, several experiments with women of different ages agreed that hormone replacement does *not* reduce the risk of heart attacks. The National Institutes of Health, after reviewing the evidence, concluded that the first studies were wrong. Taking hormones after menopause quickly fell out of favor.[3]

The most important information about any statistical study is how the data were produced. Only statistically designed opinion polls can be trusted. Only experiments can completely defeat the lurking variable and give convincing evidence that an alleged cause really does account for an observed effect.

VARIATION IS EVERYWHERE

The company's sales reps file into their monthly meeting. The sales manager rises. "Congratulations! Our sales were up 2% last month, so we're all drinking champagne this morning. You remember that when sales were down 1% last month I fired half of our reps." This picture is only slightly exaggerated. Many managers overreact to small short-term variations in key figures. Here is Arthur Nielsen, head of the country's largest market research firm, describing his experience:

> *Too many business people assign equal validity to all numbers printed on paper. They accept numbers as representing Truth and find it difficult to work with the concept of probability. They do not see a number as a kind of shorthand for a range that describes our actual knowledge of the underlying condition.*[4]

Business data such as sales and prices vary from month to month for reasons ranging from the weather to a customer's financial difficulties to the inevitable errors in gathering the data. The manager's challenge is to say when there is a real pattern behind the variation. Start by looking at the data.

Figure 2 plots the average price of a gallon of regular unleaded gasoline each month from January 1990 to February 2006.[5] There certainly is variation! But a close look shows a pattern: gas prices normally go up during the summer driving season each year, then down as demand drops in the fall. Against this regular pattern we see the effects of international events: prices rose because of the 1990 Gulf War and dropped because of the 1998 financial crisis in Asia and the September 11, 2001, terrorist attacks in the United States. The year 2005 brought the

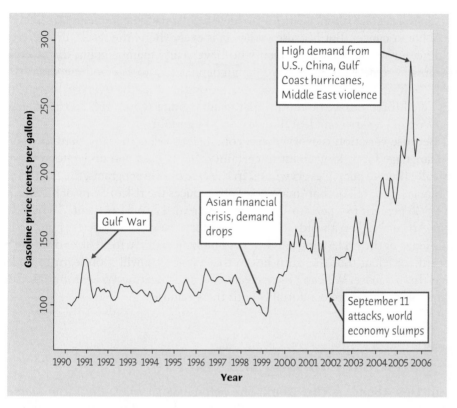

FIGURE 2 Variation is everywhere: the average retail price of regular unleaded gasoline, 1990 to early 2006.

perfect storm: the ability to produce oil and refine gasoline was overwhelmed by high demand from China and the United States, continued violence in Iraq, and hurricanes on the U.S. Gulf Coast. The data carry an important message: because the United States imports much of its oil, we can't control the price we pay for gasoline.

Variation is everywhere. Individuals vary; repeated measurements on the same individual vary; almost everything varies over time. One reason we need to know some statistics is that statistics helps us deal with variation.

CONCLUSIONS ARE NOT CERTAIN

Most women who reach middle age have regular mammograms to detect breast cancer. *Do mammograms reduce the risk of dying of breast cancer?* To defeat the lurking variable, doctors rely on experiments (called "clinical trials" in medicine) that compare different ways of screening for breast cancer. The conclusion from 13 such trials is that mammograms reduce the risk of death in women aged 50 to 64 years by 26%.[6]

AP/Wide World Photos

On the average, then, women who have regular mammograms are less likely to die of breast cancer. But because variation is everywhere, the results are different for different women. Some women who have yearly mammograms die of breast cancer, and some who never have mammograms live to 100 and die when they crash their motorcycles. Statistical conclusions are "on-the-average" statements only. Well then, can we be certain that mammograms reduce risk on the average? No. We can be very confident, but we can't be certain.

Because variation is everywhere, conclusions are uncertain. Statistics gives us a language for talking about uncertainty that is used and understood by statistically literate people everywhere. In the case of mammograms, the doctors use that language to tell us that "mammography reduces the risk of dying of breast cancer by 26 percent (95 percent confidence interval, 17 to 34 percent)." That 26% is, in Arthur Nielsen's words, a "shorthand for a range that describes our actual knowledge of the underlying condition." The range is 17% to 34%, and we are 95 percent confident that the truth lies in that range. We will soon learn to understand this language. We can't escape variation and uncertainty. Learning statistics enables us to live more comfortably with these realities.

Statistical Thinking and You

What Lies Ahead in This Book The purpose of *The Basic Practice of Statistics* (*BPS*) is to give you a working knowledge of the ideas and tools of practical statistics. We will divide practical statistics into three main areas:

1. **Data analysis** concerns methods and strategies for exploring, organizing, and describing data using graphs and numerical summaries. Only organized data can illuminate reality. Only thoughtful exploration of data can defeat the lurking variable. Part I of *BPS* (Chapters 1 to 7) discusses data analysis.

2. **Data production** provides methods for producing data that can give clear answers to specific questions. Where the data come from really is important. Basic concepts about how to select samples and design experiments are the most influential ideas in statistics. These concepts are the subject of Chapters 8 and 9.

3. **Statistical inference** moves beyond the data in hand to draw conclusions about some wider universe, taking into account that variation is everywhere and that conclusions are uncertain. To describe variation and uncertainty, inference uses the language of probability, introduced in Chapters 10 and 11. Because we are concerned with practice rather than theory, we need only a limited knowledge of probability. Chapters 12 and 13 offer more probability for those who want it. Chapters 14 to 16 discuss the reasoning of statistical inference. These chapters are the key to the rest of the book. Chapters 18 to 22 present inference as used in practice in the most common settings. Chapters 23 to 25, and the Optional Companion Chapters 26 to 29 on the text CD or online, concern more advanced or specialized kinds of inference.

Because data are numbers with a context, doing statistics means more than manipulating numbers. You must **state** a problem in its real-world context, **formulate** the problem by recognizing what specific statistical work is needed, **solve** the problem by making the necessary graphs and calculations, and **conclude** by explaining what your findings say about the real-world setting. We'll make regular use of this four-step process to encourage good habits that go beyond graphs and calculations to ask, "What do the data tell me?"

Statistics does involve lots of calculating and graphing. The text presents the techniques you need, but you should use a calculator or software to automate calculations and graphs as much as possible. Because the big ideas of statistics don't depend on any particular level of access to computing, *BPS* does not require software. Even if you make little use of technology, you should look at the "Using Technology" sections throughout the book. You will see at once that you can read and use the output from almost any technology used for statistical calculations. The ideas really are more important than the details of how to do the calculations.

You will need a calculator with some built-in statistical functions. Specifically, your calculator should find means and standard deviations and calculate correlations and regression lines. Look for a calculator that claims to do "two-variable statistics" or mentions "regression."

Because graphing and calculating are automated in statistical practice, the most important assets you can gain from the study of statistics are an understanding of the big ideas and the beginnings of good judgment in working with data. *BPS* tries to explain the most important ideas of statistics, not just teach methods. Some examples of big ideas that you will meet (one from each of the three areas of statistics) are "always plot your data," "randomized comparative experiments," and "statistical significance."

You learn statistics by doing statistical problems. As you read, you will see several levels of exercises, arranged to help you learn. Short "Apply Your Knowledge" problem sets appear after each major idea. These are straightforward exercises that help you solidify the main points as you read. Be sure you can do these exercises before going on. The end-of-chapter exercises begin with multiple-choice "Check Your Skills" exercises (with all answers in the back of the book). Use them to check your grasp of the basics. The regular "Chapter Exercises" help you combine all the ideas of a chapter. Finally, the three part review chapters look back over major blocks of learning, with many review exercises. At each step you are given less advance knowledge of exactly what statistical ideas and skills the problems will require, so each type of exercise requires more understanding.

The part review chapters (and the individual chapters in Part IV) include point-by-point lists of specific things you should be able to do. Go through that list, and be sure you can say "I can do that" to each item. Then try some of the review exercises. The book ends with a review titled "Statistical Thinking Revisited," which you should read and think about no matter where in the book your course ends.

The key to learning is persistence. The main ideas of statistics, like the main ideas of any important subject, took a long time to discover and take some time to master. The gain will be worth the pain.

Exploring Data

The first step in understanding data is to hear what the data say, to "let the statistics speak for themselves." Numbers speak clearly only when we help them speak by organizing, displaying, and summarizing. That's *data analysis*. The seven chapters in Part I present the ideas and tools of statistical data analysis. They equip you with skills that are immediately useful whenever you deal with numbers.

These chapters reflect the strong emphasis on exploring data that characterizes modern statistics. Although careful exploration of data is essential if we are to trust the results of inference, data analysis isn't just preparation for inference. To think about inference, we carefully distinguish between the data we actually have and the larger universe we want conclusions about. The Bureau of Labor Statistics, for example, has data about employment in the 60,000 households contacted by its Current Population Survey. The bureau wants to draw conclusions about employment in all 113 million U.S. households. That's a complex problem. From the viewpoint of data analysis, things are simpler. We want to explore and understand only the data in hand. The distinctions that inference requires don't concern us in Chapters 1 to 7. What does concern us is a systematic strategy for examining data and the tools that we use to carry out that strategy.

Part of that strategy is to first look at one thing at a time and then at relationships. In Chapters 1, 2, and 3 you will study **variables and their distributions.** Chapters 4, 5, and 6 concern **relationships among variables.** Chapter 7 reviews this part of the text.

"Tonight we're going to let the statistics speak for themselves."

EXPLORING DATA: Variables and Distributions

EXPLORING DATA: Relationships

Michael A. Keller/CORBIS

Picturing Distributions with Graphs

Statistics is the science of data. The volume of data available to us is overwhelming. For example, the Census Bureau's American Community Survey collects data from 250,000 households each month. The survey records facts about the household, even what type of plumbing is available. It also records facts about each person in the household—age, sex, weight, occupation, income, travel time to work, insurance, and much more. The first step in dealing with such a flood of data is to organize our thinking about data.

Individuals and variables

Any set of data contains information about some group of *individuals*. The information is organized in *variables*.

INDIVIDUALS AND VARIABLES

Individuals are the objects described by a set of data. Individuals may be people, but they may also be animals or things.

A **variable** is any characteristic of an individual. A variable can take different values for different individuals.

3

How much snow?

The TV weather report says Boston got 24 inches of white stuff. To report the value of a variable, we must first measure it. This isn't always easy. You can stick a ruler in the snow …but some snow melts, some turns to vapor, and later snow packs down earlier snow. A tree or a house in the neighborhood has a big effect. The high-tech method bounces an ultrasonic beam off the snow from a tall pole …but it works only after snow has stopped falling. So we don't really know how much snow Boston got. Let's just say "a lot."

A college's student data base, for example, includes data about every currently enrolled student. The students are the individuals described by the data set. For each individual, the data contain the values of variables such as date of birth, choice of major, and grade point average. In practice, any set of data is accompanied by background information that helps us understand the data. When you plan a statistical study or explore data from someone else's work, ask yourself the following questions:

1. **Who?** What **individuals** do the data describe? **How many** individuals appear in the data?

2. **What?** How many **variables** do the data contain? What are the **exact definitions** of these variables? In what **units of measurement** is each variable recorded? Weights, for example, might be recorded in pounds, in thousands of pounds, or in kilograms.

3. **Why? What purpose** do the data have? Do we hope to answer some specific questions? Do we want answers for just these individuals, or for some larger group that these individuals are supposed to represent? Are the individuals and variables suitable for the intended purpose?

Some variables, like a person's sex or college major, simply place individuals into categories. Others, like height and grade point average, take numerical values for which we can do arithmetic. It makes sense to give an average income for a company's employees, but it does not make sense to give an "average" sex. We can, however, count the numbers of female and male employees and do arithmetic with these counts.

CATEGORICAL AND QUANTITATIVE VARIABLES

A **categorical variable** places an individual into one of several groups or categories.

A **quantitative variable** takes numerical values for which arithmetic operations such as adding and averaging make sense. The values of a quantitative variable are usually recorded in a **unit of measurement** such as seconds or kilograms.

EXAMPLE 1.1   The American Community Survey

At the Census Bureau Web site, you can view the detailed data collected by the American Community Survey, though of course the identities of people and households are protected. If you choose the file of data on people, the *individuals* are more than one million people in households contacted by the survey. More than 120 variables are recorded for each individual. Figure 1.1 displays a very small part of the data.

Each row records data on one individual. Each column contains the values of one *variable* for all the individuals. Translated from the Census Bureau's abbreviations, the variables are

AMERICAN COMMUNITY SURVEY
U.S. CENSUS BUREAU

Courtesy U.S. Census Bureau

SERIALNO   An identifying number for the household.
PWGTP   Weight in pounds.
AGEP   Age in years.
JWMNP   Travel time to work in minutes.
SCHL   Highest level of education. The categories are designated by numbers. For example, 9 = high school graduate, 10 = some college but no degree, and 13 = bachelor's degree.
SEX   Sex, designated by 1 = male and 2 = female.
WAGP   Wage and salary income last year, in dollars.

Look at the highlighted row in Figure 1.1. This individual is a member of Household 370. He is a 53-year-old man who weighs 234 pounds, travels 10 minutes to work, has a bachelor's degree, and earned $83,000 last year. Two other people also live in Household 370, a 46-year-old woman and an 18-year-old woman.

In addition to the household serial number, there are six variables. Education and sex are categorical variables. The values for education and sex are stored as numbers, but these numbers are just labels for the categories and have no units of measurement. The other four variables are quantitative. Their values do have units. These variables are weight in pounds, age in years, travel time in minutes, and income in dollars.

The *purpose* of the American Community Survey is to collect data that represent the entire nation in order to guide government policy and business decisions. To do this, the households contacted are chosen at random from all households in the country. We will see in Chapter 8 why choosing at random is a good idea.

	A	B	C	D	E	F	G
1	SERIAL NO	PWGTP	AGEP	JWMNP	SCHL	SEX	WAGP
2	283	187	66		6	1	24000
3	283	158	66		9	2	0
4	323	176	54	10	12	2	11900
5	346	339	37	10	11	1	6000
6	346	91	27	10	10	2	30000
7	370	234	53	10	13	1	83000
8	370	181	46	15	10	2	74000
9	370	155	18		9	2	0
10	487	233	26		14	2	800
11	487	146	23		12	2	8000
12	511	236	53		9	2	0
13	511	131	53		11	1	0
14	515	213	38		11	2	12500
15	515	194	40		9	1	800
16	515	221	18	20	9	1	2500
17	515	193	11		3	1	

Each row in the spreadsheet contains data on one individual.

FIGURE 1.1 A spreadsheet displaying data from the American Community Survey.

Most data tables follow this format—each row is an individual, and each column is a variable. The data set in Figure 1.1 appears in a **spreadsheet** program that has rows and columns ready for your use. Spreadsheets are commonly used to enter and transmit data and to do simple calculations.

spreadsheet

APPLY YOUR KNOWLEDGE

1.1   **Fuel economy.** Here is a small part of a data set that describes the fuel economy (in miles per gallon) of 2006 model motor vehicles:

Make and model	Vehicle type	Transmission type	Number of cylinders	City MPG	Highway MPG
.					
.					
Audi TT Roadster	Two-seater	Manual	4	20	29
Cadillac CTS	Midsize	Automatic	6	18	27
Dodge Ram 1500	Standard pickup truck	Automatic	8	14	19
Ford Focus	Compact	Automatic	4	26	32
.					
.					
.					

(a) What are the individuals in this data set?

(b) For each individual, what variables are given? Which of these variables are categorical and which are quantitative?

1.2   **Students and TV.** You are preparing to study the television-viewing habits of college students. Describe two categorical variables and two quantitative variables that you might measure for each student. Give the units of measurement for the quantitative variables.

Categorical variables: pie charts and bar graphs

exploratory data analysis

Statistical tools and ideas help us examine data in order to describe their main features. This examination is called **exploratory data analysis.** Like an explorer crossing unknown lands, we want first to simply describe what we see. Here are two principles that help us organize our exploration of a set of data.

EXPLORING DATA

1. Begin by examining each variable by itself. Then move on to study the relationships among the variables.

2. Begin with a graph or graphs. Then add numerical summaries of specific aspects of the data.

We will also follow these principles in organizing our learning. Chapters 1 to 3 present methods for describing a single variable. We study relationships among several variables in Chapters 4 to 6. In each case, we begin with graphical displays, then add numerical summaries for more complete description.

The proper choice of graph depends on the nature of the variable. To examine a single variable, we usually want to display its *distribution*.

DISTRIBUTION OF A VARIABLE

The **distribution** of a variable tells us what values it takes and how often it takes these values.

The values of a categorical variable are labels for the categories. The **distribution of a categorical variable** lists the categories and gives either the count or the percent of individuals who fall in each category.

EXAMPLE 1.2   Radio station formats

The radio audience rating service Arbitron places the country's 13,838 radio stations into categories that describe the kind of programs they broadcast. Here is the distribution of station formats:[1]

Format	Count of stations	Percent of stations
Adult contemporary	1,556	11.2
Adult standards	1,196	8.6
Contemporary hit	569	4.1
Country	2,066	14.9
News/Talk/Information	2,179	15.7
Oldies	1,060	7.7
Religious	2,014	14.6
Rock	869	6.3
Spanish language	750	5.4
Other formats	1,579	11.4
Total	13,838	99.9

It's a good idea to check data for consistency. The counts should add to 13,838, the total number of stations. They do. The percents should add to 100%. In fact, they add to 99.9%. What happened? Each percent is rounded to the nearest tenth. The exact percents would add to 100, but the rounded percents only come close. This is **roundoff error.** Roundoff errors don't point to mistakes in our work, just to the effect of rounding off results.

roundoff error

Columns of numbers take time to read. You can use a pie chart or a bar graph to display the distribution of a categorical variable more vividly. Figure 1.2 illustrates both displays for the distribution of radio stations by format. **Pie charts** are awkward to make by hand, but software will do the job for you. *A pie chart must include all the categories that make up a whole. Use a pie chart only when you want to emphasize each category's relation to the whole.* We need the "Other" formats category in Example 1.2 to complete the whole (all radio stations) and allow us to make a pie chart. **Bar graphs** are easier to make and also easier to read, as Figure 1.2(b)

pie chart

bar graph

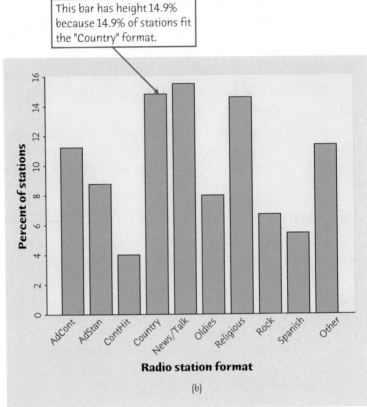

This bar has height 14.9% because 14.9% of stations fit the "Country" format.

This wedge occupies 14.9% of the pie because 14.9% of stations fit the "Country" format.

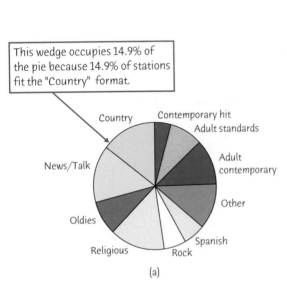

FIGURE 1.2 You can use either a pie chart or a bar graph to display the distribution of a categorical variable. Here are a pie chart and a bar graph of radio stations by format.

illustrates. Bar graphs are more flexible than pie charts. Both graphs can display the distribution of a categorical variable, but a bar graph can also compare any set of quantities that are measured in the same units.

EXAMPLE 1.3   Do you listen while you walk?

Portable MP3 music players, such as the Apple iPod, are popular—but not equally popular with people of all ages. Here are the percents of people in various age groups who own a portable MP3 player.[2]

Michael A. Keller/CORBIS

Age group (years)	Percent owning an MP3 player
12–17	27
18–24	18
25–34	20
35–44	16
45–54	10
55–64	6
65+	2

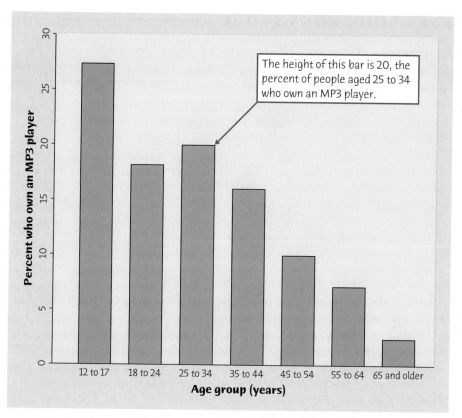

The height of this bar is 20, the percent of people aged 25 to 34 who own an MP3 player.

FIGURE 1.3 Bar graph comparing the percents of several age groups who own portable MP3 players.

It's clear that MP3 players are popular mainly among young people. We can't make a pie chart to display these data. Each percent in the table refers to a different age group, not to parts of a single whole. The bar graph in Figure 1.3 compares the seven age groups.

Bar graphs and pie charts help an audience grasp data quickly. They are, however, of limited use for data analysis because it is easy to understand data on a single categorical variable without a graph. We will move on to quantitative variables, where graphs are essential tools. But first, here is a question that you should always ask when you look at data:

EXAMPLE 1.4 Do the data tell you what you want to know?

Let's say that you plan to buy radio time to advertise your Web site for downloading MP3 music files. How helpful are the data in Example 1.2? Not very. You are interested, not in counting *stations*, but in counting *listeners*. For example, 14.6% of all stations are religious, but they have only a 5.5% share of the radio audience. In fact, you aren't even interested in the entire radio audience, because MP3 users are mostly young people. You really want to know what kinds of radio stations reach the largest numbers of young people. *Always think about whether the data you have help answer your questions.*

APPLY YOUR KNOWLEDGE ───────────────────

1.3   **The color of your car.**   News from the auto color front: fewer luxury car buyers are choosing "neutral" colors (silver, white, black). Here is the distribution of the most popular colors for 2005 model luxury cars made in North America:[3]

Color	Percent
Silver	20
White, pearl	18
Black	16
Blue	13
Light brown	10
Red	7
Yellow, gold	6

(a) What percent of vehicles are some other color?

(b) Make a bar graph of the color data. Would it be correct to make a pie chart if you added an "Other" category?

1.4   **Never on Sunday?**   Births are not, as you might think, evenly distributed across the days of the week. Here are the average numbers of babies born on each day of the week in 2003:[4]

Day	Births
Sunday	7,563
Monday	11,733
Tuesday	13,001
Wednesday	12,598
Thursday	12,514
Friday	12,396
Saturday	8,605

Present these data in a well-labeled bar graph. Would it also be correct to make a pie chart? Suggest some possible reasons why there are fewer births on weekends.

1.5   **Do the data tell you what you want to know?**   To help you plan advertising for a Web site for downloading MP3 music files, you want to know what percent of owners of portable MP3 players are 18 to 24 years old. The data in Example 1.3 do *not* tell you what you want to know. Why not?

Quantitative variables: histograms

Quantitative variables often take many values. The distribution tells us what values the variable takes and how often it takes these values. A graph of the distribution is clearer if nearby values are grouped together. The most common graph of

histogram   the distribution of one quantitative variable is a **histogram.**

EXAMPLE 1.5 *Making a histogram*

The percent of a state's adult residents who have a college degree says a lot about the state's economy. For example, states heavy in agriculture and manufacturing have fewer college graduates than states with many financial and technological employers. Table 1.1 presents the percent of each state's residents aged 25 and over who hold a bachelor's degree.[5] The *individuals* in this data set are the states. The *variable* is the percent of college graduates among a state's adults. To make a histogram of the distribution of this variable, proceed as follows:

Step 1. Choose the classes. Divide the range of the data into classes of equal width. The data in Table 1.1 range from 17.0 to 44.2, so we decide to use these classes:

$$15.0 < \text{percent with bachelor's degree} \le 20.0$$
$$20.0 < \text{percent with bachelor's degree} \le 25.0$$
$$\cdot$$
$$\cdot$$
$$\cdot$$
$$40.0 < \text{percent with bachelor's degree} \le 45.0$$

Be sure to specify the classes precisely so that each individual falls into exactly one class. Florida, with 25.0% college graduates, falls into the second class, but a state with 25.1% would fall into the third.

TABLE 1.1		**Percent of population aged 25 and over with a bachelor's degree**			
State	Percent	State	Percent	State	Percent
Alabama	21.2	Louisiana	21.3	Ohio	23.0
Alaska	26.6	Maine	25.9	Oklahoma	21.9
Arizona	24.3	Maryland	34.5	Oregon	26.4
Arkansas	19.0	Massachusetts	35.8	Pennsylvania	24.2
California	29.1	Michigan	24.3	Rhode Island	29.1
Colorado	34.7	Minnesota	30.6	South Carolina	23.2
Connecticut	34.6	Mississippi	18.7	South Dakota	23.1
Delaware	27.6	Missouri	24.1	Tennessee	21.5
Florida	25.0	Montana	25.8	Texas	24.5
Georgia	25.7	Nebraska	25.3	Utah	26.2
Hawaii	28.2	Nevada	19.5	Vermont	32.0
Idaho	24.0	New Hampshire	30.3	Virginia	32.2
Illinois	28.1	New Jersey	32.1	Washington	30.2
Indiana	21.0	New Mexico	23.7	West Virginia	17.0
Iowa	22.5	New York	29.7	Wisconsin	23.8
Kansas	28.7	North Carolina	24.3	Wyoming	23.7
Kentucky	18.6	North Dakota	25.0	District of Columbia	44.2

Step 2. Count the individuals in each class. Here are the counts:

Class	Count
15.1 to 20.0	5
20.1 to 25.0	21
25.1 to 30.0	14
30.1 to 35.0	9
35.1 to 40.0	1
40.1 to 45.0	1

Check that the counts add to 51, the number of individuals in the data (the 50 states and the District of Columbia).

Step 3. Draw the histogram. Mark the scale for the variable whose distribution you are displaying on the horizontal axis. That's the percent of a state's adults with a college degree. The scale runs from 15 to 45 because that is the span of the classes we chose. The vertical axis contains the scale of counts. Each bar represents a class. The base of the bar covers the class, and the bar height is the class count. There is no horizontal space between the bars unless a class is empty, so that its bar has height zero. Figure 1.4 is our histogram.

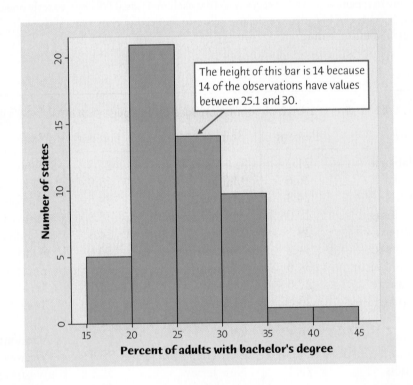

FIGURE 1.4 Histogram of the distribution of the percent of college graduates among the adult residents of the 50 states and the District of Columbia.

Although histograms resemble bar graphs, their details and uses are different. A histogram displays the distribution of a quantitative variable. The horizontal axis of a histogram is marked in the units of measurement for the variable. A bar graph compares the size of different items. The horizontal axis of a bar graph need not have any measurement scale but simply identifies the items being compared. These may be the categories of a categorical variable, but they may also be separate, like the age groups in Example 1.3. Draw bar graphs with blank space between the bars to separate the items being compared. Draw histograms with no space, to indicate that all values of the variable are covered.

Our eyes respond to the *area* of the bars in a histogram.[6] Because the classes are all the same width, area is determined by height and all classes are fairly represented. There is no one right choice of the classes in a histogram. Too few classes will give a "skyscraper" graph, with all values in a few classes with tall bars. Too many will produce a "pancake" graph, with most classes having one or no observations. Neither choice will give a good picture of the shape of the distribution. You must use your judgment in choosing classes to display the shape. Statistics software will choose the classes for you. The software's choice is usually a good one, but you can change it if you want. The histogram function in the *One Variable Statistical Calculator* applet on the text CD and Web site allows you to change the number of classes by dragging with the mouse, so that it is easy to see how the choice of classes affects the histogram.

APPLY YOUR KNOWLEDGE

1.6 **Traveling to work.** How long must you travel each day to get to work or school? Table 1.2 gives the average travel time to work for workers in each state

TABLE 1.2	Average travel time to work (minutes) for adults employed outside the home				
State	Time	State	Time	State	Time
Alabama	22.7	Louisiana	23.3	Ohio	22.1
Alaska	18.9	Maine	22.6	Oklahoma	19.1
Arizona	23.4	Maryland	30.2	Oregon	21.0
Arkansas	19.9	Massachusetts	26.0	Pennsylvania	23.8
California	26.5	Michigan	22.7	Rhode Island	21.8
Colorado	22.9	Minnesota	21.7	South Carolina	23.0
Connecticut	23.6	Mississippi	21.6	South Dakota	15.2
Delaware	22.5	Missouri	23.3	Tennessee	23.4
Florida	24.8	Montana	16.9	Texas	23.7
Georgia	26.1	Nebraska	16.5	Utah	19.7
Hawaii	24.5	Nevada	21.8	Vermont	20.3
Idaho	19.5	New Hampshire	24.6	Virginia	25.8
Illinois	27.0	New Jersey	28.5	Washington	24.8
Indiana	21.2	New Mexico	19.4	West Virginia	24.7
Iowa	18.1	New York	30.4	Wisconsin	20.4
Kansas	17.5	North Carolina	23.2	Wyoming	17.5
Kentucky	22.1	North Dakota	15.4	District of Columbia	28.4

who are at least 16 years old and don't work at home.[7] Make a histogram of the travel times using classes of width 2 minutes starting at 15 minutes. (Make this histogram by hand even if you have software, to be sure you understand the process. You may then want to compare your histogram with your software's choice.)

1.7   **Choosing classes in a histogram.** The data set menu that accompanies the *One Variable Statistical Calculator* applet includes the data on college graduates in the states from Table 1.1. Choose these data, then click on the "Histogram" tab to see a histogram.

(a) How many classes does the applet choose to use? (You can click on the graph outside the bars to get a count of classes.)

(b) Click on the graph and drag to the left. What is the smallest number of classes you can get? What are the lower and upper bounds of each class? (Click on the bar to find out.) Make a rough sketch of this histogram.

(c) Click and drag to the right. What is the greatest number of classes you can get? How many observations does the largest class have?

(d) You see that the choice of classes changes the appearance of a histogram. Drag back and forth until you get the histogram you think best displays the distribution. How many classes did you use?

Interpreting histograms

Making a statistical graph is not an end in itself. The purpose of the graph is to help us understand the data. After you make a graph, always ask, "What do I see?" Once you have displayed a distribution, you can see its important features as follows.

EXAMINING A HISTOGRAM

In any graph of data, look for the **overall pattern** and for striking **deviations** from that pattern.

You can describe the overall pattern of a histogram by its **shape, center,** and **spread.**

An important kind of deviation is an **outlier,** an individual value that falls outside the overall pattern.

One way to describe the center of a distribution is by its *midpoint,* the value with roughly half the observations taking smaller values and half taking larger values. For now, we will describe the spread of a distribution by giving the *smallest and largest values.* We will learn better ways to describe center and spread in Chapter 2.

EXAMPLE 1.6   *Describing a distribution*

Look again at the histogram in Figure 1.4. **Shape:** The distribution has a *single peak*, which represents states in which between 20% and 25% of adults have a college degree. The distribution is *skewed to the right*. Most states have no more than 30% college graduates, but several states have higher percents, so that the graph extends to the right of its peak farther than it extends to the left. **Center:** The counts in Example 1.5 show that 26 of the 51 states (including DC) have 25% or fewer college graduates. So the midpoint of the distribution is 25%. **Spread:** The spread is from 17% to 44.2%, but only two observations fall above 35%. These are Massachusetts at 35.8% and the District of Columbia at 44.2%.

Outliers: In Figure 1.4, the two observations greater than 35% are part of the long right tail but don't stand apart from the overall distribution. This histogram, with only 6 classes, hides much of the detail in the distribution. Look at Figure 1.5, a histogram of the same data with twice as many classes. It is now clear that the District of Columbia, at 44.2%, does stand apart from the other observations. It is 8.4% higher than Massachusetts, the second-highest value.

Once you have spotted possible outliers, look for an explanation. Some outliers are due to mistakes, such as typing 10.1 as 101. Other outliers point to the special nature of some observations. The District of Columbia is a city rather than a state, and we expect urban areas to have lots of college graduates.

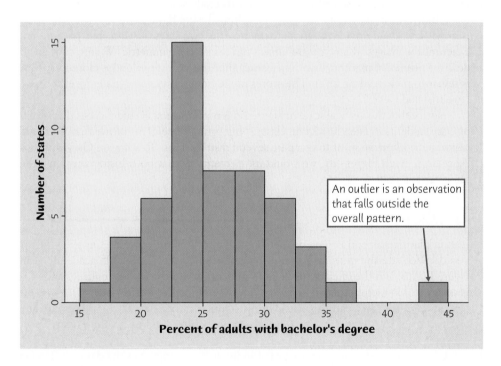

An outlier is an observation that falls outside the overall pattern.

FIGURE 1.5 Another histogram of the distribution of the percent of college graduates, with twice as many classes as Figure 1.4. Histograms with more classes show more detail but may have a less clear pattern.

Comparing Figures 1.4 and 1.5 reminds us that *the choice of classes in a histogram can influence the appearance of a distribution*. Both histograms portray a right-skewed distribution with one peak, but only Figure 1.5 shows the outlier.

When you describe a distribution, concentrate on the main features. Look for major peaks, not for minor ups and downs in the bars of the histogram. Look for

CAUTION

clear outliers, not just for the smallest and largest observations. Look for rough *symmetry* or clear *skewness*.

SYMMETRIC AND SKEWED DISTRIBUTIONS

A distribution is **symmetric** if the right and left sides of the histogram are approximately mirror images of each other.

A distribution is **skewed to the right** if the right side of the histogram (containing the half of the observations with larger values) extends much farther out than the left side. It is **skewed to the left** if the left side of the histogram extends much farther out than the right side.

Here are more examples of describing the overall pattern of a histogram.

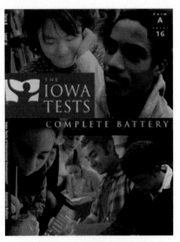

Courtesy Riverside Publishing

┌─ **EXAMPLE 1.7**   Iowa Test scores ──────────────────

Figure 1.6 displays the scores of all 947 seventh-grade students in the public schools of Gary, Indiana, on the vocabulary part of the Iowa Test of Basic Skills.[8] The distribution is *single-peaked* and *symmetric*. In mathematics, the two sides of symmetric patterns are exact mirror images. Real data are almost never exactly symmetric. We are content to describe Figure 1.6 as symmetric. The center (half above, half below) is close to 7. This is seventh-grade reading level. The scores range from 2.0 (second-grade level) to 12.1 (twelfth-grade level).

Notice that the vertical scale in Figure 1.6 is not the *count* of students but the *percent* of Gary students in each histogram class. A histogram of percents rather than counts is convenient when we want to compare several distributions. To compare Gary with Los Angeles, a much bigger city, we would use percents so that both histograms have the same vertical scale.

┌─ **EXAMPLE 1.8**   College costs ──────────────────

Jeanna plans to attend college in her home state of Massachusetts. On the College Board's Web site she finds data on tuition and fees for the 2004–2005 academic year. Figure 1.7 displays the charges for in-state students at all 59 four-year colleges and universities in Massachusetts (omitting art schools and other special colleges). As is often the case, we can't call this irregular distribution either symmetric or skewed. The big feature of the overall pattern is three peaks, corresponding to three **clusters** of colleges.

clusters

Clusters suggest that several types of individuals are mixed in the data set. Twelve colleges charge less than $10,000; 11 of these are the 11 state colleges and universities in Massachusetts. The remaining 47 colleges are all private institutions with tuition and fees exceeding $13,000. These appear to fall into two clusters, roughly described as regional institutions that charge between $15,000 and $25,000 and national institutions (think of Harvard and Mount Holyoke) with tuitions above $28,000. Only a few colleges fall between these clusters.

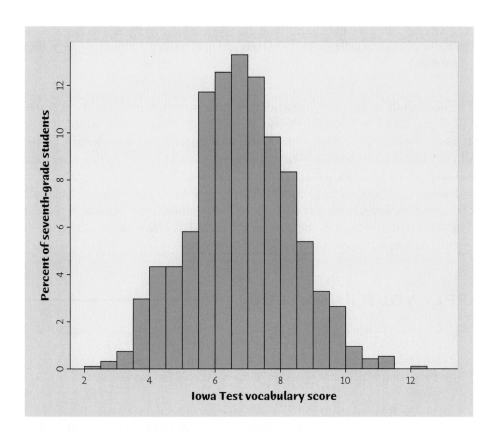

FIGURE 1.6 Histogram of the Iowa Test vocabulary scores of all seventh-grade students in Gary, Indiana. This distribution is single-peaked and symmetric.

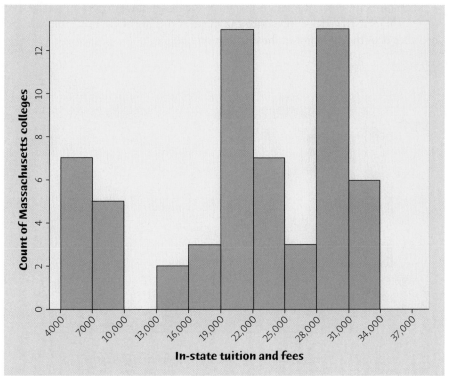

FIGURE 1.7 Histogram of the tuition and fee charges for four-year colleges in Massachusetts. The three clusters distinguish public colleges at the left from two groups of private institutions at the right.

Giving the center and spread of this distribution is not very useful because the data mix several kinds of colleges. It would be better to describe public and private colleges separately.

The overall shape of a distribution is important information about a variable. Some variables have distributions with predictable shapes. Many biological measurements on specimens from the same species and sex—lengths of bird bills, heights of young women—have symmetric distributions. On the other hand, data on people's incomes are usually strongly skewed to the right. There are many moderate incomes, some large incomes, and a few enormous incomes. Many distributions have irregular shapes that are neither symmetric nor skewed. Some data show other patterns, such as the clusters in Figure 1.7. Use your eyes, describe the pattern you see, and then try to explain the pattern.

APPLY YOUR KNOWLEDGE

1.8   **Traveling to work.**   In Exercise 1.6, you made a histogram of the average travel times to work in Table 1.2. The shape of the distribution is a bit irregular. Is it closer to symmetric or skewed? About where is the center (midpoint) of the data? What is the spread in terms of the smallest and largest values?

1.9   **Foreign-born residents.**   The states differ greatly in the percent of their residents who were born outside the United States. California leads with 26.5% foreign-born. Figure 1.8 is a histogram of the distribution of percent foreign-born residents in the states.[9] Describe the shape of this distribution. Within which class does the midpoint of the distribution lie?

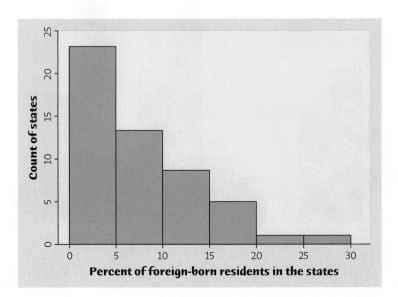

FIGURE 1.8 Histogram of the percents of state residents born outside the United States, for Exercise 1.9.

Quantitative variables: stemplots

Histograms are not the only graphical display of distributions. For small data sets, a *stemplot* is quicker to make and presents more detailed information.

STEMPLOT

To make a **stemplot:**

1. Separate each observation into a **stem,** consisting of all but the final (rightmost) digit, and a **leaf,** the final digit. Stems may have as many digits as needed, but each leaf contains only a single digit.

2. Write the stems in a vertical column with the smallest at the top, and draw a vertical line at the right of this column.

3. Write each leaf in the row to the right of its stem, in increasing order out from the stem.

The vital few

Skewed distributions can show us where to concentrate our efforts. Ten percent of the cars on the road account for half of all carbon dioxide emissions. A histogram of CO_2 emissions would show many cars with small or moderate values and a few with very high values. Cleaning up or replacing these cars would reduce pollution at a cost much lower than that of programs aimed at all cars. Statisticians who work at improving quality in industry make a principle of this: distinguish "the vital few" from "the trivial many."

┏━ **EXAMPLE 1.9**   *Making a stemplot* ━━━━━━━━━

Table 1.1 presents the percents of state residents aged 25 and over who have college degrees. To make a stemplot of these data, take the whole-number part of the percent as the stem and the final digit (tenths) as the leaf. The Kentucky entry, 18.6%, has stem 18 and leaf 6. Mississippi, at 18.7%, places leaf 7 on the same stem. These are the only observations on this stem. Arrange the leaves in order, so that **18 | 6 7** is one row in the stemplot. Figure 1.9 is the complete stemplot for the data in Table 1.1.

A stemplot looks like a histogram turned on end. Compare the stemplot in Figure 1.9 with the histograms of the same data in Figures 1.4 and 1.5. The stemplot is like a histogram with many classes. You can choose the classes in a histogram. The classes (the stems) of a stemplot are given to you. All three graphs show a distribution that has one peak and is right-skewed. Figures 1.5 and 1.9 have enough classes to make clear that the District of Columbia (44.2%) is an outlier. Histograms are more flexible than stemplots because you can choose the classes. But the stemplot, unlike the histogram, preserves the actual value of each observation. *Stemplots do not work well for large data sets, where each stem must hold a large number of leaves.* Don't try to make a stemplot of a large data set, such as the 947 Iowa Test scores in Figure 1.6.

┏━ **EXAMPLE 1.10**   *Pulling wood apart* ━━━━━━━━━

Student engineers learn that although handbooks give the strength of a material as a single number, in fact the strength varies from piece to piece. A vital lesson in all fields of study is that "variation is everywhere." The following are data from a typical student laboratory exercise: the load in pounds needed to pull apart pieces of Douglas fir 4 inches long and 1.5 inches square.

Courtesy Department of Civil Engineering, University of New Mexico

FIGURE 1.9 Stemplot of the percents of adults with college degrees in the states. Each stem is a percent and leaves are tenths of a percent.

```
17 | 0
18 | 6 7
19 | 0 5
20 |
21 | 0 2 3 5 9
22 | 5
23 | 0 1 2 7 7 8
24 | 0 1 2 3 3 3 5
25 | 0 0 3 7 8 9
26 | 2 4 6
27 | 6
28 | 1 2 7
29 | 1 1 7
30 | 2 3 6
31 |
32 | 0 1 2
33 |
34 | 5 6 7
35 | 8
36 |
37 |
38 |
39 |
40 |
41 |
42 |
43 |
44 | 2
```

The 18 stem contains the values 18.6 for Kentucky and 18.7 for Mississippi.

33,190	31,860	32,590	26,520	33,280
32,320	33,020	32,030	30,460	32,700
23,040	30,930	32,720	33,650	32,340
24,050	30,170	31,300	28,730	31,920

rounding

A stemplot of these data would have very many stems and no leaves or just one leaf on most stems. So we first **round** the data to the nearest hundred pounds. The rounded data are

332 319 326 265 333 323 330 320 305 327
230 309 327 337 323 241 302 313 287 319

Now we can make a stemplot with the first two digits (thousands of pounds) as stems and the third digit (hundreds of pounds) as leaves. Figure 1.10 is the stemplot. Rotate the stemplot counterclockwise so that it resembles a histogram, with 230 at the left end of the scale. This makes it clear that the distribution is *skewed to the left*. The *midpoint* is around 320 (32,000 pounds) and the *spread* is from 230 to 337. Because of the strong skew, we are reluctant to call the smallest observations outliers. They appear to be part of the long left tail of the distribution. Before using wood like this in construction, we should ask why some pieces are much weaker than the rest.

FIGURE 1.10 Stemplot of the breaking strength of pieces of wood, rounded to the nearest hundred pounds. Stems are thousands of pounds and leaves are hundreds of pounds.

```
23 | 0
24 | 1
25 |
26 | 5
27 |
28 | 7
29 |
30 | 2 5 9
31 | 3 9 9
32 | 0 3 3 6 7 7
33 | 0 2 3 7
```

Comparing Figures 1.9 (right-skewed) and 1.10 (left-skewed) reminds us that *the direction of skewness is the direction of the long tail, not the direction where most observations are clustered.*

You can also **split stems** in a stemplot to double the number of stems when all the leaves would otherwise fall on just a few stems. Each stem then appears twice. Leaves 0 to 4 go on the upper stem, and leaves 5 to 9 go on the lower stem. If you split the stems in the stemplot of Figure 1.10, for example, the 32 and 33 stems become

```
32 | 0 3 3
32 | 6 7 7
33 | 0 2 3
33 | 7
```

Rounding and splitting stems are matters for judgment, like choosing the classes in a histogram. The wood strength data require rounding but don't require splitting stems. The *One Variable Statistical Calculator* applet on the text CD and Web site allows you to decide whether to split stems, so that it is easy to see the effect.

splitting stems

APPLY YOUR KNOWLEDGE ———————————

1.10 **Traveling to work.** Make a stemplot of the average travel times to work in Table 1.2. Use whole minutes as your stems. Because the stemplot preserves the actual value of the observations, it is easy to find the midpoint (26th of the 51 observations in order) and the spread. What are they?

1.11 **Glucose levels.** People with diabetes must monitor and control their blood glucose level. The goal is to maintain "fasting plasma glucose" between about 90 and 130 milligrams per deciliter (mg/dl). The following are the fasting plasma glucose levels for 18 diabetics enrolled in a diabetes control class, five months after the end of the class:[10]

141	158	112	153	134	95	96	78	148
172	200	271	103	172	359	145	147	255

Make a stemplot of these data and describe the main features of the distribution. (You will want to round and also split stems.) Are there outliers? How well is the group as a whole achieving the goal for controlling glucose levels?

Karen Kasmauski/CORBIS

Time plots

Many variables are measured at intervals over time. We might, for example, measure the height of a growing child or the price of a stock at the end of each month. In these examples, our main interest is change over time. To display change over time, make a *time plot*.

> ### TIME PLOT
>
> A **time plot** of a variable plots each observation against the time at which it was measured. Always put time on the horizontal scale of your plot and the variable you are measuring on the vertical scale. Connecting the data points by lines helps emphasize any change over time.

Courtesy U.S. Geological Survey

EXAMPLE 1.11   Water levels in the Everglades

Water levels in Everglades National Park are critical to the survival of this unique region. The photo shows a water-monitoring station in Shark River Slough, the main path for surface water moving through the "river of grass" that is the Everglades. Figure 1.11 is a time plot of water levels at this station from mid-August 2000 to mid-June 2003.[11]

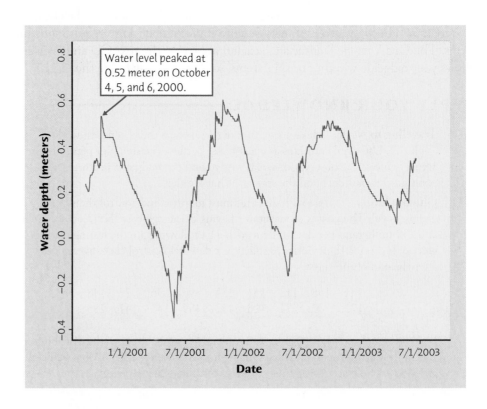

FIGURE 1.11 Time plot of water depth at a monitoring station in Everglades National Park over a period of almost three years. The yearly cycles reflect Florida's wet and dry seasons.

When you examine a time plot, look once again for an overall pattern and for strong deviations from the pattern. Figure 1.11 shows strong **cycles,** regular up-and-down movements in water level. The cycles show the effects of Florida's wet season (roughly June to November) and dry season (roughly December to May). Water levels are highest in late fall. In April and May of 2001 and 2002, water levels were less than zero—the water table was below ground level and the surface was dry. If you look closely, you can see year-to-year variation. The dry season in 2003 ended early, with the first-ever April tropical storm. In consequence, the dry-season water level in 2003 never dipped below zero.

cycles

Another common overall pattern in a time plot is a **trend,** a long-term upward or downward movement over time. Many economic variables show an upward trend. Incomes, house prices, and (alas) college tuitions tend to move generally upward over time.

trend

Histograms and time plots give different kinds of information about a variable. The time plot in Figure 1.11 presents **time series data** that show the change in water level at one location over time. A histogram displays **cross-sectional data,** such as water levels at many locations in the Everglades at the same time.

time series
cross-sectional

APPLY YOUR KNOWLEDGE

1.12 **The cost of college.** Here are data on the average tuition and fees charged by public four-year colleges and universities for the 1976 to 2005 academic years. Because almost any variable measured in dollars increases over time due to inflation (the falling buying power of a dollar), the values are given in "constant dollars," adjusted to have the same buying power that a dollar had in 2005.[12]

Year	Tuition	Year	Tuition	Year	Tuition	Year	Tuition
1976	$2,059	1984	$2,274	1992	$3,208	2000	$3,925
1977	$2,049	1985	$2,373	1993	$3,396	2001	$4,140
1978	$1,968	1986	$2,490	1994	$3,523	2002	$4,408
1979	$1,862	1987	$2,511	1995	$3,564	2003	$4,890
1980	$1,818	1988	$2,551	1996	$3,668	2004	$5,239
1981	$1,892	1989	$2,617	1997	$3,768	2005	$5,491
1982	$2,058	1990	$2,791	1998	$3,869		
1983	$2,210	1991	$2,987	1999	$3,894		

(a) Make a time plot of average tuition and fees.

(b) What overall pattern does your plot show?

(c) Some possible deviations from the overall pattern are outliers, periods of decreasing charges (in 2005 dollars), and periods of particularly rapid increase. Which are present in your plot, and during which years?

CHAPTER 1 SUMMARY

A data set contains information on a number of **individuals.** Individuals may be people, animals, or things. For each individual, the data give values for one or more **variables.** A variable describes some characteristic of an individual, such as a person's height, sex, or salary.

Some variables are **categorical** and others are **quantitative.** A categorical variable places each individual into a category, like male or female. A quantitative variable has numerical values that measure some characteristic of each individual, like height in centimeters or salary in dollars.

Exploratory data analysis uses graphs and numerical summaries to describe the variables in a data set and the relations among them.

After you understand the background of your data (individuals, variables, units of measurement), the first thing to do is almost always **plot your data.**

The **distribution** of a variable describes what values the variable takes and how often it takes these values. **Pie charts** and **bar graphs** display the distribution of a categorical variable. Bar graphs can also compare any set of quantities measured in the same units. **Histograms** and **stemplots** graph the distribution of a quantitative variable.

When examining any graph, look for an **overall pattern** and for notable **deviations** from the pattern.

Shape, center, and **spread** describe the overall pattern of the distribution of a quantitative variable. Some distributions have simple shapes, such as **symmetric** or **skewed.** Not all distributions have a simple overall shape, especially when there are few observations.

Outliers are observations that lie outside the overall pattern of a distribution. Always look for outliers and try to explain them.

When observations on a variable are taken over time, make a **time plot** that graphs time horizontally and the values of the variable vertically. A time plot can reveal **trends, cycles,** or other changes over time.

CHECK YOUR SKILLS

The Check Your Skills multiple-choice exercises ask straightforward questions about basic facts from the chapter. Answers to all of these exercises appear in the back of the book. You should expect all of your answers to be correct.

1.13   Here are the first lines of a professor's data set at the end of a statistics course:

Name	Major	Points	Grade
ADVANI, SURA	COMM	397	B
BARTON, DAVID	HIST	323	C
BROWN, ANNETTE	BIOL	446	A
CHIU, SUN	PSYC	405	B
CORTEZ, MARIA	PSYC	461	A

The individuals in these data are

(a) the students.

(b) the total points.

(c) the course grades.

1.14   To display the distribution of grades (A, B, C, D, F) in a course, it would be correct to use

(a) a pie chart but not a bar graph.

(b) a bar graph but not a pie chart.

(c) either a pie chart or a bar graph.

1.15 A study of recent college graduates records the sex and total college debt in dollars for 10,000 people a year after they graduate from college.

(a) Sex and college debt are both categorical variables.

(b) Sex and college debt are both quantitative variables.

(c) Sex is a categorical variable and college debt is a quantitative variable.

Figure 1.7 (page 17) is a histogram of the tuition and fee charges for the 2004–2005 academic year for 59 four-year colleges in Massachusetts. The following two exercises are based on this histogram.

1.16 The number of colleges with tuition and fee charges covered by the leftmost bar in the histogram is

(a) 4000.

(b) 6.

(c) 7.

1.17 The leftmost bar in the histogram covers tuition and fee charges ranging from about

(a) $3500 to $7500.

(b) $4000 to $7000.

(c) $4500 to $7500.

1.18 Here are the IQ test scores of 10 randomly chosen fifth-grade students:

145   139   126   122   125   130   96   110   118   118

To make a stemplot of these scores, you would use as stems

(a) 0 and 1.

(b) 09, 10, 11, 12, 13, and 14.

(c) 96, 110, 118, 122, 125, 126, 130, 139, and 145.

1.19 The population of the United States is aging, though less rapidly than in other developed countries. Here is a stemplot of the percents of residents aged 65 and older in the 50 states, according to the 2000 census. The stems are whole percents and the leaves are tenths of a percent.

```
 5 | 7
 6 |
 7 |
 8 | 5
 9 | 6 7 9
10 | 6
11 | 0 2 2 3 3 6 7 7
12 | 0 0 1 1 1 3 4 4 5 7 8 9
13 | 0 0 0 1 2 2 3 3 3 4 5 5 6 8
14 | 0 3 4 5 7 9
15 | 3 6
16 |
17 | 6
```

There are two outliers: Alaska has the lowest percent of older residents, and Florida has the highest. What is the percent for Florida?

(a) 5.7%

(b) 17.6%

(c) 176%

1.20   Ignoring the outliers, the shape of the distribution in Exercise 1.19 is

(a) somewhat skewed to the right.

(b) close to symmetric.

(c) somewhat skewed to the left.

1.21   The center of the distribution in Exercise 1.19 is close to

(a) 12.7%.

(b) 13.5%.

(c) 5.7% to 17.6%.

1.22   You look at real estate ads for houses in Sarasota, Florida. There are many houses ranging from $200,000 to $400,000 in price. The few houses on the water, however, have prices up to $15 million. The distribution of house prices will be

(a) skewed to the left.

(b) roughly symmetric.

(c) skewed to the right.

CHAPTER 1 EXERCISES

1.23   **Protecting wood.** How can we help wood surfaces resist weathering, especially when restoring historic wooden buildings? In a study of this question, researchers prepared wooden panels and then exposed them to the weather. Here are some of the variables recorded. Which of these variables are categorical and which are quantitative?

(a) Type of wood (yellow poplar, pine, cedar)

(b) Type of water repellent (solvent-based, water-based)

(c) Paint thickness (millimeters)

(d) Paint color (white, gray, light blue)

(e) Weathering time (months)

1.24   **Baseball players.** Here is a small part of a data set that describes Major League Baseball players as of opening day of the 2005 season:

Player	Team	Position	Age	Height	Weight	Salary
Ortiz, David	Red Sox	Outfielder	29	6-4	230	5,250,000
Nix, Laynce	Rangers	Outfielder	24	6-0	200	316,000
Perez, Antonio	Dodgers	Infielder	25	5-11	175	320,500
Piazza, Mike	Mets	Catcher	36	6-3	215	16,071,429
Rolen, Scott	Cardinals	Infielder	30	6-4	240	10,715,509

(a) What individuals does this data set describe?

(b) In addition to the player's name, how many variables does the data set contain? Which of these variables are categorical and which are quantitative?

(c) Based on the data in the table, what do you think are the units of measurement for each of the quantitative variables?

1.25 **Car colors in Europe.** Exercise 1.3 (page 10) gives data on the most popular colors for luxury cars made in North America. Here are similar data for luxury cars made in Europe:[13]

Color	Percent
Black	30
Silver	24
Gray	19
Blue	14
Green	3
White, pearl	3

What percent of European luxury cars have other colors? Make a graph of these data. What are the most important differences between color preferences in Europe and North America?

1.26 **Deaths among young people.** The number of deaths among persons aged 15 to 24 years in the United States in 2003 due to the leading causes of death for this age group were accidents, 14,966; homicide, 5148; suicide, 3921; cancer, 1628; heart disease, 1083; congenital defects, 425.[14]

(a) Make a bar graph to display these data.

(b) What additional information do you need to make a pie chart?

1.27 **Hispanic origins.** Figure 1.12 is a pie chart prepared by the Census Bureau to show the origin of the 35.3 million Hispanics in the United States, according to the 2000 census.[15] About what percent of Hispanics are Mexican? Puerto Rican? You see that it is hard to determine numbers from a pie chart. Bar graphs are much easier to use.

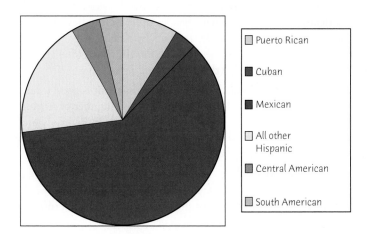

FIGURE 1.12 Pie chart of the national origins of Hispanic residents of the United States, for Exercise 1.27.

1.28   The audience for movies. Here are data on the percent of people in several age groups who attended a movie in the past 12 months:[16]

Age group	Movie attendance
18 to 24 years	83%
25 to 34 years	73%
35 to 44 years	68%
45 to 54 years	60%
55 to 64 years	47%
65 to 74 years	32%
75 years and over	20%

(a) Display these data in a bar graph. What is the main feature of the data?

(b) Would it be correct to make a pie chart of these data? Why?

(c) A movie studio wants to know what percent of the total audience for movies is 18 to 24 years old. Explain why these data do not answer this question.

1.29   Spam. Email spam is the curse of the Internet. Here is a compilation of the most common types of spam:[17]

Type of spam	Percent
Adult	14.5
Financial	16.2
Health	7.3
Leisure	7.8
Products	21.0
Scams	14.2

Pareto chart

Make two bar graphs of these percents, one with bars ordered as in the table (alphabetically) and the other with bars in order from tallest to shortest. Comparisons are easier if you order the bars by height. A bar graph ordered from tallest to shortest bar is sometimes called a **Pareto chart,** after the Italian economist who recommended this procedure.

1.30   Do adolescent girls eat fruit? We all know that fruit is good for us. Many of us don't eat enough. Figure 1.13 is a histogram of the number of servings of fruit per day claimed by 74 seventeen-year-old girls in a study in Pennsylvania.[18] Describe the shape, center, and spread of this distribution. What percent of these girls ate fewer than two servings per day?

1.31   Returns on common stocks. The return on a stock is the change in its market price plus any dividend payments made. Total return is usually expressed as a percent of the beginning price. Figure 1.14 is a histogram of the

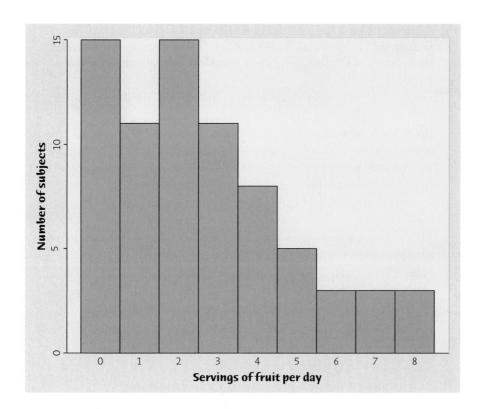

FIGURE 1.13 The distribution of fruit consumption in a sample of 74 seventeen-year-old girls, for Exercise 1.30.

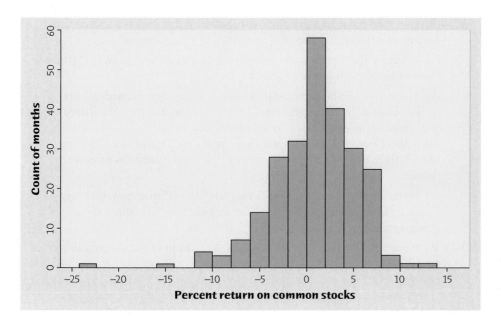

FIGURE 1.14 The distribution of monthly percent returns on U.S. common stocks from January 1985 to March 2005, for Exercise 1.31.

distribution of the monthly returns for all stocks listed on U.S. markets from January 1985 to March 2005 (243 months).[19] The extreme low outlier is the market crash of October 1987, when stocks lost 23% of their value in one month.

(a) Ignoring the outliers, describe the overall shape of the distribution of monthly returns.

(b) What is the approximate center of this distribution? (For now, take the center to be the value with roughly half the months having lower returns and half having higher returns.)

(c) Approximately what were the smallest and largest monthly returns, leaving out the outliers? (This is one way to describe the spread of the distribution.)

(d) A return less than zero means that stocks lost value in that month. About what percent of all months had returns less than zero?

1.32 **Name that variable.** A survey of a large college class asked the following questions:

1. Are you female or male? (In the data, male = 0, female = 1.)

2. Are you right-handed or left-handed? (In the data, right = 0, left = 1.)

3. What is your height in inches?

4. How many minutes do you study on a typical weeknight?

Figure 1.15 shows histograms of the student responses, in scrambled order and without scale markings. Which histogram goes with each variable? Explain your reasoning.

1.33 **Tornado damage.** The states differ greatly in the kinds of severe weather that afflict them. Table 1.3 shows the average property damage caused by tornadoes per year over the period from 1950 to 1999 in each of the 50 states and Puerto Rico.[20] (To adjust for the changing buying power of the dollar over time, all damages were restated in 1999 dollars.)

(a) What are the top five states for tornado damage? The bottom five? (Include Puerto Rico, though it is not a state.)

(b) Make a histogram of the data, by hand or using software, with classes "0 ≤ damage < 10," "10 ≤ damage < 20," and so on. Describe the shape, center, and spread of the distribution. Which states may be outliers? (To understand the outliers, note that most tornadoes in largely rural states such as Kansas cause little property damage. Damage to crops is not counted as property damage.)

(c) If you are using software, also display the "default" histogram that your software makes when you give it no instructions. How does this compare with your graph in (b)?

1.34 **Where are the doctors?** Table 1.4 gives the number of active medical doctors per 100,000 people in each state.[21]

(a) Why is the number of doctors per 100,000 people a better measure of the availability of health care than a simple count of the number of doctors in a state?

Reuters/CORBIS

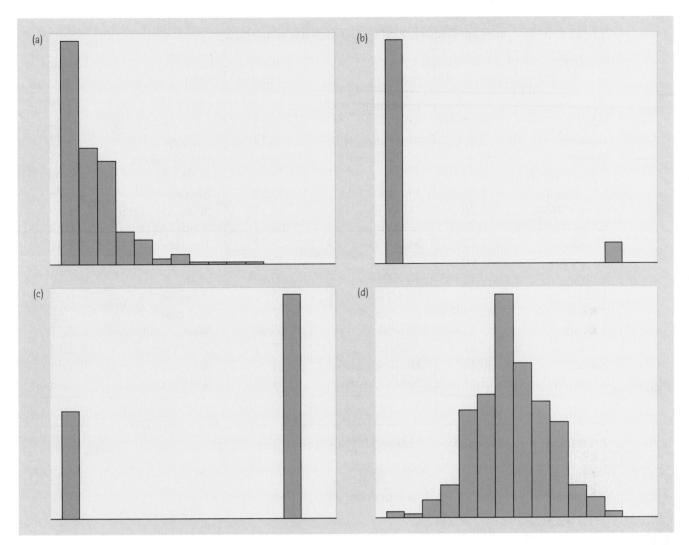

FIGURE 1.15 Histograms of four distributions, for Exercise 1.32.

(b) Make a histogram that displays the distribution of doctors per 100,000 people. Write a brief description of the distribution. Are there any outliers? If so, can you explain them?

1.35 **Carbon dioxide emissions.** Burning fuels in power plants or motor vehicles emits carbon dioxide (CO_2), which contributes to global warming. Table 1.5 displays CO_2 emissions per person from countries with populations of at least 20 million.[22]

(a) Why do you think we choose to measure emissions per person rather than total CO_2 emissions for each country?

(b) Make a stemplot to display the data of Table 1.5. Describe the shape, center, and spread of the distribution. Which countries are outliers?

TABLE 1.3   Average property damage per year due to tornadoes

State	Damage ($millions)	State	Damage ($millions)	State	Damage ($millions)
Alabama	51.88	Louisiana	27.75	Ohio	44.36
Alaska	0.00	Maine	0.53	Oklahoma	81.94
Arizona	3.47	Maryland	2.33	Oregon	5.52
Arkansas	40.96	Massachusetts	4.42	Pennsylvania	17.11
California	3.68	Michigan	29.88	Puerto Rico	0.05
Colorado	4.62	Minnesota	84.84	Rhode Island	0.09
Connecticut	2.26	Mississippi	43.62	South Carolina	17.19
Delaware	0.27	Missouri	68.93	South Dakota	10.64
Florida	37.32	Montana	2.27	Tennessee	23.47
Georgia	51.68	Nebraska	30.26	Texas	88.60
Hawaii	0.34	Nevada	0.10	Utah	3.57
Idaho	0.26	New Hampshire	0.66	Vermont	0.24
Illinois	62.94	New Jersey	2.94	Virginia	7.42
Indiana	53.13	New Mexico	1.49	Washington	2.37
Iowa	49.51	New York	15.73	West Virginia	2.14
Kansas	49.28	North Carolina	14.90	Wisconsin	31.33
Kentucky	24.84	North Dakota	14.69	Wyoming	1.78

TABLE 1.4   Medical doctors per 100,000 people, by state (2002)

State	Doctors	State	Doctors	State	Doctors
Alabama	202	Louisiana	258	Ohio	248
Alaska	194	Maine	250	Oklahoma	163
Arizona	196	Maryland	378	Oregon	242
Arkansas	194	Massachusetts	427	Pennsylvania	291
California	252	Michigan	230	Rhode Island	341
Colorado	236	Minnesota	263	South Carolina	219
Connecticut	360	Mississippi	171	South Dakota	201
Delaware	242	Missouri	233	Tennessee	250
Florida	237	Montana	215	Texas	204
Georgia	208	Nebraska	230	Utah	200
Hawaii	280	Nevada	174	Vermont	346
Idaho	161	New Hampshire	251	Virginia	253
Illinois	265	New Jersey	305	Washington	250
Indiana	207	New Mexico	222	West Virginia	221
Iowa	178	New York	385	Wisconsin	256
Kansas	210	North Carolina	241	Wyoming	176
Kentucky	219	North Dakota	228	District of Columbia	683

TABLE 1.5   Carbon dioxide emissions, metric tons per person

Country	CO_2	Country	CO_2	Country	CO_2
Algeria	2.3	Italy	7.3	Poland	8.0
Argentina	3.9	Iran	3.8	Romania	3.9
Australia	17.0	Iraq	3.6	Russia	10.2
Bangladesh	0.2	Japan	9.1	Saudi Arabia	11.0
Brazil	1.8	Kenya	0.3	South Africa	8.1
Canada	16.0	Korea, North	9.7	Spain	6.8
China	2.5	Korea, South	8.8	Sudan	0.2
Colombia	1.4	Malaysia	4.6	Tanzania	0.1
Congo	0.0	Mexico	3.7	Thailand	2.5
Egypt	1.7	Morocco	1.0	Turkey	2.8
Ethiopia	0.0	Myanmar	0.2	Ukraine	7.6
France	6.1	Nepal	0.1	United Kingdom	9.0
Germany	10.0	Nigeria	0.3	United States	19.9
Ghana	0.2	Pakistan	0.7	Uzbekistan	4.8
India	0.9	Peru	0.8	Venezuela	5.1
Indonesia	1.2	Philippines	0.9	Vietnam	0.5

1.36 **Rock sole in the Bering Sea.** "Recruitment," the addition of new members to a fish population, is an important measure of the health of ocean ecosystems. Here are data on the recruitment of rock sole in the Bering Sea from 1973 to 2000:[23]

Sarkis Images/Alamy

Year	Recruitment (millions)	Year	Recruitment (millions)	Year	Recruitment (millions)	Year	Recruitment (millions)
1973	173	1980	1411	1987	4700	1994	505
1974	234	1981	1431	1988	1702	1995	304
1975	616	1982	1250	1989	1119	1996	425
1976	344	1983	2246	1990	2407	1997	214
1977	515	1984	1793	1991	1049	1998	385
1978	576	1985	1793	1992	505	1999	445
1979	727	1986	2809	1993	998	2000	676

Make a stemplot to display the distribution of yearly rock sole recruitment. (Round to the nearest hundred and split the stems.) Describe the shape, center, and spread of the distribution and any striking deviations that you see.

1.37 **Do women study more than men?** We asked the students in a large first-year college class how many minutes they studied on a typical weeknight.

Here are the responses of random samples of 30 women and 30 men from the class:

Women					Men				
180	120	180	360	240	90	120	30	90	200
120	180	120	240	170	90	45	30	120	75
150	120	180	180	150	150	120	60	240	300
200	150	180	150	180	240	60	120	60	30
120	60	120	180	180	30	230	120	95	150
90	240	180	115	120	0	200	120	120	180

(a) Examine the data. Why are you not surprised that most responses are multiples of 10 minutes? We eliminated one student who claimed to study 30,000 minutes per night. Are there any other responses you consider suspicious?

back-to-back stemplot

(b) Make a **back-to-back stemplot** to compare the two samples. That is, use one set of stems with two sets of leaves, one to the right and one to the left of the stems. (Draw a line on either side of the stems to separate stems and leaves.) Order both sets of leaves from smallest at the stem to largest away from the stem. Report the approximate midpoints of both groups. Does it appear that women study more than men (or at least claim that they do)?

1.38   **Rock sole in the Bering Sea.**   Make a time plot of the rock sole recruitment data in Exercise 1.36. What does the time plot show that your stemplot in Exercise 1.36 did not show? When you have time series data, a time plot is often needed to understand what is happening.

1.39   **Marijuana and traffic accidents.**   Researchers in New Zealand interviewed 907 drivers at age 21. They had data on traffic accidents and they asked their subjects about marijuana use. Here are data on the numbers of accidents caused by these drivers at age 19, broken down by marijuana use at the same age:[24]

	Marijuana Use per Year			
	Never	1–10 times	11–50 times	51+ times
Drivers	452	229	70	156
Accidents caused	59	36	15	50

(a) Explain carefully why a useful graph must compare *rates* (accidents per driver) rather than *counts* of accidents in the four marijuana use classes.

(b) Make a graph that displays the accident rate for each class. What do you conclude? (You can't conclude that marijuana use *causes* accidents, because risk takers are more likely both to drive aggressively and to use marijuana.)

1.40   **Dates on coins.**   Sketch a histogram for a distribution that is skewed to the left. Suppose that you and your friends emptied your pockets of coins and recorded the year marked on each coin. The distribution of dates would be skewed to the left. Explain why.

1.41 **General Motors versus Toyota.** The J. D. Power Initial Quality Study polls more than 50,000 buyers of new motor vehicles 90 days after their purchase. A two-page questionnaire asks about "things gone wrong." Here are data on problems per 100 vehicles for vehicles made by Toyota and by General Motors in recent years. Make two time plots in the same graph to compare Toyota and GM. What are the most important conclusions you can draw from your graph?

	1998	1999	2000	2001	2002	2003	2004
GM	187	179	164	147	130	134	120
Toyota	156	134	116	115	107	115	101

1.42 **Watch those scales!** The impression that a time plot gives depends on the scales you use on the two axes. If you stretch the vertical axis and compress the time axis, change appears to be more rapid. Compressing the vertical axis and stretching the time axis make change appear slower. Make two more time plots of the college tuition data in Exercise 1.12 (page 23), one that makes tuition appear to increase very rapidly and one that shows only a gentle increase. The moral of this exercise is: pay close attention to the scales when you look at a time plot.

1.43 **Orange prices.** Figure 1.16 is a time plot of the average price of fresh oranges each month from March 1995 to March 2005.[25] The prices are "index numbers" given as percents of the average price during 1982 to 1984.

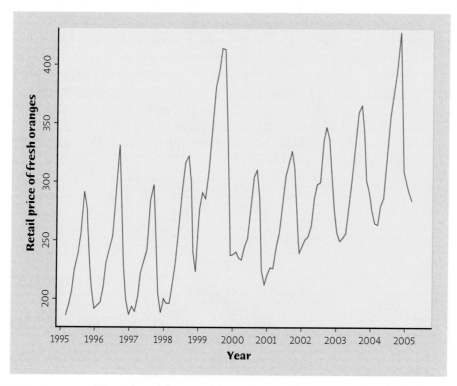

FIGURE 1.16 Time plot of the monthly retail price of fresh oranges from March 1995 to March 2005, for Exercise 1.43.

(a) The most notable pattern in this time plot is yearly cycles. At what season of the year are orange prices highest? Lowest? (To read the graph, note that the tick mark for each year is at the beginning of the year.) The cycles are explained by the time of the orange harvest in Florida.

(b) Is there a longer-term trend visible in addition to the cycles? If so, describe it.

1.44 **Alligator attacks.** Here are data on the number of unprovoked attacks by alligators on people in Florida over a 33-year period:[26]

Year	Attacks	Year	Attacks	Year	Attacks	Year	Attacks
1972	5	1981	5	1990	18	1999	15
1973	3	1982	6	1991	18	2000	23
1974	4	1983	6	1992	10	2001	17
1975	5	1984	5	1993	18	2002	14
1976	2	1985	3	1994	22	2003	6
1977	14	1986	13	1995	19	2004	11
1978	5	1987	9	1996	13		
1979	2	1988	9	1997	11		
1980	4	1989	13	1998	9		

Make two graphs of these data to illustrate why you should always make a time plot for data collected over time.

(a) Make a histogram of the counts of attacks. What is the overall shape of the distribution? What is the midpoint of the yearly counts of alligator attacks?

(b) Make a time plot. What overall pattern does your plot show? Why is the typical number of attacks from 1972 to 2004 not very useful in (say) 2006? (The main reason for the time trend is the continuing increase in Florida's population.)

1.45 **To split or not to split.** The data sets in the *One Variable Statistical Calculator* applet on the text CD and Web site include the "pulling wood apart" data from Example 1.10. The applet rounds the data in the same way as Figure 1.10 (page 21). Use the applet to make a stemplot with split stems. Do you prefer this stemplot or that in Figure 1.10? Explain your choice.

Mitchell Funk/Getty Images

Describing Distributions with Numbers

How long does it take you to get from home to work? Here are the travel times in minutes for 15 workers in North Carolina, chosen at random by the Census Bureau:[1]

30 20 10 40 25 20 10 60 15 40 5 30 12 10 10

We aren't surprised that most people estimate their travel time in multiples of 5 minutes. Here is a stemplot of these data:

```
0 | 5
1 | 000025
2 | 005
3 | 00
4 | 00
5 |
6 | 0
```

The distribution is single-peaked and right-skewed. The longest travel time (60 minutes) may be an outlier. Our goal in this chapter is to describe with numbers the center and spread of this and other distributions.

Don't hide the outliers

Data from an airliner's control surfaces, such as the vertical tail rudder, go to cockpit instruments and then to the "black box" flight data recorder. To avoid confusing the pilots, short erratic movements in the data are "smoothed" so that the instruments show overall patterns. When a crash killed 260 people, investigators suspected a catastrophic movement of the tail rudder. But the black box contained only the smoothed data. Sometimes outliers are more important than the overall pattern.

Measuring center: the mean

The most common measure of center is the ordinary arithmetic average, or *mean*.

THE MEAN $\overline{x}$

To find the **mean** of a set of observations, add their values and divide by the number of observations. If the n observations are $x_1, x_2, \ldots, x_n$, their mean is

$$\overline{x} = \frac{x_1 + x_2 + \cdots + x_n}{n}$$

or, in more compact notation,

$$\overline{x} = \frac{1}{n} \sum x_i$$

The Σ (capital Greek sigma) in the formula for the mean is short for "add them all up." The subscripts on the observations x_i are just a way of keeping the n observations distinct. They do not necessarily indicate order or any other special facts about the data. The bar over the x indicates the mean of all the x-values. Pronounce the mean $\overline{x}$ as "x-bar." This notation is very common. When writers who are discussing data use $\overline{x}$ or $\overline{y}$, they are talking about a mean.

EXAMPLE 2.1   Travel times to work

The mean travel time of our 15 North Carolina workers is

$$\overline{x} = \frac{x_1 + x_2 + \cdots + x_n}{n}$$
$$= \frac{30 + 20 + \cdots + 10}{15}$$
$$= \frac{337}{15} = 22.5 \text{ minutes}$$

In practice, you can key the data into your calculator and hit the $\overline{x}$ button. You don't have to actually add and divide. But you should know that this is what the calculator is doing.

Notice that only 6 of the 15 travel times are larger than the mean. If we leave out the longest single travel time, 60 minutes, the mean for the remaining 14 people is 19.8 minutes. That one observation raises the mean by 2.7 minutes.

Example 2.1 illustrates an important fact about the mean as a measure of center: it is sensitive to the influence of a few extreme observations. These may be outliers, but a skewed distribution that has no outliers will also pull the mean toward its long tail. Because the mean cannot resist the influence of extreme observations, *resistant measure*   we say that it is not a **resistant measure** of center.

APPLY YOUR KNOWLEDGE

2.1   **Pulling wood apart.**   Example 1.10 (page 19) gives the breaking strength in pounds of 20 pieces of Douglas fir. Find the mean breaking strength. How many of the pieces of wood have strengths less than the mean? What feature of the stemplot (Figure 1.10, page 21) explains the fact that the mean is smaller than most of the observations?

Measuring center: the median

In Chapter 1, we used the midpoint of a distribution as an informal measure of center. The *median* is the formal version of the midpoint, with a specific rule for calculation.

THE MEDIAN M

The **median M** is the midpoint of a distribution, the number such that half the observations are smaller and the other half are larger. To find the median of a distribution:

1.   Arrange all observations in order of size, from smallest to largest.

2.   If the number of observations n is odd, the median M is the center observation in the ordered list. Find the location of the median by counting $(n + 1)/2$ observations up from the bottom of the list.

3.   If the number of observations n is even, the median M is the mean of the two center observations in the ordered list. The location of the median is again $(n + 1)/2$ from the bottom of the list.

Note that the formula $(n + 1)/2$ does *not* give the median, just the location of the median in the ordered list. Medians require little arithmetic, so they are easy to find by hand for small sets of data. Arranging even a moderate number of observations in order is very tedious, however, so that finding the median by hand for larger sets of data is unpleasant. Even simple calculators have an $\bar{x}$ button, but you will need to use software or a graphing calculator to automate finding the median.

EXAMPLE 2.2   Finding the median: odd n

What is the median travel time for our 15 North Carolina workers? Here are the data arranged in order:

$$5\ 10\ 10\ 10\ 10\ 12\ 15\ \mathbf{20}\ 20\ 25\ 30\ 30\ 40\ 40\ 60$$

The count of observations $n = 15$ is odd. The bold **20** is the center observation in the ordered list, with 7 observations to its left and 7 to its right. This is the median, M = 20 minutes.

Because $n = 15$, our rule for the location of the median gives

$$\text{location of M} = \frac{n+1}{2} = \frac{16}{2} = 8$$

That is, the median is the 8th observation in the ordered list. It is faster to use this rule than to locate the center by eye.

Mitchell Funk/Getty Images

EXAMPLE 2.3   Finding the median: even *n*

Travel times to work in New York State are (on the average) longer than in North Carolina. Here are the travel times in minutes of 20 randomly chosen New York workers:

10 30 5 25 40 20 10 15 30 20 15 20 85 15 65 15 60 60 40 45

A stemplot not only displays the distribution but also makes finding the median easy because it arranges the observations in order:

```
0 | 5
1 | 0 0 5 5 5 5
2 | 0 0 0 5
3 | 0 0
4 | 0 0 5
5 |
6 | 0 0 5
7 |
8 | 5
```

The distribution is single-peaked and right-skewed, with several travel times of an hour or more. There is no center observation, but there is a center pair. These are the bold **20** and **25** in the stemplot, which have 9 observations before them in the ordered list and 9 after them. The median is midway between these two observations:

$$M = \frac{20 + 25}{2} = 22.5 \text{ minutes}$$

With $n = 20$, the rule for locating the median in the list gives

$$\text{location of M} = \frac{n+1}{2} = \frac{21}{2} = 10.5$$

The location 10.5 means "halfway between the 10th and 11th observations in the ordered list." That agrees with what we found by eye.

Comparing the mean and the median

Examples 2.1 and 2.2 illustrate an important difference between the mean and the median. The median travel time (the midpoint of the distribution) is 20 minutes. The mean travel time is higher, 22.5 minutes. The mean is pulled toward the right tail of this right-skewed distribution. The median, unlike the mean, is *resistant*. If the longest travel time were 600 minutes rather than 60 minutes, the mean would increase to more than 58 minutes but the median would not change at all. The outlier just counts as one observation above the center, no matter how far above the center it lies. The mean uses the actual value of each observation and so will chase a single large observation upward. The *Mean and Median* applet is an excellent way to compare the resistance of M and $\bar{x}$.

APPLET

COMPARING THE MEAN AND THE MEDIAN

The mean and median of a roughly symmetric distribution are close together. If the distribution is exactly symmetric, the mean and median are exactly the same. In a skewed distribution, the mean is usually farther out in the long tail than is the median.[2]

Many economic variables have distributions that are skewed to the right. For example, the median endowment of colleges and universities in 2004 was $72 million—but the mean endowment was $360 million. Most institutions have modest endowments, but a few are very wealthy. Harvard's endowment topped $22 billion. The few wealthy institutions pull the mean up but do not affect the median. Reports about incomes and other strongly skewed distributions usually give the median ("midpoint") rather than the mean ("arithmetic average"). However, a county that is about to impose a tax of 1% on the incomes of its residents cares about the mean income, not the median. The tax revenue will be 1% of total income, and the total is the mean times the number of residents. The mean and median measure center in different ways, and both are useful. *Don't confuse the "average" value of a variable (the mean) with its "typical" value, which we might describe by the median.*

APPLY YOUR KNOWLEDGE

2.2 **New York travel times.** Find the mean of the travel times to work for the 20 New York workers in Example 2.3. Compare the mean and median for these data. What general fact does your comparison illustrate?

2.3 **House prices.** The mean and median selling price of existing single-family homes sold in October 2005 were $216,200 and $265,000.[3] Which of these numbers is the mean and which is the median? Explain how you know.

2.4 **Barry Bonds.** The Major League Baseball single-season home run record is held by Barry Bonds of the San Francisco Giants, who hit 73 in 2001. Bonds played only 14 games in 2005 because of injuries, so let's look at his home run totals from 1986 (his first year) to 2004:

16 25 24 19 33 25 34 46 37 33 42 40 37 34 49 73 46 45 45

Bonds's record year is a high outlier. How do his career mean and median number of home runs change when we drop the record 73? What general fact about the mean and median does your result illustrate?

Measuring spread: the quartiles

The mean and median provide two different measures of the center of a distribution. But a measure of center alone can be misleading. The Census Bureau reports that in 2004 the median income of American households was $44,389. Half of all

Lucy Nicholson/CORBIS

households had incomes below $44,389, and half had higher incomes. The mean was higher, $60,528, because the distribution of incomes is skewed to the right. But the median and mean don't tell the whole story. The bottom 10% of households had incomes less than $10,927, and households in the top 5% took in more than $157,185.[4] We are interested in the *spread* or *variability* of incomes as well as their center. *The simplest useful numerical description of a distribution requires both a measure of center and a measure of spread.*

One way to measure spread is to give the smallest and largest observations. For example, the travel times of our 15 North Carolina workers range from 5 minutes to 60 minutes. These single observations show the full spread of the data, but they may be outliers. We can improve our description of spread by also looking at the spread of the middle half of the data. The *quartiles* mark out the middle half. Count up the ordered list of observations, starting from the smallest. The *first quartile* lies one-quarter of the way up the list. The *third quartile* lies three-quarters of the way up the list. In other words, the first quartile is larger than 25% of the observations, and the third quartile is larger than 75% of the observations. The second quartile is the median, which is larger than 50% of the observations. That is the idea of quartiles. We need a rule to make the idea exact. The rule for calculating the quartiles uses the rule for the median.

THE QUARTILES Q_1 and Q_3

To calculate the **quartiles:**

1. Arrange the observations in increasing order and locate the median M in the ordered list of observations.

2. The **first quartile Q_1** is the median of the observations whose position in the ordered list is to the left of the location of the overall median.

3. The **third quartile Q_3** is the median of the observations whose position in the ordered list is to the right of the location of the overall median.

Here are examples that show how the rules for the quartiles work for both odd and even numbers of observations.

EXAMPLE 2.4 Finding the quartiles: odd n

Our North Carolina sample of 15 workers' travel times, arranged in increasing order, is

$$5 \; 10 \; 10 \; 10 \; 10 \; 12 \; 15 \; \mathbf{20} \; 20 \; 25 \; 30 \; 30 \; 40 \; 40 \; 60$$

There is an odd number of observations, so the median is the middle one, the bold **20** in the list. The first quartile is the median of the 7 observations to the left of the median. This is the 4th of these 7 observations, so $Q_1 = 10$ minutes. If you want, you can use the rule for the location of the median with $n = 7$:

$$\text{location of } Q_1 = \frac{n+1}{2} = \frac{7+1}{2} = 4$$

The third quartile is the median of the 7 observations to the right of the median, $Q_3 = 30$ minutes. *When there is an odd number of observations, leave the overall median out of the calculation of the quartiles.*

The quartiles are resistant. For example, Q_3 would still be 30 if the outlier were 600 rather than 60.

— **EXAMPLE 2.5** Finding the quartiles: even *n* ——————

Here are the travel times to work of the 20 New Yorkers from Example 2.3, arranged in increasing order:

  5 10 10 15 15 15 15 20 20 20 | 25 30 30 40 40 45 60 60 65 85

There is an even number of observations, so the median lies midway between the middle pair, the 10th and 11th in the list. Its value is $M = 22.5$ minutes. We have marked the location of the median by |. The first quartile is the median of the first 10 observations, because these are the observations to the left of the location of the median. Check that $Q_1 = 15$ minutes and $Q_3 = 42.5$ minutes. *When the number of observations is even, use all the observations in calculating the quartiles.*

Be careful when, as in these examples, several observations take the same numerical value. Write down all of the observations and apply the rules just as if they all had distinct values.

The five-number summary and boxplots

The smallest and largest observations tell us little about the distribution as a whole, but they give information about the tails of the distribution that is missing if we know only Q_1, M, and Q_3. To get a quick summary of both center and spread, combine all five numbers.

THE FIVE-NUMBER SUMMARY

The **five-number summary** of a distribution consists of the smallest observation, the first quartile, the median, the third quartile, and the largest observation, written in order from smallest to largest. In symbols, the five-number summary is

  Minimum Q_1 M Q_3 Maximum

These five numbers offer a reasonably complete description of center and spread. The five-number summaries of travel times to work from Examples 2.4 and 2.5 are

North Carolina	5	10	20	30	60
New York	5	15	22.5	42.5	85

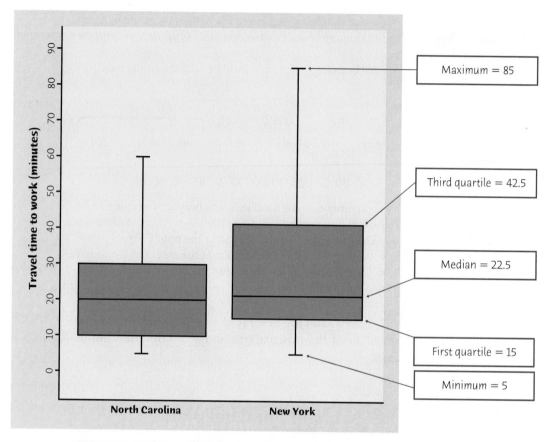

FIGURE 2.1 Boxplots comparing the travel times to work of samples of workers in North Carolina and New York.

The five-number summary of a distribution leads to a new graph, the *boxplot*. Figure 2.1 shows boxplots comparing travel times to work in North Carolina and in New York.

BOXPLOT

A **boxplot** is a graph of the five-number summary.

- A central box spans the quartiles Q_1 and Q_3.
- A line in the box marks the median M.
- Lines extend from the box out to the smallest and largest observations.

Because boxplots show less detail than histograms or stemplots, they are best used for side-by-side comparison of more than one distribution, as in Figure 2.1. Be sure to include a numerical scale in the graph. When you look at a boxplot, first locate the median, which marks the center of the distribution. Then look at the spread. The height of the box shows the spread of the middle half of the data, and the extremes (the smallest and largest observations) show the spread of the entire data set. We see from Figure 2.1 that travel times to work are in general a bit longer in New York than in North Carolina. The median, both quartiles, and the maximum are all larger in New York. New York travel times are also more variable, as shown by the height of the box and the spread between the extremes.

Finally, the New York data are more strongly right-skewed. In a symmetric distribution, the first and third quartiles are equally distant from the median. In most distributions that are skewed to the right, on the other hand, the third quartile will be farther above the median than the first quartile is below it. The extremes behave the same way, but remember that they are just single observations and may say little about the distribution as a whole.

APPLY YOUR KNOWLEDGE

2.5   **Pulling wood apart.**   Example 1.10 (page 19) gives the breaking strengths of 20 pieces of Douglas fir.

(a) Give the five-number summary of the distribution of breaking strengths. (The stemplot, Figure 1.10, helps because it arranges the data in order, but you should use the unrounded values in numerical work.)

(b) The stemplot shows that the distribution is skewed to the left. Does the five-number summary show the skew? Remember that only a graph gives a clear picture of the shape of a distribution.

2.6   **Comparing investments.**   Should you put your money into a fund that buys stocks or a fund that invests in real estate? The answer changes from time to time, and unfortunately we can't look into the future. Looking back into the past, the boxplots in Figure 2.2 compare the daily returns (in percent) on a "total stock market" fund and a real estate fund over 14 months ending in May 2005.[5]

(a) Read the graph: about what were the highest and lowest daily returns on the stock fund?

(b) Read the graph: the median return was about the same on both investments. About what was the median return?

(c) What is the most important difference between the two distributions?

Spotting suspected outliers*

Look again at the stemplot of travel times to work in New York in Example 2.3. The five-number summary for this distribution is

$$5 \quad 15 \quad 22.5 \quad 42.5 \quad 85$$

How shall we describe the spread of this distribution? The smallest and largest observations are extremes that don't describe the spread of the majority of the

---

*This short section is optional.

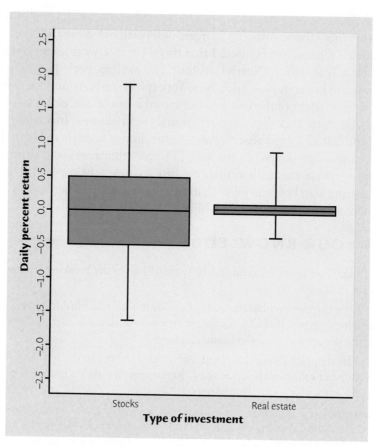

FIGURE 2.2 Boxplots comparing the distributions of daily returns on two kinds of investment, for Exercise 2.6.

data. The distance between the quartiles (the range of the center half of the data) is a more resistant measure of spread. This distance is called the *interquartile range*.

THE INTERQUARTILE RANGE *IQR*

The **interquartile range *IQR*** is the distance between the first and third quartiles:

$$IQR = Q_3 - Q_1$$

For our data on New York travel times, $IQR = 42.5 - 15 = 27.5$ minutes. However, *no single numerical measure of spread, such as IQR, is very useful for describing skewed distributions*. The two sides of a skewed distribution have different spreads, so one number can't summarize them. The interquartile range is mainly used as the basis for a rule of thumb for identifying suspected outliers.

> ### THE 1.5 × IQR RULE FOR OUTLIERS
>
> Call an observation a suspected outlier if it falls more than $1.5 \times IQR$ above the third quartile or below the first quartile.

EXAMPLE 2.6 Using the 1.5 × IQR rule

For the New York travel time data, $IQR = 27.5$ and

$$1.5 \times IQR = 1.5 \times 27.5 = 41.25$$

Any values not falling between

$$Q_1 - (1.5 \times IQR) = 15.0 - 41.25 = -26.25 \quad \text{and}$$
$$Q_3 + (1.5 \times IQR) = 42.5 + 41.25 = 83.75$$

are flagged as suspected outliers. Look again at the stemplot in Example 2.3: the only suspected outlier is the longest travel time, 85 minutes. The $1.5 \times IQR$ rule suggests that the three next-longest travel times (60 and 65 minutes) are just part of the long right tail of this skewed distribution.

The $1.5 \times IQR$ rule is not a replacement for looking at the data. It is most useful when large volumes of data are scanned automatically.

APPLY YOUR KNOWLEDGE

2.7 **Travel time to work.** In Example 2.1, we noted the influence of one long travel time of 60 minutes in our sample of 15 North Carolina workers. Does the $1.5 \times IQR$ rule identify this travel time as a suspected outlier?

2.8 **Older Americans.** The stemplot in Exercise 1.19 (page 25) displays the distribution of the percents of residents aged 65 and older in the 50 states. Stemplots help you find the five-number summary because they arrange the observations in increasing order.

(a) Give the five-number summary of this distribution.

(b) Does the $1.5 \times IQR$ rule identify Alaska and Florida as suspected outliers? Does it also flag any other states?

Measuring spread: the standard deviation

The five-number summary is not the most common numerical description of a distribution. That distinction belongs to the combination of the mean to measure center and the *standard deviation* to measure spread. The standard deviation and its close relative, the *variance*, measure spread by looking at how far the observations are from their mean.

How much is that house worth?

The town of Manhattan, Kansas, is sometimes called "the little Apple" to distinguish it from that other Manhattan. A few years ago, a house there appeared in the county appraiser's records valued at $200,059,000. That would be quite a house even on Manhattan Island. As you might guess, the entry was wrong: the true value was $59,500. But before the error was discovered, the county, the city, and the school board had based their budgets on the total appraised value of real estate, which the one outlier jacked up by 6.5%. It can pay to spot outliers before you trust your data.

THE STANDARD DEVIATION s

The **variance s²** of a set of observations is an average of the squares of the deviations of the observations from their mean. In symbols, the variance of n observations $x_1, x_2, \ldots, x_n$ is

$$s^2 = \frac{(x_1 - \overline{x})^2 + (x_2 - \overline{x})^2 + \cdots + (x_n - \overline{x})^2}{n - 1}$$

or, more compactly,

$$s^2 = \frac{1}{n - 1} \sum (x_i - \overline{x})^2$$

The **standard deviation s** is the square root of the variance s^2:

$$s = \sqrt{\frac{1}{n - 1} \sum (x_i - \overline{x})^2}$$

In practice, use software or your calculator to obtain the standard deviation from keyed-in data. Doing an example step-by-step will help you understand how the variance and standard deviation work, however.

Tom Tracy Photography/Alamy

EXAMPLE 2.7   *Calculating the standard deviation*

A person's metabolic rate is the rate at which the body consumes energy. Metabolic rate is important in studies of weight gain, dieting, and exercise. Here are the metabolic rates of 7 men who took part in a study of dieting. The units are calories per 24 hours. These are the same calories used to describe the energy content of foods.

1792   1666   1362   1614   1460   1867   1439

The researchers reported $\overline{x}$ and s for these men. First find the mean:

$$\overline{x} = \frac{1792 + 1666 + 1362 + 1614 + 1460 + 1867 + 1439}{7}$$

$$= \frac{11{,}200}{7} = 1600 \text{ calories}$$

Figure 2.3 displays the data as points above the number line, with their mean marked by an asterisk (∗). The arrows mark two of the deviations from the mean. These deviations show how spread out the data are about their mean. They are the starting point for calculating the variance and the standard deviation.

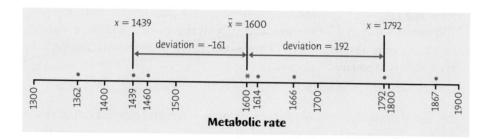

FIGURE 2.3 Metabolic rates for 7 men, with their mean (∗) and the deviations of two observations from the mean.

Observations x_i	Deviations $x_i - \bar{x}$	Squared deviations $(x_i - \bar{x})^2$
1792	$1792 - 1600 = 192$	$192^2 = 36{,}864$
1666	$1666 - 1600 = 66$	$66^2 = 4{,}356$
1362	$1362 - 1600 = -238$	$(-238)^2 = 56{,}644$
1614	$1614 - 1600 = 14$	$14^2 = 196$
1460	$1460 - 1600 = -140$	$(-140)^2 = 19{,}600$
1867	$1867 - 1600 = 267$	$267^2 = 71{,}289$
1439	$1439 - 1600 = -161$	$(-161)^2 = 25{,}921$
	sum $= 0$	sum $= 214{,}870$

The variance is the sum of the squared deviations divided by one less than the number of observations:

$$s^2 = \frac{214,870}{6} = 35{,}811.67$$

The standard deviation is the square root of the variance:

$$s = \sqrt{35{,}811.67} = 189.24 \text{ calories}$$

Notice that the "average" in the variance s^2 divides the sum by one fewer than the number of observations, that is, $n - 1$ rather than n. The reason is that the deviations $x_i - \bar{x}$ always sum to exactly 0, so that knowing $n - 1$ of them determines the last one. Only $n - 1$ of the squared deviations can vary freely, and we average by dividing the total by $n - 1$. The number $n - 1$ is called the **degrees of freedom** of the variance or standard deviation. Some calculators offer a choice between dividing by n and dividing by $n - 1$, so be sure to use $n - 1$.

degrees of freedom

More important than the details of hand calculation are the properties that determine the usefulness of the standard deviation:

- s measures *spread about the mean* and should be used only when the mean is chosen as the measure of center.

- s is *always zero or greater than zero*. $s = 0$ only when there is no spread. This happens only when all observations have the same value. Otherwise, $s > 0$. As the observations become more spread out about their mean, s gets larger.

- s has the *same units of measurement as the original observations*. For example, if you measure metabolic rates in calories, both the mean $\bar{x}$ and the standard deviation s are also in calories. This is one reason to prefer s to the variance s^2, which is in squared calories.

- Like the mean $\bar{x}$, s is *not resistant*. A few outliers can make s very large.

The use of squared deviations renders s even more sensitive than $\bar{x}$ to a few extreme observations. For example, the standard deviation of the travel times for the 15 North Carolina workers in Example 2.1 is 15.23 minutes. (Use your calculator to verify this.) If we omit the high outlier, the standard deviation drops to 11.56 minutes.

If you feel that the importance of the standard deviation is not yet clear, you are right. We will see in Chapter 3 that the standard deviation is the natural measure of spread for a very important class of symmetric distributions, the Normal distributions. The usefulness of many statistical procedures is tied to distributions of particular shapes. This is certainly true of the standard deviation.

Choosing measures of center and spread

We now have a choice between two descriptions of the center and spread of a distribution: the five-number summary, or $\bar{x}$ and s. Because $\bar{x}$ and s are sensitive to extreme observations, they can be misleading when a distribution is strongly skewed or has outliers. In fact, because the two sides of a skewed distribution have different spreads, no single number such as s describes the spread well. The five-number summary, with its two quartiles and two extremes, does a better job.

CHOOSING A SUMMARY

The five-number summary is usually better than the mean and standard deviation for describing a skewed distribution or a distribution with strong outliers. Use $\bar{x}$ and s only for reasonably symmetric distributions that are free of outliers.

Remember that a graph gives the best overall picture of a distribution. Numerical measures of center and spread report specific facts about a distribution, but they do not describe its entire shape. Numerical summaries do not disclose the presence of multiple peaks or clusters, for example. Exercise 2.10 shows how misleading numerical summaries can be. **Always plot your data.**

APPLY YOUR KNOWLEDGE ⎯⎯⎯⎯⎯

2.9   **Blood phosphate.**   The level of various substances in the blood influences our health. Here are measurements of the level of phosphate in the blood of a patient, in milligrams of phosphate per deciliter of blood, made on 6 consecutive visits to a clinic:

5.6   5.2   4.6   4.9   5.7   6.4

A graph of only 6 observations gives little information, so we proceed to compute the mean and standard deviation.

(a) Find the mean step-by-step. That is, find the sum of the 6 observations and divide by 6.

(b) Find the standard deviation step-by-step. That is, find the deviations of each observation from the mean, square the deviations, then obtain the variance and the standard deviation. Example 2.7 shows the method.

(c) Now enter the data into your calculator and use the mean and standard deviation buttons to obtain $\bar{x}$ and s. Do the results agree with your hand calculations?

2.10 $\bar{x}$ and s are not enough. The mean $\bar{x}$ and standard deviation s measure center and spread but are not a complete description of a distribution. Data sets with different shapes can have the same mean and standard deviation. To demonstrate this fact, use your calculator to find $\bar{x}$ and s for these two small data sets. Then make a stemplot of each and comment on the shape of each distribution.

Data A	9.14	8.14	8.74	8.77	9.26	8.10	6.13	3.10	9.13	7.26	4.74
Data B	6.58	5.76	7.71	8.84	8.47	7.04	5.25	5.56	7.91	6.89	12.50

2.11 Choose a summary. The shape of a distribution is a rough guide to whether the mean and standard deviation are a helpful summary of center and spread. For which of these distributions would $\bar{x}$ and s be useful? In each case, give a reason for your decision.

(a) Percents of college graduates in the states, Figure 1.5 (page 15).

(b) Iowa Test scores, Figure 1.6 (page 17).

(c) Breaking strength of wood, Figure 1.10 (page 21).

Using technology

Although a calculator with "two-variable statistics" functions will do the basic calculations we need, more elaborate tools are helpful. Graphing calculators and computer software will do calculations and make graphs as you command, freeing you to concentrate on choosing the right methods and interpreting your results. Figure 2.4 displays output describing the travel times to work of 20 people in New York State (Example 2.3). Can you find $\bar{x}$, s, and the five-number summary in each output? The big message of this section is: *Once you know what to look for, you can read output from any technological tool.*

The displays in Figure 2.4 come from the TI-83 (or TI-84) graphing calculator, two statistical programs, and the Microsoft Excel spreadsheet program. The statistical programs are CrunchIt! and Minitab. The statistical programs allow you to choose what descriptive measures you want. Excel and the TI calculators give some things we don't need. Just ignore the extras. Excel's "Descriptive Statistics" menu item doesn't give the quartiles. We used the spreadsheet's separate quartile function to get Q_1 and Q_3.

Texas Instruments TI-83

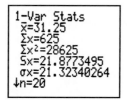

CrunchIt!

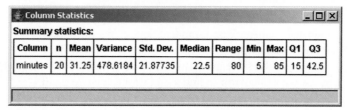

Minitab

Descriptive Statistics: NYtime

	Total								
variable	Count	Mean	StDev	Variance	Minimum	Q1	Median	Q3	Maximum
NYtime	20	31.25	21.88	478.62	5.00	15.00	22.50	43.75	85.00

Microsoft Excel

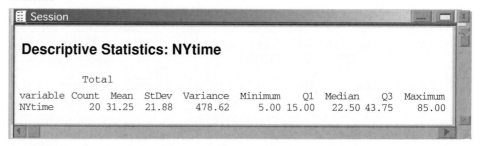

FIGURE 2.4 Output from a graphing calculator and three software packages describing the data on travel times to work in New York State.

EXAMPLE 2.8   What is the third quartile?

In Example 2.5, we saw that the quartiles of the New York travel times are $Q_1 = 15$ and $Q_3 = 42.5$. Look at the output displays in Figure 2.4. The TI-83, CrunchIt!, and Excel agree with our work. Minitab says that $Q_3 = 43.75$. What happened? *There are several rules for finding the quartiles. Some software packages use rules that give results different from ours for some sets of data.* This is true of Minitab and also of Excel, though Excel agrees with our work in this example. Our rule is simplest for hand computation. Results from the various rules are always close to each other, so *to describe data you should just use the answer your technology gives you.*

Organizing a statistical problem

Most of our examples and exercises have aimed to help you learn basic tools (graphs and calculations) for describing and comparing distributions. You have also learned principles that guide use of these tools, such as "always start with a graph" and "look for the overall pattern and striking deviations from the pattern." The data you work with are not just numbers. They describe specific settings such as water depth in the Everglades or travel time to work. Because data come from a specific setting, the final step in examining data is a conclusion for that setting. Water depth in the Everglades has a yearly cycle that reflects Florida's wet and dry seasons. Travel times to work are generally longer in New York than in North Carolina.

As you learn more statistical tools and principles, you will face more complex statistical problems. Although no framework accommodates all the varied issues that arise in applying statistics to real settings, the following four-step thought process gives useful guidance. In particular, the first and last steps emphasize that statistical problems are tied to specific real-world settings and therefore involve more than doing calculations and making graphs.

ORGANIZING A STATISTICAL PROBLEM: A FOUR-STEP PROCESS

STATE: What is the practical question, in the context of the real-world setting?

FORMULATE: What specific statistical operations does this problem call for?

SOLVE: Make the graphs and carry out the calculations needed for this problem.

CONCLUDE: Give your practical conclusion in the setting of the real-world problem.

To help you master the basics, many exercises will continue to tell you what to do—make a histogram, find the five-number summary, and so on. Real statistical problems don't come with detailed instructions. From now on, especially in the later chapters of the book, you will meet some exercises that are more realistic. Use the four-step process as a guide to solving and reporting these problems. They are marked with the four-step icon, as Example 2.9 illustrates.

STEP

EXAMPLE 2.9   *Comparing tropical flowers*

STATE: Ethan Temeles of Amherst College, with his colleague W. John Kress, studied the relationship between varieties of the tropical flower *Heliconia* on the island of Dominica and the different species of hummingbirds that fertilize the flowers.[6] Over time, the researchers believe, the lengths of the flowers and the form of the hummingbirds' beaks have evolved to match each other. If that is true, flower varieties fertilized by different hummingbird species should have distinct distributions of length.

Table 2.1 gives length measurements (in millimeters) for samples of three varieties of *Heliconia*, each fertilized by a different species of hummingbird. Do the three varieties display distinct distributions of length? How do the mean lengths compare?

Art Wolfe/Getty Images

TABLE 2.1	Flower lengths (millimeters) for three *Heliconia* varieties						
H. bihai							
47.12	46.75	46.81	47.12	46.67	47.43	46.44	46.64
48.07	48.34	48.15	50.26	50.12	46.34	46.94	48.36
H. caribaea red							
41.90	42.01	41.93	43.09	41.47	41.69	39.78	40.57
39.63	42.18	40.66	37.87	39.16	37.40	38.20	38.07
38.10	37.97	38.79	38.23	38.87	37.78	38.01	
H. caribaea yellow							
36.78	37.02	36.52	36.11	36.03	35.45	38.13	37.10
35.17	36.82	36.66	35.68	36.03	34.57	34.63	

FORMULATE: Use graphs and numerical descriptions to describe and compare these three distributions of flower length.

SOLVE: We might use boxplots to compare the distributions, but stemplots preserve more detail and work well for data sets of these sizes. Figure 2.5 displays stemplots with the stems lined up for easy comparison. The lengths have been rounded to the nearest tenth of a millimeter. The *bihai* and red varieties have somewhat skewed distributions, so we might choose to compare the five-number summaries. But because the researchers plan to use $\bar{x}$ and s for further analysis, we instead calculate these measures:

Variety	Mean length	Standard deviation
bihai	47.60	1.213
red	39.71	1.799
yellow	36.18	0.975

CONCLUDE: The three varieties differ so much in flower length that there is little overlap among them. In particular, the flowers of *bihai* are longer than either red or

```
       bihai                  red                    yellow
  34 |                   34 |                    34 | 6 6
  35 |                   35 |                    35 | 2 5 7
  36 |                   36 |                    36 | 0 0 1 5 7 8 8
  37 |                   37 | 4 8 9              37 | 0 1
  38 |                   38 | 0 0 1 1 2 2 8 9    38 | 1
  39 |                   39 | 2 6 8              39 |
  40 |                   40 | 6 7                40 |
  41 |                   41 | 5 7 9 9            41 |
  42 |                   42 | 0 2                42 |
  43 |                   43 | 1                  43 |
  44 |                   44 |                    44 |
  45 |                   45 |                    45 |
  46 | 3 4 6 7 8 8 9     46 |                    46 |
  47 | 1 1 4             47 |                    47 |
  48 | 1 2 3 4           48 |                    48 |
  49 |                   49 |                    49 |
  50 | 1 3               50 |                    50 |
```

FIGURE 2.5 Stemplots comparing the distributions of flower lengths from Table 2.1. The stems are whole millimeters and the leaves are tenths of a millimeter.

yellow. The mean lengths are 47.6 mm for *H. bihai*, 39.7 mm for *H. caribaea* red, and 36.2 mm for *H. caribaea* yellow.

APPLY YOUR KNOWLEDGE

2.12 **Logging in the rain forest.** "Conservationists have despaired over destruction of tropical rain forest by logging, clearing, and burning." These words begin a report on a statistical study of the effects of logging in Borneo.[7] Researchers compared forest plots that had never been logged (Group 1) with similar plots nearby that had been logged 1 year earlier (Group 2) and 8 years earlier (Group 3). All plots were 0.1 hectare in area. Here are the counts of trees for plots in each group:

```
Group 1:   27   22   29   21   19   33   16   20   24   27   28   19
Group 2:   12   12   15    9   20   18   17   14   14    2   17   19
Group 3:   18    4   22   15   18   19   22   12   12
```

To what extent has logging affected the count of trees? Follow the four-step process in reporting your work.

CHAPTER 2 SUMMARY

A numerical summary of a distribution should report at least its **center** and its **spread** or **variability.**

The **mean** $\bar{x}$ and the **median M** describe the center of a distribution in different ways. The mean is the arithmetic average of the observations, and the median is the midpoint of the values.

Digital Vision/Getty Images

When you use the median to indicate the center of the distribution, describe its spread by giving the **quartiles**. The **first quartile Q_1** has one-fourth of the observations below it, and the **third quartile Q_3** has three-fourths of the observations below it.

The **five-number summary** consisting of the median, the quartiles, and the smallest and largest individual observations provides a quick overall description of a distribution. The median describes the center, and the quartiles and extremes show the spread.

Boxplots based on the five-number summary are useful for comparing several distributions. The box spans the quartiles and shows the spread of the central half of the distribution. The median is marked within the box. Lines extend from the box to the extremes and show the full spread of the data.

The **variance s^2** and especially its square root, the **standard deviation s**, are common measures of spread about the mean as center. The standard deviation s is zero when there is no spread and gets larger as the spread increases.

A **resistant measure** of any aspect of a distribution is relatively unaffected by changes in the numerical value of a small proportion of the total number of observations, no matter how large these changes are. The median and quartiles are resistant, but the mean and the standard deviation are not.

The mean and standard deviation are good descriptions for symmetric distributions without outliers. They are most useful for the Normal distributions introduced in the next chapter. The five-number summary is a better description for skewed distributions.

Numerical summaries do not fully describe the shape of a distribution. Always plot your data.

A statistical problem has a real-world setting. You can organize many problems using the four steps **state, formulate, solve,** and **conclude.**

CHECK YOUR SKILLS

2.13 Here are the IQ test scores of 10 randomly chosen fifth-grade students:

> 145   139   126   122   125   130   96   110   118   118

The mean of these scores is
(a) 122.9. (b) 123.4. (c) 136.6.

2.14 The median of the 10 IQ test scores in Exercise 2.13 is
(a) 125. (b) 123.5. (c) 122.9.

2.15 The five-number summary of the 10 IQ scores in Exercise 2.13 is
(a) 96, 114, 125, 134.5, 145.
(b) 96, 118, 122.9, 130, 145.
(c) 96, 118, 123.5, 130, 145.

2.16   If a distribution is skewed to the right,

(a) the mean is less than the median.

(b) the mean and median are equal.

(c) the mean is greater than the median.

2.17   What percent of the observations in a distribution lie between the first quartile and the third quartile?

(a) 25%   (b) 50%   (c) 75%

2.18   To make a boxplot of a distribution, you must know

(a) all of the individual observations.

(b) the mean and the standard deviation.

(c) the five-number summary.

2.19   The standard deviation of the 10 IQ scores in Exercise 2.13 (use your calculator) is

(a) 13.23.   (b) 13.95.   (c) 194.6.

2.20   What are all the values that a standard deviation s can possibly take?

(a) $0 \leq s$ (b) $0 \leq s \leq 1$ (c) $-1 \leq s \leq 1$

2.21   You have data on the weights in grams of 5 baby pythons. The mean weight is 31.8 and the standard deviation of the weights is 2.39. The correct units for the standard deviation are

(a) no units—it's just a number.

(b) grams.

(c) grams squared.

2.22   Which of the following is least affected if an extreme high outlier is added to your data?

(a) The median

(b) The mean

(c) The standard deviation

CHAPTER 2 EXERCISES

2.23   **Incomes of college grads.** The Census Bureau reports that the mean and median income of people at least 25 years old who had a bachelor's degree but no higher degree were $42,087 and $53,581 in 2004. Which of these numbers is the mean and which is the median? Explain your reasoning.

2.24   **Assets of young households.** A report on the assets of American households says that the median net worth of households headed by someone younger than age 35 is $11,600. The mean net worth of these same young households is $90,700.[8] What explains the difference between these two measures of center?

2.25   **Where are the doctors?** Table 1.4 (page 32) gives the number of medical doctors per 100,000 people in each state. Exercise 1.34 asked you to plot the data. The distribution is right-skewed with several high outliers.

(a) Do you expect the mean to be greater than the median, about equal to the median, or less than the median? Why? Calculate $\bar{x}$ and M and verify your expectation.

(b) The District of Columbia, at 683 doctors per 100,000 residents, is a high outlier. If you remove D.C. because it is a city rather than a state, do you expect $\bar{x}$ or M to change more? Why? Omitting D.C., calculate both measures for the 50 states and verify your expectation.

2.26 **Making resistance visible.** In the *Mean and Median* applet, place three observations on the line by clicking below it: two close together near the center of the line, and one somewhat to the right of these two.

(a) Pull the single rightmost observation out to the right. (Place the cursor on the point, hold down a mouse button, and drag the point.) How does the mean behave? How does the median behave? Explain briefly why each measure acts as it does.

(b) Now drag the single rightmost point to the left as far as you can. What happens to the mean? What happens to the median as you drag this point past the other two (watch carefully)?

2.27 **Comparing tropical flowers.** An alternative presentation of the flower length data in Table 2.1 reports the five-number summary and uses boxplots to display the distributions. Do this. Do the boxplots fail to reveal any important information visible in the stemplots in Figure 2.5?

2.28 **University endowments.** The National Association of College and University Business Officers collects data on college endowments. In 2004, 741 colleges and universities reported the value of their endowments. When the endowment values are arranged in order, what are the positions of the median and the quartiles in this ordered list?

2.29 **How much fruit do adolescent girls eat?** Figure 1.13 (page 29) is a histogram of the number of servings of fruit per day claimed by 74 seventeen-year-old girls. With a little care, you can find the median and the quartiles from the histogram. What are these numbers? How did you find them?

2.30 **Weight of newborns.** Here is the distribution of the weight at birth for all babies born in the United States in 2002:[9]

Weight	Count	Weight	Count
Less than 500 grams	6,268	3,000 to 3,499 grams	1,521,884
500 to 999 grams	22,845	3,500 to 3,999 grams	1,125,959
1,000 to 1,499 grams	29,431	4,000 to 4,499 grams	314,182
1,500 to 1,999 grams	61,652	4,500 to 4,999 grams	48,606
2,000 to 2,499 grams	193,881	5,000 to 5,499 grams	5,396
2,500 to 2,999 grams	688,630		

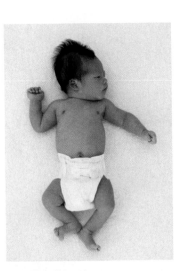

Photodisc Red/Getty Images

(a) For comparison with other years and with other countries, we prefer a histogram of the *percents* in each weight class rather than the counts. Explain why.

(b) How many babies were there? Make a histogram of the distribution, using percents on the vertical scale.

(c) What are the positions of the median and quartiles in the ordered list of all birth weights? In which weight classes do the median and quartiles fall?

TABLE 2.2		Positions and weights (pounds) for a major college football team											
QB	208	QB	195	QB	209	RB	185	RB	221	RB	221	RB	211
RB	206	RB	193	RB	235	RB	220	OL	308	OL	298	OL	285
OL	281	OL	286	OL	275	OL	293	OL	283	OL	337	OL	284
OL	325	OL	334	OL	325	OL	310	OL	290	OL	291	OL	254
WR	185	WR	183	WR	174	WR	162	WR	154	WR	188	WR	182
WR	215	WR	210	TE	224	TE	247	TE	215	KP	207	KP	192
KP	205	KP	179	KP	182	KP	207	KP	201	DB	193	DB	184
DB	177	DB	198	DB	185	DB	188	DB	188	DB	201	DB	181
DB	195	DB	187	LB	220	LB	230	LB	237	LB	237	LB	208
LB	220	LB	222	LB	199	DL	240	DL	286	DL	240	DL	232
DL	230	DL	270	DL	300	DL	246	DL	264	DL	267	DL	285
DL	263	DL	301										

2.31 More on study times. In Exercise 1.37 you examined the nightly study time claimed by first-year college men and women. The most common methods for formal comparison of two groups use $\overline{x}$ and s to summarize the data.

(a) What kinds of distributions are best summarized by $\overline{x}$ and s?

(b) One student in each group claimed to study at least 300 minutes (five hours) per night. How much does removing these observations change $\overline{x}$ and s for each group?

2.32 Behavior of the median. Place five observations on the line in the *Mean and Median* applet by clicking below it.

(a) Add one additional observation *without changing the median*. Where is your new point?

(b) Use the applet to convince yourself that when you add yet another observation (there are now seven in all), the median does not change no matter where you put the seventh point. Explain why this must be true.

2.33 A football team. The University of Miami Hurricanes have been among the more successful teams in college football. Table 2.2 gives the weights in pounds and the positions of the players on the 2005 team.[10] The positions are quarterback (QB), running back (RB), offensive line (OL), wide receiver (WR), tight end (TE), kicker/punter (KP), defensive back (DB), linebacker (LB), and defensive line (DL).

(a) Make boxplots of the weights for running backs, wide receivers, offensive linemen, defensive linemen, linebackers, and defensive backs.

(b) Briefly compare the weight distributions. Which position has the heaviest players overall? Which has the lightest?

(c) Are any individual players outliers within their position?

2.34 Guinea pig survival times. Listed on the next page are the survival times in days of 72 guinea pigs after they were injected with infectious bacteria in a medical experiment.[11] Survival times, whether of machines under stress or cancer patients after treatment, usually have distributions that are skewed to the right.

Jason Arnold/CORBIS

Dorling Kindersley/Getty Images

43	45	53	56	56	57	58	66	67	73	74	79
80	80	81	81	81	82	83	83	84	88	89	91
91	92	92	97	99	99	100	100	101	102	102	102
103	104	107	108	109	113	114	118	121	123	126	128
137	138	139	144	145	147	156	162	174	178	179	184
191	198	211	214	243	249	329	380	403	511	522	598

(a) Graph the distribution and describe its main features. Does it show the expected right skew?

(b) Which numerical summary would you choose for these data? Calculate your chosen summary. How does it reflect the skewness of the distribution?

2.35 **Never on Sunday: also in Canada?** Exercise 1.4 (page 10) gives the number of births in the United States on each day of the week during an entire year. The boxplots in Figure 2.6 are based on more detailed data from Toronto, Canada: the number of births on each of the 365 days in a year, grouped by day of the week.[12] Based on these plots, give a more detailed description of how births depend on the day of the week.

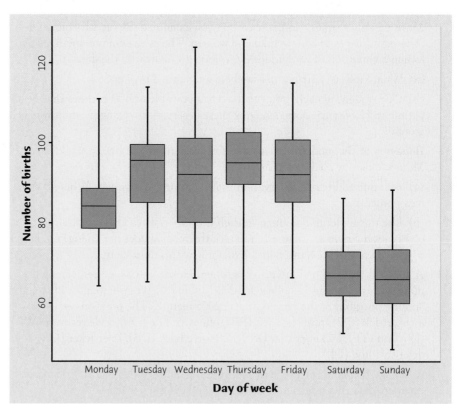

FIGURE 2.6 Boxplots of the distributions of numbers of births in Toronto, Canada, on each day of the week during a year, for Exercise 2.35.

2.36 **Does breast-feeding weaken bones?** Breast-feeding mothers secrete calcium into their milk. Some of the calcium may come from their bones, so mothers may lose bone mineral. Researchers compared 47 breast-feeding women with 22 women of similar age who were neither pregnant nor lactating. They measured the percent change in the mineral content of the women's spines over three months. Here are the data:[13]

Breast-feeding women						Other women					
−4.7	−2.5	−4.9	−2.7	−0.8	−5.3	2.4	0.0	0.9	−0.2	1.0	1.7
−8.3	−2.1	−6.8	−4.3	2.2	−7.8	2.9	−0.6	1.1	−0.1	−0.4	0.3
−3.1	−1.0	−6.5	−1.8	−5.2	−5.7	1.2	−1.6	−0.1	−1.5	0.7	−0.4
−7.0	−2.2	−6.5	−1.0	−3.0	−3.6	2.2	−0.4	−2.2	−0.1		
−5.2	−2.0	−2.1	−5.6	−4.4	−3.3						
−4.0	−4.9	−4.7	−3.8	−5.9	−2.5						
−0.3	−6.2	−6.8	1.7	0.3	−2.3						
0.4	−5.3	0.2	−2.2	−5.1							

Do the data show distinctly greater bone mineral loss among the breast-feeding women? Follow the four-step process illustrated by Example 2.9.

2.37 **Compressing soil.** Farmers know that driving heavy equipment on wet soil compresses the soil and injures future crops. Table 2.3 gives data on the "penetrability" of the same soil at three levels of compression.[14] Penetrability is a measure of the resistance plant roots meet when they grow through the soil. Low penetrability means high resistance. How does increasing compression affect penetrability? Follow the four-step process in your work.

TABLE 2.3	**Penetrability of soil at three compression levels**	
	Soil Compression Level	
Compressed	Intermediate	Loose
2.86	3.14	3.99
2.68	3.38	4.20
2.92	3.10	3.94
2.82	3.40	4.16
2.76	3.38	4.29
2.81	3.14	4.19
2.78	3.18	4.13
3.08	3.26	4.41
2.94	2.96	3.98
2.86	3.02	4.41
3.08	3.54	4.11
2.82	3.36	4.30
2.78	3.18	3.96
2.98	3.12	4.03
3.00	3.86	4.89
2.78	2.92	4.12
2.96	3.46	4.00
2.90	3.44	4.34
3.18	3.62	4.27
3.16	4.26	4.91

Player	Salary	Player	Salary	Player	Salary
TABLE 2.4		2005 salaries for the Boston Red Sox baseball team			
Player	Salary	Player	Salary	Player	Salary
Manny Ramirez	$19,806,820	Tim Wakefield	$4,670,000	Doug Mirabelli	$1,500,000
Curt Schilling	14,500,000	David Wells	4,075,000	Wade Miller	1,500,000
Johnny Damon	8,250,000	Jay Payton	3,500,000	John Halama	850,000
Edgar Renteria	8,000,000	Kevin Millar	3,500,000	Matt Mantei	750,000
Jason Varitek	8,000,000	Alan Embree	3,000,000	Ramon Vazquez	700,000
Trot Nixon	7,500,000	Mike Timlin	2,750,000	Mike Myers	600,000
Keith Foulke	7,500,000	Mark Bellhorn	2,750,000	Kevin Youkilis	323,125
Matt Clement	6,500,000	Bill Mueller	2,500,000	Adam Stern	316,000
David Ortiz	5,250,000	Bronson Arroyo	1,850,000		

Brian Snyder/CORBIS

2.38 **Athletes' salaries.** In 2004, the Boston Red Sox won the World Series for the first time in 86 years. Table 2.4 gives the salaries of the Red Sox players as of opening day of the 2005 season. Describe the distribution of salaries both with a graph and with a numerical summary. Then write a brief description of the important features of the distribution.

2.39 **Returns on stocks.** How well have stocks done over the past generation? The Standard & Poor's 500 stock index describes the average performance of the stocks of 500 leading companies. Because the average is weighted by the total market value of each company's stock, the index emphasizes larger companies. Here are the real (that is, adjusted for the changing buying power of the dollar) returns on the S&P 500 for the years 1972 to 2004:

Year	Return	Year	Return	Year	Return
1972	15.070	1983	18.075	1994	−1.316
1973	−21.522	1984	2.253	1995	34.167
1974	−34.540	1985	26.896	1996	19.008
1975	28.353	1986	17.390	1997	31.138
1976	18.177	1987	0.783	1998	26.534
1977	−12.992	1988	11.677	1999	17.881
1978	−2.264	1989	25.821	2000	−12.082
1979	4.682	1990	−8.679	2001	−13.230
1980	17.797	1991	26.594	2002	−23.909
1981	−12.710	1992	4.584	2003	26.311
1982	17.033	1993	7.127	2004	7.370

What can you say about the distribution of real returns on stocks? Follow the four-step process in your answer.

2.40 **A standard deviation contest.** This is a standard deviation contest. You must choose four numbers from the whole numbers 0 to 10, with repeats allowed.

(a) Choose four numbers that have the smallest possible standard deviation.

(b) Choose four numbers that have the largest possible standard deviation.

(c) Is more than one choice possible in either (a) or (b)? Explain.

2.41 **Test your technology.** This exercise requires a calculator with a standard deviation button or statistical software on a computer. The observations

$$10{,}001 \quad 10{,}002 \quad 10{,}003$$

have mean $\bar{x} = 10{,}002$ and standard deviation $s = 1$. Adding a 0 in the center of each number, the next set becomes

$$100{,}001 \quad 100{,}002 \quad 100{,}003$$

The standard deviation remains $s = 1$ as more 0s are added. Use your calculator or software to find the standard deviation of these numbers, adding extra 0s until you get an incorrect answer. How soon did you go wrong? This demonstrates that calculators and software cannot handle an arbitrary number of digits correctly.

2.42 **You create the data.** Create a set of 5 positive numbers (repeats allowed) that have median 10 and mean 7. What thought process did you use to create your numbers?

2.43 **You create the data.** Give an example of a small set of data for which the mean is larger than the third quartile.

Exercises 2.44 to 2.47 make use of the optional material on the $1.5 \times IQR$ rule for suspected outliers.

2.44 **Tornado damage.** Table 1.3 (page 32) shows the average property damage caused by tornadoes over a 50-year period in each of the states and Puerto Rico. The distribution is strongly skewed to the right.

(a) Give the five-number summary. Explain why you can see from these five numbers that the distribution is right-skewed.

(b) Your histogram from Exercise 1.33 suggests that a few states are outliers. Show that there are *no* suspected outliers according to the $1.5 \times IQR$ rule. You see once again that a rule is not a substitute for plotting your data.

(c) Find the mean property damage. Explain why the mean and median differ so greatly for this distribution.

2.45 **Carbon dioxide emissions.** Table 1.5 (page 33) gives carbon dioxide (CO_2) emissions per person for countries with population at least 20 million. A stemplot or histogram shows that the distribution is strongly skewed to the right. The United States and several other countries appear to be high outliers.

(a) Give the five-number summary. Explain why this summary suggests that the distribution is right-skewed.

(b) Which countries are outliers according to the $1.5 \times IQR$ rule? Make a stemplot of the data or look at your stemplot from Exercise 1.35. Do you agree with the rule's suggestions about which countries are and are not outliers?

2.46 **Athletes' salaries.** Which members of the Boston Red Sox (Table 2.4) have salaries that are suspected outliers by the $1.5 \times IQR$ rule?

2.47 **Returns on stocks.** The returns on stocks in Exercise 2.39 vary a lot: they range from a loss of more than 34% to a gain of more than 34%. Are any of these years suspected outliers by the $1.5 \times IQR$ rule?

Stone/Getty Images

The Normal Distributions

We now have a kit of graphical and numerical tools for describing distributions. What is more, we have a clear strategy for exploring data on a single quantitative variable.

EXPLORING A DISTRIBUTION

1. Always plot your data: make a graph, usually a histogram or a stemplot.
2. Look for the overall pattern (shape, center, spread) and for striking deviations such as outliers.
3. Calculate a numerical summary to briefly describe center and spread.

In this chapter, we add one more step to this strategy:

4. Sometimes the overall pattern of a large number of observations is so regular that we can describe it by a smooth curve.

Density curves

Figure 3.1 is a histogram of the scores of all 947 seventh-grade students in Gary, Indiana, on the vocabulary part of the Iowa Test of Basic Skills.[1] Scores of many students on this national test have a quite regular distribution. The histogram is

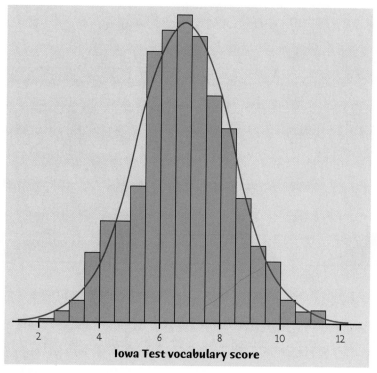

FIGURE 3.1 Histogram of the vocabulary scores of all seventh-grade students in Gary, Indiana. The smooth curve shows the overall shape of the distribution.

symmetric, and both tails fall off smoothly from a single center peak. There are no large gaps or obvious outliers. The smooth curve drawn through the tops of the histogram bars in Figure 3.1 is a good description of the overall pattern of the data.

EXAMPLE 3.1   From histogram to density curve

Our eyes respond to the *areas* of the bars in a histogram. The bar areas represent proportions of the observations. Figure 3.2(a) is a copy of Figure 3.1 with the leftmost bars shaded. The area of the shaded bars in Figure 3.2(a) represents the students with vocabulary scores 6.0 or lower. There are 287 such students, who make up the proportion $287/947 = 0.303$ of all Gary seventh-graders.

Now look at the curve drawn through the bars. In Figure 3.2(b), the area under the curve to the left of 6.0 is shaded. We can draw histogram bars taller or shorter by adjusting the vertical scale. In moving from histogram bars to a smooth curve, we make a specific choice: adjust the scale of the graph so that *the total area under the curve is exactly 1*. The total area represents the proportion 1, that is, all the observations. We can then interpret areas under the curve as proportions of the observations. The curve is now a *density curve*. The shaded area under the density curve in Figure 3.2(b) represents the proportion of students with score 6.0 or lower. This area is 0.293, only 0.010 away from the actual proportion 0.303. Areas under the density curve give quite good approximations to the actual distribution of the 947 test scores.

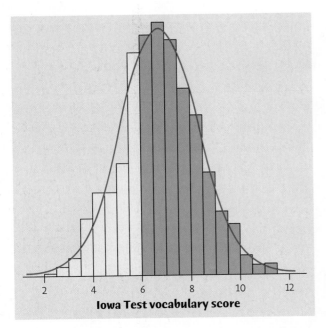

FIGURE 3.2(a) The proportion of scores less than or equal to 6.0 from the histogram is 0.303.

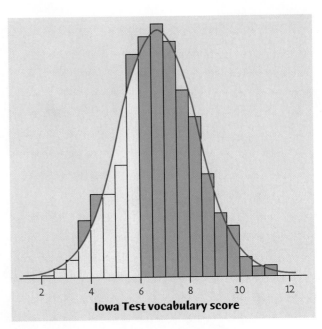

FIGURE 3.2(b) The proportion of scores less than or equal to 6.0 from the density curve is 0.293.

DENSITY CURVE

A **density curve** is a curve that

- is always on or above the horizontal axis, and
- has area exactly 1 underneath it.

A density curve describes the overall pattern of a distribution. The area under the curve and above any range of values is the proportion of all observations that fall in that range.

Density curves, like distributions, come in many shapes. Figure 3.3 shows a strongly skewed distribution, the survival times of guinea pigs from Exercise 2.34 (page 59). The histogram and density curve were both created from the data by software. Both show the overall shape and the "bumps" in the long right tail. The density curve shows a higher single peak as a main feature of the distribution. The histogram divides the observations near the peak between two bars, thus reducing the height of the peak. A density curve is often a good description of the overall pattern of a distribution. Outliers, which are deviations from the overall pattern, are not described by the curve. *Of course, no set of real data is exactly described by a density curve. The curve is an idealized description that is easy to use and accurate enough for practical use.*

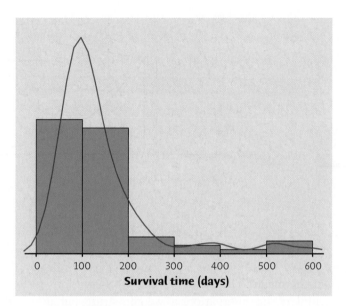

FIGURE 3.3 A right-skewed distribution pictured by both a histogram and a density curve.

APPLY YOUR KNOWLEDGE ────────────────

3.1   Sketch density curves.   Sketch density curves that describe distributions with the following shapes:

(a) Symmetric, but with two peaks (that is, two strong clusters of observations).

(b) Single peak and skewed to the left.

Describing density curves

Our measures of center and spread apply to density curves as well as to actual sets of observations. The median and quartiles are easy. Areas under a density curve represent proportions of the total number of observations. The median is the point with half the observations on either side. So *the median of a density curve is the equal-areas point,* the point with half the area under the curve to its left and the remaining half of the area to its right. The quartiles divide the area under the curve into quarters. One-fourth of the area under the curve is to the left of the first quartile, and three-fourths of the area is to the left of the third quartile. You can roughly locate the median and quartiles of any density curve by eye by dividing the area under the curve into four equal parts.

Because density curves are idealized patterns, a symmetric density curve is exactly symmetric. The median of a symmetric density curve is therefore at its center. Figure 3.4(a) shows a symmetric density curve with the median marked. It isn't so easy to spot the equal-areas point on a skewed curve. There are mathematical ways of finding the median for any density curve. That's how we marked the median on the skewed curve in Figure 3.4(b).

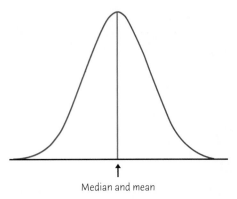

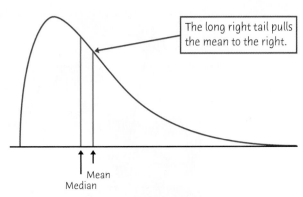

FIGURE 3.4(a) The median and mean of a symmetric density curve both lie at the center of symmetry.

FIGURE 3.4(b) The median and mean of a right-skewed density curve. The mean is pulled away from the median toward the long tail.

What about the mean? The mean of a set of observations is their arithmetic average. If we think of the observations as weights strung out along a thin rod, the mean is the point at which the rod would balance. This fact is also true of density curves. *The mean is the point at which the curve would balance if made of solid material.* Figure 3.5 illustrates this fact about the mean. A symmetric curve balances at its center because the two sides are identical. *The mean and median of a symmetric density curve are equal,* as in Figure 3.4(a). We know that the mean of a skewed distribution is pulled toward the long tail. Figure 3.4(b) shows how the mean of a skewed density curve is pulled toward the long tail more than is the median. It's hard to locate the balance point by eye on a skewed curve. There are mathematical ways of calculating the mean for any density curve, so we are able to mark the mean as well as the median in Figure 3.4(b).

MEDIAN AND MEAN OF A DENSITY CURVE

The **median** of a density curve is the equal-areas point, the point that divides the area under the curve in half.

The **mean** of a density curve is the balance point, at which the curve would balance if made of solid material.

The median and mean are the same for a symmetric density curve. They both lie at the center of the curve. The mean of a skewed curve is pulled away from the median in the direction of the long tail.

FIGURE 3.5 The mean is the balance point of a density curve.

We can roughly locate the mean, median, and quartiles of any density curve by eye. This is not true of the standard deviation. When necessary, we can once again call on more advanced mathematics to learn the value of the standard deviation. The study of mathematical methods for doing calculations with density curves is part of theoretical statistics. Though we are concentrating on statistical practice, we often make use of the results of mathematical study.

Because a density curve is an idealized description of a distribution of data, we need to distinguish between the mean and standard deviation of the density curve and the mean $\bar{x}$ and standard deviation s computed from the actual observations. The usual notation for the **mean of a density curve** is μ (the Greek letter mu). We write the **standard deviation of a density curve** as σ (the Greek letter sigma).

mean μ

standard deviation σ

APPLY YOUR KNOWLEDGE

3.2 **A uniform distribution.** Figure 3.6 displays the density curve of a *uniform distribution*. The curve takes the constant value 1 over the interval from 0 to 1 and is zero outside that range of values. This means that data described by this distribution take values that are uniformly spread between 0 and 1. Use areas under this density curve to answer the following questions.

(a) Why is the total area under this curve equal to 1?

(b) What percent of the observations lie above 0.8?

(c) What percent of the observations lie below 0.6?

(d) What percent of the observations lie between 0.25 and 0.75?

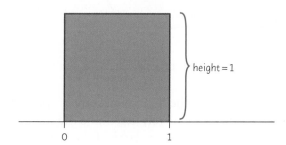

FIGURE 3.6 The density curve of a uniform distribution, for Exercises 3.2 and 3.3.

3.3 **Mean and median.** What is the mean μ of the density curve pictured in Figure 3.6? What is the median?

3.4 **Mean and median.** Figure 3.7 displays three density curves, each with three points marked on them. At which of these points on each curve do the mean and the median fall?

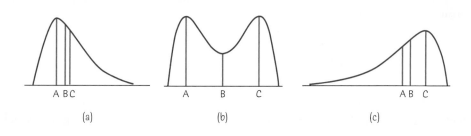

FIGURE 3.7 Three density curves, for Exercise 3.4.

Normal distributions

One particularly important class of density curves has already appeared in Figures 3.1 and 3.2. These density curves are symmetric, single-peaked, and bell-shaped. They are called *Normal curves*, and they describe *Normal distributions*. Normal distributions play a large role in statistics, but they are rather special and not at all "normal" in the sense of being usual or average. We capitalize Normal to remind you that these curves are special. All Normal distributions have the same overall shape. *The exact density curve for a particular Normal distribution is described by giving its mean μ and its standard deviation σ.* The mean is located at the center of the symmetric curve and is the same as the median. Changing μ without changing σ moves the Normal curve along the horizontal axis without changing its spread. The standard deviation σ controls the spread of a Normal curve. Figure 3.8 shows two Normal curves with different values of σ. The curve with the larger standard deviation is more spread out.

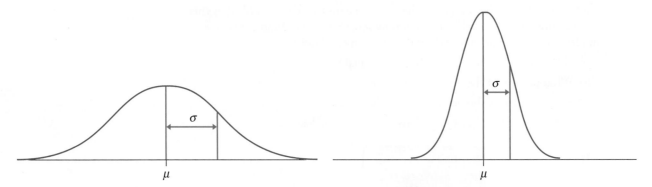

FIGURE 3.8 Two Normal curves, showing the mean μ and standard deviation σ.

The standard deviation σ is the natural measure of spread for Normal distributions. Not only do μ and σ completely determine the shape of a Normal curve, but we can locate σ by eye on the curve. Here's how. Imagine that you are skiing down a mountain that has the shape of a Normal curve. At first, you descend at an ever-steeper angle as you go out from the peak:

Fortunately, before you find yourself going straight down, the slope begins to grow flatter rather than steeper as you go out and down:

The points at which this change of curvature takes place are located at distance σ on either side of the mean μ. You can feel the change as you run a pencil along a Normal curve, and so find the standard deviation. Remember that μ and σ *alone do not specify the shape of most distributions*, and that the shape of density curves in general does not reveal σ. These are special properties of Normal distributions.

NORMAL DISTRIBUTIONS

A **Normal distribution** is described by a Normal density curve. Any particular Normal distribution is completely specified by two numbers, its mean and standard deviation.

The mean of a Normal distribution is at the center of the symmetric Normal curve. The standard deviation is the distance from the center to the change-of-curvature points on either side.

Why are the Normal distributions important in statistics? Here are three reasons. First, Normal distributions are good descriptions for some distributions of *real data*. Distributions that are often close to Normal include scores on tests taken by many people (such as Iowa Tests and SAT exams), repeated careful measurements of the same quantity, and characteristics of biological populations (such as lengths of crickets and yields of corn). Second, Normal distributions are good approximations to the results of many kinds of *chance outcomes*, such as the proportion of heads in many tosses of a coin. Third, we will see that many *statistical inference* procedures based on Normal distributions work well for other roughly symmetric distributions. However, many sets of data do not follow a Normal distribution. Most income distributions, for example, are skewed to the right and so are not Normal. Non-Normal data, like nonnormal people, not only are common but are sometimes more interesting than their Normal counterparts.

The 68-95-99.7 rule

Although there are many Normal curves, they all have common properties. In particular, all Normal distributions obey the following rule.

THE 68-95-99.7 RULE

In the Normal distribution with mean μ and standard deviation σ:

- Approximately **68%** of the observations fall within σ of the mean μ.
- Approximately **95%** of the observations fall within 2σ of μ.
- Approximately **99.7%** of the observations fall within 3σ of μ.

Figure 3.9 illustrates the 68–95–99.7 rule. By remembering these three numbers, you can think about Normal distributions without constantly making detailed calculations.

FIGURE 3.9 The
68–95–99.7 rule for Normal
distributions.

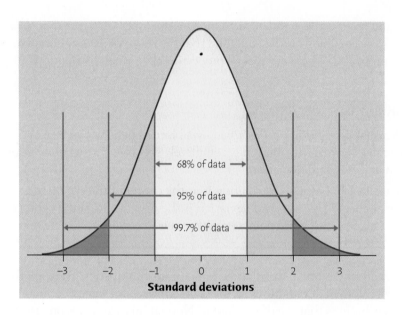

- EXAMPLE 3.2   Iowa Test scores

Figures 3.1 and 3.2 show that the distribution of Iowa Test vocabulary scores for seventh-grade students in Gary, Indiana, is close to Normal. Suppose that the distribution is exactly Normal with mean $\mu = 6.84$ and standard deviation $\sigma = 1.55$. (These are the mean and standard deviation of the 947 actual scores.)

Figure 3.10 applies the 68–95–99.7 rule to Iowa Test scores. The 95 part of the rule says that 95% of all scores are between

$$\mu - 2\sigma = 6.84 - (2)(1.55) = 6.84 - 3.10 = 3.74$$

and

$$\mu + 2\sigma = 6.84 + (2)(1.55) = 6.84 + 3.10 = 9.94$$

The other 5% of scores are outside this range. Because Normal distributions are symmetric, half these scores are lower than 3.74 and half are higher than 9.94. That is, 2.5% of the scores are below 3.74 and 2.5% are above 9.94.

The 68–95–99.7 rule describes distributions that are exactly Normal. Real data such as the actual Gary scores are never exactly Normal. For one thing, Iowa Test scores are reported only to the nearest tenth. A score can be 9.9 or 10.0, but not 9.94. We use a Normal distribution because it's a good approximation, and because we think the knowledge that the test measures is continuous rather than stopping at tenths.

How well does our work in Example 3.2 describe the actual Iowa Test scores? Well, 900 of the 947 scores are between 3.74 and 9.94. That's 95.04%, very accurate indeed. Of the remaining 47 scores, 20 are below 3.74 and 27 are above 9.94. The tails of the actual data are not quite equal, as they would be in an exactly Normal distribution. Normal distributions often describe real data better in the center of the distribution than in the extreme high and low tails.

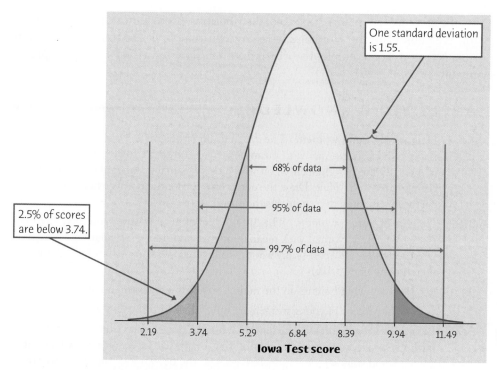

One standard deviation is 1.55.

68% of data

95% of data

2.5% of scores are below 3.74.

99.7% of data

2.19   3.74   5.29   6.84   8.39   9.94   11.49

Iowa Test score

FIGURE 3.10 The 68–95–99.7 rule applied to the distribution of Iowa Test scores in Gary, Indiana, with $\mu = 6.84$ and $\sigma = 1.55$.

EXAMPLE 3.3 Iowa Test scores

Look again at Figure 3.10. A score of 5.29 is one standard deviation below the mean. What percent of scores are higher than 5.29? Find the answer by adding areas in the figure. Here is the calculation in pictures:

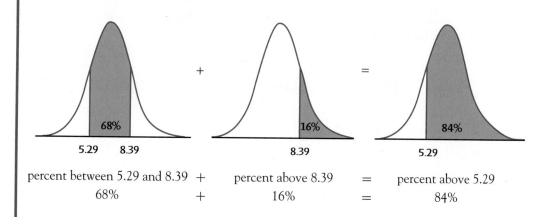

percent between 5.29 and 8.39 +   percent above 8.39   =   percent above 5.29
            68%   +   16%   =   84%

Be sure you see where the 16% came from: 32% of scores are outside the range 5.29 to 8.39, and half of these are above 8.39.

Because we will mention Normal distributions often, a short notation is helpful. We abbreviate the Normal distribution with mean μ and standard deviation σ as $N(\mu, \sigma)$. For example, the distribution of Gary Iowa Test scores is approximately $N(6.84, 1.55)$.

APPLY YOUR KNOWLEDGE

3.5 Heights of young women. The distribution of heights of women aged 20 to 29 is approximately Normal with mean 64 inches and standard deviation 2.7 inches.[2] Draw a Normal curve on which this mean and standard deviation are correctly located. (*Hint:* Draw the curve first, locate the points where the curvature changes, then mark the horizontal axis.)

3.6 Heights of young women. The distribution of heights of women aged 20 to 29 is approximately Normal with mean 64 inches and standard deviation 2.7 inches. Use the 68–95–99.7 rule to answer the following questions. (Start by making a sketch like Figure 3.10.)

(a) Between what heights do the middle 95% of young women fall?

(b) What percent of young women are taller than 61.3 inches?

3.7 Length of pregnancies. The length of human pregnancies from conception to birth varies according to a distribution that is approximately Normal with mean 266 days and standard deviation 16 days. Use the 68–95–99.7 rule to answer the following questions.

(a) Between what values do the lengths of almost all (99.7%) pregnancies fall?

(b) How short are the shortest 2.5% of all pregnancies?

Jim McGuire/Index Stock Imagery/
Picture Quest

The standard Normal distribution

As the 68–95–99.7 rule suggests, all Normal distributions share many common properties. In fact, all Normal distributions are the same if we measure in units of size σ about the mean μ as center. Changing to these units is called *standardizing*. To standardize a value, subtract the mean of the distribution and then divide by the standard deviation.

STANDARDIZING AND z-SCORES

If x is an observation from a distribution that has mean μ and standard deviation σ, the **standardized value** of x is

$$z = \frac{x - \mu}{\sigma}$$

A standardized value is often called a **z-score.**

A z-score tells us how many standard deviations the original observation falls away from the mean, and in which direction. Observations larger than the mean are positive when standardized, and observations smaller than the mean are negative.

EXAMPLE 3.4 *Standardizing women's heights*

The heights of young women are approximately Normal with $\mu = 64$ inches and $\sigma = 2.7$ inches. The standardized height is

$$z = \frac{\text{height} - 64}{2.7}$$

A woman's standardized height is the number of standard deviations by which her height differs from the mean height of all young women. A woman 70 inches tall, for example, has standardized height

$$z = \frac{70 - 64}{2.7} = 2.22$$

or 2.22 standard deviations above the mean. Similarly, a woman 5 feet (60 inches) tall has standardized height

$$z = \frac{60 - 64}{2.7} = -1.48$$

or 1.48 standard deviations less than the mean height.

He said, she said.

The height and weight distributions in this chapter come from actual measurements by a government survey. Good thing that is. When *asked* their weight, almost all women say they weigh less than they really do. Heavier men also underreport their weight—but lighter men claim to weigh more than the scale shows. We leave you to ponder the psychology of the two sexes. Just remember that "say so" is no substitute for measuring.

We often standardize observations from symmetric distributions to express them in a common scale. We might, for example, compare the heights of two children of different ages by calculating their z-scores. The standardized heights tell us where each child stands in the distribution for his or her age group.

If the variable we standardize has a Normal distribution, standardizing does more than give a common scale. It makes all Normal distributions into a single distribution, and this distribution is still Normal. Standardizing a variable that has any Normal distribution produces a new variable that has the *standard Normal distribution*.

STANDARD NORMAL DISTRIBUTION

The **standard Normal distribution** is the Normal distribution $N(0, 1)$ with mean 0 and standard deviation 1.

If a variable x has any Normal distribution $N(\mu, \sigma)$ with mean μ and standard deviation σ, then the standardized variable

$$z = \frac{x - \mu}{\sigma}$$

has the standard Normal distribution.

APPLY YOUR KNOWLEDGE

3.8 **SAT versus ACT.** Eleanor scores 680 on the mathematics part of the SAT. The distribution of SAT math scores in recent years has been Normal with mean 518

Spencer Grant/PhotoEdit

and standard deviation 114. Gerald takes the ACT Assessment mathematics test and scores 27. ACT math scores are Normally distributed with mean 20.7 and standard deviation 5.0. Find the standardized scores for both students. Assuming that both tests measure the same kind of ability, who has the higher score?

3.9   **Men's and women's heights.**   The heights of women aged 20 to 29 are approximately Normal with mean 64 inches and standard deviation 2.7 inches. Men the same age have mean height 69.3 inches with standard deviation 2.8 inches. What are the z-scores for a woman 6 feet tall and a man 6 feet tall? Say in simple language what information the z-scores give that the actual heights do not.

Finding Normal proportions

Areas under a Normal curve represent proportions of observations from that Normal distribution. There is no formula for areas under a Normal curve. Calculations use either software that calculates areas or a table of areas. The table and most software calculate one kind of area, *cumulative proportions*.

CUMULATIVE PROPORTIONS

The **cumulative proportion** for a value x in a distribution is the proportion of observations in the distribution that lie at or below x.

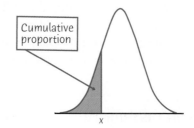

The key to calculating Normal proportions is to match the area you want with areas that represent cumulative proportions. If you make a sketch of the area you want, you will almost never go wrong. Find areas for cumulative proportions either from software or (with an extra step) from a table. The following example shows the method in a picture.

EXAMPLE 3.5   Who qualifies for college sports?

The National Collegiate Athletic Association (NCAA) requires Division I athletes to score at least 820 on the combined mathematics and verbal parts of the SAT exam in order to compete in their first college year. (Higher scores are required for students with poor high school grades.) The scores of the millions of high school seniors taking the SATs in recent years are approximately Normal with mean 1026 and standard deviation 209. What percent of high school seniors qualify for Division I college sports?

Here is the calculation in a picture: the proportion of scores above 820 is the area under the curve to the right of 820. That's the total area under the curve (which is always 1) minus the cumulative proportion up to 820.

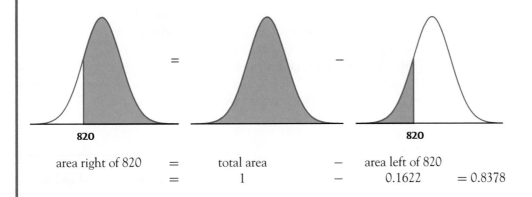

area right of 820	=	total area	−	area left of 820	
	=	1	−	0.1622	= 0.8378

About 84% of all high school seniors meet the NCAA requirement to compete in Division I college sports.

There is *no* area under a smooth curve and exactly over the point 820. Consequently, the area to the right of 820 (the proportion of scores > 820) is the same as the area at or to the right of this point (the proportion of scores ≥ 820). The actual data may contain a student who scored exactly 820 on the SAT. That the proportion of scores exactly equal to 820 is 0 for a Normal distribution is a consequence of the idealized smoothing of Normal distributions for data.

To find the numerical value 0.1622 of the cumulative proportion in Example 3.5 using software, plug in mean 1026 and standard deviation 209 and ask for the cumulative proportion for 820. Software often uses terms such as "cumulative distribution" or "cumulative probability." We will learn in Chapter 10 why the language of probability fits. Here, for example, is Minitab's output:

```
Session                                              _ □ x

Cumulative Distribution Function

Normal with mean = 1026 and standard deviation = 209

   x   P ( X <= x )
 820      0.162153
```

The *P* in the output stands for "probability," but we can read it as "proportion of the observations." CrunchIt! and the *Normal Curve* applet are even handier because they draw pictures as well as finding areas. If you are not using software, you can find cumulative proportions for Normal curves from a table. That requires an extra step.

Using the standard Normal table*

The extra step in finding cumulative proportions from a table is that we must first standardize to express the problem in the standard scale of z-scores. This allows us to get by with just one table, a table of *standard Normal cumulative proportions*. Table A in the back of the book gives cumulative proportions for the standard Normal distribution. The pictures at the top of the table remind us that the entries are cumulative proportions, areas under the curve to the left of a value z.

EXAMPLE 3.6 The standard Normal table

What proportion of observations on a standard Normal variable z take values less than 1.47?

Solution: To find the area to the left of 1.47, locate 1.4 in the left-hand column of Table A, then locate the remaining digit 7 as .07 in the top row. The entry opposite 1.4 and under .07 is 0.9292. This is the cumulative proportion we seek. Figure 3.11 illustrates this area.

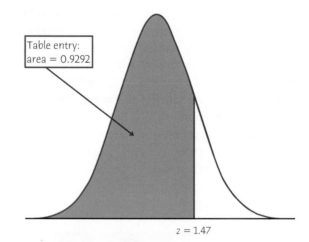

FIGURE 3.11 The area under a standard Normal curve to the left of the point $z = 1.47$ is 0.9292. Table A gives areas under the standard Normal curve.

Now that you see how Table A works, let's redo Example 3.5 using the table. We can break Normal calculations using the table into three steps.

---

*This section is unnecessary if you will always use software for Normal distribution calculations.

EXAMPLE 3.7   Who qualifies for college sports?

Scores of high school seniors on the SAT exam follow the Normal distribution with mean $\mu = 1026$ and standard deviation $\sigma = 209$. What percent of seniors score at least 820?

1. *Draw a picture.* The picture is exactly as in Example 3.5.
2. *Standardize.* Call the SAT score x. Subtract the mean, then divide by the standard deviation, to transform the problem about x into a problem about a standard Normal z:

$$x \geq 820$$
$$\frac{x - 1026}{209} \geq \frac{820 - 1026}{209}$$
$$z \geq -0.99$$

3. *Use the table.* The picture says that we want the cumulative proportion for $x = 820$. Step 2 says this is the same as the cumulative proportion for $z = -0.99$. The Table A entry for $z = -0.99$ says that this cumulative proportion is 0.1611. The area to the right of -0.99 is therefore $1 - 0.1611 = 0.8389$.

The area from the table in Example 3.7 (0.8389) is slightly less accurate than the area from software in Example 3.5 (0.8378) because we must round z to two decimal places when we use Table A. The difference is rarely important in practice. Here's the method in outline form.

USING TABLE A TO FIND NORMAL PROPORTIONS

1. State the problem in terms of the observed variable x. **Draw a picture** that shows the proportion you want in terms of cumulative proportions.
2. **Standardize** x to restate the problem in terms of a standard Normal variable z.
3. **Use Table A** and the fact that the total area under the curve is 1 to find the required area under the standard Normal curve.

EXAMPLE 3.8   Who qualifies for an athletic scholarship?

The NCAA considers a student a "partial qualifier" if the combined SAT score is at least 720. Partial qualifiers can receive athletic scholarships and practice with the team, but they can't compete during their first college year. What proportion of all students who take the SAT would be partial qualifiers?

1. *State the problem and draw a picture.* Call the SAT score x. The variable x has the $N(1026, 209)$ distribution. What proportion of SAT scores fall between 720 and 820? See the following picture.

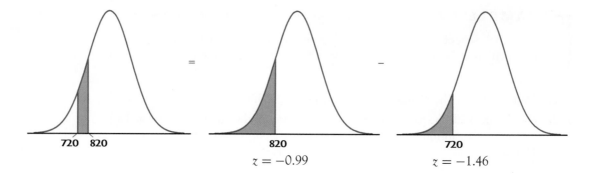

$z = -0.99$ $z = -1.46$

2. *Standardize.* Subtract the mean, then divide by the standard deviation, to turn x into a standard Normal z:

$$720 \leq x < 820$$

$$\frac{720 - 1026}{209} \leq \frac{x - 1026}{209} < \frac{820 - 1026}{209}$$

$$-1.46 \leq z < -0.99$$

3. *Use the table.* Follow the picture (we added the z-scores to the picture label to help you):

area between -1.46 and -0.99 = (area left of -0.99) − (area left of -1.46)

$$= 0.1611 - 0.0721 = 0.0890$$

About 9% of high school seniors would be partial qualifiers.

Sometimes we encounter a value of z more extreme than those appearing in Table A. For example, the area to the left of $z = -4$ is not given directly in the table. The z-values in Table A leave only area 0.0002 in each tail unaccounted for. For practical purposes, we can act as if there is zero area outside the range of Table A.

APPLY YOUR KNOWLEDGE

3.10 **Use the Normal table.** Use Table A to find the proportion of observations from a standard Normal distribution that satisfies each of the following statements. In each case, sketch a standard Normal curve and shade the area under the curve that is the answer to the question.

(a) $z < 2.85$

(b) $z > 2.85$

(c) $z > -1.66$

(d) $-1.66 < z < 2.85$

3.11 **How hard do locomotives pull?** An important measure of the performance of a locomotive is its "adhesion," which is the locomotive's pulling force as a multiple of its weight. The adhesion of one 4400-horsepower diesel locomotive model varies in actual use according to a Normal distribution with mean $\mu = 0.37$ and standard deviation $\sigma = 0.04$.

(a) What proportion of adhesions measured in use are higher than 0.40?

(b) What proportion of adhesions are between 0.40 and 0.50?

CORBIS

3.12 A better locomotive. Improvements in the locomotive's computer controls change the distribution of adhesion to a Normal distribution with mean $\mu = 0.41$ and standard deviation $\sigma = 0.02$. Find the proportions in (a) and (b) of the previous exercise after this improvement.

Finding a value given a proportion

Examples 3.5 to 3.8 illustrate the use of software or Table A to find what proportion of the observations satisfies some condition, such as "SAT score above 820." We may instead want to find the observed value with a given proportion of the observations above or below it. Statistical software will do this directly.

EXAMPLE 3.9 Find the top 10% using software

Scores on the SAT verbal test in recent years follow approximately the $N(504, 111)$ distribution. How high must a student score in order to place in the top 10% of all students taking the SAT?

We want to find the SAT score x with area 0.1 to its *right* under the Normal curve with mean $\mu = 504$ and standard deviation $\sigma = 111$. That's the same as finding the SAT score x with area 0.9 to its *left*. Figure 3.12 poses the question in graphical form. Most software will tell you x when you plug in mean 504, standard deviation 111, and cumulative proportion 0.9. Here is Minitab's output:

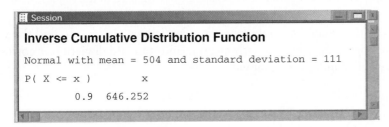

Inverse Cumulative Distribution Function

```
Normal with mean = 504 and standard deviation = 111

P( X <= x )        x
       0.9   646.252
```

Minitab gives $x = 646.252$. So scores above 647 are in the top 10%. (Round up because SAT scores can only be whole numbers.)

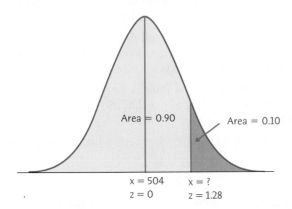

FIGURE 3.12 Locating the point on a Normal curve with area 0.10 to its right.

Without software, use Table A backward. Find the given proportion in the body of the table and then read the corresponding z from the left column and top row. There are again three steps.

EXAMPLE 3.10 Find the top 10% using Table A ———

Scores on the SAT verbal test in recent years follow approximately the $N(504, 111)$ distribution. How high must a student score in order to place in the top 10% of all students taking the SAT?

1. *State the problem and draw a picture.* This step is exactly as in Example 3.9. The picture is Figure 3.12.

2. *Use the table.* Look in the body of Table A for the entry closest to 0.9. It is 0.8997. This is the entry corresponding to $z = 1.28$. So $z = 1.28$ is the standardized value with area 0.9 to its left.

3. *Unstandardize* to transform z back to the original x scale. We know that the standardized value of the unknown x is $z = 1.28$. So x itself satisfies

$$\frac{x - 504}{111} = 1.28$$

Solving this equation for x gives

$$x = 504 + (1.28)(111) = 646.1$$

This equation should make sense: it says that x lies 1.28 standard deviations above the mean on this particular Normal curve. That is the "unstandardized" meaning of $z = 1.28$. A student must score at least 647 to place in the highest 10%.

Here is the general formula for unstandardizing a z-score. To find the value x from the Normal distribution with mean μ and standard deviation σ corresponding to a given standard Normal value z, use

$$x = \mu + z\sigma$$

EXAMPLE 3.11 Find the third quartile ———

High levels of cholesterol in the blood increase the risk of heart disease. For 14-year-old boys, the distribution of blood cholesterol is approximately Normal with mean $\mu = 170$ milligrams of cholesterol per deciliter of blood (mg/dl) and the standard deviation $\sigma = 30$ mg/dl.[3] What is the third quartile of the distribution of blood cholesterol?

1. *State the problem and draw a picture.* Call the cholesterol level x. The variable x has the $N(170, 30)$ distribution. The third quartile is the value with 75% of the distribution to its left. Figure 3.13 is the picture.

2. *Use the table.* Look in the body of Table A for the entry closest to 0.75. It is 0.7486. This is the entry corresponding to $z = 0.67$. So $z = 0.67$ is the standardized value with area 0.75 to its left.

3. *Unstandardize.* The cholesterol level corresponding to $z = 0.67$ is

$$x = \mu + z\sigma$$
$$= 170 + (0.67)(30) = 190.1$$

The third quartile of blood cholesterol levels in 14-year-old boys is about 190 mg/dl.

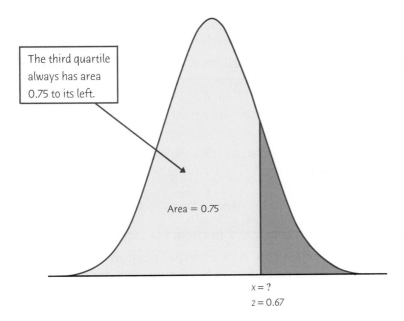

FIGURE 3.13 Locating the third quartile of a Normal curve.

The third quartile always has area 0.75 to its left.

Area = 0.75

$x = ?$
$z = 0.67$

APPLY YOUR KNOWLEDGE

3.13 Table A. Use Table A to find the value z of a standard Normal variable that satisfies each of the following conditions. (Use the value of z from Table A that comes closest to satisfying the condition.) In each case, sketch a standard Normal curve with your value of z marked on the axis.

(a) The point z with 25% of the observations falling below it.

(b) The point z with 40% of the observations falling above it.

3.14 IQ test scores. Scores on the Wechsler Adult Intelligence Scale are approximately Normally distributed with $\mu = 100$ and $\sigma = 15$.

(a) What scores fall in the lowest 25% of the distribution?

(b) How high a score is needed to be in the highest 5%?

CHAPTER 3 SUMMARY

We can sometimes describe the overall pattern of a distribution by a **density curve.** A density curve has total area 1 underneath it. An area under a density curve gives the proportion of observations that fall in a range of values.

A density curve is an idealized description of the overall pattern of a distribution that smooths out the irregularities in the actual data. We write the **mean of a density curve** as μ and the **standard deviation of a density curve** as σ to distinguish them from the mean $\bar{x}$ and standard deviation s of the actual data.

The mean, the median, and the quartiles of a density curve can be located by eye. The **mean** μ is the balance point of the curve. The **median** divides the area under the curve in half. The **quartiles** and the median divide the area under the curve into quarters. The **standard deviation** σ cannot be located by eye on most density curves.

Area = .9901

Area = .0099

$z = 2.33$

The bell curve?

Does the distribution of human intelligence follow the "bell curve" of a Normal distribution? Scores on IQ tests do roughly follow a Normal distribution. That is because a test score is calculated from a person's answers in a way that is designed to produce a Normal distribution. To conclude that intelligence follows a bell curve, we must agree that the test scores directly measure intelligence. Many psychologists don't think there is one human characteristic that we can call "intelligence" and can measure by a single test score.

The mean and median are equal for symmetric density curves. The mean of a skewed curve is located farther toward the long tail than is the median.

The **Normal distributions** are described by a special family of bell-shaped, symmetric density curves, called **Normal curves.** The mean μ and standard deviation σ completely specify a Normal distribution $N(\mu, \sigma)$. The mean is the center of the curve, and σ is the distance from μ to the change-of-curvature points on either side.

To **standardize** any observation x, subtract the mean of the distribution and then divide by the standard deviation. The resulting **z-score**

$$z = \frac{x - \mu}{\sigma}$$

says how many standard deviations x lies from the distribution mean.

All Normal distributions are the same when measurements are transformed to the standardized scale. In particular, all Normal distributions satisfy the **68–95–99.7 rule,** which describes what percent of observations lie within one, two, and three standard deviations of the mean.

If x has the $N(\mu, \sigma)$ distribution, then the **standardized variable** $z = (x - \mu)/\sigma$ has the **standard Normal distribution** $N(0, 1)$ with mean 0 and standard deviation 1. Table A gives the **cumulative proportions** of standard Normal observations that are less than z for many values of z. By standardizing, we can use Table A for any Normal distribution.

CHECK YOUR SKILLS

3.15 Which of these variables is least likely to have a Normal distribution?

(a) Income per person for 150 different countries

(b) Lengths of 50 newly hatched pythons

(c) Heights of 100 white pine trees in a forest

3.16 To completely specify the shape of a Normal distribution, you must give

(a) the mean and the standard deviation.

(b) the five-number summary.

(c) the mean and the median.

3.17 Figure 3.14 shows a Normal curve. The mean of this distribution is

(a) 0.   (b) 2.   (c) 3.

3.18 The standard deviation of the Normal distribution in Figure 3.14 is

(a) 2.   (b) 3.   (c) 5.

·3.19 The length of human pregnancies from conception to birth varies according to a distribution that is approximately Normal with mean 266 days and standard deviation 16 days. 95% of all pregnancies last between

(a) 250 and 282 days.

(b) 234 and 298 days.

(c) 218 and 314 days.

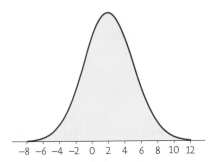

FIGURE 3.14 A Normal curve, for Exercises 3.17 and 3.18.

3.20 The scale of scores on an IQ test is approximately Normal with mean 100 and standard deviation 15. The organization MENSA, which calls itself "the high-IQ society," requires an IQ score of 130 or higher for membership. What percent of adults would qualify for membership?

(a) 95%   (b) 5%   (c) 2.5%

3.21 The scores of adults on an IQ test are approximately Normal with mean 100 and standard deviation 15. Corinne scores 118 on such a test. Her z-score is about

(a) 1.2.   (b) 7.87.   (c) 18.

3.22 The proportion of observations from a standard Normal distribution that take values less than 1.15 is about

(a) 0.1251.   (b) 0.8531.   (c) 0.8749.

3.23 The proportion of observations from a standard Normal distribution that take values larger than −0.75 is about

(a) 0.2266.   (b) 0.7734.   (c) 0.8023.

3.24 The scores of adults on an IQ test are approximately Normal with mean 100 and standard deviation 15. Corinne scores 118 on such a test. She scores higher than what percent of all adults?

(a) About 12%   (b) About 88%   (b) About 98%

CHAPTER 3 EXERCISES

3.25 **Understanding density curves.** Remember that it is areas under a density curve, not the height of the curve, that give proportions in a distribution. To illustrate this, sketch a density curve that has its peak at 0 on the horizontal axis but has greater area within 0.25 on either side of 1 than within 0.25 on either side of 0.

3.26 **Are the data Normal? Soil penetrability.** Table 2.3 (page 61) gives data on the penetrability of soil at each of three levels of compression. We might expect the penetrability of specimens of the same soil at the same level of compression to follow a Normal distribution. Make stemplots of the data for loose and for intermediate compression. Does either sample seem roughly Normal? Does either appear distinctly non-Normal? If so, what kind of departure from Normality does your stemplot show?

3.27 **IQ test scores.** The Wechsler Adult Intelligence Scale (WAIS) is the most common "IQ test." The scale of scores is set separately for each age group and is approximately Normal with mean 100 and standard deviation 15. According to the 68–95–99.7 rule, about what percent of people have WAIS scores

(a) above 100?

(b) above 145?

(c) below 85?

3.28   **Low IQ test scores.**   Scores on the Wechsler Adult Intelligence Scale (WAIS) are approximately Normal with mean 100 and standard deviation 15. People with WAIS scores below 70 are considered mentally retarded when, for example, applying for Social Security disability benefits. According to the 68–95–99.7 rule, about what percent of adults are retarded by this criterion?

3.29   **Actual IQ test scores.**   Here are the IQ test scores of 31 seventh-grade girls in a Midwest school district:[4]

114	100	104	89	102	91	114	114	103	105
108	130	120	132	111	128	118	119	86	72
111	103	74	112	107	103	98	96	112	112	93

(a) We expect IQ scores to be approximately Normal. Make a stemplot to check that there are no major departures from Normality.

(b) Nonetheless, proportions calculated from a Normal distribution are not always very accurate for small numbers of observations. Find the mean $\bar{x}$ and standard deviation s for these IQ scores. What proportions of the scores are within one standard deviation and within two standard deviations of the mean? What would these proportions be in an exactly Normal distribution?

3.30   **Standard Normal drill.**   Use Table A to find the proportion of observations from a standard Normal distribution that falls in each of the following regions. In each case, sketch a standard Normal curve and shade the area representing the region.

(a) $z \leq -2.25$

(b) $z \geq -2.25$

(c) $z > 1.77$

(d) $-2.25 < z < 1.77$

3.31   **Standard Normal drill.**

(a) Find the number z such that the proportion of observations that are less than z in a standard Normal distribution is 0.8.

(b) Find the number z such that 35% of all observations from a standard Normal distribution are greater than z.

ACT versus SAT.   *There are two major tests of readiness for college: the ACT and the SAT. ACT scores are reported on a scale from 1 to 36. The distribution of ACT scores in recent years has been roughly Normal with mean $\mu = 20.9$ and standard deviation $\sigma = 4.8$. SAT scores are reported on a scale from 400 to 1600. SAT scores have been roughly Normal with mean $\mu = 1026$ and standard deviation $\sigma = 209$. Exercises 3.32 to 3.43 are based on this information.*

3.32   Tonya scores 1318 on the SAT. Jermaine scores 27 on the ACT. Assuming that both tests measure the same thing, who has the higher score?

3.33   Jacob scores 16 on the ACT. Emily scores 670 on the SAT. Assuming that both tests measure the same thing, who has the higher score?

3.34 José scores 1287 on the SAT. Assuming that both tests measure the same thing, what score on the ACT is equivalent to José's SAT score?

3.35 Maria scores 28 on the ACT. Assuming that both tests measure the same thing, what score on the SAT is equivalent to Maria's ACT score?

3.36 Reports on a student's ACT or SAT usually give the percentile as well as the actual score. The percentile is just the cumulative proportion stated as a percent: the percent of all scores that were lower than this one. Tonya scores 1318 on the SAT. What is her percentile?

3.37 Reports on a student's ACT or SAT usually give the percentile as well as the actual score. The percentile is just the cumulative proportion stated as a percent: the percent of all scores that were lower than this one. Jacob scores 16 on the ACT. What is his percentile?

3.38 It is possible to score higher than 1600 on the SAT, but scores 1600 and above are reported as 1600. What proportion of SAT scores are reported as 1600?

3.39 It is possible to score higher than 36 on the ACT, but scores 36 and above are reported as 36. What proportion of ACT scores are reported as 36?

3.40 What SAT scores make up the top 10% of all scores?

3.41 How well must Abigail do on the ACT in order to place in the top 20% of all students?

3.42 The quartiles of any distribution are the values with cumulative proportions 0.25 and 0.75. What are the quartiles of the distribution of ACT scores?

3.43 The quintiles of any distribution are the values with cumulative proportions 0.20, 0.40, 0.60, and 0.80. What are the quintiles of the distribution of SAT scores?

3.44 **Heights of men and women.** The heights of women aged 20 to 29 follow approximately the $N(64, 2.7)$ distribution. Men the same age have heights distributed as $N(69.3, 2.8)$. What percent of young women are taller than the mean height of young men?

3.45 **Heights of men and women.** The heights of women aged 20 to 29 follow approximately the $N(64, 2.7)$ distribution. Men the same age have heights distributed as $N(69.3, 2.8)$. What percent of young men are shorter than the mean height of young women?

3.46 **A surprising calculation.** Changing the mean of a Normal distribution by a moderate amount can greatly change the percent of observations in the tails. Suppose that a college is looking for applicants with SAT math scores 750 and above.

(a) In 2004, the scores of men on the math SAT followed the $N(537, 116)$ distribution. What percent of men scored 750 or better?

(b) Women's SAT math scores that year had the $N(501, 110)$ distribution. What percent of women scored 750 or better? You see that the percent of men above 750 is almost three times the percent of women with such high scores. Why this is true is controversial.

3.47 **Grading managers.** Many companies "grade on a bell curve" to compare the performance of their managers and professional workers. This forces the use of some low performance ratings so that not all workers are listed as "above average." Ford Motor Company's "performance management process" for a time assigned 10% A grades, 80% B grades, and 10% C grades to the company's

18,000 managers. Suppose that Ford's performance scores really are Normally distributed. This year, managers with scores less than 25 received C's and those with scores above 475 received A's. What are the mean and standard deviation of the scores?

3.48   Osteoporosis. Osteoporosis is a condition in which the bones become brittle due to loss of minerals. To diagnose osteoporosis, an elaborate apparatus measures bone mineral density (BMD). BMD is usually reported in standardized form. The standardization is based on a population of healthy young adults. The World Health Organization (WHO) criterion for osteoporosis is a BMD 2.5 standard deviations below the mean for young adults. BMD measurements in a population of people similar in age and sex roughly follow a Normal distribution.

(a) What percent of healthy young adults have osteoporosis by the WHO criterion?

(b) Women aged 70 to 79 are of course not young adults. The mean BMD in this age is about -2 on the standard scale for young adults. Suppose that the standard deviation is the same as for young adults. What percent of this older population has osteoporosis?

3.49   Are the data Normal? ACT scores. Scores on the ACT test for the 2004 high school graduating class had mean 20.9 and standard deviation 4.8. In all, 1,171,460 students in this class took the test, and 1,052,490 of them had scores of 27 or lower.[5] If the distribution of scores were Normal, what percent of scores would be 27 or lower? What percent of the actual scores were 27 or lower? Does the Normal distribution describe the actual data well?

3.50   Are the data Normal? Student loans. A government report looked at the amount borrowed for college by students who graduated in 2000 and had taken out student loans.[6] The mean amount was $\overline{x} = \$17,776$ and the standard deviation was $s = \$12,034$. The quartiles were $Q_1 = \$9900$, $M = \$15,532$, and $Q_3 = \$22,500$.

(a) Compare the mean $\overline{x}$ and the median M. Also compare the distances of Q_1 and Q_3 from the median. Explain why both comparisons suggest that the distribution is right-skewed.

(b) The right skew pulls the standard deviation up. So a Normal distribution with the same mean and standard deviation would have a third quartile larger than the actual Q_3. Find the third quartile of the Normal distribution with $\mu = \$17,776$ and $\sigma = \$12,034$ and compare it with $Q_3 = \$22,500$.

The Normal Curve applet allows you to do Normal calculations quickly. It is somewhat limited by the number of pixels available for use, so that it can't hit every value exactly. In the exercises below, use the closest available values. In each case, make a sketch of the curve from the applet marked with the values you used to answer the questions.

3.51   How accurate is 68–95–99.7? The 68–95–99.7 rule for Normal distributions is a useful approximation. To see how accurate the rule is, drag one flag across the other so that the applet shows the area under the curve between the two flags.

(a) Place the flags one standard deviation on either side of the mean. What is the area between these two values? What does the 68–95–99.7 rule say this area is?

(b) Repeat for locations two and three standard deviations on either side of the mean. Again compare the 68–95–99.7 rule with the area given by the applet.

3.52 **Where are the quartiles?** How many standard deviations above and below the mean do the quartiles of any Normal distribution lie? (Use the standard Normal distribution to answer this question.)

3.53 **Grading managers.** In Exercise 3.47, we saw that Ford Motor Company grades its managers in such a way that the top 10% receive an A grade, the bottom 10% a C, and the middle 80% a B. Let's suppose that performance scores follow a Normal distribution. How many standard deviations above and below the mean do the A/B and B/C cutoffs lie? (Use the standard Normal distribution to answer this question.)

Stuart Westmorland/Getty Images

Scatterplots and Correlation

A medical study finds that short women are more likely to have heart attacks than women of average height, while tall women have the fewest heart attacks. An insurance group reports that heavier cars have fewer deaths per 10,000 vehicles registered than do lighter cars. These and many other statistical studies look at the *relationship between two variables*. Statistical relationships are overall tendencies, not ironclad rules. They allow individual exceptions. Although smokers on the average die younger than nonsmokers, some people live to 90 while smoking three packs a day.

To understand a statistical relationship between two variables, we measure both variables on the same individuals. Often, we must examine other variables as well. To conclude that shorter women have higher risk from heart attacks, for example, the researchers had to eliminate the effect of other variables such as weight and exercise habits. In this chapter we begin our study of relationships between variables. One of our main themes is that the relationship between two variables can be strongly influenced by other variables that are lurking in the background.

Explanatory and response variables

We think that car weight helps explain accident deaths and that smoking influences life expectancy. In each of these relationships, the two variables play different roles: one explains or influences the other.

RESPONSE VARIABLE, EXPLANATORY VARIABLE

A **response variable** measures an outcome of a study. An **explanatory variable** may explain or influence changes in a response variable.

You will often find explanatory variables called **independent variables,** and response variables called **dependent variables.** The idea behind this language is that the response variable depends on the explanatory variable. Because "independent" and "dependent" have other meanings in statistics that are unrelated to the explanatory-response distinction, we prefer to avoid those words.

independent variable
dependent variable

It is easiest to identify explanatory and response variables when we actually set values of one variable in order to see how it affects another variable.

┌─ EXAMPLE 4.1 Beer and blood alcohol ──────

How does drinking beer affect the level of alcohol in our blood? The legal limit for driving in all states is 0.08%. Student volunteers at The Ohio State University drank different numbers of cans of beer. Thirty minutes later, a police officer measured their blood alcohol content. Number of beers consumed is the explanatory variable, and percent of alcohol in the blood is the response variable.

When we don't set the values of either variable but just observe both variables, there may or may not be explanatory and response variables. Whether there are depends on how we plan to use the data.

┌─ EXAMPLE 4.2 College debts ──────

A college student aid officer looks at the findings of the National Student Loan Survey. She notes data on the amount of debt of recent graduates, their current income, and how stressful they feel about college debt. She isn't interested in predictions but is simply trying to understand the situation of recent college graduates. The distinction between explanatory and response variables does not apply.

A sociologist looks at the same data with an eye to using amount of debt and income, along with other variables, to explain the stress caused by college debt. Now amount of debt and income are explanatory variables and stress level is the response variable.

In many studies, the goal is to show that changes in one or more explanatory variables actually *cause* changes in a response variable. Other explanatory-response relationships do not involve direct causation. The SAT scores of high school students help predict the students' future college grades, but high SAT scores certainly don't *cause* high college grades.

Most statistical studies examine data on more than one variable. Fortunately, statistical analysis of several-variable data builds on the tools we used to examine individual variables. The principles that guide our work also remain the same:

- Plot your data. Look for overall patterns and deviations from those patterns.
- Based on what your plot shows, choose numerical summaries for some aspects of the data.

After you plot your data, think!

The statistician Abraham Wald (1902–1950) worked on war problems during World War II. Wald invented some statistical methods that were military secrets until the war ended. Here is one of his simpler ideas. Asked where extra armor should be added to airplanes, Wald studied the location of enemy bullet holes in planes returning from combat. He plotted the locations on an outline of the plane. As data accumulated, most of the outline filled up. Put the armor in the few spots with no bullet holes, said Wald. That's where bullets hit the planes that didn't make it back.

APPLY YOUR KNOWLEDGE

4.1   **Explanatory and response variables?**   You have data on a large group of college students. Here are four pairs of variables measured on these students. For each pair, is it more reasonable to simply explore the relationship between the two variables or to view one of the variables as an explanatory variable and the other as a response variable? In the latter case, which is the explanatory variable and which is the response variable?

(a) Amount of time spent studying for a statistics exam and grade on the exam.

(b) Weight in kilograms and height in centimeters.

(c) Hours per week of extracurricular activities and grade point average.

(d) Score on the SAT math exam and score on the SAT verbal exam.

4.2   **Coral reefs.**   How sensitive to changes in water temperature are coral reefs? To find out, measure the growth of corals in aquariums where the water temperature is controlled at different levels. Growth is measured by weighing the coral before and after the experiment. What are the explanatory and response variables? Are they categorical or quantitative?

4.3   **Beer and blood alcohol.**   Example 4.1 describes a study in which college students drank different amounts of beer. The response variable was their blood alcohol content (BAC). BAC for the same amount of beer might depend on other facts about the students. Name two other variables that could influence BAC.

Stuart Westmorland/Getty Images

Displaying relationships: scatterplots

The most useful graph for displaying the relationship between two quantitative variables is a *scatterplot*.

EXAMPLE 4.3   State SAT scores

Some people use average SAT scores to rank state school systems. This is not proper, because state average scores depend on more than just school quality. Following our four-step process (page 53), let's look at one influence on state SAT scores.

STATE: The percent of high school students who take the SAT varies from state to state. Does this fact help explain differences among the states in average SAT score?

FORMULATE: Examine the relationship between percent taking and state mean score. Choose the explanatory and response variables (if any). Make a *scatterplot* to display the relationship between the variables. Interpret the plot to understand the relationship.

SOLVE (first steps): We suspect that "percent taking" will help explain "mean score." So "percent taking" is the explanatory variable and "mean score" is the response variable. We want to see how mean score changes when percent taking changes, so we put percent taking (the explanatory variable) on the horizontal axis. Figure 4.1 is the scatterplot. Each point represents a single state. In Colorado, for example, 27% took the SAT, and their mean SAT score was 1107. Find 27 on the x (horizontal) axis and 1107 on the y (vertical) axis. Colorado appears as the point (27, 1107) above 27 and to the right of 1107.

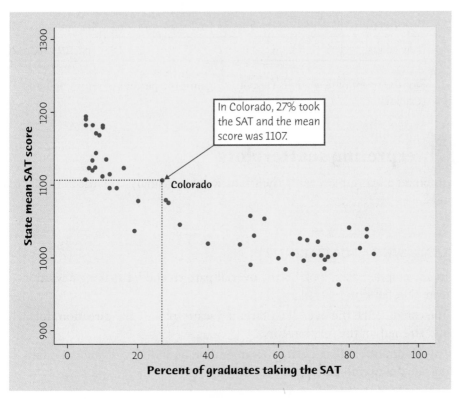

In Colorado, 27% took the SAT and the mean score was 1107.

Colorado

FIGURE 4.1 Scatterplot of the mean SAT score in each state against the percent of that state's high school graduates who take the SAT. The dotted lines intersect at the point (27, 1107), the data for Colorado.

SCATTERPLOT

A **scatterplot** shows the relationship between two quantitative variables measured on the same individuals. The values of one variable appear on the horizontal axis, and the values of the other variable appear on the vertical axis. Each individual in the data appears as the point in the plot fixed by the values of both variables for that individual.

Always plot the explanatory variable, if there is one, on the horizontal axis (the *x* axis) of a scatterplot. As a reminder, we usually call the explanatory variable *x* and the response variable *y*. If there is no explanatory-response distinction, either variable can go on the horizontal axis.

APPLY YOUR KNOWLEDGE

4.4   **Bird colonies.**   One of nature's patterns connects the percent of adult birds in a colony that return from the previous year and the number of new adults that join the colony. Following are data for 13 colonies of sparrowhawks:[1]

William S. Clark; Frank Lane Picture Agency/ CORBIS

Percent return	74	66	81	52	73	62	52	45	62	46	60	46	38
New adults	5	6	8	11	12	15	16	17	18	18	19	20	20

Plot the count of new adults (response) against the percent of returning birds (explanatory).

Interpreting scatterplots

To interpret a scatterplot, apply the strategies of data analysis learned in Chapters 1 and 2.

EXAMINING A SCATTERPLOT

In any graph of data, look for the **overall pattern** and for striking **deviations** from that pattern.

You can describe the overall pattern of a scatterplot by the **direction, form,** and **strength** of the relationship.

An important kind of deviation is an **outlier,** an individual value that falls outside the overall pattern of the relationship.

STEP

clusters

EXAMPLE 4.4   Understanding state SAT scores

SOLVE (interpret the plot): Figure 4.1 shows a clear *direction:* the overall pattern moves from upper left to lower right. That is, states in which a higher percent of high school graduates take the SAT tend to have lower mean SAT score. We call this a *negative association* between the two variables.

The *form* of the relationship is roughly a straight line with a slight curve to the right as it moves down. What is more, most states fall into two distinct **clusters.** In the cluster at the right of the plot, 49% or more of high school graduates take the SAT and the mean scores are low. The states in the cluster at the left have higher SAT scores and no more than 32% of graduates take the test. Only Nevada, where 40% take the SAT, lies between these clusters.

The *strength* of a relationship in a scatterplot is determined by how closely the points follow a clear form. The overall relationship in Figure 4.1 is moderately strong: states with similar percents taking the SAT tend to have roughly similar mean SAT scores.

What explains the clusters? There are two widely used college entrance exams, the SAT and the ACT. Each state favors one or the other. The left cluster in Figure 4.1 contains the ACT states, and the SAT states make up the right cluster. In ACT states, most students who take the SAT are applying to a selective college that requires SAT scores. This select group of students has a higher mean score than the much larger group of students who take the SAT in SAT states.

CONCLUDE: Percent taking explains much of the variation among states in average SAT score. States in which a higher percent of students take the SAT tend to have lower mean scores. SAT states as a group have lower mean SAT scores than ACT states. Average SAT score says almost nothing about quality of education in a state.

POSITIVE ASSOCIATION, NEGATIVE ASSOCIATION

Two variables are **positively associated** when above-average values of one tend to accompany above-average values of the other, and below-average values also tend to occur together.

Two variables are **negatively associated** when above-average values of one tend to accompany below-average values of the other, and vice versa.

Here is an example of a relationship with a clearer form.

EXAMPLE 4.5   Counting carnivores

Ecologists look at data to learn about nature's patterns. One pattern they have found relates the size of a carnivore and how many of those carnivores there are in an area. Measure size by body mass in kilograms. Measure "how many" by counting carnivores per 10,000 kilograms of their prey in the area. Table 4.1 gives data for 25 carnivore species.[2]

To see the pattern, plot carnivore abundance (response) against body mass (explanatory). Biologists often find that patterns involving sizes and counts are simpler when we plot the logarithms of the data. Figure 4.2 does that—you can see that 1, 10, 100, and 1000 are equally spaced on the vertical scale.

This scatterplot shows a negative association. That is, bigger carnivores are less abundant. The form of the association is **linear.** That is, the overall pattern follows a straight line from upper left to lower right. The association is quite strong because the points don't deviate a great deal from the line. It is striking that animals from many different parts of the world should fit so simple a pattern.

linear relationship

TABLE 4.1   Size and abundance of carnivores

Carnivore species	Body mass (kg)	Abundance	Carnivore species	Body mass (kg)	Abundance
Least weasel	0.14	1656.49	Eurasian lynx	20.0	0.46
Ermine	0.16	406.66	Wild dog	25.0	1.61
Small Indian mongoose	0.55	514.84	Dhole	25.0	0.81
Pine marten	1.3	31.84	Snow leopard	40.0	1.89
Kit fox	2.02	15.96	Wolf	46.0	0.62
Channel Island fox	2.16	145.94	Leopard	46.5	6.17
Arctic fox	3.19	21.63	Cheetah	50.0	2.29
Red fox	4.6	32.21	Puma	51.9	0.94
Bobcat	10.0	9.75	Spotted hyena	58.6	0.68
Canadian lynx	11.2	4.79	Lion	142.0	3.40
European badger	13.0	7.35	Tiger	181.0	0.33
Coyote	13.0	11.65	Polar bear	310.0	0.60
Ethiopian wolf	14.5	2.70			

FIGURE 4.2 Scatterplot of the abundance of 25 species of carnivores against their body mass. Larger carnivores are less abundant. (Logarithmic scales are used for both variables.)

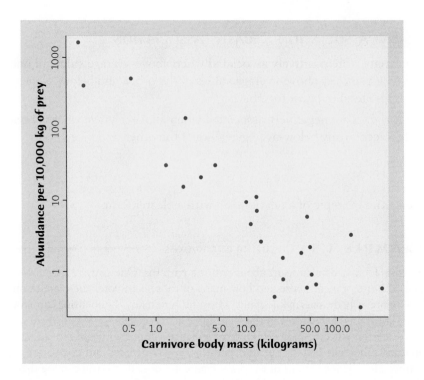

Of course, not all relationships have a simple form and a clear direction that we can describe as positive association or negative association. Exercise 4.6 gives an example that does not have a single direction.

APPLY YOUR KNOWLEDGE

4.5 **Bird colonies.** Describe the form, direction, and strength of the relationship between number of new sparrowhawks in a colony and percent of returning adults, as displayed in your plot from Exercise 4.4.

    For short-lived birds, the association between these variables is positive: changes in weather and food supply drive the populations of new and returning birds up or down together. For long-lived territorial birds, on the other hand, the association is negative because returning birds claim their territories in the colony and don't leave room for new recruits. Which type of species is the sparrowhawk?

4.6 **Does fast driving waste fuel?** How does the fuel consumption of a car change as its speed increases? Here are data for a British Ford Escort. Speed is measured in kilometers per hour, and fuel consumption is measured in liters of gasoline used per 100 kilometers traveled.[3]

Speed	10	20	30	40	50	60	70	80
Fuel	21.00	13.00	10.00	8.00	7.00	5.90	6.30	6.95

Speed	90	100	110	120	130	140	150
Fuel	7.57	8.27	9.03	9.87	10.79	11.77	12.83

(a) Make a scatterplot. (Which is the explanatory variable?)

(b) Describe the form of the relationship. It is not linear. Explain why the form of the relationship makes sense.

(c) It does not make sense to describe the variables as either positively associated or negatively associated. Why?

(d) Is the relationship reasonably strong or quite weak? Explain your answer.

Adding categorical variables to scatterplots

The Census Bureau groups the states into four broad regions, named Midwest, Northeast, South, and West. We might ask about regional patterns in SAT exam scores. Figure 4.3 repeats part of Figure 4.1, with an important difference. We have plotted only the Northeast and Midwest groups of states, using the plot symbol "+" for the northeastern states and the symbol "•" for the midwestern states.

The regional comparison is striking. The 9 northeastern states are all SAT states—in fact, at least 66% of high school graduates in each of these states take the SAT. The 12 midwestern states are mostly ACT states. In 10 of these states, the percent taking the SAT is between 5% and 11%. One midwestern state is clearly an outlier within the region. Indiana is an SAT state (64% take the SAT) that falls close to the northeastern cluster. Ohio, where 28% take the SAT, also lies outside the midwestern cluster.

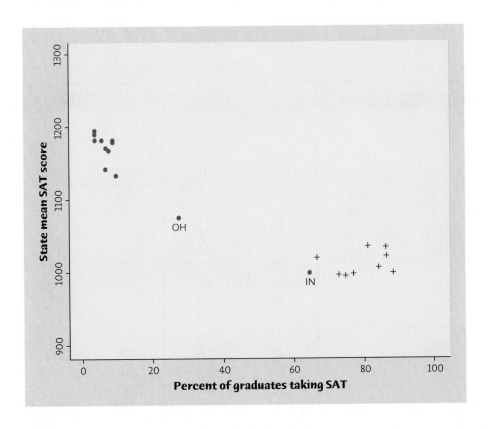

FIGURE 4.3 Mean SAT score and percent of high school graduates who take the test for only the northeastern (+) and midwestern (•) states.

Dividing the states into regions introduces a third variable into the scatterplot. "Region" is a categorical variable that has four values, although we plotted data from only two of the four regions. The two regions are identified by the two different plotting symbols.

CATEGORICAL VARIABLES IN SCATTERPLOTS

To add a categorical variable to a scatterplot, use a different plot color or symbol for each category.

APPLY YOUR KNOWLEDGE

4.7   **How fast do icicles grow?**   Japanese researchers measured the growth of icicles in a cold chamber under various conditions of temperature, wind, and water flow.[4] Table 4.2 contains data produced under two sets of conditions. In both cases, there was no wind and the temperature was set at $-11°C$. Water flowed over the icicle at a higher rate (29.6 milligrams per second) in Run 8905 and at a slower rate (11.9 mg/s) in Run 8903.

(a) Make a scatterplot of the length of the icicle in centimeters versus time in minutes, using separate symbols for the two runs.

(b) What does your plot show about the pattern of growth of icicles? What does it show about the effect of changing the rate of water flow on icicle growth?

TABLE 4.2   Growth of icicles over time

Run 8903				Run 8905			
Time (min)	Length (cm)	Time (min)	Length (cm)	Time (min)	Length (cm)	Time (min)	Length (cm)
10	0.6	130	18.1	10	0.3	130	10.4
20	1.8	140	19.9	20	0.6	140	11.0
30	2.9	150	21.0	30	1.0	150	11.9
40	4.0	160	23.4	40	1.3	160	12.7
50	5.0	170	24.7	50	3.2	170	13.9
60	6.1	180	27.8	60	4.0	180	14.6
70	7.9			70	5.3	190	15.8
80	10.1			80	6.0	200	16.2
90	10.9			90	6.9	210	17.9
100	12.7			100	7.8	220	18.8
110	14.4			110	8.3	230	19.9
120	16.6			120	9.6	240	21.1

Measuring linear association: correlation

A scatterplot displays the direction, form, and strength of the relationship between two quantitative variables. Linear (straight-line) relations are particularly important because a straight line is a simple pattern that is quite common. A linear relation is strong if the points lie close to a straight line, and weak if they are widely scattered about a line. Our eyes are not good judges of how strong a linear relationship is. The two scatterplots in Figure 4.4 depict exactly the same data, but the lower plot is drawn smaller in a large field. The lower plot seems to show a stronger linear relationship. Our eyes can be fooled by changing the plotting scales or the amount of space around the cloud of points in a scatterplot.[5] We need to follow our strategy for data analysis by using a numerical measure to supplement the graph. *Correlation* is the measure we use.

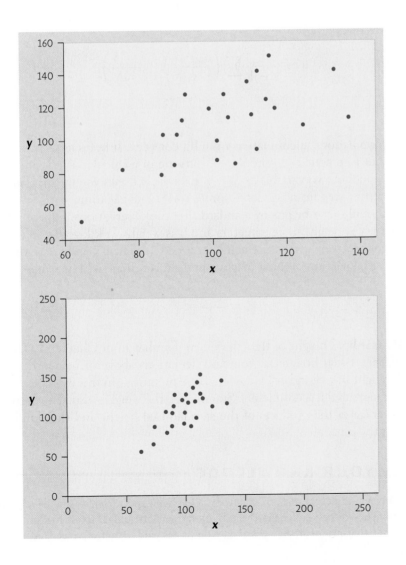

FIGURE 4.4 Two scatterplots of the same data. The straight-line pattern in the lower plot appears stronger because of the surrounding space.

> ### CORRELATION
>
> The **correlation** measures the direction and strength of the linear relationship between two quantitative variables. Correlation is usually written as r.
>
> Suppose that we have data on variables x and y for n individuals. The values for the first individual are x_1 and y_1, the values for the second individual are x_2 and y_2, and so on. The means and standard deviations of the two variables are $\overline{x}$ and s_x for the x-values, and $\overline{y}$ and s_y for the y-values. The correlation r between x and y is
>
> $$r = \frac{1}{n-1}\left[\left(\frac{x_1 - \overline{x}}{s_x}\right)\left(\frac{y_1 - \overline{y}}{s_y}\right) + \left(\frac{x_2 - \overline{x}}{s_x}\right)\left(\frac{y_2 - \overline{y}}{s_y}\right)\right.$$
> $$\left. + \cdots + \left(\frac{x_n - \overline{x}}{s_x}\right)\left(\frac{y_n - \overline{y}}{s_y}\right)\right]$$
>
> or, more compactly,
>
> $$r = \frac{1}{n-1}\sum\left(\frac{x_i - \overline{x}}{s_x}\right)\left(\frac{y_i - \overline{y}}{s_y}\right)$$

Death from superstition?

Is there a relationship between superstitious beliefs and bad things happening? Apparently there is. Chinese and Japanese people think that the number 4 is unlucky because when pronounced it sounds like the word for "death." Sociologists looked at 15 years' worth of death certificates for Chinese and Japanese Americans and for white Americans. Deaths from heart disease were notably higher on the fourth day of the month among Chinese and Japanese but not among whites. The sociologists think the explanation is increased stress on "unlucky days."

The formula for the correlation r is a bit complex. It helps us see what correlation is, but in practice you should use software or a calculator that finds r from keyed-in values of two variables x and y. Exercise 4.8 asks you to calculate a correlation step-by-step from the definition to solidify its meaning.

The formula for r begins by standardizing the observations. Suppose, for example, that x is height in centimeters and y is weight in kilograms and that we have height and weight measurements for n people. Then $\overline{x}$ and s_x are the mean and standard deviation of the n heights, both in centimeters. The value

$$\frac{x_i - \overline{x}}{s_x}$$

is the standardized height of the ith person, familiar from Chapter 3. The standardized height says how many standard deviations above or below the mean a person's height lies. Standardized values have no units—in this example, they are no longer measured in centimeters. Standardize the weights also. The correlation r is an average of the products of the standardized height and the standardized weight for the n people.

APPLY YOUR KNOWLEDGE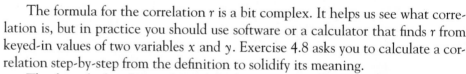

4.8 **Coffee and deforestation.** Coffee is a leading export from several developing countries. When coffee prices are high, farmers often clear forest to plant more coffee trees. Here are five years' data on prices paid to coffee growers in Indonesia and the percent of forest area lost in a national park that lies in a coffee-producing region:[6]

Price (cents per pound)	29	40	54	55	72
Forest lost (percent)	0.49	1.59	1.69	1.82	3.10

(a) Make a scatterplot. Which is the explanatory variable? What kind of pattern does your plot show?

(b) Find the correlation r step-by-step. First find the mean and standard deviation of each variable. Then find the five standardized values for each variable. Finally, use the formula for r. Explain how your value for r matches your graph in (a).

(c) Enter these data into your calculator or software and use the correlation function to find r. Check that you get the same result as in (b), up to roundoff error.

Bill Ross/CORBIS

Facts about correlation

The formula for correlation helps us see that r is positive when there is a positive association between the variables. Height and weight, for example, have a positive association. People who are above average in height tend to also be above average in weight. Both the standardized height and the standardized weight are positive. People who are below average in height tend to also have below-average weight. Then both standardized height and standardized weight are negative. In both cases, the products in the formula for r are mostly positive and so r is positive. In the same way, we can see that r is negative when the association between x and y is negative. More detailed study of the formula gives more detailed properties of r. Here is what you need to know in order to interpret correlation.

1. *Correlation makes no distinction between explanatory and response variables.* It makes no difference which variable you call x and which you call y in calculating the correlation.

2. Because r uses the standardized values of the observations, r *does not change when we change the units of measurement of x, y, or both.* Measuring height in inches rather than centimeters and weight in pounds rather than kilograms does not change the correlation between height and weight. The correlation r itself has no unit of measurement; it is just a number.

3. *Positive r indicates positive association between the variables, and negative r indicates negative association.*

4. *The correlation r is always a number between -1 and 1.* Values of r near 0 indicate a very weak linear relationship. The strength of the linear relationship increases as r moves away from 0 toward either -1 or 1. Values of r close to -1 or 1 indicate that the points in a scatterplot lie close to a straight line. The extreme values $r = -1$ and $r = 1$ occur only in the case of a perfect linear relationship, when the points lie exactly along a straight line.

EXAMPLE 4.6 *From scatterplot to correlation*

The scatterplots in Figure 4.5 illustrate how values of r closer to 1 or -1 correspond to stronger linear relationships. To make the meaning of r clearer, the standard deviations of both variables in these plots are equal, and the horizontal and vertical scales are the same. In general, it is not so easy to guess the value of r from the appearance of a scatterplot. Remember that changing the plotting scales in a scatterplot may mislead our eyes, but it does not change the correlation.

The real data we have examined also illustrate how correlation measures the strength and direction of linear relationships. Figure 4.2 shows a strong negative linear relationship between the logarithms of body mass and abundance for carnivore species. The correlation is $r = -0.912$. Figure 4.1 shows a weaker but still quite strong negative association between percent of students taking the SAT and the mean SAT score in a state. The correlation is $r = -0.876$.

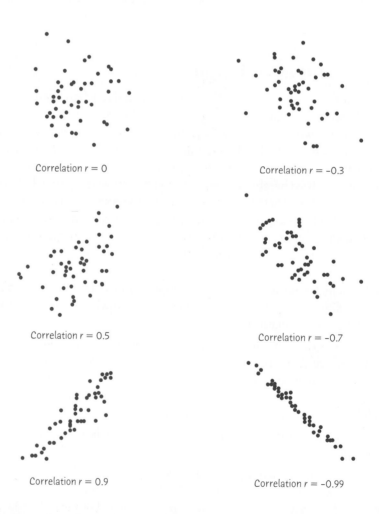

FIGURE 4.5 How correlation measures the strength of a linear relationship. Patterns closer to a straight line have correlations closer to 1 or -1.

Describing the relationship between two variables is a more complex task than describing the distribution of one variable. Here are some more facts about correlation, cautions to keep in mind when you use r.

1. *Correlation requires that both variables be quantitative*, so that it makes sense to do the arithmetic indicated by the formula for r. We cannot calculate a correlation between the incomes of a group of people and what city they live in, because city is a categorical variable.

2. Correlation measures the strength of only the linear relationship between two variables. *Correlation does not describe curved relationships between variables, no matter how strong they are.* Exercise 4.11 illustrates this important fact.

3. *Like the mean and standard deviation, the correlation is not resistant:* r is strongly affected by a few outlying observations. Use r with caution when outliers appear in the scatterplot. To explore how extreme observations can influence r, use the *Correlation and Regression* applet.

4. *Correlation is not a complete summary of two-variable data*, even when the relationship between the variables is linear. You should give the means and standard deviations of both x and y along with the correlation.

Because the formula for correlation uses the means and standard deviations, these measures are the proper choice to accompany a correlation. Here is an example in which understanding requires both means and correlation.

EXAMPLE 4.7   Scoring figure skaters

Neal Preston/CORBIS

Until a scandal at the 2002 Olympics brought change, figure skating was scored by judges on a scale from 0.0 to 6.0. The scores were often controversial. We have the scores awarded by two judges, Pierre and Elena, to many skaters. How well do they agree? We calculate that the correlation between their scores is $r = 0.9$. But the mean of Pierre's scores is 0.8 point lower than Elena's mean.

These facts do not contradict each other. They are simply different kinds of information. The mean scores show that Pierre awards lower scores than Elena. But because Pierre gives *every* skater a score about 0.8 point lower than Elena, the correlation remains high. Adding the same number to all values of either x or y does not change the correlation. If both judges score the same skaters, the competition is scored consistently because Pierre and Elena agree on which performances are better than others. The high r shows their agreement. But if Pierre scores some skaters and Elena others, we must add 0.8 points to Pierre's scores to arrive at a fair comparison.

Of course, even giving means, standard deviations, and the correlation for state SAT scores and percent taking will not point out the clusters in Figure 4.1. Numerical summaries complement plots of data, but they don't replace them.

APPLY YOUR KNOWLEDGE

4.9   **Changing the units.**   Coffee is currently priced in dollars. If it were priced in euros, and the dollar prices in Exercise 4.8 were translated into the equivalent prices in euros, would the correlation between coffee price and percent of forest loss change? Explain your answer.

4.10   **Changing the correlation.**

(a) Use your calculator or software to find the correlation between the percent of returning birds and the number of new birds from the data in Exercise 4.4.

(b) Make a scatterplot of the data with two new points added. Point A: 10% return, 25 new birds. Point B: 40% return, 5 new birds. Find two new correlations: one for the original data plus Point A, and another for the original data plus Point B.

(c) In terms of what correlation measures, explain why adding Point A makes the correlation stronger (closer to -1) and adding Point B makes the correlation weaker (closer to 0).

4.11   **Strong association but no correlation.**   The gas mileage of an automobile first increases and then decreases as the speed increases. Suppose that this relationship is very regular, as shown by the following data on speed (miles per hour) and mileage (miles per gallon):

Speed	20	30	40	50	60
MPG	24	28	30	28	24

Make a scatterplot of mileage versus speed. Show that the correlation between speed and mileage is $r = 0$. Explain why the correlation is 0 even though there is a strong relationship between speed and mileage.

CHAPTER 4 SUMMARY

To study relationships between variables, we must measure the variables on the same group of individuals.

If we think that a variable x may explain or even cause changes in another variable y, we call x an **explanatory variable** and y a **response variable.**

A **scatterplot** displays the relationship between two quantitative variables measured on the same individuals. Mark values of one variable on the horizontal axis (x axis) and values of the other variable on the vertical axis (y axis). Plot each individual's data as a point on the graph. Always plot the explanatory variable, if there is one, on the x axis of a scatterplot.

Plot points with different colors or symbols to see the effect of a categorical variable in a scatterplot.

In examining a scatterplot, look for an overall pattern showing the **direction, form,** and **strength** of the relationship, and then for **outliers** or other deviations from this pattern.

Direction: If the relationship has a clear direction, we speak of either **positive association** (high values of the two variables tend to occur together) or **negative association** (high values of one variable tend to occur with low values of the other variable).

Form: Linear relationships, where the points show a straight-line pattern, are an important form of relationship between two variables. Curved relationships and **clusters** are other forms to watch for.

Strength: The **strength** of a relationship is determined by how close the points in the scatterplot lie to a simple form such as a line.

The **correlation r** measures the strength and direction of the linear association between two quantitative variables x and y. Although you can calculate a correlation for any scatterplot, r measures only straight-line relationships.

Correlation indicates the direction of a linear relationship by its sign: $r > 0$ for a positive association and $r < 0$ for a negative association. Correlation always satisfies $-1 \leq r \leq 1$ and indicates the strength of a relationship by how close it is to -1 or 1. Perfect correlation, $r = \pm 1$, occurs only when the points on a scatterplot lie exactly on a straight line.

Correlation ignores the distinction between explanatory and response variables. The value of r is not affected by changes in the unit of measurement of either variable. Correlation is not resistant, so outliers can greatly change the value of r.

CHECK YOUR SKILLS

4.12   You have data for many families on the parents' income and the years of education their eldest child completes. When you make a scatterplot, the explanatory variable on the x axis

(a) is parents' income.

(b) is years of education.

(c) can be either income or education.

4.13   You have data for many families on the parents' income and the years of education their eldest child completes. You expect to see

(a) a positive association.

(b) very little association.

(c) a negative association.

4.14   Figure 4.6 is a scatterplot of reading test scores against IQ test scores for 14 fifth-grade children. There is one low outlier in the plot. The IQ and reading scores for this child are

(a) IQ = 10, reading = 124.

(b) IQ = 124, reading = 72.

(c) IQ = 124, reading = 10.

4.15   Removing the outlier in Figure 4.6 would

(a) increase the correlation between IQ and reading score.

(b) decrease the correlation between IQ and reading score.

(c) have little effect on the correlation.

4.16   If we leave out the low outlier, the correlation for the remaining 14 points in Figure 4.6 is closest to

(a) 0.5.   (b) −0.5.   (c) 0.95.

4.17   What are all the values that a correlation r can possibly take?

(a) $r \geq 0$ (b) $0 \leq r \leq 1$ (c) $-1 \leq r \leq 1$

FIGURE 4.6 Scatterplot of reading test score against IQ test score for fifth-grade children, for Exercises 4.14 to 4.16.

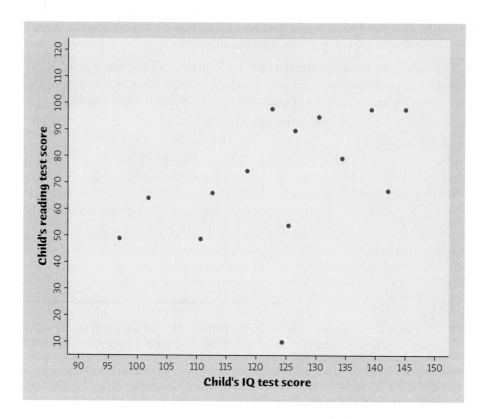

4.18 The points on a scatterplot lie very close to the line whose equation is $y = 4 - 3x$. The correlation between x and y is close to

(a) −3.   (b) −1.   (c) 1.

4.19 If women always married men who were 2 years older than themselves, the correlation between the ages of husband and wife would be

(a) 1.

(b) 0.5.

(c) Can't tell without seeing the data.

4.20 For a biology project, you measure the weight in grams and the tail length in millimeters of a group of mice. The correlation is $r = 0.7$. If you had measured tail length in centimeters instead of millimeters, what would be the correlation? (There are 10 millimeters in a centimeter.)

(a) 0.7/10 = 0.07   (b) 0.7   (c) (0.7)(10) = 7

4.21 Because elderly people may have difficulty standing to have their heights measured, a study looked at predicting overall height from height to the knee. Here are data (in centimeters) for five elderly men:

Knee height x	57.7	47.4	43.5	44.8	55.2
Height y	192.1	153.3	146.4	162.7	169.1

Use your calculator or software: the correlation between knee height and overall height is about

(a) $r = 0.88$.   (b) $r = 0.09$.   (c) $r = 0.77$.

CHAPTER 4 EXERCISES

4.22   Stocks versus T-bills.   What is the relationship between returns from buying Treasury bills and returns from buying common stocks? To buy a Treasury bill is to make a short-term loan to the U.S. government. This is much less risky than buying stock in a company, so (on the average) the returns on Treasury bills are lower than the return on stocks. Figure 4.7 plots the annual returns on stocks for the years 1950 to 2003 against the returns on Treasury bills for the same years.

(a) The best year for stocks during this period was 1954. The worst year was 1974. About what were the returns on stocks in those two years?

(b) Treasury bills are a measure of the general level of interest rates. The years around 1980 saw very high interest rates. Treasury bill returns peaked in 1981. About what was the percent return that year?

(c) Some people say that high Treasury bill returns tend to go with low returns on stocks. Does such a pattern appear clearly in Figure 4.7? Does the plot have any clear pattern?

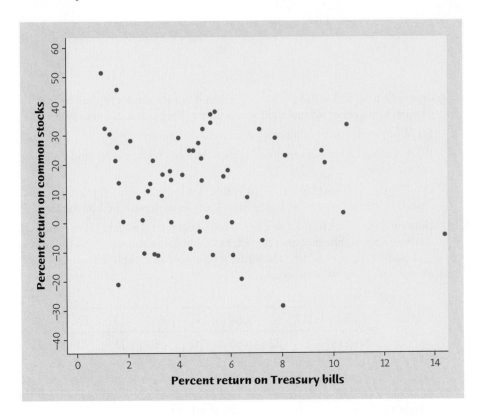

FIGURE 4.7 Scatterplot of yearly return on common stocks against return on Treasury bills, for Exercise 4.22.

4.23   Can children estimate their own reading ability?   To study this question, investigators asked 60 fifth-grade children to estimate their own reading ability,

FIGURE 4.8 Scatterplot of children's estimates of their reading ability (on a scale of 1 to 5) against their score on a reading test, for Exercise 4.23.

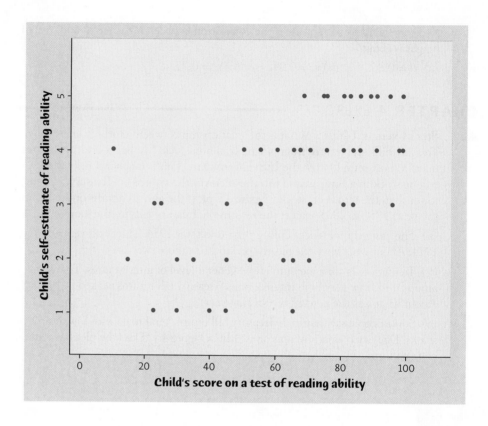

on a scale from 1 (low) to 5 (high). Figure 4.8 is a scatterplot of the children's estimates (response) against their scores on a reading test (explanatory).[7]

(a) What explains the "stair-step" pattern in the plot?

(b) Is there an overall positive association between reading score and self-estimate?

(c) There is one clear outlier. What is this child's self-estimated reading level? Does this appear to over- or underestimate the level as measured by the test?

4.24   **Data on dating.**   A student wonders if tall women tend to date taller men than do short women. She measures herself, her dormitory roommate, and the women in the adjoining rooms; then she measures the next man each woman dates. Here are the data (heights in inches):

Women (x)	66	64	66	65	70	65
Men (y)	72	68	70	68	71	65

(a) Make a scatterplot of these data. Based on the scatterplot, do you expect the correlation to be positive or negative? Near ±1 or not?

(b) Find the correlation r between the heights of the men and women. Do the data show that taller women tend to date taller men?

TABLE 4.3   World record times for the 10,000-meter run

Men				Women	
Record year	Time (seconds)	Record year	Time (seconds)	Record year	Time (seconds)
1912	1880.8	1962	1698.2	1967	2286.4
1921	1840.2	1963	1695.6	1970	2130.5
1924	1835.4	1965	1659.3	1975	2100.4
1924	1823.2	1972	1658.4	1975	2041.4
1924	1806.2	1973	1650.8	1977	1995.1
1937	1805.6	1977	1650.5	1979	1972.5
1938	1802.0	1978	1642.4	1981	1950.8
1939	1792.6	1984	1633.8	1981	1937.2
1944	1775.4	1989	1628.2	1982	1895.3
1949	1768.2	1993	1627.9	1983	1895.0
1949	1767.2	1993	1618.4	1983	1887.6
1949	1761.2	1994	1612.2	1984	1873.8
1950	1742.6	1995	1603.5	1985	1859.4
1953	1741.6	1996	1598.1	1986	1813.7
1954	1734.2	1997	1591.3	1993	1771.8
1956	1722.8	1997	1587.8		
1956	1710.4	1998	1582.7		
1960	1698.8	2004	1580.3		

4.25   World record running times.   Table 4.3 shows the progress of world record times (in seconds) for the 10,000-meter run for both men and women.

(a) Make a scatterplot of world record time against year, using separate symbols for men and women. Describe the pattern for each sex. Then compare the progress of men and women.

(b) Find the correlation between record time and year separately for men and for women. What do the correlations say about the patterns?

(c) Women began running this long distance later than men, so we might expect their improvement to be more rapid. Moreover, it is often said that men have little advantage over women in distance running as opposed to sprints, where muscular strength plays a greater role. Do the data appear to support these claims?

4.26   Thinking about correlation.   Exercise 4.24 presents data on the heights of women and of the men they date.

(a) How would r change if all the men were 6 inches shorter than the heights given in the table? Does the correlation tell us whether women tend to date men taller than themselves?

(b) If heights were measured in centimeters rather than inches, how would the correlation change? (There are 2.54 centimeters in an inch.)

Duomo/CORBIS

(c) If every woman dated a man exactly 3 inches taller than herself, what would be the correlation between male and female heights?

4.27 **Heating a home.** The Sanchez household is about to install solar panels to reduce the cost of heating their house. In order to know how much the solar panels help, they record their consumption of natural gas before the panels are installed. Gas consumption is higher in cold weather, so the relationship between outside temperature and gas consumption is important. Here are data for 16 consecutive months:[8]

Month	Nov.	Dec.	Jan.	Feb.	Mar.	Apr.	May	June
Degree-days per day	24	51	43	33	26	13	4	0
Gas used per day	6.3	10.9	8.9	7.5	5.3	4.0	1.7	1.2

Month	July	Aug.	Sept.	Oct.	Nov.	Dec.	Jan.	Feb.
Degree-days per day	0	1	6	12	30	32	52	30
Gas used per day	1.2	1.2	2.1	3.1	6.4	7.2	11.0	6.9

Outside temperature is recorded in degree-days, a common measure of demand for heating. A day's degree-days are the number of degrees its average temperature falls below 65°F. Gas used is recorded in hundreds of cubic feet. Make a plot and describe the pattern. Is correlation a helpful way to describe the pattern? Why or why not? Find the correlation if it is helpful.

4.28 **How many corn plants are too many?** How much corn per acre should a farmer plant to obtain the highest yield? Too few plants will give a low yield. On the other hand, if there are too many plants, they will compete with each other for moisture and nutrients, and yields will fall. To find the best planting rate, plant at different rates on several plots of ground and measure the harvest. (Be sure to treat all the plots the same except for the planting rate.) Here are data from such an experiment:[9]

Plants per acre	Yield (bushels per acre)			
12,000	150.1	113.0	118.4	142.6
16,000	166.9	120.7	135.2	149.8
20,000	165.3	130.1	139.6	149.9
24,000	134.7	138.4	156.1	
28,000	119.0	150.5		

(a) Is yield or planting rate the explanatory variable?

(b) Make a scatterplot of yield and planting rate. Use a scale of yields from 100 to 200 bushels per acre so that the pattern will be clear.

(c) Describe the overall pattern of the relationship. Is it linear? Is there a positive or negative association, or neither? Is correlation *r* a helpful description of this relationship? Find the correlation if it is helpful.

(d) Find the mean yield for each of the five planting rates. Plot each mean yield against its planting rate on your scatterplot and connect these five points with lines. This combination of numerical description and graphing makes the relationship clearer. What planting rate would you recommend to a farmer whose conditions were similar to those in the experiment?

4.29 **Do solar panels reduce gas usage?** After the Sanchez household gathered the information recorded in Exercise 4.27, they added solar panels to their house. They then measured their natural-gas consumption for 23 more months. Here are the data:[10]

Degree-days	19	3	3	0	0	0	8	11	27	46	38	34
Gas used	3.2	2.0	1.6	1.0	0.7	0.7	1.6	3.1	5.1	7.7	7.0	6.1

Degree-days	16	9	2	1	0	2	3	18	32	34	40
Gas used	3.0	2.1	1.3	1.0	1.0	1.0	1.2	3.4	6.1	6.5	7.5

Add the new data to your scatterplot from Exercise 4.27, using a different color or symbol. What do the before-and-after data show about the effect of solar panels?

4.30 **Hot mutual funds.** Fidelity Investments, like other large mutual-funds companies, offers many "sector funds" that concentrate their investments in narrow segments of the stock market. These funds often rise or fall by much more than the market as a whole. We can group them by broader market sector to compare returns. Here are percent total returns for 23 Fidelity "Select Portfolios" funds for the year 2003, a year in which stocks rose sharply:[11]

Market sector	Fund returns (percent)						
Consumer	23.9	14.1	41.8	43.9	31.1		
Financial services	32.3	36.5	30.6	36.9	27.5		
Natural resources	22.9	7.6	32.1	28.7	29.5	19.1	
Technology	26.1	62.7	68.1	71.9	57.0	35.0	59.4

(a) Make a plot of total return against market sector (space the four market sectors equally on the horizontal axis). Compute the mean return for each sector, add the means to your plot, and connect the means with line segments.

(b) Based on the data, which of these market sectors were the best places to invest in 2003? Hindsight is wonderful.

(c) Does it make sense to speak of a positive or negative association between market sector and total return? Why? Is correlation r a helpful description of the relationship? Why?

4.31 **Statistics for investing.** Investment reports now often include correlations. Following a table of correlations among mutual funds, a report adds: "Two funds can have perfect correlation, yet different levels of risk. For example, Fund A and Fund B may be perfectly correlated, yet Fund A moves 20% whenever Fund B moves 10%." Write a brief explanation, for someone who knows no statistics, of how this can happen. Include a sketch to illustrate your explanation.

4.32 **Statistics for investing.** A mutual-funds company's newsletter says, "A well-diversified portfolio includes assets with low correlations." The newsletter includes a table of correlations between the returns on various classes of investments. For example, the correlation between municipal bonds and large-cap stocks is 0.50, and the correlation between municipal bonds and small-cap stocks is 0.21.

(a) Rachel invests heavily in municipal bonds. She wants to diversify by adding an investment whose returns do not closely follow the returns on her bonds. Should she choose large-cap stocks or small-cap stocks for this purpose? Explain your answer.

(b) If Rachel wants an investment that tends to increase when the return on her bonds drops, what kind of correlation should she look for?

4.33 **The effect of changing units.** Changing the units of measurement can dramatically alter the appearance of a scatterplot. Return to the data on knee height and overall height in Exercise 4.21:

Knee height x	57.7	47.4	43.5	44.8	55.2
Height y	192.1	153.3	146.4	162.7	169.1

Both heights are measured in centimeters. A mad scientist prefers to measure knee height in millimeters and height in meters. The data in these units are:

Knee height x	577	474	435	448	552
Height y	1.921	1.533	1.464	1.627	1.691

(a) Make a plot with x axis extending from 0 to 600 and y axis from 0 to 250. Plot the original data on these axes. Then plot the new data using a different color or symbol. The two plots look very different.

(b) Nonetheless, the correlation is exactly the same for the two sets of measurements. Why do you know that this is true without doing any calculations? Find the two correlations to verify that they are the same.

4.34 **Teaching and research.** A college newspaper interviews a psychologist about student ratings of the teaching of faculty members. The psychologist says, "The evidence indicates that the correlation between the research productivity and teaching rating of faculty members is close to zero." The paper reports this as "Professor McDaniel said that good researchers tend to be poor teachers, and vice versa." Explain why the paper's report is wrong. Write a statement in plain language (don't use the word "correlation") to explain the psychologist's meaning.

4.35 **Sloppy writing about correlation.** Each of the following statements contains a blunder. Explain in each case what is wrong.

(a) "There is a high correlation between the gender of American workers and their income."

(b) "We found a high correlation ($r = 1.09$) between students' ratings of faculty teaching and ratings made by other faculty members."

(c) "The correlation between planting rate and yield of corn was found to be $r = 0.23$ bushel."

4.36 **Correlation is not resistant.** Go to the *Correlation and Regression* applet. Click on the scatterplot to create a group of 10 points in the lower-left corner of the scatterplot with a strong straight-line pattern (correlation about 0.9).

(a) Add one point at the upper right that is in line with the first 10. How does the correlation change?

(b) Drag this last point down until it is opposite the group of 10 points. How small can you make the correlation? Can you make the correlation negative? You see that a single outlier can greatly strengthen or weaken a correlation. Always plot your data to check for outlying points.

4.37 **Match the correlation.** You are going to use the *Correlation and Regression* applet to make scatterplots with 10 points that have correlation close to 0.7. The lesson is that many patterns can have the same correlation. Always plot your data before you trust a correlation.

(a) Stop after adding the first two points. What is the value of the correlation? Why does it have this value?

(b) Make a lower-left to upper-right pattern of 10 points with correlation about $r = 0.7$. (You can drag points up or down to adjust r after you have 10 points.) Make a rough sketch of your scatterplot.

(c) Make another scatterplot with 9 points in a vertical stack at the left of the plot. Add one point far to the right and move it until the correlation is close to 0.7. Make a rough sketch of your scatterplot.

(d) Make yet another scatterplot with 10 points in a curved pattern that starts at the lower left, rises to the right, then falls again at the far right. Adjust the points up or down until you have a quite smooth curve with correlation close to 0.7. Make a rough sketch of this scatterplot also.

*The following exercises ask you to answer questions from data without having the steps outlined as part of the exercise. Follow the **Formulate, Solve,** and **Conclude** steps of the four-step process described on page 53.*

4.38 **Brighter sunlight?** The brightness of sunlight at the earth's surface changes over time depending on whether the earth's atmosphere is more or less clear. Sunlight dimmed between 1960 and 1990. After 1990, air pollution dropped in industrial countries. Did sunlight brighten? Here are data from Boulder, Colorado, averaging over only clear days each year. (Other locations show similar trends.) The response variable is solar radiation in watts per square meter.[12]

Year	1992	1993	1994	1995	1996	1997	1998	1999	2000	2001	2002
Sun	243.2	246.0	248.0	250.3	250.9	250.9	250.0	248.9	251.7	251.4	250.9

4.39 **Merlins breeding.** Often the percent of an animal species in the wild that survive to breed again is lower following a successful breeding season. This is part of nature's self-regulation to keep population size stable. A study of merlins (small falcons) in northern Sweden observed the number of breeding pairs in an isolated area and the percent of males (banded for identification) who returned the next breeding season. Here are data for nine years:[13]

Breeding pairs	28	29	29	29	30	32	33	38	38
Percent return	82	83	70	61	69	58	43	50	47

Russell Burden/Index Stock Imagery/ PictureQuest

Do the data support the theory that a smaller percent of birds survive following a successful breeding season?

4.40 **Does social rejection hurt?** We often describe our emotional reaction to social rejection as "pain." A clever study asked whether social rejection causes activity in areas of the brain that are known to be activated by physical pain. If it does, we really do experience social and physical pain in similar ways. Subjects were first included and then deliberately excluded from a social activity while changes in brain activity were measured. After each activity, the subjects filled out questionnaires that assessed how excluded they felt. Here are data for 13 subjects:[14]

Subject	Social distress	Brain activity	Subject	Social distress	Brain activity
1	1.26	−0.055	8	2.18	0.025
2	1.85	−0.040	9	2.58	0.027
3	1.10	−0.026	10	2.75	0.033
4	2.50	−0.017	11	2.75	0.064
5	2.17	−0.017	12	3.33	0.077
6	2.67	0.017	13	3.65	0.124
7	2.01	0.021			

The explanatory variable is "social distress" measured by each subject's questionnaire score after exclusion relative to the score after inclusion. (So values greater than 1 show the degree of distress caused by exclusion.) The response variable is change in activity in a region of the brain that is activated by physical pain. Discuss what the data show.

4.41 **Hot mutual funds?** The data for 2003 in Exercise 4.30 make sector funds look attractive. Stocks rose sharply in 2003, after falling sharply in 2002 (and also in 2001 and 2000). Let's look at the percent returns for 2003 and 2002 for these same 23 funds.

2002 return	2003 return	2002 return	2003 return	2002 return	2003 return
−17.1	23.9	−0.7	36.9	−37.8	59.4
−6.7	14.1	−5.6	27.5	−11.5	22.9
−21.1	41.8	−26.9	26.1	−0.7	7.6
−12.8	43.9	−42.0	62.7	64.3	32.1
−18.9	31.1	−47.8	68.1	−9.6	28.7
−7.7	32.3	−50.5	71.9	−11.7	29.5
−17.2	36.5	−49.5	57.0	−2.3	19.1
−11.4	30.6	−23.4	35.0		

Do a careful analysis of these data: side-by-side comparison of the distributions of returns in 2002 and 2003 and also a description of the relationship between the returns of the same funds in these two years. What are your most important findings? (The outlier is Fidelity Gold Fund.)

Brendan Byrne/Agefotostock

Regression

Linear (straight-line) relationships between two quantitative variables are easy to understand and quite common. In Chapter 4, we found linear relationships in settings as varied as counting carnivores, icicle growth, and heating a home. Correlation measures the direction and strength of these relationships. When a scatterplot shows a linear relationship, we would like to summarize the overall pattern by drawing a line on the scatterplot.

Regression lines

A *regression line* summarizes the relationship between two variables, but only in a specific setting: one of the variables helps explain or predict the other. That is, regression describes a relationship between an explanatory variable and a response variable.

REGRESSION LINE

A **regression line** is a straight line that describes how a response variable y changes as an explanatory variable x changes. We often use a regression line to predict the value of y for a given value of x.

STEP

┌─ **EXAMPLE 5.1**   Does fidgeting keep you slim? ─────────

Obesity is a growing problem around the world. Here, following our four-step process (page 53), is an account of a study that sheds some light on gaining weight.

STATE: Some people don't gain weight even when they overeat. Perhaps fidgeting and other "nonexercise activity" (NEA) explains why—some people may spontaneously increase nonexercise activity when fed more. Researchers deliberately overfed 16 healthy young adults for 8 weeks. They measured fat gain (in kilograms) and, as an explanatory variable, change in energy use (in calories) from activity other than deliberate exercise—fidgeting, daily living, and the like. Here are the data:[1]

NEA change (cal)	−94	−57	−29	135	143	151	245	355
Fat gain (kg)	4.2	3.0	3.7	2.7	3.2	3.6	2.4	1.3
NEA change (cal)	392	473	486	535	571	580	620	690
Fat gain (kg)	3.8	1.7	1.6	2.2	1.0	0.4	2.3	1.1

Do people with larger increases in NEA tend to gain less fat?

FORMULATE: Make a scatterplot of the data and examine the pattern. If it is linear, use correlation to measure its strength and draw a regression line on the scatterplot to predict fat gain from change in NEA.

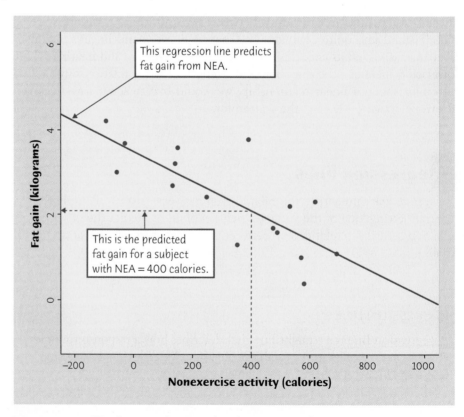

FIGURE 5.1 Weight gain after 8 weeks of overeating, plotted against increase in nonexercise activity over the same period.

SOLVE: Figure 5.1 is a scatterplot of these data. The plot shows a moderately strong negative linear association with no outliers. The correlation is $r = -0.7786$. The line on the plot is a regression line for predicting fat gain from change in NEA.

CONCLUDE: People with larger increases in nonexercise activity do indeed gain less fat. To add to this conclusion, we must study regression lines in more detail.

We can, however, already use the regression line to predict fat gain from NEA. Suppose that an individual's NEA increases by 400 calories when she overeats. Go "up and over" on the graph in Figure 5.1. From 400 calories on the x axis, go up to the regression line and then over to the y axis. The graph shows that the predicted gain in fat is a bit more than 2 kilograms.

Many calculators and software programs will give you the equation of a regression line from keyed-in data. Understanding and using the line is more important than the details of where the equation comes from.

REVIEW OF STRAIGHT LINES

Suppose that y is a response variable (plotted on the vertical axis) and x is an explanatory variable (plotted on the horizontal axis). A straight line relating y to x has an equation of the form

$$y = a + bx$$

In this equation, b is the **slope,** the amount by which y changes when x increases by one unit. The number a is the **intercept,** the value of y when $x = 0$.

EXAMPLE 5.2   *Using a regression line*

Any straight line describing the NEA data has the form

$$\text{fat gain} = a + (b \times \text{NEA change})$$

The line in Figure 5.1 is the regression line with the equation

$$\text{fat gain} = 3.505 - (0.00344 \times \text{NEA change})$$

Be sure you understand the role of the two numbers in this equation:

- The slope $b = -0.00344$ tells us that fat gained goes down by 0.00344 kilogram for each added calorie of NEA. The slope of a regression line is the *rate of change* in the response as the explanatory variable changes.
- The intercept, $a = 3.505$ kilograms, is the estimated fat gain if NEA does not change when a person overeats.

The slope of a regression line is an important numerical description of the relationship between the two variables. Although we need the value of the intercept to draw the line, this value is statistically meaningful only when, as in this example, the explanatory variable can actually take values close to zero.

The equation of the regression line makes it easy to predict fat gain. If a person's NEA increases by 400 calories when she overeats, substitute $x = 400$ in the equation. The predicted fat gain is

$$\text{fat gain} = 3.505 - (0.00344 \times 400) = 2.13 \text{ kilograms}$$

plotting a line

To **plot the line** on the scatterplot, use the equation to find the predicted y for two values of x, one near each end of the range of x in the data. Plot each y above its x and draw the line through the two points.

The slope $b = -0.00344$ in Example 5.2 is small. This does *not* mean that change in NEA has little effect on fat gain. The size of the slope depends on the units in which we measure the two variables. In this example, the slope is the change in fat gain in kilograms when NEA increases by one calorie. There are 1000 grams in a kilogram. If we measured fat gain in grams, the slope would be 1000 times larger, $b = 3.44$. *You can't say how important a relationship is by looking at the size of the slope of the regression line*.

APPLY YOUR KNOWLEDGE

5.1 **IQ and reading scores.** Data on the IQ test scores and reading test scores for a group of fifth-grade children give the regression line

$$\text{reading score} = -33.4 + (0.882 \times \text{IQ score})$$

for predicting reading score from IQ score.

(a) Say in words what the slope of this line tells you.

(b) Explain why the value of the intercept is not statistically meaningful.

(c) Find the predicted reading scores for children with IQ scores 90 and 130.

(d) Draw a graph of the regression line for IQs between 90 and 130. (Be sure to show the scales for the x and y axes.)

5.2 **The equation of a line.** An eccentric professor believes that a child with IQ 100 should have reading score 50, and that reading score should increase by 1 point for every additional point of IQ. What is the equation of the professor's regression line for predicting reading score from IQ?

The least-squares regression line

In most cases, no line will pass exactly through all the points in a scatterplot. Different people will draw different lines by eye. We need a way to draw a regression line that doesn't depend on our guess as to where the line should go. Because we use the line to predict y from x, the prediction errors we make are errors in y, the vertical direction in the scatterplot. *A good regression line makes the vertical distances of the points from the line as small as possible*.

Figure 5.2 illustrates the idea. This plot shows three of the points from Figure 5.1, along with the line, on an expanded scale. The line passes above one of the points and below two of them. The three prediction errors appear as vertical line

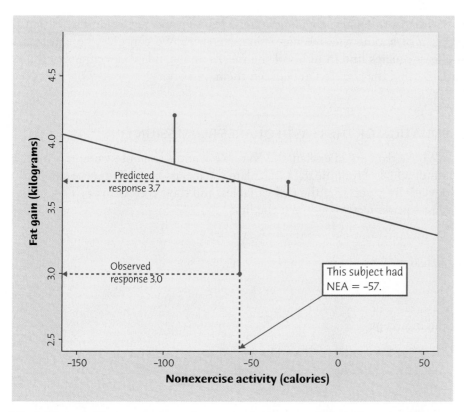

FIGURE 5.2 The least-squares idea. For each observation, find the vertical distance of each point on the scatterplot from a regression line. The least-squares regression line makes the sum of the squares of these distances as small as possible.

segments. For example, one subject had $x = -57$, a decrease of 57 calories in NEA. The line predicts a fat gain of 3.7 kilograms, but the actual fat gain for this subject was 3.0 kilograms. The prediction error is

$$\text{error} = \text{observed response} - \text{predicted response}$$
$$= 3.0 - 3.7 = -0.7 \text{ kilogram}$$

There are many ways to make the collection of vertical distances "as small as possible." The most common is the *least-squares* method.

LEAST-SQUARES REGRESSION LINE

The **least-squares regression line** of y on x is the line that makes the sum of the squares of the vertical distances of the data points from the line as small as possible.

One reason for the popularity of the least-squares regression line is that the problem of finding the line has a simple answer. We can give the equation for the least-squares line in terms of the means and standard deviations of the two variables and the correlation between them.

EQUATION OF THE LEAST-SQUARES REGRESSION LINE

We have data on an explanatory variable x and a response variable y for n individuals. From the data, calculate the means $\bar{x}$ and $\bar{y}$ and the standard deviations s_x and s_y of the two variables, and their correlation r. The least-squares regression line is the line

$$\hat{y} = a + bx$$

with **slope**

$$b = r\frac{s_y}{s_x}$$

and **intercept**

$$a = \bar{y} - b\bar{x}$$

We write $\hat{y}$ (read "y hat") in the equation of the regression line to emphasize that the line gives a *predicted* response $\hat{y}$ for any x. Because of the scatter of points about the line, the predicted response will usually not be exactly the same as the actually *observed* response y. In practice, you don't need to calculate the means, standard deviations, and correlation first. Software or your calculator will give the slope b and intercept a of the least-squares line from the values of the variables x and y. You can then concentrate on understanding and using the regression line.

Using technology

Least-squares regression is one of the most common statistical procedures. Any technology you use for statistical calculations will give you the least-squares line and related information. Figure 5.3 displays the regression output for the data of Examples 5.1 and 5.2 from a graphing calculator, two statistical programs, and a spreadsheet program. Each output records the slope and intercept of the least-squares line. The software also provides information that we do not yet need, although we will use much of it later. (In fact, we left out part of the Minitab and Excel outputs.) Be sure that you can locate the slope and intercept on all four outputs. *Once you understand the statistical ideas, you can read and work with almost any software output.*

Texas Instruments TI-83

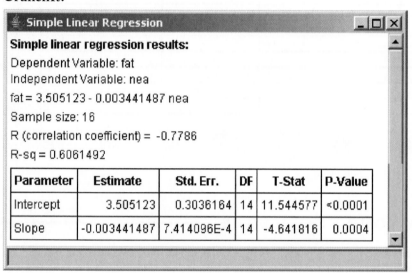

```
LinReg
 y=a+bx
 a=3.505122916
 b=-.003441487
 r²=.6061492049
 r=-.7785558457
```

CrunchIt!

Simple Linear Regression

Simple linear regression results:

Dependent Variable: fat

Independent Variable: nea

fat = 3.505123 - 0.003441487 nea

Sample size: 16

R (correlation coefficient) = -0.7786

R-sq = 0.6061492

Parameter	Estimate	Std. Err.	DF	T-Stat	P-Value
Intercept	3.505123	0.3036164	14	11.544577	<0.0001
Slope	-0.003441487	7.414096E-4	14	-4.641816	0.0004

Minitab

Session

Regression Analysis: fat versus nea

```
The regression equation is
fat = 3.51 - 0.00344 nea



Predictor          Coef      SE Coef        T        P
Constant         3.5051       0.3036    11.54    0.000
nea          -0.0034415    0.0007414    -4.64    0.000



S = 0.739853    R-Sq = 60.6%   R-Sq (adj) = 57.8%
```

FIGURE 5.3 Least-squares regression for the nonexercise activity data: output from a graphing calculator, two statistical programs, and a spreadsheet program (*continued*).

Microsoft Excel

	A	B	C	D	E	F
1	SUMMARY OUTPUT					
2						
3	*Regression statistics*					
4	Multiple R	0.778555846				
5	R Square	0.606149205				
6	Adjusted R Square	0.578017005				
7	Standard Error	0.739852874				
8	Observations	16				
9						
10		*Coefficients*	*Standard Error*	*t Stat*	*P-value*	
11	Intercept	3.505122916	0.303616403	11.54458	1.53E-08	
12	nea	-0.003441487	0.00074141	-4.64182	0.000381	
13						

Output / nea data

FIGURE 5.3 (*continued*)

APPLY YOUR KNOWLEDGE

5.3   Verify our claims. Example 5.2 gives the equation of the regression line of fat gain y on change in NEA x as

$$\hat{y} = 3.505 - 0.00344x$$

Enter the data from Example 5.1 into your software or calculator.

(a) Use the regression function to find the equation of the least-squares regression line.

(b) Also find the mean and standard deviation of both x and y and their correlation r. Calculate the slope b and intercept a of the regression line from these, using the facts in the box Equation of the Least-Squares Regression Line. Verify that in both part (a) and part (b) you get the equation in Example 5.2. (Results may differ slightly because of rounding off.)

5.4   Bird colonies. One of nature's patterns connects the percent of adult birds in a colony that return from the previous year and the number of new adults that join the colony. Here are data for 13 colonies of sparrowhawks:[2]

Percent return	74	66	81	52	73	62	52	45	62	46	60	46	38
New adults	5	6	8	11	12	15	16	17	18	18	19	20	20

As you saw in Exercise 4.4 (page 93), there is a linear relationship between the percent x of adult sparrowhawks that return to a colony from the previous year and the number y of new adult birds that join the colony.

Martin B. Withers/Frank Lane Picture
Agency/CORBIS

(a) Find the correlation r for these data. The straight-line pattern is moderately strong.

(b) Find the least-squares regression line for predicting y from x. Make a scatterplot and draw your line on the plot.

(c) Explain in words what the slope of the regression line tells us.

(d) An ecologist uses the line, based on 13 colonies, to predict how many birds will join another colony, to which 60% of the adults from the previous year return. What is the prediction?

Facts about least-squares regression

One reason for the popularity of least-squares regression lines is that they have many convenient special properties. Here are some facts about least-squares regression lines.

Fact 1. The distinction between explanatory and response variables is essential in regression. Least-squares regression makes the distances of the data points from the line small only in the y direction. If we reverse the roles of the two variables, we get a different least-squares regression line.

EXAMPLE 5.3 Predicting fat, predicting NEA ────────

Figure 5.4 repeats the scatterplot of the nonexercise activity data in Figure 5.1, but with *two* least-squares regression lines. The solid line is the regression line for predicting fat gain from change in NEA. This is the line that appeared in Figure 5.1.

We might also use the data on these 16 subjects to predict the change in NEA for another subject from that subject's fat gain when overfed for 8 weeks. Now the roles of the variables are reversed: fat gain is the explanatory variable and change in NEA is the response variable. The dashed line in Figure 5.4 is the least-squares line for predicting NEA change from fat gain. The two regression lines are not the same. *In the regression setting, you must know clearly which variable is explanatory.*

CAUTION

Fact 2. There is a close connection between correlation and the slope of the least-squares line. The slope is

$$b = r \frac{s_y}{s_x}$$

This equation says that along the regression line, **a change of one standard deviation in x corresponds to a change of r standard deviations in y.** When the variables are perfectly correlated ($r = 1$ or $r = -1$), the change in the predicted response $\hat{y}$ is the same (in standard deviation units) as the change in x. Otherwise, because $-1 \le r \le 1$, the change in $\hat{y}$ is less than the change in x. As the correlation grows less strong, the prediction $\hat{y}$ moves less in response to changes in x.

Fact 3. The least-squares regression line always passes through the point $(\overline{x}, \overline{y})$ on the graph of y against x.

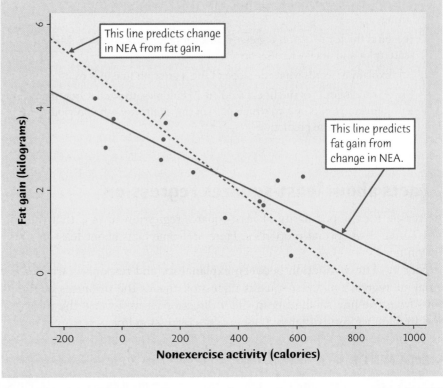

FIGURE 5.4 Two least-squares regression lines for the nonexercise activity data. The solid line predicts fat gain from change in nonexercise activity. The dashed line predicts change in nonexercise activity from fat gain.

Regression toward the mean

To "regress" means to go backward. Why are statistical methods for predicting a response from an explanatory variable called "regression"? Sir Francis Galton (1822–1911), who was the first to apply regression to biological and psychological data, looked at examples such as the heights of children versus the heights of their parents. He found that the taller-than-average parents tended to have children who were also taller than average but not as tall as their parents. Galton called this fact "regression toward the mean," and the name came to be applied to the statistical method.

Fact 4. The correlation r describes the strength of a straight-line relationship. In the regression setting, this description takes a specific form: **the square of the correlation, r^2, is the fraction of the variation in the values of y that is explained by the least-squares regression of y on x.**

The idea is that when there is a linear relationship, some of the variation in y is accounted for by the fact that as x changes it pulls y along with it. Look again at Figure 5.4, the scatterplot of the NEA data. The variation in y appears as the spread of fat gains from 0.4 kg to 4.2 kg. Some of this variation is explained by the fact that x (change in NEA) varies from a loss of 94 calories to a gain of 690 calories. As x moves from −94 to 690, it pulls y along the solid regression line. You would predict a smaller fat gain for a subject whose NEA increased by 600 calories than for someone with 0 change in NEA. But the straight-line tie of y to x doesn't explain *all* of the variation in y. The remaining variation appears as the scatter of points above and below the line.

Although we won't do the algebra, it is possible to break the variation in the observed values of y into two parts. One part measures the variation in $\hat{y}$ as x moves and pulls $\hat{y}$ with it along the regression line. The other measures the vertical scatter of the data points above and below the line. The squared correlation r^2 is the first of these as a fraction of the whole:

$$r^2 = \frac{\text{variation in } \hat{y} \text{ as } x \text{ pulls it along the line}}{\text{total variation in observed values of } y}$$

EXAMPLE 5.4 Using r^2

For the NEA data, $r = -0.7786$ and $r^2 = 0.6062$. About 61% of the variation in fat gained is accounted for by the linear relationship with change in NEA. The other 39% is individual variation among subjects that is not explained by the linear relationship.

Figure 4.2 (page 96) shows a stronger linear relationship in which the points are more tightly concentrated along a line. Here, $r = -0.9124$ and $r^2 = 0.8325$. More than 83% of the variation in carnivore abundance is explained by regression on body mass. Only 17% is variation among species with the same mass.

When you report a regression, give r^2 as a measure of how successful the regression was in explaining the response. Three of the outputs in Figure 5.3 include r^2, either in decimal form or as a percent. (CrunchIt! gives r instead.) When you see a correlation, square it to get a better feel for the strength of the association. Perfect correlation ($r = -1$ or $r = 1$) means the points lie exactly on a line. Then $r^2 = 1$ and all of the variation in one variable is accounted for by the linear relationship with the other variable. If $r = -0.7$ or $r = 0.7$, $r^2 = 0.49$ and about half the variation is accounted for by the linear relationship. In the r^2 scale, correlation ± 0.7 is about halfway between 0 and ± 1.

Facts 2, 3, and 4 are special properties of least-squares regression. They are not true for other methods of fitting a line to data.

APPLY YOUR KNOWLEDGE

5.5 **Growing corn.** Exercise 4.28 (page 110) gives data from an agricultural experiment. The purpose of the study was to see how the yield of corn changes as we change the planting rate (plants per acre).

(a) Make a scatterplot of the data. (Use a scale of yields from 100 to 200 bushels per acre.) Find the least-squares regression line for predicting yield from planting rate and add this line to your plot. Why should we *not* use the regression line for prediction in this setting?

(b) What is r^2? What does this value say about the success of the regression line in predicting yield?

(c) Even regression lines that make no practical sense obey Facts 2, 3, and 4. Use the equation of the regression line you found in (a) to show that when x is the mean planting rate, the predicted yield $\hat{y}$ is the mean of the observed yields.

5.6 **How useful is regression?** Figure 4.7 (page 107) displays the returns on common stocks and Treasury bills over a period of more than 50 years. The correlation is $r = -0.113$. Exercise 4.27 (page 110) gives data on outside temperature and natural gas used by a home during the heating season. The correlation is $r = 0.995$. Explain in simple language why knowing only these correlations enables you to say that prediction of gas used from outside temperature will be much more accurate than prediction of return on stocks from return on T-bills.

Residuals

One of the first principles of data analysis is to look for an overall pattern and also for striking deviations from the pattern. A regression line describes the overall pattern of a linear relationship between an explanatory variable and a response variable. We see deviations from this pattern by looking at the scatter of the data points about the regression line. The vertical distances from the points to the least-squares regression line are as small as possible, in the sense that they have the smallest possible sum of squares. Because they represent "left-over" variation in the response after fitting the regression line, these distances are called *residuals*.

RESIDUALS

A **residual** is the difference between an observed value of the response variable and the value predicted by the regression line. That is, a residual is the prediction error that remains after we have chosen the regression line:

$$\text{residual} = \text{observed } y - \text{predicted } y$$
$$= y - \hat{y}$$

Photodisc Green/Getty Images

EXAMPLE 5.5   I feel your pain

"Empathy" means being able to understand what others feel. To see how the brain expresses empathy, researchers recruited 16 couples in their midtwenties who were married or had been dating for at least two years. They zapped the man's hand with an electrode while the woman watched, and measured the activity in several parts of the woman's brain that would respond to her own pain. Brain activity was recorded as a fraction of the activity observed when the woman herself was zapped with the electrode. The women also completed a psychological test that measures empathy. Will women who are higher in empathy respond more strongly when their partner has a painful experience? Here are data for one brain region:[3]

Subject	1	2	3	4	5	6	7	8
Empathy score	38	53	41	55	56	61	62	48
Brain activity	−0.120	0.392	0.005	0.369	0.016	0.415	0.107	0.506
Subject	9	10	11	12	13	14	15	16
Empathy score	43	47	56	65	19	61	32	105
Brain activity	0.153	0.745	0.255	0.574	0.210	0.722	0.358	0.779

Figure 5.5 is a scatterplot, with empathy score as the explanatory variable x and brain activity as the response variable y. The plot shows a positive association. That is,

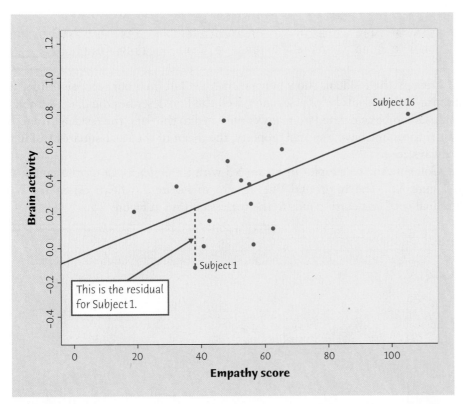

FIGURE 5.5 Scatterplot of activity in a region of the brain that responds to pain versus score on a test of empathy. Brain activity is measured as the subject watches her partner experience pain. The line is the least-squares regression line.

women who are higher in empathy do indeed react more strongly to their partner's pain. The overall pattern is moderately linear, correlation $r = 0.515$.

The line on the plot is the least-squares regression line of brain activity on empathy score. Its equation is

$$\hat{y} = -0.0578 + 0.00761x$$

For Subject 1, with empathy score 38, we predict

$$\hat{y} = -0.0578 + (0.00761)(38) = 0.231$$

This subject's actual brain activity level was -0.120. The residual is

$$\text{residual} = \text{observed } y - \text{predicted } y$$
$$= -0.120 - 0.231 = -0.351$$

The residual is negative because the data point lies below the regression line. The dashed line segment in Figure 5.5 shows the size of the residual.

There is a residual for each data point. Finding the residuals is a bit unpleasant because you must first find the predicted response for every x. Software or a graphing calculator gives you the residuals all at once. Following are the 16 residuals for the empathy study data, from software:

residuals:
```
-0.3515 -0.2494 -0.3526 -0.3072 -0.1166 -0.1136  0.1231  0.1721
 0.0463  0.0080  0.0084  0.1983  0.4449  0.1369  0.3154  0.0374
```

Because the residuals show how far the data fall from our regression line, examining the residuals helps assess how well the line describes the data. Although residuals can be calculated from any curve fitted to the data, the residuals from the least-squares line have a special property: **the mean of the least-squares residuals is always zero.**

Compare the scatterplot in Figure 5.5 with the *residual plot* for the same data in Figure 5.6. The horizontal line at zero in Figure 5.6 helps orient us. This "residual = 0" line corresponds to the regression line in Figure 5.5.

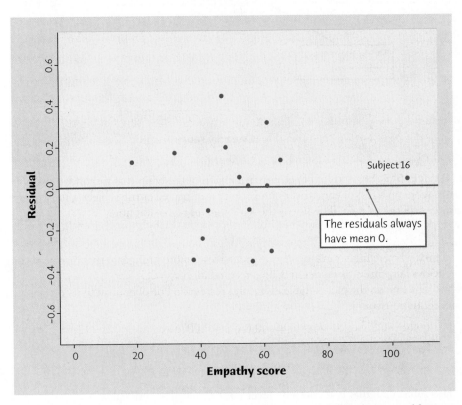

FIGURE 5.6 Residual plot for the data shown in Figure 5.5. The horizontal line at zero residual corresponds to the regression line in Figure 5.5.

RESIDUAL PLOTS

A **residual plot** is a scatterplot of the regression residuals against the explanatory variable. Residual plots help us assess how well a regression line fits the data.

A residual plot in effect turns the regression line horizontal. It magnifies the deviations of the points from the line and makes it easier to see unusual observations and patterns.

APPLY YOUR KNOWLEDGE

5.7   **Does fast driving waste fuel?**   Exercise 4.6 (page 96) gives data on the fuel consumption y of a car at various speeds x. Fuel consumption is measured in liters of gasoline per 100 kilometers driven, and speed is measured in kilometers per hour. Software tells us that the equation of the least-squares regression line is

$$\hat{y} = 11.058 - 0.01466x$$

Using this line we can add the residuals to the original data:

Speed	10	20	30	40	50	60	70	80
Fuel	21.00	13.00	10.00	8.00	7.00	5.90	6.30	6.95
Residual	10.09	2.24	−0.62	−2.47	−3.33	−4.28	−3.73	−2.94

Speed	90	100	110	120	130	140	150
Fuel	7.57	8.27	9.03	9.87	10.79	11.77	12.83
Residual	−2.17	−1.32	−0.42	0.57	1.64	2.76	3.97

(a) Make a scatterplot of the observations and draw the regression line on your plot.

(b) Would you use the regression line to predict y from x? Explain your answer.

(c) Verify the value of the first residual, for $x = 10$. Verify that the residuals have sum zero (up to roundoff error).

(d) Make a plot of the residuals against the values of x. Draw a horizontal line at height zero on your plot. How does the pattern of the residuals about this line compare with the pattern of the data points about the regression line in the scatterplot in (a)?

Influential observations

Figures 5.5 and 5.6 show one unusual observation. Subject 16 is an outlier in the x direction, with empathy score 40 points higher than any other subject. Because of its extreme position on the empathy scale, this point has a strong influence on the correlation. Dropping Subject 16 reduces the correlation from $r = 0.515$ to $r = 0.331$. You can see that this point extends the linear pattern in Figure 5.5 and so increases the correlation. We say that Subject 16 is *influential* for calculating the correlation.

INFLUENTIAL OBSERVATIONS

An observation is **influential** for a statistical calculation if removing it would markedly change the result of the calculation.

Points that are outliers in either the x or y direction of a scatterplot are often influential for the correlation. Points that are outliers in the x direction are often influential for the least-squares regression line.

EXAMPLE 5.6   An influential observation?

Subject 16 is influential for the correlation because removing it greatly reduces r. Is this observation also influential for the least-squares line? Figure 5.7 shows that it is not. The regression line calculated without Subject 16 (dashed) differs little from the line that uses all of the observations (solid). The reason that the outlier has little influence on the regression line is that it lies close to the dashed regression line calculated from the other observations.

To see why points that are outliers in the x direction are often influential, let's try an experiment. Pull Subject 16's point in the scatterplot straight down and watch the

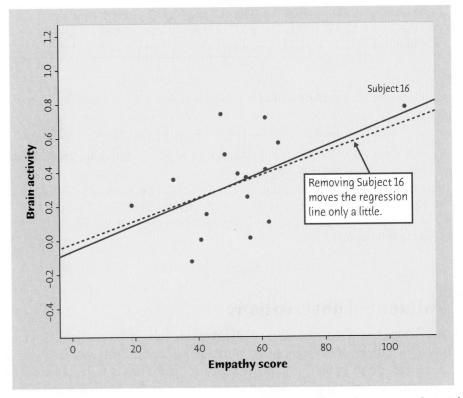

FIGURE 5.7 Subject 16 is an outlier in the x direction. The outlier is not influential for least-squares regression, because removing it moves the regression line only a little.

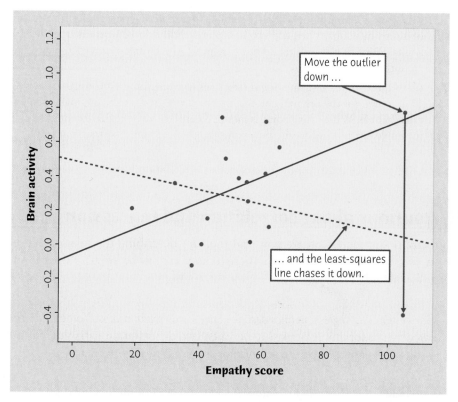

FIGURE 5.8 An outlier in the *x* direction pulls the least-squares line to itself because there are no other observations with similar values of *x* to hold the line in place. When the outlier moves down, the original regression line (solid) chases it down to the dashed line.

regression line. Figure 5.8 shows the result. The dashed line is the regression line with the outlier in its new, lower position. Because there are no other points with similar *x*-values, the line chases the outlier. An outlier in *x* pulls the least-squares line toward itself. If the outlier does not lie close to the line calculated from the other observations, it will be influential. You can use the *Correlation and Regression* applet to animate Figure 5.8.

We did not need the distinction between outliers and influential observations in Chapter 2. A single high salary that pulls up the mean salary $\bar{x}$ for a group of workers is an outlier because it lies far above the other salaries. It is also influential, because the mean changes when it is removed. In the regression setting, however, not all outliers are influential.

APPLY YOUR KNOWLEDGE

5.8   **Bird colonies.**   Return to the data of Exercise 5.4 (page 122) on sparrowhawk colonies. We will use these data to illustrate influence.

(a) Make a scatterplot of the data suitable for predicting new adults from percent of returning adults. Then add two new points. Point A: 10% return, 15 new adults. Point B: 60% return, 28 new adults. In which direction is each new point an outlier?

(b) Add three least-squares regression lines to your plot: for the original 13 colonies, for the original colonies plus Point A, and for the original colonies plus Point B. Which new point is more influential for the regression line? Explain in simple language why each new point moves the line in the way your graph shows.

Cautions about correlation and regression

Correlation and regression are powerful tools for describing the relationship between two variables. When you use these tools, you must be aware of their limitations. You already know that

- *Correlation and regression lines describe only linear relationships.* You can do the calculations for any relationship between two quantitative variables, but the results are useful only if the scatterplot shows a linear pattern.

- *Correlation and least-squares regression lines are not resistant.* Always plot your data and look for observations that may be influential.

Here are more things to keep in mind when you use correlation and regression.

Beware extrapolation. Suppose that you have data on a child's growth between 3 and 8 years of age. You find a strong linear relationship between age x and height y. If you fit a regression line to these data and use it to predict height at age 25 years, you will predict that the child will be 8 feet tall. Growth slows down and then stops at maturity, so extending the straight line to adult ages is foolish. *Few relationships are linear for all values of x. Don't make predictions far outside the range of x that actually appears in your data.*

EXTRAPOLATION

Extrapolation is the use of a regression line for prediction far outside the range of values of the explanatory variable x that you used to obtain the line. Such predictions are often not accurate.

Beware the lurking variable. Another caution is even more important: *the relationship between two variables can often be understood only by taking other variables into account. Lurking variables* can make a correlation or regression misleading.

> **LURKING VARIABLE**
>
> A **lurking variable** is a variable that is not among the explanatory or response variables in a study and yet may influence the interpretation of relationships among those variables.

You should always think about possible lurking variables before you draw conclusions based on correlation or regression.

Do left-handers die early?

Yes, said a study of 1000 deaths in California. Left-handed people died at an average age of 66 years; right-handers, at 75 years of age. Should left-handed people fear an early death? No—the lurking variable has struck again. Older people grew up in an era when many natural left-handers were forced to use their right hands. So right-handers are more common among older people, and left-handers are more common among the young. When we look at deaths, the left-handers who die are younger on the average because left-handers in general are younger. Mystery solved.

EXAMPLE 5.7   Magic Mozart?

The Kalamazoo (Michigan) Symphony once advertised a "Mozart for Minors" program with this statement: "Question: Which students scored 51 points higher in verbal skills and 39 points higher in math? Answer: Students who had experience in music."[4]

We could as well answer "Students who played soccer." Why? Children with prosperous and well-educated parents are more likely than poorer children to have experience with music and also to play soccer. They are also likely to attend good schools, get good health care, and be encouraged to study hard. These advantages lead to high test scores. Family background is a lurking variable that explains why test scores are related to experience with music.

APPLY YOUR KNOWLEDGE

5.9   The declining farm population. The number of people living on American farms has declined steadily during the last century. Here are data on the farm population (millions of persons) from 1935 to 1980:

Year	1935	1940	1945	1950	1955	1960	1965	1970	1975	1980
Population	32.1	30.5	24.4	23.0	19.1	15.6	12.4	9.7	8.9	7.2

(a) Make a scatterplot of these data and find the least-squares regression line of farm population on year.

(b) According to the regression line, how much did the farm population decline each year on the average during this period? What percent of the observed variation in farm population is accounted for by linear change over time?

(c) Use the regression equation to predict the number of people living on farms in 2000. Is this result reasonable? Why?

5.10   Is math the key to success in college? A College Board study of 15,941 high school graduates found a strong correlation between how much math minority students took in high school and their later success in college. News articles quoted the head of the College Board as saying that "math is the gatekeeper for success in college."[5] Maybe so, but we should also think about lurking variables. What might lead minority students to take more or fewer high school math courses? Would these same factors influence success in college?

Association does not imply causation

Thinking about lurking variables leads to the most important caution about correlation and regression. When we study the relationship between two variables, we often hope to show that changes in the explanatory variable *cause* changes in the response variable. *A strong association between two variables is not enough to draw conclusions about cause and effect.* Sometimes an observed association really does reflect cause and effect. A household that heats with natural gas uses more gas in colder months because cold weather requires burning more gas to stay warm. In other cases, an association is explained by lurking variables, and the conclusion that *x* causes *y* is either wrong or not proved.

> **EXAMPLE 5.8** *Does having more cars make you live longer?*
>
> A serious study once found that people with two cars live longer than people who own only one car.[6] Owning three cars is even better, and so on. There is a substantial positive correlation between number of cars *x* and length of life *y*.
>
> The basic meaning of causation is that by changing *x* we can bring about a change in *y*. Could we lengthen our lives by buying more cars? No. The study used number of cars as a quick indicator of affluence. Well-off people tend to have more cars. They also tend to live longer, probably because they are better educated, take better care of themselves, and get better medical care. The cars have nothing to do with it. There is no cause-and-effect tie between number of cars and length of life.

Correlations such as that in Example 5.8 are sometimes called "nonsense correlations." The correlation is real. What is nonsense is the conclusion that changing one of the variables causes changes in the other. A lurking variable—such as personal affluence in Example 5.8—that influences both *x* and *y* can create a high correlation even though there is no direct connection between *x* and *y*.

ASSOCIATION DOES NOT IMPLY CAUSATION

An association between an explanatory variable *x* and a response variable *y*, even if it is very strong, is not by itself good evidence that changes in *x* actually cause changes in *y*.

> **EXAMPLE 5.9** *Obesity in mothers and daughters*
>
> Obese parents tend to have obese children. The results of a study of Mexican American girls aged 9 to 12 years are typical. The investigators measured body mass index (BMI), a measure of weight relative to height, for both the girls and their mothers. People with high BMI are overweight or obese. The correlation between the BMI of daughters and the BMI of their mothers was $r = 0.506$.[7]
>
> Body type is in part determined by heredity. Daughters inherit half their genes from their mothers. There is therefore a direct causal link between the BMI of mothers and

The Super Bowl effect

The Super Bowl is the most-watched TV broadcast in the United States. Data show that on Super Bowl Sunday we consume 3 times as many potato chips as on an average day, and 17 times as much beer. What's more, the number of fatal traffic accidents goes up in the hours after the game ends. Could that be celebration? Or catching up with tasks left undone? Or maybe it's the beer.

daughters. But perhaps mothers who are overweight also set an example of little exercise, poor eating habits, and lots of television. Their daughters may pick up these habits, so the influence of heredity is mixed up with influences from the girls' environment. Both contribute to the mother-daughter correlation.

The lesson of Example 5.9 is more subtle than just "association does not imply causation." *Even when direct causation is present, it may not be the whole explanation for a correlation.* You must still worry about lurking variables. Careful statistical studies try to anticipate lurking variables and measure them. The mother-daughter study did measure TV viewing, exercise, and diet. Elaborate statistical analysis can remove the effects of these variables to come closer to the direct effect of mother's BMI on daughter's BMI. This remains a second-best approach to causation. The best way to get good evidence that x causes y is to do an **experiment** in which we change x and keep lurking variables under control. We will discuss experiments in Chapter 8.

experiment

When experiments cannot be done, explaining an observed association can be difficult and controversial. Many of the sharpest disputes in which statistics plays a role involve questions of causation that cannot be settled by experiment. Do gun control laws reduce violent crime? Does using cell phones cause brain tumors? Has increased free trade widened the gap between the incomes of more educated and less educated American workers? All of these questions have become public issues. All concern associations among variables. And all have this in common: they try to pinpoint cause and effect in a setting involving complex relations among many interacting variables.

EXAMPLE 5.10 Does smoking cause lung cancer?

Despite the difficulties, it is sometimes possible to build a strong case for causation in the absence of experiments. The evidence that smoking causes lung cancer is about as strong as nonexperimental evidence can be.

Doctors had long observed that most lung cancer patients were smokers. Comparison of smokers and "similar" nonsmokers showed a very strong association between smoking and death from lung cancer. Could the association be explained by lurking variables? Might there be, for example, a genetic factor that predisposes people both to nicotine addiction and to lung cancer? Smoking and lung cancer would then be positively associated even if smoking had no direct effect on the lungs. How were these objections overcome?

Let's answer this question in general terms: what are the criteria for establishing causation when we cannot do an experiment?

- *The association is strong.* The association between smoking and lung cancer is very strong.

- *The association is consistent.* Many studies of different kinds of people in many countries link smoking to lung cancer. That reduces the chance that a lurking variable specific to one group or one study explains the association.

- *Higher doses are associated with stronger responses.* People who smoke more cigarettes per day or who smoke over a longer period get lung cancer more often. People who stop smoking reduce their risk.

- *The alleged cause precedes the effect in time.* Lung cancer develops after years of smoking. The number of men dying of lung cancer rose as smoking became more common, with a lag of about 30 years. Lung cancer kills more men than any other form of cancer. Lung cancer was rare among women until women began to smoke. Lung cancer in women rose along with smoking, again with a lag of about 30 years, and has now passed breast cancer as the leading cause of cancer death among women.

- *The alleged cause is plausible.* Experiments with animals show that tars from cigarette smoke do cause cancer.

Medical authorities do not hesitate to say that smoking causes lung cancer. The U.S. surgeon general has long stated that cigarette smoking is "the largest avoidable cause of death and disability in the United States."[8] The evidence for causation is overwhelming—but it is not as strong as the evidence provided by well-designed experiments.

APPLY YOUR KNOWLEDGE

5.11   Education and income.   There is a strong positive association between workers' education and their income. For example, the Census Bureau reports that the median income of young adults (ages 25 to 34) who work full-time increases from \$18,508 for those with less than a ninth-grade education, to \$27,201 for high school graduates, to \$41,628 for holders of a bachelor's degree, and on up for yet more education. In part, this association reflects causation—education helps people qualify for better jobs. Suggest several lurking variables that also contribute. (Ask yourself what kinds of people tend to get more education.)

5.12   To earn more, get married?   Data show that men who are married, and also divorced or widowed men, earn quite a bit more than men the same age who have never been married. This does not mean that a man can raise his income by getting married, because men who have never been married are different from married men in many ways other than marital status. Suggest several lurking variables that might help explain the association between marital status and income.

5.13   Are big hospitals bad for you?   A study shows that there is a positive correlation between the size of a hospital (measured by its number of beds x) and the median number of days y that patients remain in the hospital. Does this mean that you can shorten a hospital stay by choosing a small hospital? Why?

CHAPTER 5 SUMMARY

A **regression line** is a straight line that describes how a response variable y changes as an explanatory variable x changes. You can use a regression line to **predict** the value of y for any value of x by substituting this x into the equation of the line.

The **slope** b of a regression line $\hat{y} = a + bx$ is the rate at which the predicted response $\hat{y}$ changes along the line as the explanatory variable x changes. Specifically, b is the change in $\hat{y}$ when x increases by 1.

The **intercept** a of a regression line $\hat{y} = a + bx$ is the predicted response $\hat{y}$ when the explanatory variable $x = 0$. This prediction is of no statistical interest unless x can actually take values near 0.

The most common method of fitting a line to a scatterplot is least squares. The **least-squares regression line** is the straight line $\hat{y} = a + bx$ that minimizes the sum of the squares of the vertical distances of the observed points from the line.

The least-squares regression line of y on x is the line with slope $r s_y/s_x$ and intercept $a = \overline{y} - b\overline{x}$. This line always passes through the point $(\overline{x}, \overline{y})$.

Correlation and regression are closely connected. The correlation r is the slope of the least-squares regression line when we measure both x and y in standardized units. The **square of the correlation** r^2 is the fraction of the variation in one variable that is explained by least-squares regression on the other variable.

Correlation and regression must be **interpreted with caution. Plot the data** to be sure the relationship is roughly linear and to detect outliers and influential observations. A plot of the **residuals** makes these effects easier to see.

Look for **influential observations,** individual points that substantially change the correlation or the regression line. Outliers in the x direction are often influential for the regression line.

Avoid **extrapolation,** the use of a regression line for prediction for values of the explanatory variable far outside the range of the data from which the line was calculated.

Lurking variables may explain the relationship between the explanatory and response variables. Correlation and regression can be misleading if you ignore important lurking variables.

Most of all, be careful not to conclude that there is a cause-and-effect relationship between two variables just because they are strongly associated. **High correlation does not imply causation.** The best evidence that an association is due to causation comes from an **experiment** in which the explanatory variable is directly changed and other influences on the response are controlled.

CHECK YOUR SKILLS

5.14 Figure 5.9 is a scatterplot of reading test scores against IQ test scores for 14 fifth-grade children. The line is the least-squares regression line for predicting reading score from IQ score. If another child in this class has IQ score 110, you predict the reading score to be close to

    (a) 50.   (b) 60.   (c) 70.

5.15 The slope of the line in Figure 5.9 is closest to

    (a) −1.   (b) 0.   (c) 1.

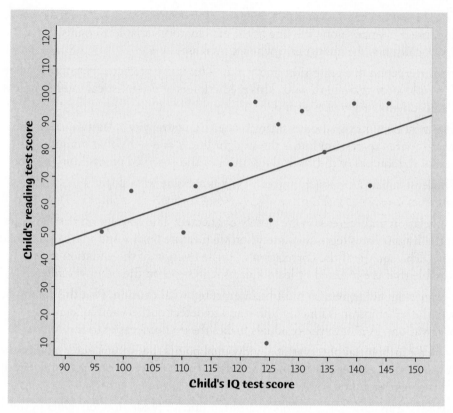

FIGURE 5.9 IQ test scores and reading test scores for 15 children, for Exercises 5.14 and 5.15.

5.16 The points on a scatterplot lie close to the line whose equation is $y = 4 - 3x$. The slope of this line is

(a) 4.   (b) 3.   (c) −3.

5.17 Fred keeps his savings in his mattress. He began with $500 from his mother and adds $100 each year. His total savings y after x years are given by the equation

(a) $y = 500 + 100x$.   (b) $y = 100 + 500x$.   (c) $y = 500 + x$.

5.18 Starting with a fresh bar of soap, you weigh the bar each day after you take a shower. Then you find the regression line for predicting weight from number of days elapsed. The slope of this line will be

(a) positive.   (b) negative.   (c) Can't tell without seeing the data.

5.19 For a biology project, you measure the weight in grams and the tail length in millimeters (mm) of a group of mice. The equation of the least-squares line for predicting tail length from weight is

$$\text{predicted tail length} = 20 + 3 \times \text{weight}$$

How much (on the average) does tail length increase for each additional gram of weight?

(a) 3 mm   (b) 20 mm   (c) 23 mm

5.20 According to the regression line in Exercise 5.19, the predicted tail length for a mouse weighing 18 grams is

(a) 74 mm.   (b) 54 mm.   (c) 34 mm.

5.21 By looking at the equation of the least-squares regression line in Exercise 5.19, you can see that the correlation between weight and tail length is

(a) greater than zero.

(b) less than zero.

(c) Can't tell without seeing the data.

5.22 If you had measured the tail length in Exercise 5.19 in centimeters instead of millimeters, what would be the slope of the regression line? (There are 10 millimeters in a centimeter.)

(a) $3/10 = 0.3$ (b) 3   (c) $(3)(10) = 30$

5.23 Because elderly people may have difficulty standing to have their heights measured, a study looked at predicting overall height from height to the knee. Here are data (in centimeters) for five elderly men:

Knee height x	57.7	47.4	43.5	44.8	55.2
Height y	192.1	153.3	146.4	162.7	169.1

Use your calculator or software: what is the equation of the least-squares regression line for predicting height from knee height?

(a) $\hat{y} = 2.4 + 44.1x$ (b) $\hat{y} = 44.1 + 2.4x$ (c) $\hat{y} = -2.5 + 0.32x$

CHAPTER 5 EXERCISES

5.24 **Penguins diving.** A study of king penguins looked for a relationship between how deep the penguins dive to seek food and how long they stay underwater.[9] For all but the shallowest dives, there is a linear relationship that is different for different penguins. The study report gives a scatterplot for one penguin titled "The relation of dive duration (DD) to depth (D)." Duration DD is measured in minutes, and depth D is in meters. The report then says, "The regression equation for this bird is: $DD = 2.69 + 0.0138D$."

Paul A. Souders/CORBIS

(a) What is the slope of the regression line? Explain in specific language what this slope says about this penguin's dives.

(b) According to the regression line, how long does a typical dive to a depth of 200 meters last?

(c) The dives varied from 40 meters to 300 meters in depth. Plot the regression line from $x = 40$ to $x = 300$.

5.25 **Measuring water quality.** Biochemical oxygen demand (BOD) measures organic pollutants in water by measuring the amount of oxygen consumed by microorganisms that break down these compounds. BOD is hard to measure accurately. Total organic carbon (TOC) is easy to measure, so it is common to measure TOC and use regression to predict BOD. A typical regression equation for water entering a municipal treatment plant is[10]

$$BOD = -55.43 + 1.507 \, TOC$$

Both BOD and TOC are measured in milligrams per liter of water.

(a) What does the slope of this line say about the relationship between BOD and TOC?

(b) What is the predicted BOD when TOC = 0? Values of BOD less than 0 are impossible. Why do you think the prediction gives an impossible value?

5.26 **Sisters and brothers.** How strongly do physical characteristics of sisters and brothers correlate? Here are data on the heights (in inches) of 11 adult pairs:[11]

Brother	71	68	66	67	70	71	70	73	72	65	66
Sister	69	64	65	63	65	62	65	64	66	59	62

(a) Use your calculator or software to find the correlation and to verify that the least-squares line for predicting sister's height from brother's height is $\hat{y} = 27.64 + 0.527x$. Make a scatterplot that includes this line.

(b) Damien is 70 inches tall. Predict the height of his sister Tonya. Based on the scatterplot and the correlation r, do you expect your prediction to be very accurate? Why?

5.27 **Heating a home.** Exercise 4.27 (page 110) gives data on degree-days and natural gas consumed by the Sanchez home for 16 consecutive months. There is a very strong linear relationship. Mr. Sanchez asks, "If a month averages 20 degree-days per day (that's 45°F), how much gas will we use?" Use your calculator or software to find the least-squares regression line and answer his question. Based on a scatterplot and r^2, do you expect your prediction from the regression line to be quite accurate? Why?

5.28 **Does social rejection hurt?** Exercise 4.40 (page 114) gives data from a study that shows that social exclusion causes "real pain." That is, activity in an area of the brain that responds to physical pain goes up as distress from social exclusion goes up. A scatterplot shows a moderately strong linear relationship. Figure 5.10 shows regression output from software for these data.

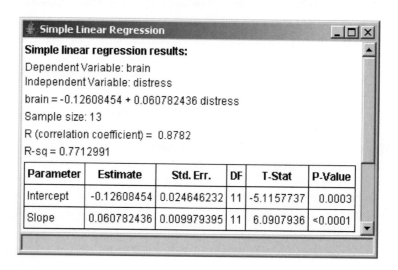

FIGURE 5.10 CrunchIt! regression output for a study of the effects of social rejection on brain activity, for Exercise 5.28.

(a) What is the equation of the least-squares regression line for predicting brain activity from social distress score? Use the equation to predict brain activity for social distress score 2.0.

(b) What percent of the variation in brain activity among these subjects is explained by the straight-line relationship with social distress score?

5.29   **Merlins breeding.**   Exercise 4.39 (page 113) gives data on the number of breeding pairs of merlins in an isolated area in each of nine years and the percent of males who returned the next year. The data show that the percent returning is lower after successful breeding seasons and that the relationship is roughly linear. Figure 5.11 shows software regression output for these data.

(a) What is the equation of the least-squares regression line for predicting the percent of males that return from the number of breeding pairs? Use the equation to predict the percent of returning males after a season with 30 breeding pairs.

(b) What percent of the year-to-year variation in percent of returning males is explained by the straight-line relationship with number of breeding pairs the previous year?

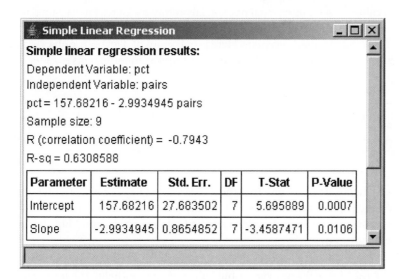

FIGURE 5.11 CrunchIt! regression output for a study of how breeding success affects survival in birds, for Exercise 5.29.

5.30   **Husbands and wives.**   The mean height of American women in their twenties is about 64 inches, and the standard deviation is about 2.7 inches. The mean height of men the same age is about 69.3 inches, with standard deviation about 2.8 inches. If the correlation between the heights of husbands and wives is about $r = 0.5$, what is the slope of the regression line of the husband's height on the wife's height in young couples? Draw a graph of this regression line. Predict the height of the husband of a woman who is 67 inches tall.

5.31   **What's my grade?**   In Professor Friedman's economics course the correlation between the students' total scores prior to the final examination and their final-examination scores is $r = 0.6$. The pre-exam totals for all students in the course have mean 280 and standard deviation 30. The final-exam scores have mean 75 and standard deviation 8. Professor Friedman has lost Julie's final exam but knows that her total before the exam was 300. He decides to predict her final-exam score from her pre-exam total.

(a) What is the slope of the least-squares regression line of final-exam scores on pre-exam total scores in this course? What is the intercept?

(b) Use the regression line to predict Julie's final-exam score.

(c) Julie doesn't think this method accurately predicts how well she did on the final exam. Use r^2 to argue that her actual score could have been much higher (or much lower) than the predicted value.

5.32 **Going to class.** A study of class attendance and grades among first-year students at a state university showed that in general students who attended a higher percent of their classes earned higher grades. Class attendance explained 16% of the variation in grade index among the students. What is the numerical value of the correlation between percent of classes attended and grade index?

5.33 **Keeping water clean.** Keeping water supplies clean requires regular measurement of levels of pollutants. The measurements are indirect—a typical analysis involves forming a dye by a chemical reaction with the dissolved pollutant, then passing light through the solution and measuring its "absorbence." To calibrate such measurements, the laboratory measures known standard solutions and uses regression to relate absorbence and pollutant concentration. This is usually done every day. Here is one series of data on the absorbence for different levels of nitrates. Nitrates are measured in milligrams per liter of water.[12]

Nitrates	50	50	100	200	400	800	1200	1600	2000	2000
Absorbence	7.0	7.5	12.8	24.0	47.0	93.0	138.0	183.0	230.0	226.0

(a) Chemical theory says that these data should lie on a straight line. If the correlation is not at least 0.997, something went wrong and the calibration procedure is repeated. Plot the data and find the correlation. Must the calibration be done again?

(b) The calibration process sets nitrate level and measures absorbence. Once established, the linear relationship will be used to estimate the nitrate level in water from a measurement of absorbence. What is the equation of the line used for estimation? What is the estimated nitrate level in a water specimen with absorbence 40?

(c) Do you expect estimates of nitrate level from absorbence to be quite accurate? Why?

5.34 **Always plot your data!** Table 5.1 presents four sets of data prepared by the statistician Frank Anscombe to illustrate the dangers of calculating without first plotting the data.[13]

(a) Without making scatterplots, find the correlation and the least-squares regression line for all four data sets. What do you notice? Use the regression line to predict y for x = 10.

(b) Make a scatterplot for each of the data sets and add the regression line to each plot.

TABLE 5.1   Four data sets for exploring correlation and regression

Data Set A

x	10	8	13	9	11	14	6	4	12	7	5
y	8.04	6.95	7.58	8.81	8.33	9.96	7.24	4.26	10.84	4.82	5.68

Data Set B

x	10	8	13	9	11	14	6	4	12	7	5
y	9.14	8.14	8.74	8.77	9.26	8.10	6.13	3.10	9.13	7.26	4.74

Data Set C

x	10	8	13	9	11	14	6	4	12	7	5
y	7.46	6.77	12.74	7.11	7.81	8.84	6.08	5.39	8.15	6.42	5.73

Data Set D

x	8	8	8	8	8	8	8	8	8	8	19
y	6.58	5.76	7.71	8.84	8.47	7.04	5.25	5.56	7.91	6.89	12.50

(c) In which of the four cases would you be willing to use the regression line to describe the dependence of y on x? Explain your answer in each case.

5.35 **Drilling into the past.** Drilling down beneath a lake in Alaska yields chemical evidence of past changes in climate. Biological silicon, left by the skeletons of single-celled creatures called diatoms, is a measure of the abundance of life in the lake. A rather complex variable based on the ratio of certain isotopes relative to ocean water gives an indirect measure of moisture, mostly from snow. As we drill down, we look further into the past. Here are data from 2300 to 12,000 years ago:[14]

Darlyne A. Murawski/National Geographic/Getty Images

Isotope (%)	Silicon (mg/g)	Isotope (%)	Silicon (mg/g)	Isotope (%)	Silicon (mg/g)
−19.90	97	−20.71	154	−21.63	224
−19.84	106	−20.80	265	−21.63	237
−19.46	118	−20.86	267	−21.19	188
−20.20	141	−21.28	296	−19.37	337

(a) Make a scatterplot of silicon (response) against isotope (explanatory). Ignoring the outlier, describe the direction, form, and strength of the relationship. The researchers say that this and relationships among other variables they measured are evidence for cyclic changes in climate that are linked to changes in the sun's activity.

(b) The researchers single out one point: "The open circle in the plot is an outlier that was excluded in the correlation analysis." Circle this outlier on your graph. What is the correlation with and without this point? The point strongly influences the correlation. Explain why the outlier moves r in the direction revealed by your calculations.

5.36 **Managing diabetes.**   People with diabetes must manage their blood sugar levels carefully. They measure their fasting plasma glucose (FPG) several times a day with a glucose meter. Another measurement, made at regular medical checkups, is called HbA. This is roughly the percent of red blood cells that have a glucose molecule attached. It measures average exposure to glucose over a period of several months. Table 5.2 gives data on both HbA and FPG for 18 diabetics five months after they had completed a diabetes education class.[15]

TABLE 5.2		Two measures of glucose level in diabetics						
Subject	HbA (%)	FPG (mg/ml)	Subject	HbA (%)	FPG (mg/ml)	Subject	HbA (%)	FPG (mg/ml)
1	6.1	141	7	7.5	96	13	10.6	103
2	6.3	158	8	7.7	78	14	10.7	172
3	6.4	112	9	7.9	148	15	10.7	359
4	6.8	153	10	8.7	172	16	11.2	145
5	7.0	134	11	9.4	200	17	13.7	147
6	7.1	95	12	10.4	271	18	19.3	255

(a) Make a scatterplot with HbA as the explanatory variable. There is a positive linear relationship, but it is surprisingly weak.

(b) Subject 15 is an outlier in the y direction. Subject 18 is an outlier in the x direction. Find the correlation for all 18 subjects, for all except Subject 15, and for all except Subject 18. Are either or both of these subjects influential for the correlation? Explain in simple language why r changes in opposite directions when we remove each of these points.

5.37 **Drilling into the past, continued.**   Is the outlier in Exercise 5.35 also strongly influential for the regression line? Calculate and draw on your graph two regression lines, and discuss what you see. Explain why adding the outlier moves the regression line in the direction shown on your graph.

5.38 **Managing diabetes, continued.**   Add three regression lines for predicting FPG from HbA to your scatterplot from Exercise 5.36: for all 18 subjects, for all except Subject 15, and for all except Subject 18. Is either Subject 15 or Subject 18 strongly influential for the least-squares line? Explain in simple language what features of the scatterplot explain the degree of influence.

5.39 **Influence in regression.**   The *Correlation and Regression* applet allows you to animate Figure 5.8. Click to create a group of 10 points in the lower-left corner of the scatterplot with a strong straight-line pattern (correlation about 0.9). Click the "Show least-squares line" box to display the regression line.

(a) Add one point at the upper right that is far from the other 10 points but exactly on the regression line. Why does this outlier have no effect on the line even though it changes the correlation?

(b) Now use the mouse to drag this last point straight down. You see that one end of the least-squares line chases this single point, while the other end remains near the middle of the original group of 10. What makes the last point so influential?

5.40 **Beavers and beetles.** Ecologists sometimes find rather strange relationships in our environment. For example, do beavers benefit beetles? Researchers laid out 23 circular plots, each 4 meters in diameter, in an area where beavers were cutting down cottonwood trees. In each plot, they counted the number of stumps from trees cut by beavers and the number of clusters of beetle larvae. Ecologists think that the new sprouts from stumps are more tender than other cottonwood growth, so that beetles prefer them. If so, more stumps should produce more beetle larvae. Here are the data:[16]

Stumps	2	2	1	3	3	4	3	1	2	5	1	3
Beetle larvae	10	30	12	24	36	40	43	11	27	56	18	40

Stumps	2	1	2	2	1	1	4	1	2	1	4
Beetle larvae	25	8	21	14	16	6	54	9	13	14	50

Analyze these data to see if they support the "beavers benefit beetles" idea. Follow the four-step process (page 53) in reporting your work.

5.41 **Climate change.** Global warming has many indirect effects on climate. For example, the summer monsoon winds in the Arabian Sea bring rain to India and are critical for agriculture. As the climate warms and winter snow cover in the vast landmass of Europe and Asia decreases, the land heats more rapidly in the summer. This may increase the strength of the monsoon. Here are data on snow cover (in millions of square kilometers) and summer wind stress (in newtons per square meter):[17]

Daniel J. Cox/Natural Exposures

Snow cover	Wind stress	Snow cover	Wind stress	Snow cover	Wind stress
6.6	0.125	16.6	0.111	26.6	0.062
5.9	0.160	18.2	0.106	27.1	0.051
6.8	0.158	15.2	0.143	27.5	0.068
7.7	0.155	16.2	0.153	28.4	0.055
7.9	0.169	17.1	0.155	28.6	0.033
7.8	0.173	17.3	0.133	29.6	0.029
8.1	0.196	18.1	0.130	29.4	0.024

Analyze these data to uncover the nature and strength of the effect of decreasing snow cover on wind stress. Follow the four-step process (page 53) in reporting your work.

TABLE 5.3   Reaction times in a computer game

Time	Distance	Hand	Time	Distance	Hand
115	190.70	right	240	190.70	left
96	138.52	right	190	138.52	left
110	165.08	right	170	165.08	left
100	126.19	right	125	126.19	left
111	163.19	right	315	163.19	left
101	305.66	right	240	305.66	left
111	176.15	right	141	176.15	left
106	162.78	right	210	162.78	left
96	147.87	right	200	147.87	left
96	271.46	right	401	271.46	left
95	40.25	right	320	40.25	left
96	24.76	right	113	24.76	left
96	104.80	right	176	104.80	left
106	136.80	right	211	136.80	left
100	308.60	right	238	308.60	left
113	279.80	right	316	279.80	left
123	125.51	right	176	125.51	left
111	329.80	right	173	329.80	left
95	51.66	right	210	51.66	left
108	201.95	right	170	201.95	left

5.42   A computer game.   A multimedia statistics learning system includes a test of skill in using the computer's mouse. The software displays a circle at a random location on the computer screen. The subject clicks in the circle with the mouse as quickly as possible. A new circle appears as soon as the subject clicks the old one. Table 5.3 gives data for one subject's trials, 20 with each hand. Distance is the distance from the cursor location to the center of the new circle, in units whose actual size depends on the size of the screen. Time is the time required to click in the new circle, in milliseconds.[18]

(a) We suspect that time depends on distance. Make a scatterplot of time against distance, using separate symbols for each hand.

(b) Describe the pattern. How can you tell that the subject is right-handed?

(c) Find the regression line of time on distance separately for each hand. Draw these lines on your plot. Which regression does a better job of predicting time from distance? Give numerical measures that describe the success of the two regressions.

5.43   Climate change: look more closely.   The report from which the data in Exercise 5.41 were taken is not clear about the time period that the data describe. Your work for Exercise 5.41 should include a scatterplot. That plot shows an odd pattern that correlation and regression don't describe. What is this pattern? On the basis of the scatterplot and rereading the report, I suspect that the data are for the months of May, June, and July over a period of 7 years. Why is the pattern in the graph consistent with this interpretation?

5.44 Using residuals. It is possible that the subject in Exercise 5.42 got better in later trials due to learning. It is also possible that he got worse due to fatigue. Plot the residuals from each regression against the time order of the trials (down the columns in Table 5.3). Is either of these systematic effects of time visible in the data?

5.45 How residuals behave. Return to the merlin data of Exercise 4.39 (page 113). Figure 5.11 shows basic regression output.

(a) Use the regression equation from the output to obtain the residuals step-by-step. That is, find the predicted percent $\hat{y}$ of returning males for each number of breeding pairs, then find the residuals $y - \hat{y}$.

(b) The residuals are the part of the response left over after the straight-line tie to the explanatory variable is removed. Find the correlation between the residuals and the explanatory variable. Your result should not be a surprise.

5.46 Using residuals. Make a residual plot (residual against explanatory variable) for the merlin regression of the previous exercise. Use a y scale from -20 to 20 or wider to better see the pattern. Add a horizontal line at $y = 0$, the mean of the residuals.

(a) Describe the pattern if we ignore the two years with $x = 38$. Do the $x = 38$ years fit this pattern?

(b) Return to the original data. Make a scatterplot with two least-squares lines: with all nine years and without the two $x = 38$ years. Although the original regression in Figure 5.11 seemed satisfactory, the two $x = 38$ years are influential. We would like more data for years with x greater than 33.

5.47 Do artificial sweeteners cause weight gain? People who use artificial sweeteners in place of sugar tend to be heavier than people who use sugar. Does this mean that artificial sweeteners cause weight gain? Give a more plausible explanation for this association.

5.48 Learning online. Many colleges offer online versions of courses that are also taught in the classroom. It often happens that the students who enroll in the online version do better than the classroom students on the course exams. This does not show that online instruction is more effective than classroom teaching, because the people who sign up for online courses are often quite different from the classroom students. Suggest some differences between online and classroom students that might explain why online students do better.

5.49 What explains grade inflation? Students at almost all colleges and universities get higher grades than was the case 10 or 20 years ago. Is grade inflation caused by lower grading standards? Suggest some lurking variables that might explain higher grades even if standards have remained the same.

5.50 Grade inflation and the SAT. The effect of a lurking variable can be surprising when individuals are divided into groups. In recent years, the mean SAT score of all high school seniors has increased. But the mean SAT score has decreased for students at each level of high school grades (A, B, C, and so on). Explain how grade inflation in high school (the lurking variable) can account for this pattern.

5.51   **Workers' incomes.**   Here is another example of the group effect cautioned about in the previous exercise. Explain how, as a nation's population grows older, median income can go down for workers in each age group, yet still go up for all workers.

5.52   **Some regression math.**   Use the equation of the least-squares regression line (box on page 120) to show that the regression line for predicting y from x always passes through the point $(\overline{x}, \overline{y})$. That is, when $x = \overline{x}$, the equation gives $\hat{y} = \overline{y}$.

5.53   **Will I bomb the final?**   We expect that students who do well on the midterm exam in a course will usually also do well on the final exam. Gary Smith of Pomona College looked at the exam scores of all 346 students who took his statistics class over a 10-year period.[19] The least-squares line for predicting final exam score from midterm-exam score was $\hat{y} = 46.6 + 0.41x$.

Octavio scores 10 points above the class mean on the midterm. How many points above the class mean do you predict that he will score on the final? (*Hint:* Use the fact that the least-squares line passes through the point $(\overline{x}, \overline{y})$ and the fact that Octavio's midterm score is $\overline{x} + 10$.) This is an example of the phenomenon that gave "regression" its name: students who do well on the midterm will on the average do less well, but still above average, on the final.

5.54   **Is regression useful?**   In Exercise 4.37 (page 113) you used the *Correlation and Regression* applet to create three scatterplots having correlation about $r = 0.7$ between the horizontal variable x and the vertical variable y. Create three similar scatterplots again, and click the "Show least-squares line" box to display the regression lines. Correlation $r = 0.7$ is considered reasonably strong in many areas of work. Because there is a reasonably strong correlation, we might use a regression line to predict y from x. In which of your three scatterplots does it make sense to use a straight line for prediction?

5.55   **Guessing a regression line.**   In the *Correlation and Regression* applet, click on the scatterplot to create a group of 15 to 20 points from lower left to upper right with a clear positive straight-line pattern (correlation around 0.7). Click the "Draw line" button and use the mouse (right-click and drag) to draw a line through the middle of the cloud of points from lower left to upper right. Note the "thermometer" above the plot. The red portion is the sum of the squared vertical distances from the points in the plot to the least-squares line. The green portion is the "extra" sum of squares for your line—it shows by how much your line misses the smallest possible sum of squares.

(a) You drew a line by eye through the middle of the pattern. Yet the right-hand part of the bar is probably almost entirely green. What does that tell you?

(b) Now click the "Show least-squares line" box. Is the slope of the least-squares line smaller (the new line is less steep) or larger (line is steeper) than that of your line? If you repeat this exercise several times, you will consistently get the same result. The least-squares line minimizes the *vertical* distances of the points from the line. It is *not* the line through the "middle" of the cloud of points. This is one reason why it is hard to draw a good regression line by eye.

Royalty-Free/CORBIS

Two-Way Tables*

We have concentrated on relationships in which at least the response variable is quantitative. Now we will describe relationships between two categorical variables. Some variables—such as sex, race, and occupation—are categorical by nature. Other categorical variables are created by grouping values of a quantitative variable into classes. Published data often appear in grouped form to save space. To analyze categorical data, we use the *counts* or *percents* of individuals that fall into various categories.

---

*This material is important in statistics, but it is needed later in this book only for Chapter 23. You may omit it if you do not plan to read Chapter 23 or delay reading it until you reach Chapter 23.

TABLE 6.1	College students by sex and age group, 2003 (thousands of persons)		
	Sex		
Age group	Female	Male	Total
15 to 17 years	89	61	150
18 to 24 years	5,668	4,697	10,365
25 to 34 years	1,904	1,589	3,494
35 years or older	1,660	970	2,630
Total	9,321	7,317	16,639

EXAMPLE 6.1   College students

two-way table
row and column variables

Table 6.1 presents Census Bureau data describing the age and sex of college students.[1] This is a **two-way table** because it describes two categorical variables. (Age is categorical here because the students are grouped into age categories.) Age group is the **row variable** because each row in the table describes students in one age group. Because age group has a natural order from youngest to oldest, the order of the rows reflects this order. Sex is the **column variable** because each column describes one sex. The entries in the table are the counts of students in each age-by-sex class.

Marginal distributions

How can we best grasp the information contained in Table 6.1? First, *look at the distribution of each variable separately.* The distribution of a categorical variable says how often each outcome occurred. The "Total" column at the right of the table contains the totals for each of the rows. These row totals give the distribution of age (the row variable) among college students: 150,000 were 15 to 17 years old, 10,365,000 were 18 to 24 years old, and so on. In the same way, the "Total" row at the bottom of the table gives the distribution of sex. The bottom row reveals a striking and important fact: women outnumber men among college students.

If the row and column totals are missing, the first thing to do in studying a two-way table is to calculate them. The distributions of sex alone and age alone are

marginal distribution

called **marginal distributions** because they appear at the right and bottom margins of the two-way table.

If you check the row and column totals in Table 6.1, you will notice a few discrepancies. For example, the sum of the entries in the "25 to 34" row is 3493. The entry in the "Total" column for that row is 3494. The explanation is **roundoff**

roundoff error

error. The table entries are in thousands of students and each is rounded to the nearest thousand. The Census Bureau obtained the "Total" entry by rounding the exact number of students aged 25 to 34 to the nearest thousand. The result was 3,494,000. Adding the row entries, each of which is already rounded, gives a slightly different result.

Percents are often more informative than counts. We can display the marginal distribution of students' age groups in terms of percents by dividing each row total by the table total and converting to a percent.

EXAMPLE 6.2 *Calculating a marginal distribution*

The percent of college students who are 18 to 24 years old is

$$\frac{\text{age 18 to 24 total}}{\text{table total}} = \frac{10,365}{16,639} = 0.623 = 62.3\%$$

Are you surprised that only about 62% of students are in the traditional college age group? Do three more such calculations to obtain the marginal distribution of age group in percents. Here it is:

	15 to 17	18 to 24	25 to 34	35 or older
Percent of college students aged	0.9	62.3	21.0	15.8

The total is 100% because everyone is in one of the four age categories.

Each marginal distribution from a two-way table is a distribution for a single categorical variable. As we saw in Chapter 1, we can use a bar graph or a pie chart to display such a distribution. Figure 6.1 is a bar graph of the distribution of age for college students.

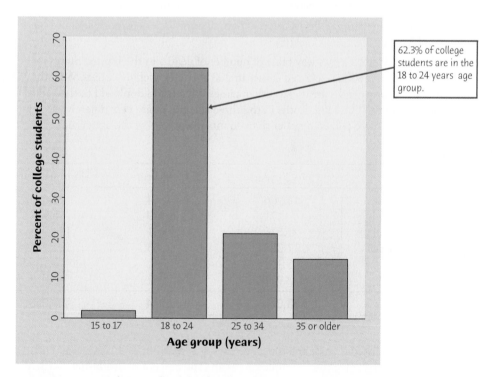

62.3% of college students are in the 18 to 24 years age group.

FIGURE 6.1 A bar graph of the distribution of age for college students. This is one of the marginal distributions for Table 6.1.

In working with two-way tables, you must calculate lots of percents. Here's a tip to help decide what fraction gives the percent you want. Ask, "What group represents the total that I want a percent of?" The count for that group is the denominator of the fraction that leads to the percent. In Example 6.2, we want a percent "of college students," so the count of college students (the table total) is the denominator.

APPLY YOUR KNOWLEDGE

Royalty-Free/CORBIS

6.1   **Risks of playing soccer.** A study in Sweden looked at former elite soccer players, people who had played soccer but not at the elite level, and people of the same age who did not play soccer. Here is a two-way table that classifies these subjects by whether or not they had arthritis of the hip or knee by their midfifties:[2]

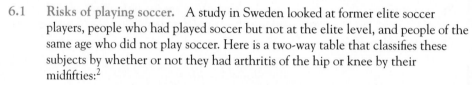

	Elite	Non-elite	Did not play
Arthritis	10	9	24
No arthritis	61	206	548

(a) How many people do these data describe?

(b) How many of these people have arthritis of the hip or knee?

(c) Give the marginal distribution of participation in soccer, both as counts and as percents.

6.2   **Deaths.** Here is a two-way table of number of deaths in the United States in three age groups from selected causes in 2003. The entries are counts of deaths.[3] Because many deaths are due to other causes, the entries don't add to the "Total deaths" count. The total deaths in the three age groups are very different, so it is important to use percents rather than counts in comparing the age groups.

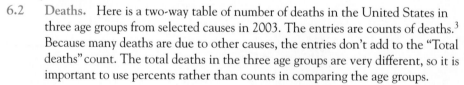

	15 to 24 years	25 to 44 years	45 to 64 years
Accidents	14,966	27,844	23,669
AIDS	171	6,879	5,917
Cancer	1,628	19,041	144,936
Heart diseases	1,083	16,283	101,713
Homicide	5,148	7,367	2,756
Suicide	3,921	11,251	10,057
Total deaths	33,022	128,924	437,058

The causes listed include the top three causes of death in each age group. For each age group, give the top three causes and the percent of deaths due to each. Use your results to explain briefly how the leading causes of death change as people get older.

Conditional distributions

Table 6.1 contains much more information than the two marginal distributions of age alone and sex alone. The nature of the relationship between the age and sex of college students cannot be deduced from the separate distributions but requires the full table. *Relationships between categorical variables are described by calculating appropriate percents from the counts given.* We use percents because counts are often hard to compare. For example, there are 5,668,000 female college students in the 18 to 24 years age group, and only 1,660,000 in the 35 years or over group. Because there are many more students overall in the 18 to 24 group, these counts don't allow us to compare how prominent women are in the two age groups. When we compare the percents of women and men in several age groups, we are comparing *conditional distributions*.

Attack of the killer TVs!

Are kids in greater danger from TV sets or alligators? Alligator attacks make the news, but they aren't high on any count of causes of death and injury. In fact, the 28 children killed by falling TV sets in the United States between 1990 and 1997 is about twice the total number of people killed by alligators in Florida since 1948.

MARGINAL AND CONDITIONAL DISTRIBUTIONS

The **marginal distribution** of one of the categorical variables in a two-way table of counts is the distribution of values of that variable among all individuals described by the table.

A **conditional distribution** of a variable is the distribution of values of that variable among only individuals who have a given value of the other variable. There is a separate conditional distribution for each value of the other variable.

EXAMPLE 6.3   Conditional distribution of sex given age

If we know that a college student is 18 to 24 years old, we need look at only the "18 to 24 years" row in the two-way table, highlighted in Table 6.2. To find the distribution of sex among only students in this age group, divide each count in the row by the row

TABLE 6.2	College students by sex and age: the 18 to 24 years age group		
	Sex		
Age group	Female	Male	Total
15 to 17 years	89	61	150
18 to 24 years	5,668	4,697	10,365
25 to 34 years	1,904	1,589	3,494
35 years or older	1,660	970	2,630
Total	9,321	7,317	16,639

total, which is 10,365. The conditional distribution of sex *given* that a student is 18 to 24 years old is

	Female	Male
Percent of 18 to 24 age group	54.7	45.3

The two percents add to 100% because all 18- to 24-year-old students are either female or male. We use the term "conditional" because these percents describe only students who satisfy the condition that they are between 18 and 24 years old.

— EXAMPLE 6.4   *Women among college students* —————————

Let's follow the four-step process (page 53), starting with a practical question of interest to college administrators.

STATE: The proportion of college students who are older than the traditional 18 to 24 years is increasing. How does the participation of women in higher education change as we look at older students?

FORMULATE: Calculate and compare the conditional distributions of sex for college students in several age groups.

SOLVE: Comparing conditional distributions reveals the nature of the association between the sex and age of college students. Look at each row in Table 6.1 (that is, at each age group) in turn. Find the numbers of women and of men as percents of each row total. Here are the four conditional distributions of sex given age group:

	Female	Male
Percent of 15 to 17 age group	59.3	40.7
Percent of 18 to 24 age group	54.7	45.3
Percent of 25 to 34 age group	54.5	45.5
Percent of 35 or older age group	63.1	36.9

Because the variable "sex" has just two values, comparing conditional distributions just amounts to comparing the percents of women in the four age groups. The bar graph in Figure 6.2 compares the percents of women in the four age groups. The heights of the bars do not add to 100% because they are not parts of a whole. Each bar describes a different age group.

CONCLUDE: Women are a majority of college students in all age groups but are somewhat more predominant among students 35 years or older. Women are more likely than men to return to college after working for a number of years. That's an important part of the relationship between the sex and age of college students.

Remember that there are two sets of conditional distributions for any two-way table. Examples 6.3 and 6.4 looked at the conditional distributions of sex for different age groups. We could also examine the conditional distributions of age for the two sexes.

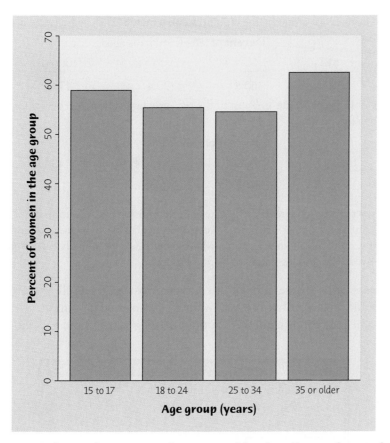

FIGURE 6.2 Bar graph comparing the percent of female college students in four age groups. There are more women than men in all age groups, but the percent of women is highest among older students.

EXAMPLE 6.5 Conditional distribution of age given sex

What is the distribution of age among female college students? Information about women students appears in the "Female" column. Look only at this column, which is highlighted in Table 6.3. To find the conditional distribution of age, divide the count of

TABLE 6.3   College students by sex and age: females

Age group	Sex		Total
	Female	Male	
15 to 17 years	89	61	150
18 to 24 years	5,668	4,697	10,365
25 to 34 years	1,904	1,589	3,494
35 years or older	1,660	970	2,630
Total	9,321	7,317	16,639

Smiling faces

Women smile more than men. The same data that produce this fact allow us to link smiling to other variables in two-way tables. For example, add as the second variable whether or not the person thinks they are being observed. If yes, that's when women smile more. If no, there's no difference between women and men. Or take the second variable to be the person's occupation or social role. Within each social category, there is very little difference in smiling between women and men.

women in each age group by the column total, which is 9321. Here is the distribution:

Percent of female students aged

15 to 17	18 to 24	25 to 34	35 or older
1.0	60.8	20.4	17.8

Looking only at the "Male" column in the two-way table gives the conditional distribution of age for men:

Percent of male students aged

15 to 17	18 to 24	25 to 34	35 or older
0.8	64.2	21.7	13.3

Each set of percents adds to 100% because each conditional distribution includes all students of one sex. Comparing these two conditional distributions shows the relationship between sex and age in another form. Male students are more likely than women to be 18 to 24 years old and less likely to be 35 or older.

Software will do these calculations for you. Most programs allow you to choose which conditional distributions you want to compare. The output in Figure 6.3 compares the four conditional distributions of sex given age and also the marginal

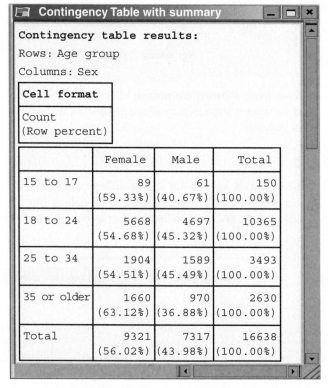

FIGURE 6.3 CrunchIt! output of the two-way table of college students by age and sex, along with each entry as a percent of its column total. The percents in the three columns give the conditional distributions of age for the two sexes and (in the third column) the marginal distribution of age for all college students.

distribution of sex for all students. The row percents in the first two columns agree (up to roundoff) with the results in Example 6.4.

No single graph (such as a scatterplot) portrays the form of the relationship between categorical variables. No single numerical measure (such as the correlation) summarizes the strength of the association. Bar graphs are flexible enough to be helpful, but you must think about what comparisons you want to display. For numerical measures, we rely on well-chosen percents. You must decide which percents you need. Here is a hint: *if there is an explanatory-response relationship, compare the conditional distributions of the response variable for the separate values of the explanatory variable.* If you think that age influences the proportions of men and women among college students, compare the conditional distributions of sex among students of different ages, as in Example 6.4.

APPLY YOUR KNOWLEDGE

6.3   **Female college students.**   Starting with Table 6.1, show the calculations to find the conditional distribution of age among female college students. Your results should agree with those in Example 6.5.

6.4   **Majors for men and women in business.**   A study of the career plans of young women and men sent questionnaires to all 722 members of the senior class in the College of Business Administration at the University of Illinois. One question asked which major within the business program the student had chosen. Here are the data from the students who responded:[4]

	Female	Male
Accounting	68	56
Administration	91	40
Economics	5	6
Finance	61	59

(a) Find the two conditional distributions of major, one for women and one for men. Based on your calculations, describe the differences between women and men with a graph and in words.

(b) What percent of the students did not respond to the questionnaire? The nonresponse weakens conclusions drawn from these data.

6.5   **Risks of playing soccer.**   The two-way table in Exercise 6.1 describes a study of arthritis of the hip or knee among people with different levels of experience playing soccer. We suspect that the more serious soccer players have more arthritis later in life. Do the data confirm this suspicion? Follow the four-step process, as illustrated in Example 6.4.

6.6   **Marginal distributions aren't the whole story.**   Here are the row and column totals for a two-way table with two rows and two columns:

a	b	50
c	d	50
60	40	100

Find *two different* sets of counts a, b, c, and d for the body of the table that give these same totals. This shows that the relationship between two variables cannot be obtained from the two individual distributions of the variables.

Simpson's paradox

As is the case with quantitative variables, the effects of lurking variables can change or even reverse relationships between two categorical variables. Here is an example that demonstrates the surprises that can await the unsuspecting user of data.

Ashley/Cooper/PICIMPACT/CORBIS

EXAMPLE 6.6 Do medical helicopters save lives?

Accident victims are sometimes taken by helicopter from the accident scene to a hospital. Helicopters save time. Do they also save lives? Let's compare the percents of accident victims who die with helicopter evacuation and with the usual transport to a hospital by road. Here are hypothetical data that illustrate a practical difficulty:[5]

	Helicopter	Road
Victim died	64	260
Victim survived	136	840
Total	200	1100

We see that 32% (64 out of 200) of helicopter patients died, but only 24% (260 out of 1100) of the others did. That seems discouraging.

The explanation is that the helicopter is sent mostly to serious accidents, so that the victims transported by helicopter are more often seriously injured. They are more likely to die with or without helicopter evacuation. Here are the same data broken down by the seriousness of the accident:

Serious Accidents

	Helicopter	Road
Died	48	60
Survived	52	40
Total	100	100

Less Serious Accidents

	Helicopter	Road
Died	16	200
Survived	84	800
Total	100	1000

Inspect these tables to convince yourself that they describe the same 1300 accident victims as the original two-way table. For example, 200 (100 + 100) were moved by helicopter, and 64 (48 + 16) of these died.

Among victims of serious accidents, the helicopter saves 52% (52 out of 100) compared with 40% for road transport. If we look only at less serious accidents, 84% of those transported by helicopter survive, versus 80% of those transported by road. Both groups of victims have a higher survival rate when evacuated by helicopter.

At first, it seems paradoxical that the helicopter does better for both groups of victims but worse when all victims are lumped together. Examining the data makes the explanation clear. Half the helicopter transport patients are from serious accidents, compared with only 100 of the 1100 road transport patients. So the helicopter carries patients who are more likely to die. The seriousness of the accident was a lurking variable that, until we uncovered it, made the relationship between survival and mode of transport to a hospital hard to interpret. Example 6.6 illustrates *Simpson's paradox*.

SIMPSON'S PARADOX

An association or comparison that holds for all of several groups can reverse direction when the data are combined to form a single group. This reversal is called **Simpson's paradox.**

The lurking variable in Simpson's paradox is categorical. That is, it breaks the individuals into groups, as when accident victims are classified as injured in a "serious accident" or a "less serious accident." Simpson's paradox is just an extreme form of the fact that observed associations can be misleading when there are lurking variables.

APPLY YOUR KNOWLEDGE

6.7   **Airline flight delays.**   Here are the numbers of flights on time and delayed for two airlines at five airports in one month. Overall on-time percents for each airline are often reported in the news. The airport that flights serve is a lurking variable that can make such reports misleading.[6]

	Alaska Airlines		America West	
	On time	Delayed	On time	Delayed
Los Angeles	497	62	694	117
Phoenix	221	12	4840	415
San Diego	212	20	383	65
San Francisco	503	102	320	129
Seattle	1841	305	201	61

(a) What percent of all Alaska Airlines flights were delayed? What percent of all America West flights were delayed? These are the numbers usually reported.

(b) Now find the percent of delayed flights for Alaska Airlines at each of the five airports. Do the same for America West.

(c) America West did worse at *every one* of the five airports, yet did better overall. That sounds impossible. Explain carefully, referring to the data, how this can happen. (The weather in Phoenix and Seattle lies behind this example of Simpson's paradox.)

6.8   **Race and the death penalty.**   Whether a convicted murderer gets the death penalty seems to be influenced by the race of the victim. Here are data on 326 cases in which the defendant was convicted of murder:[7]

White Defendant

	White victim	Black victim
Death	19	0
Not	132	9

Black Defendant

	White victim	Black victim
Death	11	6
Not	52	97

(a) Use these data to make a two-way table of defendant's race (white or black) versus death penalty (yes or no).

(b) Show that Simpson's paradox holds: a higher percent of white defendants are sentenced to death overall, but for both black and white victims a higher percent of black defendants are sentenced to death.

(c) Use the data to explain why the paradox holds in language that a judge could understand.

CHAPTER 6 SUMMARY

A **two-way table** of counts organizes data about two categorical variables. Values of the **row variable** label the rows that run across the table, and values of the **column variable** label the columns that run down the table. Two-way tables are often used to summarize large amounts of information by grouping outcomes into categories.

The **row totals** and **column totals** in a two-way table give the **marginal distributions** of the two individual variables. It is clearer to present these distributions as percents of the table total. Marginal distributions tell us nothing about the relationship between the variables.

There are two sets of **conditional distributions** for a two-way table: the distributions of the row variable for each fixed value of the column variable, and the distributions of the column variable for each fixed value of the row variable. Comparing one set of conditional distributions is one way to describe the association between the row and the column variables.

To find the **conditional distribution** of the row variable for one specific value of the column variable, look only at that one column in the table. Find each entry in the column as a percent of the column total.

Bar graphs are a flexible means of presenting categorical data. There is no single best way to describe an association between two categorical variables.

A comparison between two variables that holds for each individual value of a third variable can be changed or even reversed when the data for all values of the third variable are combined. This is **Simpson's paradox.** Simpson's paradox is an example of the effect of lurking variables on an observed association.

CHECK YOUR SKILLS

The National Survey of Adolescent Health interviewed several thousand teens (grades 7 to 12). One question asked was "What do you think are the chances you will be married in the next ten years?" Here is a two-way table of the responses by sex:[8]

	Female	Male
Almost no chance	119	103
Some chance, but probably not	150	171
A 50-50 chance	447	512
A good chance	735	710
Almost certain	1174	756

Exercises 6.9 to 6.17 are based on this table.

6.9 How many females were among the respondents?

(a) 2625   (b) 4877   (c) need more information

6.10 How many individuals are described by this table?

(a) 2625   (b) 4877   (c) need more information

6.11 The percent of females among the respondents was

(a) about 46%.   (b) about 54%.   (c) about 86%.

6.12 Your percent from the previous exercise is part of

(a) the marginal distribution of sex.

(b) the marginal distribution of chance of marriage.

(c) the conditional distribution of sex given chance of marriage.

6.13 What percent of females thought that they were almost certain to be married in the next ten years?

(a) about 40%   (b) about 45%   (c) about 61%

6.14 Your percent from the previous exercise is part of

(a) the marginal distribution of chance of marriage.

(b) the conditional distribution of sex given chance of marriage.

(c) the conditional distribution of chance of marriage given sex.

6.15 What percent of those who thought they were almost certain to be married were female?

(a) about 40%   (b) about 45%   (c) about 61%

6.16 Your percent from the previous exercise is part of

(a) the marginal distribution of chance of marriage.

(b) the conditional distribution of sex given chance of marriage.

(c) the conditional distribution of chance of marriage given sex.

6.17 A bar graph showing the conditional distribution of chance of marriage given that the respondent was female would have

(a) 2 bars.   (b) 5 bars.   (c) 10 bars.

6.18 A college looks at the grade point average (GPA) of its full-time and part-time students. Grades in science courses are generally lower than grades in other courses. There are few science majors among part-time students but many science majors among full-time students. The college finds that full-time students who are science majors have higher GPA than part-time students who are science majors. Full-time students who are not science majors also have higher GPA than part-time students who are not science majors. Yet part-time students as a group have higher GPA than full-time students. This finding is

(a) not possible: if both science and other majors who are full-time have higher GPA than those who are part-time, then all full-time students together must have higher GPA than all part-time students together.

(b) an example of Simpson's paradox: full-time students do better in both kinds of courses but worse overall because they take more science courses.

(c) due to comparing two conditional distributions that should not be compared.

CHAPTER 6 EXERCISES

Marital status and job level. *We sometimes hear that getting married is good for your career. Table 6.4 presents data from one of the studies behind this generalization. To avoid gender effects, the investigators looked only at men. The data describe the marital status and the job level of all 8235 male managers and professionals employed by a large manufacturing firm.*[9] *The firm assigns each position a grade that reflects the value of that particular job to the company. The authors of the study grouped the many job grades into quarters. Grade 1 contains jobs in the lowest quarter of the job grades, and Grade 4 contains those in the highest quarter. Exercises 6.19 to 6.23 are based on these data.*

6.19 **Marginal distributions.** Give (in percents) the two marginal distributions, for marital status and for job grade. Do each of your two sets of percents add to exactly 100%? If not, why not?

6.20 **Percents.** What percent of single men hold Grade 1 jobs? What percent of Grade 1 jobs are held by single men?

6.21 **Conditional distribution.** Give (in percents) the conditional distribution of job grade among single men. Should your percents add to 100% (up to roundoff error)?

6.22 **Marital status and job grade.** One way to see the relationship is to look at who holds Grade 1 jobs.

TABLE 6.4	Marital status and job level				
	Marital Status				
Job grade	Single	Married	Divorced	Widowed	Total
1	58	874	15	8	955
2	222	3927	70	20	4239
3	50	2396	34	10	2490
4	7	533	7	4	551
Total	337	7730	126	42	8235

(a) There are 874 married men with Grade 1 jobs, and only 58 single men with such jobs. Explain why these counts by themselves don't describe the relationship between marital status and job grade.

(b) Find the percent of men in each marital status group who have Grade 1 jobs. Then find the percent in each marital group who have Grade 4 jobs. What do these percents say about the relationship?

6.23 **Association is not causation.** The data in Table 6.4 show that single men are more likely to hold lower-grade jobs than are married men. We should not conclude that single men can help their career by getting married. What lurking variables might help explain the association between marital status and job grade?

6.24 **Attitudes toward recycled products.** Recycling is supposed to save resources. Some people think recycled products are lower in quality than other products, a fact that makes recycling less practical. People who actually use a recycled product may have different opinions from those who don't use it. Here are data on attitudes toward coffee filters made of recycled paper among people who do and don't buy these filters:[10]

	Think the quality of the recycled product is		
	Higher	The same	Lower
Buyers	20	7	9
Nonbuyers	29	25	43

(a) Find the marginal distribution of opinion about quality. Assuming that these people represent all users of coffee filters, what does this distribution tell us?

(b) How do the opinions of buyers and nonbuyers differ? Use conditional distributions as a basis for your answer. Can you conclude that using recycled filters *causes* more favorable opinions? If so, giving away samples might increase sales.

6.25 **Helping cocaine addicts.** Cocaine addiction is hard to break. Addicts need cocaine to feel any pleasure, so perhaps giving them an antidepressant drug will help. An experiment assigned 72 chronic cocaine users to take either an antidepressant drug called desipramine, lithium, or a placebo. (Lithium is a standard drug to treat cocaine addiction. A placebo is a dummy drug, used so that the effect of being in the study but not taking any drug can be seen.) One-third of the subjects, chosen at random, received each drug. Here are the results after three years:[11]

	Desipramine	Lithium	Placebo
Relapse	10	18	20
No relapse	14	6	4
Total	24	24	24

(a) Compare the effectiveness of the three treatments in preventing relapse. Use percents and draw a bar graph.

(b) Do you think that this study gives good evidence that desipramine actually *causes* a reduction in relapses?

6.26   Violent deaths. How does the impact of "violent deaths" due to accidents, homicide, and suicide change with age group? Use the data in Exercise 6.2 (page 152) and follow the four-step process (page 53) in your answer.

6.27   College degrees. Here are data on the numbers of degrees earned in 2005–2006, as projected by the National Center for Education Statistics. The table entries are counts of degrees in thousands.[12]

	Female	Male
Associate's	431	244
Bachelor's	813	584
Master's	298	215
Professional	42	47
Doctor's	21	24

Describe briefly how the participation of women changes with level of degree. Follow the four-step process, as illustrated in Example 6.4.

6.28   Do angry people have more heart disease? People who get angry easily tend to have more heart disease. That's the conclusion of a study that followed a random sample of 12,986 people from three locations for about four years. All subjects were free of heart disease at the beginning of the study. The subjects took the Spielberger Trait Anger Scale test, which measures how prone a person is to sudden anger. Here are data for the 8474 people in the sample who had normal blood pressure.[13] CHD stands for "coronary heart disease." This includes people who had heart attacks and those who needed medical treatment for heart disease.

	Low anger	Moderate anger	High anger	Total
CHD	53	110	27	190
No CHD	3057	4621	606	8284
Total	3110	4731	633	8474

Henryk Kaiser/eStock
Photography/PictureQuest

Do these data support the study's conclusion about the relationship between anger and heart disease? Follow the four-step process (page 53) in your answer.

6.29   Python eggs. How is the hatching of water python eggs influenced by the temperature of the snake's nest? Researchers assigned newly laid eggs to one of three temperatures: hot, neutral, or cold. Hot duplicates the warmth provided by the mother python. Neutral and cold are cooler, as when the mother is absent. Here are the data on the number of eggs and the number that hatched:[14]

	Cold	Neutral	Hot
Number of eggs	27	56	104
Number hatched	16	38	75

Notice that this is not a two-way table! The researchers anticipated that eggs would hatch less well at cooler temperatures. Do the data support that anticipation? Follow the four-step process (page 53) in your answer.

6.30 **Which hospital is safer?** To help consumers make informed decisions about health care, the government releases data about patient outcomes in hospitals. You want to compare Hospital A and Hospital B, which serve your community. Here are data on all patients undergoing surgery in a recent time period. The data include the condition of the patient ("good" or "poor") before the surgery. "Survived" means that the patient lived at least 6 weeks following surgery.

Good Condition

	Hospital A	Hospital B
Died	6	8
Survived	594	592
Total	600	600

Poor Condition

	Hospital A	Hospital B
Died	57	8
Survived	1443	192
Total	1500	200

(a) Compare percents to show that Hospital A has a higher survival rate for both groups of patients.

(b) Combine the data into a single two-way table of outcome ("survived" or "died") by hospital (A or B). The local paper reports just these overall survival rates. Which hospital has the higher rate?

(c) Explain from the data, in language that a reporter can understand, how Hospital B can do better overall even though Hospital A does better for both groups of patients.

6.31 **Discrimination?** Wabash Tech has two professional schools, business and law. Here are two-way tables of applicants to both schools, categorized by gender and admission decision. (Although these data are made up, similar situations occur in reality.)[15]

Business

	Admit	Deny
Male	480	120
Female	180	20

Law

	Admit	Deny
Male	10	90
Female	100	200

(a) Make a two-way table of gender by admission decision for the two professional schools together by summing entries in these tables.

(b) From the two-way table, calculate the percent of male applicants who are admitted and the percent of female applicants who are admitted. Wabash admits a higher percent of male applicants.

(c) Now compute separately the percents of male and female applicants admitted by the business school and by the law school. Each school admits a higher percent of female applicants.

(d) This is Simpson's paradox: both schools admit a higher percent of the women who apply, but overall Wabash admits a lower percent of female applicants than of male applicants. Explain carefully, as if speaking to a skeptical reporter, how it can happen that Wabash appears to favor males when each school individually favors females.

6.32 **Obesity and health.** Recent studies have shown that earlier reports underestimated the health risks associated with being overweight. The error was due to overlooking lurking variables. In particular, smoking tends both to reduce weight and to lead to earlier death. Illustrate Simpson's paradox by a simplified version of this situation. That is, make up two-way tables of overweight (yes or no) by early death (yes or no) separately for smokers and nonsmokers such that

- Overweight smokers and overweight nonsmokers both tend to die earlier than those not overweight.

- But when smokers and nonsmokers are combined into a two-way table of overweight by early death, persons who are not overweight tend to die earlier.

Gallo Images–Anthony Bannister/Getty Images

Exploring Data: Part I Review

Data analysis is the art of describing data using graphs and numerical summaries. The purpose of data analysis is to help us see and understand the most important features of a set of data. Chapter 1 commented on graphs to display distributions: pie charts and bar graphs for categorical variables, histograms and stemplots for quantitative variables. In addition, time plots show how a quantitative variable changes over time. Chapter 2 presented numerical tools for describing the center and spread of the distribution of one variable. Chapter 3 discussed density curves for describing the overall pattern of a distribution, with emphasis on the Normal distributions.

The first STATISTICS IN SUMMARY figure on the next page organizes the big ideas for exploring a quantitative variable. Plot your data, then describe their center and spread using either the mean and standard deviation or the five-number summary. The last step, which makes sense only for some data, is to summarize the data in compact form by using a Normal curve as a description of the overall pattern. The question marks at the last two stages remind us that the usefulness of numerical summaries and Normal distributions depends on what we find when we examine graphs of our data. No short summary does justice to irregular shapes or to data with several distinct clusters.

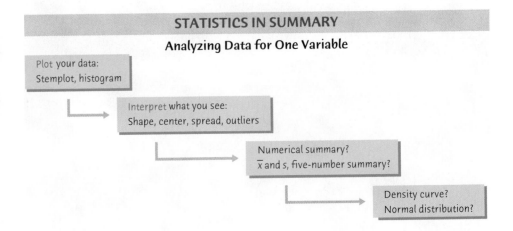

Chapters 4 and 5 applied the same ideas to relationships between two quanti-tative variables. The second STATISTICS IN SUMMARY figure retraces the big ideas, with details that fit the new setting. Always begin by making graphs of your data. In the case of a scatterplot, we have learned a numerical summary only for data that show a roughly linear pattern on the scatterplot. The summary is then the means and standard deviations of the two variables and their correlation. A regression line drawn on the plot gives a compact description of the overall pat-tern that we can use for prediction. Once again there are question marks at the last two stages to remind us that correlation and regression describe only straight-line relationships. Chapter 6 shows how to understand relationships between two categorical variables; comparing well-chosen percents is the key.

You can organize your work in any open-ended data analysis setting by follow-ing the four-step State, Formulate, Solve, and Conclude process first introduced in Chapter 2. After we have mastered the extra background needed for statistical inference, this process will also guide practical work on inference later in the book.

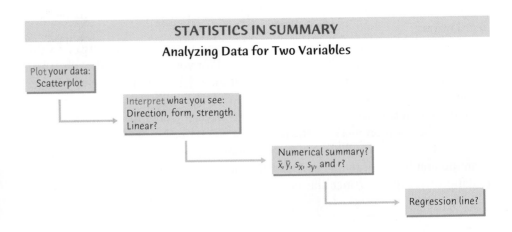

PART I SUMMARY

Here are the most important skills you should have acquired from reading Chapters 1 to 6.

A. DATA

1. Identify the individuals and variables in a set of data.
2. Identify each variable as categorical or quantitative. Identify the units in which each quantitative variable is measured.
3. Identify the explanatory and response variables in situations where one variable explains or influences another.

B. DISPLAYING DISTRIBUTIONS

1. Recognize when a pie chart can and cannot be used.
2. Make a bar graph of the distribution of a categorical variable, or in general to compare related quantities.
3. Interpret pie charts and bar graphs.
4. Make a time plot of a quantitative variable over time. Recognize patterns such as trends and cycles in time plots.
5. Make a histogram of the distribution of a quantitative variable.
6. Make a stemplot of the distribution of a small set of observations. Round leaves or split stems as needed to make an effective stemplot.

C. DESCRIBING DISTRIBUTIONS (QUANTITATIVE VARIABLE)

1. Look for the overall pattern and for major deviations from the pattern.
2. Assess from a histogram or stemplot whether the shape of a distribution is roughly symmetric, distinctly skewed, or neither. Assess whether the distribution has one or more major peaks.
3. Describe the overall pattern by giving numerical measures of center and spread in addition to a verbal description of shape.
4. Decide which measures of center and spread are more appropriate: the mean and standard deviation (especially for symmetric distributions) or the five-number summary (especially for skewed distributions).
5. Recognize outliers and give plausible explanations for them.

D. NUMERICAL SUMMARIES OF DISTRIBUTIONS

1. Find the median M and the quartiles Q_1 and Q_3 for a set of observations.
2. Find the five-number summary and draw a boxplot; assess center, spread, symmetry, and skewness from a boxplot.
3. Find the mean $\overline{x}$ and the standard deviation s for a set of observations.
4. Understand that the median is more resistant than the mean. Recognize that skewness in a distribution moves the mean away from the median toward the long tail.

5. Know the basic properties of the standard deviation: $s \geq 0$ always; $s = 0$ only when all observations are identical and increases as the spread increases; s has the same units as the original measurements; s is pulled strongly up by outliers or skewness.

E. DENSITY CURVES AND NORMAL DISTRIBUTIONS

1. Know that areas under a density curve represent proportions of all observations and that the total area under a density curve is 1.

2. Approximately locate the median (equal-areas point) and the mean (balance point) on a density curve.

3. Know that the mean and median both lie at the center of a symmetric density curve and that the mean moves farther toward the long tail of a skewed curve.

4. Recognize the shape of Normal curves and estimate by eye both the mean and standard deviation from such a curve.

5. Use the 68–95–99.7 rule and symmetry to state what percent of the observations from a Normal distribution fall between two points when both points lie at the mean or one, two, or three standard deviations on either side of the mean.

6. Find the standardized value (z-score) of an observation. Interpret z-scores and understand that any Normal distribution becomes standard Normal $N(0, 1)$ when standardized.

7. Given that a variable has a Normal distribution with a stated mean μ and standard deviation σ, calculate the proportion of values above a stated number, below a stated number, or between two stated numbers.

8. Given that a variable has a Normal distribution with a stated mean μ and standard deviation σ, calculate the point having a stated proportion of all values above it or below it.

F. SCATTERPLOTS AND CORRELATION

1. Make a scatterplot to display the relationship between two quantitative variables measured on the same subjects. Place the explanatory variable (if any) on the horizontal scale of the plot.

2. Add a categorical variable to a scatterplot by using a different plotting symbol or color.

3. Describe the direction, form, and strength of the overall pattern of a scatterplot. In particular, recognize positive or negative association and linear (straight-line) patterns. Recognize outliers in a scatterplot.

4. Judge whether it is appropriate to use correlation to describe the relationship between two quantitative variables. Find the correlation r.

5. Know the basic properties of correlation: r measures the direction and strength of only straight-line relationships; r is always a number between -1 and 1; $r = \pm 1$ only for perfect straight-line relationships; r moves away from 0 toward ± 1 as the straight-line relationship gets stronger.

G. REGRESSION LINES

1. Understand that regression requires an explanatory variable and a response variable. Use a calculator or software to find the least-squares regression line of a response variable y on an explanatory variable x from data.

2. Explain what the slope b and the intercept a mean in the equation $\hat{y} = a + bx$ of a regression line.

3. Draw a graph of a regression line when you are given its equation.

4. Use a regression line to predict y for a given x. Recognize extrapolation and be aware of its dangers.

5. Find the slope and intercept of the least-squares regression line from the means and standard deviations of x and y and their correlation.

6. Use r^2, the square of the correlation, to describe how much of the variation in one variable can be accounted for by a straight-line relationship with another variable.

7. Recognize outliers and potentially influential observations from a scatterplot with the regression line drawn on it.

8. Calculate the residuals and plot them against the explanatory variable x. Recognize that a residual plot magnifies the pattern of the scatterplot of y versus x.

H. CAUTIONS ABOUT CORRELATION AND REGRESSION

1. Understand that both r and the least-squares regression line can be strongly influenced by a few extreme observations.

2. Recognize possible lurking variables that may explain the observed association between two variables x and y.

3. Understand that even a strong correlation does not mean that there is a cause-and-effect relationship between x and y.

4. Give plausible explanations for an observed association between two variables: direct cause and effect, the influence of lurking variables, or both.

I. CATEGORICAL DATA (Optional)

1. From a two-way table of counts, find the marginal distributions of both variables by obtaining the row sums and column sums.

2. Express any distribution in percents by dividing the category counts by their total.

3. Describe the relationship between two categorical variables by computing and comparing percents. Often this involves comparing the conditional distributions of one variable for the different categories of the other variable.

4. Recognize Simpson's paradox and be able to explain it.

Driving in Canada

Canada is a civilized and restrained nation, at least in the eyes of Americans. A survey sponsored by the Canada Safety Council suggests that driving in Canada may be more adventurous than expected. Of the Canadian drivers surveyed, 88% admitted to aggressive driving in the past year, and 76% said that sleep-deprived drivers were common on Canadian roads. What really alarms us is the name of the survey: the Nerves of Steel Aggressive Driving Study.

REVIEW EXERCISES

Review exercises help you solidify the basic ideas and skills in Chapters 1 to 6.

7.1   **Describing colleges.** Popular magazines rank colleges and universities on their "academic quality" in serving undergraduate students. Give one categorical variable and two quantitative variables that you would like to see measured for each college if you were choosing where to study.

7.2   **Affording college.** From time to time, the Department of Education estimates the "average unmet need" for undergraduate students—the cost of school minus estimated family contributions and financial aid. Here are the averages for full-time students at four types of institution in the most recent study, for the 1999–2000 academic year:[1]

Public 2-year	Public 4-year	Private nonprofit 4-year	Private for-profit
$2747	$2369	$4931	$6548

Make a bar graph of these data. Write a one-sentence conclusion about the unmet needs of students. Explain clearly why it is incorrect to make a pie chart.

7.3   **Changes in how we watch.** Movies earn income from many sources other than theater showings. Here are data on the income of movie studios from two sources over time, in billions of dollars (the amounts have been adjusted to the same buying power that a dollar had in 2004):[2]

	1948	1980	1985	1990	1995	2000	2004
Theater showings	7.8	4.5	3.04	5.28	5.72	6.02	7.40
Video/DVD sales	0	0.2	2.40	6.02	10.90	11.97	20.90

Make two time plots on the same scales to compare the two sources of income. (Use one dashed and one solid line to keep them separate.) What pattern does your plot show?

7.4   **What we watch now.** The previous exercise looked at movie studio income from theaters and video/DVD sales over time. Here are data on studio income in 2004, in billions of dollars:

Source	Income
Theaters	7.4
Video/DVD	20.9
Pay TV	4.0
Free TV	12.6

Make a graph that compares these amounts. What percent of studio income comes from theater showings of movies?

7.5   **Growing icicles.** Table 4.2 (page 98) gives data on the growth of icicles over time. Let's look again at Run 8903, for which a slower flow of water produces faster growth.

(a) How can you tell from a calculation, without drawing a scatterplot, that the pattern of growth is very close to a straight line?

(b) What is the equation of the least-squares regression line for predicting an icicle's length from time in minutes under these conditions?

(c) Predict the length of an icicle after one full day. This prediction can't be trusted. Why not?

7.6 **Weights aren't Normal.** The heights of people of the same sex and similar ages follow a Normal distribution reasonably closely. Weights, on the other hand, are not Normally distributed. The weights of women aged 20 to 29 have mean 141.7 pounds and median 133.2 pounds. The first and third quartiles are 118.3 pounds and 157.3 pounds. What can you say about the shape of the weight distribution? Why?

7.7 **Returns on stocks aren't Normal.** The 99.7 part of the 68–95–99.7 rule says that in practice Normal distributions are about 6 standard deviations wide. Exercise 2.39 (page 62) gives the real returns for the S&P 500 stock index over a 33-year period. The shape of the distribution is not close to Normal. Find the mean and standard deviation of the real returns. What are the values 3 standard deviations above and below the mean, which would span the distribution if it were Normal? How do these values compare with the actual lowest and highest returns? Remember that the 68–95–99.7 rule applies only to Normal distributions.

7.8 **Remember what you ate.** How well do people remember their past diet? Data are available for 91 people who were asked about their diet when they were 18 years old. Researchers asked them at about age 55 to describe their eating habits at age 18. For each subject, the researchers calculated the correlation between actual intakes of many foods at age 18 and the intakes the subjects now remember. The median of the 91 correlations was $r = 0.217$. The authors say, "We conclude that memory of food intake in the distant past is fair to poor."[3] Explain why $r = 0.217$ points to this conclusion.

7.9 **Cicadas as fertilizer?** Every 17 years, swarms of cicadas emerge from the ground in the eastern United States, live for about six weeks, then die. (There are several "broods," so we experience cicada eruptions more often than every 17 years.) There are so many cicadas that their dead bodies can serve as fertilizer and increase plant growth. In an experiment, a researcher added 10 cicadas under some plants in a natural plot of American bellflowers in a forest, leaving other plants undisturbed. One of the response variables was the size of seeds produced by the plants. Here are data (seed mass in milligrams) for 39 cicada plants and 33 undisturbed (control) plants:[4]

Cicada plants				Control plants			
0.237	0.277	0.241	0.142	0.212	0.188	0.263	0.253
0.109	0.209	0.238	0.277	0.261	0.265	0.135	0.170
0.261	0.227	0.171	0.235	0.203	0.241	0.257	0.155
0.276	0.234	0.255	0.296	0.215	0.285	0.198	0.266
0.239	0.266	0.296	0.217	0.178	0.244	0.190	0.212
0.238	0.210	0.295	0.193	0.290	0.253	0.249	0.253
0.218	0.263	0.305	0.257	0.268	0.190	0.196	0.220
0.351	0.245	0.226	0.276	0.246	0.145	0.247	0.140
0.317	0.310	0.223	0.229	0.241			
0.192	0.201	0.211					

Alastair Shay; Papilio/CORBIS

4 STEP

Do the data support the idea that dead cicadas can serve as fertilizer? Follow the four-step process (page 53) in your work.

7.10 **Hot mutual funds?** Investment advertisements always warn that "past performance does not guarantee future results." Here is an example that shows why you should pay attention to this warning. The table below gives the percent returns from 23 Fidelity Investments "sector funds" in 2002 (a down year for stocks) and 2003 (an up year). Sector funds invest in narrow segments of the stock market. They often rise and fall faster than the market as a whole.

2002 return	2003 return	2002 return	2003 return	2002 return	2003 return
−17.1	23.9	−0.7	36.9	−37.8	59.4
−6.7	14.1	−5.6	27.5	−11.5	22.9
−21.1	41.8	−26.9	26.1	−0.7	36.9
−12.8	43.9	−42.0	62.7	64.3	32.1
−18.9	31.1	−47.8	68.1	−9.6	28.7
−7.7	32.3	−50.5	71.9	−11.7	29.5
−17.2	36.5	−49.5	57.0	−2.3	19.1
−11.4	30.6	−23.4	35.0		

(a) Make a scatterplot of 2003 return (response) against 2002 return (explanatory). The funds with the best performance in 2002 tend to have the worst performance in 2003. Fidelity Gold Fund, the only fund with a positive return in both years, is an extreme outlier.

(b) To demonstrate that correlation is not resistant, find r for all 23 funds and then find r for the 22 funds other than Gold. Explain from Gold's position in your plot why omitting this point makes r more negative.

7.11 **More about cicadas.** Let's examine the distribution of seed mass for plants in the cicada group of Exercise 7.9 in more detail.

(a) Make a stemplot. Is the overall shape roughly symmetric or clearly skewed? There are both low and high observations that we might call outliers.

(b) Find the mean and standard deviation of the seed masses. Then remove both the smallest and largest masses and find the mean and standard deviation of the remaining 37 seeds. Why does removing these two observations reduce s? Why does it have little effect on $\bar{x}$?

7.12 **More on hot funds.** Continue your study of the returns for Fidelity sector funds from Exercise 7.10. The least-squares line, like the correlation, is not resistant.

(a) Find the equations of two least-squares lines for predicting 2003 return from 2002 return, one for all 23 funds and one omitting Fidelity Gold Fund. Make a scatterplot with both lines drawn on it. The two lines are very different.

(b) Starting with the least-squares idea, explain why adding Fidelity Gold Fund to the other 22 funds moves the line in the direction that your graph shows.

7.13 **Outliers?** In Exercise 7.11, you noticed that the smallest and largest observations might be called outliers. Are either of these observations suspected outliers by the $1.5 \times IQR$ rule (page 47)?

7.14 **Where does the water go?** Here are data on the amounts of water withdrawn from natural sources, including rivers, lakes, and wells, in 2000. The units are millions of gallons per day.[5]

Use	Water withdrawn
Public water supplies	43,300
Domestic water supplies	3,590
Irrigation	137,000
Industry	19,780
Power plant cooling	195,500
Fish farming	3,700

Make a bar graph to present these data. For clarity, order the bars by amount of water used. The total water withdrawn is about 408,000 million gallons per day. About how much is withdrawn for uses not mentioned above?

7.15 **Best-selling soft drinks.** Here are data on the market share of the best-selling brands of carbonated soft drinks in 2003:[6]

Brand	Market share
Coke Classic	18.6%
Pepsi-Cola	11.9%
Diet Coke	9.4%
Mountain Dew	6.3%
Sprite	5.9%
Diet Pepsi	5.8%
Dr. Pepper	5.7%

AP Photo/Mark Lennihan

Display these data in a graph. What percent of the soft drink market is held by other brands?

7.16 **Presidential elections.** Here are the percents of the popular vote won by the successful candidate in each of the presidential elections from 1948 to 2004.

Year	1948	1952	1956	1960	1964	1968	1972	1976
Percent	49.6	55.1	57.4	49.7	61.1	43.4	60.7	50.1

Year	1980	1984	1988	1992	1996	2000	2004
Percent	50.7	58.8	53.9	43.2	49.2	47.9	51.2

(a) Make a stemplot of the winners' percents.

(b) What is the median percent of the vote won by the successful candidate in presidential elections?

(c) Call an election a landslide if the winner's percent falls at or above the third quartile. Find the third quartile. Which elections were landslides?

7.17   **The Mississippi River.**   Table 7.1 gives the volume of water discharged by the Mississippi River into the Gulf of Mexico for each year from 1954 to 2001.[7]   The units are cubic kilometers of water—the Mississippi is a big river.

(a) Make a graph of the distribution of water volume. Describe the overall shape of the distribution and any outliers.

(b) Based on the shape of the distribution, do you expect the mean to be close to the median, clearly less than the median, or clearly greater than the median? Why? Find the mean and the median to check your answer.

(c) Based on the shape of the distribution, does it seem reasonable to use $\bar{x}$ and s to describe the center and spread of this distribution? Why? Find $\bar{x}$ and s if you think they are a good choice. Otherwise, find the five-number summary.

TABLE 7.1	Yearly discharge (cubic kilometers of water) of the Mississippi River						
Year	Discharge	Year	Discharge	Year	Discharge	Year	Discharge
1954	290	1966	410	1978	560	1990	680
1955	420	1967	460	1979	800	1991	700
1956	390	1968	510	1980	500	1992	510
1957	610	1969	560	1981	420	1993	900
1958	550	1970	540	1982	640	1994	640
1959	440	1971	480	1983	770	1995	590
1960	470	1972	600	1984	710	1996	670
1961	600	1973	880	1985	680	1997	680
1962	550	1974	710	1986	600	1998	690
1963	360	1975	670	1987	450	1999	580
1964	390	1976	420	1988	420	2000	390
1965	500	1977	430	1989	630	2001	580

7.18   **More on the Mississippi River.**   The data in Table 7.1 are a time series. Make a time plot that shows how the volume of water in the Mississippi changed between 1954 and 2001. What does the time plot reveal that the histogram from the previous exercise does not? It is a good idea to always make a time plot of time series data because a histogram cannot show changes over time.

7.19   **A big toe problem.**   Hallux abducto valgus (call it HAV) is a deformation of the big toe that is not common in youth and often requires surgery. Doctors used X-rays to measure the angle (in degrees) of deformity in 38 consecutive patients under the age of 21 who came to a medical center for surgery to correct HAV.[8] The angle is a measure of the seriousness of the deformity. The data appear in Table 7.2 as "HAV angle." Make a graph and give a numerical description of this distribution. Are there any outliers? Write a brief discussion of the shape, center, and spread of the angle of deformity among young patients needing surgery for this condition.

7.20   **More on a big toe problem.**   The HAV angle data in the previous exercise contain one high outlier. Calculate the median, the mean, and the standard deviation for the full data set and also for the 37 observations remaining when you remove the outlier. How strongly does the outlier affect each of these measures?

TABLE 7.2   Angle of deformity (degrees) for two types of foot deformity

HAV angle	MA angle	HAV angle	MA angle	HAV angle	MA angle
28	18	21	15	16	10
32	16	17	16	30	12
25	22	16	10	30	10
34	17	21	7	20	10
38	33	23	11	50	12
26	10	14	15	25	25
25	18	32	12	26	30
18	13	25	16	28	22
30	19	21	16	31	24
26	10	22	18	38	20
28	17	20	10	32	37
13	14	18	15	21	23
20	20	26	16		

7.21   Predicting foot problems.   Metatarsus adductus (call it MA) is a turning in of the front part of the foot that is common in adolescents and usually corrects itself. Table 7.2 gives the severity of MA ("MA angle") as well. Doctors speculate that the severity of MA can help predict the severity of HAV.

(a) Make a scatterplot of the data. (Which is the explanatory variable?)

(b) Describe the form, direction, and strength of the relationship between MA angle and HAV angle. Are there any clear outliers in your graph?

(c) Do you think the data confirm the doctors' speculation? Why or why not?

7.22   Predicting foot problems, continued.

(a) Find the equation of the least-squares regression line for predicting HAV angle from MA angle. Add this line to the scatterplot you made in the previous exercise.

(b) A new patient has MA angle 25 degrees. What do you predict this patient's HAV angle to be?

(c) Does knowing MA angle allow doctors to predict HAV angle accurately? Explain your answer from the scatterplot, then calculate a numerical measure to support your finding.

7.23   Data on mice.   For a biology project, you measure the tail length (centimeters) and weight (grams) of 12 mice of the same variety. What units of measurement do each of the following have?

(a) The mean length of the tails.

(b) The first quartile of the tail lengths.

(c) The standard deviation of the tail lengths.

(d) The correlation between tail length and weight.

7.24   Catalog shopping (optional).   What is the most important reason that students buy from catalogs? The answer may differ for different groups of students. Here are

Beer in South Dakota

Take a break from doing exercises to apply your math to beer cans in South Dakota. A newspaper there reported that every year an average of 650 beer cans per mile are tossed onto the state's highways. South Dakota has about 83,000 miles of roads. How many beer cans is that in all? The Census Bureau says that there are about 770,000 people in South Dakota. How many beer cans does each man, woman, and child in the state toss on the road each year? That's pretty impressive. Maybe the paper got its numbers wrong.

results for samples of American and East Asian students at a large midwestern university:[9]

	American	Asian
Save time	29	10
Easy	28	11
Low price	17	34
Live far from stores	11	4
No pressure to buy	10	3
Other reason	20	7
Total	115	69

(a) Give the marginal distribution of reasons for all students, in percents.

(b) Give the two conditional distributions of reasons, for American and for East Asian students. What are the most important differences between the two groups of students?

7.25 **How are schools doing? (optional)**   The nonprofit group Public Agenda conducted telephone interviews with parents of high school children. Interviewers chose equal numbers of black, white, and Hispanic parents at random. One question asked was "Are the high schools in your state doing an excellent, good, fair or poor job, or don't you know enough to say?" Here are the survey results:[10]

	Black parents	Hispanic parents	White parents
Excellent	12	34	22
Good	69	55	81
Fair	75	61	60
Poor	24	24	24
Don't know	22	28	14
Total	202	202	201

Write a brief analysis of these results that focuses on the relationship between parent group and opinions about schools.

7.26 **Weighing bean seeds.**   Biological measurements on the same species often follow a Normal distribution quite closely. The weights of seeds of a variety of winged bean are approximately Normal with mean 525 milligrams (mg) and standard deviation 110 mg.

(a) What percent of seeds weigh more than 500 mg?

(b) If we discard the lightest 10% of these seeds, what is the smallest weight among the remaining seeds?

7.27 Breaking bolts. Mechanical measurements on supposedly identical objects usually vary. The variation often follows a Normal distribution. The stress required to break a type of bolt varies Normally with mean 75 kilopounds per square inch (ksi) and standard deviation 8.3 ksi.

(a) What percent of these bolts will withstand a stress of 90 ksi without breaking?

(b) What range covers the middle 50% of breaking strengths for these bolts?

Soap in the shower. *From Rex Boggs in Australia comes an unusual data set: before showering in the morning, he weighed the bar of soap in his shower stall. The weight goes down as the soap is used. The data appear in Table 7.3 (weights in grams). Notice that Mr. Boggs forgot to weigh the soap on some days. Exercises 7.28 to 7.30 are based on the soap data set.*

TABLE 7.3	Weight (grams) of a bar of soap used to shower				
Day	Weight	Day	Weight	Day	Weight
1	124	8	84	16	27
2	121	9	78	18	16
5	103	10	71	19	12
6	96	12	58	20	8
7	90	13	50	21	6

7.28 Scatterplot. Plot the weight of the bar of soap against day. Is the overall pattern roughly linear? Based on your scatterplot, is the correlation between day and weight close to 1, positive but not close to 1, close to 0, negative but not close to −1, or close to −1? Explain your answer.

7.29 Regression. Find the equation of the least-squares regression line for predicting soap weight from day.

(a) What is the equation? Explain what it tells us about the rate at which the soap lost weight.

(b) Mr. Boggs did not measure the weight of the soap on day 4. Use the regression equation to predict that weight.

(c) Draw the regression line on your scatterplot from the previous exercise.

7.30 Prediction? Use the regression equation in the previous exercise to predict the weight of the soap after 30 days. Why is it clear that your answer makes no sense? What's wrong with using the regression line to predict weight after 30 days?

7.31 Statistics for investing. Joe's retirement plan invests in stocks through an "index fund" that follows the behavior of the stock market as a whole, as measured by the S&P 500 stock index. Joe wants to buy a mutual fund that does not track the index closely. He reads that monthly returns from Fidelity Technology Fund have correlation $r = 0.77$ with the S&P 500 index and that Fidelity Real Estate Fund has correlation $r = 0.37$ with the index.

(a) Which of these funds has the closer relationship to returns from the stock market as a whole? How do you know?

(b) Does the information given tell Joe anything about which fund has had higher returns?

7.32   **Initial public offerings.**   The business magazine *Forbes* reports that 4567 companies sold their first stock to the public between 1990 and 2000. The *mean* change in the stock price of these companies since the first stock was issued was +111%. The *median* change was −31%.[11]   Explain how this could happen. (*Hint:* Start with the fact that Cisco Systems stock went up 60,600%.)

7.33   **Moving in step?**   One reason to invest abroad is that markets in different countries don't move in step. When American stocks go down, foreign stocks may go up. So an investor who holds both bears less risk. That's the theory. Now we read: "The correlation between changes in American and European share prices has risen from 0.4 in the mid-1990s to 0.8 in 2000."[12]   Explain to an investor who knows no statistics why this fact reduces the protection provided by buying European stocks.

7.34   **Interpreting correlation.**   The same article that claims that the correlation between changes in stock prices in Europe and the United States was 0.8 in 2000 goes on to say: "Crudely, that means that movements on Wall Street can explain 80% of price movements in Europe." Is this true? What is the correct percent explained if $r = 0.8$?

7.35   **Coaching for the SATs.**   A study finds that high school students who take the SAT, enroll in an SAT coaching course, and then take the SAT a second time raise their SAT mathematics scores from a mean of 521 to a mean of 561.[13]   What factors other than "taking the course causes higher scores" might explain this improvement?

SUPPLEMENTARY EXERCISES

Supplementary exercises apply the skills you have learned in ways that require more thought or more elaborate use of technology.

7.36   **Change in the Serengeti.**   Long-term records from the Serengeti National Park in Tanzania show interesting ecological relationships. When wildebeest are more abundant, they graze the grass more heavily, so there are fewer fires and more trees grow. Lions feed more successfully when there are more trees, so the lion population increases. Here are data on one part of this cycle, wildebeest abundance (in thousands of animals) and the percent of the grass area that burned in the same year:[14]

Gallo Images–Anthony Bannister/Getty Images

Wildebeest (1000s)	Percent burned	Wildebeest (1000s)	Percent burned	Wildebeest (1000s)	Percent burned
396	56	360	88	1147	32
476	50	444	88	1173	31
698	25	524	75	1178	24
1049	16	622	60	1253	24
1178	7	600	56	1249	53
1200	5	902	45		
1302	7	1440	21		

To what extent do these data support the claim that more wildebeest reduce the percent of grasslands that burn? How rapidly does burned area decrease as the number of wildebeest increases? Include a graph and suitable calculations. Follow the four-step process (page 53) in your answer.

7.37 **Prey attract predators.**   Here is one way in which nature regulates the size of animal populations: high population density attracts predators, who remove a higher proportion of the population than when the density of the prey is low. One study looked at kelp perch and their common predator, the kelp bass. The researcher set up four large circular pens on sandy ocean bottom in southern California. He chose young perch at random from a large group and placed 10, 20, 40, and 60 perch in the four pens. Then he dropped the nets protecting the pens, allowing bass to swarm in, and counted the perch left after 2 hours. Here are data on the proportions of perch eaten in four repetitions of this setup:[15]

Perch	Proportion killed			
10	0.0	0.1	0.3	0.3
20	0.2	0.3	0.3	0.6
40	0.075	0.3	0.6	0.725
60	0.517	0.55	0.7	0.817

Do the data support the principle that "more prey attract more predators, who drive down the number of prey"? Follow the four-step process (page 53) in your answer.

7.38 **Extrapolation.**   Your work in Exercise 7.36 no doubt included a regression line. Use the equation of this line to illustrate the danger of extrapolation, taking advantage of the fact that the percent of grasslands burned cannot be less than zero.

Falling through the ice.   *The Nenana Ice Classic is an annual contest to guess the exact time in the spring thaw when a tripod erected on the frozen Tanana River near Nenana, Alaska, will fall through the ice. The 2005 jackpot prize was $285,000. The contest has been run since 1917. Table 7.4 gives simplified data that record only the date on which the tripod fell each year. The earliest date so far is April 20. To make the data easier to use, the table gives the date each year in days starting with April 20. That is, April 20 is 1, April 21 is 2, and so on. You will need software or a graphing calculator to analyze these data in Exercises 7.39 to 7.41.[16]*

7.39 **When does the ice break up?**   We have 89 years of data on the date of ice breakup on the Tanana River. Describe the distribution of the breakup date with both a graph or graphs and appropriate numerical summaries. What is the median date (month and day) for ice breakup?

7.40 **Global warming?**   Because of the high stakes, the falling of the tripod has been carefully observed for many years. If the date the tripod falls has been getting earlier, that may be evidence for the effects of global warming.

(a) Make a time plot of the date the tripod falls against year.

2006 Bill Watkins/AlaskaStock.com

TABLE 7.4		Days from April 20 for the Tanana River tripod to fall									
Year	Day	Year	Day	Year	Day	Year	Day	Year	Day	Year	Day
1917	11	1932	12	1947	14	1962	23	1977	17	1992	25
1918	22	1933	19	1948	24	1963	16	1978	11	1993	4
1919	14	1934	11	1949	25	1964	31	1979	11	1994	10
1920	22	1935	26	1950	17	1965	18	1980	10	1995	7
1921	22	1936	11	1951	11	1966	19	1981	11	1996	16
1922	23	1937	23	1952	23	1967	15	1982	21	1997	11
1923	20	1938	17	1953	10	1968	19	1983	10	1998	1
1924	22	1939	10	1954	17	1969	9	1984	20	1999	10
1925	16	1940	1	1955	20	1970	15	1985	23	2000	12
1926	7	1941	14	1956	12	1971	19	1986	19	2001	19
1927	23	1942	11	1957	16	1972	21	1987	16	2002	18
1928	17	1943	9	1958	10	1973	15	1988	8	2003	10
1929	16	1944	15	1959	19	1974	17	1989	12	2004	5
1930	19	1945	27	1960	13	1975	21	1990	5	2005	9
1931	21	1946	16	1961	16	1976	13	1991	12		

(b) There is a great deal of year-to-year variation. Fitting a regression line to the data may help us see the trend. Fit the least-squares line and add it to your time plot. What do you conclude?

(c) There is much variation about the line. Give a numerical description of how much of the year-to-year variation in ice breakup time is accounted for by the time trend represented by the regression line.

7.41 **More on global warming.** Side-by-side boxplots offer a different look at the data. Group the data into periods of roughly equal length: 1917 to 1939, 1940 to 1959, 1960 to 1979, and 1980 to 2005. Make boxplots to compare ice breakup dates in these four time periods. Write a brief description of what the plots show.

7.42 **Save the eagles.** The pesticide DDT was especially threatening to bald eagles. Here are data on the productivity of the eagle population in northwestern Ontario, Canada.[17] The eagles nest in an area free of DDT but migrate south and eat prey contaminated with the pesticide. DDT was banned at the end of 1972. The researcher observed every nesting area he could reach every year between 1966 and 1981. He measured productivity by the count of young eagles per nesting area.

Ron Sanford/CORBIS

Year	Count	Year	Count	Year	Count	Year	Count
1966	1.26	1970	0.54	1974	0.46	1978	0.82
1967	0.73	1971	0.60	1975	0.77	1979	0.98
1968	0.89	1972	0.54	1976	0.86	1980	0.93
1969	0.84	1973	0.78	1977	0.96	1981	1.12

(a) Make a time plot of the data. Does the plot support the claim that banning DDT helped save the eagles?

(b) It appears that the overall pattern might be described by *two* straight lines. Find the least-squares line for 1966 to 1972 (pre-ban) and also the least-squares line for 1975 to 1981 (allowing a few years for DDT to leave the environment after the ban). Draw these lines on your plot. Would you use the second line to predict young per nesting area in the several years after 1981?

7.43   **Thin monkeys, fat monkeys.**   Animals and people that take in more energy than they expend will get fatter. Here are data on 12 rhesus monkeys: 6 lean monkeys (4% to 9% body fat) and 6 obese monkeys (13% to 44% body fat). The data report the energy expended in 24 hours (kilojoules per minute) and the lean body mass (kilograms, leaving out fat) for each monkey.[18]

Lean		Obese	
Mass	Energy	Mass	Energy
6.6	1.17	7.9	0.93
7.8	1.02	9.4	1.39
8.9	1.46	10.7	1.19
9.8	1.68	12.2	1.49
9.7	1.06	12.1	1.29
9.3	1.16	10.8	1.31

(a) What is the mean lean body mass of the lean monkeys? Of the obese monkeys? Because animals with higher lean mass usually expend more energy, we can't directly compare energy expended.

(b) Instead, look at how energy expended is related to body mass. Make a scatterplot of energy versus mass, using different plot symbols for lean and obese monkeys. Then add to the plot two regression lines, one for lean monkeys and one for obese monkeys. What do these lines suggest about the monkeys?

7.44   **Casting aluminum.**   In casting metal parts, molten metal flows through a "gate" into a die that shapes the part. The gate velocity (the speed at which metal is forced through the gate) plays a critical role in die casting. A firm that casts cylindrical aluminum pistons examined 12 types formed from the same alloy. How does the cylinder wall thickness (inches) influence the gate velocity (feet per second) chosen by the skilled workers who do the casting? If there is a clear pattern, it can be used to direct new workers or to automate the process. Analyze these data and report your findings, following the four-step process.[19]

Thickness	Velocity	Thickness	Velocity	Thickness	Velocity
0.248	123.8	0.524	228.6	0.697	145.2
0.359	223.9	0.552	223.8	0.752	263.1
0.366	180.9	0.628	326.2	0.806	302.4
0.400	104.8	0.697	302.4	0.821	302.4

7.45   **Weeds among the corn.**   Lamb's-quarter is a common weed that interferes with the growth of corn. An agriculture researcher planted corn at the same rate in 16 small plots of ground, then weeded the plots by hand to allow a fixed number of lamb's-quarter plants to grow in each meter of corn row. No other weeds were allowed to grow. Following are the yields of corn (bushels per acre) in each of the plots:[20]

Weeds per meter	Corn yield	Weeds per meter	Corn yield	Weeds per meter	Corn yield	Weeds per meter	Corn yield
0	166.7	1	166.2	3	158.6	9	162.8
0	172.2	1	157.3	3	176.4	9	142.4
0	165.0	1	166.7	3	153.1	9	162.8
0	176.9	1	161.1	3	156.0	9	162.4

Blickwinkel/Alamy

(a) What are the explanatory and response variables in this experiment?

(b) Make side-by-side stemplots of the yields, after rounding to the nearest bushel. Give the median yield for each group (using the unrounded data). What do you conclude about the effect of this weed on corn yield?

7.46   **Weeds among the corn, continued.**   We can also use regression to analyze the data on weeds and corn yield. The advantage of regression over the side-by-side comparison in the previous exercise is that we can use the fitted line to draw conclusions for counts of weeds other than the ones the researcher actually used.

(a) Make a scatterplot of corn yield against weeds per meter. Find the least-squares regression line and add it to your plot. What does the slope of the fitted line tell us about the effect of lamb's-quarter on corn yield?

(b) Predict the yield for corn grown under these conditions with 6 lamb's-quarter plants per meter of row.

EESEE CASE STUDIES

The Electronic Encyclopedia of Statistical Examples and Exercises (EESEE) is available on the text CD and Web site. These more elaborate stories, with data, provide settings for longer case studies. Here are some suggestions for EESEE stories that apply the ideas you have learned in Chapters 1 to 6.

7.47   **Is Old Faithful Faithful?**   Write a response to Questions 1 and 3 for this case study. (Describing a distribution, scatterplots, and regression.)

7.48   **Checkmating and Reading Skills.**   Write a report based on Question 1 in this case study. (Describing a distribution.)

7.49   **Counting Calories.**   Respond to Questions 1, 4, and 6 for this case study. (Describing and comparing distributions.)

7.50   **Mercury in Florida's Bass.**   Respond to Question 5. (Scatterplots, form of relationships. By the way, "homoscedastic" means that the scatter of points about the overall pattern is roughly the same from one side of the scatterplot to the other.)

7.51   **Brain Size and Intelligence.**   Write a response to Question 3. (Scatterplots, correlation, and lurking variables.)

7.52   **Acorn Size and Oak Tree Range.**   Write a report based on Questions 1 and 2. (Scatterplots, correlation, and regression.)

7.53   **Surviving the *Titanic*.**   Answer Questions 1, 2, and 3. (Two-way tables.)

From Exploration to Inference

The purpose of statistics is to gain understanding from data. We can seek understanding in different ways, depending on the circumstances. We have studied one approach to data, *exploratory data analysis*, in some detail. Now we move from data analysis toward *statistical inference*. Both types of reasoning are essential to effective work with data. Here is a brief sketch of the differences between them.

EXPLORATORY DATA ANALYSIS	STATISTICAL INFERENCE
Purpose is unrestricted exploration of the data, searching for interesting patterns.	Purpose is to answer specific questions, posed before the data were produced.
Conclusions apply only to the individuals and circumstances for which we have data in hand.	Conclusions apply to a larger group of individuals or a broader class of circumstances.
Conclusions are informal, based on what we see in the data.	Conclusions are formal, backed by a statement of our confidence in them.

Our journey toward inference begins in Chapters 8 and 9 with *data production*, statistical ideas for producing data to answer specific questions. Chapters 10 and 11 (and the optional Chapters 12 and 13) concern *probability*, the language of formal statistical conclusions. Finally, Chapters 14, 15, and 16 present the core concepts of inference. Chapter 17 reviews the material of Chapters 8 to 16. In practice, data analysis and inference cooperate. Successful inference requires good data production, data analysis to ensure that the data are regular enough, and the language of probability to state conclusions.

"I was an eight, too, until the number crunchers got hold of me."

PART II

Robert Daly/Getty Images

Producing Data: Sampling

Statistics, the science of data, provides ideas and tools that we can use in many settings. Sometimes we have data that describe a group of individuals and want to learn what the data say. That's the job of exploratory data analysis. Sometimes we have specific questions but no data to answer them. To get sound answers, we must *produce data* in a way that is designed to answer our questions.

Suppose our question is "What percent of college students think that people should not obey laws that violate their personal values?" To answer the question, we interview undergraduate college students. We can't afford to ask all students, so we put the question to a *sample* chosen to represent the entire student *population*. How shall we choose a sample that truly represents the opinions of the entire population? Statistical designs for choosing samples are the topic of this chapter.

Observation versus experiment

Our goal in choosing a sample is a picture of the population, disturbed as little as possible by the act of gathering information. Samples are one kind of *observational study*. In other settings, we gather data from an *experiment*. In doing an experiment, we don't just observe individuals or ask them questions. We actively impose some treatment in order to observe the response. Experiments can answer questions such as "Does aspirin reduce the chance of a heart attack?" and "Do a

You just don't understand

A sample survey of journalists and scientists found quite a communications gap. Journalists think that scientists are arrogant, while scientists think that journalists are ignorant. We won't take sides, but here is one interesting result from the survey: 82% of the scientists agree that the "media do not understand statistics well enough to explain new findings" in medicine and other fields.

majority of college students prefer Pepsi to Coke when they taste both without knowing which they are drinking?" Experiments, like samples, provide useful data only when properly designed. We will discuss statistical design of experiments in Chapter 9. The distinction between experiments and observational studies is one of the most important ideas in statistics.

OBSERVATION VERSUS EXPERIMENT

An **observational study** observes individuals and measures variables of interest but does not attempt to influence the responses. The purpose of an observational study is to describe some group or situation.

An **experiment,** on the other hand, deliberately imposes some treatment on individuals in order to observe their responses. The purpose of an experiment is to study whether the treatment causes a change in the response.

Observational studies are essential sources of data about topics from the opinions of voters to the behavior of animals in the wild. But an observational study, even one based on a statistical sample, is a poor way to gauge the effect of an intervention. To see the response to a change, we must actually impose the change. When our goal is to understand cause and effect, experiments are the only source of fully convincing data.

EXAMPLE 8.1   *The rise and fall of hormone replacement*

Should women take hormones such as estrogen after menopause, when natural production of these hormones ends? In 1992, several major medical organizations said "Yes." In particular, women who took hormones seemed to reduce their risk of a heart attack by 35% to 50%. The risks of taking hormones appeared small compared with the benefits.

The evidence in favor of hormone replacement came from a number of observational studies that compared women who were taking hormones with others who were not. But women who choose to take hormones are very different from women who do not: they are richer and better educated and see doctors more often. These women do many things to maintain their health. It isn't surprising that they have fewer heart attacks.

Experiments don't let women decide what to do. They assign women to either hormone replacement or to dummy pills that look and taste the same as the hormone pills. The assignment is done by a coin toss, so that all kinds of women are equally likely to get either treatment. By 2002, several experiments with women of different ages agreed that hormone replacement does *not* reduce the risk of heart attacks. The National Institutes of Health, after reviewing the evidence, concluded that the observational studies were wrong. Taking hormones after menopause quickly fell out of favor.[1]

When we simply observe women, the effects of actually taking hormones are *confounded* with (mixed up with) the characteristics of women who choose to take hormones.

> **CONFOUNDING**
>
> Two variables (explanatory variables or lurking variables) are **confounded** when their effects on a response variable cannot be distinguished from each other.

Observational studies of the effect of one variable on another often fail because the explanatory variable is confounded with lurking variables. We will see that well-designed experiments take steps to defeat confounding.

EXAMPLE 8.2   Wine, beer, or spirits?

Moderate use of alcohol is associated with better health. Observational studies suggest that drinking wine rather than beer or spirits confers added health benefits. But people who prefer wine are different from those who drink mainly beer or stronger stuff. Wine drinkers as a group are richer and better educated. They eat more fruits and vegetables and less fried food. Their diets contain less fat, less cholesterol, and also less alcohol. They are less likely to smoke. The explanatory variable (What type of alcoholic beverage do you drink most often?) is confounded with many lurking variables (education, wealth, diet, and so on). A large study therefore concludes: "The apparent health benefits of wine compared with other alcoholic beverages, as described by others, may be a result of confounding by dietary habits and other lifestyle factors."[2]   Figure 8.1 shows the confounding in picture form.

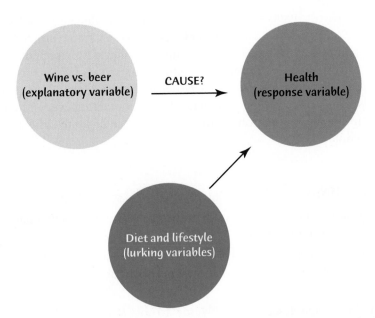

FIGURE 8.1 Confounding: We can't distinguish the effects of what people drink from the effects of their overall diet and lifestyle.

APPLY YOUR KNOWLEDGE

AB/Getty Images

8.1   **Cell phones and brain cancer.**   A study of cell phones and the risk of brain cancer looked at a group of 469 people who have brain cancer. The investigators matched each cancer patient with a person of the same sex, age, and race who did not have brain cancer, then asked about use of cell phones.[3] Result: "Our data suggest that use of handheld cellular telephones is not associated with risk of brain cancer." Is this an observational study or an experiment? Why? What are the explanatory and response variables?

8.2   **Teaching economics.**   An educational software company wants to compare the effectiveness of its computer animation for teaching about supply and demand curves with that of a textbook presentation. The company tests the economic knowledge of a number of first-year college students, then divides them into two groups. One group uses the animation, and the other studies the text. The company retests all the students and compares the increase in economic understanding in the two groups. Is this an experiment? Why or why not? What are the explanatory and response variables?

8.3   **TV viewing and aggression.**   A typical hour of prime-time television shows three to five violent acts. Research shows that there is a clear association between time spent watching TV and aggressive behavior by adolescents. Nonetheless, it is hard to conclude that watching TV *causes* aggression. Suggest several lurking variables describing an adolescent's home life that may be confounded with how much TV he or she watches.[4]

Sampling

A political scientist wants to know what percent of college-age adults consider themselves conservatives. An automaker hires a market research firm to learn what percent of adults aged 18 to 35 recall seeing television advertisements for a new gas-electric hybrid car. Government economists inquire about average household income. In all these cases, we want to gather information about a large group of individuals. Time, cost, and inconvenience forbid contacting every individual. So we gather information about only part of the group in order to draw conclusions about the whole.

> ### POPULATION, SAMPLE, SAMPLING DESIGN
>
> The **population** in a statistical study is the entire group of individuals about which we want information.
>
> A **sample** is a part of the population from which we actually collect information. We use a sample to draw conclusions about the entire population.
>
> A **sampling design** describes exactly how to choose a sample from the population.

Pay careful attention to the details of the definitions of "population" and "sample." Look at Exercise 8.4 right now to check your understanding.

We often draw conclusions about a whole on the basis of a sample. Everyone has sipped a spoonful of soup and judged the entire bowl on the basis of that taste. But a bowl of soup is uniform, so that the taste of a single spoonful represents the whole. Choosing a representative sample from a large and varied population is not so easy. The first step in a proper **sample survey** is to say exactly *what population* we want to describe. The second step is to say exactly *what we want to measure*, that is, to give exact definitions of our variables. These preliminary steps can be complicated, as the following example illustrates.

sample survey

— **EXAMPLE 8.3**   The Current Population Survey ——

The most important government sample survey in the United States is the monthly Current Population Survey (CPS). The CPS contacts about 60,000 households each month. It produces the monthly unemployment rate and much other economic and social information (see Figure 8.2). To measure unemployment, we must first specify the population we want to describe. Which age groups will we include? Will we include illegal aliens or people in prisons? The CPS defines its population as all U.S. residents (whether citizens or not) 16 years of age and over who are civilians and are not in an institution such as a prison. The unemployment rate announced in the news refers to this specific population.

The second question is harder: what does it mean to be "unemployed"? Someone who is not looking for work—for example, a full-time student—should not be called unemployed just because she is not working for pay. If you are chosen for the CPS sample, the interviewer first asks whether you are available to work and whether you actually looked for work in the past four weeks. If not, you are neither employed nor unemployed—you are not in the labor force.

If you are in the labor force, the interviewer goes on to ask about employment. If you did any work for pay or in your own business during the week of the survey, you

FIGURE 8.2 The Web page of the Current Population Survey, www.bls.census.gov/cps.

are employed. If you worked at least 15 hours in a family business without pay, you are employed. You are also employed if you have a job but didn't work because of vacation, being on strike, or other good reason. An unemployment rate of 4.7% means that 4.7% of the sample was unemployed, using the exact CPS definitions of both "labor force" and "unemployed."

APPLY YOUR KNOWLEDGE

8.4 **Sampling students.** A political scientist wants to know how college students feel about the Social Security system. She obtains a list of the 3456 undergraduates at her college and mails a questionnaire to 250 students selected at random. Only 104 questionnaires are returned.

(a) What is the population in this study? Be careful: what group does she *want information about?*

(b) What is the sample? Be careful: from what group does she *actually obtain information?*

8.5 **The American Community Survey.** The American Community Survey (ACS) is replacing the "long form" sent to some households in the every-ten-years national census. Each month, the Census Bureau mails survey forms to 250,000 households. Telephone calls are made to households that don't return the form. In the end, the Census Bureau gets responses from about 97% of the households it tries to contact. The survey asks questions about the people living in the household and about such things as plumbing, motor vehicles, and housing costs. What is the population for the ACS? What is the sample from which information is actually obtained?

8.6 **Customer satisfaction.** A department store mails a customer satisfaction survey to people who make credit card purchases at the store. This month, 45,000 people made credit card purchases. Surveys are mailed to 1000 of these people, chosen at random, and 137 people return the survey form. What is the population for this survey? What is the sample from which information was actually obtained?

How to sample badly

How can we choose a sample that we can trust to represent the population? A sampling design is a specific method for choosing a sample from the population. The easiest—but not the best—design just chooses individuals close at hand. If we are interested in finding out how many people have jobs, for example, we might go to a shopping mall and ask people passing by if they are employed. A sample selected by taking the members of the population that are easiest to reach is called a

convenience sample **convenience sample.** Convenience samples often produce unrepresentative data.

┌─ **EXAMPLE 8.4** Sampling at the mall ─────────────────

A sample of mall shoppers is fast and cheap. But people at shopping malls tend to be more prosperous than typical Americans. They are also more likely to be teenagers or retired. Moreover, unless interviewers are carefully trained, they tend to question well-dressed, respectable people and avoid poorly dressed or tough-looking individuals. In short, mall interviews will not contact a sample that is representative of the entire population.

Interviews at shopping malls will almost surely overrepresent middle-class and retired people and underrepresent the poor. This will happen almost every time we take such a sample. That is, it is a systematic error caused by a bad sampling design, not just bad luck on one sample. This is *bias:* the outcomes of mall surveys will repeatedly miss the truth about the population in the same ways.

BIAS

The design of a statistical study is **biased** if it systematically favors certain outcomes.

EXAMPLE 8.5   Online polls

The American Family Association (AFA) is a conservative group that claims to stand for "traditional family values." It regularly posts online poll questions on its Web site—just click on a response to take part. Because the respondents are people who visit this site, the poll results always support AFA's positions. Well, almost always. In 2004, AFA's online poll asked about the heated issue of allowing same-sex marriage. Soon, email lists and social network sites favored mostly by young liberals pointed to the AFA poll. Almost 850,000 people responded, and 60% of them favored legalizing same-sex marriage. AFA claimed that homosexual rights groups had skewed its poll.

Online polls are now everywhere—some sites will even provide help in conducting your own online poll. As the AFA poll illustrates, you can't trust the results. *People who take the trouble to respond to an open invitation are usually not representative of any clearly defined population.* That's true of regular visitors to AFA's site, of the activists who made a special effort to vote in the marriage poll, and of the people who bother to respond to write-in, call-in, or online polls in general. Polls like these are examples of *voluntary response sampling.*

CAUTION

VOLUNTARY RESPONSE SAMPLE

A **voluntary response sample** consists of people who choose themselves by responding to a broad appeal. Voluntary response samples are biased because people with strong opinions are most likely to respond.

APPLY YOUR KNOWLEDGE

8.7   **Sampling on campus.**   You see a woman student standing in front of the student center, now and then stopping other students to ask them questions. She says that she is collecting student opinions for a class assignment. Explain why this sampling method is almost certainly biased.

8.8   **More sampling on campus.**   Your college wants to gather student opinion about parking for students on campus. It isn't practical to contact all students.

(a) Give an example of a way to choose a sample of students that is poor practice because it depends on voluntary response.

(b) Give another example of a bad way to choose a sample that doesn't use voluntary response.

Simple random samples

In a voluntary response sample, people choose whether to respond. In a convenience sample, the interviewer makes the choice. In both cases, personal choice produces bias. The statistician's remedy is to allow impersonal chance to choose the sample. A sample chosen by chance allows neither favoritism by the sampler nor self-selection by respondents. Choosing a sample by chance attacks bias by giving all individuals an equal chance to be chosen. Rich and poor, young and old, black and white, all have the same chance to be in the sample.

The simplest way to use chance to select a sample is to place names in a hat (the population) and draw out a handful (the sample). This is the idea of *simple random sampling*.

SIMPLE RANDOM SAMPLE

A **simple random sample (SRS)** of size n consists of n individuals from the population chosen in such a way that every set of n individuals has an equal chance to be the sample actually selected.

An SRS not only gives each individual an equal chance to be chosen but also gives every possible sample an equal chance to be chosen. There are other random sampling designs that give each individual, but not each sample, an equal chance. Exercise 8.44 describes one such design.

When you think of an SRS, picture drawing names from a hat to remind yourself that an SRS doesn't favor any part of the population. That's why an SRS is a better method of choosing samples than convenience or voluntary response sampling. But writing names on slips of paper and drawing them from a hat is slow and inconvenient. That's especially true if, like the Current Population Survey, we must draw a sample of size 60,000. In practice, samplers use software. The *Simple Random Sample* applet makes the choosing of an SRS very fast. If you don't use the applet or other software, you can randomize by using a *table of random digits*.

RANDOM DIGITS

A **table of random digits** is a long string of the digits 0, 1, 2, 3, 4, 5, 6, 7, 8, 9 with these two properties:

1. Each entry in the table is equally likely to be any of the 10 digits 0 through 9.

2. The entries are independent of each other. That is, knowledge of one part of the table gives no information about any other part.

Table B at the back of the book is a table of random digits. Table B begins with the digits 19223950340575628713. To make the table easier to read, the digits appear in groups of five and in numbered rows. The groups and rows have no meaning—the table is just a long list of randomly chosen digits. There are two steps in using the table to choose a simple random sample.

USING TABLE B TO CHOOSE AN SRS

Step 1. Label. Give each member of the population a numerical label of the *same length*.

Step 2. Table. To choose an SRS, read from Table B successive groups of digits of the length you used as labels. Your sample contains the individuals whose labels you find in the table.

Are these random digits really random?

Not a chance. The random digits in Table B were produced by a computer program. Computer programs do exactly what you tell them to do. Give the program the same input and it will produce exactly the same "random" digits. Of course, clever people have devised computer programs that produce output that *looks* like random digits. These are called "pseudo-random numbers," and that's what Table B contains. Pseudo-random numbers work fine for statistical randomizing, but they have hidden nonrandom patterns that can mess up more refined uses.

You can label up to 100 items with two digits: 01, 02, ..., 99, 00. Up to 1000 items can be labeled with three digits, and so on. Always use the shortest labels that will cover your population. As standard practice, we recommend that you begin with label 1 (or 01 or 001, as needed). Reading groups of digits from the table gives all individuals the same chance to be chosen because all labels of the same length have the same chance to be found in the table. For example, any pair of digits in the table is equally likely to be any of the 100 possible labels 01, 02, ..., 99, 00. Ignore any group of digits that was not used as a label or that duplicates a label already in the sample. You can read digits from Table B in any order—across a row, down a column, and so on—because the table has no order. As standard practice, we recommend reading across rows.

EXAMPLE 8.6 Sampling spring break resorts

A campus newspaper plans a major article on spring break destinations. The authors intend to call four randomly chosen resorts at each destination to ask about their attitudes toward groups of students as guests. Here are the resorts listed in one city:

01	Aloha Kai	08	Captiva	15	Palm Tree	22	Sea Shell
02	Anchor Down	09	Casa del Mar	16	Radisson	23	Silver Beach
03	Banana Bay	10	Coconuts	17	Ramada	24	Sunset Beach
04	Banyan Tree	11	Diplomat	18	Sandpiper	25	Tradewinds
05	Beach Castle	12	Holiday Inn	19	Sea Castle	26	Tropical Breeze
06	Best Western	13	Lime Tree	20	Sea Club	27	Tropical Shores
07	Cabana	14	Outrigger	21	Sea Grape	28	Veranda

Robert Daly/Getty Images

Step 1. Label. Because two digits are needed to label the 28 resorts, all labels will have two digits. We have added labels 01 to 28 in the list of resorts. Always say how you labeled the members of the population. To sample from the 1240 resorts in a major vacation area, you would label the resorts 0001, 0002, ..., 1239, 1240.

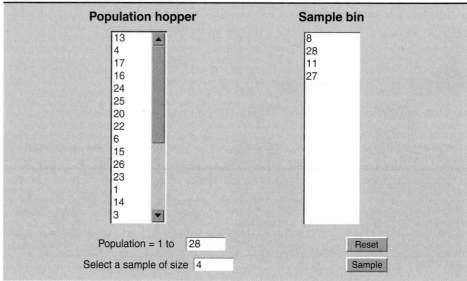

FIGURE 8.3 The *Simple Random Sample* applet used to choose an SRS of size $n = 4$ from a population of size 28.

Step 2. Table. To use the *Simple Random Sample* applet, just enter 28 in the "Population =" box and 4 in the "Select a sample" box, click "Reset," and click "Sample." Figure 8.3 shows the result of one sample.

To use Table B, read two-digit groups until you have chosen four resorts. Starting at line 130 (any line will do), we find

69051   64817   87174   09517   84534   06489   87201   97245

Because the labels are two digits long, read successive two-digit groups from the table. Ignore groups not used as labels, like the initial 69. Also ignore any repeated labels, like the second and third 17s in this row, because you can't choose the same resort twice. Your sample contains the resorts labeled 05, 16, 17, and 20. These are Beach Castle, Radisson, Ramada, and Sea Club.

We can trust results from an SRS, because it uses impersonal chance to avoid bias. Online polls and mall interviews also produce samples. We can't trust results from these samples, because they are chosen in ways that invite bias. *The first question to ask about any sample is whether it was chosen at random.*

EXAMPLE 8.7   Do you avoid soda?

A Gallup Poll on the American diet asked subjects about their attitudes toward various foods. The press release mentioned "the increasing proportion of Americans who say they try to avoid 'soda or pop' (51%, up from 41% in 2002)." Can we trust that 51%?

Ask first how Gallup selected its sample. Later in the press release we read this: "These results are based on telephone interviews with a randomly selected national sample of 1,005 adults, aged 18 and older, conducted July 8–11, 2004."[5]

This is a good start toward gaining our confidence. Gallup tells us what population it has in mind (people at least 18 years old who live anywhere in the United States). We know that the sample from this population was of size 1005 and, most important, that it was chosen at random. There is more to say, but we have at least heard the comforting words "randomly selected."

APPLY YOUR KNOWLEDGE

8.9 **Apartment living.** You are planning a report on apartment living in a college town. You decide to select three apartment complexes at random for in-depth interviews with residents. Use the *Simple Random Sample* applet, other software, or Table B to select a simple random sample of three of the following apartment complexes. If you use Table B, start at line 117.

Ashley Oaks	Country View	Mayfair Village
Bay Pointe	Country Villa	Nobb Hill
Beau Jardin	Crestview	Pemberly Courts
Bluffs	Del-Lynn	Peppermill
Brandon Place	Fairington	Pheasant Run
Briarwood	Fairway Knolls	River Walk
Brownstone	Fowler	Sagamore Ridge
Burberry Place	Franklin Park	Salem Courthouse
Cambridge	Georgetown	Village Square
Chauncey Village	Greenacres	Waterford Court
Country Squire	Lahr House	Williamsburg

8.10 **Minority managers.** A firm wants to understand the attitudes of its minority managers toward its system for assessing management performance. Below is a list of all the firm's managers who are members of minority groups. Use the *Simple Random Sample* applet, other software, or Table B at line 139 to choose six to be interviewed in detail about the performance appraisal system.

Abdulhamid	Duncan	Huang	Puri
Agarwal	Fernandez	Kim	Richards
Baxter	Fleming	Liao	Rodriguez
Bonds	Gates	Mourning	Santiago
Brown	Goel	Naber	Shen
Castillo	Gomez	Peters	Vega
Cross	Hernandez	Pliego	Wang

Bill Lai/Index Stock Imagery/PictureQuest

8.11 **Sampling the forest.** To gather data on a 1200-acre pine forest in Louisiana, the U.S. Forest Service laid a grid of 1410 equally spaced circular plots over a map of the forest. A ground survey visited a sample of 10% of these plots.[6]

(a) How would you label the plots?

(b) Use Table B, beginning at line 105, to choose the first 5 plots in an SRS of 141 plots.

Do not call!

People who do sample surveys hate telemarketing. We all get so many unwanted sales pitches by phone that many people hang up before learning that the caller is conducting a survey rather than selling vinyl siding. You can eliminate calls from commercial telemarketers by placing your phone number on the National Do Not Call Registry. Sign up at www.donotcall.gov.

Other sampling designs

The general framework for statistical sampling is a *probability sample*.

PROBABILITY SAMPLE

A **probability sample** is a sample chosen by chance. We must know what samples are possible and what chance, or probability, each possible sample has.

Some probability sampling designs (such as an SRS) give each member of the population an equal chance to be selected. This may not be true in more elaborate sampling designs. In every case, however, the use of chance to select the sample is the essential principle of statistical sampling.

Designs for sampling from large populations spread out over a wide area are usually more complex than an SRS. For example, it is common to sample important groups within the population separately, then combine these samples. This is the idea of a *stratified random sample*.

STRATIFIED RANDOM SAMPLE

To select a **stratified random sample,** first classify the population into groups of similar individuals, called **strata.** Then choose a separate SRS in each stratum and combine these SRSs to form the full sample.

Choose the strata based on facts known before the sample is taken. For example, a population of election districts might be divided into urban, suburban, and rural strata. A stratified design can produce more precise information than an SRS of the same size by taking advantage of the fact that individuals in the same stratum are similar to one another.

Ryan McVay/Photo Disc/Getty Images

EXAMPLE 8.8 Seat belt use in Hawaii

Each state conducts an annual survey of seat belt use by drivers, following guidelines set by the federal government. The guidelines require probability samples. Seat belt use is observed at randomly chosen road locations at random times during daylight hours. The locations are not an SRS of all locations in the state but rather a stratified sample using the state's counties as strata.

In Hawaii, the counties are the islands that make up the state's territory. The seat belt survey sample consists of 135 road locations in the four most populated islands: 66 in Oahu, 24 in Maui, 23 in Hawaii, and 22 in Kauai. The sample sizes on the islands are proportional to the amount of road traffic.[7]

multistage sample   Seat belt surveys in larger states often use **multistage samples.** Counties are grouped into strata by population size. At the first stage, choose a stratified sample of counties that includes all of the most populated counties and a selection of smaller counties. The second stage selects locations at random within each county chosen at the first stage. These are also stratified samples, with locations grouped into strata by, for example, high, medium and low traffic volume.

Most large-scale sample surveys use multistage samples. The samples at individual stages may be SRSs but are often stratified. Analysis of data from sampling designs more complex than an SRS takes us beyond basic statistics. But the SRS is the building block of more elaborate designs, and analysis of other designs differs more in complexity of detail than in fundamental concepts.

APPLY YOUR KNOWLEDGE

8.12 **A stratified sample.** A club has 30 student members and 10 faculty members. The students are

Abel	Fisher	Huber	Miranda	Reinmann
Carson	Ghosh	Jimenez	Moskowitz	Santos
Chen	Griswold	Jones	Neyman	Shaw
David	Hein	Kim	O'Brien	Thompson
Deming	Hernandez	Klotz	Pearl	Utts
Elashoff	Holland	Liu	Potter	Varga

The faculty members are

Andrews	Fernandez	Kim	Moore	West
Besicovitch	Gupta	Lightman	Vicario	Yang

The club can send 4 students and 2 faculty members to a convention. It decides to choose those who will go by random selection. Use software or Table B to choose a stratified random sample of 4 students and 2 faculty members.

8.13 **Sampling by accountants.** Accountants use stratified samples during audits to verify a company's records of such things as accounts receivable. The stratification is based on the dollar amount of the item and often includes 100% sampling of the largest items. One company reports 5000 accounts receivable. Of these, 100 are in amounts over $50,000; 500 are in amounts between $1000 and $50,000; and the remaining 4400 are in amounts under $1000. Using these groups as strata, you decide to verify all of the largest accounts and to sample 5% of the midsize accounts and 1% of the small accounts. How would you label the two strata from which you will sample? Use software or Table B, starting at line 115, to select *only the first 5* accounts from each of these strata.

Cautions about sample surveys

Random selection eliminates bias in the choice of a sample from a list of the population. When the population consists of human beings, however, accurate information from a sample requires more than a good sampling design.

To begin, we need an accurate and complete list of the population. Because such a list is rarely available, most samples suffer from some degree of *undercoverage*. A sample survey of households, for example, will miss not only homeless people but prison inmates and students in dormitories. An opinion poll conducted by telephone will miss the 5% of American households without residential phones. The results of national sample surveys therefore have some bias if the people not covered—who most often are poor people—differ from the rest of the population.

A more serious source of bias in most sample surveys is *nonresponse*, which occurs when a selected individual cannot be contacted or refuses to cooperate. Nonresponse to sample surveys often reaches 50% or more, even with careful planning and several callbacks. Because nonresponse is higher in urban areas, most sample surveys substitute other people in the same area to avoid favoring rural areas in the final sample. If the people contacted differ from those who are rarely at home or who refuse to answer questions, some bias remains.

UNDERCOVERAGE AND NONRESPONSE

Undercoverage occurs when some groups in the population are left out of the process of choosing the sample.

Nonresponse occurs when an individual chosen for the sample can't be contacted or refuses to participate.

EXAMPLE 8.9 How bad is nonresponse?

The Current Population Survey has the lowest nonresponse rate of any poll we know: only about 6% or 7% of the households in the sample don't respond. People are more likely to respond to a government survey, and the CPS contacts its sample in person before doing later interviews by phone.

The University of Chicago's General Social Survey (GSS) is the nation's most important social science survey. (See Figure 8.4.) The GSS also contacts its sample in person, and it is run by a university. Despite these advantages, its most recent survey had a 30% rate of nonresponse.

What about opinion polls by news media and opinion-polling firms? We don't know their rates of nonresponse because they won't say. That itself is a bad sign. The Pew Research Center for the People and the Press imitated a careful telephone survey and published the results: out of 2879 households called, 1658 were never at home, refused, or would not finish the interview. That's a nonresponse rate of 58%.[8]

response bias In addition, the behavior of the respondent or of the interviewer can cause **response bias** in sample results. People know that they should take the trouble to vote, for example, so many who didn't vote in the last election will tell an interviewer that they did. The race or sex of the interviewer can influence responses to questions about race relations or attitudes toward feminism. Answers to questions that ask respondents to recall past events are often inaccurate because of faulty memory. For example, many people "telescope" events in the past, bringing them

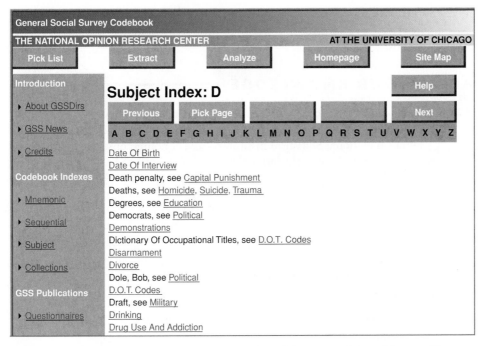

FIGURE 8.4 A small part of the subject index of the General Social Survey. The GSS has tracked opinions about a wide variety of issues since 1972.

forward in memory to more recent time periods. "Have you visited a dentist in the last 6 months?" will often draw a "Yes" from someone who last visited a dentist 8 months ago.[9] Careful training of interviewers and careful supervision to avoid variation among the interviewers can reduce response bias. Good interviewing technique is another aspect of a well-done sample survey.

The **wording of questions** is the most important influence on the answers given to a sample survey. Confusing or leading questions can introduce strong bias, and even minor changes in wording can change a survey's outcome. Here are some examples.[10]

wording effects

EXAMPLE 8.10 Help the poor?

How do Americans feel about government help for the poor? Only 13% think we are spending too much on "assistance to the poor," but 44% think we are spending too much on "welfare."

EXAMPLE 8.11 Independence for Scotland?

How do the Scots feel about the movement to become independent from England? Well, 51% would vote for "independence for Scotland," but only 34% support "an independent Scotland separate from the United Kingdom."

It seems that "assistance to the poor" and "independence" are nice, hopeful words. "Welfare" and "separate" are negative words. *You can't trust the results of a sample survey until you have read the exact questions asked. The amount of nonresponse and the date of the survey are also important.* Good statistical design is a part, but only a part, of a trustworthy survey.

APPLY YOUR KNOWLEDGE

8.14   Ring-no-answer.   A common form of nonresponse in telephone surveys is "ring-no-answer." That is, a call is made to an active number but no one answers. The Italian National Statistical Institute looked at nonresponse to a government survey of households in Italy during the periods January 1 to Easter and July 1 to August 31. All calls were made between 7 and 10 P.M., but 21.4% gave "ring-no-answer" in one period versus 41.5% "ring-no-answer" in the other period.[11] Which period do you think had the higher rate of no answers? Why? Explain why a high rate of nonresponse makes sample results less reliable.

8.15   Question wording.   In 2000, when the federal budget showed a large surplus, the Pew Research Center asked two questions of random samples of adults. Both questions stated that Social Security would be "fixed." Here are the uses suggested for the remaining surplus:

> *Should the money be used for a tax cut, or should it be used to fund new government programs?*

> *Should the money be used for a tax cut, or should it be spent on programs for education, the environment, health care, crime-fighting and military defense?*

One of these questions drew 60% favoring a tax cut. The other drew only 22%. Which wording pulls respondents toward a tax cut? Why?

Inference about the population

Despite the many practical difficulties in carrying out a sample survey, using chance to choose a sample does eliminate bias in the actual selection of the sample from the list of available individuals. But it is unlikely that results from a sample are exactly the same as for the entire population. Sample results, like the official unemployment rate obtained from the monthly Current Population Survey, are only estimates of the truth about the population. If we select two samples at random from the same population, we will draw different individuals. So the sample results will almost certainly differ somewhat. Properly designed samples avoid systematic bias, but their results are rarely exactly correct and they vary from sample to sample.

How accurate is a sample result like the monthly unemployment rate? We can't say for sure, because the result would be different if we took another sample. But the results of random sampling don't change haphazardly from sample to sample. Because we deliberately use chance, the results obey the laws of probability that govern chance behavior. We can say how large an error we are likely to make in drawing conclusions about the population from a sample. Results from a sample survey usually come with a margin of error that sets bounds on the size of the likely error. How to do this is part of the business of statistical inference. We will describe the reasoning in Chapter 14.

One point is worth making now: **larger random samples give more accurate results than smaller samples.** By taking a very large sample, you can be confident that the sample result is very close to the truth about the population. The Current Population Survey contacts about 60,000 households, so it estimates the national unemployment rate very accurately. Opinion polls that contact 1000 or 1500 people give less accurate results. Of course, only probability samples carry this guarantee. The AFA's voluntary response sample on same-sex marriage is worthless even though 850,000 people clicked a response. Using a probability sampling design and taking care to deal with practical difficulties reduce bias in a sample. The size of the sample then determines how close to the population truth the sample result is likely to fall.

APPLY YOUR KNOWLEDGE

8.16 **Ask more people.** Just before a presidential election, a national opinion-polling firm increases the size of its weekly sample from the usual 1500 people to 4000 people. Why do you think the firm does this?

CHAPTER 8 SUMMARY

We can produce data intended to answer specific questions by **observational studies** or **experiments. Sample surveys** that select a part of a population of interest to represent the whole are one type of observational study. **Experiments,** unlike observational studies, actively impose some treatment on the subjects of the experiment.

Observational studies often fail to show that changes in an explanatory variable actually cause changes in a response variable, because the explanatory variable is **confounded** with lurking variables. Variables are confounded when their effects on a response can't be distinguished from each other.

A sample survey selects a **sample** from the **population** of all individuals about which we desire information. We base conclusions about the population on data from the sample.

The **design** of a sample describes the method used to select the sample from the population. **Probability sampling** designs use chance to select a sample.

The basic probability sample is a **simple random sample (SRS).** An SRS gives every possible sample of a given size the same chance to be chosen.

Choose an SRS by labeling the members of the population and using a **table of random digits** to select the sample. Software can automate this process.

To choose a **stratified random sample,** classify the population into **strata,** groups of individuals that are similar in some way that is important to the response. Then choose a separate SRS from each stratum.

Failure to use probability sampling often results in **bias,** or systematic errors in the way the sample represents the population. **Voluntary response samples,** in which the respondents choose themselves, are particularly prone to large bias.

In human populations, even probability samples can suffer from bias due to **undercoverage** or **nonresponse,** from **response bias,** or from misleading results due to **poorly worded questions.** Sample surveys must deal expertly with these potential problems in addition to using a probability sampling design.

CHECK YOUR SKILLS

8.17   The Nurses' Health Study has interviewed a sample of more than 100,000 female registered nurses every two years since 1976. The study finds that "light-to-moderate drinkers had a significantly lower risk of death" than either nondrinkers or heavy drinkers. The Nurses' Health Study is

(a) an observational study.

(b) an experiment.

(c) Can't tell without more information.

8.18   How strong is the evidence from the Nurses' Health Study (see the previous exercise) that moderate drinking lowers the risk of death?

(a) Quite strong because it comes from an experiment.

(b) Quite strong because it comes from a large random sample.

(c) Weak, because drinking habits are confounded with many other variables.

8.19   An opinion poll contacts 1161 adults and asks them, "Which political party do you think has better ideas for leading the country in the twenty-first century?" In all, 696 of the 1161 say, "The Democrats." The sample in this setting is

(a) all 225 million adults in the United States.

(b) the 1161 people interviewed.

(c) the 696 people who chose the Democrats.

8.20   A committee on community relations in a college town plans to survey local businesses about the importance of students as customers. From telephone book listings, the committee chooses 150 businesses at random. Of these, 73 return the questionnaire mailed by the committee. The population for this study is

(a) all businesses in the college town.

(b) the 150 businesses chosen.

(c) the 73 businesses that returned the questionnaire.

8.21   The sample in the setting of the previous exercise is

(a) all businesses in the college town.

(b) the 150 businesses chosen.

(c) the 73 businesses that returned the questionnaire.

8.22   You can find the Excite Poll online at `poll.excite.com`. You simply click on a response to become part of the sample. The poll question for June 19, 2005, was "Do you prefer watching first-run movies at a movie theater, or waiting until they are available on home video or pay-per-view?" In all, 8896 people responded, with only 13% (1118 people) saying they preferred theaters. You can conclude that

(a) American adults strongly prefer watching movies at home.

(b) the poll uses voluntary response, so the results tell us little about the population of all adults.

(c) the sample is too small to draw any conclusion.

8.23   You must choose an SRS of 10 of the 440 retail outlets in New York that sell your company's products. How would you label this population in order to use Table B?

(a) 001, 002, 003, ..., 439, 440

(b) 000, 001, 002, ..., 439, 440

(c) 1, 2, ..., 439, 440

8.24   You are using the table of random digits to choose a simple random sample of 6 students from a class of 30 students. You label the students 01 to 30 in alphabetical order. Go to line 133 of Table B. Your sample contains the students labeled

(a) 45, 74, 04, 18, 07, 65.

(b) 04, 18, 07, 13, 02, 07.

(c) 04, 18, 07, 13, 02, 05.

8.25   You want to choose an SRS of 5 of the 7200 salaried employees of a corporation. You label the employees 0001 to 7200 in alphabetical order. Using line 111 of Table B, your sample contains the employees labeled

(a) 6694, 5130, 0041, 2712, 3827.

(b) 6694, 0513, 0929, 7004, 1271.

(c) 8148, 6694, 8760, 5130, 9297.

8.26   A sample of households in a community is selected at random from the telephone directory. In this community, 4% of households have no telephone and another 35% have unlisted telephone numbers. The sample will certainly suffer from

(a) nonresponse.

(b) undercoverage.

(c) false responses.

CHAPTER 8 EXERCISES

In all exercises asking for an SRS, you may use Table B, the Simple Random Sample applet, or other software.

8.27   **Alcohol and heart attacks.**   Many studies have found that people who drink alcohol in moderation have lower risk of heart attacks than either nondrinkers or heavy drinkers. Does alcohol consumption also improve survival after a heart attack? One study followed 1913 people who were hospitalized after severe heart attacks. In the year before their heart attacks, 47% of these people did not drink, 36% drank moderately, and 17% drank heavily. After four years, fewer of the moderate drinkers had died.[12]   Is this an observational study or an experiment? Why? What are the explanatory and response variables?

8.28   Reducing nonresponse.   How can we reduce the rate of refusals in telephone surveys? Most people who answer at all listen to the interviewer's introductory remarks and then decide whether to continue. One study made telephone calls to randomly selected households to ask opinions about the next election. In some calls, the interviewer gave her name, in others she identified the university she was representing, and in still others she identified both herself and the university. The study recorded what percent of each group of interviews was completed. Is this an observational study or an experiment? Why? What are the explanatory and response variables?

8.29   Safety of anesthetics.   The National Halothane Study was a major investigation of the safety of anesthetics used in surgery. Records of over 850,000 operations performed in 34 major hospitals showed the following death rates for four common anesthetics:[13]

Anesthetic	A	B	C	D
Death rate	1.7%	1.7%	3.4%	1.9%

There is a clear association between the anesthetic used and the death rate of patients. Anesthetic C appears dangerous.

(a) Explain why we call the National Halothane Study an observational study rather than an experiment, even though it compared the results of using different anesthetics in actual surgery.

(b) When the study looked at other variables that are confounded with a doctor's choice of anesthetic, it found that Anesthetic C was not causing extra deaths. Suggest important lurking variables that are confounded with what anesthetic a patient receives.

Jeremy Hoare/Alamy

8.30   Movie viewing.   An opinion poll calls 2000 randomly chosen residential telephone numbers, then asks to speak with an adult member of the household. The interviewer asks, "How many movies have you watched in a movie theater in the past 12 months?"

(a) What population do you think the poll has in mind?

(b) In all, 1131 people respond. What is the rate (percent) of nonresponse?

(c) What source of response error is likely for the question asked?

8.31   The United States in world affairs.   A Gallup Poll asked, "Do you think the U.S. should take the leading role in world affairs, take a major role but not the leading role, take a minor role, or take no role at all in world affairs?" Gallup's report said, "Results are based on telephone interviews with 1,002 national adults, aged 18 and older, conducted Feb. 9–12, 2004."[14]

(a) What is the population for this sample survey? What was the sample?

(b) Gallup notes that the order of the four possible responses was rotated when the question was read over the phone. Why was this done?

8.32   Same-sex marriage.   Example 8.5 reports an online poll in which 60% of the respondents favored making same-sex marriage legal. National random samples taken at the same time showed 55% to 60% of the respondents opposed to legalizing same-sex marriage. (The results varied a bit depending on the exact question asked.) Explain briefly to someone who knows no statistics why the random samples report public opinion more reliably than the online poll.

8.33 **Ann Landers takes a sample.** Advice columnist Ann Landers once asked her female readers whether they would be content with affectionate treatment by men, with no sex ever. Over 90,000 women wrote in, with 72% answering "Yes." Many of the letters described unfeeling treatment at the hands of men. Explain why this sample is certainly biased. What is the likely direction of the bias? That is, is 72% probably higher or lower than the truth about the population of all adult women?

8.34 **Seat belt use.** A study in El Paso, Texas, looked at seat belt use by drivers. Drivers were observed at randomly chosen convenience stores. After they left their cars, they were invited to answer questions that included questions about seat belt use. In all, 75% said they always used seat belts, yet only 61.5% were wearing seat belts when they pulled into the store parking lots.[15] Explain the reason for the bias observed in responses to the survey. Do you expect bias in the same direction in most surveys about seat belt use?

8.35 **Do you trust the Internet?** You want to ask a sample of college students the question "How much do you trust information about health that you find on the Internet—a great deal, somewhat, not much, or not at all?" You try out this and other questions on a pilot group of 10 students chosen from your class. The class members are

Anderson	Deng	Glaus	Nguyen	Samuels
Arroyo	De Ramos	Helling	Palmiero	Shen
Batista	Drasin	Husain	Percival	Tse
Bell	Eckstein	Johnson	Prince	Velasco
Burke	Fernandez	Kim	Puri	Wallace
Cabrera	Fullmer	Molina	Richards	Washburn
Calloway	Gandhi	Morgan	Rider	Zabidi
Delluci	Garcia	Murphy	Rodriguez	Zhao

Choose an SRS of 10 students. If you use Table B, start at line 117.

8.36 **Telephone area codes.** There are approximately 371 active telephone area codes covering Canada, the United States, and some Caribbean areas. (More are created regularly.) You want to choose an SRS of 25 of these area codes for a study of available telephone numbers. Label the codes 001 to 371 and use the *Simple Random Sample* applet or other software to choose your sample. (If you use Table B, start at line 129 and choose only the first 5 codes in the sample.)

8.37 **Nonresponse.** Academic sample surveys, unlike commercial polls, often discuss nonresponse. A survey of drivers began by randomly sampling all listed residential telephone numbers in the United States. Of 45,956 calls to these numbers, 5029 were completed.[16] What was the rate of nonresponse for this sample? (Only one call was made to each number. Nonresponse would be lower if more calls were made.)

8.38 **Running red lights.** The sample described in the previous exercise produced a list of 5024 licensed drivers. The investigators then chose an SRS of 880 of these drivers to answer questions about their driving habits.

Altrendo Images/Getty Images

(a) How would you assign labels to the 5024 drivers? Use Table B, starting at line 104, to choose the first 5 drivers in the sample.

(b) One question asked was "Recalling the last ten traffic lights you drove through, how many of them were red when you entered the intersections?" Of the 880 respondents, 171 admitted that at least one light had been red. A practical problem with this survey is that people may not give truthful answers. What is the likely direction of the bias: do you think more or fewer than 171 of the 880 respondents really ran a red light? Why?

8.39 **Sampling at a party.** At a party there are 30 students over age 21 and 20 students under age 21. You choose at random 3 of those over 21 and separately choose at random 2 of those under 21 to interview about attitudes toward alcohol. You have given every student at the party the same chance to be interviewed: what is that chance? Why is your sample not an SRS?

8.40 **Random digits.** In using Table B repeatedly to choose random samples, you should not always begin at the same place, such as line 101. Why not?

8.41 **Random digits.** Which of the following statements are true of a table of random digits, and which are false? Briefly explain your answers.

(a) There are exactly four 0s in each row of 40 digits.

(b) Each pair of digits has chance 1/100 of being 00.

(c) The digits 0000 can never appear as a group, because this pattern is not random.

8.42 **Sampling at a party.** At a large block party there are 290 men and 110 women. You want to ask opinions about how to improve the next party. To be sure that women's opinions are adequately represented, you decide to choose a stratified random sample of 20 men and 20 women. Explain how you will assign labels to the names of the people at the party. Give the labels of the first 3 men and the first 3 women in your sample. If you use Table B, start at line 130.

8.43 **Sampling Amazon forests.** Stratified samples are widely used to study large areas of forest. Based on satellite images, a forest area in the Amazon basin is divided into 14 types. Foresters studied the four most commercially valuable types: alluvial climax forests of quality levels 1, 2, and 3, and mature secondary forest. They divided the area of each type into large parcels, chose parcels of each type at random, and counted tree species in a 20- by 25-meter rectangle randomly placed within each parcel selected. Here is some detail:

Wolfgang Kaehler/CORBIS

Forest type	Total parcels	Sample size
Climax 1	36	4
Climax 2	72	7
Climax 3	31	3
Secondary	42	4

Choose the stratified sample of 18 parcels. Be sure to explain how you assigned labels to parcels. If you use Table B, start at line 102.

systematic random sample

8.44 **Systematic random samples.** *Systematic random samples* are often used to choose a sample of apartments in a large building or dwelling units in a block at the last stage of a multistage sample. An example will illustrate the idea of a systematic sample. Suppose that we must choose 4 addresses out of 100. Because 100/4 = 25, we can think of the list as four lists of 25 addresses. Choose 1 of the first 25 at random, using Table B. The sample contains this address and the addresses 25, 50, and 75 places down the list from it. If 13 is chosen, for example, then the systematic random sample consists of the addresses numbered 13, 38, 63, and 88.

(a) Use Table B to choose a systematic random sample of 5 addresses from a list of 200. Enter the table at line 120.

(b) Like an SRS, a systematic sample gives all individuals the same chance to be chosen. Explain why this is true, then explain carefully why a systematic sample is nonetheless *not* an SRS.

8.45   **Random digit dialing.**   The list of individuals from which a sample is actually selected is called the *sampling frame*. Ideally, the frame should list every individual in the population, but in practice this is often difficult. A frame that leaves out part of the population is a common source of undercoverage.

(a) Suppose that a sample of households in a community is selected at random from the telephone directory. What households are omitted from this frame? What types of people do you think are likely to live in these households? These people will probably be underrepresented in the sample.

(b) It is usual in telephone surveys to use random digit dialing equipment that selects the last four digits of a telephone number at random after being given the exchange (the first three digits). Which of the households you mentioned in your answer to (a) will be included in the sampling frame by random digit dialing?

8.46   **Wording survey questions.**   Comment on each of the following as a potential sample survey question. Is the question clear? Is it slanted toward a desired response?

(a) "Some cell phone users have developed brain cancer. Should all cell phones come with a warning label explaining the danger of using cell phones?"

(b) "Do you agree that a national system of health insurance should be favored because it would provide health insurance for everyone and would reduce administrative costs?"

(c) "In view of the negative externalities in parent labor force participation and pediatric evidence associating increased group size with morbidity of children in day care, do you support government subsidies for day care programs?"

8.47   **Regulating guns.**   The National Gun Policy Survey asked respondents' opinions about government regulation of firearms. A report from the survey says, "Participating households were identified through random digit dialing; the respondent in each household was selected by the most-recent-birthday method."[17]

(a) What is "random digit dialing?" Why is it a practical method for obtaining (almost) an SRS of households?

(b) The survey wants the opinion of an individual adult. Several adults may live in a household. In that case, the survey interviewed the adult with the most recent birthday. Why is this preferable to simply interviewing the person who answers the phone?

8.48   **Your own bad questions.**   Write your own examples of bad sample survey questions.

(a) Write a biased question designed to get one answer rather than another.

(b) Write a question that is confusing, so that it is hard to answer.

8.49   **Canada's national health care.**   The Ministry of Health in the Canadian province of Ontario wants to know whether the national health care system is achieving its goals in the province. Much information about health care comes from patient records, but that source doesn't allow us to compare people who use health services with those who don't. So the Ministry of Health conducted the Ontario Health Survey, which interviewed a random sample of 61,239 people who live in Ontario.[18]

(a) What is the population for this sample survey? What is the sample?

(b) The survey found that 76% of males and 86% of females in the sample had visited a general practitioner at least once in the past year. Do you think these estimates are close to the truth about the entire population? Why?

8.50   **Polling Hispanics.**   A New York Times News Service article on a poll concerned with the opinions of Hispanics includes this paragraph:

> The poll was conducted by telephone from July 13 to 27, with 3,092 adults nationwide, 1,074 of whom described themselves as Hispanic. It has a margin of sampling error of plus or minus three percentage points for the entire poll and plus or minus four percentage points for Hispanics. Sample sizes for most Hispanic nationalities, like Cubans or Dominicans, were too small to break out the results separately.[19]

(a) Why is the "margin of sampling error" larger for Hispanics than for all 3092 respondents?

(b) Why would a very small sample size prevent a responsible news organization from breaking out results for Cubans separately?

Royalty-Free/CORBIS

Producing Data: Experiments

A study is an experiment when we actually do something to people, animals, or objects in order to observe the response. Because the purpose of an experiment is to reveal the response of one variable to changes in other variables, the distinction between explanatory and response variables is essential.

Experiments

Here is the basic vocabulary of experiments.

SUBJECTS, FACTORS, TREATMENTS

The **individuals** studied in an experiment are often called **subjects,** particularly when they are people.

The explanatory variables in an experiment are often called **factors.**

A **treatment** is any specific experimental condition applied to the subjects. If an experiment has several factors, a treatment is a combination of specific values of each factor.

Royalty-Free/CORBIS

EXAMPLE 9.1   Effects of good day care

Does day care help low-income children stay in school and hold good jobs later in life? The Carolina Abecedarian Project (the name suggests the ABCs) has followed a group of children since 1972. The *subjects* are 111 people who in 1972 were healthy but low-income black infants in Chapel Hill, North Carolina. All the infants received nutritional supplements and help from social workers. Half, chosen at random, were also placed in an intensive preschool program. The experiment compares these two *treatments*. There is a single *factor*, "preschool, yes or no." There are many *response variables*, recorded over more than 20 years, including academic test scores, college attendance, and employment.[1]

EXAMPLE 9.2   Effects of TV advertising

What are the effects of repeated exposure to an advertising message? The answer may depend both on the length of the ad and on how often it is repeated. An experiment investigated this question using undergraduate students as *subjects*. All subjects viewed a 40-minute television program that included ads for a digital camera. Some subjects saw a 30-second commercial; others, a 90-second version. The same commercial was shown either 1, 3, or 5 times during the program.

This experiment has two *factors:* length of the commercial, with 2 values, and repetitions, with 3 values. The 6 combinations of one value of each factor form 6 *treatments*. Figure 9.1 shows the layout of the treatments. After viewing, all of the subjects answered questions about their recall of the ad, their attitude toward the camera, and their intention to purchase it. These are the *response variables*.[2]

Examples 9.1 and 9.2 illustrate the advantages of experiments over observational studies. In an experiment, we can study the effects of the specific treatments we are interested in. By assigning subjects to treatments, we can avoid confounding. If, for example, we simply compare children whose parents did and did not choose an intensive preschool program, we may find that children in the program come from richer and better-educated parents. Example 9.1 avoids that. Moreover,

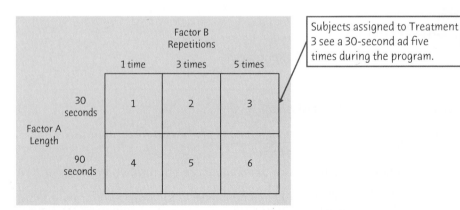

FIGURE 9.1 The treatments in the experimental design of Example 9.2. Combinations of values of the two factors form six treatments.

we can control the environment of the subjects to hold constant factors that are of no interest to us, such as the specific product advertised in Example 9.2.

Another advantage of experiments is that we can study the combined effects of several factors simultaneously. The interaction of several factors can produce effects that could not be predicted from looking at the effect of each factor alone. Perhaps longer commercials increase interest in a product, and more commercials also increase interest, but if we both make a commercial longer and show it more often, viewers get annoyed and their interest in the product drops. The two-factor experiment in Example 9.2 will help us find out.

APPLY YOUR KNOWLEDGE

9.1   **Internet telephone calls.**   You can use your computer to make long-distance telephone calls over the Internet. How will the cost affect the use of this service? A university plans an experiment to find out. It will offer voice over Internet service to all 350 students in one of its dormitories. Some students will pay a low flat rate. Others will pay higher rates at peak periods and very low rates off-peak. The university is interested in how the payment plan affects the amount and time of use. What are the subjects, the factors, the treatments, and the response variables in this experiment?

9.2   **Growing in the shade.**   Ability to grow in shade may help pines found in the dry forests of Arizona resist drought. How well do these pines grow in shade? Investigators planted pine seedlings in a greenhouse in either full light, light reduced to 25% of normal by shade cloth, or light reduced to 5% of normal. At the end of the study, they dried the young trees and weighed them. What are the individuals, the treatments, and the response variable in this experiment?

9.3   **Improving adolescents' habits.**   Most American adolescents don't eat well and don't exercise enough. Can middle schools increase physical activity among their students? Can they persuade students to eat better? Investigators designed a "physical activity intervention" to increase activity in physical education classes and during leisure periods throughout the school day. They also designed a "nutrition intervention" that improved school lunches and offered ideas for healthy home-packed lunches. Each participating school was randomly assigned to one of the interventions, both interventions, or no intervention. The investigators observed physical activity and lunchtime consumption of fat. Identify the individuals, the factors, and the response variables in this experiment. Use a diagram like that in Figure 9.1 to display the treatments.

How to experiment badly

Experiments are the preferred method for examining the effect of one variable on another. By imposing the specific treatment of interest and controlling other influences, we can pin down cause and effect. Statistical designs are often essential for effective experiments, just as they are for sampling. To see why, let's start with an example of a bad design.

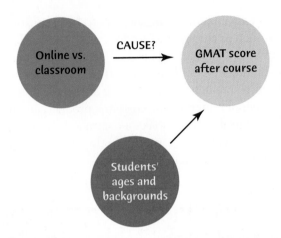

FIGURE 9.2 Confounding. We can't distinguish the effect of the treatment from the effects of lurking variables.

EXAMPLE 9.3   An uncontrolled experiment ⎯⎯⎯⎯⎯⎯⎯

A college regularly offers a review course to prepare candidates for the Graduate Management Admission Test (GMAT), which is required by most graduate business schools. This year, it offers only an online version of the course. The average GMAT score of students in the online course is 10% higher than the longtime average for those who took the classroom review course. Is the online course more effective?

This experiment has a very simple design. A group of subjects (the students) were exposed to a treatment (the online course), and the outcome (GMAT scores) was observed. Here is the design:

$$\text{Subjects} \longrightarrow \text{Online course} \longrightarrow \text{GMAT scores}$$

A closer look at the GMAT review course showed that the students in the online review course were quite different from the students who in past years took the classroom course. In particular, they were older and more likely to be employed. An online course appeals to these mature people, but we can't compare their performance with that of the undergraduates who previously dominated the course. The online course might even be less effective than the classroom version. The effect of online versus in-class instruction is confounded with the effect of lurking variables. Figure 9.2 shows the confounding in picture form. As a result of confounding, the experiment is biased in favor of the online course.

Most laboratory experiments use a design like that in Example 9.3:

$$\text{Subjects} \longrightarrow \text{Treatment} \longrightarrow \text{Measure response}$$

In the controlled environment of the laboratory, simple designs often work well. *Field experiments and experiments with human subjects are exposed to more variable conditions and deal with more variable subjects. A simple design often yields worthless results because of confounding with lurking variables.*

APPLY YOUR KNOWLEDGE ⎯⎯⎯⎯⎯⎯⎯⎯⎯⎯⎯⎯⎯⎯⎯

9.4   **Reducing unemployment.**   Will cash bonuses speed the return to work of unemployed people? A state department of employment security notes that last year 68% of people who filed claims for unemployment insurance found a new job within 15 weeks. As an experiment, the state offers $500 to people filing unemployment claims if they find a job within 15 weeks. The percent who do so increases to 77%. Explain why confounding with lurking variables makes it impossible to say whether the treatment really caused the increase.

Randomized comparative experiments

The remedy for the confounding in Example 9.3 is to do a *comparative experiment* in which some students are taught in the classroom and other, similar students take the course online. The first group is called a **control group.** Most well-designed experiments compare two or more treatments. Part of the design of an experiment is a description of the factors (explanatory variables) and the layout of the treatments, with comparison as the leading principle.

control group

Comparison alone isn't enough to produce results we can trust. If the treatments are given to groups that differ markedly when the experiment begins, bias will result. For example, if we allow students to elect online or classroom instruction, students who are older and employed are likely to sign up for the online course. Personal choice will bias our results in the same way that volunteers bias the results of online opinion polls. The solution to the problem of bias is the same for experiments and for samples: use impersonal chance to select the groups.

> **RANDOMIZED COMPARATIVE EXPERIMENT**
>
> An experiment that uses both comparison of two or more treatments and chance assignment of subjects to treatments is a **randomized comparative experiment.**

Golfing at random

Random drawings give everyone the same chance to be chosen, so they offer a fair way to decide who gets a scarce good—like a round of golf. Lots of golfers want to play the famous Old Course at St. Andrews, Scotland. Some can reserve in advance, at considerable expense. Most must hope that chance favors them in the daily random drawing for tee times. At the height of the summer season, only 1 in 6 wins the right to pay $200 for a round.

EXAMPLE 9.4   *On-campus versus online*

The college decides to compare the progress of 25 on-campus students taught in the classroom with that of 25 students taught the same material online. Select the students who will be taught online by taking a simple random sample of size 25 from the 50 available subjects. The remaining 25 students form the control group. They will receive classroom instruction. The result is a randomized comparative experiment with two groups. Figure 9.3 outlines the design in graphical form.

The selection procedure is exactly the same as it is for sampling: label and table. **Step 1. Label** the 50 students 01 to 50. **Step 2. Table.** Go to the table of random digits and read successive two-digit groups. The first 25 labels encountered select the online group. As usual, ignore repeated labels and groups of digits not used as labels. For example, if you begin at line 125 in Table B, the first five students chosen are those labeled 21, 49, 37, 18, and 44. Software such as the *Simple Random Sample* applet makes it particularly easy to choose treatment groups at random.

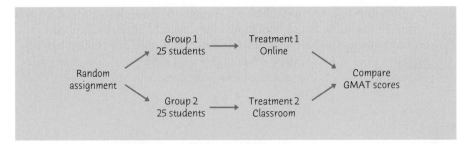

FIGURE 9.3 Outline of a randomized comparative experiment to compare online and classroom instruction, for Example 9.4.

The design in Figure 9.3 is *comparative* because it compares two treatments (the two instructional settings). It is *randomized* because the subjects are assigned to the treatments by chance. This "flowchart" outline presents all the essentials: randomization, the sizes of the groups and which treatment they receive, and the response variable. There are, as we will see later, statistical reasons for generally using treatment groups about equal in size. We call designs like that in Figure 9.3 *completely randomized.*

COMPLETELY RANDOMIZED DESIGN

In a **completely randomized** experimental design, all the subjects are allocated at random among all the treatments.

Completely randomized designs can compare any number of treatments. Here is an example that compares three treatments.

EXAMPLE 9.5   *Conserving energy*

Many utility companies have introduced programs to encourage energy conservation among their customers. An electric company considers placing electronic meters in households to show what the cost would be if the electricity use at that moment continued for a month. Will meters reduce electricity use? Would cheaper methods work almost as well? The company decides to conduct an experiment.

One cheaper approach is to give customers a chart and information about monitoring their electricity use. The experiment compares these two approaches (meter, chart) and also a control. The control group of customers receives information about energy conservation but no help in monitoring electricity use. The response variable is total electricity used in a year. The company finds 60 single-family residences in the same city willing to participate, so it assigns 20 residences at random to each of the three treatments. Figure 9.4 outlines the design.

To carry out the random assignment, label the 60 households 01 to 60. Enter Table B (or use software) to select an SRS of 20 to receive the meters. Continue in Table B, selecting 20 more to receive charts. The remaining 20 form the control group.

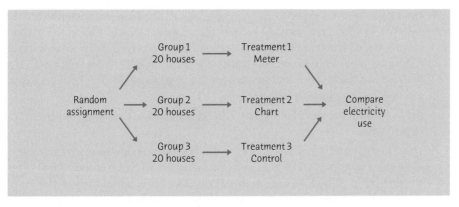

FIGURE 9.4 Outline of a completely randomized design comparing three energy-saving programs, for Example 9.5.

Examples 9.4 and 9.5 describe completely randomized designs that compare values of a single factor. In Example 9.4, the factor is the type of instruction. In Example 9.5, it is the method used to encourage energy conservation. Completely randomized designs can have more than one factor. The advertising experiment of Example 9.2 has two factors: the length and the number of repetitions of a television commercial. Their combinations form the six treatments outlined in Figure 9.1. A completely randomized design assigns subjects at random to these six treatments. Once the layout of treatments is set, the randomization needed for a completely randomized design is tedious but straightforward.

APPLY YOUR KNOWLEDGE

9.5   **Does ginkgo improve memory?** The law allows marketers of herbs and other natural substances to make health claims that are not supported by evidence. Brands of ginkgo extract claim to "improve memory and concentration." A randomized comparative experiment found no evidence for such effects.[3] The subjects were 230 healthy people over 60 years old. They were randomly assigned to ginkgo or a placebo pill (a dummy pill that looks and tastes the same). All the subjects took a battery of tests for learning and memory before treatment started and again after six weeks.

Blickwinkel/Alamy

(a) Following the model of Figure 9.3, outline the design of this experiment.

(b) Use the *Simple Random Sample* applet, other software, or Table B to assign half the subjects to the ginkgo group. If you use software, report the first 20 members of the ginkgo group (in the applet's "Sample bin") and the first 20 members of the placebo group (those left in the "Population hopper"). If you use Table B, start at line 103 and choose only the first 5 members of the ginkgo group.

APPLET

9.6   **Can tea prevent cataracts?** Eye cataracts are responsible for over 40% of blindness around the world. Can drinking tea regularly slow the growth of cataracts? We can't experiment on people, so we use rats as subjects. Researchers injected 18 young rats with a substance that causes cataracts. One group of the rats also received black tea extract; a second group received green tea extract; and a third got a placebo, a substance with no effect on the body. The response variable was the growth of cataracts over the next six weeks. Yes, both tea extracts did slow cataract growth.[4]

(a) Following the model of Figures 9.3 and 9.4, outline the design of this experiment.

(b) The *Simple Random Sample* applet allows you to randomly assign subjects to more than two groups. Use the applet to choose an SRS of 6 of the 18 rats to form the first group. Which rats are in this group? The "Population hopper" now contains the 12 remaining rats, in scrambled order. Click "Sample" again to choose an SRS of 6 of these to make up the second group. Which rats were chosen? The 6 rats remaining in the "Population hopper" form the third group.

9.7 **Growing in the shade.** You have 45 pine seedlings available for the experiment described in Exercise 9.2. Outline the design of this experiment. Use software or Table B to randomly assign seedlings to the three treatment groups.

The logic of randomized comparative experiments

Randomized comparative experiments are designed to give good evidence that differences in the treatments actually *cause* the differences we see in the response. The logic is as follows:

- Random assignment of subjects forms groups that should be similar in all respects before the treatments are applied. Exercise 9.48 uses the *Simple Random Sample* applet to demonstrate this.

- Comparative design ensures that influences other than the experimental treatments operate equally on all groups.

- Therefore, differences in average response must be due either to the treatments or to the play of chance in the random assignment of subjects to the treatments.

That "either-or" deserves more thought. In Example 9.4, we cannot say that *any* difference between the average GMAT scores of students enrolled online and in the classroom must be caused by a difference in the effectiveness of the two types of instruction. There would be some difference even if both groups received the same instruction, because of variation among students in background and study habits. Chance assigns students to one group or the other, and this creates a chance difference between the groups. We would not trust an experiment with just one student in each group, for example. The results would depend too much on which group got lucky and received the stronger student. If we assign many subjects to each group, however, the effects of chance will average out and there will be little difference in the average responses in the two groups unless the treatments themselves cause a difference. "Use enough subjects to reduce chance variation" is the third big idea of statistical design of experiments.

PRINCIPLES OF EXPERIMENTAL DESIGN

The basic principles of statistical design of experiments are

1. Control the effects of lurking variables on the response, most simply by comparing two or more treatments.

2. Randomize—use impersonal chance to assign subjects to treatments.

3. Use enough subjects in each group to reduce chance variation in the results.

We hope to see a difference in the responses so large that it is unlikely to happen just because of chance variation. We can use the laws of probability, which give a mathematical description of chance behavior, to learn if the treatment effects are larger than we would expect to see if only chance were operating. If they are, we call them *statistically significant*.

STATISTICAL SIGNIFICANCE

An observed effect so large that it would rarely occur by chance is called **statistically significant.**

If we observe statistically significant differences among the groups in a randomized comparative experiment, we have good evidence that the treatments actually caused these differences. You will often see the phrase "statistically significant" in reports of investigations in many fields of study. The great advantage of randomized comparative experiments is that they can produce data that give good evidence for a cause-and-effect relationship between the explanatory and response variables. We know that in general a strong association does not imply causation. A statistically significant association in data from a well-designed experiment *does* imply causation.

What's news?
Randomized comparative experiments provide the best evidence for medical advances. Do newspapers care? Maybe not. University researchers looked at 1192 articles in medical journals, of which 7% were turned into stories by the two newspapers examined. Of the journal articles, 37% concerned observational studies and 25% described randomized experiments. Among the articles publicized by the newspapers, 58% were observational studies and only 6% were randomized experiments. Conclusion: the newspapers want exciting stories, especially bad news stories, whether or not the evidence is good.

APPLY YOUR KNOWLEDGE

9.8 **Conserving energy.** Example 9.5 describes an experiment to learn whether providing households with electronic meters or charts will reduce their electricity consumption. An executive of the electric company objects to including a control group. He says: "It would be simpler to just compare electricity use last year (before the meter or chart was provided) with consumption in the same

Scratch my furry ears

Rats and rabbits, specially bred to be uniform in their inherited characteristics, are the subjects in many experiments. Animals, like people, are quite sensitive to how they are treated. This can create opportunities for hidden bias. For example, human affection can change the cholesterol level of rabbits. Choose some rabbits at random and regularly remove them from their cages to have their heads scratched by friendly people. Leave other rabbits unloved. All the rabbits eat the same diet, but the rabbits that receive affection have lower cholesterol.

placebo

period this year. If households use less electricity this year, the meter or chart must be working." Explain clearly why this design is inferior to that in Example 9.5.

9.9 **Exercise and heart attacks.** Does regular exercise reduce the risk of a heart attack? Here are two ways to study this question. Explain clearly why the second design will produce more trustworthy data.

1. A researcher finds 2000 men over 40 who exercise regularly and have not had heart attacks. She matches each with a similar man who does not exercise regularly, and she follows both groups for 5 years.

2. Another researcher finds 4000 men over 40 who have not had heart attacks and are willing to participate in a study. She assigns 2000 of the men to a regular program of supervised exercise. The other 2000 continue their usual habits. The researcher follows both groups for 5 years.

9.10 **The Monday effect.** Puzzling but true: stocks tend to go down on Mondays. There is no convincing explanation for this fact. A study looked at this "Monday effect" in more detail, using data on the daily returns of stocks over a 30-year period. Here are some of the findings:

> To summarize, our results indicate that the well-known Monday effect is caused largely by the Mondays of the last two weeks of the month. The mean Monday return of the first three weeks of the month is, in general, not significantly different from zero and is generally significantly higher than the mean Monday return of the last two weeks. Our finding seems to make it more difficult to explain the Monday effect.[5]

A friend thinks that "significantly" in this article has its plain English meaning, roughly "I think this is important." Explain in simple language what "significantly higher" and "not significantly different from zero" tell us here.

Cautions about experimentation

The logic of a randomized comparative experiment depends on our ability to treat all the subjects identically in every way except for the actual treatments being compared. Good experiments therefore require careful attention to details.

The experiment on the effects of ginkgo on memory (Exercise 9.5) is a typical medical experiment. All of the subjects took the same tests and received the same medical attention. All of them took a pill every day, ginkgo in the treatment group and a placebo in the control group. A **placebo** is a dummy treatment. Many patients respond favorably to any treatment, even a placebo, perhaps because they trust the doctor. The response to a dummy treatment is called the *placebo effect.* If the control group did not take any pills, the effect of ginkgo in the treatment group would be confounded with the placebo effect, the effect of simply taking pills.

In addition, the study was *double-blind.* The subjects didn't know whether they were taking ginkgo or a placebo. Neither did the investigators who worked with them. The double-blind method avoids unconscious bias by, for example, a doctor who is convinced that a new medical treatment must be better than a placebo.

In many medical studies, only the statistician who does the randomization knows which treatment each patient is receiving.

DOUBLE-BLIND EXPERIMENTS

In a **double-blind** experiment, neither the subjects nor the people who interact with them know which treatment each subject is receiving.

The most serious potential weakness of experiments is **lack of realism:** *the subjects or treatments or setting of an experiment may not realistically duplicate the conditions we really want to study.* Here are two examples.

EXAMPLE 9.6   Response to advertising

The study of television advertising in Example 9.2 showed a 40-minute videotape to students who knew an experiment was going on. We can't be sure that the results apply to everyday television viewers. Many behavioral science experiments use as subjects students or other volunteers who know they are subjects in an experiment. That's not a realistic setting.

EXAMPLE 9.7   Center brake lights

Do those high center brake lights, required on all cars sold in the United States since 1986, really reduce rear-end collisions? Randomized comparative experiments with fleets of rental and business cars, done before the lights were required, showed that the third brake light reduced rear-end collisions by as much as 50%. Alas, requiring the third light in all cars led to only a 5% drop.

What happened? Most cars did not have the extra brake light when the experiments were carried out, so it caught the eye of following drivers. Now that almost all cars have the third light, they no longer capture attention.

Lightworks Media/Alamy

Lack of realism can limit our ability to apply the conclusions of an experiment to the settings of greatest interest. Most experimenters want to generalize their conclusions to some setting wider than that of the actual experiment. *Statistical analysis of an experiment cannot tell us how far the results will generalize.* Nonetheless, the randomized comparative experiment, because of its ability to give convincing evidence for causation, is one of the most important ideas in statistics.

APPLY YOUR KNOWLEDGE

9.11 **Dealing with pain.** Health care providers are giving more attention to relieving the pain of cancer patients. An article in the journal *Cancer* surveyed a number of studies and concluded that controlled-release morphine tablets, which release the painkiller gradually over time, are more effective than giving standard morphine when the patient needs it.[6] The "methods" section of the article begins: "Only those published studies that were controlled (i.e., randomized, double blind, and comparative), repeated-dose studies with CR morphine tablets in cancer pain

Digital Vision/Getty Images

patients were considered for this review." Explain the terms in parentheses to someone who knows nothing about medical experiments.

9.12   **Does meditation reduce anxiety?** An experiment that claimed to show that meditation reduces anxiety proceeded as follows. The experimenter interviewed the subjects and rated their level of anxiety. Then the subjects were randomly assigned to two groups. The experimenter taught one group how to meditate and they meditated daily for a month. The other group was simply told to relax more. At the end of the month, the experimenter interviewed all the subjects again and rated their anxiety level. The meditation group now had less anxiety. Psychologists said that the results were suspect because the ratings were not blind. Explain what this means and how lack of blindness could bias the reported results.

Matched pairs and other block designs

Completely randomized designs are the simplest statistical designs for experiments. They illustrate clearly the principles of control, randomization, and adequate number of subjects. However, completely randomized designs are often inferior to more elaborate statistical designs. In particular, matching the subjects in various ways can produce more precise results than simple randomization.

matched pairs design

One common design that combines matching with randomization is the **matched pairs design.** A matched pairs design compares just two treatments. Choose pairs of subjects that are as closely matched as possible. Use chance to decide which subject in a pair gets the first treatment. The other subject in that pair gets the other treatment. That is, the random assignment of subjects to treatments is done within each matched pair, not for all subjects at once. Sometimes each "pair" in a matched pairs design consists of just one subject, who gets both treatments one after the other. Each subject serves as his or her own control. The *order* of the treatments can influence the subject's response, so we randomize the order for each subject.

Royalty-Free/CORBIS

> **EXAMPLE 9.8**   *Cell phones and driving*
>
> Does talking on a hands-free cell phone distract drivers? Undergraduate students "drove" in a high-fidelity driving simulator equipped with a hands-free cell phone. The car ahead brakes: how quickly does the subject react? Let's compare two designs for this experiment. There are 40 student subjects available.
>
> In a *completely randomized design,* all 40 subjects are assigned at random, 20 to simply drive and the other 20 to talk on the cell phone while driving. In the *matched pairs design* that was actually used, all subjects drive both with and without using the cell phone. The two drives are on separate days to reduce carryover effects. The *order* of the two treatments is assigned at random: 20 subjects are chosen to drive first with the phone, and the remaining 20 drive first without the phone.[7]
>
> Some subjects naturally react faster than others. The completely randomized design relies on chance to distribute the faster subjects roughly evenly between the two groups. The matched pairs design compares each subject's reaction time with and without the cell phone. This makes it easier to see the effects of using the phone.

Matched pairs designs use the principles of comparison of treatments and randomization. However, the randomization is not complete—we do not randomly assign all the subjects at once to the two treatments. Instead, we randomize only within each matched pair. This allows matching to reduce the effect of variation among the subjects. Matched pairs are one kind of *block design*, with each pair forming a *block*.

BLOCK DESIGN

A **block** is a group of individuals that are known before the experiment to be similar in some way that is expected to affect the response to the treatments.

In a **block design,** the random assignment of individuals to treatments is carried out separately within each block.

A block design combines the idea of creating equivalent treatment groups by matching with the principle of forming treatment groups at random. Blocks are another form of *control*. They control the effects of some outside variables by bringing those variables into the experiment to form the blocks. Here are some typical examples of block designs.

EXAMPLE 9.9   Men, women, and advertising

Women and men respond differently to advertising. An experiment to compare the effectiveness of three advertisements for the same product will want to look separately at the reactions of men and women, as well as assess the overall response to the ads.

A completely randomized design considers all subjects, both men and women, as a single pool. The randomization assigns subjects to three treatment groups without regard to their sex. This ignores the differences between men and women. A better design considers women and men separately. Randomly assign the women to three groups, one to view each advertisement. Then separately assign the men at random to three groups. Figure 9.5 outlines this improved design.

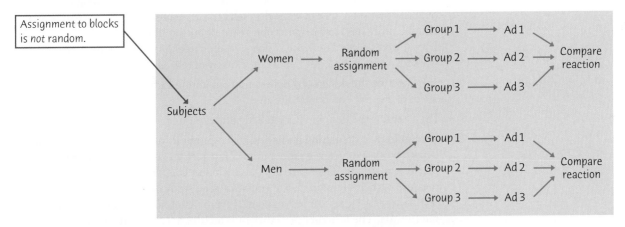

FIGURE 9.5 Outline of a block design, for Example 9.9. The blocks consist of male and female subjects. The treatments are three advertisements for the same product.

┌─ **EXAMPLE 9.10**   Comparing welfare policies ──────────

A social policy experiment will assess the effect on family income of several proposed new welfare systems and compare them with the present welfare system. Because the future income of a family is strongly related to its present income, the families who agree to participate are divided into blocks of similar income levels. The families in each block are then allocated at random among the welfare systems.

A block design allows us to draw separate conclusions about each block, for example, about men and women in Example 9.9. Blocking also allows more precise overall conclusions, because the systematic differences between men and women can be removed when we study the overall effects of the three advertisements. The idea of blocking is an important additional principle of statistical design of experiments. A wise experimenter will form blocks based on the most important unavoidable sources of variability among the subjects. Randomization will then average out the effects of the remaining variation and allow an unbiased comparison of the treatments.

Like the design of samples, the design of complex experiments is a job for experts. Now that we have seen a bit of what is involved, we will concentrate for the most part on completely randomized experiments.

APPLY YOUR KNOWLEDGE ───────────────────────

9.13   **Comparing hand strength.**   Is the right hand generally stronger than the left in right-handed people? You can crudely measure hand strength by placing a bathroom scale on a shelf with the end protruding, then squeezing the scale between the thumb below and the four fingers above it. The reading of the scale shows the force exerted. Describe the design of a matched pairs experiment to compare the strength of the right and left hands, using 10 right-handed people as subjects. (You need not actually do the randomization.)

9.14   **How long did I work?**   A psychologist wants to know if the difficulty of a task influences our estimate of how long we spend working at it. She designs two sets of mazes that subjects can work through on a computer. One set has easy mazes and the other has hard mazes. Subjects work until told to stop (after 6 minutes, but subjects do not know this). They are then asked to estimate how long they worked. The psychologist has 30 students available to serve as subjects.

(a) Describe the design of a completely randomized experiment to learn the effect of difficulty on estimated time.

(b) Describe the design of a matched pairs experiment using the same 30 subjects.

9.15   **Technology for teaching statistics.**   The Brigham Young University statistics department is performing randomized comparative experiments to compare teaching methods. Response variables include students' final-exam scores and a measure of their attitude toward statistics. One study compares two levels of technology for large lectures: standard (overhead projectors and chalk) and multimedia. The individuals in the study are the 8 lectures in a basic statistics course. There are four instructors, each of whom teaches two lectures. Because the lecturers differ, their lectures form four blocks.[8] Suppose the lectures and lecturers are as follows:

Lecture	Lecturer	Lecture	Lecturer
1	Hilton	5	Tolley
2	Christensen	6	Hilton
3	Hadfield	7	Tolley
4	Hadfield	8	Christensen

Outline a block design and do the randomization that your design requires.

CHAPTER 9 SUMMARY

In an experiment, we impose one or more **treatments** on individuals, often called **subjects.** Each treatment is a combination of values of the explanatory variables, which we call **factors.**

The **design** of an experiment describes the choice of treatments and the manner in which the subjects are assigned to the treatments.

The basic principles of statistical design of experiments are **control** and **randomization** to combat bias and **using enough subjects** to reduce chance variation.

The simplest form of control is **comparison.** Experiments should compare two or more treatments in order to avoid **confounding** of the effect of a treatment with other influences, such as lurking variables.

Randomization uses chance to assign subjects to the treatments. Randomization creates treatment groups that are similar (except for chance variation) before the treatments are applied. Randomization and comparison together prevent **bias,** or systematic favoritism, in experiments.

You can carry out randomization by using software or by giving numerical labels to the subjects and using a **table of random digits** to choose treatment groups.

Applying each treatment to many subjects reduces the role of chance variation and makes the experiment more sensitive to differences among the treatments.

Good experiments require attention to detail as well as good statistical design. Many behavioral and medical experiments are **double-blind.** Some give a **placebo** to a control group. **Lack of realism** in an experiment can prevent us from generalizing its results.

In addition to comparison, a second form of control is to restrict randomization by forming **blocks** of individuals that are similar in some way that is important to the response. Randomization is then carried out separately within each block.

Matched pairs are a common form of blocking for comparing just two treatments. In some matched pairs designs, each subject receives both treatments in a random order. In others, the subjects are matched in pairs as closely as possible, and each subject in a pair receives one of the treatments.

CHECK YOUR SKILLS

9.16 A study of cell phones and the risk of brain cancer looked at a group of 469 people who have brain cancer. The investigators matched each cancer patient with a person of the same sex, age, and race who did not have brain cancer, then asked about use of cell phones. This is

(a) an observational study.

(b) an uncontrolled experiment.

(c) a randomized comparative experiment.

9.17 What electrical changes occur in muscles as they get tired? Student subjects hold their arms above their shoulders until they have to drop them. Meanwhile, the electrical activity in their arm muscles is measured. This is

(a) an observational study.

(b) an uncontrolled experiment.

(c) a randomized comparative experiment.

9.18 Can changing diet reduce high blood pressure? Vegetarian diets and low-salt diets are both promising. Men with high blood pressure are assigned at random to four diets: (1) normal diet with unrestricted salt; (2) vegetarian with unrestricted salt; (3) normal with restricted salt; and (4) vegetarian with restricted salt. This experiment has

(a) one factor, the choice of diet.

(b) two factors, normal/vegetarian diet and unrestricted/restricted salt.

(c) four factors, the four diets being compared.

9.19 In the experiment of the previous exercise, the 240 subjects are labeled 001 to 240. Software assigns an SRS of 60 subjects to Diet 1, an SRS of 60 of the remaining 180 to Diet 2, and an SRS of 60 of the remaining 120 to Diet 3. The 60 who are left get Diet 4. This is a

(a) completely randomized design.

(b) block design, with four blocks.

(c) matched pairs design.

9.20 An important response variable in the experiment described in Exercise 9.18 must be

(a) the amount of salt in the subject's diet.

(b) which of the four diets a subject is assigned to.

(c) change in blood pressure after 8 weeks on the assigned diet.

9.21 A medical experiment compares an antidepression medicine with a placebo for relief of chronic headaches. There are 36 headache patients available to serve as subjects. To choose 18 patients to receive the medicine, you would

(a) assign labels 01 to 36 and use Table B to choose 18.

(b) assign labels 01 to 18, because only 18 need be chosen.

(c) assign the first 18 who signed up to get the medicine.

9.22 The Community Intervention Trial for Smoking Cessation asked whether a community-wide advertising campaign would reduce smoking. The researchers located 11 pairs of communities, each pair similar in location, size, economic status, and so on. One community in each pair participated in the advertising campaign and the other did not. This is

(a) an observational study.

(b) a matched pairs experiment.

(c) a completely randomized experiment.

9.23   To decide which community in each pair in the previous exercise should get the advertising campaign, it is best to

(a) toss a coin.

(b) choose the community that will help pay for the campaign.

(c) choose the community with a mayor who will participate.

9.24   A marketing class designs two videos advertising an expensive Mercedes sports car. They test the videos by asking fellow students to view both (in random order) and say which makes them more likely to buy the car. Mercedes should be reluctant to agree that the video favored in this study will sell more cars because

(a) the study used a matched pairs design instead of a completely randomized design.

(b) results from students may not generalize to the older and richer customers who might buy a Mercedes.

(c) this is an observational study, not an experiment.

CHAPTER 9 EXERCISES

In all exercises that require randomization, you may use Table B, the Simple Random Sample *applet, or other software. See Exercise 9.6 for directions on using the applet for more than two treatment groups.*

9.25   **Wine, beer, or spirits?**   Example 8.2 (page 191) describes a study that compared three groups of people: the first group drinks mostly wine, the second drinks mostly beer, and the third drinks mostly spirits. This study is comparative, but it is not an experiment. Why not?

9.26   **Treating breast cancer.**   The most common treatment for breast cancer discovered in its early stages was once removal of the breast. It is now usual to remove only the tumor and nearby lymph nodes, followed by radiation. To study whether these treatments differ in their effectiveness, a medical team examines the records of 25 large hospitals and compares the survival times after surgery of all women who have had either treatment.

(a) What are the explanatory and response variables?

(b) Explain carefully why this study is not an experiment.

(c) Explain why confounding will prevent this study from discovering which treatment is more effective. (The current treatment was in fact recommended after several large randomized comparative experiments.)

9.27   **Wine, beer, or spirits?**   You have recruited 300 adults aged 45 to 65 who are willing to follow your orders about alcohol consumption over the next five years. You want to compare the effects on heart disease of moderate drinking of just wine, just beer, or just spirits. Outline the design of a completely randomized experiment to do this. (No such experiment has been done because subjects aren't willing to have their drinking regulated for years.)

9.28   **Marijuana and work.**   How does smoking marijuana affect willingness to work? Canadian researchers persuaded young adult men who used marijuana to live for 98 days in a "planned environment." The men earned money by weaving belts. They used their earnings to pay for meals and other consumption and could keep any money left over. One group smoked two potent marijuana cigarettes every evening. The other group smoked two weak marijuana cigarettes. All subjects could buy more cigarettes but were given strong or weak cigarettes depending on their group. Did the weak and strong groups differ in work output and earnings?[9]

(a) Outline the design of this experiment.

(b) Here are the names of the 20 subjects. Use software or Table B at line 131 to carry out the randomization your design requires.

Abate	Dubois	Gutierrez	Lucero	Rosen
Afifi	Engel	Huang	McNeill	Thompson
Brown	Fluharty	Iselin	Morse	Travers
Cheng	Gerson	Kaplan	Quinones	Ullmann

9.29   **The benefits of red wine.**   Does red wine protect moderate drinkers from heart disease better than other alcoholic beverages? Red wine contains substances called polyphenols that may change blood chemistry in a desirable way. This calls for a randomized comparative experiment. The subjects were healthy men aged 35 to 65. They were randomly assigned to drink red wine (9 subjects), drink white wine (9 subjects), drink white wine and also take polyphenols from red wine (6 subjects), take polyphenols alone (9 subjects), or drink vodka and lemonade (6 subjects).[10] Outline the design of the experiment and randomly assign the 39 subjects to the 5 groups. If you use Table B, start at line 107.

9.30   **Response to TV ads.**   You decide to use a completely randomized design in the two-factor experiment on response to advertising described in Example 9.2 (page 214). The 36 students named below will serve as subjects. (Ignore the asterisks.) Outline the design and randomly assign the subjects to the 6 treatments. If you use Table B, start at line 130.

Alomar	Denman	Han	Liang	Padilla*	Valasco
Asihiro*	Durr*	Howard*	Maldonado	Plochman	Vaughn
Bennett	Edwards*	Hruska	Marsden	Rosen*	Wei
Bikalis	Farouk	Imrani	Montoya*	Solomon	Wilder*
Chao*	Fleming	James	O'Brian	Trujillo	Willis
Clemente	George	Kaplan*	Ogle*	Tullock	Zhang*

9.31   **Improving adolescents' habits.**   Twenty-four public middle schools agree to participate in the experiment described in Exercise 9.3 (page 215). Use a diagram to outline a completely randomized design for this experiment. Do the randomization required to assign schools to treatments. If you use the *Simple Random Sample* applet or other software, choose all four treatment groups. If you use Table B, start at line 105 and choose only the first two groups.

9.32   **Relieving headaches.**   Doctors identify "chronic tension–type headaches" as headaches that occur almost daily for at least six months. Can antidepressant medications or stress management training reduce the number and severity of these headaches? Are both together more effective than either alone?

(a) Use a diagram like Figure 9.1 to display the treatments in a design with two factors: "medication, yes or no" and "stress management, yes or no." Then outline the design of a completely randomized experiment to compare these treatments.

(b) The headache sufferers named below have agreed to participate in the study. Randomly assign the subjects to the treatments. If you use the *Simple Random Sample* applet or other software, assign all the subjects. If you use Table B, start at line 130 and assign subjects to only the first treatment group.

Abbott	Decker	Herrera	Lucero	Richter
Abdalla	Devlin	Hersch	Masters	Riley
Alawi	Engel	Hurwitz	Morgan	Samuels
Broden	Fuentes	Irwin	Nelson	Smith
Chai	Garrett	Jiang	Nho	Suarez
Chuang	Gill	Kelley	Ortiz	Upasani
Cordoba	Glover	Kim	Ramdas	Wilson
Custer	Hammond	Landers	Reed	Xiang

9.33 **Fabric finishing.** A maker of fabric for clothing is setting up a new line to "finish" the raw fabric. The line will use either metal rollers or natural-bristle rollers to raise the surface of the fabric; a dyeing cycle time of either 30 minutes or 40 minutes; and a temperature of either 150°C or 175°C. An experiment will compare all combinations of these choices. Three specimens of fabric will be subjected to each treatment and scored for quality.

(a) What are the factors and the treatments? How many individuals (fabric specimens) does the experiment require?

(b) Outline a completely randomized design for this experiment. (You need not actually do the randomization.)

9.34 **Frappuccino light?** Here's the opening of a press release from June 2004: "Starbucks Corp. on Monday said it would roll out a line of blended coffee drinks intended to tap into the growing popularity of reduced-calorie and reduced-fat menu choices for Americans." You wonder if Starbucks customers like the new "Mocha Frappuccino Light" as well as the regular Mocha Frappuccino coffee.

(a) Describe a matched pairs design to answer this question. Be sure to include proper blinding of your subjects.

(b) You have 20 regular Starbucks customers on hand. Use the *Simple Random Sample* applet or Table B at line 141 to do the randomization that your design requires.

9.35 **Growing trees faster.** The concentration of carbon dioxide (CO_2) in the atmosphere is increasing rapidly due to our use of fossil fuels. Because green plants use CO_2 to fuel photosynthesis, more CO_2 may cause trees to grow faster. An elaborate apparatus allows researchers to pipe extra CO_2 to a 30-meter circle of forest. We want to compare the growth in base area of trees in treated and untreated areas to see if extra CO_2 does in fact increase growth. We can afford to treat three circular areas.[11]

(a) Describe the design of a completely randomized experiment using six well-separated 30-meter circular areas in a pine forest. Sketch the circles and carry out the randomization your design calls for.

(b) Areas within the forest may differ in soil fertility. Describe a matched pairs design using three pairs of circles that will reduce the extra variation due to different fertility. Sketch the circles and carry out the randomization your design calls for.

9.36   **Athletes taking oxygen.** We often see players on the sidelines of a football game inhaling oxygen. Their coaches think this will speed their recovery. We might measure recovery from intense exertion as follows: Have a football player run 100 yards three times in quick succession. Then allow three minutes to rest before running 100 yards again. Time the final run. Because players vary greatly in speed, you plan a matched pairs experiment using 25 football players as subjects. Discuss the design of such an experiment to investigate the effect of inhaling oxygen during the rest period.

9.37   **Protecting ultramarathon runners.**   An ultramarathon, as you might guess, is a footrace longer than the 26.2 miles of a marathon. Runners commonly develop respiratory infections after an ultramarathon. Will taking 600 milligrams of vitamin C daily reduce these infections? Researchers randomly assigned ultramarathon runners to receive either vitamin C or a placebo. Separately, they also randomly assigned these treatments to a group of nonrunners the same age as the runners. All subjects were watched for 14 days after the big race to see if infections developed.[12]

(a) What is the name for this experimental design?

(b) Use a diagram to outline the design.

9.38   **Reducing spine fractures.**   Fractures of the spine are common and serious among women with advanced osteoporosis (low mineral density in the bones). Can taking strontium renelate help? A large medical experiment assigned 1649 women to take either strontium renelate or a placebo each day. All of the subjects had osteoporosis and had suffered at least one fracture. All were taking calcium supplements and receiving standard medical care. The response variables were measurements of bone density and counts of new fractures over three years. The subjects were treated at 10 medical centers in 10 different countries.[13]   Outline a block design for this experiment, with the medical centers as blocks. Explain why this is the proper design.

9.39   **Wine, beer, or spirits?**   Women as a group develop heart disease much later than men. We can improve the completely randomized design of Exercise 9.27 by using women and men as blocks. Your 300 subjects include 120 women and 180 men. Outline a block design for comparing wine, beer, and spirits. Be sure to say how many subjects you will put in each group in your design.

9.40   **Response to TV ads, continued.**   We can improve on the completely randomized design you outlined in Exercise 9.30. The 36 subjects include 24 women and 12 men. Men and women often react differently to advertising. You therefore decide to use a block design with the two genders as blocks. You must assign the 6 treatments at random within each block separately.

(a) Outline the design with a diagram.

(b) The 12 men are marked with asterisks in the list in Exercise 9.30. Use Table B, beginning at line 140, to do the randomization. Report your result in a table that lists the 24 women and 12 men and the treatment you assigned to each.

9.41   **Prayer and meditation.**   You read in a magazine that "nonphysical treatments such as meditation and prayer have been shown to be effective in controlled scientific studies for such ailments as high blood pressure, insomnia, ulcers, and asthma." Explain in simple language what the article means by "controlled scientific studies." Why can such studies in principle provide good evidence that, for example, meditation is an effective treatment for high blood pressure?

9.42   **College students.**   Give an example of a question about college students, their behavior, or their opinions that would best be answered by

(a) a sample survey.

(b) an experiment.

9.43   **Quick randomizing.**   Here's a quick and easy way to randomize. You have 100 subjects, 50 women and 50 men. Toss a coin. If it's heads, assign the men to the treatment group and the women to the control group. If the coin comes up tails, assign the women to treatment and the men to control. This gives every individual subject a 50-50 chance of being assigned to treatment or control. Why isn't this a good way to randomly assign subjects to treatment groups?

9.44   **Daytime running lights.**   Canada requires that cars be equipped with "daytime running lights," headlights that automatically come on at a low level when the car is started. Many manufacturers are now equipping cars sold in the United States with running lights. Will running lights reduce accidents by making cars more visible?

(a) Briefly discuss the design of an experiment to help answer this question. In particular, what response variables will you examine?

(b) Example 9.7 (page 223) discusses center brake lights. What cautions do you draw from that example that apply to an experiment on the effects of running lights?

9.45   **Do antioxidants prevent cancer?**   People who eat lots of fruits and vegetables have lower rates of colon cancer than those who eat little of these foods. Fruits and vegetables are rich in "antioxidants" such as vitamins A, C, and E. Will taking antioxidants help prevent colon cancer? A medical experiment studied this question with 864 people who were at risk of colon cancer. The subjects were divided into four groups: daily beta-carotene, daily vitamins C and E, all three vitamins every day, or daily placebo. After four years, the researchers were surprised to find no significant difference in colon cancer among the groups.[14]

(a) What are the explanatory and response variables in this experiment?

(b) Outline the design of the experiment. Use your judgment in choosing the group sizes.

(c) The study was double-blind. What does this mean?

(d) What does "no significant difference" mean in describing the outcome of the study?

(e) Suggest some lurking variables that could explain why people who eat lots of fruits and vegetables have lower rates of colon cancer. The experiment suggests that these variables, rather than the antioxidants, may be responsible for the observed benefits of fruits and vegetables.

9.46   An herb for depression?   Does the herb Saint-John's-wort relieve major depression? Here are some excerpts from the report of a study of this issue.[15] The study concluded that the herb is no more effective than a placebo.

(a) "Design: Randomized, double-blind, placebo-controlled clinical trial...." A clinical trial is a medical experiment using actual patients as subjects. Explain the meaning of each of the other terms in this description.

(b) "Participants ... were randomly assigned to receive either Saint-John's-wort extract ($n = 98$) or placebo ($n = 102$).... The primary outcome measure was the rate of change in the Hamilton Rating Scale for Depression over the treatment period." Based on this information, use a diagram to outline the design of this clinical trial.

9.47   Explaining medical research.   Observational studies had suggested that vitamin E reduces the risk of heart disease. Careful experiments, however, showed that vitamin E has no effect, at least for women. According to a commentary in the *Journal of the American Medical Association*:

> *Thus, vitamin E enters the category of therapies that were promising in epidemiologic and observational studies but failed to deliver in adequately powered randomized controlled trials. As in other studies, the "healthy user" bias must be considered, ie, the healthy lifestyle behaviors that characterize individuals who care enough about their health to take various supplements are actually responsible for the better health, but this is minimized with the rigorous trial design.*[16]

A friend who knows no statistics asks you to explain this.

(a) What is the difference between observational studies and experiments?

(b) What is a "randomized controlled trial"? (We'll discuss "adequately powered" in Chapter 16.)

(c) How does "healthy user bias" explain how people who take vitamin E supplements have better health in observational studies but not in controlled experiments?

9.48   Randomization avoids bias.   Suppose that the 25 even-numbered students among the 50 students available for the comparison of on-campus and online instruction (Example 9.4) are older, employed students. We hope that randomization will distribute these students roughly equally between the on-campus and online groups. Use the *Simple Random Sample* applet to take 20 samples of size 25 from the 50 students. (Be sure to click "Reset" after each sample.) Record the counts of even-numbered students in each of your 20 samples. You see that there is considerable chance variation but no systematic bias in favor of one or the other group in assigning the older students. Larger samples from a larger population will on the average do an even better job of creating two similar groups.

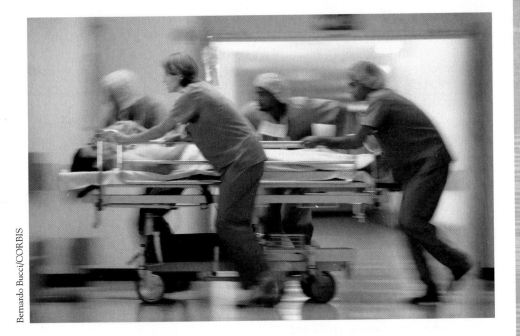

Bernardo Bucci/CORBIS

Data Ethics*

The production and use of data, like all human endeavors, raise ethical questions. We won't discuss the telemarketer who begins a telephone sales pitch with "I'm conducting a survey." Such deception is clearly unethical. It enrages legitimate survey organizations, which find the public less willing to talk with them. Neither will we discuss those few researchers who, in the pursuit of professional advancement, publish fake data. There is no ethical question here—faking data to advance your career is just wrong. It will end your career when uncovered. But just how honest must researchers be about real, unfaked data? Here is an example that suggests the answer is "More honest than they often are."

EXAMPLE 1   The whole truth?

Papers reporting scientific research are supposed to be short, with no extra baggage. Brevity, however, can allow researchers to avoid complete honesty about their data. Did they choose their subjects in a biased way? Did they report data on only some of their subjects? Did they try several statistical analyses and report only the ones that looked best? The statistician John Bailar screened more than 4000 medical papers in more than a decade as consultant to the *New England Journal of Medicine*. He says, "When it came to the statistical review, it was often clear that critical information was lacking, and the gaps nearly always had the practical effect of making the authors' conclusions look stronger than they should have."[1] The situation is no doubt worse in fields that screen published work less carefully.

This commentary
discusses . . .

Institutional review boards

Informed consent

Confidentiality

Clinical trials

**Behavioral and social
  science experiments**

---

*This short essay concerns a very important topic, but the material is not needed to read the rest of the book.

The most complex issues of data ethics arise when we collect data from people. The ethical difficulties are more severe for experiments that impose some treatment on people than for sample surveys that simply gather information. Trials of new medical treatments, for example, can do harm as well as good to their subjects. Here are some basic standards of data ethics that must be obeyed by any study that gathers data from human subjects, whether sample survey or experiment.

BASIC DATA ETHICS

The organization that carries out the study must have an **institutional review board** that reviews all planned studies in advance in order to protect the subjects from possible harm.

All individuals who are subjects in a study must give their **informed consent** before data are collected.

All individual data must be kept **confidential.** Only statistical summaries for groups of subjects may be made public.

The law requires that studies carried out or funded by the federal government obey these principles.[2] But neither the law nor the consensus of experts is completely clear about the details of their application.

Institutional review boards

The purpose of an institutional review board is not to decide whether a proposed study will produce valuable information or whether it is statistically sound. The board's purpose is, in the words of one university's board, "to protect the rights and welfare of human subjects (including patients) recruited to participate in research activities." The board reviews the plan of the study and can require changes. It reviews the consent form to ensure that subjects are informed about the nature of the study and about any potential risks. Once research begins, the board monitors its progress at least once a year.

The most pressing issue concerning institutional review boards is whether their workload has become so large that their effectiveness in protecting subjects drops. When the government temporarily stopped human subject research at Duke University Medical Center in 1999 due to inadequate protection of subjects, more than 2000 studies were going on. That's a lot of review work. There are shorter review procedures for projects that involve only minimal risks to subjects, such as most sample surveys. When a board is overloaded, there is a temptation to put more proposals in the minimal risk category to speed the work.

Informed consent

Both words in the phrase "informed consent" are important, and both can be controversial. Subjects must be *informed* in advance about the nature of a study and any risk of harm it may bring. In the case of a sample survey, physical harm is not possible. The subjects should be told what kinds of questions the survey will ask and about how much of their time it will take. Experimenters must tell subjects the nature and purpose of the study and outline possible risks. Subjects must then *consent* in writing.

EXAMPLE 2   Who can consent?

Are there some subjects who can't give informed consent? It was once common, for example, to test new vaccines on prison inmates who gave their consent in return for good-behavior credit. Now we worry that prisoners are not really free to refuse, and the law forbids almost all medical research in prisons.

Children can't give fully informed consent, so the usual procedure is to ask their parents. A study of new ways to teach reading is about to start at a local elementary school, so the study team sends consent forms home to parents. Many parents don't return the forms. Can their children take part in the study because the parents did not say "No," or should we allow only children whose parents returned the form and said "Yes"?

What about research into new medical treatments for people with mental disorders? What about studies of new ways to help emergency room patients who may be unconscious? In most cases, there is not time to get the consent of the family. Does the principle of informed consent bar realistic trials of new treatments for unconscious patients?

These are questions without clear answers. Reasonable people differ strongly on all of them. There is nothing simple about informed consent.[3]

Bernardo Bucci/CORBIS

The difficulties of informed consent do not vanish even for capable subjects. Some researchers, especially in medical trials, regard consent as a barrier to getting patients to participate in research. They may not explain all possible risks; they may not point out that there are other therapies that might be better than those being studied; they may be too optimistic in talking with patients even when the consent form has all the right details. On the other hand, mentioning every possible risk leads to very long consent forms that really are barriers. "They are like rental car contracts," one lawyer said. Some subjects don't read forms that run five or six printed pages. Others are frightened by the large number of possible (but unlikely) disasters that might happen and so refuse to participate. Of course, unlikely disasters sometimes happen. When they do, lawsuits follow and the consent forms become yet longer and more detailed.

Confidentiality

Ethical problems do not disappear once a study has been cleared by the review board, has obtained consent from its subjects, and has actually collected data about the subjects. It is important to protect the subjects' privacy by keeping all data about individuals confidential. The report of an opinion poll may say what percent of the 1200 respondents felt that legal immigration should be reduced. It may not report what *you* said about this or any other issue.

anonymity

Confidentiality is not the same as **anonymity.** Anonymity means that subjects are anonymous—their names are not known even to the director of the study. Anonymity is rare in statistical studies. Even where it is possible (mainly in surveys conducted by mail), anonymity prevents any follow-up to improve nonresponse or inform subjects of results.

Any breach of confidentiality is a serious violation of data ethics. The best practice is to separate the identity of the subjects from the rest of the data at once. Sample surveys, for example, use the identification only to check on who did or did not respond. In an era of advanced technology, however, it is no longer enough to be sure that each individual set of data protects people's privacy. The government, for example, maintains a vast amount of information about citizens in many separate data bases—census responses, tax returns, Social Security information, data from surveys such as the Current Population Survey, and so on. Many of these data bases can be searched by computers for statistical studies. A clever computer search of several data bases might be able, by combining information, to identify you and learn a great deal about you even if your name and other identification have been removed from the data available for search. A colleague from Germany once remarked that "female full professor of statistics with PhD from the United States" was enough to identify her among all the 83 million residents of Germany. Privacy and confidentiality of data are hot issues among statisticians in the computer age.

EXAMPLE 3   Uncle Sam knows

Citizens are required to give information to the government. Think of tax returns and Social Security contributions. The government needs these data for administrative purposes—to see if you paid the right amount of tax and how large a Social Security benefit you are owed when you retire. Some people feel that individuals should be able to forbid any other use of their data, even with all identification removed. This would prevent using government records to study, say, the ages, incomes, and household sizes of Social Security recipients. Such a study could well be vital to debates on reforming Social Security.

Clinical trials

Clinical trials are experiments that study the effectiveness of medical treatments on actual patients. Medical treatments can harm as well as heal, so clinical trials spotlight the ethical problems of experiments with human subjects. Here are the starting points for a discussion:

• Randomized comparative experiments are the only way to see the true effects of new treatments. Without them, risky treatments that are no more effective than placebos will become common.

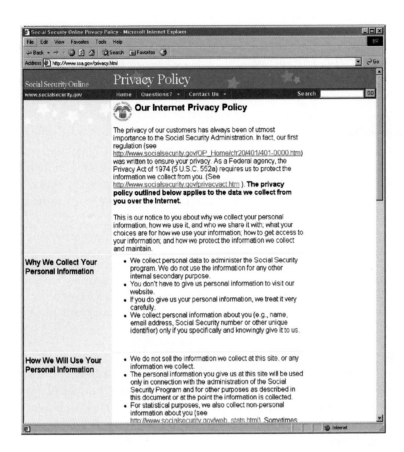

The privacy policy of the government's Social Security Administration, available online at www.ssa.gov.

- Clinical trials produce great benefits, but most of these benefits go to future patients. The trials also pose risks, and these risks are borne by the subjects of the trial. So we must balance future benefits against present risks.

- Both medical ethics and international human rights standards say that "the interests of the subject must always prevail over the interests of science and society."

The quoted words are from the 1964 Helsinki Declaration of the World Medical Association, the most respected international standard. The most outrageous examples of unethical experiments are those that ignore the interests of the subjects.

EXAMPLE 4 The Tuskegee study

In the 1930s, syphilis was common among black men in the rural South, a group that had almost no access to medical care. The Public Health Service Tuskegee study recruited 399 poor black sharecroppers with syphilis and 201 others without the disease in order to observe how syphilis progressed when no treatment was given. Beginning in 1943, penicillin became available to treat syphilis. The study subjects were not treated. In fact, the Public Health Service prevented any treatment until word leaked out and forced an end to the study in the 1970s.

The Tuskegee study is an extreme example of investigators following their own interests and ignoring the well-being of their subjects. A 1996 review said, "It has come to symbolize racism in medicine, ethical misconduct in human research, paternalism by physicians, and government abuse of vulnerable people." In 1997, President Clinton formally apologized to the surviving participants in a White House ceremony.[4]

Because "the interests of the subject must always prevail," medical treatments can be tested in clinical trials only when there is reason to hope that they will help the patients who are subjects in the trials. Future benefits aren't enough to justify experiments with human subjects. Of course, if there is already strong evidence that a treatment works and is safe, it is unethical *not* to give it. Here are the words of Dr. Charles Hennekens of the Harvard Medical School, who directed the large clinical trial that showed that aspirin reduces the risk of heart attacks:

> There's a delicate balance between when to do or not do a randomized trial. On the one hand, there must be sufficient belief in the agent's potential to justify exposing half the subjects to it. On the other hand, there must be sufficient doubt about its efficacy to justify withholding it from the other half of subjects who might be assigned to placebos.[5]

Why is it ethical to give a control group of patients a placebo? Well, we know that placebos often work. Moreover, placebos have no harmful side effects. So in the state of balanced doubt described by Dr. Hennekens, the placebo group may be getting a better treatment than the drug group. If we *knew* which treatment was better, we would give it to everyone. When we don't know, it is ethical to try both and compare them.

Behavioral and social science experiments

When we move from medicine to the behavioral and social sciences, the direct risks to experimental subjects are less acute, but so are the possible benefits to the subjects. Consider, for example, the experiments conducted by psychologists in their study of human behavior.

David Pollack/CORBIS

EXAMPLE 5   Psychologists in the men's room

Psychologists observe that people have a "personal space" and are uneasy if others come too close to them. We don't like strangers to sit at our table in a coffee shop if other tables are available, and we see people move apart in elevators if there is room to do so. Americans tend to require more personal space than people in most other cultures. Can violations of personal space have physical, as well as emotional, effects?

Investigators set up shop in a men's public restroom. They blocked off urinals to force men walking in to use either a urinal next to an experimenter (treatment group) or a urinal separated from the experimenter (control group). Another experimenter, using a periscope from a toilet stall, measured how long the subject took to start urinating and how long he continued.[6]

This personal space experiment illustrates the difficulties facing those who plan and review behavioral studies.

- There is no risk of harm to the subjects, although they would certainly object to being watched through a periscope. What should we protect subjects from when physical harm is unlikely? Possible emotional harm? Undignified situations? Invasion of privacy?

- What about informed consent? The subjects did not even know they were participating in an experiment. Many behavioral experiments rely on hiding the true purpose of the study. The subjects would change their behavior if told in advance what the investigators were looking for. Subjects are asked to consent on the basis of vague information. They receive full information only after the experiment.

The "Ethical Principles" of the American Psychological Association require consent unless a study merely observes behavior in a public place. They allow deception only when it is necessary to the study, does not hide information that might influence a subject's willingness to participate, and is explained to subjects as soon as possible. The personal space study (from the 1970s) does not meet current ethical standards.

We see that the basic requirement for informed consent is understood differently in medicine and psychology. Here is an example of another setting with yet another interpretation of what is ethical. The subjects get no information and give no consent. They don't even know that an experiment may be sending them to jail for the night.

EXAMPLE 6 Reducing domestic violence ─────────

How should police respond to domestic violence calls? In the past, the usual practice was to remove the offender and order him to stay out of the household overnight. Police were reluctant to make arrests because the victims rarely pressed charges. Women's groups argued that arresting offenders would help prevent future violence even if no charges were filed. Is there evidence that arrest will reduce future offenses? That's a question that experiments have tried to answer.

A typical domestic violence experiment compares two treatments: arrest the suspect and hold him overnight, or warn the suspect and release him. When police officers reach the scene of a domestic violence call, they calm the participants and investigate. Weapons or death threats require an arrest. If the facts permit an arrest but do not require it, an officer radios headquarters for instructions. The person on duty opens the next envelope in a file prepared in advance by a statistician. The envelopes contain the treatments in random order. The police either arrest the suspect or warn and release him, depending on the contents of the envelope. The researchers then watch police records and visit the victim to see if the domestic violence reoccurs.

Such experiments show that arresting domestic violence suspects does reduce their future violent behavior.[7] As a result of this evidence, arrest has become the common police response to domestic violence.

The domestic violence experiments shed light on an important issue of public policy. Because there is no informed consent, the ethical rules that govern clinical trials and most social science studies would forbid these experiments. They were cleared by review boards because, in the words of one domestic violence researcher, "These people became subjects by committing acts that allow the police to arrest them. You don't need consent to arrest someone."

DISCUSSION EXERCISES

Most of these exercises pose issues for discussion. There are no right or wrong answers, but there are more and less thoughtful answers.

1. **Minimal risk?** You are a member of your college's institutional review board. You must decide whether several research proposals qualify for lighter review because they involve only minimal risk to subjects. Federal regulations say that "minimal risk" means the risks are no greater than "those ordinarily encountered in daily life or during the performance of routine physical or psychological examinations or tests." That's vague. Which of these do you think qualifies as "minimal risk"?

    (a) Draw a drop of blood by pricking a finger in order to measure blood sugar.

    (b) Draw blood from the arm for a full set of blood tests.

    (c) Insert a tube that remains in the arm, so that blood can be drawn regularly.

2. **Who reviews?** Government regulations require that institutional review boards consist of at least five people, including at least one scientist, one nonscientist, and one person from outside the institution. Most boards are larger, but many contain just one outsider.

    (a) Why should review boards contain people who are not scientists?

    (b) Do you think that one outside member is enough? How would you choose that member? (For example, would you prefer a medical doctor? A member of the clergy? An activist for patients' rights?)

3. **Getting consent.** A researcher suspects that traditional religious beliefs tend to be associated with an authoritarian personality. She prepares a questionnaire that measures authoritarian tendencies and also asks many religious questions. Write a description of the purpose of this research to be read by subjects in order to obtain their informed consent. You must balance the conflicting goals of not deceiving the subjects as to what the questionnaire will tell about them and of not biasing the sample by scaring off religious people.

4. **No consent needed?** In which of the circumstances below would you allow collecting personal information without the subjects' consent?

    (a) A government agency takes a random sample of income tax returns to obtain information on the average income of people in different occupations. Only the incomes and occupations are recorded from the returns, not the names.

    (b) A social psychologist attends public meetings of a religious group to study the behavior patterns of members.

    (c) The social psychologist pretends to be converted to membership in a religious group and attends private meetings to study the behavior patterns of members.

5. **Studying your blood.** Long ago, doctors drew a blood specimen from you as part of treating minor anemia. Unknown to you, the sample was stored. Now researchers plan to use stored samples from you and many other people to look for genetic factors that may influence anemia. It is no longer possible to ask your consent. Modern technology can read your entire genetic makeup from the blood sample.

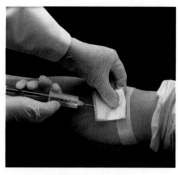

Lester Lefkowitz/CORBIS

(a) Do you think it violates the principle of informed consent to use your blood sample if your name is on it but you were not told that it might be saved and studied later?

(b) Suppose that your identity is not attached. The blood sample is known only to come from (say) "a 20-year-old white female being treated for anemia." Is it now OK to use the sample for research?

(c) Perhaps we should use biological materials such as blood samples only from patients who have agreed to allow the material to be stored for later use in research. It isn't possible to say in advance what kind of research, so this falls short of the usual standard for informed consent. Is it nonetheless acceptable, given complete confidentiality and the fact that using the sample can't physically harm the patient?

6. **Anonymous? Confidential?** One of the most important nongovernment surveys in the United States is the National Opinion Research Center's General Social Survey. The GSS regularly monitors public opinion on a wide variety of political and social issues. Interviews are conducted in person in the subject's home. Are a subject's responses to GSS questions anonymous, confidential, or both? Explain your answer.

7. **Anonymous? Confidential?** Texas A&M, like many universities, offers free screening for HIV, the virus that causes AIDS. The announcement says, "Persons who sign up for the HIV Screening will be assigned a number so that they do not have to give their name." They can learn the results of the test by telephone, still without giving their name. Does this practice offer *anonymity* or just *confidentiality?*

8. **Political polls.** The presidential election campaign is in full swing, and the candidates have hired polling organizations to take sample surveys to find out what the voters think about the issues. What information should the pollsters be required to give out?

(a) What does the standard of informed consent require the pollsters to tell potential respondents?

(b) The standards accepted by polling organizations also require giving respondents the name and address of the organization that carries out the poll. Why do you think this is required?

(c) The polling organization usually has a professional name such as "Samples Incorporated," so respondents don't know that the poll is being paid for by a political party or candidate. Would revealing the sponsor to respondents bias the poll? Should the sponsor always be announced whenever poll results are made public?

9. **Making poll results public.** Some people think that the law should require that all political poll results be made public. Otherwise, the possessors of poll results can use the information to their own advantage. They can act on the

information, release only selected parts of it, or time the release for best effect. A candidate's organization replies that they are paying for the poll in order to gain information for their own use, not to amuse the public. Do you favor requiring complete disclosure of political poll results? What about other private surveys, such as market research surveys of consumer tastes?

10. **Student subjects.** Students taking Psychology 001 are required to serve as experimental subjects. Students in Psychology 002 are not required to serve, but they are given extra credit if they do so. Students in Psychology 003 are required either to sign up as subjects or to write a term paper. Serving as an experimental subject may be educational, but current ethical standards frown on using "dependent subjects" such as prisoners or charity medical patients. Students are certainly somewhat dependent on their teachers. Do you object to any of these course policies? If so, which ones, and why?

11. **Unequal benefits.** Researchers on aging proposed to investigate the effect of supplemental health services on the quality of life of older people. Eligible patients on the rolls of a large medical clinic were to be randomly assigned to treatment and control groups. The treatment group would be offered hearing aids, dentures, transportation, and other services not available without charge to the control group. The review board felt that providing these services to some but not other persons in the same institution raised ethical questions. Do you agree?

12. **How many have HIV?** Researchers from Yale, working with medical teams in Tanzania, wanted to know how common infection with HIV, the virus that causes AIDS, is among pregnant women in that African country. To do this, they planned to test blood samples drawn from pregnant women.

Yale's institutional review board insisted that the researchers get the informed consent of each woman and tell her the results of the test. This is the usual procedure in developed nations. The Tanzanian government did not want to tell the women why blood was drawn or tell them the test results. The government feared panic if many people turned out to have an incurable disease for which the country's medical system could not provide care. The study was canceled. Do you think that Yale was right to apply its usual standards for protecting subjects?

13. **AIDS trials in Africa.** Effective drugs for treating AIDS are very expensive, so some African nations cannot afford to give them to large numbers of people. Yet AIDS is more common in parts of Africa than anywhere else. Several clinical trials are looking at ways to prevent pregnant mothers infected with HIV from passing the infection to their unborn children, a major source of HIV infections in Africa. Some people say these trials are unethical because they do not give effective AIDS drugs to their subjects, as would be required in rich nations. Others reply that the trials are looking for treatments that can work in the real world in Africa and that they promise benefits at least to the children of their subjects. What do you think?

14. **AIDS trials in Africa.** One of the most important goals of AIDS research is to find a vaccine that will protect against HIV infection. Because AIDS is so common in parts of Africa, that is the easiest place to test a vaccine. It is likely, however, that a vaccine would be so expensive that it could not (at least at first) be widely used in Africa. Is it ethical to test in Africa if the benefits go mainly to rich countries? The treatment group of subjects would get the vaccine and the placebo group would later be given the vaccine if it proved effective. So the

actual subjects would benefit—it is the future benefits that would go elsewhere. What do you think?

15. **Asking teens about sex.**   The Centers for Disease Control and Prevention, in a survey of teenagers, asked the subjects if they were sexually active. Those who said "Yes" were then asked, "How old were you when you had sexual intercourse for the first time?" Should consent of parents be required to ask minors about sex, drugs, and other such issues, or is consent of the minors themselves enough? Give reasons for your opinion.

16. **Deceiving subjects.**   Students sign up to be subjects in a psychology experiment. When they arrive, they are told that interviews are running late and are taken to a waiting room. The experimenters then stage a theft of a valuable object left in the waiting room. Some subjects are alone with the thief, and others are in pairs—these are the treatments being compared. Will the subject report the theft?

The students had agreed to take part in an unspecified study, and the true nature of the experiment is explained to them afterward. Do you think this study is ethically OK?

17. **Deceiving subjects.**   A psychologist conducts the following experiment: she measures the attitude of subjects toward cheating, then has them play a game rigged so that winning without cheating is impossible. The computer that organizes the game also records—unknown to the subjects—whether or not they cheat. Then attitude toward cheating is retested.

Subjects who cheat tend to change their attitudes to find cheating more acceptable. Those who resist the temptation to cheat tend to condemn cheating more strongly on the second test of attitude. These results confirm the psychologist's theory.

This experiment tempts subjects to cheat. The subjects are led to believe that they can cheat secretly when in fact they are observed. Is this experiment ethically objectionable? Explain your position.

Cut and Deal Ltd./Alamy

Introducing Probability

Why is probability, the mathematics of chance behavior, needed to understand statistics, the science of data? Let's look at a typical sample survey.

EXAMPLE 10.1 Do you lotto?

What proportion of all adults bought a lottery ticket in the past 12 months? We don't know, but we do have results from the Gallup Poll. Gallup took a random sample of 1523 adults. The poll found that 868 of the people in the sample bought tickets. The proportion who bought tickets was

$$\text{sample proportion} = \frac{868}{1523} = 0.57 \ \text{(that is, 57\%)}$$

Because all adults had the same chance to be among the chosen 1523, it seems reasonable to use this 57% as an estimate of the unknown proportion in the population. It's a *fact* that 57% of the sample bought lottery tickets—we know because Gallup asked them. We don't know what percent of all adults bought tickets, but we *estimate* that about 57% did. This is a basic move in statistics: use a result from a sample to estimate something about a population.

What if Gallup took a second random sample of 1523 adults? The new sample would have different people in it. It is almost certain that there would not be exactly 868 positive responses. That is, Gallup's estimate of the proportion of adults who bought a lottery ticket will vary from sample to sample. Could it happen that one random sample finds that 57% of adults recently bought a lottery ticket and a second random sample finds that only 37% had done so? *Random samples eliminate bias from the act of choosing a sample, but they can still be wrong because of the variability that results when we choose at random.* If the variation when we take repeat samples from the same population is too great, we can't trust the results of any one sample.

This is where we need facts about probability to make progress in statistics. Because Gallup uses chance to choose its samples, the laws of probability govern the behavior of the samples. Gallup says that the probability is 0.95 that an estimate from one of their samples comes within ±3 percentage points of the truth about the population of all adults. The first step toward understanding this statement is to understand what "probability 0.95" means. Our purpose in this chapter is to understand the language of probability, but without going into the mathematics of probability theory.

The idea of probability

To understand why we can trust random samples and randomized comparative experiments, we must look closely at chance behavior. The big fact that emerges is this: **chance behavior is unpredictable in the short run but has a regular and predictable pattern in the long run.**

Toss a coin, or choose an SRS. The result can't be predicted in advance, because the result will vary when you toss the coin or choose the sample repeatedly. But there is still a regular pattern in the results, a pattern that emerges clearly only after many repetitions. This remarkable fact is the basis for the idea of probability.

SuperStock

━ EXAMPLE 10.2   *Coin tossing* ━

When you toss a coin, there are only two possible outcomes, heads or tails. Figure 10.1 shows the results of tossing a coin 5000 times twice. For each number of tosses from 1 to 5000, we have plotted the proportion of those tosses that gave a head. Trial A (solid blue line) begins tail, head, tail, tail. You can see that the proportion of heads for Trial A starts at 0 on the first toss, rises to 0.5 when the second toss gives a head, then falls to 0.33 and 0.25 as we get two more tails. Trial B, on the other hand, starts with five straight heads, so the proportion of heads is 1 until the sixth toss.

The proportion of tosses that produce heads is quite variable at first. Trial A starts low and Trial B starts high. As we make more and more tosses, however, the proportion of heads for both trials gets close to 0.5 and stays there. If we made yet a third trial at tossing the coin a great many times, the proportion of heads would again settle down to 0.5 in the long run. This is the intuitive idea of probability. Probability 0.5 means "occurs half the time in a very large number of trials." The probability 0.5 appears as a horizontal line on the graph.

We might suspect that a coin has probability 0.5 of coming up heads just because the coin has two sides. But we can't be sure. The coin might be unbalanced. In fact, spinning a penny or nickel on a flat surface, rather than tossing the coin, doesn't give heads probability 0.5. The idea of probability is empirical. That is, it is based on observation rather than theorizing. Probability describes what happens in very many trials, and we must observe many trials to pin down a

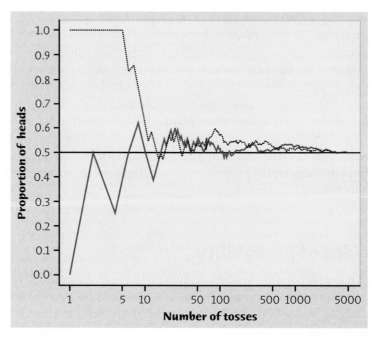

FIGURE 10.1 The proportion of tosses of a coin that give a head changes as we make more tosses. Eventually, however, the proportion approaches 0.5, the probability of a head. This figure shows the results of two trials of 5000 tosses each.

probability. In the case of tossing a coin, some diligent people have in fact made thousands of tosses.

EXAMPLE 10.3   Some coin tossers

The French naturalist Count Buffon (1707–1788) tossed a coin 4040 times. Result: 2048 heads, or proportion 2048/4040 = 0.5069 for heads.

Around 1900, the English statistician Karl Pearson heroically tossed a coin 24,000 times. Result: 12,012 heads, a proportion of 0.5005.

While imprisoned by the Germans during World War II, the South African mathematician John Kerrich tossed a coin 10,000 times. Result: 5067 heads, a proportion of 0.5067.

RANDOMNESS AND PROBABILITY

We call a phenomenon **random** if individual outcomes are uncertain but there is nonetheless a regular distribution of outcomes in a large number of repetitions.

The **probability** of any outcome of a random phenomenon is the proportion of times the outcome would occur in a very long series of repetitions.

Does God play dice?

Few things in the world are truly random in the sense that no amount of information will allow us to predict the outcome. We could in principle apply the laws of physics to a tossed coin, for example, and calculate whether it will land heads or tails. But randomness does rule events inside individual atoms. Albert Einstein didn't like this feature of the new quantum theory. "I shall never believe that God plays dice with the world," said the great scientist. Eighty years later, it appears that Einstein was wrong.

That some things are random is an observed fact about the world. The outcome of a coin toss, the time between emissions of particles by a radioactive source, and the sexes of the next litter of lab rats are all random. So is the outcome of a random sample or a randomized experiment. Probability theory is the branch of mathematics that describes random behavior. Of course, we can never observe a probability exactly. We could always continue tossing the coin, for example. Mathematical probability is an idealization based on imagining what would happen in an indefinitely long series of trials.

The best way to understand randomness is to observe random behavior, as in Figure 10.1. You can do this with physical devices like coins, but computer simulations (imitations) of random behavior allow faster exploration. The *Probability* applet is a computer simulation that animates Figure 10.1. It allows you to choose the probability of a head and simulate any number of tosses of a coin with that probability. Experience shows that the proportion of heads gradually settles down close to the probability. Equally important, it also shows that *the proportion in a small or moderate number of tosses can be far from the probability. Probability describes only what happens in the long run.*

Computer simulations like the *Probability* applet start with given probabilities and imitate random behavior, but we can estimate a real-world probability only by actually observing many trials. Nonetheless, computer simulations are very useful because we need long runs of trials. In situations such as coin tossing, the proportion of an outcome often requires several hundred trials to settle down to the probability of that outcome. Short runs give only rough estimates of a probability.

APPLY YOUR KNOWLEDGE

10.1 Texas Hold'em. In the popular Texas Hold'em variety of poker, players make their best five-card poker hand by combining the two cards they are dealt with three of five cards available to all players. You read in a book on poker that if you hold a pair (two cards of the same rank) in your hand, the probability of getting four of a kind is 88/1000. Explain carefully what this means. In particular, explain why it does *not* mean that if you play 1000 such hands, exactly 88 will be four of a kind.

10.2 Tossing a thumbtack. Toss a thumbtack on a hard surface 100 times. How many times did it land with the point up? What is the approximate probability of landing point up?

10.3 Random digits. The table of random digits (Table B) was produced by a random mechanism that gives each digit probability 0.1 of being a 0.

(a) What proportion of the first 50 digits in the table are 0s? This proportion is an estimate, based on 50 repetitions, of the true probability, which in this case is known to be 0.1.

(b) The *Probability* applet can imitate random digits. Set the probability of heads in the applet to 0.1. Check "Show true probability" to show this value on the graph. A head stands for a 0 in the random digit table and a tail stands for any other digit. Simulate 200 digits (40 at a time—don't click "Reset"). If you kept going forever, presumably you would get 10% heads. What was the result of your 200 tosses?

Cut and Deal Ltd./Alamy

10.4 Probability says.... Probability is a measure of how likely an event is to occur. Match one of the probabilities that follow with each statement of likelihood given. (The probability is usually a more exact measure of likelihood than is the verbal statement.)

$$0 \qquad 0.01 \qquad 0.3 \qquad 0.6 \qquad 0.99 \qquad 1$$

(a) This event is impossible. It can never occur.

(b) This event is certain. It will occur on every trial.

(c) This event is very unlikely, but it will occur once in a while in a long sequence of trials.

(d) This event will occur more often than not.

Probability models

Gamblers have known for centuries that the fall of coins, cards, and dice displays clear patterns in the long run. The idea of probability rests on the observed fact that the average result of many thousands of chance outcomes can be known with near certainty. How can we give a mathematical description of long-run regularity?

To see how to proceed, think first about a very simple random phenomenon, tossing a coin once. When we toss a coin, we cannot know the outcome in advance. What *do* we know? We are willing to say that the outcome will be either heads or tails. We believe that each of these outcomes has probability 1/2. This description of coin tossing has two parts:

- A list of possible outcomes.
- A probability for each outcome.

Such a description is the basis for all probability models. Here is the basic vocabulary we use.

PROBABILITY MODELS

The **sample space** S of a random phenomenon is the set of all possible outcomes.

An **event** is an outcome or a set of outcomes of a random phenomenon. That is, an event is a subset of the sample space.

A **probability model** is a mathematical description of a random phenomenon consisting of two parts: a sample space S and a way of assigning probabilities to events.

A sample space S can be very simple or very complex. When we toss a coin once, there are only two outcomes, heads and tails. The sample space is $S = \{H, T\}$. When Gallup draws a random sample of 1523 adults, the sample space contains all possible choices of 1523 of the 225 million adults in the country. This S is extremely large. Each member of S is a possible sample, which explains the term *sample space*.

EXAMPLE 10.4   Rolling dice

Rolling two dice is a common way to lose money in casinos. There are 36 possible outcomes when we roll two dice and record the up-faces in order (first die, second die). Figure 10.2 displays these outcomes. They make up the sample space S. "Roll a 5" is an event, call it A, that contains four of these 36 outcomes:

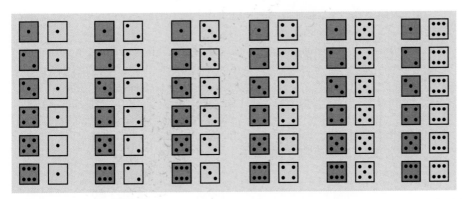

How can we assign probabilities to this sample space? We can find the actual probabilities for two specific dice only by actually tossing the dice many times, and even then only approximately. So we will give a probability model that assumes ideal, perfectly balanced dice. This model will be quite accurate for carefully made casino dice and less accurate for the cheap dice that come with a board game.

If the dice are perfectly balanced, all 36 outcomes in Figure 10.2 will be *equally likely*. That is, each of the 36 outcomes will come up on one thirty-sixth of all rolls in the long run. So each outcome has probability 1/36. There are 4 outcomes in the event A ("roll a 5"), so this event has probability 4/36. In this way we can assign a probability to any event. So we have a complete probability model.

FIGURE 10.2 The 36 possible outcomes in rolling two dice. If the dice are carefully made, all of these outcomes have the same probability.

EXAMPLE 10.5   Rolling dice and counting the spots

Gamblers care only about the total number of spots on the up-faces of the dice. The sample space for rolling two dice and counting the spots is

$$S = \{2, 3, 4, 5, 6, 7, 8, 9, 10, 11, 12\}$$

CAUTION

Comparing this S with Figure 10.2 reminds us that *we can change S by changing the detailed description of the random phenomenon we are describing.*

What are the probabilities for this new sample space? The 11 possible outcomes are *not* equally likely, because there are six ways to roll a 7 and only one way to roll a 2 or a 12. That's the key: each outcome in Figure 10.2 has probability 1/36. So "roll a 7" has probability 6/36 because this event contains 6 of the 36 outcomes. Similarly, "roll a 2" has probability 1/36, and "roll a 5" (4 outcomes from Figure 10.2) has probability 4/36. Here is the complete probability model:

Number of spots	2	3	4	5	6	7	8	9	10	11	12
Probability	1/36	2/36	3/36	4/36	5/36	6/36	5/36	4/36	3/36	2/36	1/36

APPLY YOUR KNOWLEDGE

10.5 Sample space. Choose a student at random from a large statistics class. Describe a sample space S for each of the following. (In some cases you may have some freedom in specifying S.)

(a) Ask how much time the student spent studying during the past 24 hours.

(b) Ask how much money in coins (not bills) the student is carrying.

(c) Record the student's letter grade at the end of the course.

(d) Ask whether the student did or did not take a math class in each of the two previous years of school.

10.6 Dungeons & Dragons. Role-playing games such as Dungeons & Dragons use many different types of dice. A four-sided die has faces with 1, 2, 3, and 4 spots.

(a) What is the sample space for rolling the die twice (spots on first and second rolls)? Follow the example of Figure 10.2.

(b) What is the assignment of probabilities to outcomes in this sample space? Assume that the die is perfectly balanced, and follow the method of Example 10.4.

10.7 Dungeons & Dragons. The intelligence of a character in the game is determined by rolling the four-sided die twice and adding 1 to the sum of the spots. Start with your work in the previous exercise to give a probability model (sample space and probabilities of outcomes) for the character's intelligence. Follow the method of Example 10.5.

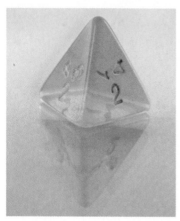
Fabio Pili/Alamy

Probability rules

In Examples 10.4 and 10.5 we found probabilities for perfectly balanced dice. As random phenomena go, dice are pretty simple. Even so, we had to assume idealized dice rather than working with real dice. In most situations, it isn't easy to give a "correct" probability model. We can make progress by listing some facts that must be true for *any* assignment of probabilities. These facts follow from the idea of probability as "the long-run proportion of repetitions on which an event occurs."

1. **Any probability is a number between 0 and 1.** Any proportion is a number between 0 and 1, so any probability is also a number between 0 and 1. An event with probability 0 never occurs, and an event with probability 1 occurs on every trial. An event with probability 0.5 occurs in half the trials in the long run.

2. **All possible outcomes together must have probability 1.** Because some outcome must occur on every trial, the sum of the probabilities for all possible outcomes must be exactly 1.

3. **If two events have no outcomes in common, the probability that one or the other occurs is the sum of their individual probabilities.** If one event occurs in 40% of all trials, a different event occurs in 25% of all trials, and the two can never occur together, then one or the other occurs on 65% of all trials because 40% + 25% = 65%.

4. **The probability that an event does not occur is 1 minus the probability that the event does occur.** If an event occurs in (say) 70% of all trials, it fails to occur in the other 30%. The probability that an event occurs and the probability that it does not occur always add to 100%, or 1.

We can use mathematical notation to state Facts 1 to 4 more concisely. Capital letters near the beginning of the alphabet denote events. If A is any event, we write its probability as $P(A)$. Here are our probability facts in formal language. As you apply these rules, remember that they are just another form of intuitively true facts about long-run proportions.

PROBABILITY RULES

Rule 1. The probability $P(A)$ of any event A satisfies $0 \leq P(A) \leq 1$.

Rule 2. If S is the sample space in a probability model, then $P(S) = 1$.

Rule 3. Two events A and B are **disjoint** if they have no outcomes in common and so can never occur together. If A and B are disjoint,

$$P(A \text{ or } B) = P(A) + P(B)$$

This is the **addition rule for disjoint events.**

Rule 4. For any event A,

$$P(A \text{ does not occur}) = 1 - P(A)$$

Equally likely?

A game of bridge begins by dealing all 52 cards in the deck to the four players, 13 to each. If the deck is well shuffled, all of the immense number of possible hands will be equally likely. But don't expect the hands that appear in newspaper bridge columns to reflect the equally likely probability model. Writers on bridge choose "interesting" hands, especially those that lead to high bids that are rare in actual play.

The addition rule extends to more than two events that are disjoint in the sense that no two have any outcomes in common. If events A, B, and C are disjoint, the probability that one of these events occurs is $P(A) + P(B) + P(C)$.

Image Source/Alamy

EXAMPLE 10.6   Using the probability rules

We already used the addition rule, without calling it by that name, to find the probabilities in Example 10.5. The event "roll a 5" contains the four disjoint outcomes displayed in Example 10.4, so the addition rule (Rule 3) says that its probability is

$$P(\text{roll a 5}) = P\left(\boxed{\cdot}\ \boxed{\because}\right) + P\left(\boxed{\because}\ \boxed{\cdot}\right) + P\left(\boxed{\therefore}\ \boxed{\cdot}\right) + P\left(\boxed{\vdots}\ \boxed{\cdot}\right)$$

$$= \frac{1}{36} + \frac{1}{36} + \frac{1}{36} + \frac{1}{36}$$

$$= \frac{4}{36} = 0.111$$

Check that the probabilities in Example 10.5, found using the addition rule, are all between 0 and 1 and add to exactly 1. That is, this probability model obeys Rules 1 and 2.

What is the probability of rolling anything other than a 5? By Rule 4,

$$P(\text{roll does not give a 5}) = 1 - P(\text{roll a 5})$$

$$= 1 - 0.111 = 0.889$$

Our model assigns probabilities to individual outcomes. To find the probability of an event, just add the probabilities of the outcomes that make up the event. For example:

$$P(\text{outcome is odd}) = P(3) + P(5) + P(7) + P(9) + P(11)$$

$$= \frac{2}{36} + \frac{4}{36} + \frac{6}{36} + \frac{4}{36} + \frac{2}{36}$$

$$= \frac{18}{36} = \frac{1}{2}$$

APPLY YOUR KNOWLEDGE

10.8   **Preparing for the GMAT.**   A company that offers courses to prepare students for the Graduate Management Admission test (GMAT) has the following information about its customers: 20% are currently undergraduate students in business; 15% are undergraduate students in other fields of study; 60% are college graduates who are currently employed; and 5% are college graduates who are not employed.

(a) Does this assignment of probabilities to customer backgrounds satisfy Rules 1 and 2?

(b) What percent of customers are currently undergraduates?

10.9   **Languages in Canada.**   Canada has two official languages, English and French. Choose a Canadian at random and ask, "What is your mother tongue?" Here is the distribution of responses, combining many separate languages from the broad Asian/Pacific region:[1]

Language	English	French	Asian/Pacific	Other
Probability	0.59	0.23	0.07	?

(a) What probability should replace "?" in the distribution?

(b) What is the probability that a Canadian's mother tongue is not English?

Discrete probability models

Examples 10.4, 10.5, and 10.6 illustrate one way to assign probabilities to events: assign a probability to every individual outcome, then add these probabilities to find the probability of any event. This idea works well when there are only a finite (fixed and limited) number of outcomes.

DISCRETE PROBABILITY MODEL

A probability model with a finite sample space is called **discrete.**

To assign probabilities in a discrete model, list the probabilities of all the individual outcomes. These probabilities must be numbers between 0 and 1 and must have sum 1. The probability of any event is the sum of the probabilities of the outcomes making up the event.

EXAMPLE 10.7   Benford's law

Faked numbers in tax returns, invoices, or expense account claims often display patterns that aren't present in legitimate records. Some patterns, like too many round numbers, are obvious and easily avoided by a clever crook. Others are more subtle. It is a striking fact that the first digits of numbers in legitimate records often follow a model known as Benford's law.[2] Call the first digit of a randomly chosen record X for short. Benford's law gives this probability model for X (note that a first digit can't be 0):

First digit X	1	2	3	4	5	6	7	8	9
Probability	0.301	0.176	0.125	0.097	0.079	0.067	0.058	0.051	0.046

Check that the probabilities of the outcomes sum to exactly 1. This is therefore a legitimate discrete probability model. Investigators can detect fraud by comparing the first digits in records such as invoices paid by a business with these probabilities.

The probability that a first digit is equal to or greater than 6 is

$$P(X \geq 6) = P(X = 6) + P(X = 7) + P(X = 8) + P(X = 9)$$
$$= 0.067 + 0.058 + 0.051 + 0.046 = 0.222$$

This is less than the probability that a record has first digit 1,

$$P(X = 1) = 0.301$$

Fraudulent records tend to have too few 1s and too many higher first digits.

Note that the probability that a first digit is greater than or equal to 6 is not the same as the probability that a first digit is strictly greater than 6. The latter probability is

$$P(X > 6) = 0.058 + 0.051 + 0.046 = 0.155$$

The outcome $X = 6$ is included in "greater than or equal to" and is not included in "strictly greater than."

APPLY YOUR KNOWLEDGE

10.10 Rolling a die. Figure 10.3 displays several discrete probability models for rolling a die. We can learn which model is actually *accurate* for a particular die only by rolling the die many times. However, some of the models are not *legitimate*. That is, they do not obey the rules. Which are legitimate and which are not? In the case of the illegitimate models, explain what is wrong.

		Probability		
Outcome	Model 1	Model 2	Model 3	Model 4
⚀	1/7	1/3	1/3	1
⚁	1/7	1/6	1/6	1
⚂	1/7	1/6	1/6	2
⚃	1/7	0	1/6	1
⚄	1/7	1/6	1/6	1
⚅	1/7	1/6	1/6	2

FIGURE 10.3 Four assignments of probabilities to the six faces of a die, for Exercise 10.10.

10.11 Benford's law. The first digit of a randomly chosen expense account claim follows Benford's law (Example 10.7). Consider the events

$$A = \{\text{first digit is 7 or greater}\} \qquad B = \{\text{first digit is odd}\}$$

(a) What outcomes make up the event A? What is $P(A)$?

(b) What outcomes make up the event B? What is $P(B)$?

(c) What outcomes make up the event "A or B"? What is $P(A \text{ or } B)$? Why is this probability not equal to $P(A) + P(B)$?

10.12 Watching TV. Choose a young person (age 19 to 25) at random and ask, "In the past seven days, how many days did you watch television?" Call the response X for short. Here is a probability model for the response:[3]

Days X	0	1	2	3	4	5	6	7
Probability	0.04	0.03	0.06	0.08	0.09	0.08	0.05	0.57

(a) Verify that this is a legitimate discrete probability model.

(b) Describe the event $X < 7$ in words. What is $P(X < 7)$?

(c) Express the event "watched TV at least once" in terms of X. What is the probability of this event?

Continuous probability models

When we use the table of random digits to select a digit between 0 and 9, the discrete probability model assigns probability 1/10 to each of the 10 possible outcomes. Suppose that we want to choose a number at random between 0 and 1, allowing *any* number between 0 and 1 as the outcome. Software random number generators will do this. The sample space is now an entire interval of numbers:

$$S = \{\text{all numbers between 0 and 1}\}$$

Call the outcome of the random number generator Y for short. How can we assign probabilities to such events as $\{0.3 \leq Y \leq 0.7\}$? As in the case of selecting a random digit, we would like all possible outcomes to be equally likely. But we cannot assign probabilities to each individual value of Y and then add them, because there are infinitely many possible values.

We use a new way of assigning probabilities directly to events—as *areas under a density curve*. Any density curve has area exactly 1 underneath it, corresponding to total probability 1. We first met density curves as models for data in Chapter 3 (page 64).

Really random digits

For purists, the RAND Corporation long ago published a book titled *One Million Random Digits*. The book lists 1,000,000 digits that were produced by a very elaborate physical randomization and really are random. An employee of RAND once told me that this is not the most boring book that RAND has ever published.

CONTINUOUS PROBABILITY MODEL

A **continuous probability model** assigns probabilities as areas under a density curve. The area under the curve and above any range of values is the probability of an outcome in that range.

EXAMPLE 10.8 *Random numbers*

The random number generator will spread its output uniformly across the entire interval from 0 to 1 as we allow it to generate a long sequence of numbers. The results of many trials are represented by the uniform density curve shown in Figure 10.4. This density curve has height 1 over the interval from 0 to 1. The area under the curve is 1, and the probability of any event is the area under the curve and above the event in question.

As Figure 10.4(a) illustrates, the probability that the random number generator produces a number between 0.3 and 0.7 is

$$P(0.3 \leq Y \leq 0.7) = 0.4$$

because the area under the density curve and above the interval from 0.3 to 0.7 is 0.4. The height of the curve is 1 and the area of a rectangle is the product of height and length, so the probability of any interval of outcomes is just the length of the interval.

Similarly,

$$P(Y \leq 0.5) = 0.5$$
$$P(Y > 0.8) = 0.2$$
$$P(Y \leq 0.5 \text{ or } Y > 0.8) = 0.7$$

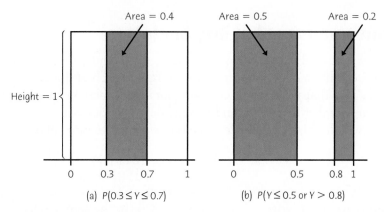

(a) $P(0.3 \leq Y \leq 0.7)$ (b) $P(Y \leq 0.5 \text{ or } Y > 0.8)$

FIGURE 10.4 Probability as area under a density curve. The uniform density curve spreads probability evenly between 0 and 1.

The last event consists of two nonoverlapping intervals, so the total area above the event is found by adding two areas, as illustrated by Figure 10.4(b). This assignment of probabilities obeys all of our rules for probability.

The probability model for a continuous random variable assigns probabilities to intervals of outcomes rather than to individual outcomes. In fact, *all continuous probability models assign probability 0 to every individual outcome.* Only intervals of values have positive probability. To see that this is true, consider a specific outcome such as $P(Y = 0.8)$ in Example 10.8. The probability of any interval is the same as its length. The point 0.8 has no length, so its probability is 0.

We can use any density curve to assign probabilities. The density curves that are most familiar to us are the Normal curves. So **Normal distributions are probability models.** There is a close connection between a Normal distribution as an idealized description for data and a Normal probability model. If we look at the heights of all young women, we find that they closely follow the Normal distribution with mean $\mu = 64$ inches and standard deviation $\sigma = 2.7$ inches. That is a distribution for a large set of data. Now choose one young woman at random. Call her height X. If we repeat the random choice very many times, the distribution of values of X is the same Normal distribution.

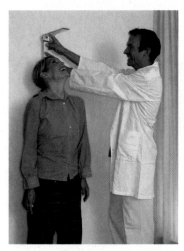

Henrik Sorensen/Getty Images

─ **EXAMPLE 10.9**   *The heights of young women* ─

What is the probability that a randomly chosen young woman has height between 68 and 70 inches? The height X of the woman we choose has the $N(64, 2.7)$ distribution. We want $P(68 \leq X \leq 70)$. Software or the *Normal Curve* applet will give us the answer at once.

We can also find the probability by standardizing and using Table A, the table of standard Normal probabilities. We will reserve capital Z for a standard Normal variable.

$$P(68 \leq X \leq 70) = P\left(\frac{68 - 64}{2.7} \leq \frac{X - 64}{2.7} \leq \frac{70 - 64}{2.7}\right)$$
$$= P(1.48 \leq Z \leq 2.22)$$
$$= 0.9868 - 0.9306 = 0.0562$$

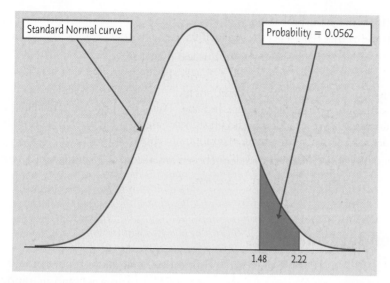

FIGURE 10.5 The probability in Example 10.9 as an area under the standard Normal curve.

Figure 10.5 shows the area under the standard Normal curve. The calculation is the same as those we did in Chapter 3. Only the language of probability is new.

APPLY YOUR KNOWLEDGE

10.13 Random numbers. Let X be a random number between 0 and 1 produced by the idealized random number generator described in Example 10.8 and Figure 10.4. Find the following probabilities:

(a) $P(X \le 0.4)$

(b) $P(X < 0.4)$

(c) $P(0.3 \le X \le 0.5)$

10.14 Adding random numbers. Generate two random numbers between 0 and 1 and take Y to be their sum. The sum Y can take any value between 0 and 2. The density curve of Y is the triangle shown in Figure 10.6.

(a) Verify by geometry that the area under this curve is 1.

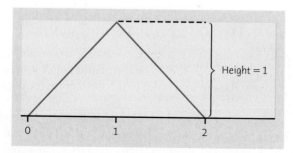

FIGURE 10.6 The density curve for the sum of two random numbers, for Exercise 10.14. This density curve spreads probability between 0 and 2.

(b) What is the probability that Y is less than 1? (Sketch the density curve, shade the area that represents the probability, then find that area. Do this for (c) also.)

(c) What is the probability that Y is less than 0.5?

10.15 **Iowa Test scores.** The Normal distribution with mean $\mu = 6.8$ and standard deviation $\sigma = 1.6$ is a good description of the Iowa Test vocabulary scores of seventh-grade students in Gary, Indiana. This is a continuous probability model for the score of a randomly chosen student. Figure 3.1 (page 65) pictures the density curve. Call the score of a randomly chosen student X for short.

(a) Write the event "the student chosen has a score of 10 or higher" in terms of X.

(b) Find the probability of this event.

Random variables

Examples 10.7 to 10.9 use a shorthand notation that is often convenient. In Example 10.9, we let X stand for the result of choosing a woman at random and measuring her height. We know that X would take a different value if we made another random choice. Because its value changes from one random choice to another, we call the height X a *random variable*.

RANDOM VARIABLE

A **random variable** is a variable whose value is a numerical outcome of a random phenomenon.

The **probability distribution** of a random variable X tells us what values X can take and how to assign probabilities to those values.

We usually denote random variables by capital letters near the end of the alphabet, such as X or Y. Of course, the random variables of greatest interest to us are outcomes such as the mean $\bar{x}$ of a random sample, for which we will keep the familiar notation. There are two main types of random variables, corresponding to two types of probability models: *discrete* and *continuous*.

EXAMPLE 10.10 Discrete and continuous random variables

The first digit X in Example 10.7 is a random variable whose possible values are the whole numbers {1, 2, 3, 4, 5, 6, 7, 8, 9}. The distribution of X assigns a probability to each of these outcomes. Random variables that have a finite list of possible outcomes are called **discrete**.

discrete random variable

Compare the output Y of the random number generator in Example 10.8. The values of Y fill the entire interval of numbers between 0 and 1. The probability distribution of Y is given by its density curve, shown in Figure 10.4. Random variables that can take on any value in an interval, with probabilities given as areas under a density curve, are called **continuous**.

continuous random variable

APPLY YOUR KNOWLEDGE

10.16 Grades in a statistics course. North Carolina State University posts the grade distributions for its courses online.[4] Students in Statistics 302 in the Spring 2005 semester received 45% A's, 35% B's, 16% C's, 2% D's, and 2% F's. Choose a Statistics 302 student at random. To "choose at random" means to give every student the same chance to be chosen. The student's grade on a four-point scale (with A = 4) is a discrete random variable X with this probability distribution:

Value of X	0	1	2	3	4
Probability	0.02	0.02	0.16	0.35	0.45

(a) Say in words what the meaning of $P(X \geq 3)$ is. What is this probability?

(b) Write the event "the student got a grade poorer than C" in terms of values of the random variable X. What is the probability of this event?

10.17 ACT scores. ACT scores for the 1,171,460 members of the 2004 high school graduating class who took the test closely follow the Normal distribution with mean 20.9 and standard deviation 4.8. Choose a student at random from this group and let Y be his or her ACT score. Write the event "the student's score was higher than 25" in terms of Y and find its probability.

Personal probability*

We began our discussion of probability with one idea: the probability of an outcome of a random phenomenon is the proportion of times that outcome would occur in a very long series of repetitions. This idea ties probability to actual outcomes. It allows us, for example, to estimate probabilities by simulating random phenomena. Yet we often meet another, quite different, idea of probability.

What are the odds?

Gamblers often express chance in terms of *odds* rather than probability. Odds of A to B against an outcome means that the probability of that outcome is $B/(A+B)$. So "odds of 5 to 1" is another way of saying "probability 1/6." A probability is always between 0 and 1, but odds range from 0 to infinity. Although odds are mainly used in gambling, they give us a way to make very small probabilities clearer. "Odds of 999 to 1" may be easier to understand than "probability 0.001."

─ **EXAMPLE 10.11** Joe and the Chicago Cubs ─

Joe sits staring into his beer as his favorite baseball team, the Chicago Cubs, loses another game. The Cubbies have some good young players, so let's ask Joe, "What's the chance that the Cubs will go to the World Series next year?" Joe brightens up. "Oh, about 10%," he says.

Does Joe assign probability 0.10 to the Cubs' appearing in the World Series? The outcome of next year's pennant race is certainly unpredictable, but we can't reasonably ask what would happen in many repetitions. Next year's baseball season will happen only once and will differ from all other seasons in players, weather, and many other ways. If probability measures "what would happen if we did this many times," Joe's 0.10 is not a probability. Probability is based on data about many repetitions of the same random phenomenon. Joe is giving us something else, his personal judgment.

*This section is optional.

Although Joe's 0.10 isn't a probability in our usual sense, it gives useful information about Joe's opinion. More seriously, a company asking, "How likely is it that building this plant will pay off within five years?" can't employ an idea of probability based on many repetitions of the same thing. The opinions of company officers and advisers are nonetheless useful information, and these opinions can be expressed in the language of probability. These are *personal probabilities*.

PERSONAL PROBABILITY

A **personal probability** of an outcome is a number between 0 and 1 that expresses an individual's judgment of how likely the outcome is.

Rachel's opinion about the Cubs may differ from Joe's, and the opinions of several company officers about the new plant may differ. Personal probabilities are indeed personal: they vary from person to person. Moreover, a personal probability can't be called right or wrong. If we say, "In the long run, this coin will come up heads 60% of the time," we can find out if we are right by actually tossing the coin several thousand times. If Joe says, "I think the Cubs have a 10% chance of going to the World Series next year," that's just Joe's opinion. Why think of personal probabilities as probabilities? Because any set of personal probabilities that makes sense obeys the same basic Rules 1 to 4 that describe any legitimate assignment of probabilities to events. If Joe thinks there's a 10% chance that the Cubs will go to the World Series, he must also think that there's a 90% chance that they won't go. There is just one set of rules of probability, even though we now have two interpretations of what probability means.

APPLY YOUR KNOWLEDGE

10.18 **Will you have an accident?**   The probability that a randomly chosen driver will be involved in an accident in the next year is about 0.2. This is based on the proportion of millions of drivers who have accidents. "Accident" includes things like crumpling a fender in your own driveway, not just highway accidents.

(a) What do you think is your own probability of being in an accident in the next year? This is a personal probability.

(b) Give some reasons why your personal probability might be a more accurate prediction of your "true chance" of having an accident than the probability for a random driver.

(c) Almost everyone says their personal probability is lower than the random driver probability. Why do you think this is true?

CHAPTER 10 SUMMARY

A **random phenomenon** has outcomes that we cannot predict but that nonetheless have a regular distribution in very many repetitions.

The **probability** of an event is the proportion of times the event occurs in many repeated trials of a random phenomenon.

A **probability model** for a random phenomenon consists of a sample space S and an assignment of probabilities P.

The **sample space** S is the set of all possible outcomes of the random phenomenon. Sets of outcomes are called **events.** P assigns a number $P(A)$ to an event A as its probability.

Any assignment of probability must obey the rules that state the basic properties of probability:

1. $0 \le P(A) \le 1$ for any event A.
2. $P(S) = 1$.
3. **Addition rule:** Events A and B are **disjoint** if they have no outcomes in common. If A and B are disjoint, then $P(A \text{ or } B) = P(A) + P(B)$.
4. For any event A, $P(A \text{ does not occur}) = 1 - P(A)$.

When a sample space S contains finitely many possible values, a **discrete probability model** assigns each of these values a probability between 0 and 1 such that the sum of all the probabilities is exactly 1. The probability of any event is the sum of the probabilities of all the values that make up the event.

A sample space can contain all values in some interval of numbers. A **continuous probability model** assigns probabilities as areas under a density curve. The probability of any event is the area under the curve above the values that make up the event.

A **random variable** is a variable taking numerical values determined by the outcome of a random phenomenon. The **probability distribution** of a random variable X tells us what the possible values of X are and how probabilities are assigned to those values.

A random variable X and its distribution can be **discrete** or **continuous.** A **discrete random variable** has finitely many possible values. Its distribution gives the probability of each value. A **continuous random variable** takes all values in some interval of numbers. A density curve describes the probability distribution of a continuous random variable.

CHECK YOUR SKILLS

10.19 You read in a book on poker that the probability of being dealt three of a kind in a five-card poker hand is 1/50. This means that

(a) if you deal thousands of poker hands, the fraction of them that contain three of a kind will be very close to 1/50.

(b) if you deal 50 poker hands, exactly 1 of them will contain three of a kind.

(c) if you deal 10,000 poker hands, exactly 200 of them will contain three of a kind.

10.20 A basketball player shoots 8 free throws during a game. The sample space for counting the number she makes is

(a) S = any number between 0 and 1.

(b) S = whole numbers 0 to 8.

(c) S = all sequences of 8 hits or misses, like HMMHHHMH.

Here is the probability model for the blood type of a randomly chosen person in the United States. Exercises 10.21 to 10.24 use this information.

Blood type	O	A	B	AB
Probability	0.45	0.40	0.11	?

10.21 This probability model is

(a) continuous.　(b) discrete.　(c) equally likely.

10.22 The probability that a randomly chosen American has type AB blood must be

(a) any number between 0 and 1.　(b) 0.04.　(c) 0.4.

10.23 Maria has type B blood. She can safely receive blood transfusions from people with blood types O and B. What is the probability that a randomly chosen American can donate blood to Maria?

(a) 0.11　(b) 0.44　(c) 0.56

10.24 What is the probability that a randomly chosen American does not have type O blood?

(a) 0.55　(b) 0.45　(c) 0.04

10.25 In a table of random digits such as Table B, each digit is equally likely to be any of 0, 1, 2, 3, 4, 5, 6, 7, 8, or 9. What is the probability that a digit in the table is a 0?

(a) 1/9　(b) 1/10　(c) 9/10

10.26 In a table of random digits such as Table B, each digit is equally likely to be any of 0, 1, 2, 3, 4, 5, 6, 7, 8, or 9. What is the probability that a digit in the table is 7 or greater?

(a) 7/10　(b) 4/10　(c) 3/10

10.27 Choose an American household at random and let the random variable X be the number of cars (including SUVs and light trucks) they own. Here is the probability model if we ignore the few households that own more than 5 cars:

Number of cars X	0	1	2	3	4	5
Probability	0.09	0.36	0.35	0.13	0.05	0.02

A housing company builds houses with two-car garages. What percent of households have more cars than the garage can hold?

(a) 20%　(b) 45%　(c) 55%

10.28 Choose a person at random and give him or her an IQ test. The result is a random variable Y. The probability distribution of Y is the Normal distribution with mean $\mu = 100$ and standard deviation $\sigma = 15$. The probability $P(Y > 120)$ that the person chosen has IQ score higher than 120 is about

(a) 0.908.　(b) 0.184.　(c) 0.092.

CHAPTER 10 EXERCISES

10.29 Nickels falling over. You may feel that it is obvious that the probability of a head in tossing a coin is about 1/2 because the coin has two faces. Such opinions are not always correct. Stand a nickel on edge on a hard, flat surface. Pound the surface with your hand so that the nickel falls over. What is the probability that it falls with heads upward? Make at least 50 trials to estimate the probability of a head.

10.30 Sample space. In each of the following situations, describe a sample space S for the random phenomenon.

(a) A basketball player shoots four free throws. You record the sequence of hits and misses.

(b) A basketball player shoots four free throws. You record the number of baskets she makes.

10.31 Probability models? In each of the following situations, state whether or not the given assignment of probabilities to individual outcomes is legitimate, that is, satisfies the rules of probability. If not, give specific reasons for your answer.

(a) Roll a die and record the count of spots on the up-face: $P(1) = 0$, $P(2) = 1/6$, $P(3) = 1/3$, $P(4) = 1/3$, $P(5) = 1/6$, $P(6) = 0$.

(b) Choose a college student at random and record sex and enrollment status: $P(\text{female full-time}) = 0.56$, $P(\text{female part-time}) = 0.24$, $P(\text{male full-time}) = 0.44$, $P(\text{male part-time}) = 0.17$.

(c) Deal a card from a shuffled deck: $P(\text{clubs}) = 12/52$, $P(\text{diamonds}) = 12/52$, $P(\text{hearts}) = 12/52$, $P(\text{spades}) = 16/52$.

10.32 Education among young adults. Choose a young adult (age 25 to 34) at random. The probability is 0.12 that the person chosen did not complete high school, 0.31 that the person has a high school diploma but no further education, and 0.29 that the person has at least a bachelor's degree.

(a) What must be the probability that a randomly chosen young adult has some education beyond high school but does not have a bachelor's degree?

(b) What is the probability that a randomly chosen young adult has at least a high school education?

10.33 Deaths on the job. Government data on job-related deaths assign a single occupation to each such death that occurs in the United States. The data show that the probability is 0.134 that a randomly chosen death was agriculture-related, and 0.119 that it was manufacturing-related. What is the probability that a death was either agriculture-related or manufacturing-related? What is the probability that the death was related to some other occupation?

10.34 Loaded dice. There are many ways to produce crooked dice. To *load* a die so that 6 comes up too often and 1 (which is opposite 6) comes up too seldom, add a bit of lead to the filling of the spot on the 1 face. If a die is loaded so that 6 comes up with probability 0.2 and the probabilities of the 2, 3, 4, and 5 faces are not affected, what is the assignment of probabilities to the six faces?

10.35 What probability doesn't say. The idea of probability is that the *proportion* of heads in many tosses of a balanced coin eventually gets close to 0.5. But does the actual *count* of heads get close to one-half the number of tosses? Let's find out. Set the "Probability of heads" in the *Probability* applet to 0.5 and the number of tosses

APPLET

to 40. You can extend the number of tosses by clicking "Toss" again to get 40 more. Don't click "Reset" during this exercise.

(a) After 40 tosses, what is the proportion of heads? What is the count of heads? What is the difference between the count of heads and 20 (one-half the number of tosses)?

(b) Keep going to 120 tosses. Again record the proportion and count of heads and the difference between the count and 60 (half the number of tosses).

(c) Keep going. Stop at 240 tosses and again at 480 tosses to record the same facts. Although it may take a long time, the laws of probability say that the proportion of heads will always get close to 0.5 and also that the difference between the count of heads and half the number of tosses will always grow without limit.

10.36 **A door prize.** A party host gives a door prize to one guest chosen at random. There are 48 men and 42 women at the party. What is the probability that the prize goes to a woman? Explain how you arrived at your answer.

10.37 **Land in Canada.** Canada's national statistics agency, Statistics Canada, says that the land area of Canada is 9,094,000 square kilometers. Of this land, 4,176,000 square kilometers are forested. Choose a square kilometer of land in Canada at random.

(a) What is the probability that the area you choose is forested?

(b) What is the probability that it is not forested?

10.38 **Foreign language study.** Choose a student in grades 9 to 12 at random and ask if he or she is studying a language other than English. Here is the distribution of results:

Keith Gunnar/Getty Images

Language	Spanish	French	German	All others	None
Probability	0.26	0.09	0.03	0.03	0.59

(a) Explain why this is a legitimate probability model.

(b) What is the probability that a randomly chosen student is studying a language other than English?

(c) What is the probability that a randomly chosen student is studying French, German, or Spanish?

10.39 **Car colors.** Choose a new car or light truck at random and note its color. Here are the probabilities of the most popular colors for vehicles made in North America in 2005:[5]

Color	Silver	White	Gray	Blue	Black	Red
Probability	0.18	0.17	0.15	0.12	0.11	0.11

(a) What is the probability that the vehicle you choose has any color other than the six listed?

(b) What is the probability that a randomly chosen vehicle is neither silver nor white?

10.40 **Colors of M&M's.**   If you draw an M&M candy at random from a bag of the candies, the candy you draw will have one of six colors. The probability of drawing each color depends on the proportion of each color among all candies made. Here is the distribution for milk chocolate M&M's:[6]

Color	Yellow	Red	Orange	Brown	Green	Blue
Probability	0.14	0.13	0.20	0.13	0.16	?

(a) What must be the probability of drawing a blue candy?

(b) What is the probability that you do not draw a brown candy?

(c) What is the probability that the candy you draw is either yellow, orange, or red?

10.41 **More M&M's.**   You can create your own custom blend of M&M's, with 21 colors to choose from. Cindy chooses equal numbers of teal, aqua green, light blue, dark blue, and light purple. When you choose a candy at random from Cindy's custom blend, what is the probability for each color?

10.42 **Race and ethnicity.**   The 2000 census allowed each person to choose from a long list of races. That is, in the eyes of the Census Bureau, you belong to whatever race you say you belong to. "Hispanic/Latino" is a separate category; Hispanics may be of any race. If we choose a resident of the United States at random, the 2000 census gives these probabilities:

	Hispanic	Not Hispanic
Asian	0.000	0.036
Black	0.003	0.121
White	0.060	0.691
Other	0.062	0.027

(a) Verify that this is a legitimate assignment of probabilities.

(b) What is the probability that a randomly chosen American is Hispanic?

(c) Non-Hispanic whites are the historical majority in the United States. What is the probability that a randomly chosen American is not a member of this group?

10.43 **Spelling errors.**   Spell-checking software catches "nonword errors" that result in a string of letters that is not a word, as when "the" is typed as "teh." When undergraduates are asked to type a 250-word essay (without spell-checking), the number X of nonword errors has the following distribution:

Value of X	0	1	2	3	4
Probability	0.1	0.2	0.3	0.3	0.1

(a) Is the random variable X discrete or continuous? Why?

(b) Write the event "at least one nonword error" in terms of X. What is the probability of this event?

(c) Describe the event $X \le 2$ in words. What is its probability? What is the probability that $X < 2$?

10.44 First digits again. A crook who never heard of Benford's law might choose the first digits of his faked invoices so that all of 1, 2, 3, 4, 5, 6, 7, 8, and 9 are equally likely. Call the first digit of a randomly chosen fake invoice W for short.

(a) Write the probability distribution for the random variable W.

(b) Find $P(W \ge 6)$ and compare your result with the Benford's law probability from Example 10.7.

10.45 Who goes to Paris? Abby, Deborah, Mei-Ling, Sam, and Roberto work in a firm's public relations office. Their employer must choose two of them to attend a conference in Paris. To avoid unfairness, the choice will be made by drawing two names from a hat. (This is an SRS of size 2.)

(a) Write down all possible choices of two of the five names. This is the sample space.

(b) The random drawing makes all choices equally likely. What is the probability of each choice?

(c) What is the probability that Mei-Ling is chosen?

(d) What is the probability that neither of the two men (Sam and Roberto) is chosen?

10.46 Birth order. A couple plans to have three children. There are 8 possible arrangements of girls and boys. For example, GGB means the first two children are girls and the third child is a boy. All 8 arrangements are (approximately) equally likely.

(a) Write down all 8 arrangements of the sexes of three children. What is the probability of any one of these arrangements?

(b) Let X be the number of girls the couple has. What is the probability that $X = 2$?

(c) Starting from your work in (a), find the distribution of X. That is, what values can X take, and what are the probabilities for each value?

10.47 Unusual dice. Nonstandard dice can produce interesting distributions of outcomes. You have two balanced, six-sided dice. One is a standard die, with faces having 1, 2, 3, 4, 5, and 6 spots. The other die has three faces with 0 spots and three faces with 6 spots. Find the probability distribution for the total number of spots Y on the up-faces when you roll these two dice. (*Hint:* Start with a picture like Figure 10.2 for the possible up-faces. Label the three 0 faces on the second die 0a, 0b, 0c in your picture, and similarly distinguish the three 6 faces.)

10.48 Random numbers. Many random number generators allow users to specify the range of the random numbers to be produced. Suppose that you specify that the random number Y can take any value between 0 and 2. Then the density curve of the outcomes has constant height between 0 and 2, and height 0 elsewhere.

(a) Is the random variable Y discrete or continuous? Why?

(b) What is the height of the density curve between 0 and 2? Draw a graph of the density curve.

(c) Use your graph from (b) and the fact that probability is area under the curve to find $P(Y \le 1)$.

10.49 Did you vote?   A sample survey contacted an SRS of 663 registered voters in Oregon shortly after an election and asked respondents whether they had voted. Voter records show that 56% of registered voters had actually voted. We will see later that in this situation the proportion of the sample who voted (call this proportion $\hat{p}$) has approximately the Normal distribution with mean $\mu = 0.56$ and standard deviation $\sigma = 0.019$.

(a) If the respondents answer truthfully, what is $P(0.52 \leq \hat{p} \leq 0.60)$? This is the probability that the sample proportion $\hat{p}$ estimates the population proportion 0.56 within plus or minus 0.04.

(b) In fact, 72% of the respondents said they had voted ($\hat{p} = 0.72$). If respondents answer truthfully, what is $P(\hat{p} \geq 0.72)$? This probability is so small that it is good evidence that some people who did not vote claimed that they did vote.

10.50 More random numbers.   Find these probabilities as areas under the density curve you sketched in Exercise 10.48.

(a) $P(0.5 < Y < 1.3)$.

(b) $P(Y \geq 0.8)$.

10.51 NAEP math scores.   Scores on the latest National Assessment of Educational Progress 12th-grade mathematics test were approximately Normal with mean 300 points (out of 500 possible) and standard deviation 35 points. Let Y stand for the score of a randomly chosen student. Express each of the following events in terms of Y and use the 68–95–99.7 rule to give the approximate probability.

(a) The student has a score above 300.

(b) The student's score is above 370.

10.52 Playing Pick 4.   The Pick 4 games in many state lotteries announce a four-digit winning number each day. The winning number is essentially a four-digit group from a table of random digits. You win if your choice matches the winning digits. Suppose your chosen number is 5974.

(a) What is the probability that your number matches the winning number exactly?

(b) What is the probability that your number matches the digits in the winning number *in any order*?

AP Photo/Nick Ut

10.53 Friends.   How many close friends do you have? Suppose that the number of close friends adults claim to have varies from person to person with mean $\mu = 9$ and standard deviation $\sigma = 2.5$. An opinion poll asks this question of an SRS of 1100 adults. We will see later that in this situation the sample mean response $\bar{x}$ has approximately the Normal distribution with mean 9 and standard deviation 0.075. What is $P(8.9 \leq \bar{x} \leq 9.1)$, the probability that the sample result $\bar{x}$ estimates the population truth $\mu = 9$ to within ± 0.1?

10.54 Playing Pick 4, continued.   The Wisconsin version of Pick 4 pays out $5000 on a $1 bet if your number matches the winning number exactly. It pays $200 on a $1 bet if the digits in your number match those of the winning number in any order. You choose which of these two bets to make. On the average over many bets, your winnings will be

$$\text{mean amount won} = \text{payout amount} \times \text{probability of winning}$$

What are the mean payout amounts for these two bets? Is one of the two bets a better choice?

10.55 Shaq's free throws. The basketball player Shaquille O'Neal makes about half of his free throws over an entire season. Use the *Probability* applet or software to simulate 100 free throws shot by a player who has probability 0.5 of making each shot. (In most software, the key phrase to look for is "Bernoulli trials." This is the technical term for independent trials with Yes/No outcomes. Our outcomes here are "Hit" and "Miss.")

(a) What percent of the 100 shots did he hit?

(b) Examine the sequence of hits and misses. How long was the longest run of shots made? Of shots missed? (Sequences of random outcomes often show runs longer than our intuition thinks likely.)

10.56 Simulating an opinion poll. A recent opinion poll showed that about 65% of the American public have a favorable opinion of the software company Microsoft. Suppose that this is exactly true. Choosing a person at random then has probability 0.65 of getting one who has a favorable opinion of Microsoft. Use the *Probability* applet or your statistical software to simulate choosing many people at random. (In most software, the key phrase to look for is "Bernoulli trials." This is the technical term for independent trials with Yes/No outcomes. Our outcomes here are "Favorable" or not.)

(a) Simulate drawing 20 people, then 80 people, then 320 people. What proportion has a favorable opinion of Microsoft in each case? We expect (but because of chance variation we can't be sure) that the proportion will be closer to 0.65 in longer runs of trials.

(b) Simulate drawing 20 people 10 times and record the percents in each sample who have a favorable opinion of Microsoft. Then simulate drawing 320 people 10 times and again record the 10 percents. Which set of 10 results is less variable? We expect the results of samples of size 320 to be more predictable (less variable) than the results of samples of size 20. That is "long-run regularity" showing itself.

Gandee Vasan/Getty Images

Sampling Distributions

How much on the average do American households earn? The government's Current Population Survey contacted a sample of 113,146 households in March 2005. Their mean income in 2004 was $\bar{x} = \$60,528$.[1] That \$60,528 describes the sample, but we use it to estimate the mean income of all households. This is an example of statistical inference: we use information from a sample to infer something about a wider population.

Because the results of random samples and randomized comparative experiments include an element of chance, we can't guarantee that our inferences are correct. What we can guarantee is that our methods usually give correct answers. We will see that the reasoning of statistical inference rests on asking, "How often would this method give a correct answer if I used it very many times?" If our data come from random sampling or randomized comparative experiments, the laws of probability answer the question "What would happen if we did this many times?" This chapter presents some facts about probability that help answer this question.

Parameters and statistics

As we begin to use sample data to draw conclusions about a wider population, we must take care to keep straight whether a number describes a sample or a population. Here is the vocabulary we use.

PARAMETER, STATISTIC

A **parameter** is a number that describes the population. In statistical practice, the value of a parameter is not known because we cannot examine the entire population.

A **statistic** is a number that can be computed from the sample data without making use of any unknown parameters. In practice, we often use a statistic to estimate an unknown parameter.

EXAMPLE 11.1   Household income

The mean income of the sample of households contacted by the Current Population Survey was $\overline{x} = \$60,528$. The number $60,528 is a *statistic* because it describes this one Current Population Survey sample. The population that the poll wants to draw conclusions about is all 113 million U.S. households. The *parameter* of interest is the mean income of all of these households. We don't know the value of this parameter.

Remember: **s**tatistics come from **s**amples, and **p**arameters come from **p**opulations. As long as we were just doing data analysis, the distinction between population and sample was not important. Now, however, it is essential. The notation we use must reflect this distinction. We write μ (the Greek letter mu) for the **mean of a population.** This is a fixed parameter that is unknown when we use a sample for inference. The **mean of the sample** is the familiar $\overline{x}$, the average of the observations in the sample. This is a statistic that would almost certainly take a different value if we chose another sample from the same population. The sample mean $\overline{x}$ from a sample or an experiment is an estimate of the mean μ of the underlying population.

population mean μ

sample mean $\overline{x}$

Simon Marcus/CORBIS

APPLY YOUR KNOWLEDGE

11.1 **Effects of caffeine.**   How does caffeine affect our bodies? In a matched pairs experiment, subjects pushed a button as quickly as they could after taking a caffeine pill and also after taking a placebo pill. The mean pushes per minute were **283** for the placebo and **311** for caffeine. Is each of the boldface numbers a parameter or a statistic?

11.2 **Indianapolis voters.**   Voter registration records show that **68%** of all voters in Indianapolis are registered as Republicans. To test a random digit dialing device, you use the device to call 150 randomly chosen residential telephones in Indianapolis. Of the registered voters contacted, **73%** are registered Republicans. Is each of the boldface numbers a parameter or a statistic?

11.3 **Inspecting bearings.**   A carload lot of bearings has mean diameter **2.5003** centimeters (cm). This is within the specifications for acceptance of the lot by the purchaser. By chance, an inspector chooses 100 bearings from the lot that have mean diameter **2.5009** cm. Because this is outside the specified limits, the lot is mistakenly rejected. Is each of the boldface numbers a parameter or a statistic?

Statistical estimation and the law of large numbers

Statistical inference uses sample data to draw conclusions about the entire population. Because good samples are chosen randomly, statistics such as $\bar{x}$ are random variables. We can describe the behavior of a sample statistic by a probability model that answers the question "What would happen if we did this many times?" Here is an example that will lead us toward the probability ideas most important for statistical inference.

High-tech gambling

There are more than 640,000 slot machines in the United States. Once upon a time, you put in a coin and pulled the lever to spin three wheels, each with 20 symbols. No longer. Now the machines are video games with flashy graphics and outcomes produced by random number generators. Machines can accept many coins at once, can pay off on a bewildering variety of outcomes, and can be networked to allow common jackpots. Gamblers still search for systems, but in the long run the law of large numbers guarantees the house its 5% profit.

EXAMPLE 11.2 Does this wine smell bad?

Sulfur compounds such as dimethyl sulfide (DMS) are sometimes present in wine. DMS causes "off-odors" in wine, so winemakers want to know the odor threshold, the lowest concentration of DMS that the human nose can detect. Different people have different thresholds, so we start by asking about the mean threshold μ in the population of all adults. The number μ is a parameter that describes this population.

To estimate μ, we present tasters with both natural wine and the same wine spiked with DMS at different concentrations to find the lowest concentration at which they identify the spiked wine. Here are the odor thresholds (measured in micrograms of DMS per liter of wine) for 10 randomly chosen subjects:

$$28 \quad 40 \quad 28 \quad 33 \quad 20 \quad 31 \quad 29 \quad 27 \quad 17 \quad 21$$

The mean threshold for these subjects is $\bar{x} = 27.4$. It seems reasonable to use the sample result $\bar{x} = 27.4$ to estimate the unknown μ. An SRS should fairly represent the population, so the mean $\bar{x}$ of the sample should be somewhere near the mean μ of the population. Of course, we don't expect $\bar{x}$ to be exactly equal to μ. We realize that if we choose another SRS, the luck of the draw will probably produce a different $\bar{x}$.

If $\bar{x}$ is rarely exactly right and varies from sample to sample, why is it nonetheless a reasonable estimate of the population mean μ? Here is one answer: if we keep on taking larger and larger samples, the statistic $\bar{x}$ is *guaranteed* to get closer and closer to the parameter μ. We have the comfort of knowing that if we can afford to keep on measuring more subjects, eventually we will estimate the mean odor threshold of all adults very accurately. This remarkable fact is called the *law of large numbers*. It is remarkable because it holds for *any* population, not just for some special class such as Normal distributions.

LAW OF LARGE NUMBERS

Draw observations at random from any population with finite mean μ. As the number of observations drawn increases, the mean $\bar{x}$ of the observed values gets closer and closer to the mean μ of the population.

The law of large numbers can be proved mathematically starting from the basic laws of probability. The behavior of $\bar{x}$ is similar to the idea of probability. In the long run, the *proportion* of outcomes taking any value gets close to the probability of that value, and the *average* outcome gets close to the population mean. Figure 10.1 (page 248) shows how proportions approach probability in one example. Here is an example of how sample means approach the population mean.

EXAMPLE 11.3   The law of large numbers in action

In fact, the distribution of odor thresholds among all adults has mean 25. The mean $\mu = 25$ is the true value of the parameter we seek to estimate. Figure 11.1 shows how the sample mean $\bar{x}$ of an SRS drawn from this population changes as we add more subjects to our sample.

The first subject in Example 11.2 had threshold 28, so the line in Figure 11.1 starts there. The mean for the first two subjects is

$$\bar{x} = \frac{28 + 40}{2} = 34$$

This is the second point on the graph. At first, the graph shows that the mean of the sample changes as we take more observations. Eventually, however, the mean of the observations gets close to the population mean $\mu = 25$ and settles down at that value.

If we started over, again choosing people at random from the population, we would get a different path from left to right in Figure 11.1. The law of large numbers says that whatever path we get will always settle down at 25 as we draw more and more people.

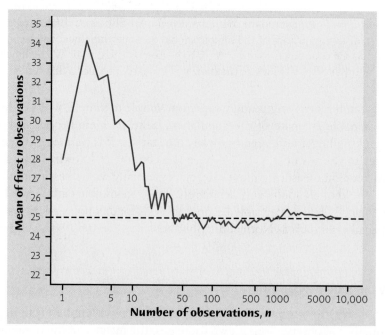

FIGURE 11.1 The law of large numbers in action: as we take more observations, the sample mean $\bar{x}$ always approaches the mean μ of the population.

The *Law of Large Numbers* applet animates Figure 11.1 in a different setting. You can use the applet to watch $\overline{x}$ change as you average more observations until it eventually settles down at the mean μ.

The law of large numbers is the foundation of such business enterprises as gambling casinos and insurance companies. The winnings (or losses) of a gambler on a few plays are uncertain—that's why gambling is exciting. In Figure 11.1, the mean of even 100 observations is not yet very close to μ. It is only *in the long run* that the mean outcome is predictable. The house plays tens of thousands of times. So the house, unlike individual gamblers, can count on the long-run regularity described by the law of large numbers. The average winnings of the house on tens of thousands of plays will be very close to the mean of the distribution of winnings. Needless to say, this mean guarantees the house a profit. That's why gambling can be a business.

APPLY YOUR KNOWLEDGE

11.4　Means in action.　Figure 11.1 shows how the mean of n observations behaves as we keep adding more observations to those already in hand. The first 10 observations are given in Example 11.2. Demonstrate that you grasp the idea of Figure 11.1: find the means of the first one, two, three, four, and five of these observations and plot the successive means against n. Verify that your plot agrees with the first part of the plot in Figure 11.1.

11.5　Insurance.　The idea of insurance is that we all face risks that are unlikely but carry high cost. Think of a fire destroying your home. Insurance spreads the risk: we all pay a small amount, and the insurance policy pays a large amount to those few of us whose homes burn down. An insurance company looks at the records for millions of homeowners and sees that the mean loss from fire in a year is $\mu = \$250$ per person. (Most of us have no loss, but a few lose their homes. The $250 is the average loss.) The company plans to sell fire insurance for $250 plus enough to cover its costs and profit. Explain clearly why it would be unwise to sell only 12 policies. Then explain why selling thousands of such policies is a safe business.

Sampling distributions

The law of large numbers assures us that if we measure enough subjects, the statistic $\overline{x}$ will eventually get very close to the unknown parameter μ. But our study in Example 11.2 had just 10 subjects. What can we say about $\overline{x}$ from 10 subjects as an estimate of μ? We ask: "What would happen if we took many samples of 10 subjects from this population?" Here's how to answer this question:

- Take a large number of samples of size 10 from the population.
- Calculate the sample mean $\overline{x}$ for each sample.
- Make a histogram of the values of $\overline{x}$.
- Examine the distribution displayed in the histogram for shape, center, and spread, as well as outliers or other deviations.

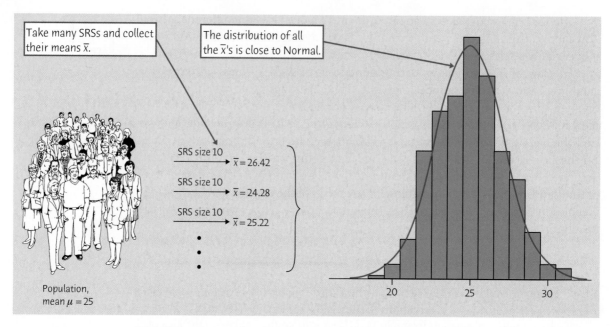

FIGURE 11.2 The idea of a sampling distribution: take many samples from the same population, collect the $\bar{x}$'s from all the samples, and display the distribution of the $\bar{x}$'s. The histogram shows the results of 1000 samples.

simulation

In practice it is too expensive to take many samples from a large population such as all adult U.S. residents. But we can imitate many samples by using software. Using software to imitate chance behavior is called **simulation.**

> **EXAMPLE 11.4**   What would happen in many samples?
>
> Extensive studies have found that the DMS odor threshold of adults follows roughly a Normal distribution with mean $\mu = 25$ micrograms per liter and standard deviation $\sigma = 7$ micrograms per liter. With this information, we can simulate many repetitions of Example 11.2 with different subjects drawn at random from the population.
>
> Figure 11.2 illustrates the process of choosing many samples and finding the sample mean threshold $\bar{x}$ for each one. Follow the flow of the figure from the population at the left, to choosing an SRS and finding the $\bar{x}$ for this sample, to collecting together the $\bar{x}$'s from many samples. The first sample has $\bar{x} = 26.42$. The second sample contains a different 10 people, with $\bar{x} = 24.28$, and so on. The histogram at the right of the figure shows the distribution of the values of $\bar{x}$ from 1000 separate SRSs of size 10. This histogram displays the *sampling distribution* of the statistic $\bar{x}$.

SAMPLING DISTRIBUTION

The **sampling distribution** of a statistic is the distribution of values taken by the statistic in all possible samples of the same size from the same population.

Strictly speaking, the sampling distribution is the ideal pattern that would emerge if we looked at all possible samples of size 10 from our population. A distribution obtained from a fixed number of trials, like the 1000 trials in Figure 11.2, is only an approximation to the sampling distribution. One of the uses of probability theory in statistics is to obtain exact sampling distributions without simulation. The interpretation of a sampling distribution is the same, however, whether we obtain it by simulation or by the mathematics of probability.

We can use the tools of data analysis to describe any distribution. Let's apply those tools to Figure 11.2. What can we say about the shape, center, and spread of this distribution?

- **Shape:** It looks Normal! Detailed examination confirms that the distribution of $\bar{x}$ from many samples does have a distribution that is very close to Normal.
- **Center:** The mean of the 1000 $\bar{x}$'s is 24.95. That is, the distribution is centered very close to the population mean $\mu = 25$.
- **Spread:** The standard deviation of the 1000 $\bar{x}$'s is 2.217, notably smaller than the standard deviation $\sigma = 7$ of the population of individual subjects.

Although these results describe just one simulation of a sampling distribution, they reflect facts that are true whenever we use random sampling.

APPLY YOUR KNOWLEDGE

11.6 **Generating a sampling distribution.** Let's illustrate the idea of a sampling distribution in the case of a very small sample from a very small population. The population is the scores of 10 students on an exam:

Student	0	1	2	3	4	5	6	7	8	9
Score	82	62	80	58	72	73	65	66	74	62

The parameter of interest is the mean score μ in this population. The sample is an SRS of size $n = 4$ drawn from the population. Because the students are labeled 0 to 9, a single random digit from Table B chooses one student for the sample.

(a) Find the mean of the 10 scores in the population. This is the population mean μ.

(b) Use the first digits in row 116 of Table B to draw an SRS of size 4 from this population. What are the four scores in your sample? What is their mean $\bar{x}$? This statistic is an estimate of μ.

(c) Repeat this process 9 more times, using the first digits in rows 117 to 125 of Table B. Make a histogram of the 10 values of $\bar{x}$. You are

Rigging the lottery

We have all seen televised lottery drawings in which numbered balls bubble about and are randomly popped out by air pressure. How might we rig such a drawing? In 1980, when the Pennsylvania lottery used just three balls, a drawing was rigged by the host and several stagehands. They injected paint into all balls bearing 8 of the 10 digits. This weighed them down and guaranteed that all three balls for the winning number would have the remaining 2 digits. The perps then bet on all combinations of these digits. When 6-6-6 popped out, they won $1.2 million. Yes, they were caught.

unbiased estimator

constructing the sampling distribution of $\overline{x}$. Is the center of your histogram close to μ?

The sampling distribution of $\overline{x}$

Figure 11.2 suggests that when we choose many SRSs from a population, the sampling distribution of the sample means is centered at the mean of the original population and less spread out than the distribution of individual observations. Here are the facts.

MEAN AND STANDARD DEVIATION OF A SAMPLE MEAN [2]

Suppose that $\overline{x}$ is the mean of an SRS of size n drawn from a large population with mean μ and standard deviation σ. Then the sampling distribution of $\overline{x}$ has **mean μ** and **standard deviation $\sigma/\sqrt{n}$.**

These facts about the mean and the standard deviation of the sampling distribution of $\overline{x}$ are true for *any* population, not just for some special class such as Normal distributions. Both facts have important implications for statistical inference.

- The mean of the statistic $\overline{x}$ is always equal to the mean μ of the population. That is, the sampling distribution of $\overline{x}$ is centered at μ. In repeated sampling, $\overline{x}$ will sometimes fall above the true value of the parameter μ and sometimes below, but there is no systematic tendency to overestimate or underestimate the parameter. This makes the idea of lack of bias in the sense of "no favoritism" more precise. Because the mean of $\overline{x}$ is equal to μ, we say that the statistic $\overline{x}$ is an **unbiased estimator** of the parameter μ.

- An unbiased estimator is "correct on the average" in many samples. How close the estimator falls to the parameter in most samples is determined by the spread of the sampling distribution. If individual observations have standard deviation σ, then sample means $\overline{x}$ from samples of size n have standard deviation $\sigma/\sqrt{n}$. That is, **averages are less variable than individual observations.**

We have described the center and spread of the sampling distribution of a sample mean $\overline{x}$, but not its shape. The shape of the distribution of $\overline{x}$ depends on the shape of the population. Here is one important case: if measurements in the population follow a Normal distribution, then so does the sample mean.

SAMPLING DISTRIBUTION OF A SAMPLE MEAN

If individual observations have the $N(\mu, \sigma)$ distribution, then the sample mean $\overline{x}$ of an SRS of size n has the $N(\mu, \sigma/\sqrt{n})$ distribution.

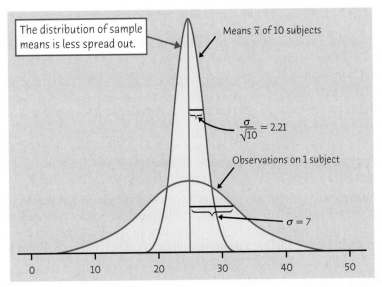

The distribution of sample means is less spread out.

Means $\overline{x}$ of 10 subjects

$\dfrac{\sigma}{\sqrt{10}} = 2.21$

Observations on 1 subject

$\sigma = 7$

FIGURE 11.3 The distribution of single observations compared with the distribution of the means $\overline{x}$ of 10 observations. Averages are less variable than individual observations.

EXAMPLE 11.5 *Population distribution, sampling distribution*

If we measure the DMS odor thresholds of individual adults, the values follow the Normal distribution with mean $\mu = 25$ micrograms per liter and standard deviation $\sigma = 7$ micrograms per liter. We call this the **population distribution** because it shows how measurements vary within the population.

population distribution

    Take many SRSs of size 10 from this population and find the sample mean $\overline{x}$ for each sample, as in Figure 11.2. The *sampling distribution* describes how the values of $\overline{x}$ vary among samples. That sampling distribution is also Normal, with mean $\mu = 25$ and standard deviation

$$\frac{\sigma}{\sqrt{n}} = \frac{7}{\sqrt{10}} = 2.2136$$

Figure 11.3 contrasts these two Normal distributions. Both are centered at the population mean, but sample means are much less variable than individual observations.

    Not only is the standard deviation of the distribution of $\overline{x}$ smaller than the standard deviation of individual observations, but it gets smaller as we take larger samples. **The results of large samples are less variable than the results of small samples.** If n is large, the standard deviation of $\overline{x}$ is small, and almost all samples will give values of $\overline{x}$ that lie very close to the true parameter μ. That is, the sample mean from a large sample can be trusted to estimate the population mean accurately. *However, the standard deviation of the sampling distribution gets smaller only at the rate $\sqrt{n}$. To cut the standard deviation of $\overline{x}$ in half, we must take four times as many observations, not just twice as many.*

CAUTION

APPLY YOUR KNOWLEDGE

11.7   A sample of teens.   A study of the health of teenagers plans to measure the blood cholesterol level of an SRS of youths aged 13 to 16. The researchers will report the mean $\bar{x}$ from their sample as an estimate of the mean cholesterol level μ in this population.

(a) Explain to someone who knows no statistics what it means to say that $\bar{x}$ is an "unbiased" estimator of μ.

(b) The sample result $\bar{x}$ is an unbiased estimator of the population truth μ no matter what size SRS the study uses. Explain to someone who knows no statistics why a large sample gives more trustworthy results than a small sample.

11.8   Measurements in the lab.   Juan makes a measurement in a chemistry laboratory and records the result in his lab report. The standard deviation of students' lab measurements is $\sigma = 10$ milligrams. Juan repeats the measurement 3 times and records the mean $\bar{x}$ of his 3 measurements.

(a) What is the standard deviation of Juan's mean result? (That is, if Juan kept on making 3 measurements and averaging them, what would be the standard deviation of all his $\bar{x}$'s?)

(b) How many times must Juan repeat the measurement to reduce the standard deviation of $\bar{x}$ to 5? Explain to someone who knows no statistics the advantage of reporting the average of several measurements rather than the result of a single measurement.

11.9   National math scores.   The scores of 12th-grade students on the National Assessment of Educational Progress year 2000 mathematics test have a distribution that is approximately Normal with mean $\mu = 300$ and standard deviation $\sigma = 35$.

(a) Choose one 12th-grader at random. What is the probability that his or her score is higher than 300? Higher than 335?

(b) Now choose an SRS of four 12th-graders and calculate their mean score $\bar{x}$. If you did this many times, what would be the mean and standard deviation of all the $\bar{x}$-values?

(c) What is the probability that the mean score for your SRS is higher than 300? Higher than 335?

The central limit theorem

The facts about the mean and standard deviation of $\bar{x}$ are true no matter what the shape of the population distribution may be. But what is the shape of the sampling distribution when the population distribution is not Normal? It is a remarkable fact that as the sample size increases, the distribution of $\bar{x}$ changes shape: it looks less like that of the population and more like a Normal distribution. When the sample is large enough, the distribution of $\bar{x}$ is very close to Normal. This is true no matter what shape the population distribution has, as long as the population has a finite standard deviation σ. This famous fact of probability theory is called the *central limit theorem*. It is much more useful than the fact that the distribution of $\bar{x}$ is exactly Normal if the population is exactly Normal.

> ## CENTRAL LIMIT THEOREM
>
> Draw an SRS of size n from any population with mean μ and finite standard deviation σ. When n is large, the sampling distribution of the sample mean $\overline{x}$ is approximately Normal:
>
> $$\overline{x} \text{ is approximately } N\left(\mu, \frac{\sigma}{\sqrt{n}}\right)$$
>
> The central limit theorem allows us to use Normal probability calculations to answer questions about sample means from many observations even when the population distribution is not Normal.

More general versions of the central limit theorem say that the distribution of any sum or average of many small random quantities is close to Normal. This is true even if the quantities are correlated with each other (as long as they are not too highly correlated) and even if they have different distributions (as long as no one random quantity is so large that it dominates the others). The central limit theorem suggests why the Normal distributions are common models for observed data. Any variable that is a sum of many small influences will have approximately a Normal distribution.

How large a sample size n is needed for $\overline{x}$ to be close to Normal depends on the population distribution. More observations are required if the shape of the population distribution is far from Normal. Here are two examples in which the population is far from Normal.

EXAMPLE 11.6 The central limit theorem in action ————

In March 2004, the Current Population Survey contacted 98,789 households. Figure 11.4(a) is a histogram of the earnings of the 62,101 households that had earned income greater than zero in 2003. As we expect, the distribution of earned incomes is strongly skewed to the right and very spread out. The right tail of the distribution is longer than the histogram shows because there are too few high incomes for their bars to be visible on this scale. In fact, we cut off the earnings scale at $300,000 to save space—a few households earned even more than $300,000. The mean earnings for these 62,101 households was $57,085.

Regard these 62,101 households as a population. Take an SRS of 100 households. The mean earnings in this sample is $\overline{x} = \$48,600$. That's less than the mean of the population. Take another SRS of size 100. The mean for this sample is $\overline{x} = \$64,766$. That's higher than the mean of the population. *What would happen if we did this many times?* Figure 11.4(b) is a histogram of the mean earnings for 500 samples, each of size 100. The scales in Figures 11.4(a) and 11.4(b) are the same, for easy comparison. Although the distribution of individual earnings is skewed and very spread out, the distribution of sample means is roughly symmetric and much less spread out.

Figure 11.4(c) zooms in on the center part of the axis for another histogram of the same 500 values of $\overline{x}$. Although $n = 100$ is not a very large sample size and the

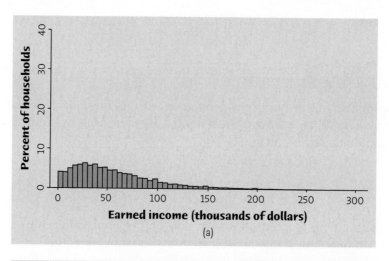

(a)

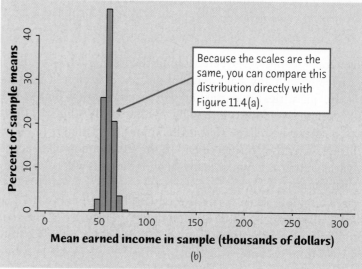

Because the scales are the same, you can compare this distribution directly with Figure 11.4(a).

(b)

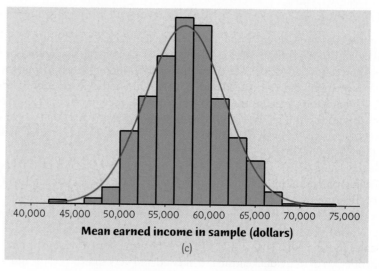

(c)

FIGURE 11.4 The central limit theorem in action. **(a)** The distribution of earned income in a population of 62,101 households. **(b)** The distribution of the mean earnings for 500 SRSs of 100 households each from this population. **(c)** The distribution of the sample means in more detail: the shape is close to Normal.

population distribution is extremely skewed, we can see that the distribution of sample means is close to Normal.

Comparing Figures 11.4(a) and 11.4(b) illustrates the two most important ideas of this chapter.

THINKING ABOUT SAMPLE MEANS

Means of random samples are **less variable** than individual observations.

Means of random samples are **more Normal** than individual observations.

EXAMPLE 11.7   The central limit theorem in action

The *Central Limit Theorem* applet allows you to watch the central limit theorem in action. Figure 11.5 presents snapshots from the applet. Figure 11.5(a) shows the density curve of a single observation, that is, of the population. The distribution is strongly

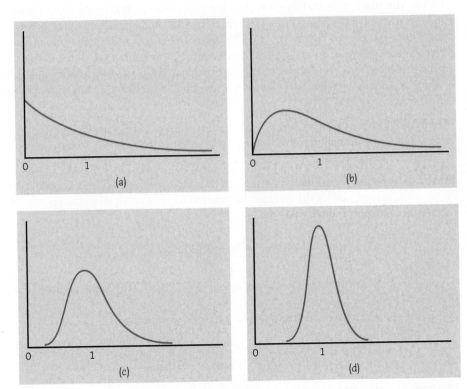

FIGURE 11.5 The central limit theorem in action: the distribution of sample means $\bar{x}$ from a strongly non-Normal population becomes more Normal as the sample size increases. **(a)** The distribution of 1 observation. **(b)** The distribution of $\bar{x}$ for 2 observations. **(c)** The distribution of $\bar{x}$ for 10 observations. **(d)** The distribution of $\bar{x}$ for 25 observations.

right-skewed, and the most probable outcomes are near 0. The mean μ of this distribution is 1, and its standard deviation σ is also 1. This particular distribution is called an *exponential distribution*. Exponential distributions are used as models for the lifetime in service of electronic components and for the time required to serve a customer or repair a machine.

Figures 11.5(b), (c), and (d) are the density curves of the sample means of 2, 10, and 25 observations from this population. As n increases, the shape becomes more Normal. The mean remains at $\mu = 1$, and the standard deviation decreases, taking the value $1/\sqrt{n}$. The density curve for 10 observations is still somewhat skewed to the right but already resembles a Normal curve having $\mu = 1$ and $\sigma = 1/\sqrt{10} = 0.32$. The density curve for $n = 25$ is yet more Normal. The contrast between the shapes of the population distribution and of the distribution of the mean of 10 or 25 observations is striking.

Let's use Normal calculations based on the central limit theorem to answer a question about the very non-Normal distribution in Figure 11.5(a).

4
STEP

EXAMPLE 11.8 Maintaining air conditioners

STATE: The time (in hours) that a technician requires to perform preventive maintenance on an air-conditioning unit is governed by the exponential distribution whose density curve appears in Figure 11.5(a). The mean time is $\mu = 1$ hour and the standard deviation is $\sigma = 1$ hour. Your company has a contract to maintain 70 of these units in an apartment building. You must schedule technicians' time for a visit to this building. Is it safe to budget an average of 1.1 hours for each unit? Or should you budget an average of 1.25 hours?

FORMULATE: We can treat these 70 air conditioners as an SRS from all units of this type. What is the probability that the average maintenance time for 70 units exceeds 1.1 hours? That the average time exceeds 1.25 hours?

SOLVE: The central limit theorem says that the sample mean time $\bar{x}$ spent working on 70 units has approximately the Normal distribution with mean equal to the population mean $\mu = 1$ hour and standard deviation

$$\frac{\sigma}{\sqrt{70}} = \frac{1}{\sqrt{70}} = 0.12 \text{ hour}$$

The distribution of $\bar{x}$ is therefore approximately $N(1, 0.12)$. This Normal curve is the solid curve in Figure 11.6.

Using this Normal distribution, the probabilities we want are

$$P(\bar{x} > 1.10 \text{ hours}) = 0.2014$$
$$P(\bar{x} > 1.25 \text{ hours}) = 0.0182$$

(Software gives these probabilities immediately, or you can standardize and use Table A. Don't forget to use standard deviation 0.12 in your software or when you standardize $\bar{x}$.)

CONCLUDE: If you budget 1.1 hours per unit, there is a 20% chance that the technicians will not complete the work in the building within the budgeted time. This chance drops to 2% if you budget 1.25 hours. You therefore budget 1.25 hours per unit.

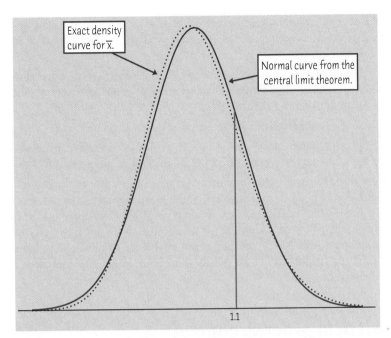

FIGURE 11.6 The exact distribution (dashed) and the Normal approximation from the central limit theorem (solid) for the average time needed to maintain an air conditioner, for Example 11.8. The probability we want is the area to the right of 1.1.

Using more mathematics, we can start with the exponential distribution and find the actual density curve of $\bar{x}$ for 70 observations. This is the dashed curve in Figure 11.6. You can see that the solid Normal curve is a good approximation. The exactly correct probability for 1.1 hours is an area to the right of 1.1 under the dashed density curve. It is 0.1977. The central limit theorem Normal approximation 0.2014 is off by only about 0.004.

APPLY YOUR KNOWLEDGE

11.10 What does the central limit theorem say? Asked what the central limit theorem says, a student replies, "As you take larger and larger samples from a population, the histogram of the sample values looks more and more Normal." Is the student right? Explain your answer.

11.11 Detecting gypsy moths. The gypsy moth is a serious threat to oak and aspen trees. A state agriculture department places traps throughout the state to detect the moths. When traps are checked periodically, the mean number of moths trapped is only 0.5, but some traps have several moths. The distribution of moth counts is discrete and strongly skewed, with standard deviation 0.7.

(a) What are the mean and standard deviation of the average number of moths $\bar{x}$ in 50 traps?

(b) Use the central limit theorem to find the probability that the average number of moths in 50 traps is greater than 0.6.

Bruce Coleman/Alamy

11.12 **SAT scores.**   The total SAT scores of high school seniors in recent years have mean $\mu = 1026$ and standard deviation $\sigma = 209$. The distribution of SAT scores is roughly Normal.

(a) Ramon scored 1100. If scores have a Normal distribution, what percentile of the distribution is this? (That is, what percent of scores are lower than Ramon's?)

(b) Now consider the mean $\overline{x}$ of the scores of 70 randomly chosen students. If $\overline{x} = 1100$, what percentile of the sampling distribution of $\overline{x}$ is this?

(c) Which of your calculations, (a) or (b), is less accurate because SAT scores do not have an exactly Normal distribution? Explain your answer.

11.13 **More on insurance.**   An insurance company knows that in the entire population of millions of homeowners, the mean annual loss from fire is $\mu = \$250$ and the standard deviation of the loss is $\sigma = \$1000$. The distribution of losses is strongly right-skewed: most policies have \$0 loss, but a few have large losses. If the company sells 10,000 policies, can it safely base its rates on the assumption that its average loss will be no greater than \$275? Follow the four-step process in your answer.

Statistical process control*

The sampling distribution of the sample mean $\overline{x}$ has an immediate application to *statistical process control*. The goal of statistical process control is to make a process stable over time and then keep it stable unless planned changes are made. You might want, for example, to keep your weight constant over time. A manufacturer of machine parts wants the critical dimensions to be the same for all parts. "Constant over time" and "the same for all" are not realistic requirements. They ignore the fact that *all processes have variation*. Your weight fluctuates from day to day; the critical dimension of a machined part varies a bit from item to item; the time to process a college admission application is not the same for all applications. Variation occurs in even the most precisely made product due to small changes in the raw material, the adjustment of the machine, the behavior of the operator, and even the temperature in the plant. Because variation is always present, we can't expect to hold a variable exactly constant over time. The statistical description of stability over time requires that the *pattern of variation* remain stable, not that there be no variation in the variable measured.

> **STATISTICAL CONTROL**
>
> A variable that continues to be described by the same distribution when observed over time is said to be in statistical control, or simply **in control.**
>
> **Control charts** are statistical tools that monitor a process and alert us when the process has been disturbed so that it is now **out of control.** This is a signal to find and correct the cause of the disturbance.

*The rest of this chapter is optional. A more complete treatment of process control appears in Companion Chapter 27.

Control charts work by distinguishing the natural variation in the process from the additional variation that suggests that the process has changed. A control chart sounds an alarm when it sees too much variation. The most common application of control charts is to monitor the performance of an industrial process. The same methods, however, can be used to check the stability of quantities as varied as the ratings of a television show, the level of ozone in the atmosphere, and the gas mileage of your car. Control charts combine graphical and numerical descriptions of data with use of sampling distributions. They therefore provide a natural bridge between exploratory data analysis and formal statistical inference.

$\overline{x}$ charts*

The population in the control chart setting is all items that would be produced by the process if it ran on forever in its present state. The items actually produced form samples from this population. We generally speak of the process rather than the population. Choose a quantitative variable, such as a diameter or a voltage, that is an important measure of the quality of an item. The process mean μ is the long-term average value of this variable; μ describes the center or aim of the process. The sample mean $\overline{x}$ of several items estimates μ and helps us judge whether the center of the process has moved away from its proper value. The most common control chart plots the means $\overline{x}$ of small samples taken from the process at regular intervals over time.

When you first apply control charts to a process, the process may not be in control. Even if it is in control, you don't yet understand its behavior. You must collect data from the process, establish control by uncovering and removing the reasons for disturbances, and then set up control charts to maintain control. To quickly explain the main ideas, we'll assume that you know the usual behavior of the process from long experience. Here are the conditions we will work with.

PROCESS-MONITORING CONDITIONS

Measure a quantitative variable x that has a **Normal distribution.** The process has been operating in control for a long period, so that we know the **process mean μ** and the **process standard deviation σ** that describe the distribution of x as long as the process remains in control.

EXAMPLE 11.9   Making computer monitors

A manufacturer of computer monitors must control the tension on the mesh of fine wires that lies behind the surface of the viewing screen. Too much tension will tear the mesh, and too little will allow wrinkles. Tension is measured by an electrical device with output readings in millivolts (mV). The proper tension is 275 mV. Some variation is always present in the production process. When the process is operating properly, the standard deviation of the tension readings is $\sigma = 43$ mV.

TABLE 11.1	Twenty control chart samples of mesh tension				
Sample	Tension measurements				$\bar{x}$
1	234.5	272.3	234.5	272.3	253.4
2	311.1	305.8	238.5	286.2	285.4
3	247.1	205.3	252.6	316.1	255.3
4	215.4	296.8	274.2	256.8	260.8
5	327.9	247.2	283.3	232.6	272.7
6	304.3	236.3	201.8	238.5	245.2
7	268.9	276.2	275.6	240.2	265.2
8	282.1	247.7	259.8	272.8	265.6
9	260.8	259.9	247.9	345.3	278.5
10	329.3	231.8	307.2	273.4	285.4
11	266.4	249.7	231.5	265.2	253.2
12	168.8	330.9	333.6	318.3	287.9
13	349.9	334.2	292.3	301.5	319.5
14	235.2	283.1	245.9	263.1	256.8
15	257.3	218.4	296.2	275.2	261.8
16	235.1	252.7	300.6	297.6	271.5
17	286.3	293.8	236.2	275.3	272.9
18	328.1	272.6	329.7	260.1	297.6
19	316.4	287.4	373.0	286.0	315.7
20	296.8	350.5	280.6	259.8	296.9

The operator measures the tension on a sample of 4 monitors each hour. The mean $\bar{x}$ of each sample estimates the mean tension μ for the process at the time of the sample. Table 11.1 shows the samples and their means for 20 consecutive hours of production. How can we use these data to keep the process in control?

A time plot helps us see whether or not the process is stable. Figure 11.7 is a plot of the successive sample means against the order in which the samples were taken. We have plotted each sample mean from the table against its sample number. For example, the mean of the first sample is 253.4 mV, and this is the value plotted for sample 1. Because the target value for the process mean is $\mu = 275$ mV, we draw a *center line* at that level across the plot. How much variation about this center line do we expect to see? For example, are samples 13 and 19 so high that they suggest lack of control?

The tension measurements are roughly Normal, and we know that sample means are more Normal than individual measurements. So the $\bar{x}$-values from successive samples will follow a Normal distribution. If the standard deviation of the individual screens remains at $\sigma = 43$ mV, the standard deviation of $\bar{x}$ from 4 screens is

$$\frac{\sigma}{\sqrt{n}} = \frac{43}{\sqrt{4}} = 21.5 \text{ mV}$$

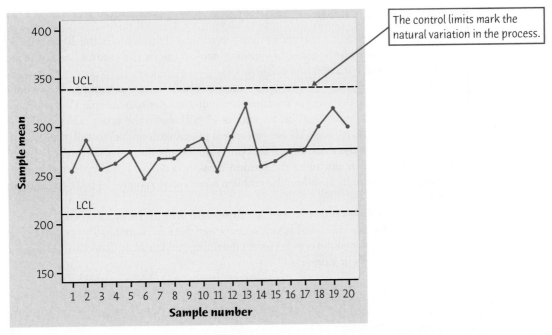

FIGURE 11.7 $\bar{x}$ chart for the mesh tension data of Table 11.1. The control limits are labeled UCL for upper control limit and LCL for lower control limit. No points lie outside the control limits.

As long as the mean remains at its target value $\mu = 275$ mV, the 99.7 part of the 68–95–99.7 rule says that almost all values of $\bar{x}$ will lie between

$$\mu - 3\frac{\sigma}{\sqrt{n}} = 275 - (3)(21.5) = 210.5$$

$$\mu + 3\frac{\sigma}{\sqrt{n}} = 275 + (3)(21.5) = 339.5$$

We therefore draw dashed *control limits* at these two levels on the plot. The control limits show the extent of the natural variation of $\bar{x}$-values when the process is in control. We now have an $\bar{x}$ *control chart*.

$\bar{x}$ CONTROL CHART

To evaluate the control of a process with given standards μ and σ, make an **$\bar{x}$ control chart** as follows:

- Plot the means $\bar{x}$ of regular samples of size n against time.
- Draw a horizontal **center line** at μ.
- Draw horizontal **control limits** at $\mu \pm 3\sigma/\sqrt{n}$.

Any $\bar{x}$ that does not fall between the control limits is evidence that the process is out of control.

EXAMPLE 11.10   Interpreting x̄ charts

Figure 11.7 is a typical x̄ chart for a process in control. The means of the 20 samples do vary, but all lie within the range of variation marked out by the control limits. We are seeing the natural variation of a stable process.

Figures 11.8 and 11.9 illustrate two ways in which the process can go out of control. In Figure 11.8, the process was disturbed sometime between sample 12 and sample 13. As a result, the mean tension for sample 13 falls above the upper control limit. It is common practice to mark all out-of-control points with an "x" to call attention to them. A search for the cause begins as soon as we see a point out of control. Investigation finds that the mounting of the tension-measuring device has slipped, resulting in readings that are too high. When the problem is corrected, samples 14 to 20 are again in control.

Figure 11.9 shows the effect of a steady upward drift in the process center, starting at sample 11. You see that some time elapses before the x̄ for sample 18 is out of control. The one-point-out signal works better for detecting sudden large disturbances than for detecting slow drifts in a process.

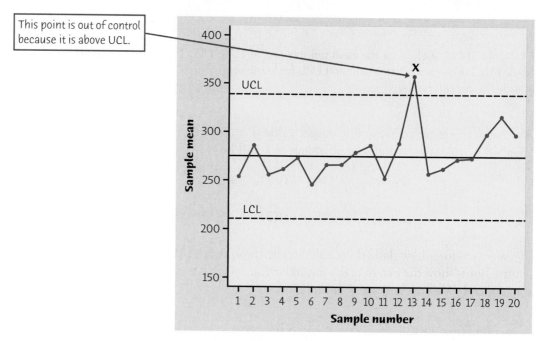

FIGURE 11.8 This x̄ chart is identical to that in Figure 11.7, except that a disturbance has driven x̄ for sample 13 above the upper control limit. The out-of-control point is marked with an x.

x̄ chart   An x̄ control chart is often called simply an **x̄ chart.** Because a control chart is a warning device, it is not necessary that our probability calculations be exactly correct. Approximate Normality is good enough. In that same spirit, control charts use the approximate Normal probabilities given by the 68–95–99.7 rule rather than more exact calculations using Table A.

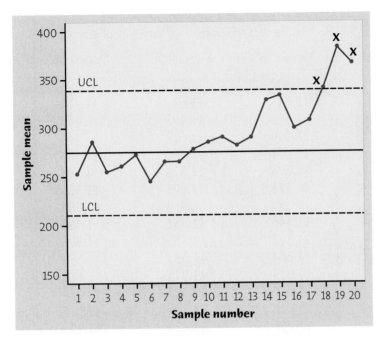

FIGURE 11.9 The first 10 points on this $\bar{x}$ chart are as in Figure 11.7. The process mean drifts upward after sample 10, and the sample means $\bar{x}$ reflect this drift. The points for samples 18, 19, and 20 are out of control.

APPLY YOUR KNOWLEDGE

11.14 Auto thermostats. A maker of auto air conditioners checks a sample of 4 thermostatic controls from each hour's production. The thermostats are set at 75°F and then placed in a chamber where the temperature rises gradually. The temperature at which the thermostat turns on the air conditioner is recorded. The process mean should be $\mu = 75°$. Past experience indicates that the response temperature of properly adjusted thermostats varies with $\sigma = 0.5°$. The mean response temperature $\bar{x}$ for each hour's sample is plotted on an $\bar{x}$ control chart. Calculate the center line and control limits for this chart.

11.15 Tablet hardness. A pharmaceutical manufacturer forms tablets by compressing a granular material that contains the active ingredient and various fillers. The hardness of a sample from each lot of tablets is measured in order to control the compression process. The process has been operating in control with mean at the target value $\mu = 11.5$ and estimated standard deviation $\sigma = 0.2$. Table 11.2 gives three sets of data, each representing $\bar{x}$ for 20 successive samples of $n = 4$ tablets. One set remains in control at the target value. In a second set, the process mean μ shifts suddenly to a new value. In a third, the process mean drifts gradually.

(a) What are the center line and control limits for an $\bar{x}$ chart for this process?

(b) Draw a separate $\bar{x}$ chart for each of the three data sets. Mark any points that are beyond the control limits.

TABLE 11.2	Three sets of $\bar{x}$'s from 20 samples of size 4		
Sample	Data set A	Data set B	Data set C
1	11.602	11.627	11.495
2	11.547	11.613	11.475
3	11.312	11.493	11.465
4	11.449	11.602	11.497
5	11.401	11.360	11.573
6	11.608	11.374	11.563
7	11.471	11.592	11.321
8	11.453	11.458	11.533
9	11.446	11.552	11.486
10	11.522	11.463	11.502
11	11.664	11.383	11.534
12	11.823	11.715	11.624
13	11.629	11.485	11.629
14	11.602	11.509	11.575
15	11.756	11.429	11.730
16	11.707	11.477	11.680
17	11.612	11.570	11.729
18	11.628	11.623	11.704
19	11.603	11.472	12.052
20	11.816	11.531	11.905

(c) Based on your work in (b) and the appearance of the control charts, which set of data comes from a process that is in control? In which case does the process mean shift suddenly, and at about which sample do you think that the mean changed? Finally, in which case does the mean drift gradually?

Thinking about process control*

The purpose of a control chart is not to ensure good quality by inspecting most of the items produced. **Control charts focus on the process itself rather than on the individual products.** By checking the process at regular intervals, we can detect disturbances and correct them quickly. Statistical process control achieves high quality at a lower cost than inspecting all of the products. Small samples of 4 or 5 items are usually adequate for process control.

A process that is in control is stable over time, but stability alone does not guarantee good quality. The natural variation in the process may be so large that many of the products are unsatisfactory. Nonetheless, establishing control brings a number of advantages.

• In order to assess whether the process quality is satisfactory, we must observe the process when it is operating in control, free of breakdowns and other disturbances.

11.21 Scores on the SAT college entrance test in a recent year were roughly Normal with mean 1026 and standard deviation 209. You choose an SRS of 100 students and average their SAT scores. If you do this many times, the standard deviation of the average scores you get will be close to

(a) 209.   (b) $100/\sqrt{209} = 6.92$.   (c) $209/\sqrt{100} = 20.9$.

11.22 A newborn baby has extremely low birth weight (ELBW) if it weighs less than 1000 grams. A study of the health of such children in later years examined a random sample of 219 children. Their mean weight at birth was $\bar{x} = 810$ grams. This sample mean is an *unbiased estimator* of the mean weight μ in the population of all ELBW babies. This means that

(a) in many samples from this population, the mean of the many values of $\bar{x}$ will be equal to μ.

(b) as we take larger and larger samples from this population, $\bar{x}$ will get closer and closer to μ.

(c) in many samples from this population, the many values of $\bar{x}$ will have a distribution that is close to Normal.

11.23 The number of hours a light bulb burns before failing varies from bulb to bulb. The distribution of burnout times is strongly skewed to the right. The central limit theorem says that

(a) as we look at more and more bulbs, their average burnout time gets ever closer to the mean μ for all bulbs of this type.

(b) the average burnout time of a large number of bulbs has a distribution of the same shape (strongly skewed) as the distribution for individual bulbs.

(c) the average burnout time of a large number of bulbs has a distribution that is close to Normal.

11.24 A machine manufactures parts whose diameters vary according to the Normal distribution with mean $\mu = 40.150$ millimeters (mm) and standard deviation $\sigma = 0.003$ mm. An inspector measures a random sample of 4 parts. The probability that the average diameter of these 4 parts is less than 40.148 mm is about

(a) 0.092.   (b) 0.251.   (c) 0.908.

CHAPTER 11 EXERCISES

11.25 **Women's heights.** A random sample of female college students has a mean height of **65** inches, which is greater than the **64**-inch mean height of all young women. Is each of the bold numbers a parameter or a statistic? Explain your answer.

11.26 **Small classes in school.** The Tennessee STAR experiment randomly assigned children to regular or small classes during their first four years of school. When these children reached high school, **40.2%** of blacks from small classes took the ACT or SAT college entrance exams. Only **31.7%** of blacks from regular classes took one of these exams. Is each of the boldface numbers a parameter or a statistic? Explain your answer.

11.27 Playing the numbers. The numbers racket is a well-entrenched illegal gambling operation in most large cities. One version works as follows: you choose one of the 1000 three-digit numbers 000 to 999 and pay your local numbers runner a dollar to enter your bet. Each day, one three-digit number is chosen at random and pays off $600. The mean payoff for the population of thousands of bets is $\mu = 60$ cents. Joe makes one bet every day for many years. Explain what the law of large numbers says about Joe's results as he keeps on betting.

11.28 Roulette. A roulette wheel has 38 slots, of which 18 are black, 18 are red, and 2 are green. When the wheel is spun, the ball is equally likely to come to rest in any of the slots. One of the simplest wagers chooses red or black. A bet of $1 on red returns $2 if the ball lands in a red slot. Otherwise, the player loses his dollar. When gamblers bet on red or black, the two green slots belong to the house. Because the probability of winning $2 is 18/38, the mean payoff from a $1 bet is twice 18/38, or 94.7 cents. Explain what the law of large numbers tells us about what will happen if a gambler makes very many bets on red.

Matthias Kulka/CORBIS

11.29 The law of large numbers. Suppose that you roll two balanced dice and look at the spots on the up-faces. There are 36 possible outcomes, displayed in Figure 10.2 (page 251). Because the dice are balanced, all 36 outcomes are equally likely. The average number of spots is 7. This is the population mean μ for the idealized population that contains the results of rolling two dice forever. The law of large numbers says that the average $\overline{x}$ from a finite number of rolls gets closer and closer to 7 as we do more and more rolls.

APPLET

(a) Click "More dice" once in the *Law of Large Numbers* applet to get two dice. Click "Show mean" to see the mean 7 on the graph. Leaving the number of rolls at 1, click "Roll dice" three times. How many spots did each roll produce? What is the average for the three rolls? You see that the graph displays at each point the average number of spots for all rolls up to the last one. Now you understand the display.

(b) Set the number of rolls to 100 and click "Roll dice." The applet rolls the two dice 100 times. The graph shows how the average count of spots changes as we make more rolls. That is, the graph shows $\overline{x}$ as we continue to roll the dice. Make a rough sketch of the final graph.

(c) Repeat your work from (b). Click "Reset" to start over, then roll two dice 100 times. Make a sketch of the final graph of the mean $\overline{x}$ against the number of rolls. Your two graphs will often look very different. What they have in common is that the average eventually gets close to the population mean $\mu = 7$. The law of large numbers says that this will *always* happen if you keep on rolling the dice.

11.30 What's the mean? Suppose that you roll three balanced dice. We wonder what the mean number of spots on the up-faces of the three dice is. The law of large numbers says that we can find out by experience: roll three dice many times, and the average number of spots will eventually approach the true mean. Set up the *Law of Large Numbers* applet to roll three dice. Don't click "Show mean" yet. Roll the dice until you are confident you know the mean quite closely, then click "Show mean" to verify your discovery. What is the mean? Make a rough sketch of the path the averages $\overline{x}$ followed as you kept adding more rolls.

11.31 Lightning strikes. The number of lightning strikes on a square kilometer of open ground in a year has mean 6 and standard deviation 2.4. (These values are typical of much of the United States.) The National Lightning Detection

Gandee Vasan/Getty Images

Network uses automatic sensors to watch for lightning in a sample of 10 square kilometers. What are the mean and standard deviation of $\overline{x}$, the mean number of strikes per square kilometer?

11.32 **Heights of male students.** To estimate the mean height μ of male students on your campus, you will measure an SRS of students. You know from government data that the standard deviation of the heights of young men is about 2.8 inches. How large an SRS must you take to reduce the standard deviation of the sample mean to one-half inch? Use the four-step process to outline your work.

11.33 **Heights of male students, continued.** To estimate the mean height μ of male students on your campus, you will measure an SRS of students. You know from government data that heights of young men are approximately Normal with standard deviation about 2.8 inches. You want your sample mean $\overline{x}$ to estimate μ with an error of no more than one-half inch in either direction.

(a) What standard deviation must $\overline{x}$ have so that 99.7% of all samples give an $\overline{x}$ within one-half inch of μ? (Use the 68–95–99.7 rule.)

(b) How large an SRS do you need to reduce the standard deviation of $\overline{x}$ to the value you found in part (a)?

11.34 **More on heights of male students.** In Exercise 11.32, you decided to measure n male students. Suppose that the distribution of heights of all male students on your campus is Normal with mean 70 inches and standard deviation 2.8 inches.

(a) If you choose one student at random, what is the probability that he is between 69 and 71 inches tall?

(b) What is the probability that the mean height of your sample is between 69 and 71 inches?

11.35 **Durable press fabrics.** "Durable press" cotton fabrics are treated to improve their recovery from wrinkles after washing. Unfortunately, the treatment also reduces the strength of the fabric. The breaking strength of untreated fabric is Normally distributed with mean 58 pounds and standard deviation 2.3 pounds. The same type of fabric after treatment has Normally distributed breaking strength with mean 30 pounds and standard deviation 1.6 pounds.[3] A clothing manufacturer tests an SRS of 5 specimens of each fabric.

(a) What is the probability that the mean breaking strength of the 5 untreated specimens exceeds 50 pounds?

(b) What is the probability that the mean breaking strength of the 5 treated specimens exceeds 50 pounds?

11.36 **Glucose testing.** Shelia's doctor is concerned that she may suffer from gestational diabetes (high blood glucose levels during pregnancy). There is variation both in the actual glucose level and in the blood test that measures the level. A patient is classified as having gestational diabetes if the glucose level is above 140 milligrams per deciliter (mg/dl) one hour after a sugary drink. Shelia's measured glucose level one hour after the sugary drink varies according to the Normal distribution with $\mu = 125$ mg/dl and $\sigma = 10$ mg/dl.

(a) If a single glucose measurement is made, what is the probability that Shelia is diagnosed as having gestational diabetes?

(b) If measurements are made on 4 separate days and the mean result is compared with the criterion 140 mg/dl, what is the probability that Shelia is diagnosed as having gestational diabetes?

Alan Hicks/Getty Images

11.37 Pollutants in auto exhausts. The level of nitrogen oxides (NOX) in the exhaust of cars of a particular model varies Normally with mean 0.2 grams per mile (g/mi) and standard deviation 0.05 g/mi. Government regulations call for NOX emissions no higher than 0.3 g/mi.

(a) What is the probability that a single car of this model fails to meet the NOX requirement?

(b) A company has 25 cars of this model in its fleet. What is the probability that the average NOX level $\bar{x}$ of these cars is above the 0.3 g/mi limit?

11.38 Glucose testing, continued. Shelia's measured glucose level one hour after a sugary drink varies according to the Normal distribution with $\mu = 125$ mg/dl and $\sigma = 10$ mg/dl. What is the level L such that there is probability only 0.05 that the mean glucose level of 4 test results falls above L? (*Hint:* This requires a backward Normal calculation. See page 81 in Chapter 3 if you need to review.)

11.39 Pollutants in auto exhausts, continued. The level of nitrogen oxides (NOX) in the exhaust of cars of a particular model varies Normally with mean 0.2 g/mi and standard deviation 0.05 g/mi. A company has 25 cars of this model in its fleet. What is the level L such that the probability that the average NOX level $\bar{x}$ for the fleet is greater than L is only 0.01? (*Hint:* This requires a backward Normal calculation. See page 81 in Chapter 3 if you need to review.)

11.40 Returns on stocks. Andrew plans to retire in 40 years. He is thinking of investing his retirement funds in stocks, so he seeks out information on past returns. He learns that over the 101 years from 1900 to 2000, the real (that is, adjusted for inflation) returns on U.S. common stocks had mean 8.7% and standard deviation 20.2%.[4] The distribution of annual returns on common stocks is roughly symmetric, so the mean return over even a moderate number of years is close to Normal. What is the probability (assuming that the past pattern of variation continues) that the mean annual return on common stocks over the next 40 years will exceed 10%? What is the probability that the mean return will be less than 5%? Follow the four-step process in your answer.

11.41 Auto accidents. The number of accidents per week at a hazardous intersection varies with mean 2.2 and standard deviation 1.4. This distribution takes only whole-number values, so it is certainly not Normal.

(a) Let $\bar{x}$ be the mean number of accidents per week at the intersection during a year (52 weeks). What is the approximate distribution of $\bar{x}$ according to the central limit theorem?

(b) What is the approximate probability that $\bar{x}$ is less than 2?

(c) What is the approximate probability that there are fewer than 100 accidents at the intersection in a year? (*Hint:* Restate this event in terms of $\bar{x}$.)

11.42 Airline passengers get heavier. In response to the increasing weight of airline passengers, the Federal Aviation Administration in 2003 told airlines to assume that passengers average 190 pounds in the summer, including clothing and carry-on baggage. But passengers vary, and the FAA did not specify a standard deviation. A reasonable standard deviation is 35 pounds. Weights are not Normally distributed, especially when the population includes both men and women, but they are not very non-Normal. A commuter plane carries 19 passengers. What is the approximate probability that the total weight of the passengers exceeds 4000 pounds? Use the four-step process to guide your work.

Jeff Greenberg/The Image Works

(*Hint:* To apply the central limit theorem, restate the problem in terms of the mean weight.)

11.43 **Generating a sampling distribution.** We want to know what percent of American adults approve of legal gambling. This population proportion p is a parameter. To estimate p, take an SRS and find the proportion $\hat{p}$ in the sample who approve of gambling. If we take many SRSs of the same size, the proportion $\hat{p}$ will vary from sample to sample. The distribution of its values in all SRSs is the sampling distribution of this statistic.

Figure 11.10 is a small population. Each circle represents an adult. The colored circles are people who disapprove of legal gambling, and the white circles are people who approve. You can check that 60 of the 100 circles are white, so in this population the proportion who approve of gambling is $p = 60/100 = 0.6$.

(a) The circles are labeled 00, 01, ..., 99. Use line 101 of Table B to draw an SRS of size 5. What is the proportion $\hat{p}$ of the people in your sample who approve of gambling?

(b) Take 9 more SRSs of size 5 (10 in all), using lines 102 to 110 of Table B, a different line for each sample. You now have 10 values of the sample proportion $\hat{p}$. What are they?

(c) Because your samples have only 5 people, the only values $\hat{p}$ can take are 0/5, 1/5, 2/5, 3/5, 4/5, and 5/5. That is, $\hat{p}$ is always 0, 0.2, 0.4, 0.6, 0.8, or 1. Mark these numbers on a line and make a histogram of your 10 results by putting a bar above each number to show how many samples had that outcome. (You have begun to construct the sampling distribution of $\hat{p}$, although just 10 samples is a small start.)

(d) Taking samples of size 5 from a population of size 100 is not a practical setting, but let's look at your results anyway. How many of your 10 samples estimated the population proportion $p = 0.6$ exactly correctly? Is the true value 0.6 roughly in the center of your sample values?

11.44 **A better way to generate a sampling distribution.**   You can use the *Probability* applet to speed up and improve Exercise 11.43. You have a population in which 60% of the individuals approve of legal gambling. You want to take many samples from this population to observe how the sample proportion who approve of gambling varies from sample to sample. Set the "Probability of heads" in the applet to 0.6 and the number of tosses to 40. This simulates an SRS of size 40 from a large population. Each head in the sample is a person who approves of legal gambling and each tail is a person who disapproves. By alternating between "Toss" and "Reset" you can take many samples quickly.

APPLET

(a) Take 50 samples, recording the proportion who approve of gambling in each sample. (The applet gives this proportion at the top left of its display.) Make a histogram of the 50 sample proportions.

(b) Another population contains only 20% who approve of legal gambling. Take 50 samples of size 40 from this population, record the number in each sample who approve, and make a histogram of the 50 sample proportions. How do the centers of your two histograms reflect the differing truths about the two populations?

The following exercises concern the optional material on statistical process control.

11.45 **Dyeing yarn.** The unique colors of the cashmere sweaters your firm makes result from heating undyed yarn in a kettle with a dye liquor. The pH (acidity) of the

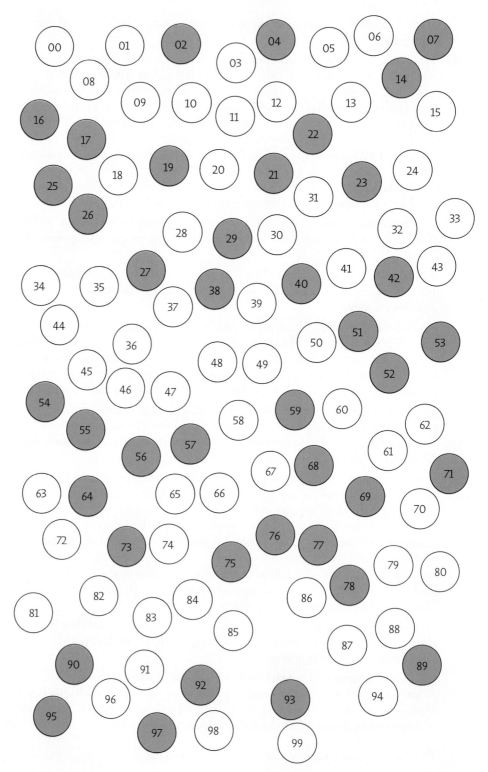

FIGURE 11.10 A population of 100 people, for Exercise 11.43. The white circles represent people who approve of legal gambling. The colored circles represent people who oppose gambling.

liquor is critical for regulating dye uptake and hence the final color. There are 5 kettles, all of which receive dye liquor from a common source. Twice each day, the pH of the liquor in each kettle is measured, giving a sample of size 5. The process has been operating in control with $\mu = 4.22$ and $\sigma = 0.127$. Give the center line and control limits for the $\bar{x}$ chart.

11.46 Hospital losses. A hospital struggling to contain costs investigates procedures on which it loses money. Government standards place medical procedures into Diagnostic Related Groups (DRGs). For example, major joint replacements are DRG 209. The hospital takes from its records a random sample of 8 DRG 209 patients each month. The losses incurred per patient have been in control, with mean $6400 and standard deviation $700. Here are the mean losses $\bar{x}$ for the samples taken in the next 15 months:

4
STEP

| 6244 | 6534 | 6080 | 6476 | 6469 | 6544 | 6415 | 6697 |
| 6497 | 6912 | 6638 | 6857 | 6659 | 7509 | 7374 |

What does an $\bar{x}$ chart suggest about the hospital's losses on major joint replacements? Follow the four-step process in your answer.

11.47 Dyeing yarn, continued. What are the natural tolerances for the pH of an individual dye kettle in the setting of Exercise 11.45?

11.48 Milling. The width of a slot cut by a milling machine is important to the proper functioning of a hydraulic system for large tractors. The manufacturer checks the control of the milling process by measuring a sample of 5 consecutive items during each hour's production. The target width for the slot is $\mu = 0.8750$ inch. The process has been operating in control with center close to the target and $\sigma = 0.0012$ inch. What center line and control limits should be drawn on the $\bar{x}$ chart?

11.49 Is the quality OK? Statistical control means that a process is stable. It doesn't mean that this stable process produces high-quality items. Return to the mesh-tensioning process described in Examples 11.9 and 11.11. This process is in control with mean $\mu = 275$ mV and standard deviation $\sigma = 43$ mV.

(a) The current specifications set by customers for mesh tension are 100 to 400 mV. What percent of monitors meet these specifications?

(b) The customers now set tighter specifications, 150 to 350 mV. What percent meet the new specifications? The process has not changed, but product quality, measured by percent meeting the specifications, is no longer good.

11.50 Improving the process. The center of the mesh tensions for the process in the previous exercise is 275 mV. The center of the specifications is 250 mV, so we should be able to improve the process by adjusting the center to 250 mV. This is an easy adjustment that does not change the process variation. What percent of monitors now meet the new specifications?

Jim Craigmyle/CORBIS

General Rules of Probability*

The mathematics of probability can provide models to describe the flow of traffic through a highway system, a telephone interchange, or a computer processor; the genetic makeup of populations; the energy states of subatomic particles; the spread of epidemics or rumors; and the rate of return on risky investments. Although we are interested in probability because of its usefulness in statistics, the mathematics of chance is important in many fields of study. Our study of probability in Chapter 10 concentrated on basic ideas and facts. Now we look at some details. With more probability at our command, we can model more complex random phenomena. We have already met and used four rules.

---

*This more advanced chapter gives more detail about probability. The material is not needed to read the rest of the book.

PROBABILITY RULES

Rule 1. For any event A, $0 \leq P(A) \leq 1$.

Rule 2. If S is the sample space, $P(S) = 1$.

Rule 3. Addition rule: If A and B are **disjoint** events,

$$P(A \text{ or } B) = P(A) + P(B)$$

Rule 4. For any event A,

$$P(A \text{ does not occur}) = 1 - P(A)$$

Independence and the multiplication rule

Rule 3, the addition rule for disjoint events, describes the probability that *one or the other* of two events A and B occurs in the special situation when A and B cannot occur together. Now we will describe the probability that *both* events A and B occur, again only in a special situation.

Venn diagram

You may find it helpful to draw a picture to display relations among several events. A picture like Figure 12.1 that shows the sample space S as a rectangular area and events as areas within S is called a **Venn diagram.** The events A and B in Figure 12.1 are disjoint because they do not overlap. The Venn diagram in Figure 12.2 illustrates two events that are not disjoint. The event $\{A \text{ and } B\}$ appears as the overlapping area that is common to both A and B.

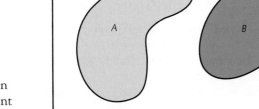

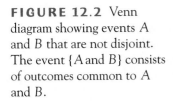

FIGURE 12.1 Venn diagram showing disjoint events A and B.

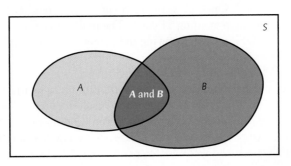

FIGURE 12.2 Venn diagram showing events A and B that are not disjoint. The event $\{A \text{ and } B\}$ consists of outcomes common to A and B.

Suppose that you toss a balanced coin twice. You are counting heads, so two events of interest are

$$A = \text{first toss is a head}$$
$$B = \text{second toss is a head}$$

The events A and B are not disjoint. They occur together whenever both tosses give heads. We want to find the probability of the event $\{A \text{ and } B\}$ that *both* tosses are heads.

The coin tossing of Buffon, Pearson, and Kerrich described at the beginning of Chapter 10 makes us willing to assign probability 1/2 to a head when we toss a coin. So

$$P(A) = 0.5$$
$$P(B) = 0.5$$

What is $P(A \text{ and } B)$? Common sense says that it is 1/4. The first coin will give a head half the time and then the second will give a head on half of those tosses, so both coins will give heads on $1/2 \times 1/2 = 1/4$ of all tosses in the long run. This reasoning assumes that the second coin still has probability 1/2 of a head after the first has given a head. This is true—we can verify it by tossing two coins many times and observing the proportion of heads on the second toss after the first toss has produced a head. We say that the events "head on the first toss" and "head on *independence*   the second toss" are **independent.** Independence means that the outcome of the first toss cannot influence the outcome of the second toss.

EXAMPLE 12.1   Independent or not?

Because a coin has no memory and most coin tossers cannot influence the fall of the coin, it is safe to assume that successive coin tosses are independent. For a balanced coin this means that after we see the outcome of the first toss, we still assign probability 1/2 to heads on the second toss.

On the other hand, the colors of successive cards dealt from the same deck are not independent. A standard 52-card deck contains 26 red and 26 black cards. For the first card dealt from a shuffled deck, the probability of a red card is $26/52 = 0.50$ (equally likely outcomes). Once we see that the first card is red, we know that there are only 25 reds among the remaining 51 cards. The probability that the second card is red is therefore only $25/51 = 0.49$. Knowing the outcome of the first deal changes the probabilities for the second.

If a nurse measures your height twice, it is reasonable to assume that the two results are independent observations. Each records your actual height plus a measurement error, and the size of the error in the first result does not influence the instrument that makes the second reading. But if you take an IQ test or other mental test twice in succession, the two test scores are not independent. The learning that occurs on the first attempt influences your second attempt.

MULTIPLICATION RULE FOR INDEPENDENT EVENTS

Two events A and B are **independent** if knowing that one occurs does not change the probability that the other occurs. If A and B are independent,

$$P(A \text{ and } B) = P(A)P(B)$$

The multiplication rule also extends to collections of more than two events, provided that all are independent. Independence of events A, B, and C means that no information about any one or any two can change the probability of the remaining events. Independence is often assumed in setting up a probability model when the events we are describing seem to have no connection.

Condemned by independence

Assuming independence when it isn't true can lead to disaster. Several mothers in England were convicted of murder simply because two of their children had died in their cribs with no visible cause. An "expert witness" for the prosecution said that the probability of an unexplained crib death in a nonsmoking middle-class family is 1/8500. He then multiplied 1/8500 by 1/8500 to claim that there is only a 1 in 73 million chance that two children in the same family could have died naturally. This is nonsense: it assumes that crib deaths are independent, and data suggest that they are not. Some common genetic or environmental cause, not murder, probably explains the deaths.

EXAMPLE 12.2 Surviving?

During World War II, the British found that the probability that a bomber is lost through enemy action on a mission over occupied Europe was 0.05. The probability that the bomber returns safely from a mission was therefore 0.95. It is reasonable to assume that missions are independent. Take A_i to be the event that a bomber survives its ith mission. The probability of surviving 2 missions is

$$P(A_1 \text{ and } A_2) = P(A_1)P(A_2)$$
$$= (0.95)(0.95) = 0.9025$$

The multiplication rule also applies to more than two independent events, so the probability of surviving 3 missions is

$$P(A_1 \text{ and } A_2 \text{ and } A_3) = P(A_1)P(A_2)P(A_3)$$
$$= (0.95)(0.95)(0.95) = 0.8574$$

The probability of surviving 20 missions is only

$$P(A_1 \text{ and } A_2 \text{ and } \ldots \text{ and } A_{20}) = P(A_1)P(A_2)\cdots P(A_{20})$$
$$= (0.95)(0.95)\cdots(0.95)$$
$$= (0.95)^{20} = 0.3585$$

The tour of duty for an airman was 30 missions.

If two events A and B are independent, the event that A does not occur is also independent of B, and so on. Suppose, for example, that 75% of all registered voters in a rural district are Republicans. If an opinion poll interviews two voters chosen independently, the probability that the first is a Republican and the second is not a Republican is $(0.75)(0.25) = 0.1875$.

EXAMPLE 12.3 Rapid HIV testing

STATE: Many people who come to clinics to be tested for HIV, the virus that causes AIDS, don't come back to learn the test results. Clinics now use "rapid HIV tests" that give a result while the client waits. In a clinic in Malawi, for example, use of rapid tests increased the percent of clients who learned their test results from 69% to 99.7%.

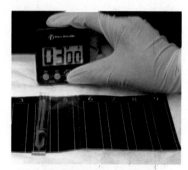

CDC/Cheryl Tryon; Stacy Howard

The trade-off for fast results is that rapid tests are less accurate than slower laboratory tests. Applied to people who have no HIV antibodies, one rapid test has probability about 0.004 of producing a false positive (that is, of falsely indicating that antibodies are present).[1] If a clinic tests 200 people who are free of HIV antibodies, what is the chance that at least one false positive will occur?

FORMULATE: It is reasonable to assume that the test results for different individuals are independent. We have 200 independent events, each with probability 0.004. What is the probability that at least one of these events occurs?

SOLVE: The probability of a negative result for any one person is $1 - 0.004 = 0.996$. The probability of at least one false positive among the 200 people tested is therefore

$$P(\text{at least one positive}) = 1 - P(\text{no positives})$$
$$= 1 - P(\text{200 negatives})$$
$$= 1 - 0.996^{200}$$
$$= 1 - 0.4486 = 0.5514$$

CONCLUDE: The probability is greater than 1/2 that at least one of the 200 people will test positive for HIV, even though no one has the virus.

The multiplication rule $P(A \text{ and } B) = P(A)P(B)$ holds if A and B are independent but not otherwise. The addition rule $P(A \text{ or } B) = P(A) + P(B)$ holds if A and B are disjoint but not otherwise. Resist the temptation to use these simple rules when the circumstances that justify them are not present. *You must also be careful not to confuse disjointness and independence.* If A and B are disjoint, then the fact that A occurs tells us that B cannot occur—look again at Figure 12.1. So disjoint events are not independent. Unlike disjointness, we cannot picture independence in a Venn diagram, because it involves the probabilities of the events rather than just the outcomes that make up the events.

APPLY YOUR KNOWLEDGE

12.1 **Lost Internet sites.** Internet sites often vanish or move, so that references to them can't be followed. In fact, 13% of Internet sites referenced in major scientific journals are lost within two years after publication.[2] If a paper contains seven Internet references, what is the probability that all seven are still good two years later? What specific assumptions did you make in order to calculate this probability?

12.2 **Playing the slots.** Slot machines are now video games, with outcomes determined by random number generators. In the old days, slot machines were like this: you pull the lever to spin three wheels; each wheel has 20 symbols, all equally likely to show when the wheel stops spinning; the three wheels are independent of each other. Suppose that the middle wheel has 9 bells among its 20 symbols, and the left and right wheels have 1 bell each.

(a) You win the jackpot if all three wheels show bells. What is the probability of winning the jackpot?

(b) There are three ways that the three wheels can show two bells and one symbol other than a bell. Find the probability of each of these ways.

(c) What is the probability that the wheels stop with exactly two bells showing among them?

12.3 **Common names.** The Census Bureau says that the 10 most common names in the United States are (in order) Smith, Johnson, Williams, Jones, Brown, Davis, Miller, Wilson, Moore, and Taylor. These names account for 5.6% of all U.S. residents. Out of curiosity, you look at the authors of the textbooks for your current courses. There are 9 authors in all. Would you be surprised if none of the names of these authors were among the 10 most common? Give a probability to support your answer and explain the reasoning behind your calculation.

12.4 **College-educated construction workers?** Government data show that 28% of employed people have at least 4 years of college and that 6% of employed people are construction workers. Nonetheless, we can't conclude that, because $(0.28)(0.06) = 0.017$, about 1.7% of employed people are college-educated construction workers. Why not?

The general addition rule

We know that if A and B are disjoint events, then $P(A \text{ or } B) = P(A) + P(B)$. If events A and B are *not* disjoint, they can occur together. The probability that one or the other occurs is then *less* than the sum of their probabilities. As Figure 12.3 illustrates, outcomes common to both are counted twice when we add probabilities, so we must subtract this probability once. Here is the addition rule for any two events, disjoint or not.

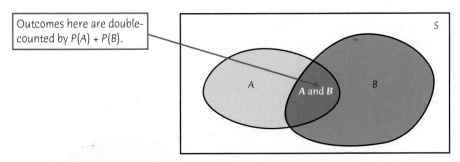

FIGURE 12.3 The general addition rule: $P(A \text{ or } B) = P(A) + P(B) - P(A \text{ and } B)$ for any events A and B.

GENERAL ADDITION RULE FOR ANY TWO EVENTS

For any two events A and B,

$$P(A \text{ or } B) = P(A) + P(B) - P(A \text{ and } B)$$

If A and B are disjoint, the event $\{A \text{ and } B\}$ that both occur contains no outcomes and therefore has probability 0. So the general addition rule includes Rule 3, the addition rule for disjoint events.

EXAMPLE 12.4 Motor vehicle sales

Motor vehicles sold in the United States are classified as either cars or light trucks and as either domestic or imported. "Light trucks" include SUVs and minivans. "Domestic" means made in North America, so that a Toyota made in Canada counts as domestic.

In a recent year, 80% of the new vehicles sold to individuals were domestic, 54% were light trucks, and 47% were domestic light trucks. Choose a vehicle sale at random. Then

$$P(\text{domestic or light truck}) = P(\text{domestic}) + P(\text{light truck}) - P(\text{domestic light truck})$$
$$= 0.80 + 0.54 - 0.47 = 0.87$$

That is, 87% of vehicles sold were either domestic or light trucks. A vehicle is an imported car if it is *neither* domestic nor a light truck. So

$$P(\text{imported car}) = 1 - 0.87 = 0.13$$

Venn diagrams are a great help in finding probabilities because you can just think of adding and subtracting areas. Look carefully at Figure 12.4, which shows some events and their probabilities for Example 12.4. What is the probability that a randomly chosen vehicle sale is a domestic car? The Venn diagram shows that this is the probability that the vehicle is domestic minus the probability that it is a domestic light truck, $0.8 - 0.47 = 0.33$. The four probabilities that appear in the figure add to 1 because they refer to four disjoint events that make up the entire sample space.

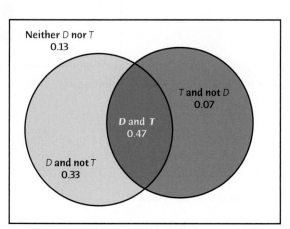

FIGURE 12.4 Venn diagram and probabilities for motor vehicle sales, Example 12.4.

D = vehicle is domestic T = vehicle is a light truck

APPLY YOUR KNOWLEDGE

12.5   Tastes in music.   Musical styles other than rock and pop are becoming more popular. A survey of college students finds that 40% like country music, 30% like gospel music, and 10% like both. Make a Venn diagram and use it to answer these questions.

(a) What percent of college students like country but not gospel?

(b) What percent like neither country nor gospel?

12.6   Distance learning.   A study of the students taking distance learning courses at a university finds that they are mostly older students not living in the university town. Choose a distance learning student at random. Let A be the event that the student is 25 years old or older and B the event that the student is local. The study finds that $P(A) = 0.7$, $P(B) = 0.25$, and $P(A \text{ and } B) = 0.05$.

(a) What is the probability that the student is less than 25 years old?

(b) What is the probability that the student is at least 25 years old and not local?

Mark C. Burnett/Stock, Boston

Conditional probability

The probability we assign to an event can change if we know that some other event has occurred. This idea is the key to many applications of probability.

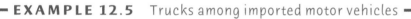

EXAMPLE 12.5   *Trucks among imported motor vehicles*

Figure 12.4, based on the information in Example 12.4, gives the following probabilities for a randomly chosen motor vehicle sold at retail in the United States:

	Domestic	Imported	Total
Light truck	0.47	0.07	0.54
Car	0.33	0.13	0.46
Total	0.80	0.20	

The "Total" row and column are obtained from the probabilities in the body of the table by the addition rule. For example, the probability that a randomly chosen vehicle is a light truck is

$$P(\text{truck}) = P(\text{truck and domestic}) + P(\text{truck and imported})$$
$$= 0.47 + 0.07 = 0.54$$

Now we are told that the vehicle chosen is imported. That is, it is one of the 20% in the "Imported" column of the table. The probability that a vehicle is a truck, *given the information that it is imported*, is the proportion of trucks in the "Imported" column,

$$P(\text{truck} \mid \text{imported}) = \frac{0.07}{0.20} = 0.35$$

This is a **conditional probability.** You can read the bar | as "given the information that."

Politically correct

In 1950, the Soviet mathematician B. V. Gnedenko (1912–1995) wrote *The Theory of Probability*, a text that was popular around the world. The introduction contains a mystifying paragraph that begins, "We note that the entire development of probability theory shows evidence of how its concepts and ideas were crystallized in a severe struggle between materialistic and idealistic conceptions." It turns out that "materialistic" is jargon for "Marxist-Leninist." It was good for the health of Soviet scientists in the Stalin era to add such statements to their books.

conditional probability

Although 54% of the vehicles sold are trucks, only 35% of imported vehicles are trucks. It's common sense that knowing that one event (the vehicle is imported) occurs often changes the probability of another event (the vehicle is a truck). The example also shows how we should define conditional probability. The idea of a conditional probability $P(B \mid A)$ of one event B given that another event A occurs is the proportion *of all occurrences of A* for which B also occurs.

CONDITIONAL PROBABILITY

When $P(A) > 0$, the **conditional probability** of B given A is

$$P(B \mid A) = \frac{P(A \text{ and } B)}{P(A)}$$

The conditional probability $P(B \mid A)$ makes no sense if the event A can never occur, so we require that $P(A) > 0$ whenever we talk about $P(B \mid A)$. *Be sure to keep in mind the distinct roles of the events A and B in* $P(B \mid A)$. Event A represents the information we are given, and B is the event whose probability we are calculating. Here is an example that emphasizes this distinction.

EXAMPLE 12.6   Imports among trucks

What is the conditional probability that a randomly chosen vehicle is imported, *given the information that it is a truck?* Using the definition of conditional probability,

$$P(\text{imported} \mid \text{truck}) = \frac{P(\text{imported and truck})}{P(\text{truck})}$$

$$= \frac{0.07}{0.54} = 0.13$$

Only 13% of trucks sold are imports.

Be careful not to confuse the two different conditional probabilities

$$P(\text{truck} \mid \text{imported}) = 0.35$$
$$P(\text{imported} \mid \text{truck}) = 0.13$$

The first answers the question "What proportion of imports are trucks?" The second answers "What proportion of trucks are imports?"

APPLY YOUR KNOWLEDGE

12.7   **Tastes in music.** In the setting of Exercise 12.5, what is the conditional probability that a student likes gospel music, given that he or she likes country music?

12.8   **Distance learning.** In the setting of Exercise 12.6, what is the conditional probability that a student is local, given that he or she is less than 25 years old?

12.9   Computer games.   Here is the distribution of computer games sold in 2004 by type of game:[3]

Game type	Probability
Strategy	0.269
Family and children's	0.203
Shooters	0.163
Role playing	0.100
Sports	0.054
Other	0.211

What is the conditional probability that a computer game is a strategy game, given that it is not a family or children's game?

The general multiplication rule

The definition of conditional probability reminds us that in principle all probabilities, including conditional probabilities, can be found from the assignment of probabilities to events that describes a random phenomenon. More often, however, conditional probabilities are part of the information given to us in a probability model. The definition of conditional probability then turns into a rule for finding the probability that both of two events occur.

GENERAL MULTIPLICATION RULE FOR ANY TWO EVENTS

The probability that both of two events A and B happen together can be found by

$$P(A \text{ and } B) = P(A)P(B \mid A)$$

Here $P(B \mid A)$ is the conditional probability that B occurs, given the information that A occurs.

In words, this rule says that for both of two events to occur, first one must occur and then, given that the first event has occurred, the second must occur. This is often just common sense expressed in the language of probability, as the following example illustrates.

EXAMPLE 12.7   Instant messaging

The Pew Internet and American Life Project finds that 87% of teenagers (ages 12 to 17) are online, and that 75% of online teens use instant messaging (IM).[4] What percent of teens are online *and* use IM?

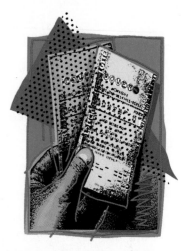

Winning the lottery twice

In 1986, Evelyn Marie Adams won the New Jersey lottery for the second time, adding $1.5 million to her previous $3.9 million jackpot. The *New York Times* claimed that the odds of one person winning the big prize twice were 1 in 17 trillion. Nonsense, said two statisticians in a letter to the *Times*. The chance that Evelyn Marie Adams would win twice is indeed tiny, but it is almost certain that *someone* among the millions of lottery players would win two jackpots. Sure enough, Robert Humphries won his second Pennsylvania lottery jackpot ($6.8 million total) in 1988.

Use the general multiplication rule:

$$P(\text{online}) = 0.87$$

$$P(\text{use IM} \mid \text{online}) = 0.75$$

$$P(\text{online and use IM}) = P(\text{online}) \times P(\text{use IM} \mid \text{online})$$

$$= (0.87)(0.75) = 0.6525$$

That is, about 65% of teens are online and use IM.

You should think your way through this: if 87% of teens are online and 75% *of these* use instant messaging, then 75% of 87% are both online and users of IM.

The multiplication rule extends to the probability that all of several events occur. The key is to condition each event on the occurrence of *all* of the preceding events. For example, we have for three events A, B, and C that

$$P(A \text{ and } B \text{ and } C) = P(A)P(B \mid A)P(C \mid A \text{ and } B)$$

— **EXAMPLE 12.8**   *Fundraising by telephone* —————————

STATE: A charity raises funds by calling a list of prospective donors to ask for pledges. It is able to talk with 40% of the names on its list. Of those the charity reaches, 30% make a pledge. But only half of those who pledge actually make a contribution. What percent of the donor list contributes?

FORMULATE: Express the information we are given in terms of events and their probabilities:

If $A = \{$the charity reaches a prospect$\}$ then $P(A) = 0.4$
If $B = \{$the prospect makes a pledge$\}$ then $P(B \mid A) = 0.3$
If $C = \{$the prospect makes a contribution$\}$ then $P(C \mid A \text{ and } B) = 0.5$

We want to find $P(A \text{ and } B \text{ and } C)$.

SOLVE: Use the general multiplication rule:

$$P(A \text{ and } B \text{ and } C) = P(A)P(B \mid A)P(C \mid A \text{ and } B)$$

$$= 0.4 \times 0.3 \times 0.5 = 0.06$$

CONCLUDE: Only 6% of the prospective donors make a contribution.

As Example 12.8 illustrates, formulating a problem in the language of probability is often the key to success in applying probability ideas.

Independence

The conditional probability $P(B \mid A)$ is generally not equal to the unconditional probability $P(B)$. That's because the occurrence of event A generally gives us some additional information about whether or not event B occurs. If knowing that A occurs gives no additional information about B, then A and B are independent events. The precise definition of independence is expressed in terms of conditional probability.

INDEPENDENT EVENTS

Two events A and B that both have positive probability are **independent** if

$$P(B \mid A) = P(B)$$

We now see that the multiplication rule for independent events, $P(A \text{ and } B) = P(A)P(B)$, is a special case of the general multiplication rule, $P(A \text{ and } B) = P(A)P(B \mid A)$, just as the addition rule for disjoint events is a special case of the general addition rule. We rarely use the definition of independence, because most often independence is part of the information given to us in a probability model.

APPLY YOUR KNOWLEDGE

12.10 At the gym. Suppose that 10% of adults belong to health clubs, and 40% of these health club members go to the club at least twice a week. What percent of all adults go to a health club at least twice a week? Write the information given in terms of probabilities and use the general multiplication rule.

12.11 Education and income. Call a person educated if he or she holds at least a bachelor's degree. Call a person who earns at least $100,000 a year prosperous. The Census Bureau says that in 2004, 28% of American adults (age 25 and older) were educated. Among these educated adults, 13% were prosperous. What percent of adults were both educated and prosperous? Follow the four-step process.

12.12 The probability of a flush. A poker player holds a flush when all 5 cards in the hand belong to the same suit (clubs, diamonds, hearts, or spades). We will find the probability of a flush when 5 cards are dealt. Remember that a deck contains 52 cards, 13 of each suit, and that when the deck is well shuffled, each card dealt is equally likely to be any of those that remain in the deck.

(a) Concentrate on spades. What is the probability that the first card dealt is a spade? What is the conditional probability that the second card is a spade, given that the first is a spade? (*Hint:* How many cards remain? How many of these are spades?)

(b) Continue to count the remaining cards to find the conditional probabilities of a spade on the third, the fourth, and the fifth card, given in each case that all previous cards are spades.

(c) The probability of being dealt 5 spades is the product of the 5 probabilities you have found. Why? What is this probability?

(d) The probability of being dealt 5 hearts or 5 diamonds or 5 clubs is the same as the probability of being dealt 5 spades. What is the probability of being dealt a flush?

Tree diagrams

Probability problems often require us to combine several of the basic rules into a more elaborate calculation. Here is an example that illustrates how to solve problems that have several stages.

EXAMPLE 12.9 *Adults in the chat room?*

STATE: Online chat rooms are dominated by the young. Let's look only at adult Internet users, age 18 and over. The Pew Internet and American Life Project finds that 29% of adult Internet users are age 18 to 29, another 47% are 30 to 49 years old, and the remaining 24% are age 50 and over. Moreover, 47% of the 18 to 29 age group chat, as do 21% of those aged 30 to 49 and just 7% of those 50 and over. What percent of all adult Internet users chat?

FORMULATE: To use the tools of probability, restate Pew's percents as probabilities. If we choose an online adult at random,

$$P(\text{age 18 to 29}) = 0.29$$
$$P(\text{age 30 to 49}) = 0.47$$
$$P(\text{age 50 and older}) = 0.24$$

Jim Craigmyle/CORBIS

These three probabilities add to 1 because all adult Internet users are in one of the three age groups. The percents of each group who chat are *conditional* probabilities:

$$P(\text{chat} \mid \text{age 18 to 29}) = 0.47$$
$$P(\text{chat} \mid \text{age 30 to 49}) = 0.21$$
$$P(\text{chat} \mid \text{age 50 and older}) = 0.07$$

We want to find the unconditional probability $P(\text{chat})$.

tree diagram

SOLVE: The **tree diagram** in Figure 12.5 organizes this information. Each segment in the tree is one stage of the problem. Each complete branch shows a path through the two stages. The probability written on each segment is the conditional probability of an Internet user following that segment given that he or she has reached the node from which it branches.

Starting at the left, an Internet user falls into one of the three age groups. The probabilities of these groups mark the leftmost segments in the tree. Look at age 18 to 29, the top branch. The two segments going out from the "18 to 29" branch point carry the conditional probabilities

$$P(\text{chat} \mid \text{age 18 to 29}) = 0.47$$
$$P(\text{no chat} \mid \text{age 18 to 29}) = 0.53$$

The full tree shows the probabilities for all three age groups.

Now use the multiplication rule. The probability that a randomly chosen Internet user is an 18- to 29-year-old who chats is

$$P(\text{18 to 29 and chat}) = P(\text{18 to 29})P(\text{chat} \mid \text{18 to 29})$$
$$= (0.29)(0.47) = 0.1363$$

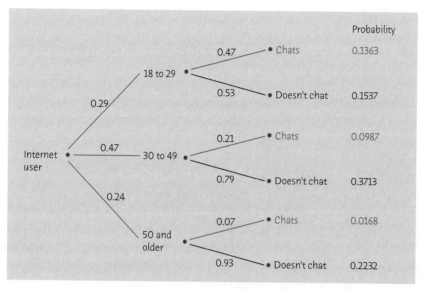

FIGURE 12.5 Tree diagram for chat room participants, Example 12.9. The three disjoint paths to the outcome that an adult Internet user participates in chat rooms are colored red.

This probability appears at the end of the topmost branch. You see that the probability of any complete branch in the tree is the product of the probabilities of the segments in that branch.

There are three disjoint paths to chatting, starting with the three age groups. These paths are colored red in Figure 12.5. Because the three paths are disjoint, the probability that an Internet user chats is the sum of their probabilities,

$$P(\text{chat}) = (0.29)(0.47) + (0.47)(0.21) + (0.24)(0.07)$$
$$= 0.1363 + 0.0987 + 0.0168 = 0.2518$$

CONCLUDE: About 25% of all adult Internet users take part in chat rooms.

It takes longer to explain a tree diagram than it does to use it. Once you have understood a problem well enough to draw the tree, the rest is easy. Here is another question about online chat that the tree diagram helps us answer.

EXAMPLE 12.10   *Young adults in the chat room*

STATE: What percent of adult chat room participants are age 18 to 29?

FORMULATE: In probability language, we want the conditional probability

$$P(18 \text{ to } 29 \mid \text{chat}) = \frac{P(18 \text{ to } 29 \text{ and chat})}{P(\text{chat})}$$

SOLVE: Look again at the tree diagram. $P(\text{chat})$ is the overall outcome. $P(18 \text{ to } 29$ and chat) is the result of following the top branch of the tree diagram. So

$$P(18 \text{ to } 29 \mid \text{chat}) = \frac{0.1363}{0.2518} = 0.5413$$

> **CONCLUDE**: Over half of adult chat room participants are between 18 and 29 years old. Compare this conditional probability with the original information (unconditional) that 29% of adult Internet users are between 18 and 29 years old. Knowing that a person chats increases the probability that he or she is young.

Examples 12.9 and 12.10 illustrate a common setting for tree diagrams. Some outcome (such as participating in chat rooms) has several sources (such as the three age groups). Starting from

- the probability of each source, and
- the conditional probability of the outcome given each source

the tree diagram leads to the overall probability of the outcome. Example 12.9 does this. You can then use the probability of the outcome and the definition of conditional probability to find the conditional probability of one of the sources given that the outcome occurred. Example 12.10 shows how.

APPLY YOUR KNOWLEDGE

12.13 Spelling errors. Spelling errors in a text are either "nonword errors" or "word errors." A nonword error produces a string of letters that is not a word, as when "the" is typed as "teh." Word errors produce the wrong word, as when "loose" is typed as "lose." Nonword errors make up 25% of all errors. A human proofreader will catch 90% of nonword errors and 70% of word errors. What percent of all errors will the proofreader catch? Follow the four-step process as illustrated in Example 12.9.

12.14 Testing for HIV. Enzyme immunoassay tests are used to screen blood specimens for the presence of antibodies to HIV, the virus that causes AIDS. Antibodies indicate the presence of the virus. The test is quite accurate but is not always correct. Here are approximate probabilities of positive and negative test results when the blood tested does and does not actually contain antibodies to HIV:[5]

	Test Result	
	+	−
Antibodies present	0.9985	0.0015
Antibodies absent	0.0060	0.9940

Suppose that 1% of a large population carries antibodies to HIV in their blood.

(a) Draw a tree diagram for selecting a person from this population (outcomes: antibodies present or absent) and for testing his or her blood (outcomes: test positive or negative).

(b) What is the probability that the test is positive for a randomly chosen person from this population?

12.15 Nonword spelling errors. Continue your work from Exercise 12.13. Of all errors that the proofreader catches, what percent are nonword errors?

12.16 False HIV positives. Continue your work from Exercise 12.14. What is the probability that a person has the antibody, given that the test is positive? (Your result illustrates a fact that is important when considering proposals for widespread testing for HIV, illegal drugs, or agents of biological warfare: if the condition being tested is uncommon in the population, most positives will be false positives.)

CHAPTER 12 SUMMARY

Events A and B are **disjoint** if they have no outcomes in common. In that case, $P(A \text{ or } B) = P(A) + P(B)$.

The **conditional probability** $P(B \mid A)$ of an event B given an event A is defined by

$$P(B \mid A) = \frac{P(A \text{ and } B)}{P(A)}$$

when $P(A) > 0$. In practice, we most often find conditional probabilities from directly available information rather than from the definition.

Events A and B are **independent** if knowing that one event occurs does not change the probability we would assign to the other event; that is, $P(B \mid A) = P(B)$. In that case, $P(A \text{ and } B) = P(A)P(B)$.

Any assignment of probability obeys these general rules:

Addition rule: If events $A, B, C, \ldots$ are all **disjoint** in pairs, then

$P(\text{at least one of these events occurs}) = P(A) + P(B) + P(C) + \cdots$

Multiplication rule: If events $A, B, C, \ldots$ are **independent,** then

$P(\text{all of the events occur}) = P(A)P(B)P(C)\cdots$

General addition rule: For any two events A and B,

$P(A \text{ or } B) = P(A) + P(B) - P(A \text{ and } B)$

General multiplication rule: For any two events A and B,

$P(A \text{ and } B) = P(A)P(B \mid A)$

CHECK YOUR SKILLS

12.17 An instant lottery game gives you probability 0.02 of winning on any one play. Plays are independent of each other. If you play 3 times, the probability that you win on none of your plays is about

(a) 0.98.   (b) 0.94.   (c) 0.000008.

12.18 The probability that you win on one or more of your 3 plays of the game in the previous exercise is about

(a) 0.02.   (b) 0.06.   (c) 0.999992.

12.19 An athlete suspected of having used steroids is given two tests that operate independently of each other. Test A has probability 0.9 of being positive if steroids have been used. Test B has probability 0.8 of being positive if steroids have been used. What is the probability that *neither* test is positive if steroids have been used?

(a) 0.72   (b) 0.38   (c) 0.02

Government data give the following counts of violent deaths in a recent year among people 20 to 24 years of age by sex and cause of death:

	Female	Male
Accidents	1818	6457
Homicide	457	2870
Suicide	345	2152

Exercises 12.20 to 12.23 are based on this table.

12.20 Choose a violent death in this age group at random. The probability that the victim was male is about

(a) 0.81.   (b) 0.78.   (c) 0.19.

12.21 The conditional probability that the victim was male, given that the death was accidental, is about

(a) 0.81.   (b) 0.78.   (c) 0.56.

12.22 The conditional probability that the death was accidental, given that the victim was male, is about

(a) 0.81.   (b) 0.78.   (c) 0.56.

12.23 Let A be the event that a victim of violent death was a woman and B the event that the death was a suicide. The proportion of suicides among violent deaths of women is expressed in probability notation as

(a) $P(A \text{ and } B)$.   (b) $P(A \mid B)$.   (c) $P(B \mid A)$.

12.24 Choose an American adult at random. The probability that you choose a woman is 0.52. The probability that the person you choose has never married is 0.24. The probability that you choose a woman who has never married is 0.11. The probability that the person you choose is either a woman or never married (or both) is therefore about

(a) 0.76.   (b) 0.65.   (c) 0.12.

12.25 Of people who died in the United States in a recent year, 86% were white, 12% were black, and 2% were Asian. (This ignores a small number of deaths among other races.) Diabetes caused 2.8% of deaths among whites, 4.4% among blacks, and 3.5% among Asians. The probability that a randomly chosen death is a white who died of diabetes is about

(a) 0.107.   (b) 0.030.   (c) 0.024.

12.26 Using the information in the previous exercise, the probability that a randomly chosen death was due to diabetes is about

(a) 0.107.   (b) 0.030.   (c) 0.024.

CHAPTER 12 EXERCISES

12.27 Playing the lottery. New York State's "Quick Draw" lottery moves right along. Players choose between one and ten numbers from the range 1 to 80; 20 winning numbers are displayed on a screen every four minutes. If you choose just one number, your probability of winning is 20/80, or 0.25. Lester plays one number 8 times as he sits in a bar. What is the probability that all 8 bets lose?

12.28 Universal blood donors. People with type O-negative blood are universal donors. That is, any patient can receive a transfusion of O-negative blood. Only 7.2% of the American population have O-negative blood. If 10 people appear at random to give blood, what is the probability that at least one of them is a universal donor?

12.29 Telemarketing. Telephone marketers and opinion polls use random digit dialing equipment to call residential telephone numbers at random. The polling firm Zogby International reports that just 20% of calls reach a live person.[6] Calls are independent.

(a) A telemarketer places 5 calls. What is the probability that none of them reaches a person?

(b) Only 8% of calls made to residential numbers in New York City reach a person. What is the probability that none of 5 calls made to New York City reaches a person?

12.30 A random walk on Wall Street? The random walk theory of stock prices holds that price movements in disjoint time periods are independent of each other. Suppose that we record only whether the price is up or down each year, and that the probability that our portfolio rises in price in any one year is 0.65. (This probability is approximately correct for a portfolio containing equal dollar amounts of all common stocks listed on the New York Stock Exchange.)

(a) What is the probability that our portfolio goes up for three consecutive years?

(b) What is the probability that the portfolio's value moves in the same direction (either up or down) for three consecutive years?

12.31 Older women. Government data show that 6% of the American population are at least 75 years of age and that about 52% of Americans are women. Explain why it is wrong to conclude that because $(0.06)(0.52) = 0.0312$ about 3% of the population are women aged 75 or over.

12.32 Foreign-born Californians. The Census Bureau reports that 27% of California residents are foreign-born. Suppose that you choose three Californians at random, so that each has probability 0.27 of being foreign-born and the three choices are independent of each other. Let the random variable X be the number of foreign-born people you chose.

(a) What are the possible values of X?

(b) Look at your three people in order. There are eight possible arrangements of foreign (F) and domestic (D) birth. For example, FFD means the first two are foreign-born and the third is not. Write down all eight arrangements and find the probability of each arrangement.

(c) What is the value of X for each arrangement in (b)? What is the probability of each possible value of X? (You have found the distribution of a Yes/No response for an SRS of size 3. In principle, the same idea works for an SRS of any size.)

12.33 **Getting into college.** Ramon has applied to both Princeton and Stanford. He thinks the probability that Princeton will admit him is 0.4, the probability that Stanford will admit him is 0.5, and the probability that both will admit him is 0.2. Make a Venn diagram. Then answer these questions.

(a) What is the probability that neither university admits Ramon?

(b) What is the probability that he gets into Stanford but not Princeton?

(c) Are admission to Princeton and admission to Stanford independent events?

12.34 **Tendon surgery.** You have torn a tendon and are facing surgery to repair it. The surgeon explains the risks to you: infection occurs in 3% of such operations, the repair fails in 14%, and both infection and failure occur together in 1%. What percent of these operations succeed and are free from infection? Follow the four-step process in your answer.

12.35 **Screening job applicants.** A company retains a psychologist to assess whether job applicants are suited for assembly-line work. The psychologist classifies applicants as one of A (well suited), B (marginal), or C (not suited). The company is concerned about the event D that an employee leaves the company within a year of being hired. Data on all people hired in the past five years give these probabilities:

$$P(A) = 0.4 \qquad P(B) = 0.3 \qquad P(C) = 0.3$$
$$P(A \text{ and } D) = 0.1 \qquad P(B \text{ and } D) = 0.1 \qquad P(C \text{ and } D) = 0.2$$

Sketch a Venn diagram of the events A, B, C, and D and mark on your diagram the probabilities of all combinations of psychological assessment and leaving (or not) within a year. What is $P(D)$, the probability that an employee leaves within a year?

12.36 **Foreign-language study.** Choose a student in grades 9 to 12 at random and ask if he or she is studying a language other than English. Here is the distribution of results:

Language	Spanish	French	German	All others	None
Probability	0.26	0.09	0.03	0.03	0.59

What is the conditional probability that a student is studying Spanish, given that he or she is studying some language other than English?

12.37 **Income tax returns.** Here is the distribution of the adjusted gross income (in thousands of dollars) reported on individual federal income tax returns in 2003:

Income	< 25	25–49	50–99	100–199	≥ 200
Probability	0.454	0.252	0.206	0.068	0.020

(a) What is the probability that a randomly chosen return shows an adjusted gross income of $50,000 or more?

(b) Given that a return shows an income of at least $50,000, what is the conditional probability that the income is at least $100,000?

12.38 **Geometric probability.** Choose a point at random in the square with sides $0 \leq x \leq 1$ and $0 \leq y \leq 1$. This means that the probability that the point falls in any region within the square is equal to the area of that region. Let X be the x coordinate and Y the y coordinate of the point chosen. Find the conditional probability $P(Y < 1/2 \mid Y > X)$. (*Hint:* Draw a diagram of the square and the events $Y < 1/2$ and $Y > X$.)

12.39 **A probability teaser.** Suppose (as is roughly correct) that each child born is equally likely to be a boy or a girl and that the sexes of successive children are independent. If we let BG mean that the older child is a boy and the younger child is a girl, then each of the combinations BB, BG, GB, GG has probability 0.25. Ashley and Brianna each have two children.

(a) You know that at least one of Ashley's children is a boy. What is the conditional probability that she has two boys?

(b) You know that Brianna's older child is a boy. What is the conditional probability that she has two boys?

12.40 **The probability of a royal flush.** A royal flush is the highest hand possible in poker. It consists of the ace, king, queen, jack, and ten of the same suit. Modify the calculation outlined in Exercise 12.12 (page 313) to find the probability of being dealt a royal flush in a five-card hand.

12.41 **College degrees.** Here are the counts (in thousands) of earned degrees in the United States in the 2005–2006 academic year, classified by level and by the sex of the degree recipient:[7]

	Bachelor's	Master's	Professional	Doctorate	Total
Female	784	276	39	20	1119
Male	559	197	44	25	825
Total	1343	473	83	45	1944

(a) If you choose a degree recipient at random, what is the probability that the person you choose is a woman?

(b) What is the conditional probability that you choose a woman, given that the person chosen received a professional degree?

(c) Are the events "choose a woman" and "choose a professional degree recipient" independent? How do you know?

12.42 **College degrees.** Exercise 12.41 gives the counts (in thousands) of earned degrees in the United States in the 2005–2006 academic year. Use these data to answer the following questions.

(a) What is the probability that a randomly chosen degree recipient is a man?

(b) What is the conditional probability that the person chosen received a bachelor's degree, given that he is a man?

(c) Use the multiplication rule to find the probability of choosing a male bachelor's degree recipient. Check your result by finding this probability directly from the table of counts.

12.43 Julie's job prospects. Julie is graduating from college. She has studied biology, chemistry, and computing and hopes to use her science background in crime investigation. Late one night she thinks about some jobs for which she has applied. Let A, B, and C be the events that Julie is offered a job by

A = the Connecticut Office of the Chief Medical Examiner
B = the New Jersey Division of Criminal Justice
C = the federal Disaster Mortuary Operations Response Team

Julie writes down her personal probabilities for being offered these jobs:

$P(A) = 0.6$ $P(B) = 0.4$ $P(C) = 0.2$
$P(A \text{ and } B) = 0.1$ $P(A \text{ and } C) = 0.05$ $P(B \text{ and } C) = 0.05$
$P(A \text{ and } B \text{ and } C) = 0$

Make a Venn diagram of the events A, B, and C. As in Figure 12.4, mark the probabilities of every intersection involving these events. Use this diagram for Exercises 12.44 to 12.46.

12.44 What is the probability that Julie is offered at least one of the three jobs?

12.45 What is the probability that Julie is offered both the Connecticut and New Jersey jobs, but not the federal job?

12.46 If Julie is offered the federal job, what is the conditional probability that she is also offered the New Jersey job? If Julie is offered the New Jersey job, what is the conditional probability that she is also offered the federal job?

12.47 The geometric distributions. You are tossing a balanced die that has probability 1/6 of coming up 1 on each toss. Tosses are independent. We are interested in how long we must wait to get the first 1.

(a) The probability of a 1 on the first toss is 1/6. What is the probability that the first toss is not a 1 and the second toss is a 1?

(b) What is the probability that the first two tosses are not 1s and the third toss is a 1? This is the probability that the first 1 occurs on the third toss.

(c) Now you see the pattern. What is the probability that the first 1 occurs on the fourth toss? On the fifth toss? Give the general result: what is the probability that the first 1 occurs on the kth toss?

Comment: The distribution of the number of trials to the first success is called a **geometric distribution.** In this problem you have found geometric distribution probabilities when the probability of a success on each trial is 1/6. The same idea works for any probability of success.

geometric distribution

12.48 Urban voters. The voters in a large city are 40% white, 40% black, and 20% Hispanic. (Hispanics may be of any race in official statistics, but here we are speaking of political blocs.) A black mayoral candidate anticipates attracting 30% of the white vote, 90% of the black vote, and 50% of the Hispanic vote. Draw a tree diagram with probabilities for the race (white, black, or Hispanic) and vote (for or against the candidate) of a randomly chosen voter. What percent of the overall vote does the candidate expect to get? Use the four-step process to guide your work.

12.49 At the gas pump. At a self-service gas station, 40% of the customers pump regular gas, 35% pump midgrade gas, and 25% pump premium gas. Of those who pump regular, 30% pay at least $30. Of those who pump midgrade, 50% pay at least $30. And of those who pump premium, 60% pay at least $30. What is the probability that the next customer pays at least $30? Follow the four-step process.

12.50 Where do the votes come from? In the election described in Exercise 12.48, what percent of the candidate's votes come from black voters? (Write this as a conditional probability and use the definition of conditional probability.)

12.51 Who pays $30 for gas? In the setting of Exercise 12.49, what percent of customers who pay at least $30 pump premium? (Write this as a conditional probability and use your result from the previous exercise.)

12.52 Fundraising by telephone. Tree diagrams can organize problems having more than two stages. Figure 12.6 shows probabilities for a charity calling potential donors by telephone.[8] Each person called is either a recent donor, a past donor, or a new prospect. At the next stage, the person called either does or does not pledge to contribute, with conditional probabilities that depend on the donor class the person belongs to. Finally, those who make a pledge either do or don't actually make a contribution.

(a) What percent of calls result in a contribution?

(b) What percent of those who contribute are recent donors?

Maya Barnes/The Image Works

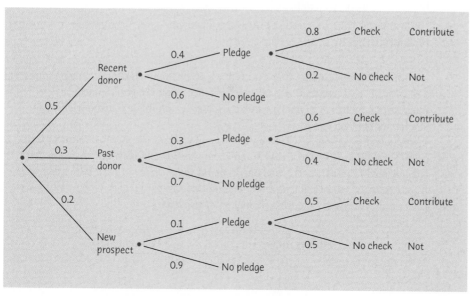

FIGURE 12.6 Tree diagram for fundraising by telephone, Exercise 12.52. The three stages are the type of prospect called, whether or not the person makes a pledge, and whether or not a person who pledges actually makes a contribution.

Working. In the language of government statistics, you are "in the labor force" if you are available for work and either working or actively seeking work. The unemployment rate is the proportion of the labor force (not of the entire population) who are unemployed. Here are data from the Current Population Survey for the civilian population aged 25 years and over in 2004. The table entries are counts in thousands of people. Exercises 12.53 to 12.55 make use of these data.

Highest education	Total population	In labor force	Employed
Did not finish high school	27,669	12,470	11,408
High school but no college	59,860	37,834	35,857
Less than bachelor's degree	47,556	34,439	32,977
College graduate	51,852	40,390	39,293

12.53 Find the unemployment rate for people with each level of education. (This is the conditional probability of being unemployed, given an education level.) How does the unemployment rate change with education? Explain carefully why your results show that level of education and being employed are not independent.

12.54 (a) What is the probability that a randomly chosen person 25 years of age or older is in the labor force?

(b) If you know that the person chosen is a college graduate, what is the conditional probability that he or she is in the labor force?

(c) Are the events "in the labor force" and "college graduate" independent? How do you know?

12.55 (a) You know that a person is employed. What is the conditional probability that he or she is a college graduate?

(b) You know that a second person is a college graduate. What is the conditional probability that he or she is employed?

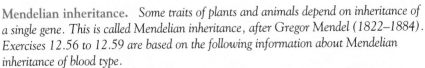

Mendelian inheritance.   Some traits of plants and animals depend on inheritance of a single gene. This is called Mendelian inheritance, after Gregor Mendel (1822–1884). Exercises 12.56 to 12.59 are based on the following information about Mendelian inheritance of blood type.

*   Each of us has an ABO blood type, which describes whether two characteristics called A and B are present. Every human being has two blood type alleles (gene forms), one inherited from our mother and one from our father. Each of these alleles can be A, B, or O. Which two we inherit determines our blood type. Here is a table that shows what our blood type is for each combination of two alleles:*

Alleles inherited	Blood type
A and A	A
A and B	AB
A and O	A
B and B	B
B and O	B
O and O	O

We inherit each of a parent's two alleles with probability 0.5. We inherit independently from our mother and father.

12.56 Rachel and Jonathan both have alleles A and B.

(a) What blood types can their children have?

(b) What is the probability that their next child has each of these blood types?

12.57 Sarah and David both have alleles B and O.

(a) What blood types can their children have?

(b) What is the probability that their next child has each of these blood types?

12.58 Isabel has alleles A and O. Carlos has alleles A and B. They have two children.

(a) What is the probability that both children have blood type A?

(b) What is the probability that both children have the same blood type?

12.59 Jasmine has alleles A and O. Tyrone has alleles B and O.

(a) What is the probability that a child of these parents has blood type O?

(b) If Jasmine and Tyrone have three children, what is the probability that all three have blood type O?

(c) What is the probability that the first child has blood type O and the next two do not?

B. Neumann/zefa/CORBIS

Binomial Distributions*

A basketball player shoots 5 free throws. How many does she make? A new treatment for pancreatic cancer is tried on 250 patients. How many survive for five years? You plant 10 dogwood trees. How many live through the winter? In all these situations, we want a probability model for a *count* of successful outcomes.

The binomial setting and binomial distributions

The distribution of a count depends on how the data are produced. Here is a common situation.

THE BINOMIAL SETTING

1. There are a fixed number n of observations.

2. The n observations are all **independent.** That is, knowing the result of one observation does not change the probabilities we assign to other observations.

3. Each observation falls into one of just two categories, which for convenience we call "success" and "failure."

4. The probability of a success, call it p, is the same for each observation.

---

*This more advanced chapter concerns a special topic in probability. The material is not needed to read the rest of the book.

Think of tossing a coin n times as an example of the binomial setting. Each toss gives either heads or tails. Knowing the outcome of one toss doesn't change the probability of a head on any other toss, so the tosses are independent. If we call heads a success, then p is the probability of a head and remains the same as long as we toss the same coin. The number of heads we count is a discrete random variable X. The distribution of X is called a *binomial distribution*.

BINOMIAL DISTRIBUTION

The count X of successes in the binomial setting has the **binomial distribution** with parameters n and p. The parameter n is the number of observations, and p is the probability of a success on any one observation. The possible values of X are the whole numbers from 0 to n.

The binomial distributions are an important class of probability distributions. *Pay attention to the binomial setting, because not all counts have binomial distributions.*

CAUTION

EXAMPLE 13.1   Blood types

Genetics says that children receive genes from their parents independently. Each child of a particular pair of parents has probability 0.25 of having type O blood. If these parents have 5 children, the number who have type O blood is the count X of successes in 5 independent observations with probability 0.25 of a success on each observation. So X has the binomial distribution with $n = 5$ and $p = 0.25$.

EXAMPLE 13.2   Dealing cards

Deal 10 cards from a shuffled deck and count the number X of red cards. There are 10 observations, and each gives either a red or a black card. A "success" is a red card. But the observations are *not* independent. If the first card is black, the second is more likely to be red because there are more red cards than black cards left in the deck. The count X does *not* have a binomial distribution.

Binomial distributions in statistical sampling

The binomial distributions are important in statistics when we wish to make inferences about the proportion p of "successes" in a population. Here is a typical example.

EXAMPLE 13.3   Choosing an SRS of CDs

A music distributor inspects an SRS of 10 CDs from a shipment of 10,000 music CDs. Suppose that (unknown to the distributor) 10% of the CDs in the shipment have defective copy-protection schemes that will harm personal computers. Count the number X of bad CDs in the sample.

Was he good or was he lucky?

When a baseball player hits .300, everyone applauds. A .300 hitter gets a hit in 30% of times at bat. Could a .300 year just be luck? Typical major leaguers bat about 500 times a season and hit about .260. A hitter's successive tries seem to be independent, so we have a binomial setting. From this model, we can calculate or simulate the probability of hitting .300. It is about 0.025. Out of 100 run-of-the-mill major league hitters, two or three each year will bat .300 because they were lucky.

This is not quite a binomial setting. Just as removing one card in Example 13.2 changes the makeup of the deck, removing one CD changes the proportion of bad CDs remaining in the shipment. So the probability that the second CD chosen is bad changes when we know that the first is bad. But removing one CD from a shipment of 10,000 changes the makeup of the remaining 9999 CDs very little. In practice, the distribution of X is very close to the binomial distribution with $n = 10$ and $p = 0.1$.

Example 13.3 shows how we can use the binomial distributions in the statistical setting of selecting an SRS. When the population is much larger than the sample, a count of successes in an SRS of size n has approximately the binomial distribution with n equal to the sample size and p equal to the proportion of successes in the population.

SAMPLING DISTRIBUTION OF A COUNT

Choose an SRS of size n from a population with proportion p of successes. When the population is much larger than the sample, the count X of successes in the sample has approximately the binomial distribution with parameters n and p.

APPLY YOUR KNOWLEDGE

In each of Exercises 13.1 to 13.3, X is a count. Does X have a binomial distribution? Give your reasons in each case.

13.1 Random digit dialing. When an opinion poll calls residential telephone numbers at random, only 20% of the calls reach a live person. You watch the random dialing machine make 15 calls. X is the number that reach a live person.

13.2 Logging in. At peak periods, 15% of attempted log-ins to an online email service fail. Log-in attempts are independent and each has the same probability of failing. Darci logs in repeatedly until she succeeds. X is the number of the log-in attempt that finally succeeds.

13.3 Computer instruction. A student studies binomial distributions using computer-assisted instruction. After the lesson, the computer presents 10 problems. The student solves each problem and enters her answer. The computer gives additional instruction between problems if the answer is wrong. The count X is the number of problems that the student gets right.

13.4 I can't relax. Opinion polls find that 14% of Americans "never have time to relax."[1] If you take an SRS of 500 adults, what is the approximate distribution of the number in your sample who say they never have time to relax?

B. Neumann/zefa/CORBIS

Binomial probabilities

We can find a formula for the probability that a binomial random variable takes any value by adding probabilities for the different ways of getting exactly that many successes in n observations. Here is the example that illustrates the idea.

EXAMPLE 13.4 Inheriting blood type

Each child born to a particular set of parents has probability 0.25 of having blood type O. If these parents have 5 children, what is the probability that exactly 2 of them have type O blood?

   The count of children with type O blood is a binomial random variable X with $n = 5$ tries and probability $p = 0.25$ of a success on each try. We want $P(X = 2)$.

Because the method doesn't depend on the specific example, let's use "S" for success and "F" for failure for short. Do the work in two steps.

Step 1. Find the probability that a specific 2 of the 5 tries, say the first and the third, give successes. This is the outcome SFSFF. Because tries are independent, the multiplication rule for independent events applies. The probability we want is

$$P(SFSFF) = P(S)P(F)P(S)P(F)P(F)$$
$$= (0.25)(0.75)(0.25)(0.75)(0.75)$$
$$= (0.25)^2(0.75)^3$$

Step 2. Observe that *any one arrangement* of 2 S's and 3 F's has this same probability. This is true because we multiply together 0.25 twice and 0.75 three times whenever we have 2 S's and 3 F's. The probability that $X = 2$ is the probability of getting 2 S's and 3 F's in any arrangement whatsoever. Here are all the possible arrangements:

SSFFF   SFSFF   SFFSF   SFFFS   FSSFF
FSFSF   FSFFS   FFSSF   FFSFS   FFFSS

There are 10 of them, all with the same probability. The overall probability of 2 successes is therefore

$$P(X = 2) = 10(0.25)^2(0.75)^3 = 0.2637$$

The pattern of this calculation works for any binomial probability. To use it, we must count the number of arrangements of k successes in n observations. We use the following fact to do the counting without actually listing all the arrangements.

What looks random?

Toss a coin six times and record heads (H) or tails (T) on each toss. Which of these outcomes is more probable: HTHTTH or TTTHHH? Almost everyone says that HTHTTH is more probable, because TTTHHH does not "look random." In fact, both are equally probable. That heads has probability 0.5 says that about half of a very long sequence of tosses will be heads. It doesn't say that heads and tails must come close to alternating in the short run. The coin doesn't know what past outcomes were, and it can't try to create a balanced sequence.

BINOMIAL COEFFICIENT

The number of ways of arranging k successes among n observations is given by the **binomial coefficient**

$$\binom{n}{k} = \frac{n!}{k!\,(n-k)!}$$

for $k = 0, 1, 2, \ldots, n$.

factorial   The formula for binomial coefficients uses the **factorial** notation. For any positive whole number n, its factorial $n!$ is

$$n! = n \times (n-1) \times (n-2) \times \cdots \times 3 \times 2 \times 1$$

Also, $0! = 1$.

The larger of the two factorials in the denominator of a binomial coefficient will cancel much of the $n!$ in the numerator. For example, the binomial coefficient we need for Example 13.4 is

$$\binom{5}{2} = \frac{5!}{2!\,3!}$$
$$= \frac{(5)(4)(3)(2)(1)}{(2)(1) \times (3)(2)(1)}$$
$$= \frac{(5)(4)}{(2)(1)} = \frac{20}{2} = 10$$

CAUTION

The notation $\binom{n}{k}$ is not related to the fraction $\frac{n}{k}$. A helpful way to remember its meaning is to read it as "binomial coefficient n choose k." Binomial coefficients have many uses, but we are interested in them only as an aid to finding binomial probabilities. The binomial coefficient $\binom{n}{k}$ counts the number of different ways in which k successes can be arranged among n observations. The binomial probability $P(X = k)$ is this count multiplied by the probability of any one specific arrangement of the k successes. Here is the result we seek.

BINOMIAL PROBABILITY

If X has the binomial distribution with n observations and probability p of success on each observation, the possible values of X are $0, 1, 2, \ldots, n$. If k is any one of these values,

$$P(X = k) = \binom{n}{k} p^k (1-p)^{n-k}$$

EXAMPLE 13.5   Inspecting CDs

The number X of CDs with defective copy protection in Example 13.3 has approximately the binomial distribution with $n = 10$ and $p = 0.1$.

The probability that the sample contains no more than 1 defective CD is

$$P(X \le 1) = P(X = 1) + P(X = 0)$$
$$= \binom{10}{1}(0.1)^1(0.9)^9 + \binom{10}{0}(0.1)^0(0.9)^{10}$$

$$= \frac{10!}{1!\,9!}(0.1)(0.3874) + \frac{10!}{0!\,10!}(1)(0.3487)$$

$$= (10)(0.1)(0.3874) + (1)(1)(0.3487)$$

$$= 0.3874 + 0.3487 = 0.7361$$

This calculation uses the facts that $0! = 1$ and that $a^0 = 1$ for any number a other than 0. We see that about 74% of all samples will contain no more than 1 bad CD. In fact, 35% of the samples will contain no bad CDs. A sample of size 10 cannot be trusted to alert the distributor to the presence of unacceptable CDs in the shipment.

Using technology

The binomial probability formula is awkward to use, particularly for the probabilities of events that contain many outcomes. You can find tables of binomial probabilities $P(X = k)$ and cumulative probabilities $P(X \le k)$ for selected values of n and p.

The most efficient way to do binomial calculations is to use technology. Figure 13.1 shows output for the calculation in Example 13.5 from a graphing calculator, two statistical programs, and a spreadsheet program. We asked all four to give cumulative probabilities. The TI-83, CrunchIt!, and Minitab have menu entries for binomial cumulative probabilities. Excel has no menu entry, but the worksheet function BINOMDIST is available. All of the outputs agree with the result 0.7361 of Example 13.5.

APPLY YOUR KNOWLEDGE

13.5   **Proofreading.**   Typing errors in a text are either nonword errors (as when "the" is typed as "teh") or word errors that result in a real but incorrect word. Spell-checking software will catch nonword errors but not word errors. Human proofreaders catch 70% of word errors. You ask a fellow student to proofread an essay in which you have deliberately made 10 word errors.

(a) If the student matches the usual 70% rate, what is the distribution of the number of errors caught? What is the distribution of the number of errors missed?

(b) Missing 3 or more out of 10 errors seems a poor performance. What is the probability that a proofreader who catches 70% of word errors misses exactly 3 out of 10? If you use software, also find the probability of missing 3 or more out of 10.

13.6   **Random digit dialing.**   When an opinion poll calls residential telephone numbers at random, only 20% of the calls reach a live person. You watch the random dialing machine make 15 calls.

(a) What is the probability that exactly 3 calls reach a person?

(b) What is the probability that 3 or fewer calls reach a person?

13.7   **Tax returns.**   The Internal Revenue Service reports that 8.7% of individual tax returns in 2003 showed an adjusted gross income of $100,000 or more. A random audit chooses 20 tax returns for careful study. What is the probability that more than 1 return shows an income of $100,000 or more? (*Hint:* It is easier to first find the probability that only 0 or 1 of the returns chosen shows an income this high.)

Texas Instruments TI-83 Plus

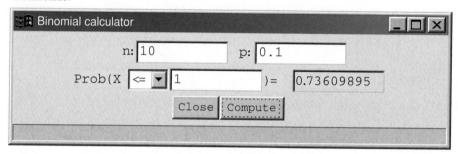

CrunchIt!

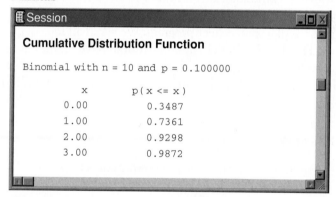

Minitab

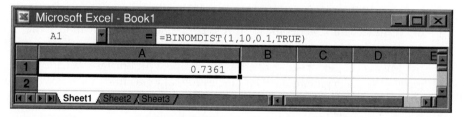

Microsoft Excel

FIGURE 13.1 The binomial probability $P(X \leq 1)$ for Example 13.5: output from a graphing calculator, two statistical programs, and a spreadsheet program.

Binomial mean and standard deviation

If a count X has the binomial distribution based on n observations with probability p of success, what is its mean μ? That is, in very many repetitions of the binomial setting, what will be the average count of successes? We can guess the answer. If a basketball player makes 80% of her free throws, the mean number made in 10 tries should be 80% of 10, or 8. In general, the mean of a binomial distribution should be $\mu = np$. Here are the facts.

BINOMIAL MEAN AND STANDARD DEVIATION

If a count X has the binomial distribution with number of observations n and probability of success p, the **mean** and **standard deviation** of X are

$$\mu = np$$
$$\sigma = \sqrt{np(1 - p)}$$

Remember that these short formulas are good only for binomial distributions. They can't be used for other distributions.

EXAMPLE 13.6   Inspecting CDs

Continuing Example 13.5, the count X of bad CDs is binomial with $n = 10$ and $p = 0.1$. The histogram in Figure 13.2 displays this probability distribution. (Because probabilities are long-run proportions, using probabilities as the heights of the bars shows what the distribution of X would be in very many repetitions.) The distribution is strongly skewed. Although X can take any whole-number value from 0 to 10, the probabilities of values larger than 5 are so small that they do not appear in the histogram.

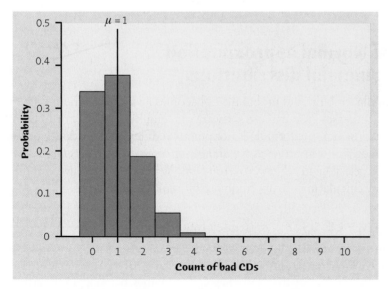

FIGURE 13.2 Probability histogram for the binomial distribution with $n = 10$ and $p = 0.1$.

The probability of rain is …

You work all week. Then it rains on the weekend. Can there really be a statistical truth behind our perception that the weather is against us? At least on the east coast of the United States, the answer is "Yes." Going back to 1946, it seems that Sundays receive 22% more precipitation than Mondays. The likely explanation is that the pollution from all those workday cars and trucks forms the seeds for raindrops—with just enough delay to cause rain on the weekend.

The mean and standard deviation of the binomial distribution in Figure 13.2 are

$$\mu = np$$
$$= (10)(0.1) = 1$$
$$\sigma = \sqrt{np(1-p)}$$
$$= \sqrt{(10)(0.1)(0.9)} = \sqrt{0.9} = 0.9487$$

The mean is marked on the probability histogram in Figure 13.2.

APPLY YOUR KNOWLEDGE

13.8 Random digit dialing. (a) What is the mean number of calls that reach a person in Exercise 13.6?

(b) What is the standard deviation σ of the count of calls that reach a person?

(c) If calls are made to New York City rather than nationally, the probability that a call reaches a person is only $p = 0.08$. How does this new p affect the standard deviation? What would be the standard deviation if $p = 0.01$? What does your work show about the behavior of the standard deviation of a binomial distribution as the probability of a success gets closer to 0?

13.9 Proofreading. Return to the proofreading setting of Exercise 13.5.

(a) What is the mean number of errors caught? What is the mean number of errors missed? You see that these two means must add to 10, the total number of errors.

(b) What is the standard deviation σ of the number of errors caught?

(c) Suppose that a proofreader catches 90% of word errors, so that $p = 0.9$. What is σ in this case? What is σ if $p = 0.99$? What happens to the standard deviation of a binomial distribution as the probability of a success gets close to 1?

The Normal approximation to binomial distributions

The formula for binomial probabilities becomes awkward as the number of observations n increases. You can use software or a graphing calculator to handle many problems for which the formula is not practical. If technology does not rescue you, there is another alternative: *as the number of observations n gets larger, the binomial distribution gets close to a Normal distribution*. When n is large, we can use Normal probability calculations to approximate binomial probabilities.

EXAMPLE 13.7 Attitudes toward shopping

Are attitudes toward shopping changing? Sample surveys show that fewer people enjoy shopping than in the past. A survey asked a nationwide random sample of 2500 adults if they agreed or disagreed that "I like buying new clothes, but shopping is often frustrating and time-consuming."[2] The population that the poll wants to draw conclusions about is all U.S. residents aged 18 and over. Suppose that in fact 60% of all adult U.S. residents

Erica Shires/zefa/CORBIS

would say "Agree" if asked the same question. What is the probability that 1520 or more of the sample agree?

Because there are almost 225 million adults in the United States, we can take the responses of 2500 randomly chosen adults to be independent. So the number in our sample who agree that shopping is frustrating is a random variable X having the binomial distribution with $n = 2500$ and $p = 0.6$. To find the probability that at least 1520 of the people in the sample find shopping frustrating, we must add the binomial probabilities of all outcomes from $X = 1520$ to $X = 2500$. This isn't practical. Here are three ways to do this problem.

1. Use technology, as in Figure 13.1. The result is

$$P(X \geq 1520) = 0.2131$$

This answer is exactly correct to four decimal places.

2. Simulate a large number of samples. Figure 13.3 displays a histogram of the counts X from 1000 samples of size 2500 when the truth about the population is $p = 0.6$. Because 221 of these 1000 samples have X at least 1520, the probability estimated from the simulation is

$$P(X \geq 1520) = \frac{221}{1000} = 0.221$$

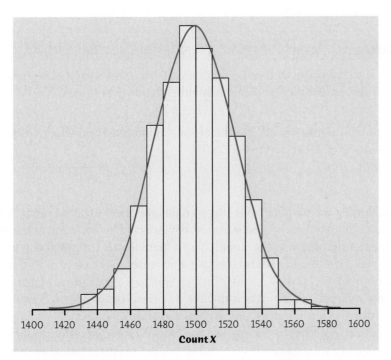

Count X

FIGURE 13.3 Histogram of 1000 binomial counts ($n = 2500$, $p = 0.6$) and the Normal density curve that approximates this binomial distribution.

This answer is only approximately correct. The law of large numbers says that the results of such simulations always get closer to the true probability as we simulate larger numbers of samples.

3. Both of the previous methods require software. Instead, look at the Normal curve in Figure 13.3. This is the density curve of the Normal distribution with the same mean and standard deviation as the binomial variable X:

$$\mu = np = (2500)(0.6) = 1500$$

$$\sigma = \sqrt{np(1-p)} = \sqrt{(2500)(0.6)(0.4)} = 24.49$$

As the figure shows, this Normal distribution approximates the binomial distribution quite well. So we can do a Normal calculation.

EXAMPLE 13.8 Normal calculation of a binomial probability

Act as though the count X has the $N(1500, 24.49)$ distribution. Standardizing X gives a standard Normal variable Z. The probability we want is

$$P(X \geq 1520) = P\left(\frac{X - 1500}{24.49} \geq \frac{1520 - 1500}{24.49}\right)$$
$$= P(Z \geq 0.82)$$
$$= 1 - 0.7939 = 0.2061$$

The Normal approximation 0.2061 differs from the software result 0.2131 by only 0.007.

NORMAL APPROXIMATION FOR BINOMIAL DISTRIBUTIONS

Suppose that a count X has the binomial distribution with n observations and success probability p. When n is large, the distribution of X is approximately Normal, $N(np, \sqrt{np(1-p)}\,)$.

As a rule of thumb, we will use the Normal approximation when n is so large that $np \geq 10$ and $n(1-p) \geq 10$.

The Normal approximation is easy to remember because it says that X is Normal with its binomial mean and standard deviation. The accuracy of the Normal approximation improves as the sample size n increases. It is most accurate for any fixed n when p is close to 1/2 and least accurate when p is near 0 or 1. This is why the rule of thumb in the box depends on p as well as n. The *Normal Approximation to Binomial* applet shows in visual form how well the Normal approximation fits the binomial distribution for any n and p. You can slide n and watch the approximation get better. Whether or not you use the Normal approximation should depend on how accurate your calculations need to be. For most statistical purposes great accuracy is not required. Our rule of thumb for use of the Normal approximation reflects this judgment.

APPLY YOUR KNOWLEDGE

13.10 Using Benford's law. According to Benford's law (Example 10.7, page 255), the probability that the first digit of the amount of a randomly chosen invoice is a 1 or a 2 is 0.477. You examine 90 invoices from a vendor and find that 29 have first digits 1 or 2. If Benford's law holds, the count of 1s and 2s will have the binomial distribution with $n = 90$ and $p = 0.477$. Too few 1s and 2s suggests fraud. What is the approximate probability of 29 or fewer if the invoices follow Benford's law? Do you suspect that the invoice amounts are not genuine?

13.11 Mark McGwire's home runs. In 1998, Mark McGwire of the St. Louis Cardinals hit 70 home runs, a new major league record. Was this feat as surprising as most of us thought? In the three seasons before 1998, McGwire hit a home run in 11.6% of his times at bat. He went to bat 509 times in 1998. McGwire's home run count in 509 times at bat has approximately the binomial distribution with $n = 509$ and $p = 0.116$. What is the mean number of home runs he will hit in 509 times at bat? What is the probability of 70 or more home runs? (Use the Normal approximation.)

13.12 Checking for survey errors. One way of checking the effect of undercoverage, nonresponse, and other sources of error in a sample survey is to compare the sample with known facts about the population. About 12% of American adults are black. The number X of blacks in a random sample of 1500 adults should therefore vary with the binomial ($n = 1500$, $p = 0.12$) distribution.

(a) What are the mean and standard deviation of X?

(b) Use the Normal approximation to find the probability that the sample will contain between 165 and 195 blacks. Be sure to check that you can safely use the approximation.

CHAPTER 13 SUMMARY

A count X of successes has a **binomial distribution** in the **binomial setting:** there are n observations; the observations are independent of each other; each observation results in a success or a failure; and each observation has the same probability p of a success.

The binomial distribution with n observations and probability p of success gives a good approximation to the sampling distribution of the count of successes in an SRS of size n from a large population containing proportion p of successes.

If X has the binomial distribution with parameters n and p, the possible values of X are the whole numbers 0, 1, 2, ..., n. The **binomial probability** that X takes any value is

$$P(X = k) = \binom{n}{k} p^k (1 - p)^{n-k}$$

Binomial probabilities in practice are best found using software.

The **binomial coefficient**

$$\binom{n}{k} = \frac{n!}{k!\,(n-k)!}$$

counts the number of ways k successes can be arranged among n observations. Here the **factorial $n!$** is

$$n! = n \times (n-1) \times (n-2) \times \cdots \times 3 \times 2 \times 1$$

for positive whole numbers n, and $0! = 1$.

The **mean** and **standard deviation** of a binomial count X are

$$\mu = np$$
$$\sigma = \sqrt{np(1-p)}$$

The **Normal approximation** to the binomial distribution says that if X is a count having the binomial distribution with parameters n and p, then when n is large, X is approximately $N(np, \sqrt{np(1-p)}\,)$. Use this approximation only when $np \geq 10$ and $n(1-p) \geq 10$.

CHECK YOUR SKILLS

13.13 Joe reads that 1 out of 4 eggs contains salmonella bacteria. So he never uses more than 3 eggs in cooking. If eggs do or don't contain salmonella independently of each other, the number of contaminated eggs when Joe uses 3 chosen at random has the distribution

(a) binomial with $n = 4$ and $p = 1/4$.

(b) binomial with $n = 3$ and $p = 1/4$.

(c) binomial with $n = 3$ and $p = 1/3$.

13.14 In the previous exercise, the probability that at least one of Joe's 3 eggs contains salmonella is about

(a) 0.68.　　(b) 0.58.　　(c) 0.30.

13.15 In a group of 10 college students, 4 are business majors. You choose 3 of the 10 students at random and ask their major. The distribution of the number of business majors you choose is

(a) binomial with $n = 10$ and $p = 0.4$.

(b) binomial with $n = 3$ and $p = 0.4$.

(c) not binomial.

13.16 If a basketball player makes 5 free throws and misses 2 free throws during a game, in how many ways can you arrange the sequence of hits and misses?

(a) $\binom{7}{5} = 42$　　(b) $\binom{7}{5} = 21$　　(c) $\binom{5}{2} = 10$

13.17 A basketball player makes 70% of her free throws. She takes 7 free throws in a game. If the shots are independent of each other, the probability that she makes the first 5 and misses the last 2 is about

(a) 0.635.　　(b) 0.318.　　(c) 0.015.

13.18 A basketball player makes 70% of her free throws. She takes 7 free throws in a game. If the shots are independent of each other, the probability that she makes 5 out of the 7 shots is about

(a) 0.635.　　(b) 0.318.　　(c) 0.015.

Each entry in a table of random digits like Table B has probability 0.1 of being a 0, and digits are independent of each other. Exercises 13.19 to 13.21 use this setting.

13.19 The probability of finding exactly 4 0s in a line 40 digits long is about

(a) 0.0000225.   (b) 0.0225.   (c) 0.2059.

13.20 The mean number of 0s in a line 40 digits long is

(a) 4.   (b) 3.098.   (c) 0.4.

13.21 Ten lines in the table contain 400 digits. The count of 0s in these lines is approximately Normal with

(a) mean 40 and standard deviation 36.

(b) mean 40 and standard deviation 6.

(c) mean 36 and standard deviation 6.

CHAPTER 13 EXERCISES

13.22 Binomial setting? In each situation below, is it reasonable to use a binomial distribution for the random variable X? Give reasons for your answer in each case.

(a) An auto manufacturer chooses one car from each hour's production for a detailed quality inspection. One variable recorded is the count X of finish defects (dimples, ripples, etc.) in the car's paint.

(b) The pool of potential jurors for a murder case contains 100 persons chosen at random from the adult residents of a large city. Each person in the pool is asked whether he or she opposes the death penalty; X is the number who say "Yes."

(c) Joe buys a ticket in his state's Pick 3 lottery game every week; X is the number of times in a year that he wins a prize.

13.23 Binomial setting?   In which of these two sports settings is a binomial distribution more likely to be at least approximately correct? Explain your answer.

(a) A National Football League kicker has made 80% of his field goal attempts in the past. This season he attempts 20 field goals. The attempts differ widely in distance, angle, wind, and so on.

(b) A National Basketball Association player has made 80% of his free-throw attempts in the past. This season he takes 150 free throws. Basketball free throws are always attempted from 15 feet away with no interference from other players.

David Bergman/CORBIS

13.24 On the Web.   What kinds of Web sites do males aged 18 to 34 visit? About 50% of male Internet users in this age group visit an auction site such as eBay at least once a month.[3] Interview a random sample of 12 male Internet users aged 18 to 34.

(a) What is the distribution of the number who have visited an online auction site in the past month?

(b) What is the probability that exactly 8 of the 12 have visited an auction site in the past month? If you have software, also find the probability that at least 8 of the 12 have visited an auction site in the past month.

13.25 Testing ESP. In a test for ESP (extrasensory perception), a subject is told that cards the experimenter can see but he cannot contain either a star, a circle, a wave, or a square. As the experimenter looks at each of 20 cards in turn, the subject names the shape on the card. A subject who is just guessing has probability 0.25 of guessing correctly on each card.

(a) The count of correct guesses in 20 cards has a binomial distribution. What are n and p?

(b) What is the mean number of correct guesses in many repetitions of the experiment?

(c) What is the probability of exactly 5 correct guesses?

13.26 Random stock prices. A believer in the random walk theory of stock markets thinks that an index of stock prices has probability 0.65 of increasing in any year. Moreover, the change in the index in any given year is not influenced by whether it rose or fell in earlier years. Let X be the number of years among the next 5 years in which the index rises.

(a) X has a binomial distribution. What are n and p?

(b) What are the possible values that X can take?

(c) Find the probability of each value of X. Draw a probability histogram for the distribution of X. (See Figure 13.2 for an example of a probability histogram.)

(d) What are the mean and standard deviation of this distribution? Mark the location of the mean on your histogram.

Kayte Deioma/Photo Edit

13.27 How many cars? Twenty percent of American households own three or more motor vehicles. You choose 12 households at random.

(a) What is the probability that none of the chosen households owns three or more vehicles? What is the probability that at least one household owns three or more vehicles?

(b) What are the mean and standard deviation of the number of households in your sample that own three or more vehicles?

(c) What is the probability that your sample count is greater than the mean?

13.28 False positives in testing for HIV. A rapid test for the presence in the blood of antibodies to HIV, the virus that causes AIDS, gives a positive result with probability about 0.004 when a person who is free of HIV antibodies is tested. A clinic tests 1000 people who are all free of HIV antibodies.

(a) What is the distribution of the number of positive tests?

(b) What is the mean number of positive tests?

(c) You cannot safely use the Normal approximation for this distribution. Explain why.

13.29 Reaching dropouts. High school dropouts make up 12.3% of all Americans aged 18 to 24. A vocational school that wants to attract dropouts mails an advertising flyer to 25,000 persons between the ages of 18 and 24.

(a) If the mailing list can be considered a random sample of the population, what is the mean number of high school dropouts who will receive the flyer?

(b) What is the approximate probability that at least 3500 dropouts will receive the flyer?

13.30 Multiple-choice tests.   Here is a simple probability model for multiple-choice tests. Suppose that each student has probability p of correctly answering a question chosen at random from a universe of possible questions. (A strong student has a higher p than a weak student.) Answers to different questions are independent. Jodi is a good student for whom $p = 0.75$.

(a) Use the Normal approximation to find the probability that Jodi scores 70% or lower on a 100-question test.

(b) If the test contains 250 questions, what is the probability that Jodi will score 70% or lower?

13.31 Survey demographics.   According to the Census Bureau, 12.4% of American adults (age 18 and over) are Hispanic (data for 2004). An opinion poll plans to contact an SRS of 1200 adults.

(a) What is the mean number of Hispanics in such samples? What is the standard deviation?

(b) According to the 68–95–99.7 rule, what range will include the counts of Hispanics in 95% of all such samples?

(c) How large a sample is required to make the mean number of Hispanics at least 200?

13.32 Leaking gas tanks.   Leakage from underground gasoline tanks at service stations can damage the environment. It is estimated that 25% of these tanks leak. You examine 15 tanks chosen at random, independently of each other.

(a) What is the mean number of leaking tanks in such samples of 15?

(b) What is the probability that 10 or more of the 15 tanks leak?

(c) Now you do a larger study, examining a random sample of 1000 tanks nationally. What is the probability that at least 275 of these tanks are leaking?

13.33 Genetics.   According to genetic theory, the blossom color in the second generation of a certain cross of sweet peas should be red or white in a 3:1 ratio. That is, each plant has probability 3/4 of having red blossoms, and the blossom colors of separate plants are independent.

(a) What is the probability that exactly 6 out of 8 of these plants have red blossoms?

(b) What is the mean number of red-blossomed plants when 80 plants of this type are grown from seeds?

(c) What is the probability of obtaining at least 50 red-blossomed plants when 80 plants are grown from seeds?

13.34 Language study.   Of American high school students, 41% are studying a language other than English. An opinion poll plans to ask high school students about foreign affairs. Perhaps language study will influence attitudes. If the poll interviews an SRS of 500 students, what is the probability that between 35% and 50% of the sample are studying a foreign language? (*Hint:* First translate these percents into counts of the 500 students in the sample.)

13.35 Is this coin balanced?   While he was a prisoner of war during World War II, John Kerrich tossed a coin 10,000 times. He got 5067 heads. If the coin is perfectly balanced, the probability of a head is 0.5. Is there reason to think that Kerrich's coin gave too many heads to be balanced? To answer this question, find the probability that a balanced coin would give 5067 or more heads in 10,000 tosses. What do you conclude?

13.36 **Inspecting CDs.** Example 13.5 concerns the count of bad CDs in inspection samples of size 10. The count has the binomial distribution with $n = 10$ and $p = 0.1$. Set these values for the number of tosses and probability of heads in the *Probability* applet. In the example, we calculated that the probability of getting a sample with exactly 1 bad CD is 0.3874. Of course, when we inspect only a few lots, the proportion of samples with exactly 1 bad CD will differ from this probability. Click "Toss" and "Reset" repeatedly to simulate inspecting 20 lots. Record the number of bad CDs (the count of heads) in each of the 20 samples. What proportion of the 20 lots had exactly 1 bad CD? Remember that probability tells us only what happens in the long run.

APPLET

Confidence Intervals: The Basics

After we have selected a sample, we know the responses of the individuals in the sample. The usual reason for taking a sample is not to learn about the individuals in the sample but to *infer* from the sample data some conclusion about the wider population that the sample represents.

> **STATISTICAL INFERENCE**
>
> **Statistical inference** provides methods for drawing conclusions about a population from sample data.

Because a different sample might lead to different conclusions, we can't be certain that our conclusions are correct. Statistical inference uses the language of probability to say how trustworthy our conclusions are. This chapter and the following chapter introduce the two most common types of inference. This chapter concerns *confidence intervals* for estimating the value of a population parameter. Chapter 15 introduces *tests of significance*, which assess the evidence for a claim about a population. Both types of inference are based on the sampling distributions of statistics. That is, both report probabilities that state what would happen if we used the inference method many times.

343

In these chapters, we concentrate on the reasoning of inference. To present the reasoning clearly, we start with a setting that is too simple to be realistic. Here is the setting for our work in Chapters 14 and 15.

SIMPLE CONDITIONS FOR INFERENCE ABOUT A MEAN

1. We have an SRS from the population of interest. There is no nonresponse or other practical difficulty.

2. The variable we measure has a perfectly Normal distribution $N(\mu, \sigma)$ in the population.

3. We don't know the population mean μ. But we do know the population standard deviation σ.

The conditions that we have a perfect SRS, that the population is perfectly Normal, and that we know the population σ are all unrealistic. After you have mastered the basic reasoning of inference, later chapters will show how practical inference deals with more realistic settings.

Estimating with confidence

Young people have a better chance of good jobs and high incomes if they are good with numbers. How strong are the quantitative skills of young Americans of working age? One source of data is the National Assessment of Educational Progress (NAEP) Young Adult Literacy Assessment Survey, which is based on a nationwide probability sample of households.

Ranges are for statistics?

Many people like to think that statistical estimates are exact. The Nobel prize–winning economist Daniel McFadden tells a story of his time on the Council of Economic Advisers. Presented with a range of forecasts for economic growth, President Lyndon Johnson replied: "Ranges are for cattle; give me one number."

EXAMPLE 14.1 NAEP quantitative scores

The NAEP survey includes a short test of quantitative skills, covering mainly basic arithmetic and the ability to apply it to realistic problems. Scores on the test range from 0 to 500. A person who scores 233 can add the amounts of two checks appearing on a bank deposit slip; someone scoring 325 can determine the price of a meal from a menu; a person scoring 375 can transform a price in cents per ounce into dollars per pound.

In a recent year, 840 men 21 to 25 years of age were in the NAEP sample. Their mean quantitative score was $\bar{x} = 272$. On the basis of this sample, we want to estimate the mean score μ in the population of more than 10 million young men of these ages.[1]

To match the "simple conditions," we will treat the NAEP sample as a perfect SRS of young men and NAEP scores in the population of all young men as having an exactly Normal distribution with standard deviation $\sigma = 60$.

Here is the reasoning of statistical estimation in a nutshell.

1. To estimate the unknown population mean μ, use the mean $\bar{x} = 272$ of the random sample. We don't expect $\bar{x}$ to be exactly equal to μ, so we want to say how accurate this estimate is.

2. We know the sampling distribution of $\bar{x}$. In repeated samples, $\bar{x}$ has the Normal distribution with mean μ and standard deviation $\sigma/\sqrt{n}$. So the average score $\bar{x}$ of 840 young men has standard deviation

$$\frac{\sigma}{\sqrt{n}} = \frac{60}{\sqrt{840}} = 2.1 \quad \text{(rounded off)}$$

3. The 95 part of the 68–95–99.7 rule for Normal distributions says that $\bar{x}$ and its mean μ are within 4.2 (that's two standard deviations) of each other in 95% of all samples. So if we estimate that μ lies somewhere in the interval from $\bar{x} - 4.2$ to $\bar{x} + 4.2$, we'll be right 95% of the times we take a sample. For this particular sample, this interval is

$$\bar{x} - 4.2 = 272 - 4.2 = 267.8$$

to

$$\bar{x} + 4.2 = 272 + 4.2 = 276.2$$

The big idea is that the sampling distribution of $\bar{x}$ tells us how close to μ the sample mean $\bar{x}$ is likely to be. A confidence interval just turns that information around to say how close to $\bar{x}$ the unknown population mean μ is likely to be.

EXAMPLE 14.2   Statistical estimation in pictures

Figures 14.1 and 14.2 illustrate the reasoning of estimation in graphical form. Figure 14.1 summarizes the idea of the sampling distribution. Starting with the population, imagine taking many SRSs of 840 young men. The first sample has mean NAEP score $\bar{x} = 272$, the second has mean $\bar{x} = 268$, the third has mean $\bar{x} = 273$, and so on. If we collect all

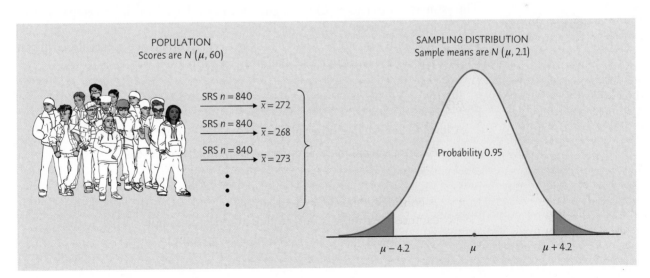

FIGURE 14.1 The sampling distribution of the mean NAEP quantitative score $\bar{x}$ of an SRS of 840 young men. In 95% of all samples, $\bar{x}$ lies within ± 4.2 of the unknown population mean μ.

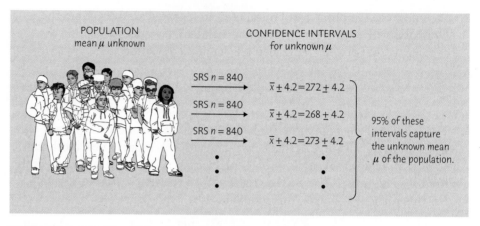

FIGURE 14.2 To say that $\overline{x} \pm 4.2$ is a 95% confidence interval for the population mean μ is to say that, in repeated samples, 95% of these intervals capture μ.

these sample means and display their distribution, we get the Normal distribution with mean equal to the unknown μ and standard deviation 2.1.

The 68–95–99.7 rule says that in 95% of all samples, the sample mean $\overline{x}$ lies within 4.2 (two standard deviations) of the population mean μ. Whenever this happens, the interval $\overline{x} \pm 4.2$ captures μ.

Figure 14.2 summarizes the behavior of this interval. Starting with the population, imagine taking many SRSs of 840 young men. The formula $\overline{x} \pm 4.2$ gives an interval based on each sample; *95% of these intervals capture the unknown population mean* μ.

The interval of numbers between the values $\overline{x} \pm 4.2$ is called a 95% *confidence interval* for μ. Like most confidence intervals we will meet, this one has the form

$$\text{estimate} \pm \text{margin of error}$$

margin of error   The estimate ($\overline{x}$ in this case) is our guess for the value of the unknown parameter. The **margin of error** ± 4.2 shows how accurate we believe our guess is, based on the variability of the estimate. This is a 95% confidence interval because it catches the unknown μ in 95% of all possible samples.

CONFIDENCE INTERVAL

A **level C confidence interval** for a parameter has two parts:

• An interval calculated from the data, usually of the form

$$\text{estimate} \pm \text{margin of error}$$

• A **confidence level** C, which gives the probability that the interval will capture the true parameter value in repeated samples. That is, the confidence level is the success rate for the method.

Users can choose the confidence level, usually 90% or higher because we usually want to be quite sure of our conclusions. The most common confidence level is 95%.

INTERPRETING A CONFIDENCE INTERVAL

The confidence level is the success rate of the method that produces the interval. We don't know whether the 95% confidence interval from a particular sample is one of the 95% that capture μ or one of the unlucky 5% that miss.

To say that we are **95% confident** that the unknown μ lies between 267.8 and 276.2 is shorthand for **"We got these numbers using a method that gives correct results 95% of the time."**

Figure 14.2 is one way to picture the idea of a 95% confidence interval. Figure 14.3 illustrates the idea in a different form. Study these figures carefully. If you understand what they say, you have mastered one of the big ideas of statistics. Figure 14.3 shows the result of drawing many SRSs from the same population and

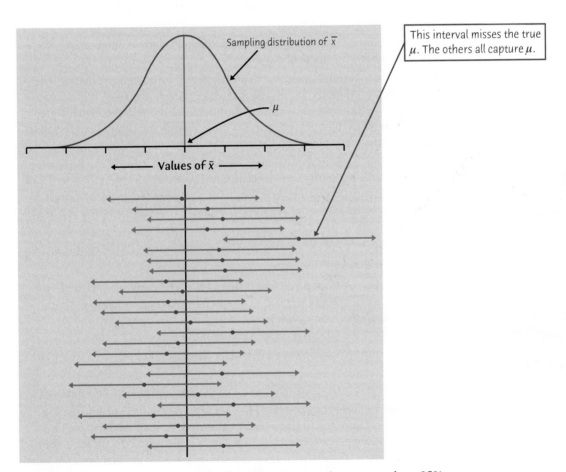

FIGURE 14.3 Twenty-five samples from the same population gave these 95% confidence intervals. In the long run, 95% of all samples give an interval that contains the population mean μ.

calculating a 95% confidence interval from each sample. The center of each interval is at $\bar{x}$ and therefore varies from sample to sample. The sampling distribution of $\bar{x}$ appears at the top of the figure to show the long-term pattern of this variation. The 95% confidence intervals from 25 SRSs appear below. The center $\bar{x}$ of each interval is marked by a dot. The arrows on either side of the dot span the confidence interval. All except one of these 25 intervals cover the true value of μ. In a very large number of samples, 95% of the confidence intervals would contain μ. The *Confidence Interval* applet animates Figure 14.3. You can use the applet to watch confidence intervals from one sample after another capture or fail to capture the true parameter.

APPLY YOUR KNOWLEDGE

14.1   More on NAEP test scores.   Suppose that you give the NAEP test to an SRS of 1000 people from a large population in which the scores have mean 280 and standard deviation $\sigma = 60$. The mean $\bar{x}$ of the 1000 scores will vary if you take repeated samples.

(a) The sampling distribution of $\bar{x}$ is approximately Normal. It has mean $\mu = 280$. What is its standard deviation?

(b) Sketch the Normal curve that describes how $\bar{x}$ varies in many samples from this population. Mark the mean $\mu = 280$. According to the 68–95–99.7 rule, about 95% of all the values of $\bar{x}$ fall within _____ of the mean. What is the missing number? Call it m for "margin of error." Shade the region from the mean minus m to the mean plus m on the axis of your sketch, as in Figure 14.1.

(c) Whenever $\bar{x}$ falls in the region you shaded, the true value of the population mean, $\mu = 280$, lies in the confidence interval between $\bar{x} - m$ and $\bar{x} + m$. Draw the confidence interval below your sketch for one value of $\bar{x}$ inside the shaded region and one value of $\bar{x}$ outside the shaded region. (Use Figure 14.3 as a model for your drawing.)

(d) In what percent of all samples will the true mean $\mu = 280$ be caught by the confidence interval $\bar{x} \pm m$?

14.2   Losing weight.   A Gallup Poll found that 51% of the people in its sample said "Yes" when asked, "Would you like to lose weight?" Gallup announced: "For results based on the total sample of national adults, one can say with 95% confidence that the margin of sampling error is ±3 percentage points."[2]

(a) What is the 95% confidence interval for the percent of all adults who want to lose weight?   (48 , 54)

(b) What does it mean to say that we have "95% confidence" in this interval?

14.3   Confidence intervals in action.   The idea of an 80% confidence interval is that the interval captures the true parameter value in 80% of all samples. That's not high enough confidence for practical use, but 80% hits and 20% misses make it easy to see how a confidence interval behaves in repeated samples from the same population. Go to the *Confidence Interval* applet.

(a) Set the confidence level to 80%. Click "Sample" to choose an SRS and calculate the confidence interval. Do this 10 times to simulate 10 SRSs with their

Jim Naughten/CORBIS

10 confidence intervals. How many of the 10 intervals captured the true mean μ? How many missed?

(b) You see that we can't predict whether the next sample will hit or miss. The confidence level, however, tells us what percent will hit in the long run. Reset the applet and click "Sample 50" to get the confidence intervals from 50 SRSs. How many hit? Keep clicking "Sample 50" and record the percent of hits among 100, 200, 300, 400, 500, 600, 700, 800, and 1000 SRSs. Even 1000 samples is not truly "the long run," but we expect the percent of hits in 1000 samples to be fairly close to the confidence level, 80%.

Confidence intervals for the mean μ

To find a 95% confidence interval for the mean NAEP score of young men, we first caught the central 95% of a Normal curve by going out two standard deviations in both directions from the mean. To find a level C confidence interval, we first catch the central area C under a Normal curve. Because all Normal distributions are the same in the standard scale, we can obtain everything we need from the standard Normal curve.

Figure 14.4 shows how the central area C under a standard Normal curve is marked off by two points z^* and $-z^*$. Numbers like z^* that mark off specified areas are called **critical values** of the standard Normal distribution. Values of z^* for many choices of C appear in the bottom row of Table C in the back of the book. This row is labeled z^*. Here are the entries for the most common confidence levels:

critical value

Confidence level C	90%	95%	99%
Critical value z^*	1.645	1.960	2.576

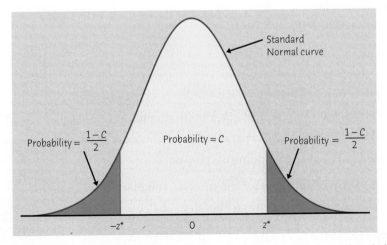

FIGURE 14.4 The critical value z^* is the number that catches central probability C under a standard Normal curve between $-z^*$ and z^*.

Notice that for C = 95% the table gives $z^* = 1.960$. This is slightly more precise than the value $z^* = 2$ based on the 68–95–99.7 rule. You can of course use software to find critical values z^*, as well as the entire confidence interval.

Figure 14.4 shows that there is area C under the standard Normal curve between $-z^*$ and z^*. If we start at the sample mean $\bar{x}$ and go out z^* standard deviations, we get an interval that contains the population mean μ in a proportion C of all samples. This interval is

$$\text{from} \quad \bar{x} - z^* \frac{\sigma}{\sqrt{n}} \quad \text{to} \quad \bar{x} + z^* \frac{\sigma}{\sqrt{n}}$$

or

$$\bar{x} \pm z^* \frac{\sigma}{\sqrt{n}}$$

It is a level C confidence interval for μ.

CONFIDENCE INTERVAL FOR THE MEAN OF A NORMAL POPULATION

Draw an SRS of size n from a Normal population having unknown mean μ and known standard deviation σ. A level C **confidence interval for μ** is

$$\bar{x} \pm z^* \frac{\sigma}{\sqrt{n}}$$

The critical value z^* is illustrated in Figure 14.4 and found in Table C.

The steps in finding a confidence interval mirror the overall four-step process for organizing statistical problems.

CONFIDENCE INTERVALS: THE FOUR-STEP PROCESS

STATE: What is the practical question that requires estimating a parameter?

FORMULATE: Identify the parameter and choose a level of confidence.

SOLVE: Carry out the work in two phases:

(a) Check the conditions for the interval you plan to use.
(b) Calculate the confidence interval.

CONCLUDE: Return to the practical question to describe your results in this setting.

EXAMPLE 14.3 Healing of skin wounds

STATE: Biologists studying the healing of skin wounds measured the rate at which new cells closed a razor cut made in the skin of an anesthetized newt. Here are data from 18 newts, measured in micrometers (millionths of a meter) per hour:[3]

$$29 \quad 27 \quad 34 \quad 40 \quad 22 \quad 28 \quad 14 \quad 35 \quad 26$$
$$35 \quad 12 \quad 30 \quad 23 \quad 18 \quad 11 \quad 22 \quad 23 \quad 33$$

This is one of several sets of measurements made under different conditions. We want to estimate the mean healing rate for comparison with rates under other conditions.

FORMULATE: We will estimate the mean rate μ for all newts of this species by giving a 95% confidence interval.

SOLVE: We should start by checking the conditions for inference. For this first example, we will find the interval, then discuss how statistical practice deals with conditions that are never perfectly satisfied.

The mean of the sample is

$$\bar{x} = \frac{29 + 27 + 34 + \cdots + 33}{18} = 25.67$$

Royalty-Free/CORBIS

As part of the "simple conditions," suppose that from past experience with this species of newts we know that the standard deviation of healing rates is 8 micrometers per hour. For 95% confidence, the critical value is $z^* = 1.960$. A 95% confidence interval for μ is therefore

$$\bar{x} \pm z^* \frac{\sigma}{\sqrt{n}} = 25.67 \pm 1.960 \frac{8}{\sqrt{18}}$$
$$= 25.67 \pm 3.70$$
$$= 21.97 \text{ to } 29.37$$

CONCLUDE: We are 95% confident that the mean healing rate for all newts of this species is between 21.97 and 29.37 micrometers per hour.

In practice, the first part of the *Solve* step is to check the conditions for inference. The "simple conditions" are:

1. **SRS:** We don't have an actual SRS from the population of all newts of this species. Scientists usually act as if animal subjects are SRSs from their species or genetic type if there is nothing special about how the subjects were obtained. This study was a randomized comparative experiment in which these 18 newts were assigned at random from a larger group of newts to get one of the treatments being compared.

2. **Normal distribution:** The biologists expect from past experience that measurements like this on several animals of the same species under the same conditions will follow approximately a Normal distribution. We can't look at the population, but we can examine the sample. Figure 14.5 is a stemplot, with split stems. The shape is irregular, but there are no outliers or strong skewness. Shapes like this often occur in small samples from Normal populations, so we have no reason to doubt that the population distribution is Normal.

FIGURE 14.5 Stemplot of the healing rates in Example 14.3.

```
1 | 1 2 4
1 | 8
2 | 2 2 3 3
2 | 6 7 8 9
3 | 0 3 4
3 | 5 5
4 | 0
```

3. **Known σ:** It really is unrealistic to suppose that we know that $\sigma = 8$. We will see in Chapter 18 that it is easy to do away with the need to know σ.

As this discussion suggests, inference methods are often used when conditions like SRS and Normal population are not exactly satisfied. Wise use requires judgment. Later chapters will give you a better basis for judgment. For now, just act as though the "simple conditions" are satisfied.

APPLY YOUR KNOWLEDGE

14.4 Find a critical value. The critical value z^* for confidence level 97.5% is not in Table C. Use software or Table A of standard Normal probabilities to find z^*. Include in your answer a copy of Figure 14.4 with C = 0.975 that shows how much area is left in each tail when the central area is 0.975.

14.5 Analyzing pharmaceuticals. A manufacturer of pharmaceutical products analyzes each batch of a product to verify the concentration of the active ingredient. The chemical analysis is not perfectly precise. In fact, repeated measurements follow a Normal distribution with mean μ equal to the true concentration and standard deviation $\sigma = 0.0068$ grams per liter. Three analyses of one batch give concentrations 0.8403, 0.8363, and 0.8447 grams per liter. To estimate the true concentration, give a 95% confidence interval for μ. Follow the four-step process as illustrated in Example 14.3.

14.6 IQ test scores. Here are the IQ test scores of 31 seventh-grade girls in a Midwest school district:[4]

114	100	104	89	102	91	114	114	103	105
108	130	120	132	111	128	118	119	86	72
111	103	74	112	107	103	98	96	112	112	93

(a) These 31 girls are an SRS of all seventh-grade girls in the school district. Suppose that the standard deviation of IQ scores in this population is known to be $\sigma = 15$. We expect the distribution of IQ scores to be close to Normal. Make a stemplot of the distribution of these 31 scores (split the stems) to verify that there are no major departures from Normality. You have now checked the "simple conditions" to the extent possible.

(b) Estimate the mean IQ score for all seventh-grade girls in the school district, using a 99% confidence interval. Follow the four-step process as illustrated in Example 14.3.

How confidence intervals behave

The confidence interval $\bar{x} \pm z^* \sigma / \sqrt{n}$ for the mean of a Normal population illustrates several important properties that are shared by all confidence intervals in common use. The user chooses the confidence level, and the margin of error follows from this choice. We would like high confidence and also a small margin of error. High confidence says that our method almost always gives correct answers. A small margin of error says that we have pinned down the parameter quite precisely. The margin of error is

$$\text{margin of error} = z^* \frac{\sigma}{\sqrt{n}}$$

This expression has z^* and σ in the numerator and $\sqrt{n}$ in the denominator. So the margin of error gets smaller when

- z^* gets smaller. Smaller z^* is the same as lower confidence level C (look at Figure 14.4 again). *There is a trade-off between the confidence level and the margin of error. To obtain a smaller margin of error from the same data, you must be willing to accept lower confidence.*

- σ is smaller. The standard deviation σ measures the variation in the population. You can think of the variation among individuals in the population as noise that obscures the average value μ. It is easier to pin down μ when σ is small.

- n gets larger. Increasing the sample size n reduces the margin of error for any confidence level. *Because n appears under a square root sign, we must take four times as many observations in order to cut the margin of error in half.*

EXAMPLE 14.4   *Changing the margin of error*

Example 14.3 gives the 95% confidence interval

$$25.67 \pm 3.70$$

for the mean healing rate of newt skin. The 90% confidence interval based on the same data replaces the 95% critical value $z^* = 1.960$ by the 90% critical value $z^* = 1.645$. The interval is

$$\bar{x} \pm z^* \frac{\sigma}{\sqrt{n}} = 25.67 \pm 1.645 \frac{8}{\sqrt{18}}$$
$$= 25.67 \pm 3.10$$

Lower confidence results in a smaller margin of error, ± 3.10 in place of ± 3.70. In the same way, you can calculate that the margin of error for 99% confidence is larger, ± 4.86. Figure 14.6 compares these three confidence intervals.

Decreasing the number of measurements from 18 to 9 will increase the margin of error for 95% confidence. Check that replacing $\sqrt{18}$ by $\sqrt{9}$ increases the margin of error from ± 3.70 to ± 5.23.

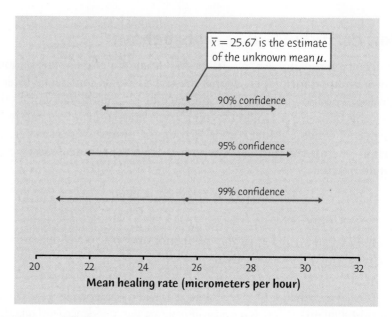

FIGURE 14.6 The lengths of three confidence intervals for Example 14.4. All three are centered at the estimate $\bar{x} = 25.67$. When the data and the sample size remain the same, higher confidence requires a larger margin of error.

APPLY YOUR KNOWLEDGE

14.7 **Sample size and margin of error.** High school students who take the SAT mathematics exam a second time generally score higher than on their first try. The change in score has a Normal distribution with standard deviation $\sigma = 50$. A random sample of 1000 students gains an average of $\bar{x} = 22$ points on their second try.[5]

(a) Give a 95% confidence interval for the mean score gain μ in the population of all students.

(b) Suppose that the same result, $\bar{x} = 22$, had come from a sample of 250 students. Give the 95% confidence interval for the population mean μ in this case.

(c) Suppose that a sample of 4000 students had produced the sample mean $\bar{x} = 22$. Again give the 95% confidence interval for μ.

(d) What are the margins of error for samples of size 250, 1000, and 4000? How does increasing the sample size change the margin of error of a confidence interval?

14.8 **Confidence level and margin of error.** A random sample of 1000 high school students gains an average of $\bar{x} = 22$ points in their second attempt at the SAT mathematics exam. The change in score has a Normal distribution with standard deviation $\sigma = 50$.

(a) Give a 95% confidence interval for the mean score gain μ in the population of all students.

(b) Give the 90% and 99% confidence intervals for μ.

(c) What are the margins of error for 90%, 95%, and 99% confidence? How does increasing the confidence level change the margin of error of a confidence interval?

Choosing the sample size

A wise user of statistics never plans a sample or an experiment without at the same time planning the inference. You can arrange to have both high confidence and a small margin of error by taking enough observations. The margin of error of the confidence interval for the mean of a Normally distributed population is $m = z^*\sigma/\sqrt{n}$. To obtain a desired margin of error m, put in the value of z^* for your desired confidence level, and solve for the sample size n. Here is the result.

SAMPLE SIZE FOR DESIRED MARGIN OF ERROR

The confidence interval for the mean of a Normal population will have a specified margin of error m when the sample size is

$$n = \left(\frac{z^*\sigma}{m}\right)^2$$

This formula is not the proverbial free lunch. Taking observations costs time and money. The required sample size may be impossibly expensive. *Notice that it is the size of the sample that determines the margin of error. The size of the population does not influence the sample size we need.* (This is true as long as the population is much larger than the sample.)

CAUTION

— EXAMPLE 14.5 How many observations? —

The biologists in Example 14.3 would like to estimate the mean healing rate μ within no more than ± 3 micrometers per hour with 90% confidence. How many newts must they measure?

The desired margin of error is $m = 3$. For 90% confidence, Table C gives $z^* = 1.645$. We know that $\sigma = 8$. Therefore,

$$n = \left(\frac{z^*\sigma}{m}\right)^2 = \left(\frac{1.645 \times 8}{3}\right)^2 = 19.2$$

Because 19 newts will give a slightly larger margin of error than desired, and 20 newts a slightly smaller margin of error, the biologists must measure 20 newts. *Always round up to the next higher whole number when finding n.*

CAUTION

APPLY YOUR KNOWLEDGE

14.9 **Improving SAT scores.** How large a sample of high school students in Exercise 14.7 would be needed to estimate the mean change μ in SAT score to within ± 2 points with 95% confidence?

14.10 Estimating mean IQ. How large a sample of schoolgirls in Exercise 14.6 would be needed to estimate the mean IQ score μ within ±5 points with 99% confidence?

CHAPTER 14 SUMMARY

A **confidence interval** uses sample data to estimate an unknown population parameter with an indication of how accurate the estimate is and of how confident we are that the result is correct.

Any confidence interval has two parts: an interval calculated from the data and a confidence level C. The **interval** often has the form

$$\text{estimate} \pm \text{margin of error}$$

The **confidence level** is the success rate of the method that produces the interval. That is, C is the probability that the method will give a correct answer. If you use 95% confidence intervals often, in the long run 95% of your intervals will contain the true parameter value. You do not know whether a 95% confidence interval calculated from a particular set of data contains the true parameter value.

A level C **confidence interval for the mean μ** of a Normal population with known standard deviation σ, based on an SRS of size n, is given by

$$\bar{x} \pm z^* \frac{\sigma}{\sqrt{n}}$$

The **critical value** z^* is chosen so that the standard Normal curve has area C between $-z^*$ and z^*.

Other things being equal, the **margin of error** of a confidence interval gets smaller as

- the confidence level C decreases,
- the population standard deviation σ decreases, and
- the sample size n increases.

The sample size required to obtain a confidence interval with specified margin of error m for a Normal mean is

$$n = \left(\frac{z^* \sigma}{m}\right)^2$$

where z^* is the critical value for the desired level of confidence. Always round n up when you use this formula.

CHECK YOUR SKILLS

14.11 To give a 98% confidence interval for a population mean μ, you would use the critical value

(a) 1.960.   (b) 2.054.   (c) 2.326.

14.12 An opinion poll says that the result of their latest sample has a margin of error of plus or minus three percentage points. This means that

(a) we can be certain that the poll result is within three percentage points of the truth about the population.

(b) we could be certain that the poll result is within three percentage points of the truth if there were no nonresponse.

(c) the poll used a method that gives a result within three percentage points of the truth in 95% of all samples.

14.13 A laboratory scale is known to have a standard deviation of $\sigma = 0.001$ gram in repeated weighings. Scale readings in repeated weighings are Normally distributed, with mean equal to the true weight of the specimen. If you weigh a specimen three times on this scale, the mean result $\bar{x}$ has standard deviation

(a) 0.001 gram.   (b) 0.000577 gram.   (c) 0.000333 gram.

14.14 Three weighings of a specimen on the scale described in Exercise 14.13 give (in grams) 3.412, 3.416, and 3.414. A 95% confidence interval for the true weight is

(a) 3.414 ± 0.00113.   (b) 3.414 ± 0.00065.   (c) 3.414 ± 0.00196.

14.15 Another specimen is weighed 8 times on the same scale as in the previous exercises. The average weight is 4.1602 grams. A 99% confidence interval for the true weight of this specimen is

(a) 4.1602 ± 0.00032.   (b) 4.1602 ± 0.00069.   (c) 4.1602 ± 0.00091.

14.16 How many times must you weigh a specimen on the scale in Exercise 14.13 in order to get a margin of error no larger than ± 0.0005 with 95% confidence?

(a) 4 times   (b) 15 times   (c) 16 times

14.17 A government report says that a 90% confidence interval for the mean income of American households is $59,067 \pm 356. This is based on a random sample of 60,000 households. If the same sample results had come from a sample of 15,000 households, the new margin of error would be

(a) $\pm 712.   (b) $\pm 356.   (c) $\pm 178.

14.18 Suppose that the survey in the previous exercise had obtained the result $\bar{x} = $59,067$ from a sample of 60,000 households in New York State (population 19.5 million) instead of from all households in the United States (population 300 million). The margin of error for 90% confidence would be

(a) about $\pm 356.   (b) greater than $\pm 356.   (c) less than $\pm 356.

14.19 Suppose that the report in Exercise 14.17 had used 95% confidence rather than 90% confidence. The margin of error would be

(a) $\pm 356.   (b) greater than $\pm 356.   (c) less than $\pm 356.

14.20 A Gallup Poll asked 1060 randomly selected adults, "How would you rate the overall quality of the environment in this country today—as excellent, good, only fair, or poor?" In all, 46% of the sample rated the environment as good or excellent. Gallup said that "one can say with 95% confidence that the margin of sampling error is ± 3 percentage points." If the poll had interviewed 1500 persons rather than 1060, the margin of error for 95% confidence would be

(a) ± 3 percentage points.

(b) greater than ± 3 percentage points.

(c) less than ± 3 percentage points.

CHAPTER 14 EXERCISES

M. Thomsen/zefa/CORBIS

14.21 Hotel managers' personalities. Successful hotel managers must have personality characteristics often thought of as feminine (such as "compassionate") as well as those often thought of as masculine (such as "forceful"). The Bem Sex-Role Inventory (BSRI) is a personality test that gives separate ratings for female and male stereotypes, both on a scale of 1 to 7. A sample of 148 male general managers of three-star and four-star hotels had mean BSRI masculinity score $\overline{x} = 5.91$.[6] The standard deviation of masculinity scores for all adult males is $\sigma = 0.79$. Assume that this σ is also true in the population of male hotel managers. Give a 99% confidence interval for the mean masculinity score of all male managers of hotels in this class.

14.22 More about hotel managers. The hotel managers described in the previous exercise had mean BSRI femininity score $\overline{y} = 5.29$. Assume that the standard deviation of femininity scores in the population of all hotel managers is the same as the $\sigma = 0.78$ for the adult male population. Give a 90% confidence interval for the mean femininity score of all male managers of hotels in this class.

14.23 Length of a confidence interval. Your confidence interval in Exercise 14.22 is shorter than your interval in Exercise 14.21, even though the intervals come from the same sample and the two measures have very similar standard deviations. Why does the interval in Exercise 14.22 have a smaller margin of error?

14.24 How large a sample? You would be satisfied to estimate the BSRI masculinity score of hotel managers to within ±0.2 with 99% confidence. The standard deviation of the scores is probably close to the value $\sigma = 0.79$ for the adult male population. How large a sample of hotel managers do you need?

STEP

14.25 Bone loss by nursing mothers. Breast-feeding mothers secrete calcium into their milk. Some of the calcium may come from their bones, so mothers may lose bone mineral. Researchers measured the percent change in mineral content of the spines of 47 mothers during three months of breast-feeding.[7] Here are the data:

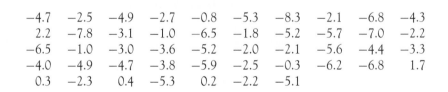

−4.7	−2.5	−4.9	−2.7	−0.8	−5.3	−8.3	−2.1	−6.8	−4.3
2.2	−7.8	−3.1	−1.0	−6.5	−1.8	−5.2	−5.7	−7.0	−2.2
−6.5	−1.0	−3.0	−3.6	−5.2	−2.0	−2.1	−5.6	−4.4	−3.3
−4.0	−4.9	−4.7	−3.8	−5.9	−2.5	−0.3	−6.2	−6.8	1.7
0.3	−2.3	0.4	−5.3	0.2	−2.2	−5.1			

SW Productions/Photo Disc/Getty Images

(a) The researchers are willing to consider these 47 women as an SRS from the population of all nursing mothers. Suppose that the percent change in this population has standard deviation $\sigma = 2.5\%$. Make a stemplot of the data to see that they appear to follow a Normal distribution quite closely. (Don't forget that you need both a 0 and a −0 stem because there are both positive and negative values.)

(b) Use a 99% confidence to estimate the mean percent change in the population. Follow the four-step process in your answer.

14.26 Pulling wood apart.   How heavy a load (pounds) is needed to pull apart pieces of Douglas fir 4 inches long and 1.5 inches square? Here are data from students doing a laboratory exercise:

33,190	31,860	32,590	26,520	33,280
32,320	33,020	32,030	30,460	32,700
23,040	30,930	32,720	33,650	32,340
24,050	30,170	31,300	28,730	31,920

(a) We are willing to regard the wood pieces prepared for the lab session as an SRS of all similar pieces of Douglas fir. Engineers also commonly assume that characteristics of materials vary Normally. Make a graph to show the shape of the distribution for these data. Does the Normality condition appear safe? Suppose that the strength of pieces of wood like these follows a Normal distribution with standard deviation 3000 pounds.

(b) Give a 90% confidence interval for the mean load required to pull the wood apart. Follow the four-step process in your work.

14.27 This wine stinks.   Sulfur compounds cause "off-odors" in wine, so winemakers want to know the odor threshold, the lowest concentration of a compound that the human nose can detect. The odor threshold for dimethyl sulfide (DMS) in trained wine tasters is about 25 micrograms per liter of wine (μg/l). The untrained noses of consumers may be less sensitive, however. Here are the DMS odor thresholds for 10 untrained students:

$$31 \quad 31 \quad 43 \quad 36 \quad 23 \quad 34 \quad 32 \quad 30 \quad 20 \quad 24$$

(a) Assume that the standard deviation of the odor threshold for untrained noses is known to be $\sigma = 7$ μg/l. Briefly discuss the other two "simple conditions," using a stemplot to verify that the distribution is roughly symmetric with no outliers.

(b) Following the four-step process, give a 95% confidence interval for the mean DMS odor threshold among all students.

14.28 Pulling wood apart, continued.   You want to estimate the mean load needed to pull apart the pieces of wood in Exercise 14.26 to within ±1000 pounds with 95% confidence. How large a sample is needed?

14.29 Engine crankshafts.   Here are measurements (in millimeters) of a critical dimension on a sample of auto engine crankshafts:

224.120	224.001	224.017	223.982	223.989	223.961
223.960	224.089	223.987	223.976	223.902	223.980
224.098	224.057	223.913	223.999		

The data come from a production process that is known to have standard deviation $\sigma = 0.060$ mm. The process mean is supposed to be $\mu = 224$ mm but can drift away from this target during production.

(a) We expect the distribution of the dimension to be close to Normal. Make a stemplot or histogram of these data and describe the shape of the distribution.

(b) Give a 95% confidence interval for the process mean at the time these crankshafts were produced.

14.30 **Student study times.** A class survey in a large class for first-year college students asked, "About how many minutes do you study on a typical weeknight?" The mean response of the 269 students was $\bar{x} = 137$ minutes. Suppose that we know that the study time follows a Normal distribution with standard deviation $\sigma = 65$ minutes in the population of all first-year students at this university.

(a) Use the survey result to give a 99% confidence interval for the mean study time of all first-year students.

(b) What condition not yet mentioned is needed for your confidence interval to be valid?

14.31 **A big toe deformity.** Table 7.2 (page 177) gives data on 38 consecutive patients who came to a medical center for treatment of hallux abducto valgus (HAV), a deformation of the big toe. It is reasonable to consider these patients as an SRS of people suffering from HAV. The seriousness of the deformity is measured by the angle (in degrees) of deformity.

(a) The data contain one high outlier. What is the angle for this outlier? The presence of the outlier violates the conditions for our confidence interval. Suppose that there is a good medical reason for removing the outlier.

(b) The remaining 37 observations follow a Normal distribution closely. Assume that angle has a Normal distribution with standard deviation $\sigma = 6.3$ degrees. Based on these 37 observations, give a 95% confidence interval for the mean angle of deformity in the population.

14.32 **An outlier strikes.** There were actually 270 responses to the class survey in Exercise 14.30. One student claimed to study 30,000 minutes per night. We know he's joking, so we left out this value. If we did a calculation without looking at the data, we would get $\bar{x} = 248$ minutes for all 270 students. Now what is the 99% confidence interval for the population mean? (Continue to use $\sigma = 65$.) Compare the new interval with that in Exercise 14.30. The message is clear: always look at your data, because outliers can greatly change your result.

14.33 **Calibrating a scale.** To assess the accuracy of a laboratory scale, a standard weight known to weigh 10 grams is weighed repeatedly. The scale readings are Normally distributed with unknown mean (this mean is 10 grams if the scale has no bias). The standard deviation of the scale readings is known to be 0.0002 gram.

(a) The weight is weighed five times. The mean result is 10.0023 grams. Give a 98% confidence interval for the mean of repeated measurements of the weight.

(b) How many measurements must be averaged to get a margin of error of ±0.0001 with 98% confidence?

14.34 **Explaining confidence.** A student reads that a 95% confidence interval for the mean NAEP quantitative score for men of ages 21 to 25 is 267.8 to 276.2. Asked to explain the meaning of this interval, the student says, "95% of all young men have scores between 267.8 and 276.2." Is the student right? Explain your answer.

14.35 **Explaining confidence.** Here is an explanation from the Associated Press concerning one of its opinion polls. Explain briefly but clearly in what way this explanation is incorrect.

> For a poll of 1,600 adults, the variation due to sampling error is no more than three percentage points either way. The error margin is said to be valid

at the 95 percent confidence level. This means that, if the same questions were repeated in 20 polls, the results of at least 19 surveys would be within three percentage points of the results of this survey.

14.36 Crime. A Gallup Poll of 1002 adults found that 25% of the respondents said that their household had experienced a crime in the past year. Among respondents aged 18 to 29 years, 43% had been victims of a crime. Gallup says, "For results based on the total sample of national adults, one can say with 95% confidence that the margin of sampling error is ±3 percentage points." Is the margin of error for adults aged 18 to 29 smaller or larger than ±3 percentage points? Why?

14.37 A newspaper poll. A *New York Times* poll on women's issues interviewed 1025 women and 472 men randomly selected from the United States, excluding Alaska and Hawaii. The poll announced a margin of error of ±3 percentage points for 95% confidence in conclusions about women. The margin of error for results concerning men was ±4 percentage points. Why is this larger than the margin of error for women?

14.38 What confidence means. Confidence tells us how often our method will produce an interval that captures the true population parameter if we use the method a very large number of times. The *Confidence Interval* applet allows us to actually use the method many times.

(a) Set the confidence level to 90%. Click "Sample 50" to choose 50 SRSs and calculate the confidence intervals. How many captured the true population mean μ? Keep clicking "Sample 50" until you have 1000 samples. What percent of the 1000 confidence intervals captured the true μ?

(b) Now choose 95% confidence. Look carefully when you first click "Sample 50." Are these intervals longer or shorter than the 90% confidence intervals? Again take 1000 samples. What percent of the intervals captured the true μ?

(c) Do the same thing for 99% confidence. What percent of 1000 samples gave confidence intervals that caught the true mean? Did the behavior of many intervals for the three confidence levels closely reflect the choice of confidence level?

14.39 An interactive table of critical values. The bottom row of Table C shows critical values for the standard Normal distribution. The *Normal Curve* applet can find the critical value for any level of confidence. First, verify that the critical value for 95% confidence is $z = 1.96$. To do this, drag one of the flags in the applet across the other so that the applet tells you the area between them, then find the position that makes this central area 0.95. Use the same method to find the critical value for 92.5% confidence. Make a sketch of the applet display for 92.5% confidence.

Ramin/Talaie/CORBIS

Tests of Significance: The Basics

Confidence intervals are one of the two most common types of statistical inference. Use a confidence interval when your goal is to estimate a population parameter. The second common type of inference, called *tests of significance*, has a different goal: to assess the evidence provided by data about some claim concerning a population. Here is the reasoning of statistical tests in a nutshell.

EXAMPLE 15.1 *I'm a great free-throw shooter*

I claim that I make 80% of my basketball free throws. To test my claim, you ask me to shoot 20 free throws. I make only 8 of the 20. "Aha!" you say. "Someone who makes 80% of his free throws would almost never make only 8 out of 20. So I don't believe your claim."

Your reasoning is based on asking what would happen if my claim were true and we repeated the sample of 20 free throws many times—I would almost never make as few as 8. This outcome is so unlikely that it gives strong evidence that my claim is not true.

You can say how strong the evidence against my claim is by giving the probability that I would make as few as 8 out of 20 free throws if I really make 80% in the long run. This probability is 0.0001. I would make as few as 8 of 20 only once in 10,000 tries in the long run if my claim to make 80% is true. The small probability convinces you that my claim is false.

The *Reasoning of a Statistical Test* applet animates Example 15.1. You can ask a player to shoot free throws until the data do (or don't) convince you that he makes fewer than 80%. Significance tests use an elaborate vocabulary, but the basic idea is simple: *an outcome that would rarely happen if a claim were true is good evidence that the claim is not true*.

The reasoning of tests of significance

The reasoning of statistical tests, like that of confidence intervals, is based on asking what would happen if we repeated the sample or experiment many times. We will act as if the "simple conditions" listed on page 344 are true: we have a perfect SRS from an exactly Normal population with standard deviation σ known to us. Here is an example we will explore.

Ramin/Talaie/CORBIS

EXAMPLE 15.2   Sweetening colas

Diet colas use artificial sweeteners to avoid sugar. These sweeteners gradually lose their sweetness over time. Manufacturers therefore test new colas for loss of sweetness before marketing them. Trained tasters sip the cola along with drinks of standard sweetness and score the cola on a "sweetness score" of 1 to 10. The cola is then stored for a month at high temperature to imitate the effect of four months' storage at room temperature. Each taster scores the cola again after storage. This is a matched pairs experiment. Our data are the differences (score before storage minus score after storage) in the tasters' scores. The bigger these differences, the bigger the loss of sweetness.

Suppose we know that for any cola, the sweetness loss scores vary from taster to taster according to a Normal distribution with standard deviation $\sigma = 1$. The mean μ for all tasters measures loss of sweetness and is different for different colas.

Here are the sweetness losses for a new cola, as measured by 10 trained tasters:

$$2.0 \quad 0.4 \quad 0.7 \quad 2.0 \quad -0.4 \quad 2.2 \quad -1.3 \quad 1.2 \quad 1.1 \quad 2.3$$

Most are positive. That is, most tasters found a loss of sweetness. But the losses are small, and two tasters (the negative scores) thought the cola gained sweetness. The average sweetness loss is given by the sample mean,

$$\bar{x} = \frac{2.0 + 0.4 + \cdots + 2.3}{10} = 1.02$$

Are these data good evidence that the cola lost sweetness in storage?

The reasoning is the same as in Example 15.1. We make a claim and ask if the data give evidence *against* it. We seek evidence that there *is* a sweetness loss, so the claim we test is that there *is not* a loss. In that case, the mean loss for the population of all trained testers would be $\mu = 0$.

- If the claim that $\mu = 0$ is true, the sampling distribution of $\bar{x}$ from 10 tasters is Normal with mean $\mu = 0$ and standard deviation

$$\frac{\sigma}{\sqrt{n}} = \frac{1}{\sqrt{10}} = 0.316$$

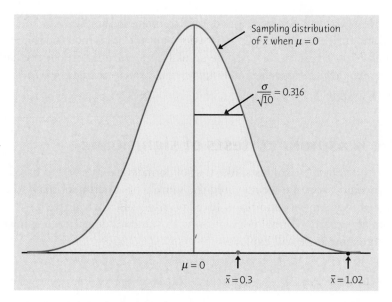

Sampling distribution of x̄ when μ = 0

$\frac{\sigma}{\sqrt{10}} = 0.316$

μ = 0

x̄ = 0.3

x̄ = 1.02

FIGURE 15.1 If the cola does not lose sweetness in storage, the mean score x̄ for 10 tasters will have this sampling distribution. The actual result for one cola was x̄ = 0.3. That could easily happen just by chance. Another cola had x̄ = 1.02. That's so far out on the Normal curve that it is good evidence that this cola did lose sweetness.

Figure 15.1 shows this sampling distribution. We can judge whether any observed x̄ is surprising by locating it on this distribution.

- Suppose that the 10 tasters had mean loss x̄ = 0.3. It is clear from Figure 15.1 that an x̄ this large could easily occur just by chance when the population mean is μ = 0. That 10 tasters find x̄ = 0.3 is not evidence of a sweetness loss.

- In fact, the taste test produced x̄ = 1.02. That's way out on the Normal curve in Figure 15.1—so far out that *an observed value this large would rarely occur just by chance if the true μ were 0.* This observed value is good evidence that in fact the true μ is greater than 0, that is, that the cola lost sweetness. The manufacturer must reformulate the cola and try again.

APPLY YOUR KNOWLEDGE

15.1   **Anemia.**   Hemoglobin is a protein in red blood cells that carries oxygen from the lungs to body tissues. People with less than 12 grams of hemoglobin per deciliter of blood (g/dl) are anemic. A public health official in Jordan suspects that the mean μ for all children in Jordan is less than 12. He measures a sample of 50 children. Suppose that the "simple conditions" hold: the 50 children are an SRS from all Jordanian children and the hemoglobin level in this population follows a Normal distribution with standard deviation σ = 1.6 g/dl.

(a) We seek evidence *against* the claim that μ = 12. What is the sampling distribution of x̄ in many samples of size 50 if in fact μ = 12? Make a sketch of the Normal curve for this distribution. (Sketch a Normal curve, then mark the axis using what you know about locating the mean and standard deviation on a Normal curve.)

(b) The sample mean was $\bar{x} = 11.3$. Mark this outcome on the sampling distribution. Also mark the outcome $\bar{x} = 11.8$ g/dl of a different study of 50 children. Explain carefully from your sketch why one of these outcomes is good evidence that μ is lower than 12, and also why the other outcome is not good evidence for this conclusion.

15.2 **Student attitudes.** The Survey of Study Habits and Attitudes (SSHA) is a psychological test that measures students' study habits and attitudes toward school. Scores range from 0 to 200. The mean score for college students is about 115, and the standard deviation is about 30. A teacher suspects that the mean μ for older students is higher than 115. She gives the SSHA to an SRS of 25 students who are at least 30 years old. Suppose we know that scores in the population of older students are Normally distributed with standard deviation $\sigma = 30$.

James Marshall/The Image Works

(a) We seek evidence *against* the claim that $\mu = 115$. What is the sampling distribution of the mean score $\bar{x}$ of a sample of 25 students if the claim is true? Sketch the density curve of this distribution. (Sketch a Normal curve, then mark the axis using what you know about locating the mean and standard deviation on a Normal curve.)

(b) Suppose that the sample data give $\bar{x} = 118.6$. Mark this point on the axis of your sketch. In fact, the result was $\bar{x} = 125.8$. Mark this point on your sketch. Using your sketch, explain in simple language why one result is good evidence that the mean score of all older students is greater than 115 and why the other outcome is not.

Stating hypotheses

A statistical test starts with a careful statement of the claims we want to compare. In Example 15.2, we saw that the taste test data are not plausible if the cola loses no sweetness. Because the reasoning of tests looks for evidence *against* a claim, we start with the claim we seek evidence against, such as "no loss of sweetness."

NULL AND ALTERNATIVE HYPOTHESES

The statement being tested in a statistical test is called the **null hypothesis.** The test is designed to assess the strength of the evidence *against* the null hypothesis. Usually the null hypothesis is a statement of "no effect" or "no difference."

The claim about the population that we are trying to find evidence *for* is the **alternative hypothesis.** The alternative hypothesis is **one-sided** if it states that a parameter is *larger than* or *smaller than* the null hypothesis value. It is **two-sided** if it states that the parameter is *different from* the null value.

Honest hypotheses?

Chinese and Japanese, for whom the number 4 is unlucky, die more often on the fourth day of the month than on other days. The authors of a study did a statistical test of the claim that the fourth day has more deaths than other days and found good evidence in favor of this claim. Can we trust this? Not if the authors looked at all days, picked the one with the most deaths, then made "this day is different" the claim to be tested. A critic raised that issue, and the authors replied: No, we had day 4 in mind in advance, so our test was legitimate.

We abbreviate the null hypothesis as H_0 and the alternative hypothesis as H_a. *Hypotheses always refer to a population, not to a particular outcome. Be sure to state H_0 and H_a in terms of population parameters.* Because H_a expresses the effect that we hope to find evidence *for*, it is sometimes easier to begin by stating H_a and then set up H_0 as the statement that the hoped-for effect is not present.

In Example 15.2, we are seeking evidence *for* loss in sweetness. The null hypothesis says "no loss" on the average in a large population of tasters. The alternative hypothesis says "there is a loss." So the hypotheses are

$$H_0: \mu = 0$$
$$H_a: \mu > 0$$

The alternative hypothesis is *one-sided* because we are interested only in whether the cola *lost* sweetness.

EXAMPLE 15.3 Studying job satisfaction

Does the job satisfaction of assembly workers differ when their work is machine-paced rather than self-paced? Assign workers either to an assembly line moving at a fixed pace or to a self-paced setting. All subjects work in both settings, in random order. This is a matched pairs design. After two weeks in each work setting, the workers take a test of job satisfaction. The response variable is the difference in satisfaction scores, self-paced minus machine-paced.

The parameter of interest is the mean μ of the differences in scores in the population of all assembly workers. The null hypothesis says that there is no difference between self-paced and machine-paced work, that is,

$$H_0: \mu = 0$$

The authors of the study wanted to know if the two work conditions have different levels of job satisfaction. They did not specify the direction of the difference. The alternative hypothesis is therefore *two-sided*:

$$H_a: \mu \neq 0$$

The hypotheses should express the hopes or suspicions we have before we see the data. It is cheating to first look at the data and then frame hypotheses to fit what the data show. Thus, the fact that the workers in the study of Example 15.3 were more satisfied with self-paced work should not influence our choice of H_a. If you do not have a specific direction firmly in mind in advance, use a two-sided alternative.

APPLY YOUR KNOWLEDGE

15.3 **Anemia.** State the null and alternative hypotheses for the anemia study described in Exercise 15.1.

15.4 **Student attitudes.** State the null and alternative hypotheses for the study of older students' attitudes described in Exercise 15.2.

15.5 **Fuel economy.** According to the Environmental Protection Agency (EPA), the Honda Civic hybrid car gets 51 miles per gallon (mpg) on the highway. The EPA ratings often overstate true fuel economy. Larry keeps careful records of the gas mileage of his new Civic hybrid for 3000 miles of highway driving. His result is $\bar{x} = 47.2$ mpg. Larry wonders whether the data show that his true long-term average highway mileage is less than 51 mpg. What are his null and alternative hypotheses?

15.6 **Travel times to work.** A labor specialist thinks that the mean travel time to work for all workers in North Carolina is 20 minutes. A random sample of 15 workers finds that their mean travel time is $\bar{x} = 22.5$ minutes. What are the null and alternative hypotheses for testing whether the true mean is different from 20 minutes?

15.7 **Stating hypotheses.** In planning a study of the birth weights of babies whose mothers did not see a doctor before delivery, a researcher states the hypotheses as

$$H_0: \bar{x} = 1000 \text{ grams}$$
$$H_a: \bar{x} < 1000 \text{ grams}$$

What's wrong with this?

Test statistics

A significance test uses data in the form of a **test statistic.** Here are some principles that apply to most tests: *test statistic*

- The test is based on a statistic that compares the value of the parameter stated by the null hypothesis with an estimate of the parameter from the sample data. The estimate is usually the same one used in a confidence interval for the parameter.

- Large values of the test statistic indicate that the estimate is far from the parameter value specified by H_0. These values give evidence against H_0. The alternative hypothesis determines which directions count against H_0.

EXAMPLE 15.4   Sweetening colas: the test statistic

In Example 15.2, the null hypothesis is $H_0: \mu = 0$ and the estimate of μ is $\bar{x} = 1.02$. The test statistic for hypotheses about the mean μ of a Normal distribution is the standardized version of $\bar{x}$:

$$z = \frac{\bar{x} - \mu}{\sigma/\sqrt{n}}$$

The statistic z says how far $\bar{x}$ is from the value of μ given by the null hypothesis, in standard deviation units. For Example 15.2,

$$z = \frac{1.02 - 0}{1/\sqrt{10}} = 3.23$$

Because the sample result is more than 3 standard deviations above the hypothesized mean 0, it gives good evidence that the mean sweetness loss is not 0, but positive.

APPLY YOUR KNOWLEDGE

15.8 Sweetening colas. Figure 15.1 compares two possible results for the taste test of Example 15.2. Mean $\bar{x} = 1.02$ is far out on the Normal curve and so is good evidence against $H_0: \mu = 0$. Mean $\bar{x} = 0.3$ is not far enough out to convince us that the population mean is greater than 0. Example 15.4 shows that the test statistic is $z = 3.23$ for $\bar{x} = 1.02$. What is z for $\bar{x} = 0.3$? The standard scale makes it easier to compare the two results.

15.9 Anemia. What are the values of the test statistic z for the two outcomes in the anemia study of Exercise 15.1?

15.10 Student attitudes. What are the values of the test statistic z for the two outcomes for mean SSHA of older students in Exercise 15.2?

P-values

The null hypothesis H_0 states the claim we are seeking evidence *against*. The test statistic measures how far the sample data diverge from the null hypothesis. If the test statistic is large and is in the direction suggested by the alternative hypothesis H_a, we have data that would be unlikely if H_0 were true. We make "unlikely" precise by calculating a probability.

P-VALUE

The probability, computed assuming that H_0 is true, that the test statistic would take a value as extreme or more extreme than that actually observed is called the **P-value** of the test. The smaller the P-value, the stronger the evidence against H_0 provided by the data.

Small P-values are evidence against H_0, because they say that the observed result is unlikely to occur when H_0 is true. Large P-values fail to give evidence against H_0.

EXAMPLE 15.5   Sweetening colas: one-sided P-value

The study of sweetness loss in Example 15.2 tests the hypotheses

$$H_0: \mu = 0$$
$$H_a: \mu > 0$$

Because the alternative hypothesis says that $\mu > 0$, values of $\bar{x}$ greater than 0 favor H_a over H_0. The 10 tasters found mean sweetness loss $\bar{x} = 1.02$. *The P-value is the probability of getting an $\bar{x}$ at least as large as 1.02 when the null hypothesis is really true.*

The test statistic z is the standardized version of the sample mean $\bar{x}$ using $\mu = 0$, the value specified by H_0. That is,

$$z = \frac{1.02 - 0}{1/\sqrt{10}} = 3.23$$

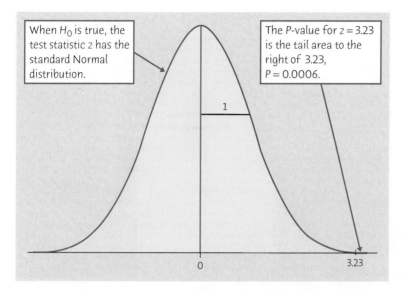

When H_0 is true, the test statistic z has the standard Normal distribution.

The P-value for $z = 3.23$ is the tail area to the right of 3.23, $P = 0.0006$.

1

0   3.23

FIGURE 15.2 The P-value for the value $z = 3.23$ of the test statistic in Example 15.5. The P-value is the probability (when H_0 is true) that z takes a value as large or larger than the actually observed value.

Because $\overline{x}$ has a Normal distribution, z has the standard Normal distribution when H_0 is true. So *the P-value is also the probability of getting a z at least as large as 3.23*. Figure 15.2 shows this P-value on the standard Normal curve that displays the distribution of z. Using Table A or software,

$$P\text{-value} = P(Z > 3.23) = 1 - 0.9994 = 0.0006$$

We would very rarely observe a mean sweetness loss of 1.02 or larger if H_0 were true. The small P-value provides strong evidence against H_0 and in favor of the alternative $H_a: \mu > 0$.

The alternative hypothesis sets the direction that counts as evidence against H_0. In Example 15.5, only large values count because the alternative is one-sided on the high side. If the alternative is two-sided, both directions count.

EXAMPLE 15.6 Job satisfaction: two-sided P-value

Suppose we know that differences in job satisfaction scores in Example 15.3 follow a Normal distribution with standard deviation $\sigma = 60$. If there is no difference in job satisfaction between the two work environments, the mean is $\mu = 0$. This is H_0. The alternative hypothesis says simply "there is a difference," $H_a: \mu \neq 0$.

Data from 18 workers gave $\overline{x} = 17$. That is, these workers preferred the self-paced environment on the average. The test statistic is

$$z = \frac{\overline{x} - 0}{\sigma/\sqrt{n}}$$

$$= \frac{17 - 0}{60/\sqrt{18}} = 1.20$$

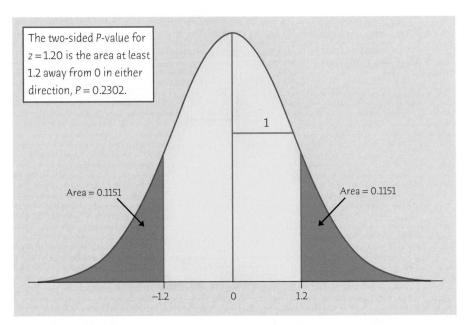

The two-sided P-value for $z = 1.20$ is the area at least 1.2 away from 0 in either direction, $P = 0.2302$.

Area = 0.1151   Area = 0.1151

-1.2 0 1.2

FIGURE 15.3 The P-value for the two-sided test in Example 15.6. The observed value of the test statistic is $z = 1.20$.

Because the alternative is two-sided, the P-value is the probability of getting a z at least as far from 0 in either direction as the observed z = 1.20. As always, calculate the P-value taking H_0 *to be true. When* H_0 *is true,* $\mu = 0$ *and z has the standard Normal distribution. Figure 15.3 shows the P-value as an area under the standard Normal curve. It is*

$$P\text{-value} = P(Z < -1.20 \text{ or } Z > 1.20) = 2P(Z < -1.20)$$
$$= (2)(0.1151) = 0.2302$$

Values as far from 0 as $\overline{x} = 17$ would happen 23% of the time when the true population mean is $\mu = 0$. An outcome that would occur so often when H_0 is true is not good evidence against H_0.

The conclusion of Example 15.6 is *not* that H_0 is true. The study looked for evidence against H_0: $\mu = 0$ and failed to find strong evidence. That is all we can say. No doubt the mean μ for the population of all assembly workers is not exactly equal to 0. A large enough sample would give evidence of the difference, even if it is very small. Tests of significance assess the evidence *against* H_0. If the evidence is strong, we can confidently reject H_0 in favor of the alternative. *Failing to find evidence against* H_0 *means only that the data are consistent with* H_0, *not that we have clear evidence that* H_0 *is true.*

The *P-Value of a Test of Significance* applet automates the work of finding P-values for samples of size 50 or smaller. The applet even displays P-values as areas under a Normal curve, just like Figures 15.2 and 15.3.

APPLY YOUR KNOWLEDGE

15.11 P-value automated. Go to the *P-Value of a Test of Significance* applet. Enter the information for Example 15.6: hypotheses, n, σ, and $\bar{x}$. Click "Show P." The applet tells you that $P = 0.2302$. Make a sketch of how the applet shows the P-value as an area under a Normal curve. The sketch differs from Figure 15.3 only in that the applet shows the original scale of $\bar{x}$ rather than the standard scale of z.

15.12 Sweetening colas. Figure 15.1 shows that the outcome $\bar{x} = 0.3$ from the cola taste test is not good evidence that the mean sweetness loss is greater than 0. What is the P-value for this outcome? This P-value says, "A sample outcome this large or larger would often occur just by chance when the true mean is really 0."

15.13 Anemia. What are the P-values for the two outcomes of the anemia study in Exercise 15.1? Explain briefly why these values tell us that one outcome is strong evidence against the null hypothesis and that the other outcome is not.

15.14 Student attitudes. What are the P-values for the two outcomes of the study of SSHA scores of older students in Exercise 15.2? Explain briefly why these values tell us that one outcome is strong evidence against the null hypothesis and that the other outcome is not.

Statistical significance

We sometimes take one final step to assess the evidence against H_0. We can compare the P-value with a fixed value that we regard as decisive. This amounts to announcing in advance how much evidence against H_0 we will insist on. The decisive value of P is called the **significance level.** We write it as α, the Greek letter alpha. If we choose $\alpha = 0.05$, we are requiring that the data give evidence against H_0 so strong that it would happen no more than 5% of the time (1 time in 20 samples in the long run) when H_0 is true. If we choose $\alpha = 0.01$, we are insisting on stronger evidence against H_0, evidence so strong that it would appear only 1% of the time (1 time in 100 samples) if H_0 is in fact true.

significance level

STATISTICAL SIGNIFICANCE

If the P-value is as small or smaller than α, we say that the data are **statistically significant at level α.**

"Significant" in the statistical sense does not mean "important." It means simply "not likely to happen just by chance." The significance level α makes "not likely" more exact. Significance at level 0.01 is often expressed by the statement "The results were significant ($P < 0.01$)." Here P stands for the P-value. The actual P-value is more informative than a statement of significance because it allows us to assess significance at any level we choose. For example, a result with $P = 0.03$ is significant at the $\alpha = 0.05$ level but is not significant at the $\alpha = 0.01$ level.

APPLY YOUR KNOWLEDGE

15.15 Anemia. In Exercises 15.9 and 15.13, you found the z test statistic and the P-value for the outcome $\bar{x} = 11.8$ in the anemia study of Exercise 15.1. Is this outcome statistically significant at the $\alpha = 0.05$ level? At the $\alpha = 0.01$ level?

15.16 Student attitudes. In Exercises 15.10 and 15.14, you found the z test statistic and the P-value for the outcome $\bar{x} = 125.8$ in the attitudes study of Exercise 15.2. Is this outcome statistically significant at the $\alpha = 0.05$ level? At the $\alpha = 0.01$ level?

15.17 Protecting ultramarathon runners. Exercise 9.37 (page 232) describes an experiment designed to learn whether taking vitamin C reduces respiratory infections among ultramarathon runners. The report of the study said:

Sixty-eight percent of the runners in the placebo group reported the development of symptoms of upper respiratory tract infection after the race; this was significantly more ($P < 0.01$) than that reported by the vitamin C–supplemented group (33%).

(a) Explain to someone who knows no statistics why "significantly more" means there is good reason to think that vitamin C works.

(b) Now explain more exactly: what does $P < 0.01$ mean?

Down with driver ed!

Who could object to driver-training courses in schools? The killjoy who looks at data, that's who. Careful studies show no significant effect of driver training on the behavior of teenage drivers. Because many states allow those who take driver ed to get a license at a younger age, the programs may actually increase accidents and road deaths by increasing the number of young and risky drivers.

Tests for a population mean

The steps in carrying out a significance test mirror the overall four-step process for organizing realistic statistical problems.

TESTS OF SIGNIFICANCE: THE FOUR-STEP PROCESS

STATE: What is the practical question that requires a statistical test?

FORMULATE: Identify the parameter and state null and alternative hypotheses.

SOLVE: Carry out the test in three phases:

(a) Check the conditions for the test you plan to use.

(b) Calculate the test statistic.

(c) Find the P-value.

CONCLUDE: Return to the practical question to describe your results in this setting.

Once you have stated your question, formulated hypotheses, and checked the conditions for your test, you or your software can find the test statistic and P-value by following a rule. Here is the rule for the test we have used in our examples.

z TEST FOR A POPULATION MEAN

Draw an SRS of size n from a Normal population that has unknown mean μ and known standard deviation σ. To **test the null hypothesis that μ has a specified value,**

$$H_0: \mu = \mu_0$$

calculate the **one-sample z test statistic**

$$z = \frac{\bar{x} - \mu_0}{\sigma/\sqrt{n}}$$

In terms of a variable Z having the standard Normal distribution, the P-value for a test of H_0 against

$H_a: \mu > \mu_0$ is $P(Z \geq z)$

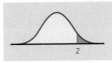

$H_a: \mu < \mu_0$ is $P(Z \leq z)$

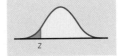

$H_a: \mu \neq \mu_0$ is $2P(Z \geq |z|)$

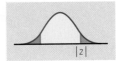

EXAMPLE 15.7   Executives' blood pressures

STATE: The National Center for Health Statistics reports that the systolic blood pressure for males 35 to 44 years of age has mean 128 and standard deviation 15. The medical director of a large company looks at the medical records of 72 executives in this age group and finds that the mean systolic blood pressure in this sample is $\bar{x} = 126.07$. Is this evidence that the company's executives have a different mean blood pressure from the general population?

FORMULATE: The null hypothesis is "no difference" from the national mean $\mu_0 = 128$. The alternative is two-sided, because the medical director did not have a particular direction in mind before examining the data. So the hypotheses about the unknown mean μ of the executive population are

$$H_0: \mu = 128$$
$$H_a: \mu \neq 128$$

SOLVE: As part of the "simple conditions," suppose we know that executives' blood pressures follow a Normal distribution with standard deviation $\sigma = 15$. The one-sample

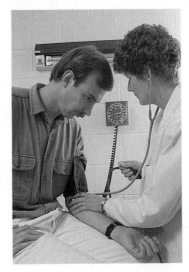

W&D Mcintyre/Photo Researchers

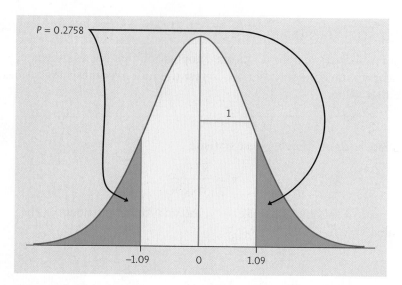

FIGURE 15.4 The P-value for the two-sided test in Example 15.7. The observed value of the test statistic is $z = -1.09$.

z **test statistic** is

$$z = \frac{\overline{x} - \mu_0}{\sigma/\sqrt{n}} = \frac{126.07 - 128}{15/\sqrt{72}}$$
$$= -1.09$$

To help find a **P-value,** sketch the standard Normal curve and mark on it the observed value of z. Figure 15.4 shows that the P-value is the probability that a standard Normal variable Z takes a value at least 1.09 away from zero. From Table A or software, this probability is

$$P = 2P(Z \geq 1.09) = 2(1 - 0.8621) = 0.2758$$

CONCLUDE: More than 27% of the time, an SRS of size 72 from the general male population would have a mean blood pressure at least as far from 128 as that of the executive sample. The observed $\overline{x} = 126.07$ is therefore not good evidence that executives differ from other men.

In this chapter we are acting as if the "simple conditions" stated on page 344 are true. In practice, you must verify these conditions.

1. **SRS:** The most important condition is that the 72 executives in the sample are an SRS from the population of all middle-aged male executives in the company. We should check this requirement by asking how the data were produced. If medical records are available only for executives with recent medical problems, for example, the data are of little value for our purpose. It turns out that all executives are given a free annual medical exam, and that the medical director selected 72 exam results at random.

2. **Normal distribution:** We should also examine the distribution of the 72 observations to look for signs that the population distribution is not Normal.

3. **Known σ:** It really is unrealistic to suppose that we know that $\sigma = 15$. We will see in Chapter 18 that it is easy to do away with the need to know σ.

— EXAMPLE 15.8   *Can you balance your checkbook?* —

STATE: In a discussion of the education level of the American workforce, someone says, "The average young person can't even balance a checkbook." The National Assessment of Educational Progress says that a score of 275 or higher on its quantitative test reflects the skill needed to balance a checkbook. The NAEP random sample of 840 young men had a mean score of $\bar{x} = 272$, a bit below the checkbook-balancing level. Is this sample result good evidence that the mean for *all* young men is less than 275?

FORMULATE: The hypotheses are

$$H_0\text{: } \mu = 275$$
$$H_a\text{: } \mu < 275$$

SOLVE: Suppose we know that NAEP scores have a Normal distribution with $\sigma = 60$. The z **test statistic** is

$$z = \frac{\bar{x} - \mu_0}{\sigma/\sqrt{n}} = \frac{272 - 275}{60/\sqrt{840}}$$
$$= -1.45$$

Because H_a is one-sided on the low side, small values of z count against H_0. Figure 15.5 illustrates the **P-value.** Using Table A or software, the P-value is

$$P = P(Z \leq -1.45) = 0.0735$$

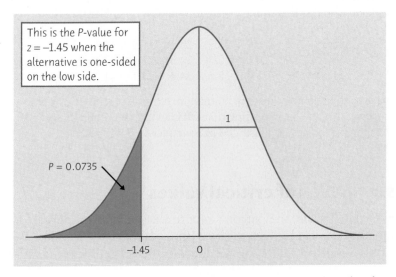

This is the P-value for z = −1.45 when the alternative is one-sided on the low side.

P = 0.0735

−1.45   0

FIGURE 15.5 The P-value for the one-sided test in Example 15.8. The observed value of the test statistic is $z = -1.45$.

CONCLUDE: A mean score as low as 272 would occur about 7 times in 100 samples if the population mean were 275. This is modest evidence that the mean NAEP score for all young men is less than 275. It is significant at the $\alpha = 0.10$ level but not at the $\alpha = 0.05$ level.

APPLY YOUR KNOWLEDGE

15.18 Water quality. An environmentalist group collects a liter of water from each of 45 random locations along a stream and measures the amount of dissolved oxygen in each specimen. The mean is 4.62 milligrams (mg). Is this strong evidence that the stream has a mean oxygen content of less than 5 mg per liter? (Suppose we know that dissolved oxygen varies among locations according to a Normal distribution with $\sigma = 0.92$ mg.)

15.19 Improving your SAT score. We suspect that on the average students will score higher on their second attempt at the SAT mathematics exam than on their first attempt. Suppose we know that the changes in score (second try minus first try) follow a Normal distribution with standard deviation $\sigma = 50$. Here are the results for 46 randomly chosen high school students:

−30	24	47	70	−62	55	−41	−32	128	−11
−43	122	−10	56	32	−30	−28	−19	1	17
57	−14	−58	77	27	−33	51	17	−67	29
94	−11	2	12	−53	−49	49	8	−24	96
120	2	−33	−2	−39	99				

Do these data give good evidence that the mean change in the population is greater than zero? Follow the four-step process as illustrated in Examples 15.7 and 15.8.

15.20 Reading a computer screen. Does the use of fancy type fonts slow down the reading of text on a computer screen? Adults can read four paragraphs of text in an average time of 22 seconds in the common Times New Roman font. Ask 25 adults to read this text in the ornate font named Gigi. Here are their times:[1]

23.2	21.2	28.9	27.7	29.1	27.3	16.1	22.6	25.6
34.2	23.9	26.8	20.5	34.3	21.4	32.6	26.2	34.1
31.5	24.6	23.0	28.6	24.4	28.1	41.3		

Suppose that reading times are Normal with $\sigma = 6$ seconds. Is there good evidence that the mean reading time for Gigi is greater than 22 seconds? Follow the four-step process as illustrated in Examples 15.7 and 15.8.

Robert Daly/Getty Images

Using tables of critical values*

In terms of the *P*-value, the outcome of a test is significant at level α if $P \leq \alpha$. Significance at any level is easy to assess once you have the *P*-value. When you do not use software, *P*-values can be difficult to calculate. Fortunately, you can

---

*This section is optional. It is useful only if you do not use software that gives *P*-values.

decide whether a result is statistically significant by using a table of critical values, the same table we use for confidence intervals. The table also allows you to approximate the *P*-value without calculation. Here are two examples.

EXAMPLE 15.9   Is it significant (one-sided)?

In Example 15.8, we examined whether the mean NAEP quantitative score of young men is less than 275. The hypotheses are

$$H_0: \mu = 275$$
$$H_a: \mu < 275$$

The z statistic takes the value $z = -1.45$. How significant is the evidence against H_0?

To determine significance, compare the observed $z = -1.45$ with the critical values z^* in the last row of Table C. The values z^* correspond to the one-sided and two-sided *P*-values given at the bottom of the table. The value $z = -1.45$ (ignoring its sign) falls between the critical values 1.282 and 1.645. Because z is farther from 0 than 1.282, the critical value for one-sided *P*-value 0.10, the test *is* significant at level $\alpha = 0.10$. Because $z = 1.45$ is *not* farther from 0 than the critical value 1.645 for *P*-value 0.05, the test is *not* significant at level $\alpha = 0.05$. So we know that $0.05 < P < 0.10$.

Figure 15.6 locates $z = -1.45$ between the two tabled critical values, with minus signs added because the alternative is one-sided on the low side. The figure also

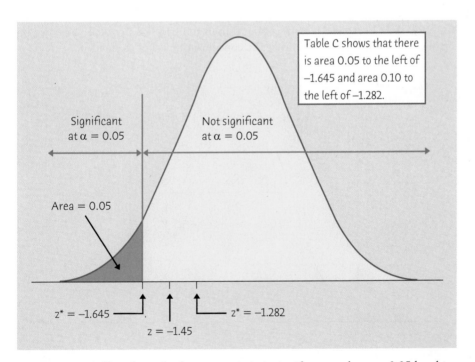

Table C shows that there is area 0.05 to the left of −1.645 and area 0.10 to the left of −1.282.

Significant at $\alpha = 0.05$

Not significant at $\alpha = 0.05$

Area = 0.05

$z^* = -1.645$

$z^* = -1.282$

$z = -1.45$

FIGURE 15.6 Deciding whether a z statistic is significant at the $\alpha = 0.05$ level in the one-sided test of Example 15.9. The observed value $z = -1.45$ of the test statistic is not significant because it is not in the extreme 5% of the standard Normal distribution.

shows how the critical value $z^* = -1.645$ separates values of z that are significant at the $\alpha = 0.05$ level from values that are not significant.

STEP

EXAMPLE 15.10 Is it significant (two-sided)?

STATE: An analytical laboratory is asked to evaluate the claim that the concentration of the active ingredient in a specimen is 0.86 grams per liter (g/l). The lab makes 3 repeated analyses of the specimen. The mean result is $\bar{x} = 0.8404$ g/l. The true concentration is the mean μ of the population of all analyses of the specimen. Is there significant evidence at the 1% level that $\mu \neq 0.86$ g/l?

FORMULATE: The hypotheses are

$$H_0: \mu = 0.86$$
$$H_a: \mu \neq 0.86$$

SOLVE: Suppose that the standard deviation of the analysis process is known to be $\sigma = 0.0068$ g/l. The z statistic is

$$z = \frac{0.8404 - 0.86}{0.0068/\sqrt{3}} = -4.99$$

Because the alternative is two-sided, the P-value is the area under the standard Normal curve below -4.99 and above 4.99. Compare $z = -4.99$ (ignoring its sign) with the critical value for two-sided P-value 0.01 from Table C. This critical value is $z^* = 2.576$. Figure 15.7 locates $z = -4.99$ and the critical values on the standard Normal curve.

CONCLUDE: Because z is farther from 0 than the two-sided critical value, we have significant evidence ($P < 0.01$) that the concentration is not as claimed.

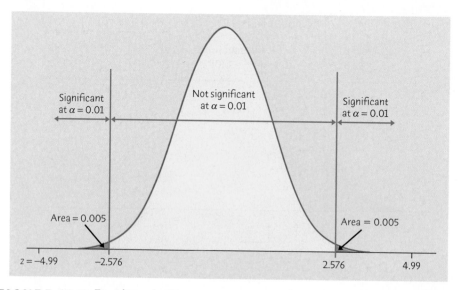

FIGURE 15.7 Deciding whether a z statistic is significant at the $\alpha = 0.01$ level in the two-sided test of Example 15.10. The observed value $z = -4.99$ is significant because it is in the extreme 1% of the standard Normal distribution.

In fact, $z = -4.99$ lies beyond all the critical values in Table C. The largest critical value is 3.291, for two-sided P-value 0.001. So we can say that the two-sided test is significant at the 0.001 level, not just at the 0.01 level. Software gives the exact P-value as

$$P = 2P(Z \geq 4.99) = 0.0000006$$

No wonder Figure 15.7 places $z = -4.99$ so far out that the Normal curve is not visible above the axis.

Because the practice of statistics almost always employs software that calculates P-values automatically, tables of critical values are becoming outdated. Tables of critical values such as Table C appear in this book for learning purposes and to rescue students without good computing facilities.

APPLY YOUR KNOWLEDGE

15.21 Significance. You are testing H_0: $\mu = 0$ against H_a: $\mu > 0$ based on an SRS of 20 observations from a Normal population. What values of the z statistic are statistically significant at the $\alpha = 0.005$ level?

15.22 Significance. You are testing H_0: $\mu = 0$ against H_a: $\mu \neq 0$ based on an SRS of 20 observations from a Normal population. What values of the z statistic are statistically significant at the $\alpha = 0.005$ level?

15.23 Testing a random number generator. A random number generator is supposed to produce random numbers that are uniformly distributed on the interval from 0 to 1. If this is true, the numbers generated come from a population with $\mu = 0.5$ and $\sigma = 0.2887$. A command to generate 100 random numbers gives outcomes with mean $\bar{x} = 0.4365$. Assume that the population σ remains fixed. We want to test

$$H_0: \mu = 0.5$$
$$H_a: \mu \neq 0.5$$

(a) Calculate the value of the z test statistic.

(b) Is the result significant at the 5% level ($\alpha = 0.05$)?

(c) Is the result significant at the 1% level ($\alpha = 0.01$)?

(d) Between which two Normal critical values in the bottom row of Table C does z lie? Between what two numbers does the P-value lie? What do you conclude?

Tests from confidence intervals

Both tests and confidence intervals for a population mean μ start by using the sample mean $\bar{x}$ to estimate μ. Both rely on probabilities calculated from Normal distributions. In fact, a two-sided test at significance level α can be carried out from a confidence interval with confidence level $C = 1 - \alpha$.

> ### CONFIDENCE INTERVALS AND TWO-SIDED TESTS
>
> A level α two-sided significance test rejects a hypothesis $H_0: \mu = \mu_0$ exactly when the value μ_0 falls outside a level $1 - \alpha$ confidence interval for μ.

EXAMPLE 15.11 Tests from a confidence interval

In Example 15.7, a medical director found mean blood pressure $\bar{x} = 126.07$ for an SRS of 72 executives. Is this value significantly different from the national mean $\mu_0 = 128$ at the 10% significance level?

We can answer this question directly by a two-sided test or indirectly from a 90% confidence interval. The confidence interval is

$$\bar{x} \pm z^* \frac{\sigma}{\sqrt{n}} = 126.07 \pm 1.645 \frac{15}{\sqrt{72}}$$

$$= 126.07 \pm 2.91$$

$$= 123.16 \text{ to } 128.98$$

The hypothesized value $\mu_0 = 128$ falls *inside* this confidence interval, so we *cannot* reject

$$H_0: \mu = 128$$

at the 10% significance level. On the other hand, a two-sided test *can* reject

$$H_0: \mu = 129$$

at the 10% level, because 129 lies *outside* the confidence interval.

APPLY YOUR KNOWLEDGE

15.24 Test and confidence interval. The P-value for a two-sided test of the null hypothesis $H_0: \mu = 10$ is 0.06.
(a) Does the 95% confidence interval include the value 10? Why?
(b) Does the 90% confidence interval include the value 10? Why?

15.25 Confidence interval and test. A 95% confidence interval for a population mean is 31.5 ± 3.5.
(a) Can you reject the null hypothesis that $\mu = 34$ at the 5% significance level? Why?
(b) Can you reject the null hypothesis that $\mu = 36$ at the 5% significance level? Why?

CHAPTER 15 SUMMARY

A **test of significance** assesses the evidence provided by data against a **null hypothesis** H_0 in favor of an **alternative hypothesis** H_a.

Hypotheses are always stated in terms of population parameters. Usually H_0 is a statement that no effect is present, and H_a says that a parameter differs from its null value in a specific direction (**one-sided alternative**) or in either direction (**two-sided alternative**).

The essential reasoning of a significance test is as follows. Suppose for the sake of argument that the null hypothesis is true. If we repeated our data production many times, would we often get data as inconsistent with H_0 as the data we actually have? If the data are unlikely when H_0 is true, they provide evidence against H_0.

A test is based on a **test statistic** that measures how far the sample outcome is from the value stated by H_0.

The **P-value** of a test is the probability, computed supposing H_0 to be true, that the test statistic will take a value at least as extreme as that actually observed. Small P-values indicate strong evidence against H_0. To calculate a P-value we must know the sampling distribution of the test statistic when H_0 is true.

If the P-value is as small or smaller than a specified value α, the data are **statistically significant** at significance level α.

Significance tests for the null hypothesis H_0: $\mu = \mu_0$ concerning the unknown mean μ of a population are based on the **one-sample z test statistic**

$$z = \frac{\overline{x} - \mu_0}{\sigma/\sqrt{n}}$$

The z test assumes an SRS of size n from a Normal population with known population standard deviation σ. P-values are computed from the standard Normal distribution.

CHECK YOUR SKILLS

15.26 The mean score of adult men on a psychological test that measures "masculine stereotypes" is 4.88. A researcher studying hotel managers suspects that successful managers score higher than adult men in general. A random sample of 48 managers of large hotels has mean $\overline{x} = 5.91$. The null hypothesis for the researcher's test is
(a) H_0: $\mu = 4.88$.   (b) H_0: $\mu = 5.91$.   (c) H_0: $\mu > 4.88$.

15.27 The researcher's alternative hypothesis for the test in Exercise 15.26 is
(a) H_a: $\mu \neq 5.91$.   (b) H_a: $\mu > 4.88$.   (c) H_a: $\mu > 5.91$.

15.28 Suppose that scores of hotel managers on the psychological test of Exercise 15.26 are Normal with standard deviation $\sigma = 0.79$. The value of the z statistic for the researcher's test is
(a) $z = 1.30$.   (b) $z = -1.30$.   (c) $z = 9.03$.

15.29 If a z statistic has value $z = 1.30$, the two-sided P-value is
(a) 0.9032.   (b) 0.1936.   (c) 0.0968.

15.30 If a z statistic has value $z = -1.30$, the two-sided P-value is
(a) 0.9032.   (b) 0.1936.   (c) 0.0968.

15.31 If a z statistic has value $z = 1.30$ and H_a says that the population mean is greater than its value under H_0, the one-sided P-value is
(a) 0.9032.   (b) 0.1936.   (c) 0.0968.

15.32 If a z statistic has value $z = -1.30$ and H_a says that the population mean is greater than its value under H_0, the one-sided P-value is
(a) 0.9032.   (b) 0.1936.   (c) 0.0968.

15.33 If a z statistic has value $z = 9.03$, the two-sided P-value is
(a) very close to 0.   (b) very close to 1.   (c) Can't tell from the table.

15.34 You use software to do a test. The program tells you that the P-value is $P = 0.031$. This result is

(a) not significant at the 5% level.

(b) significant at the 5% level but not at the 1% level.

(c) significant at the 1% level.

15.35 A government report says that a 90% confidence interval for the mean income of American households is $59,067 \pm \$356$. Is the mean income significantly different from $59,000?

(a) It is not significantly different at the 10% level and therefore is also not significantly different at the 5% level.

(b) It is not significantly different at the 10% level but might be significantly different at the 5% level.

(c) It is significantly different at the 10% level.

CHAPTER 15 EXERCISES

In all exercises that call for P-values, give the actual value if you use software or the P-value applet. Otherwise, use Table C to give values between which P must fall.

15.36 This wine stinks. Sulfur compounds cause "off-odors" in wine, so winemakers want to know the odor threshold, the lowest concentration of a compound that the human nose can detect. The odor threshold for dimethyl sulfide (DMS) in trained wine tasters is about 25 micrograms per liter of wine (μg/l). The untrained noses of consumers may be less sensitive, however. Here are the DMS odor thresholds for 10 untrained students:

$$31 \quad 31 \quad 43 \quad 36 \quad 23 \quad 34 \quad 32 \quad 30 \quad 20 \quad 24$$

Assume that the odor threshold for untrained noses is Normally distributed with $\sigma = 7$ μg/l. Is there evidence that the mean threshold for untrained tasters is greater than 25 μg/l? Follow the four-step process, as illustrated in Example 15.8, in your answer.

15.37 IQ test scores. Exercise 14.6 (page 352) gives the IQ test scores of 31 seventh-grade girls in a Midwest school district. IQ scores follow a Normal distribution with standard deviation $\sigma = 15$. Treat these 31 girls as an SRS of all seventh-grade girls in this district. IQ scores in a broad population are supposed to have mean $\mu = 100$. Is there evidence that the mean in this district differs from 100? Follow the four-step process, as illustrated in Example 15.7, in your answer.

15.38 Hotel managers' personalities. Successful hotel managers must have personality characteristics often thought of as feminine (such as "compassionate") as well as those often thought of as masculine (such as "forceful"). The Bem Sex-Role Inventory (BSRI) is a personality test that gives separate ratings for female and male stereotypes, both on a scale of 1 to 7. A sample of 148 male general mangers of three-star and four-star hotels had mean BSRI femininity score $\overline{y} = 5.29$.[2] The mean score for the general male population is $\mu = 5.19$. Do hotel managers on the average differ significantly in femininity score from men in general? Assume that the standard deviation of scores in the population of all male hotel managers is the same as the $\sigma = 0.78$ for the adult male population. Follow the four-step process in your work.

15.39 Bone loss by nursing mothers. Exercise 14.25 (page 358) gives the percent change in the mineral content of the spine for 47 mothers during three months of nursing a baby. As in that exercise, suppose that the percent change in the population of all nursing mothers has a Normal distribution with standard deviation $\sigma = 2.5\%$. Do these data give good evidence that on the average nursing mothers lose bone mineral? Use the four-step process to organize your work.

15.40 Sample size affects the P-value. In Example 15.6, a sample of $n = 18$ workers had mean response $\bar{x} = 17$. Using $\sigma = 60$, the example shows that for testing $H_0: \mu = 0$ against the two-sided alternative, $z = 1.20$ and $P = 0.2302$. Suppose that $\bar{x} = 17$ had come from a sample of 75 workers rather than 18 workers. Find the test statistic z and its two-sided P-value. Do the data give good evidence that the population mean is not zero? (The P-value is smaller for larger n because the sampling distribution of $\bar{x}$ becomes less spread out as n increases. So the tail area beyond $\bar{x} = 17$ gets smaller as n increases.)

15.41 Tests and confidence intervals. In Exercise 14.22 you found a confidence interval for the mean μ based on the same data used in Exercise 15.38. Explain why the confidence interval is more informative than the test result.

15.42 The Supreme Court speaks. Court cases in such areas as employment discrimination often involve tests of significance. The Supreme Court has said that z-scores beyond $z^* = 2$ or 3 are generally convincing statistical evidence. For a two-sided test, what significance level α corresponds to $z^* = 2$? To $z^* = 3$?

15.43 The wrong alternative. One of your friends is comparing movie ratings by female and male students for a class project. She starts with no expectations as to which sex will rate a movie more highly. After seeing that women rate a particular movie more highly than men, she tests a one-sided alternative about the mean ratings:

$$H_0: \mu_F = \mu_M$$
$$H_a: \mu_F > \mu_M$$

Joe Sohm/The Image Works

She finds $z = 2.1$ with one-sided P-value $P = 0.0179$.

(a) Explain why your friend should have used the two-sided alternative hypothesis.

(b) What is the correct P-value for $z = 2.1$?

15.44 The wrong P. The report of a study of seat belt use by drivers says, "Hispanic drivers were not significantly more likely than White/non-Hispanic drivers to overreport safety belt use (27.4 vs. 21.1%, respectively; $z = 1.33$, $P > 1.0$)."[3] How do you know that the P-value given is incorrect? What is the correct one-sided P-value for test statistic $z = 1.33$?

15.45 Tracking the placebo effect. The placebo effect is particularly strong in patients with Parkinson's disease. To understand the workings of the placebo effect, scientists measure activity at a key point in the brain when patients receive a placebo that they think is an active drug and also when no treatment is given.[4] The response variable is the difference in brain activity, placebo minus no treatment. Does the placebo reduce activity on the average? State clearly what

the parameter μ is for this matched pairs setting. Then state H_0 and H_a for the significance test.

15.46 Fortified breakfast cereals. The Food and Drug Administration recommends that breakfast cereals be fortified with folic acid. In a matched pairs study, volunteers ate either fortified or unfortified cereal for some time, then switched to the other cereal. The response variable is the difference in blood folic acid, fortified minus unfortified. Does eating fortified cereal raise the level of folic acid in the blood? State H_0 and H_a for a test to answer this question. State carefully what the parameter μ in your hypotheses is.

15.47 How to show that you are rich. Every society has its own marks of wealth and prestige. In ancient China, it appears that owning pigs was such a mark. Evidence comes from examining burial sites. The skulls of sacrificed pigs tend to appear along with expensive ornaments, which suggests that the pigs, like the ornaments, signal the wealth and prestige of the person buried. A study of burials from around 3500 B.C. concluded that "there are striking differences in grave goods between burials with pig skulls and burials without them.... A test indicates that the two samples of total artifacts are significantly different at the 0.01 level."[5] Explain clearly why "significantly different at the 0.01 level" gives good reason to think that there really is a systematic difference between burials that contain pig skulls and those that lack them.

15.48 Cicadas as fertilizer? Every 17 years, swarms of cicadas emerge from the ground in the eastern United States, live for about six weeks, then die. There are so many cicadas that their dead bodies can serve as fertilizer. In an experiment, a researcher added cicadas under some plants in a natural plot of bellflowers on the forest floor, leaving other plants undisturbed. "In this experiment, cicada-supplemented bellflowers from a natural field population produced foliage with 12% greater nitrogen content relative to controls ($P = 0.031$)."[6] A colleague who knows no statistics says that an increase of 12% isn't a lot—maybe it's just an accident due to natural variation among the plants. Explain in simple language how "$P = 0.031$" answers this objection.

15.49 Forests and windstorms. Does the destruction of large trees in a windstorm change forests in any important way? Here is the conclusion of a study that found that the answer is no:

We found surprisingly little divergence between treefall areas and adjacent control areas in the richness of woody plants ($P = 0.62$), in total stem densities ($P = 0.98$), or in population size or structure for any individual shrub or tree species.[7]

The two P-values refer to null hypotheses that say "no change" in measurements between treefall and control areas. Explain clearly why these values provide no evidence of change.

15.50 Diet and bowel cancer. It has long been thought that eating a healthier diet reduces the risk of bowel cancer. A large study cast doubt on this advice. The subjects were 2079 people who had polyps removed from their bowels in the past six months. Such polyps may lead to cancer. The subjects were randomly assigned to a low-fat, high-fiber diet or to a control group in which subjects ate their usual diets. All subjects were checked for polyps over the next four years.[8]

(a) Outline the design of this experiment.

(b) Surprisingly, the occurrence of new polyps "did not differ significantly between the two groups." Explain clearly what this finding means.

15.51 **5% versus 1%.** Sketch the standard Normal curve for the z test statistic and mark off areas under the curve to show why a value of z that is significant at the 1% level in a one-sided test is always significant at the 5% level. If z is significant at the 5% level, what can you say about its significance at the 1% level?

15.52 **Is this what P means?** When asked to explain the meaning of "the P-value was $P = 0.03$," a student says, "This means there is only probability 0.03 that the null hypothesis is true." Is this an essentially correct explanation? Explain your answer.

15.53 **Is this what significance means?** Another student, when asked why statistical significance appears so often in research reports, says, "Because saying that results are significant tells us that they cannot easily be explained by chance variation alone." Do you think that this statement is essentially correct? Explain your answer.

15.54 **Pulling wood apart.** In Exercise 14.26 (page 359), you found a 90% confidence interval for the mean load required to pull apart pieces of Douglas fir. Use this interval (or calculate it anew here) to answer these questions:

(a) Is there significant evidence at the $\alpha = 0.10$ level against the hypothesis that the mean is 32,000 pounds for the two-sided alternative?

(b) Is there significant evidence at the $\alpha = 0.10$ level against the hypothesis that the mean is 31,500 pounds for the two-sided alternative?

15.55 **I'm a great free-throw shooter.** The *Reasoning of a Statistical Test* applet animates Example 15.1. That example asks if a basketball player's actual performance gives evidence against the claim that he or she makes 80% of free throws. The parameter in question is the percent p of free throws that the player will make if he or she shoots free throws forever. The population is all free throws the player will ever shoot. The null hypothesis is always the same, that the player makes 80% of shots taken:

$$H_0 : p = 80\%$$

The applet does not do a formal statistical test. Instead, it allows you to ask the player to shoot until you are reasonably confident that the true percent of hits is or is not very close to 80%.

    I claim that I make 80% of my free throws. To test my claim, we go to the gym and I shoot 20 free throws. Set the applet to take 20 shots. Check "Show null hypothesis" so that my claim is visible in the graph.

(a) Click "Shoot." How many of the 20 shots did I make? Are you convinced that I really make less than 80%?

(b) If you are not convinced, click "Shoot" again for 20 more shots. Keep going until *either* you are convinced that I don't make 80% of my shots *or* it appears that my true percent made is pretty close to 80%. How many shots did you watch me shoot? How many did I make? What did you conclude? Then click "Show true %" to reveal the truth. Was your conclusion correct?

    Comment: You see why statistical tests say how strong the evidence is *against* some claim. If I make only 10 of 40 shots, you are pretty sure I can't make 80% in the long run. But even if I make exactly 80 of 100, my true long-term percent

David Madison/The Image Bank/Getty Images

might be 78% or 81% instead of 80%. It's hard to be convinced that I make exactly 80%.

15.56 **Significance at the 0.0125 level.**   The *Normal Curve* applet allows you to find critical values of the standard Normal distribution and to visualize the values of the z statistic that are significant at any level. Max is interested in whether a one-sided z test is statistically significant at the $\alpha = 0.0125$ level. Use the *Normal Curve* applet to tell Max what values of z are significant. Sketch the standard Normal curve marked with the values that led to your result.

Left Lane Productions/CORBIS

Inference in Practice

To this point, we have met just two procedures for statistical inference. Both concern inference about the mean μ of a population when the "simple conditions" (page 344) are true: the data are an SRS, the population has a Normal distribution, and we know the standard deviation σ of the population. Under these conditions, a confidence interval for the mean μ is

$$\bar{x} \pm z^* \frac{\sigma}{\sqrt{n}}$$

To test a hypothesis H_0: $\mu = \mu_0$ we use the one-sample z statistic:

$$z = \frac{\bar{x} - \mu_0}{\sigma/\sqrt{n}}$$

We call these **z procedures** because they both start with the one-sample z statistic and use the standard Normal distribution.

In later chapters we will modify these procedures for inference about a population mean to make them useful in practice. We will also introduce procedures for confidence intervals and tests in most of the settings we met in learning to explore data. There are libraries—both of books and of software—full of more elaborate statistical techniques. The reasoning of confidence intervals and tests is the same, no matter how elaborate the details of the procedure are.

There is a saying among statisticians that "mathematical theorems are true; statistical methods are effective when used with judgment." That the one-sample z statistic has the standard Normal distribution when the null hypothesis is true is a mathematical theorem. Effective use of statistical methods requires more than

Don't touch the plants

We know that confounding can distort inference. We don't always recognize how easy it is to confound data. Consider the innocent scientist who visits plants in the field once a week to measure their size. A study of six plant species found that one touch a week significantly increased leaf damage by insects in two species and significantly decreased damage in another species.

knowing such facts. It requires even more than understanding the underlying reasoning.

This chapter begins the process of helping you develop the judgment needed to use statistics in practice. That process will continue in examples and exercises through the rest of this book.

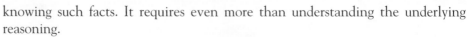

Where did the data come from?

The most important requirement for any inference procedure is that the data come from a process to which the laws of probability apply. Inference is most reliable when the data come from a probability sample or a randomized comparative experiment. Probability samples use chance to choose respondents. Randomized comparative experiments use chance to assign subjects to treatments. The deliberate use of chance ensures that the laws of probability apply to the outcomes, and this in turn ensures that statistical inference makes sense.

WHERE THE DATA COME FROM MATTERS

When you use statistical inference, you are acting as if your data are a probability sample or come from a randomized experiment.

Statistical confidence intervals and tests cannot remedy basic flaws in producing the data, such as voluntary response samples or uncontrolled experiments.

If your data don't come from a probability sample or a randomized comparative experiment, your conclusions may be challenged. To answer the challenge, you must usually rely on subject-matter knowledge, not on statistics. It is common to apply statistics to data that are not produced by random selection. When you see such a study, ask whether the data can be trusted as a basis for the conclusions of the study.

> **EXAMPLE 16.1**   *The psychologist and the sociologist*

A psychologist is interested in how our visual perception can be fooled by optical illusions. Her subjects are students in Psychology 101 at her university. Most psychologists would agree that it's safe to treat the students as an SRS of all people with normal vision. There is nothing special about being a student that changes visual perception.

A sociologist at the same university uses students in Sociology 101 to examine attitudes toward poor people and antipoverty programs. Students as a group are younger than the adult population as a whole. Even among young people, students as a group come from more prosperous and better-educated homes. Even among students, this university isn't typical of all campuses. Even on this campus, students in a sociology course may have opinions that are quite different from those of engineering students. The sociologist can't reasonably act as if these students are a random sample from any interesting population.

EXAMPLE 16.2 Mammary artery ligation

Angina is the severe pain caused by inadequate blood supply to the heart. Perhaps we can relieve angina by tying off the mammary arteries to force the body to develop other routes to supply blood to the heart. Surgeons tried this procedure, called "mammary artery ligation." Patients reported a statistically significant reduction in angina pain.

Statistical significance says that something other than chance is at work, but it does not say what that something is. The mammary artery ligation experiment was uncontrolled, so that the reduction in pain might be nothing more than the placebo effect. Sure enough, a randomized comparative experiment showed that ligation was no more effective than a placebo. Surgeons abandoned the operation at once.[1]

APPLY YOUR KNOWLEDGE

16.1 **A TV station takes a poll.** A local television station announces a question for a call-in opinion poll on the six o'clock news and then gives the response on the eleven o'clock news. Today's question is "What yearly pay do you think members of the City Council should get? Call us with your number." In all, 958 people call. The mean pay they suggest is $\bar{x} = \$8740$ per year, and the standard deviation of the responses is $s = \$1125$. For a large sample such as this, s is very close to the unknown population σ, so take $\sigma = \$1125$. The station calculates the 95% confidence interval for the mean pay μ that all citizens would propose for council members to be $8669 to $8811.

(a) Is the station's calculation correct?

(b) Does their conclusion describe the population of all the city's citizens? Explain your answer.

Cautions about the z procedures

Any confidence interval or significance test can be used only under specific conditions. It's up to you to understand these conditions and judge whether they fit your problem. If statistical procedures carried warning labels like those on drugs, most inference methods would have long labels indeed. With that in mind, let's look back at the "simple conditions" for the z confidence interval and test.

CAUTION

- *The data must be an SRS from the population.* We are safest if we actually carried out the random selection of an SRS. The NAEP scores in Example 14.1 (page 344) and the executive blood pressures in Example 15.7 (page 373) come from actual random samples. Remember, though, that in some cases an attempt to choose an SRS can be frustrated by nonresponse and other practical problems. There are many settings in which we don't have an actual random sample but the data can nonetheless be thought of as observations taken at random from a population. Biologists regard the 18 newts in Example 14.3 (page 351) as if they were randomly chosen from all newts of the same variety.

The status of data as roughly an SRS from an interesting population is often not clear. Subjects in medical studies, for example, are most often patients at one or several medical centers. This is a kind of convenience sample. We may hesitate to regard these patients as an SRS from all patients everywhere with the same medical condition. Yet it isn't possible to actually choose an SRS, and a randomized clinical trial with real patients surely gives useful information. *When an actual SRS is not possible, results are tentative. It is wise to wait until several studies produce similar results before coming to a conclusion.* Don't trust an excited news report of a medical trial until other studies confirm the finding.

- *Different methods are needed for different designs.* The z procedures aren't correct for probability samples more complex than an SRS. Later chapters give methods for some other designs, but we won't discuss inference for really complex settings. Always be sure that you (or your statistical consultant) know how to carry out the inference your design calls for.

- *Outliers can distort the result.* Because $\bar{x}$ is strongly influenced by a few extreme observations, outliers can have a large effect on the z confidence interval and test. Always explore your data before doing inference. In particular, you should search for outliers and try to correct them or justify their removal before performing the z procedures. If the outliers cannot be removed, ask your statistical consultant about procedures that are not sensitive to outliers.

- *The shape of the population distribution matters.* Our "simple conditions" state that the population distribution is Normal. Outliers or extreme skewness make the z procedures untrustworthy unless the sample is large. Other violations of Normality are often not critical in practice. The z procedures use Normality of the sample mean $\bar{x}$, not Normality of individual observations. The central limit theorem tells us that $\bar{x}$ is more Normal than the individual observations. In practice, the z procedures are reasonably accurate for any reasonably symmetric distribution for samples of even moderate size. If the sample is large, $\bar{x}$ will be close to Normal even if individual measurements are strongly skewed, as Figures 11.4 (page 282) and 11.5 (page 283) illustrate. Chapter 18 gives practical guidelines.

- *You must know the standard deviation σ of the population.* This condition is rarely satisfied in practice. Because of it, the z procedures are of little use. We will see in Chapter 18 that simple changes give very useful procedures that don't require that σ be known. When the sample is very large, the sample standard deviation s will be close to σ, so in effect we do know σ. Even in this situation, it is better to use the procedures of Chapter 18.

Every inference procedure that we will meet has its own list of warnings. Because many of the warnings are similar to those above, we will not print the full warning label each time. It is easy to state (from the mathematics of probability) conditions under which a method of inference is exactly correct. These conditions are never fully met in practice. For example, no population is exactly Normal. Deciding when a statistical procedure should be used often requires judgment assisted by exploratory analysis of the data.

Dropping out

An experiment found that weight loss is significantly more effective than exercise for reducing high cholesterol and high blood pressure. The 170 subjects were randomly assigned to a weight-loss program, an exercise program, or a control group. Only 111 of the 170 subjects completed their assigned treatment, and the analysis used data from these 111. Did the dropouts create bias? Always ask about details of the data before trusting inference.

APPLY YOUR KNOWLEDGE

16.2 **Running red lights.** A survey of licensed drivers inquired about running red lights. One question asked, "Of every ten motorists who run a red light, about how many do you think will be caught?" The mean result for 880 respondents was $\bar{x} = 1.92$ and the standard deviation was $s = 1.83$.[2] For this large sample, s will be close to the population standard deviation σ, so suppose we know that $\sigma = 1.83$.

(a) Give a 95% confidence interval for the mean opinion in the population of all licensed drivers.

(b) The distribution of responses is skewed to the right rather than Normal. This will not strongly affect the z confidence interval for this sample. Why not?

(c) The 880 respondents are an SRS from completed calls among 45,956 calls to randomly chosen residential telephone numbers listed in telephone directories. Only 5029 of the calls were completed. This information gives two reasons to suspect that the sample may not represent all licensed drivers. What are these reasons?

Helen King/CORBIS

Cautions about confidence intervals

The most important caution about confidence intervals in general is a consequence of the use of a sampling distribution. A sampling distribution shows how a statistic such as $\bar{x}$ varies in repeated sampling. This variation causes "random sampling error" because the statistic misses the true parameter by a random amount. No other source of variation or bias in the sample data influences the sampling distribution. So *the margin of error in a confidence interval ignores everything except the sample-to-sample variation due to choosing the sample randomly.*

CAUTION

> ### THE MARGIN OF ERROR DOESN'T COVER ALL ERRORS
>
> The margin of error in a confidence interval covers only random sampling errors.
>
> Practical difficulties such as undercoverage and nonresponse are often more serious than random sampling error. The margin of error does not take such difficulties into account.

Remember this unpleasant fact when reading the results of an opinion poll or other sample survey. The practical conduct of the survey influences the trustworthiness of its results in ways that are not included in the announced margin of error.

APPLY YOUR KNOWLEDGE

16.3 **Rating the environment.** A Gallup Poll asked the question "How would you rate the overall quality of the environment in this country today—as excellent, good, only fair, or poor?" In all, 46% of the sample rated the environment as good or excellent. Gallup announced the poll's margin of error for 95% confidence as ± 3 percentage points. Which of the following sources of error are included in the margin of error?

(a) The poll dialed telephone numbers at random and so missed all people without phones.

(b) Nonresponse—some people whose numbers were chosen never answered the phone in several calls or answered but refused to participate in the poll.

(c) There is chance variation in the random selection of telephone numbers.

16.4   **Holiday spending.** "How much do you plan to spend for gifts this holiday season?" An interviewer asks this question of 250 customers at a large shopping mall. The sample mean and standard deviation of the responses are $\bar{x} = \$237$ and $s = \$65$.

(a) The distribution of spending is skewed, but we can act as though $\bar{x}$ is Normal. Why?

(b) For this large sample, we can act as if $\sigma = \$65$ because the sample s will be close to the population σ. Use the sample result to give a 99% confidence interval for the mean gift spending of all adults.

(c) This confidence interval can't be trusted to give information about the spending plans of all adults. Why not?

Cautions about significance tests

Significance tests are widely used in reporting the results of research in many fields of applied science and in industry. New pharmaceutical products require significant evidence of effectiveness and safety. Courts inquire about statistical significance in hearing class action discrimination cases. Marketers want to know whether a new ad campaign significantly outperforms the old one, and medical researchers want to know whether a new therapy performs significantly better. In all these uses, statistical significance is valued because it points to an effect that is unlikely to occur simply by chance.

The reasoning of tests is less straightforward than the reasoning of confidence intervals, and the cautions needed are more elaborate. Here are some points to keep in mind when using or interpreting significance tests.

How small a P is convincing? The purpose of a test of significance is to describe the degree of evidence provided by the sample against the null hypothesis. The P-value does this. But how small a P-value is convincing evidence against the null hypothesis? This depends mainly on two circumstances:

* *How plausible is* H_0? If H_0 represents an assumption that the people you must convince have believed for years, strong evidence (small P) will be needed to persuade them.

* *What are the consequences of rejecting* H_0? If rejecting H_0 in favor of H_a means making an expensive changeover from one type of product

packaging to another, you need strong evidence that the new packaging will boost sales.

These criteria are a bit subjective. Different people will often insist on different levels of significance. Giving the P-value allows each of us to decide individually if the evidence is sufficiently strong.

Users of statistics have often emphasized standard levels of significance such as 10%, 5%, and 1%. For example, courts have tended to accept 5% as a standard in discrimination cases.[3] This emphasis reflects the time when tables of critical values rather than software dominated statistical practice. The 5% level ($\alpha = 0.05$) is particularly common. *There is no sharp border between "significant" and "insignificant," only increasingly strong evidence as the P-value decreases. There is no practical distinction between the P-values 0.049 and 0.051. It makes no sense to treat $P \leq 0.05$ as a universal rule for what is significant.*

APPLY YOUR KNOWLEDGE

16.5 **Is it significant?** In the absence of special preparation SAT mathematics (SATM) scores in recent years have varied Normally with mean $\mu = 518$ and $\sigma = 114$. Fifty students go through a rigorous training program designed to raise their SATM scores by improving their mathematics skills. Either by hand or by using the *P-Value of a Test of Significance* applet, carry out a test of

$$H_0: \mu = 518$$

$$H_a: \mu > 518$$

(with $\sigma = 114$) in each of the following situations:

(a) The students' average score is $\bar{x} = 544$. Is this result significant at the 5% level?

(b) The average score is $\bar{x} = 545$. Is this result significant at the 5% level?

The difference between the two outcomes in (a) and (b) is of no importance. Beware attempts to treat $\alpha = 0.05$ as sacred.

Statistical significance and practical significance When a null hypothesis ("no effect" or "no difference") can be rejected at the usual levels, $\alpha = 0.05$ or $\alpha = 0.01$, there is good evidence that an effect is present. But that effect may be very small. When large samples are available, even tiny deviations from the null hypothesis will be significant.

EXAMPLE 16.3 It's significant. Or not. So what?

We are testing the hypothesis of no correlation between two variables. With 1000 observations, an observed correlation of only $r = 0.08$ is significant evidence at the 1%

level that the correlation in the population is not zero but positive. *The small P-value does not mean there is a strong association, only that there is strong evidence of some association.* The true population correlation is probably quite close to the observed sample value, $r = 0.08$. We might well conclude that for practical purposes we can ignore the association between these variables, even though we are confident (at the 1% level) that the correlation is positive.

On the other hand, if we have only 10 observations, a correlation of $r = 0.5$ is not significantly greater than zero even at the 5% level. Small samples vary so much that a large r is needed if we are to be confident that we aren't just seeing chance variation at work. So a small sample will often fall short of significance even if the true population correlation is quite large.

Should tests be banned?

Significance tests don't tell us how large or how important an effect is. Research in psychology has emphasized tests, so much so that some think their weaknesses should ban them from use. The American Psychological Association asked a group of experts. They said: Use anything that sheds light on your study. Use more data analysis and confidence intervals. But: "The task force does not support any action that could be interpreted as banning the use of null hypothesis significance testing or *P*-values in psychological research and publication."

SAMPLE SIZE AFFECTS STATISTICAL SIGNIFICANCE

Because large random samples have small chance variation, very small population effects can be highly significant if the sample is large.

Because small random samples have a lot of chance variation, even large population effects can fail to be significant if the sample is small.

Statistical significance does not tell us whether an effect is large enough to be important. That is, **statistical significance is not the same thing as practical significance.**

Keep in mind that statistical significance means "the sample showed an effect larger than would often occur just by chance." The extent of chance variation changes with the size of the sample, so sample size does matter. Exercises 16.6 and 16.7 demonstrate in detail how increasing the sample size drives down the *P*-value.

The remedy for attaching too much importance to statistical significance is to pay attention to the actual data as well as to the *P*-value. Plot your data and examine them carefully. Outliers can either produce highly significant results or destroy the significance of otherwise convincing data. If an effect is highly significant, is it also large enough to be important in practice? Or is the effect significant even though it is small simply because you have a large sample? On the other hand, even important effects can fail to be significant in a small sample. Because an important-looking effect in a small sample might just be chance variation, you should gather more data before you jump to conclusions.

It's a good idea to give a confidence interval for the parameter in which you are interested. A confidence interval actually estimates the size of an effect rather than simply asking if it is too large to reasonably occur by chance alone. Confidence intervals are not used as often as they should be, while tests of significance are perhaps overused.

APPLY YOUR KNOWLEDGE ━━━━━━━━━━━━━━━━━━━

16.6   **Detecting acid rain.**   Emissions of sulfur dioxide by industry set off chemical changes in the atmosphere that result in "acid rain." The acidity of liquids is measured by pH on a scale of 0 to 14. Distilled water has pH 7.0, and lower pH values indicate acidity. Normal rain is somewhat acidic, so acid rain is sometimes defined as rainfall with a pH below 5.0. Suppose that pH measurements of rainfall on different days in a Canadian forest follow a Normal distribution with standard deviation $\sigma = 0.5$. A sample of n days finds that the mean pH is $\bar{x} = 4.8$. Is this good evidence that the mean pH μ for all rainy days is less than 5.0? The answer depends on the size of the sample.

Use the *P-Value of a Test of Significance* applet. Enter

$$H_0: \mu = 5.0$$
$$H_a: \mu < 5.0$$

$\sigma = 0.5$, and $\bar{x} = 4.8$. Then enter $n = 5$, $n = 15$, and $n = 40$ one after the other, clicking "Show P" each time to get the three P-values. What are they? Sketch the three Normal curves displayed by the applet, with $\bar{x} = 4.8$ marked on each curve. *The P-value of the same result $\bar{x} = 4.8$ gets smaller (more significant) as the sample size increases.*

16.7 **Detecting acid rain, by hand.** The previous exercise is very important to your understanding of tests of significance. If you don't use the applet, you should do the calculations by hand. Find the P-value in each of the following situations:

(a) We measure the acidity of rainfall on 5 days. The average pH is $\bar{x} = 4.8$.

(b) Use a larger sample of 15 days. The average pH is $\bar{x} = 4.8$.

(c) Finally, measure acidity for a sample of 40 days. The average pH is $\bar{x} = 4.8$.

16.8 **Confidence intervals help.** Give a 95% confidence interval for the mean pH μ in each part of the previous two exercises. The intervals, unlike the P-values, give a clear picture of what mean pH values are plausible for each sample.

16.9 **How far do rich parents take us?** How much education children get is strongly associated with the wealth and social status of their parents. In social science jargon, this is "socioeconomic status," or SES. But the SES of parents has little influence on whether children who have graduated from college go on to yet more education. One study looked at whether college graduates took the graduate admissions tests for business, law, and other graduate programs. The effects of the parents' SES on taking the LSAT test for law school were "both statistically insignificant and small."

(a) What does "statistically insignificant" mean?

(b) Why is it important that the effects were small in size as well as insignificant?

Beware of multiple analyses Statistical significance ought to mean that you have found an effect that you were looking for. The reasoning behind statistical significance works well if you decide what effect you are seeking, design a study to search for it, and use a test of significance to weigh the evidence you get. In other settings, significance may have little meaning.

EXAMPLE 16.4 *Cell phones and brain cancer*

Might the radiation from cell phones be harmful to users? Many studies have found little or no connection between using cell phones and various illnesses. Here is part of a news account of one study:

Edward Bock/CORBIS

A hospital study that compared brain cancer patients and a similar group without brain cancer found no statistically significant association between cell phone use and a group of brain cancers known as gliomas. But when 20 types of glioma were considered separately an association was found between phone use and one rare form. Puzzlingly, however, this risk appeared to decrease rather than increase with greater mobile phone use.[4]

Think for a moment: Suppose that the 20 null hypotheses (no association) for these 20 significance tests are all true. Then each test has a 5% chance of being significant at the 5% level. That's what $\alpha = 0.05$ means: results this extreme occur 5% of the time just by chance when the null hypothesis is true. Because 5% is 1/20, we expect about 1 of 20 tests to give a significant result just by chance. That's what the study observed.

Running one test and reaching the 5% level of significance is reasonably good evidence that you have found something. Running 20 tests and reaching that level only once is not. The caution about multiple analyses applies to confidence intervals as well. A single 95% confidence interval has probability 0.95 of capturing the true parameter each time you use it. The probability that all of 20 confidence intervals will capture their parameters is much less than 95%. If you think that multiple tests or intervals may have discovered an important effect, you need to gather new data to do inference about that specific effect.

APPLY YOUR KNOWLEDGE

16.10 **Searching for ESP.**   A researcher looking for evidence of extrasensory perception (ESP) tests 500 subjects. Four of these subjects do significantly better ($P < 0.01$) than random guessing.

(a) Is it proper to conclude that these four people have ESP? Explain your answer.

(b) What should the researcher now do to test whether any of these four subjects have ESP?

The power of a test*

One of the most important questions in planning a study is "How large a sample?" We know that if our sample is too small, even large effects in the population will often fail to give statistically significant results. Here are the questions we must answer to decide how large a sample we must take.

Significance level. How much protection do we want against getting a significant result from our sample when there really is no effect in the population?

Effect size. How large an effect in the population is important in practice?

Power. How confident do we want to be that our study will detect an effect of the size we think is important?

---

*The remainder of this chapter presents more advanced material that is not needed to read the rest of the book. The idea of the power of a test is, however, important in practice.

The three boldface terms are statistical shorthand for three pieces of information. *Power* is a new idea.

EXAMPLE 16.5   Sweetening colas: planning a study

Let's illustrate typical answers to these questions in the example of testing a new cola for loss of sweetness in storage (Example 15.2, page 363). Ten trained tasters rated the sweetness on a 10-point scale before and after storage, so that we have each taster's judgment of loss of sweetness. From experience, we know that sweetness loss scores vary from taster to taster according to a Normal distribution with standard deviation about $\sigma = 1$. To see if the taste test gives reason to think that the cola does lose sweetness, we will test

$$H_0: \mu = 0$$
$$H_a: \mu > 0$$

Are 10 tasters enough, or should we use more?

Significance level. Requiring significance at the 5% level is enough protection against declaring there is a loss in sweetness when in fact there is no change if we could look at the entire population. This means that when there is no change in sweetness in the population, 1 out of 20 samples of tasters will wrongly find a significant loss.

Effect size. A mean sweetness loss of 0.8 point on the 10-point scale will be noticed by consumers and so is important in practice. This isn't enough to specify effect size for statistical purposes. A 0.8-point mean loss is big if sweetness scores don't vary much, say $\sigma = 0.2$. The same loss is small if scores vary a lot among tasters, say $\sigma = 5$. The proper measure of effect size is the *standardized* sweetness loss:

$$\text{effect size} = \frac{\text{true mean response} - \text{hypothesized response}}{\text{standard deviation of response}}$$
$$= \frac{\mu - \mu_0}{\sigma}$$
$$= \frac{0.8 - 0}{1} = 0.8$$

In this example, the effect size is the same as the mean sweetness loss because $\sigma = 1$.

Power. We want to be 90% confident that our test will detect a mean loss of 0.8 point in the population of all tasters. We agreed to use significance at the 5% level as our standard for detecting an effect. So we want probability at least 0.9 that a test at the $\alpha = 0.05$ level will reject the null hypothesis $H_0: \mu = 0$ when the true population mean is $\mu = 0.8$.

The probability that the test successfully detects a sweetness loss of the specified size is the *power* of the test. You can think of tests with high power as being highly sensitive to deviations from the null hypothesis. In Example 16.5, we decided that we want power 90% when the truth about the population is that $\mu = 0.8$.

> ## POWER
>
> The probability that a fixed level α significance test will reject H_0 when a particular alternative value of the parameter is true is called the **power** of the test against that alternative.

For most statistical tests, calculating power is a job for professional statisticians. The z test is easier, but we will nonetheless skip the details. Here is the answer in practical terms: how large a sample do we need for a z test at the 5% significance level to have power 90% against various effect sizes?[5]

Effect size	0.1	0.2	0.3	0.4	0.5	0.6	0.7	0.8	0.9	1.0
Sample size	857	215	96	54	35	24	18	14	11	9

Remember that "effect size" is the standardized value of the true population mean. Our earlier sample of 10 tasters is large enough that we can be 90% confident of detecting (at the 5% significance level) an effect of size 1, but not an effect of size 0.8. If we want 90% power against effect size 0.8 we need at least 14 tasters.

You can see that smaller effects require larger samples to reach 90% power. Here is an overview of influences on "How large a sample do I need?"

- If you insist on a smaller significance level (such as 1% rather than 5%), you will need a larger sample. A smaller significance level requires stronger evidence to reject the null hypothesis.
- If you insist on higher power (such as 99% rather than 90%), you will need a larger sample. Higher power gives a better chance of detecting an effect when it is really there.
- At any significance level and desired power, a two-sided alternative requires a larger sample than a one-sided alternative.
- At any significance level and desired power, detecting a small effect requires a larger sample than detecting a large effect.

Serious statistical studies always try to answer "How large a sample do I need?" as part of planning the study. If your study concerns the mean μ of a population, you need at least a rough idea of the size of the population standard deviation σ and of how big a deviation $\mu - \mu_0$ of the population mean from its hypothesized value you want to be able to detect. More elaborate settings, such as comparing the mean effects of several treatments, require more elaborate advance information. You can leave the details to experts, but you should understand the idea of power and the factors that determine how large a sample you need.

Fish, fishermen, and power

Are the stocks of cod in the ocean off eastern Canada declining? Studies over many years failed to find significant evidence of a decline. These studies had low power—that is, they might fail to find a decline even if one was present. When it became clear that the cod were vanishing, quotas on fishing ravaged the economy in parts of Canada. If the earlier studies had had high power, they would likely have seen the decline. Quick action might have reduced the economic and environmental costs.

APPLY YOUR KNOWLEDGE

16.11 **Student attitudes: planning a study.** The Survey of Study Habits and Attitudes (SSHA) is a psychological test that measures students' study habits and attitudes toward school. Scores range from 0 to 200. The mean score for college students is about 115, and the standard deviation is about 30. A teacher suspects that the mean μ for older students is higher than 115. Suppose that $\sigma = 30$ and the teacher uses the 5% level of significance in a test of the hypotheses

$$H_0: \mu = 115$$

$$H_a: \mu > 115$$

How large a sample of older students must she test in order to have power 90% in each of the following situations? (Use the small table that follows the definition of power.)

(a) The true mean SSHA score for older students is 130.

(b) The true mean SSHA score for older students is 139.

16.12 **What is power?** Example 15.8 (page 375) describes a test of the hypotheses

$$H_0: \mu = 275$$

$$H_a: \mu < 275$$

Here μ is the mean score of all young men on the NAEP test of quantitative skills. We know that $\sigma = 60$ and we have the NAEP scores of a random sample of 840 young men. A statistician tells you that the power of the z test with $\alpha = 0.05$ against the alternative that the true mean score is $\mu = 270$ is 0.78. Explain in simple language what "power = 0.78" means.

16.13 **Thinking about power.** Answer these questions in the setting of the previous exercise.

(a) To get higher power against the same alternative with the same α, what must we do?

(b) If we decide to use $\alpha = 0.10$ in place of $\alpha = 0.05$, does the power increase or decrease?

(c) If we shift our interest to the alternative $\mu = 265$ with no other changes, does the power increase or decrease?

Type I and Type II errors*

We can assess the performance of a test by giving two probabilities: the significance level α and the power for an alternative that we want to be able to detect. In practice, part of planning a study is to calculate power against a range of alternatives to learn which alternatives the test is likely to detect and which it is likely to miss. If the test does not have high enough power against alternatives that we want to detect, the remedy is to increase the size of the sample. That can be expensive, so the planning process must balance good statistical properties against cost.

The significance level of a test is the probability of making the *wrong* decision when the null hypothesis is true. The power for a specific alternative is the probability of making the *right* decision when that alternative is true. We can just as well describe the test by giving the probability of a *wrong* decision under both conditions.

TYPE I AND TYPE II ERRORS

If we reject H_0 when in fact H_0 is true, this is a **Type I error.**

If we fail to reject H_0 when in fact H_a is true, this is a **Type II error.**

The **significance level** α of any fixed level test is the probability of a Type I error.

The **power** of a test against any alternative is 1 minus the probability of a Type II error for that alternative.

The possibilities are summed up in Figure 16.1. If H_0 is true, our decision is correct if we accept H_0 and is a Type I error if we reject H_0. If H_a is true, our decision is either correct or a Type II error. Only one error is possible at one time.

Given a test, we could try to calculate both error probabilities. In practice, it is much more common to specify a significance level and calculate power. This amounts to specifying the probability of a Type I error and then calculating the probability of a Type II error. Here is an example of such a calculation.

FIGURE 16.1 The two types of error in testing hypotheses.

		Truth about the population	
		H_0 true	H_a true
Decision based on sample	Reject H_0	Type I error	Correct decision
	Accept H_0	Correct decision	Type II error

EXAMPLE 16.6 Sweetening colas: calculating power

The cola maker of Example 16.5 wants to test

$$H_0: \mu = 0$$
$$H_a: \mu > 0$$

The z test rejects H_0 in favor of H_a at the 5% significance level if the z statistic exceeds 1.645, the critical value for $\alpha = 0.05$. If we use $n = 10$ tasters, what is the power of this test when the true mean sweetness loss is $\mu = 0.8$?

Step 1. *Write the rule for rejecting H_0 in terms of $\overline{x}$.* We know that $\sigma = 1$, so the z test rejects H_0 at the $\alpha = 0.05$ level when

$$z = \frac{\overline{x} - 0}{1/\sqrt{10}} \geq 1.645$$

This is the same as

$$\overline{x} \geq 0 + 1.645 \frac{1}{\sqrt{10}}$$

or, doing the arithmetic,

$$\text{Reject } H_0 \text{ when } \overline{x} \geq 0.5202$$

This step just restates the rule for the test. It pays no attention to the specific alternative we have in mind.

Step 2. *The power is the probability of this event under the condition that the alternative $\mu = 0.8$ is true.* Software gives a precise answer,

$$\text{power} = P(\overline{x} \geq 0.5202 \text{ when } \mu = 0.8) = 0.8119$$

To get an approximate answer from Table A, standardize $\overline{x}$ using $\mu = 0.8$:

$$\text{power} = P(\overline{x} \geq 0.5202 \text{ when } \mu = 0.8)$$

$$= P\left(\frac{\overline{x} - 0.8}{1/\sqrt{10}} \geq \frac{0.5202 - 0.8}{1/\sqrt{10}}\right)$$

$$= P(Z \geq -0.88)$$

$$= 1 - 0.1894 = 0.8106$$

The test will declare that the cola loses sweetness only 5% of the time when it actually does not ($\alpha = 0.05$) and 81% of the time when the true mean sweetness loss is 0.8 (power $= 0.81$). This is consistent with our finding in the previous section that sample size 10 isn't enough to achieve power 0.90.

The calculations in Example 16.6 show that the two error probabilities are

$$P(\text{Type I error}) = P(\text{reject } H_0 \text{ when } \mu = 0)$$
$$= 0.05$$
$$P(\text{Type II error}) = P(\text{fail to reject } H_0 \text{ when } \mu = 0.8)$$
$$= 0.19$$

The idea behind the calculation in Example 16.6 is that the z test statistic is standardized taking the null hypothesis to be true. If an alternative is true, this is no longer the correct standardization. So we go back to $\overline{x}$ and standardize again taking the alternative to be true. Figure 16.2 illustrates the rule for the test and the two sampling distributions, one under the null hypothesis $\mu = 0$ and the other under the alternative $\mu = 0.8$. The level α is the probability of rejecting H_0 when H_0 is true, so it is an area under the top curve. The power is the probability of rejecting H_0 when H_a is true, so it is an area under the bottom curve. The *Power of a Test* applet draws a picture like Figure 16.2 and calculates the power of the z test for sample sizes of 50 or smaller.

APPLET

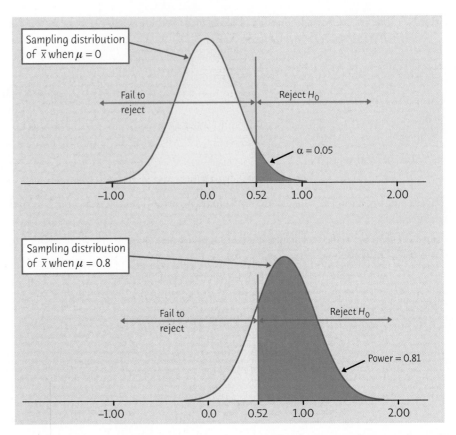

FIGURE 16.2 Significance level and power for the test of Example 16.6. The test rejects H_0 when $\bar{x} \geq 0.52$. The level α is the probability of this event when the null hypothesis is true. The power is the probability of the same event when the alternative hypothesis is true.

Calculations of power (or of error probabilities) are useful for planning studies because we can make these calculations before we have any data. Once we actually have data, it is more common to report a *P*-value rather than a reject-or-not decision at a fixed significance level α. The *P*-value measures the strength of the evidence provided by the data against H_0 and in favor of H_a. It leaves any action or decision based on that evidence up to each individual. Different people may require different strengths of evidence.

APPLY YOUR KNOWLEDGE

16.14 **Two types of error.** In a criminal trial, the defendant is held to be innocent until shown to be guilty beyond a reasonable doubt. If we consider hypotheses

$$H_0: \text{defendant is innocent}$$

$$H_a: \text{defendant is guilty}$$

we can reject H_0 only if the evidence strongly favors H_a.

(a) Is this goal better served by a test with $\alpha = 0.20$ or a test with $\alpha = 0.01$? Explain your answer.

(b) Make a diagram like Figure 16.1 that shows the truth about the defendant, the possible verdicts, and identifies the two types of error.

16.15 **Two types of error.** Your company markets a computerized medical diagnostic program used to evaluate thousands of people. The program scans the results of routine medical tests (pulse rate, blood tests, etc.) and refers the case to a doctor if there is evidence of a medical problem. The program makes a decision about each person.

(a) What are the two hypotheses and the two types of error that the program can make? Describe the two types of error in terms of "false positive" and "false negative" test results.

(b) The program can be adjusted to decrease one error probability, at the cost of an increase in the other error probability. Which error probability would you choose to make smaller, and why? (This is a matter of judgment. There is no single correct answer.)

16.16 **Detecting acid rain: power.** Exercise 16.6 (page 394) concerned detecting acid rain (rainfall with pH less than 5) from measurements made on a sample of n days for several sample sizes n. That exercise shows how the P-value for an observed sample mean $\bar{x}$ changes with n. It would be wise to do power calculations before deciding on the sample size. Suppose that pH measurements follow a Normal distribution with standard deviation $\sigma = 0.5$. You plan to test the hypotheses

$$H_0: \mu = 5$$

$$H_a: \mu < 5$$

at the 5% level of significance. You want to use a test that will almost always reject H_0 when the true mean pH is 4.7. Use the *Power of a Test* applet to find the power against the alternative $\mu = 4.7$ for samples of size $n = 5, n = 15$, and $n = 40$. What happens to the power as the size of the sample increases? Which of these sample sizes are adequate for use in this setting?

16.17 **Detecting acid rain: power by hand.** Even though software is used in practice to calculate power, doing the work by hand in a few examples builds your understanding. Find the power of the test in the previous exercise for a sample of size $n = 15$ by following these steps.

(a) Write the z test statistic for a sample of size 15. What values of z lead to rejecting H_0 at the 5% significance level?

(b) Starting from your result in (a), what values of $\bar{x}$ lead to rejecting H_0?

(c) What is the probability of rejecting H_0 when $\mu = 4.7$? This probability is the power against this alternative.

16.18 **Find the error probabilities.** You have an SRS of size $n = 9$ from a Normal distribution with $\sigma = 1$. You wish to test

$$H_0: \mu = 0$$

$$H_a: \mu > 0$$

You decide to reject H_0 if $\bar{x} > 0$ and to accept H_0 otherwise.

(a) Find the probability of a Type I error. That is, find the probability that the test rejects H_0 when in fact $\mu = 0$.

(b) Find the probability of a Type II error when $\mu = 0.3$. This is the probability that the test accepts H_0 when in fact $\mu = 0.3$.

(c) Find the probability of a Type II error when $\mu = 1$.

CHAPTER 16 SUMMARY

A specific confidence interval or test is correct only under specific conditions. The most important conditions concern the method used to produce the data. Other factors such as the shape of the population distribution may also be important.

Whenever you use statistical inference, you are acting as if your data are a probability sample or come from a randomized comparative experiment.

Always do data analysis before inference to detect outliers or other problems that would make inference untrustworthy.

The margin of error in a confidence interval accounts for only the chance variation due to random sampling. In practice, errors due to nonresponse or undercoverage are often more serious.

There is no universal rule for how small a *P*-value is convincing. Beware of placing too much weight on traditional significance levels such as $\alpha = 0.05$.

Very small effects can be highly significant (small P) when a test is based on a large sample. A statistically significant effect need not be practically important. Plot the data to display the effect you are seeking, and use confidence intervals to estimate the actual values of parameters.

On the other hand, lack of significance does not imply that H_0 is true. Even a large effect can fail to be significant when a test is based on a small sample.

Many tests run at once will probably produce some significant results by chance alone, even if all the null hypotheses are true.

The **power** of a significance test measures its ability to detect an alternative hypothesis. The power against a specific alternative is the probability that the test will reject H_0 when that alternative is true.

We can describe the performance of a test at fixed level α by giving the probabilities of two types of error. A **Type I error** occurs if we reject H_0 when it is in fact true. A **Type II error** occurs if we fail to reject H_0 when in fact H_a is true.

In a fixed level α significance test, the significance level α is the probability of a Type I error, and the power against a specific alternative is 1 minus the probability of a Type II error for that alternative.

Increasing the size of the sample increases the power (reduces the probability of a Type II error) when the significance level remains fixed.

CHECK YOUR SKILLS

16.19 A professor interested in the opinions of college-age adults about a new hit movie asks students in her course on documentary filmmaking to rate the entertainment value of the movie on a scale of 0 to 5. A confidence interval for the mean rating by all college-age adults based on these data is of little use because

(a) the course is small, so the margin of error will be large.

(b) many of the students in the course will probably refuse to respond.

(c) the students in the course can't be considered a random sample from the population.

16.20 Here's a quote from a medical journal: "An uncontrolled experiment in 17 women found a significantly improved mean clinical symptom score after treatment. Methodologic flaws make it difficult to interpret the results of this study." The authors of this paper are skeptical about the significant improvement because

(a) there is no control group, so the improvement might be due to the placebo effect or to the fact that many medical conditions improve over time.

(b) the P-value given was $P = 0.03$, which is too large to be convincing.

(c) the response variable might not have an exactly Normal distribution in the population.

16.21 You turn your Web browser to the online Excite Poll. You see that yesterday's question was "Do you support or oppose state laws allowing illegal immigrants to have driver's licenses?" In all, 10,282 people responded, with 8138 (79%) saying they were opposed. You should refuse to calculate any 95% confidence interval based on this sample because

(a) yesterday's responses are meaningless today.

(b) inference from a voluntary response sample can't be trusted.

(c) the sample is too large.

16.22 Many sample surveys use well-designed random samples but half or more of the original sample can't be contacted or refuse to take part. Any errors due to this nonresponse

(a) have no effect on the accuracy of confidence intervals.

(b) are included in the announced margin of error.

(c) are in addition to the random variation accounted for by the announced margin of error.

16.23 You ask a random sample of students at your school if they have ever used the Internet to plagiarize a paper for an assignment. Despite your use of a really random sample, your results will probably underestimate the extent of plagiarism at your school in ways not covered by your margin of error. This bias occurs because

(a) some students don't tell the truth about improper behavior such as plagiarism.

(b) you sampled only students at your school.

(c) 95% confidence isn't high enough.

16.24 Vigorous exercise helps people live several years longer (on the average). Whether mild activities like slow walking extend life is not clear. Suppose that the added life expectancy from regular slow walking is just 2 months. A statistical test is more likely to find a significant increase in mean life if

(a) it is based on a very large random sample.

(b) it is based on a very small random sample.

(c) The size of the sample doesn't have any effect on the significance of the test.

16.25 The most important condition for sound conclusions from statistical inference is usually

(a) that the data can be thought of as a random sample from the population of interest.

(b) that the population distribution is exactly Normal.

(c) that no calculation errors are made in the confidence interval or test statistic.

16.26 An opinion poll reports that 60% of adults have tried to lose weight. It adds that the margin of error for 95% confidence is ±3%. The true probability that such polls give results within ±3% of the truth is

(a) 0.95 because the poll uses 95% confidence intervals.

(b) less than 0.95 because of nonresponse and other errors not included in the margin of error ±3%.

(c) only approximately 0.95 because the sampling distribution is only approximately Normal.

16.27 A medical experiment compared the herb echinacea with a placebo for preventing colds. One response variable was "volume of nasal secretions" (if you have a cold, you blow your nose a lot). Take the average volume of nasal secretions in people without colds to be $\mu = 1$. An increase to $\mu = 3$ indicates a cold. The significance level of a test of $H_0: \mu = 1$ versus $H_a: \mu > 1$ is

(a) the probability that the test rejects H_0 when $\mu = 1$ is true.

(b) the probability that the test rejects H_0 when $\mu = 3$ is true.

(c) the probability that the test fails to reject H_0 when $\mu = 3$ is true.

16.28 (Optional) The power of the test in the previous exercise against the specific alternative $\mu = 3$ is

(a) the probability that the test rejects H_0 when $\mu = 1$ is true.

(b) the probability that the test rejects H_0 when $\mu = 3$ is true.

(c) the probability that the test fails to reject H_0 when $\mu = 3$ is true.

CHAPTER 16 EXERCISES

16.29 **Hotel managers.** In Exercises 14.21 and 14.22 (page 358) you gave confidence intervals based on data from 148 general managers of three-star and four-star hotels. Before you trust your results, you would like more information about the data. What facts would you most like to know?

16.30 **Comparing statistics texts.** A publisher wants to know which of two statistics textbooks better helps students learn the z procedures. The company finds 10 colleges that use each text and gives randomly chosen statistics students at those colleges a quiz on the z procedures. You should refuse to use these data to compare the effectiveness of the two texts. Why?

16.31 Sampling at the mall. A market researcher chooses at random from women entering a large suburban shopping mall. One outcome of the study is a 95% confidence interval for the mean of "the highest price you would pay for a pair of casual shoes."

(a) Explain why this confidence interval does not give useful information about the population of all women.

(b) Explain why it may give useful information about the population of women who shop at large suburban malls.

16.32 When to use pacemakers. A medical panel prepared guidelines for when cardiac pacemakers should be implanted in patients with heart problems. The panel reviewed a large number of medical studies to judge the strength of the evidence supporting each recommendation. For each recommendation, they ranked the evidence as level A (strongest), B, or C (weakest). Here, in scrambled order, are the panel's descriptions of the three levels of evidence.[6] Which is A, which B, and which C? Explain your ranking.

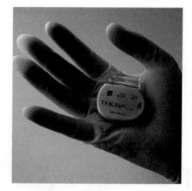

Layne Kennedy/CORBIS

Evidence was ranked as level _____ when data were derived from a limited number of trials involving comparatively small numbers of patients or from well-designed data analysis of nonrandomized studies or observational data registries.

Evidence was ranked as level _____ if the data were derived from multiple randomized clinical trials involving a large number of individuals.

Evidence was ranked as level _____ when consensus of expert opinion was the primary source of recommendation.

16.33 Nuke terrorists? A recent Gallup Poll found that 27% of adult Americans support "using nuclear weapons to attack terrorist facilities." Gallup says:

For results based on samples of this size, one can say with 95 percent confidence that the maximum error attributable to sampling and other random effects is plus or minus 3 percentage points.

Give one example of a source of error in the poll result that is *not* included in this margin of error.

16.34 Why are larger samples better? Statisticians prefer large samples. Describe briefly the effect of increasing the size of a sample (or the number of subjects in an experiment) on each of the following:

(a) The margin of error of a 95% confidence interval.

(b) The *P*-value of a test, when H_0 is false and all facts about the population remain unchanged as n increases.

(c) (Optional) The power of a fixed level α test, when α, the alternative hypothesis, and all facts about the population remain unchanged.

16.35 What is significance good for? Which of the following questions does a test of significance answer? Briefly explain your replies.

(a) Is the sample or experiment properly designed?

(b) Is the observed effect due to chance?

(c) Is the observed effect important?

16.36 Sensitive questions. The National AIDS Behavioral Surveys found that 170 individuals in its random sample of 2673 adult heterosexuals said they had multiple sexual partners in the past year. That's 6.36% of the sample. Why is this estimate likely to be biased? Does the margin of error of a 95% confidence interval for the proportion of all adults with multiple partners allow for this bias?

16.37 College degrees. Table 1.1 (page 11) gives the percent of each state's residents aged 25 and over who hold a bachelor's degree. It makes no sense to find $\bar{x}$ for these data and use it to get a confidence interval for the mean percent μ in the states. Why not?

16.38 Effect of an outlier. Examining data on how long students take to complete their degree program, you find one outlier. Will this outlier have a greater effect on a confidence interval for mean completion time if your sample is small or large? Why?

16.39 Supermarket shoppers. A marketing consultant observes 50 consecutive shoppers at a supermarket. Here are the amounts (in dollars) spent in the store by these shoppers:

3.11	8.88	9.26	10.81	12.69	13.78	15.23	15.62	17.00	17.39
18.36	18.43	19.27	19.50	19.54	20.16	20.59	22.22	23.04	24.47
24.58	25.13	26.24	26.26	27.65	28.06	28.08	28.38	32.03	34.98
36.37	38.64	39.16	41.02	42.97	44.08	44.67	45.40	46.69	48.65
50.39	52.75	54.80	59.07	61.22	70.32	82.70	85.76	86.37	93.34

Left Lane Productions/CORBIS

(a) Why is it risky to regard these 50 shoppers as an SRS from the population of all shoppers at this store? Name some factors that might make 50 consecutive shoppers at a particular time unrepresentative of all shoppers.

(b) Make a stemplot of the data. The stemplot suggests caution in using the z procedures for these data. Why?

16.40 Predicting success of trainees. What distinguishes managerial trainees who eventually become executives from those who don't succeed and leave the company? We have abundant data on past trainees—data on their personalities and goals, their college preparation and performance, even their family backgrounds and their hobbies. Statistical software makes it easy to perform dozens of significance tests on these dozens of variables to see which ones best predict later success. We find that future executives are significantly more likely than washouts to have an urban or suburban upbringing and an undergraduate degree in a technical field. Explain clearly why using these "significant" variables to select future trainees is not wise.

16.41 What distinguishes schizophrenics? A group of psychologists once measured 77 variables on a sample of schizophrenic people and a sample of people who were not schizophrenic. They compared the two samples using 77 separate significance tests. Two of these tests were significant at the 5% level. Suppose that there is in fact no difference in any of the variables between people who are and people who are not schizophrenic, so that all 77 null hypotheses are true.

(a) What is the probability that one specific test shows a difference significant at the 5% level?

(b) Why is it not surprising that 2 of the 77 tests were significant at the 5% level?

16.42 Internet users.   A survey of users of the Internet found that males outnumbered females by nearly 2 to 1. This was a surprise, because earlier surveys had put the ratio of men to women closer to 9 to 1. Later in the article we find this information:

Detailed surveys were sent to more than 13,000 organizations on the Internet; 1,468 usable responses were received. According to Mr. Quarterman, the margin of error is 2.8 percent, with a confidence level of 95 percent.[7]

(a) What was the *response rate* for this survey? (The response rate is the percent of the planned sample that responded.)

(b) Do you think that the small margin of error is a good measure of the accuracy of the survey's results? Explain your answer.

16.43 Comparing package designs.   A company compares two package designs for a laundry detergent by placing bottles with both designs on the shelves of several markets. Checkout scanner data on more than 5000 bottles bought show that more shoppers bought Design A than Design B. The difference is statistically significant ($P = 0.02$). Can we conclude that consumers strongly prefer Design A? Explain your answer.

16.44 Island life.   When human settlers bring new plants and animals to an island, they may drive out native plants and animals. A study of 220 oceanic islands far from other land counted "exotic" (introduced from outside) bird species and the number of bird species that have become extinct since Europeans arrived on the islands. The study report says, "Numbers of exotic bird species and native bird extinctions are also positively correlated ($r = 0.62$, $n = 220$ islands, $P < 0.01$)."[8]

(a) The hypotheses concern the correlation for all oceanic islands, the population from which these 220 islands are a sample. Call this population correlation ρ. The hypotheses tested are

$$H_0 {:}\ \rho = 0$$
$$H_a {:}\ \rho > 0$$

In simple language, explain what $P < 0.01$ tells us.

(b) Before drawing practical conclusions from a P-value, we must look at the sample size and at the size of the observed effect. If the sample is large, effects too small to be important may be statistically significant. Do you think that is the case here? Why?

16.45 Helping welfare mothers.   A study compares two groups of mothers with young children who were on welfare two years ago. One group attended a voluntary training program that was offered free of charge at a local vocational school and was advertised in the local news media. The other group did not choose to attend the training program. The study finds a significant difference ($P < 0.01$) between the proportions of the mothers in the two groups who are still on welfare. The difference is not only significant but quite large. The report says that with 95% confidence the percent of the nonattending group still on welfare is 21% ± 4% higher than that of the group who attended the program. You are on the staff of a member of Congress who is interested in the plight of welfare mothers and who asks you about the report.

(a) Explain in simple language what "a significant difference $(P < 0.01)$" means.

(b) Explain clearly and briefly what "95% confidence" means.

(c) Is this study good evidence that requiring job training of all welfare mothers would greatly reduce the percent who remain on welfare for several years?

The following exercises concern the optional material on power and error probabilities for tests.

16.46 **Island life.** Exercise 16.44 describes a study that tested the null hypothesis that there is 0 correlation between the number of exotic bird species on an island and the number of native bird extinctions. Describe in words what it means to make a Type I and a Type II error in this setting.

16.47 **Is the stock market efficient?** You are reading an article in a business journal that discusses the "efficient market hypothesis" for the behavior of securities prices. The author admits that most tests of this hypothesis have failed to find significant evidence against it. But he says this failure is a result of the fact that the tests used have low power. "The widespread impression that there is strong evidence for market efficiency may be due just to a lack of appreciation of the low power of many statistical tests."[9]

Explain in simple language why tests having low power often fail to give evidence against a null hypothesis even when the hypothesis is really false.

16.48 **Error probabilities.** Exercise 16.12 describes a test at significance level $\alpha = 0.05$ that has power 0.78. What are the probabilities of Type I and Type II errors for this test?

16.49 **Power.** You read that a statistical test at the $\alpha = 0.01$ level has probability 0.14 of making a Type II error when a specific alternative is true. What is the power of the test against this alternative?

16.50 **Power of a two-sided test.** Power calculations for two-sided tests follow the same outline as for one-sided tests. Example 15.10 (page 378) presents a test of

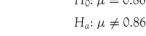

$$H_0: \mu = 0.86$$

$$H_a: \mu \neq 0.86$$

at the 1% level of significance. The sample size is $n = 3$ and $\sigma = 0.0068$. We will find the power of this test against the alternative $\mu = 0.845$. (The *Power of a Test* applet will do this for you, but it may help your understanding to go through the details.)

APPLET

(a) The test in Example 15.10 rejects H_0 when $|z| \geq 2.576$. The test statistic z is

$$z = \frac{\bar{x} - 0.86}{0.0068/\sqrt{3}}$$

Write the rule for rejecting H_0 in terms of the values of $\bar{x}$. (Because the test is two-sided, it rejects when $\bar{x}$ is either too large or too small.)

(b) Now find the probability that $\bar{x}$ takes values that lead to rejecting H_0 if the true mean is $\mu = 0.845$. This probability is the power.

(c) What is the probability that this test makes a Type II error when $\mu = 0.845$?

16.51 **Find the power.** In Example 15.7 (page 373), a company medical director failed to find significant evidence that the mean blood pressure of a population of executives differed from the national mean $\mu = 128$. The medical director now wonders if the test used would detect an important difference if one were present. For the SRS of size 72 from a population with standard deviation $\sigma = 15$, the z statistic is

$$z = \frac{\bar{x} - 128}{15/\sqrt{72}}$$

The two-sided test rejects H_0: $\mu = 128$ at the 5% level of significance when $|z| \geq 1.96$.

(a) Find the power of the test against the alternative $\mu = 134$.

(b) Find the power of the test against $\mu = 122$. Can the test be relied on to detect a mean that differs from 128 by 6?

(c) If the alternative were farther from H_0, say $\mu = 136$, would the power be higher or lower than the values calculated in (a) and (b)?

Peter Lilja/Getty Images

17

From Exploration to Inference: Part II Review

Designs for producing data are essential parts of statistics in practice. Figures 17.1 and 17.2 display the big ideas visually. Random sampling and randomized comparative experiments are perhaps the most important statistical inventions of the twentieth century. Both were slow to gain acceptance, and you will still see many voluntary response samples and uncontrolled experiments. You should now understand good techniques for producing data and also why bad techniques often produce worthless data. The deliberate use of chance in producing data is a central idea in statistics. It not only reduces bias but allows use of the laws of probability to analyze data. Fortunately, we need only some basic facts about probability in order to understand statistical inference.

Statistical inference draws conclusions about a population on the basis of sample data and uses probability to indicate how reliable the conclusions are. A confidence interval estimates an unknown parameter. A significance test shows how strong the evidence is for some claim about a parameter.

Figure 17.1 STATISTICS IN SUMMARY

Simple Random Sample

Population

All samples of size n
are equally likely

Sample data
$x_1, x_2, \ldots, x_n$

Figure 17.2 STATISTICS IN SUMMARY
Randomized Comparative Experiment

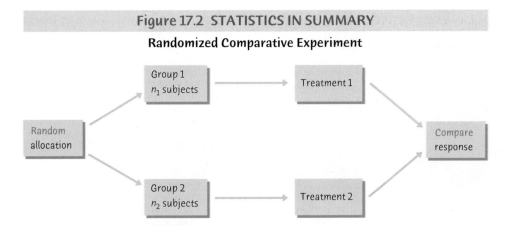

The probabilities in both confidence intervals and tests tell us what would happen if we used the method for the interval or test very many times.

- A confidence level is the success rate of the method for a confidence interval. This is the probability that the method actually produces an interval that contains the unknown parameter. A 95% confidence interval gives a correct result 95% of the time when we use it repeatedly.

- A *P*-value tells us how surprising the observed outcome would be if the null hypothesis were true. That is, *P* is the probability that the test would produce a result at least as extreme as the observed result if the null hypothesis really were true. Very surprising outcomes (small *P*-values) are good evidence that the null hypothesis is not true.

Figures 17.3 and 17.4 use the z procedures introduced in Chapters 14 and 15 to present in picture form the big ideas of confidence intervals and significance

Figure 17.3 STATISTICS IN SUMMARY
The Idea of a Confidence Interval

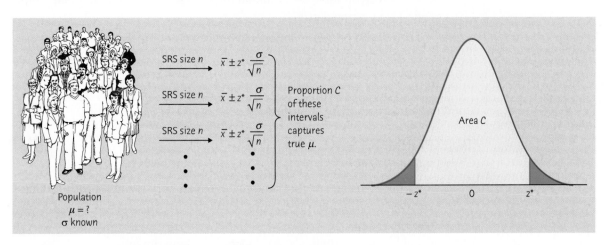

Figure 17.4 STATISTICS IN SUMMARY

The Idea of a Significance Test

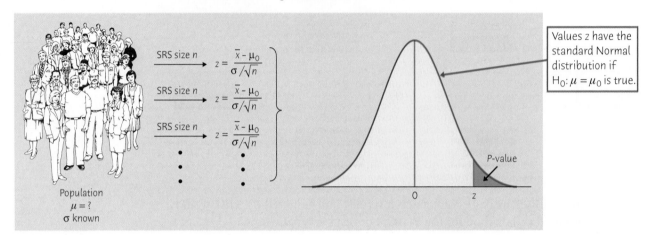

tests. These ideas are the foundation for the rest of this book. We will have much to say about many statistical methods and their use in practice. In every case, the basic reasoning of confidence intervals and significance tests remains the same.

PART II SUMMARY

Here are the most important skills you should have acquired from reading Chapters 8 to 16.

A. SAMPLING

1. Identify the population in a sampling situation.

2. Recognize bias due to voluntary response samples and other inferior sampling methods.

3. Use software or Table B of random digits to select a simple random sample (SRS) from a population.

4. Recognize the presence of undercoverage and nonresponse as sources of error in a sample survey. Recognize the effect of the wording of questions on the responses.

5. Use random digits to select a stratified random sample from a population when the strata are identified.

B. EXPERIMENTS

1. Recognize whether a study is an observational study or an experiment.

2. Recognize bias due to confounding of explanatory variables with lurking variables in either an observational study or an experiment.

3. Identify the factors (explanatory variables), treatments, response variables, and individuals or subjects in an experiment.

4. Outline the design of a completely randomized experiment using a diagram like that in Figure 17.2. The diagram in a specific case should show the sizes of the groups, the specific treatments, and the response variable.

5. Use software or Table B of random digits to carry out the random assignment of subjects to groups in a completely randomized experiment.

6. Recognize the placebo effect. Recognize when the double-blind technique should be used.

7. Explain why randomized comparative experiments can give good evidence for cause-and-effect relationships.

C. PROBABILITY

1. Recognize that some phenomena are random. Probability describes the long-run regularity of random phenomena.

2. Understand that the probability of an event is the proportion of times the event occurs in very many repetitions of a random phenomenon. Use the idea of probability as long-run proportion to think about probability.

3. Use basic probability rules to detect illegitimate assignments of probability: Any probability must be a number between 0 and 1, and the total probability assigned to all possible outcomes must be 1.

4. Use basic probability rules to find the probabilities of events that are formed from other events. The probability that an event does not occur is 1 minus its probability. If two events are disjoint, the probability that one or the other occurs is the sum of their individual probabilities.

5. Find probabilities in a discrete probability model by adding the probabilities of their outcomes. Find probabilities in a continuous probability model as areas under a density curve.

6. Use the notation of random variables to make compact statements about random outcomes, such as $P(\overline{x} \leq 4) = 0.3$. Be able to interpret such statements.

D. SAMPLING DISTRIBUTIONS

1. Identify parameters and statistics in a statistical study.

2. Recognize the fact of sampling variability: a statistic will take different values when you repeat a sample or experiment.

3. Interpret a sampling distribution as describing the values taken by a statistic in all possible repetitions of a sample or experiment under the same conditions.

4. Interpret the sampling distribution of a statistic as describing the probabilities of its possible values.

Icing the kicker

The football team lines up for what they hope will be the winning field goal ... and the other team calls time out. "Make the kicker think about it" is their motto. Does "icing the kicker" really work? That is, does the probability of making a field goal go down when the kicker must wait around during the time out? This isn't a simple question. A detailed statistical study considered the distance, the weather, the kicker's skill, and so on. But the conclusion is cheering to coaches: yes, icing the kicker does reduce the probability of success.

E. THE SAMPLING DISTRIBUTION OF A SAMPLE MEAN

1. Recognize when a problem involves the mean $\bar{x}$ of a sample. Understand that $\bar{x}$ estimates the mean μ of the population from which the sample is drawn.

2. Use the law of large numbers to describe the behavior of $\bar{x}$ as the size of the sample increases.

3. Find the mean and standard deviation of a sample mean $\bar{x}$ from an SRS of size n when the mean μ and standard deviation σ of the population are known.

4. Understand that $\bar{x}$ is an unbiased estimator of μ and that the variability of $\bar{x}$ about its mean μ gets smaller as the sample size increases.

5. Understand that $\bar{x}$ has approximately a Normal distribution when the sample is large (central limit theorem). Use this Normal distribution to calculate probabilities that concern $\bar{x}$.

F. GENERAL RULES OF PROBABILITY (Optional)

1. Use Venn diagrams to picture relationships among several events.

2. Use the general addition rule to find probabilities that involve overlapping events.

3. Understand the idea of independence. Judge when it is reasonable to assume independence as part of a probability model.

4. Use the multiplication rule for independent events to find the probability that all of several independent events occur.

5. Use the multiplication rule for independent events in combination with other probability rules to find the probabilities of complex events.

6. Understand the idea of conditional probability. Find conditional probabilities for individuals chosen at random from a table of counts of possible outcomes.

7. Use the general multiplication rule to find $P(A \text{ and } B)$ from $P(A)$ and the conditional probability $P(B \mid A)$.

8. Use tree diagrams to organize several-stage probability models.

G. BINOMIAL DISTRIBUTIONS (Optional)

1. Recognize the binomial setting: a fixed number n of independent success-failure trials with the same probability p of success on each trial.

2. Recognize and use the binomial distribution of the count of successes in a binomial setting.

3. Use the binomial probability formula to find probabilities of events involving the count X of successes in a binomial setting for small values of n.

4. Find the mean and standard deviation of a binomial count X.

5. Recognize when you can use the Normal approximation to a binomial distribution. Use the Normal approximation to calculate probabilities that concern a binomial count X.

H. CONFIDENCE INTERVALS

1. State in nontechnical language what is meant by "95% confidence" or other statements of confidence in statistical reports.
2. Know the four-step process (page 350) for any confidence interval.
3. Calculate a confidence interval for the mean μ of a Normal population with known standard deviation σ, using the formula $\bar{x} \pm z^* \sigma / \sqrt{n}$.
4. Understand how the margin of error of a confidence interval changes with the sample size and the level of confidence C.
5. Find the sample size required to obtain a confidence interval of specified margin of error m when the confidence level and other information are given.
6. Identify sources of error in a study that are *not* included in the margin of error of a confidence interval, such as undercoverage or nonresponse.

I. SIGNIFICANCE TESTS

1. State the null and alternative hypotheses in a testing situation when the parameter in question is a population mean μ.
2. Explain in nontechnical language the meaning of the P-value when you are given the numerical value of P for a test.
3. Know the four-step process (page 372) for any significance test.

4. Calculate the one-sample z test statistic and the P-value for both one-sided and two-sided tests about the mean μ of a Normal population.
5. Assess statistical significance at standard levels α, either by comparing P with α or by comparing z with standard Normal critical values.
6. Recognize that significance testing does not measure the size or importance of an effect. Explain why a small effect can be significant in a large sample and why a large effect can fail to be significant in a small sample.
7. Recognize that any inference procedure acts as if the data were properly produced. The z confidence interval and test require that the data be an SRS from the population.

REVIEW EXERCISES

Review exercises help you solidify the basic ideas and skills in Chapters 8 to 16.

17.1 **Consumer behavior.** A researcher studying the effect of price cuts on consumers' expectations makes up two different histories of the store price of a hypothetical brand of laundry detergent for the past year. Students in a marketing course view one or the other price history on a computer. Some students see a steady price, while others see regular sales that temporarily cut the price. Next, the students are asked what price they would expect to pay for the detergent. Is this study an experiment? Why? What are the explanatory and response variables?

17.2   **Tom Clancy's writing.**   Different types of writing can sometimes be distinguished by the lengths of the words used. A student interested in this fact wants to study the lengths of words used by Tom Clancy in his novels. She opens a Clancy novel at random and records the lengths of each of the first 250 words on the page. What is the population in this study? What is the sample? What is the variable measured?

17.3   **How much do students earn?**   A university's financial aid office wants to know how much it can expect students to earn from summer employment. This information will be used to set the level of financial aid. The population contains 3478 students who have completed at least one year of study but have not yet graduated. The university will send a questionnaire to an SRS of 100 of these students, drawn from an alphabetized list.

(a) Describe how you will label the students in order to select the sample.

(b) Use Table B, beginning at line 105, to select the first 5 students in the sample.

(c) What is the response variable in this study?

17.4   **California area codes.**   A sample survey of California households uses random digit dialing to choose telephone numbers at random. Numbers are selected separately within area codes. California area codes are

209	213	310	323	408	415	424	510	530
559	562	619	626	650	661	707	714	760
805	818	831	858	909	916	925	949	951

Use software, the *Simple Random Sample* applet, or Table B to choose an SRS of 7 of these area codes. If you use Table B, start at line 111.

17.5   **Elephants and bees.**   Elephants sometimes damage crops in Africa. It turns out that elephants dislike bees. They recognize beehives in areas where they are common and avoid them. Can this be used to keep elephants away from trees? A group in Kenya placed active beehives in some trees and empty beehives in others. Will elephant damage be less in trees with hives? Will even empty hives keep elephants away?[1]

Peter Lilja/Getty Images

(a) Outline the design of an experiment to answer these questions using 72 acacia trees (be sure to include a control group).

(b) Use software or the *Simple Random Sample* applet to choose the trees for the active hive group, or Table B at line 137 to choose the first 4 trees in that group.

(c) What is the response variable in this experiment?

17.6   **Support groups for breast cancer.**   Does participating in a support group extend the lives of women with breast cancer? There is no good evidence for this claim, but it was hard to carry out randomized comparative experiments because breast cancer patients believe that support groups help and want to be in one. When the first such experiment was finally completed, it showed that support groups have no effect on survival time. The experiment assigned 235 women with advanced breast cancer to two groups: 158 to "expressive group therapy" and 77 to a control group.[2]

(a) Outline the design of this experiment.

(b) Use software or the *Simple Random Sample* applet to choose the 77 members of the control group (list only the first 10), or use Table B at line 110 to choose the first 5 members of the control group.

APPLET

17.7 Effects of day care.   The Carolina Abecedarian Project investigated the effect of high-quality preschool programs on children from poor families. Children were randomly assigned to two groups. One group participated in a year-round preschool program from the age of three months. The control group received social services but no preschool. At age 21, **35%** of the treatment group and **14%** of the control group were attending a four-year college or had already graduated from college. Is each of the boldface numbers a parameter or a statistic? Why?

17.8 TV programming.   Your local television station wonders if its viewers would rather watch your college basketball team play or an NBA game scheduled at the same time. It schedules the NBA game and receives 89 calls asking that it show the local game instead. The 89 callers are a sample. What population does the station want information about? Does the sample give trustworthy information about the sample? Explain your answer.

17.9 Marijuana and driving.   Questioning a sample of young people in New Zealand revealed a positive association between use of marijuana (cannabis) and traffic accidents caused by the members of the sample. Both cannabis use and accidents were measured by interviewing the young people themselves. The study report says, "It is unlikely that self reports of cannabis use and accident rates will be perfectly accurate."[3] Is the response bias likely to make the reported association stronger or weaker than the true association? Why?

17.10 Estimating blood cholesterol.   The distribution of blood cholesterol level in the population of young men aged 20 to 34 years is close to Normal with standard deviation $\sigma = 41$ milligrams per deciliter (mg/dl). You measure the blood cholesterol of 14 cross-country runners. The mean level is $\bar{x} = 172$ mg/dl. Assuming that σ is the same as in the general population, give a 90% confidence interval for the mean level μ among cross-country runners.

17.11 Testing blood cholesterol.   The mean blood cholesterol level for all men aged 20 to 34 years is $\mu = 188$ mg/dl. We suspect that the mean for cross-country runners is lower. State hypotheses, use the information in Exercise 17.10 to find the test statistic, and give the P-value. Is the result significant at the $\alpha = 0.10$ level? At $\alpha = 0.05$? At $\alpha = 0.01$?

17.12 Smaller margin of error.   How large a sample is needed to cut the margin of error in Exercise 17.10 in half? How large a sample is needed to cut the margin of error to ± 5 mg/dl?

17.13 More significant results.   You increase the sample of cross-country runners from 14 to 56. Suppose that this larger sample gives the same mean level, $\bar{x} = 172$ mg/dl. Redo the test in Exercise 17.11. What is the P-value now? At which of the levels $\alpha = 0.10$, $\alpha = 0.05$, $\alpha = 0.01$ is the result significant? What general fact about significance tests does comparing your results here and in Exercise 17.11 illustrate?

Pete Atkinson/Getty Images

17.14 Pesticides in whale blubber.   The level of pesticides found in the blubber of whales is a measure of pollution of the oceans by runoff from land and can also be used to identify different populations of whales. A sample of 8 male minke whales in the West Greenland area of the North Atlantic found the mean concentration

4
STEP

of the insecticide dieldrin to be $\bar{x} = 357$ nanograms per gram of blubber (ng/g).[4] Suppose that the concentration in all such whales varies Normally with standard deviation $\sigma = 50$ ng/g. Use a 95% confidence interval to estimate the mean level. Follow the four-step process for confidence intervals (page 350) in your work.

17.15 Testing pesticide level. The Food and Drug Administration regulates the amount of dieldrin in raw food. For some foods, no more than 100 ng/g is allowed. Using the information in Exercise 17.14, is there good evidence that the mean concentration in whale blubber is above this level? Follow the four-step process for significance tests (page 372) in your work.

17.16 Other confidence levels. Use the information in Exercise 17.14 to give an 80% confidence interval and a 90% confidence interval for the mean concentration of dieldrin in the whale population. What general fact about confidence intervals do the margins of error of your three intervals illustrate?

17.17 Birth weight and IQ: estimation. Infants weighing less than 1500 grams at birth are classed as "very low birth weight." Low birth weight carries many risks. One study followed 113 male infants with very low birth weight to adulthood. At age 20, the mean IQ score for these men was $\bar{x} = 87.6$.[5] IQ scores vary Normally with standard deviation $\sigma = 15$. Give a 95% confidence interval for the mean IQ score at age 20 for all very-low-birth-weight males. Use the four-step process for confidence intervals (page 350) as a guide.

17.18 Birth weight and IQ: testing. IQ tests are scaled so that the mean score in a large population should be $\mu = 100$. We suspect that the very-low-birth-weight population has mean score less than 100. Does the study described in the previous exercise give good evidence that this is true? Use the four-step process for significance tests (page 372) as a guide.

17.19 Birth weight and IQ: causation? Very-low-birth-weight babies are more likely to be born to unmarried mothers and to mothers who did not complete high school.

(a) Explain why the study of Exercise 17.17 was not an experiment.

(b) Explain clearly why confounding prevents us from concluding that very low birth weight in itself reduces adult IQ.

17.20 Sample space. A randomly chosen subject arrives for a study of exercise and fitness. Describe a sample space for each of the following. (In some cases, you may have some freedom in your choice of S.)

(a) The subject is either female or male.

(b) After 10 minutes on an exercise bicycle, you ask the subject to rate his or her effort on the Rate of Perceived Exertion (RPE) scale. RPE ranges in whole-number steps from 6 (no exertion at all) to 20 (maximal exertion).

(c) You measure VO2, the maximum volume of oxygen consumed per minute during exercise. VO2 is generally between 2.5 and 6.1 liters per minute.

(d) You measure the maximum heart rate (beats per minute).

17.21 Spam email. More than 75% of email messages are now "spam." Choose a spam email message at random. Here is the distribution of topics:[6]

Topic	Adult	Financial	Health	Leisure	Products	Scams
Probability	0.145	0.162	0.073	0.078	0.210	0.142

(a) What is the probability that a spam email does not concern one of these topics?

(b) Corinne is particularly annoyed by spam offering "adult" content (that is, pornography) and scams. What is the probability that a randomly chosen spam email falls into one or the other of these categories?

17.22 **How many in the house?** In government data, a household consists of all occupants of a dwelling unit. Here is the distribution of household size in the United States:

Number of persons	1	2	3	4	5	6	7
Probability	0.27	0.33	0.16	0.14	0.06	0.03	0.01

Choose an American household at random and let the random variable Y be the number of persons living in the household.

(a) Express "more than one person lives in this household" in terms of Y. What is the probability of this event?

(b) What is $P(2 < Y \leq 4)$?

(c) What is $P(Y \neq 2)$?

17.23 **Moving up.** A study of social mobility in England looked at the social class reached by the sons of lower-class fathers. Social classes are numbered from 1 (low) to 5 (high). Take the random variable X to be the class of a randomly chosen son of a father in Class 1. The study found that the distribution of X is

Son's class	1	2	3	4	5
Probability	0.48	0.38	0.08	0.05	0.01

(a) Check that this distribution satisfies the two requirements for a legitimate discrete probability model.

(b) What is $P(X \leq 3)$?

(c) What is $P(X < 3)$?

(d) Write the event "a son of a lower-class father reaches one of the two highest classes" in terms of values of X. What is the probability of this event?

17.24 **The addition rule.** The addition rule for probabilities, $P(A \text{ or } B) = P(A) + P(B)$, is not always true. Give (in words) an example of real-world events A and B for which this rule is not true.

17.25 **Internet access.** The amount that households pay service providers for access to the Internet varies quite a bit, but the mean monthly fee is $38 and the standard deviation is $10. The distribution is not Normal: some households pay about $10 for limited dial-up access or about $25 for unlimited dial-up access, but a majority pay more for broadband connections. A sample survey asks an SRS of 500 households with Internet access how much they pay. What is the probability that the average fee paid by the sample households exceeds $39?

17.26 **An IQ test.** The Wechsler Adult Intelligence Scale (WAIS) is a common "IQ test" for adults. The distribution of WAIS scores for persons over 16 years of age is approximately Normal with mean 100 and standard deviation 15.

(a) What is the probability that a randomly chosen individual has a WAIS score of 105 or higher?

(b) What are the mean and standard deviation of the average WAIS score $\bar{x}$ for an SRS of 60 people?

(c) What is the probability that the average WAIS score of an SRS of 60 people is 105 or higher?

(d) Would your answers to any of (a), (b), or (c) be affected if the distribution of WAIS scores in the adult population were distinctly non-Normal?

17.27 Distributions: means versus individuals. The z confidence interval and test are based on the sampling distribution of the sample mean $\bar{x}$. Suppose that the distribution of the scores of young men on the National Assessment of Educational Progress quantitative test is Normal with mean $\mu = 272$ and standard deviation $\sigma = 60$.

(a) You take an SRS of 100 young men. According to the 99.7 part of the 68–95–99.7 rule, about what range of scores do you expect to see in your sample?

(b) You look at many SRSs of size 100. About what range of sample mean scores $\bar{x}$ do you expect to see?

17.28 Distributions: larger samples. In the setting of the previous exercise, how many men must you sample to cut the range of values of $\bar{x}$ in half? This will also cut the margin of error of a confidence interval for μ in half. Do you expect the range of individual scores in the new sample to also be much less than in a sample of size 100? Why?

17.29 Size of apartments. The mean area of the several thousand apartments in a new development is advertised to be 1250 square feet. A tenant group thinks that the apartments are smaller than advertised. They hire an engineer to measure a random sample of apartments to test their suspicion. Here are the data:

1244	1245	1242	1245	1237	1245	1246	1232	1237
1247	1245	1240	1234	1244	1243	1234	1238	1237

Suppose that apartment sizes in the development vary Normally with standard deviation 5 square feet due to variation during construction. Is there good reason to think that the mean is less than 1250 square feet? Follow the four-step process for significance tests (page 372).

17.30 Normal body temperature? Here are the daily average body temperatures (degrees Fahrenheit) for 20 healthy adults.[7] Do these data give evidence that the mean body temperature for all healthy adults is not equal to the traditional 98.6 degrees? Follow the four-step process for significance tests (page 372). (Suppose that body temperature varies Normally with standard deviation 0.7 degree.)

98.74	98.83	96.80	98.12	97.89	98.09	97.87	97.42	97.30	97.84
100.27	97.90	99.64	97.88	98.54	98.33	97.87	97.48	98.92	98.33

Dann Tardiff/CORBIS

17.31 Size of apartments. Use the data in Exercise 17.29 to estimate the mean size of apartments in this complex with 95% confidence. Follow the four-step process for confidence intervals (page 350).

17.32 Normal body temperature. Use the data in Exercise 17.30 to estimate mean body temperature with 90% confidence. Follow the four-step process for confidence intervals (page 350).

17.33 Cash to find work? Will cash bonuses speed the return to work of unemployed people? The Illinois Department of Employment Security designed an experiment to find out. The subjects were 10,065 people aged 20 to 54 who were filing claims for unemployment insurance. Some were offered $500 if they found a job within 11 weeks and held it for at least 4 months. Others could tell potential employers that the state would pay the employer $500 for hiring them. A control group got neither kind of bonus.[8]

(a) Suggest two response variables of interest to the state and outline the design of the experiment.

(b) How will you label the subjects for random assignment? Use Table B at line 127 to choose the first 3 subjects for the first treatment.

17.34 Surviving a layoff. Workers who survive a layoff of other employees at their location may suffer from "survivor guilt." A study of survivor guilt and its effects used as subjects 120 students who were offered an opportunity to earn extra course credit by doing proofreading. Each subject worked in the same cubicle as another student, who was an accomplice of the experimenters. At a break midway through the work, one of three things happened:

> Treatment 1: The accomplice was told to leave; it was explained that this was because she performed poorly.

> Treatment 2: It was explained that unforeseen circumstances meant there was only enough work for one person. By "chance," the accomplice was chosen to be laid off.

> Treatment 3: Both students continued to work after the break.

The subjects' work performance after the break was compared with performance before the break.[9]

(a) Outline the design of this completely randomized experiment.

(b) If you are using software or the *Simple Random Sample* applet, choose the subjects for Treatment 1 and list the first 10. If not, use Table B at line 123 to choose the first 4 subjects for Treatment 1.

17.35 Brains at work. When our brains store information, complicated chemical changes take place. In trying to understand these changes, researchers blocked some processes in brain cells taken from rats and compared these cells with a control group of normal cells. They say that "no differences were seen" between the two groups in four response variables. They give P-values 0.45, 0.83, 0.26, and 0.84 for these four comparisons.[10]

(a) Say clearly what P-value $P = 0.45$ says about the response that was observed.

(b) It isn't literally true that "no differences were seen." That is, the mean responses were not exactly alike in the two groups. Explain what the researchers mean when they give $P = 0.45$ and say "no difference was seen."

17.36 Support groups for breast cancer, continued. Here are some of the results of the medical study described in Exercise 17.6. Women in the treatment group reported less pain ($P = 0.04$), but there was no significant difference between the groups in median survival time ($P = 0.72$). Explain carefully why $P = 0.04$ is evidence that the treatment *does* make a difference and why $P = 0.72$ means that there is no evidence that support groups prolong life.

17.37 California brushfires. We often see televised reports of brushfires threatening homes in California. Some people argue that the modern practice of quickly putting out small fires allows fuel to accumulate and so increases the damage done by large fires. A detailed study of historical data suggests that this is wrong—the damage has risen simply because there are more houses in risky areas.[11] As usual, the study report gives statistical information tersely. Here is the summary of a regression of number of fires on decade (9 data points, for the 1910s to the 1990s): "Collectively, since 1910, there has been a highly significant increase ($r^2 = 0.61$, $P < 0.01$) in the number of fires per decade." How would you explain this statement to someone who knows no statistics? Include an explanation of both the description given by r^2 and its statistical significance.

CORBIS

SUPPLEMENTARY EXERCISES

Supplementary exercises apply the skills you have learned in ways that require more thought or more elaborate use of technology.

17.38 Sampling students. You want to investigate the attitudes of students at your school toward the school's policy on sexual harassment. You have a grant that will pay the costs of contacting about 500 students.

(a) Specify the exact population for your study. For example, will you include part-time students?

(b) Describe your sample design. Will you use a stratified sample?

(c) Briefly discuss the practical difficulties that you anticipate. For example, how will you contact the students in your sample?

17.39 The placebo effect. A survey of physicians found that some doctors give a placebo to a patient who complains of pain for which the physician can find no cause. If the patient's pain improves, these doctors conclude that it had no physical basis. The medical school researchers who conducted the survey claimed that these doctors do not understand the placebo effect. Why?

17.40 Informed consent. The requirement that human subjects give their informed consent to participate in an experiment can greatly reduce the number of available subjects. For example, a study of new teaching methods asks the consent of parents for their children to be taught by either a new method or the standard method. Many parents do not return the forms, so their children must continue to follow the standard curriculum. Why is it not correct to consider these children as part of the control group along with children who are randomly assigned to the standard method?

17.41 Missile defense. The question of whether the United States should develop a system intended to protect against a missile attack is controversial. Opinion polls give quite different results depending on the wording of the question asked. For each of the following items of information, say whether including it in the question would *increase* or *decrease* the percent of a poll sample who support missile defense.[12]

(a) The system is intended to protect the nation against a nuclear attack.

(b) The system would cost $60 billion.

(c) Deploying a missile defense system would interfere with existing arms-control treaties.

(d) Many scientists say such a system is unlikely to work.

17.42 Market research. Stores advertise price reductions to attract customers. What type of price cut is most attractive? Market researchers prepared ads for athletic shoes announcing different levels of discounts (20%, 40%, or 60%). The student subjects who read the ads were also given "inside information" about the fraction of shoes on sale (50% or 100%). Each subject then rated the attractiveness of the sale on a scale of 1 to 7.[13]

(a) There are two factors. Make a sketch like Figure 9.1 (page 214) that displays the treatments formed by all combinations of levels of the factors.

(b) Outline a completely randomized design using 60 student subjects. Use software or Table B at line 111 to choose the subjects for the first treatment.

17.43 Making french fries. Few people want to eat discolored french fries. Potatoes are kept refrigerated before being cut for french fries to prevent spoiling and preserve flavor. But immediate processing of cold potatoes causes discoloring due to complex chemical reactions. The potatoes must therefore be brought to room temperature before processing. Design an experiment in which tasters will rate the color and flavor of french fries prepared from several groups of potatoes. The potatoes will be fresh picked or stored for a month at room temperature or stored for a month refrigerated. They will then be sliced and cooked either immediately or after an hour at room temperature.

(a) What are the factors and their levels, the treatments, and the response variables?

(b) Describe and outline the design of this experiment.

(c) It is efficient to have each taster rate fries from all treatments. How will you use randomization in presenting fries to the tasters?

17.44 Comparing wine tasters. Two wine tasters rate each wine they taste on a scale of 1 to 5. From data on their ratings of a large number of wines, we obtain the following probabilities for both tasters' ratings of a randomly chosen wine:

		Taster 2			
Taster 1	1	2	3	4	5
1	0.03	0.02	0.01	0.00	0.00
2	0.02	0.08	0.05	0.02	0.01
3	0.01	0.05	0.25	0.05	0.01
4	0.00	0.02	0.05	0.20	0.02
5	0.00	0.01	0.01	0.02	0.06

(a) Why is this a legitimate discrete probability model?

(b) What is the probability that the tasters agree when rating a wine?

(c) What is the probability that Taster 1 rates a wine higher than Taster 2? What is the probability that Taster 2 rates a wine higher than Taster 1?

David Moore

17.45 A 14-sided die. An ancient Korean drinking game involves a 14-sided die. The players roll the die in turn and must submit to whatever humiliation is written on the up-face: something like, "Keep still when tickled on face." Six of the 14 faces are squares. Let's call them A, B, C, D, E, and F for short. The other eight faces are triangles, which we will call 1, 2, 3, 4, 5, 6, 7, and 8. Each of the squares is equally likely. Each of the triangles is also equally likely, but the triangle probability differs from the square probability. The probability of getting a square is 0.72. Give the probability model for the 14 possible outcomes.

17.46 Alcohol and mortality. It appears that people who drink alcohol in moderation have lower death rates than either people who drink heavily or people who do not drink at all. The protection offered by moderate drinking is concentrated among people over 50 and on deaths from heart disease. The Nurses' Health Study played an essential role in establishing these facts for women. This part of the study followed 85,709 female nurses for 12 years, during which time 2658 of the subjects died. The nurses completed a questionnaire that described their diet, including their use of alcohol. They were reexamined every two years. Conclusion: "As compared with nondrinkers and heavy drinkers, light-to-moderate drinkers had a significantly lower risk of death."[14]

(a) Was this study an experiment? Explain your answer.

(b) What does "significantly lower risk of death" mean in simple language?

(c) Suggest some lurking variables that might be confounded with how much a person drinks. The investigators used advanced statistical methods to adjust for many such variables before concluding that the moderate drinkers really have a lower risk of death.

17.47 Tests from confidence intervals. You read in a Census Bureau report that a 99% confidence interval for the mean income of the top 20% of American households in 2004 is $151,593 ± $2125. Based on this interval, can you reject the null hypothesis that the mean income in this group is $150,000? What is the alternative hypothesis of the test? What is its significance level?

17.48 Low power? (optional) It appears that eating oat bran lowers cholesterol slightly. At a time when oat bran was something of a fad, a paper in the *New England Journal of Medicine* found that it had no significant effect on cholesterol.[15] The paper reported a study with just 20 subjects. Letters to the journal denounced publication of a negative finding from a study with very low power. Explain why lack of significance in a study with low power gives no reason to accept the null hypothesis that oat bran has no effect.

17.49 Type I and Type II errors (optional). Exercise 17.18 asks for a significance test of the null hypothesis that the mean IQ of very-low-birth-weight male babies is 100 against the alternative hypothesis that the mean is less than 100. State in words what it means to make a Type I error and a Type II error in this setting.

OPTIONAL EXERCISES

These exercises concern the optional material in Chapters 12 and 13.

17.50 Tax returns. The Internal Revenue Service received 130,424,000 individual income tax returns for 2003. Of these, 11,415,000 reported an adjusted gross income of at least $100,000, and 181,000 reported at least $1 million.[16] If you know that a randomly chosen return shows an income of $100,000 or more, what is the conditional probability that the income is at least $1 million?

17.51 Comparing wine tasters. In the setting of Exercise 17.44, Taster 1's rating for a wine is 3. What is the conditional probability that Taster 2's rating is higher than 3?

17.52 A baseball cliché. How often have you heard a baseball radio or TV announcer say something like "Scott has hit safely in 9 of the last 12 games," as if this were an impressive performance? Let's find out how impressive. Major league starting players (leaving out pitchers) hit safely in about 67% of their games.[17]

(a) It's reasonable to take games as independent. What is the distribution of the number of games out of 12 in which a typical player hits safely?

(b) What is the probability that a player hits safely in 9 or more out of 12 games? In 8 or more out of 12?

17.53 Posting photos online. Suppose (as is roughly true) that 20% of all Internet users have posted photos online. A sample survey interviews an SRS of 1555 Internet users.

(a) What is the actual distribution of the number X in the sample who have posted photos online?

(b) What is the probability that 300 or fewer of the people in the sample have posted photos online? (Use software or a suitable approximation.)

17.54 Many tests. Long ago, a group of psychologists carried out 77 separate significance tests and found that 2 were significant at the 5% level. Suppose that these tests are independent of each other. (In fact, they were not independent, because all involved the same subjects.) If all of the null hypotheses are true, each test has probability 0.05 of being significant at the 5% level. Use the binomial distribution to find the probability that 2 or more of the tests are significant.

17.55 Is business success just chance? Investors like to think that some companies are consistently successful. Academic researchers looked at data for many companies to determine whether each firm's sales growth was above the median for all firms in each year. They found that a simple "just chance" model fit well: years are independent, and the probability of being above the median in any one year is 1/2.[18] If this model holds, what is the probability that a particular firm is above average for two consecutive years? For all of four years?

17.56 Admitting students to college. A selective college would like to have an entering class of 1200 students. Because not all students who are offered admission accept, the college admits more than 1200 students. Past experience shows that about 70% of the students admitted will accept. The college decides to admit 1500 students. Assuming that students make their decisions independently, the number who accept has the $B(1500, 0.7)$ distribution. If this number is less than 1200, the college will admit students from its waiting list.

(a) What are the mean and the standard deviation of the number X of students who accept?

(b) Use the Normal approximation to find the probability that at least 1000 students accept.

17.57 Admitting students to college, continued. What is the approximate probability that the college in the previous exercise admits the top 110 students on its waiting list?

17.58 Life tables. The National Center for Health Statistics produces a "life table" for the American population. For each year of age, the table gives the probability that a randomly chosen U.S. resident will die during that year of life. These are *conditional* probabilities, given that the person lived to the birthday that marks the beginning of the year. Here is an excerpt from the table:

Year of life	Probability of death
51	0.00439
52	0.00473
53	0.00512
54	0.00557
55	0.00610

What is the probability that a person who lives to age 50 (the beginning of the 51st year) will live to age 55?

17.59 Cystic fibrosis. Cystic fibrosis is a lung disorder that often results in death. It is inherited but can be inherited only if both parents are carriers of an abnormal gene. In 1989, the CF gene that is abnormal in carriers of cystic fibrosis was identified. The probability that a randomly chosen person of European ancestry carries an abnormal CF gene is 1/25. (The probability is less in other ethnic groups.) The CF20m test detects most but not all harmful mutations of the CF gene. The test is positive for 90% of people who are carriers. It is (ignoring human error) never positive for people who are not carriers. What is the probability that a randomly chosen person of European ancestry tests positive?

17.60 Cystic fibrosis, continued. Jason tests positive on the CF20m test. What is the probability that he is a carrier of the abnormal CF gene?

17.61 Students online. Students have different patterns of Internet use than other adults. Among adult Internet users, 4.1% are full-time students and another 2.9% are part-time students. Students are much more likely to access the Internet from someplace other than work or home: 58% of full-time students do so, as do 30% of part-time students, but only 21% of other users.[19] What percent of all adult users reach the Internet from someplace other than home or work?

17.62 Teenage drivers. An insurance company has the following information about drivers aged 16 to 18 years: 20% are involved in accidents each year; 10% in this age group are A students; among those involved in an accident, 5% are A students.

(a) Let A be the event that a young driver is an A student and C the event that a young driver is involved in an accident this year. State the information given in terms of probabilities and conditional probabilities for the events A and C.

(b) What is the probability that a randomly chosen young driver is an A student and is involved in an accident?

17.63 Teenage drivers, continued. Use your work from the previous exercise to find the percent of A students who are involved in accidents. (Start by expressing this as a conditional probability.)

17.64 Do the rich stay that way? We like to think that anyone can rise to the top. That's possible, but it's easier if you start near the top. Divide families by the income of the parents into the top 20%, the bottom 20%, and the middle 60%.

Tom & Dee Ann McCarthy/CORBIS

Here are the conditional probabilities that a child of each class of parents ends up in each income class as an adult.[20] For example, a child of parents in the top 20% has probability 0.42 of also being in the top 20%.

	Child's Class		
Parent's class	Top 20%	Middle 60%	Bottom 20%
Top 20%	0.42	0.52	0.06
Middle 60%	0.15	0.68	0.17
Bottom 20%	0.07	0.56	0.37

Suppose that these probabilities stay the same for three generations. Draw a tree diagram to show the path of a child and grandchild of parents in the top 20% of incomes. For example, the child might drop to the middle and the grandchild might then rise back to the top. What is the probability that the grandchild of people in the top 20% is also in the top 20%?

EESEE CASE STUDIES

The Electronic Encyclopedia of Statistical Examples and Exercises (EESEE) is available on the text CD and Web site. These more elaborate stories, with data, provide settings for longer case studies. Here are some suggestions for EESEE stories that apply the ideas you have learned in Chapters 8 to 16.

17.65 **Fear of Buildings on Campus.** Respond to Questions 1, 2, and 3 for this case study. (Sample surveys.)

17.66 **Puerto Rican vs. U.S. Consumers.** Write a report that answers all three questions. (Cautions about sample surveys.)

17.67 **Anecdotes of Bias.** Answer all of the questions posed about these incidents. (Cautions about sample surveys.)

17.68 **Checkmating and Reading Skills.** Respond to Questions 1 and 3 for this story. (Sampling, data analysis.)

17.69 **Surgery in a Blanket.** Write a response to Questions 1 and 2. (Design of experiments.)

17.70 **Visibility of Highway Signs.** Answer Questions 1, 2, and 3(a) for this study. (Design of experiments, data analysis.)

17.71 **Columbus's 1993 Election Poll.** Write a report that responds to Questions 1 to 5. (Sample surveys, cautions about sample surveys, interpreting confidence intervals.)

17.72 **Anecdotes of Significance Testing.** Answer all three questions. (Interpreting P-values.)

17.73 **Blinded Knee Doctors.**

(a) Outline the design of this experiment.

(b) You read that "the patients, physicians, and physical therapists were blinded" during the study. What does this mean?

(c) You also read that "the pain scores for Group A were significantly lower than Group C but not significantly lower than Group B." What does this mean? What does this finding lead you to conclude about the use of NSAIDs?

Inference about Variables

With the principles in hand, we proceed to practice, that is, to inference in fully realistic settings. In the remaining chapters of this book, you will meet many of the most commonly used statistical procedures. We have grouped these procedures into two classes, corresponding to our division of data analysis into exploring variables and distributions and exploring relationships. The five chapters of Part III concern inference about the distribution of a single variable and inference for comparing the distributions of two variables. Part IV deals with inference for relationships among variables. In Chapters 18 and 19, we analyze data on quantitative variables. We begin with the familiar Normal distribution for a quantitative variable. Chapters 20 and 21 concern categorical variables, so that inference begins with counts and proportions of outcomes. Chapter 22 reviews this part of the text.

The four-part process for approaching a statistical problem can guide much of your work in these chapters. You should review the outlines of the four-part process for a confidence interval (page 350) and for a test of significance (page 372). The statement of an exercise usually does the *State* step for you, leaving the *Formulate*, *Solve*, and *Conclude* steps for you to complete. We recommend that you first summarize the *State* step in your own words to help organize your thinking. Many examples and exercises in these chapters involve both carrying out inference and thinking about inference in practice. Remember that any inference method is useful only under certain conditions, and that you must judge these conditions before rushing to inference.

QUANTITATIVE RESPONSE VARIABLE

CATEGORICAL RESPONSE VARIABLE

Image State Royalty Free/Alamy

Inference about a Population Mean

This chapter describes confidence intervals and significance tests for the mean μ of a population. We used the z procedures in exactly this setting to introduce the ideas of confidence intervals and tests. Now we discard the unrealistic condition that we know the population standard deviation σ and present procedures for practical use. We also pay more attention to the real-data setting of our work. The details of confidence intervals and tests change only slightly when you don't know σ. More important, you can interpret your results exactly as before. To emphasize this, Examples 18.2 and 18.3 repeat the most important examples of Chapters 14 and 15.

Conditions for inference

Confidence intervals and tests of significance for the mean μ of a Normal population are based on the sample mean $\bar{x}$. Confidence levels and P-values are probabilities calculated from the sampling distribution of $\bar{x}$. Here are the conditions needed for realistic inference about a population mean.

> ## CONDITIONS FOR INFERENCE ABOUT A MEAN
>
> - We can regard our data as a **simple random sample** (SRS) from the population. This condition is very important.
> - Observations from the population have a **Normal distribution** with mean μ and standard deviation σ. In practice, it is enough that the distribution be symmetric and single-peaked unless the sample is very small. Both μ and σ are unknown parameters.

There is another condition that applies to all of the inference methods in this book: *the population must be much larger than the sample, say at least 20 times as large.*[1] All of our examples and exercises satisfy this condition. Practical settings in which the sample is a large part of the population are rather special, and we will not discuss them.

When the conditions for inference are satisfied, the sample mean $\overline{x}$ has the Normal distribution with mean μ and standard deviation $\sigma/\sqrt{n}$. Because we don't know σ, we estimate it by the sample standard deviation s. We then estimate the standard deviation of $\overline{x}$ by $s/\sqrt{n}$. This quantity is called the *standard error* of the sample mean $\overline{x}$.

> ## STANDARD ERROR
>
> When the standard deviation of a statistic is estimated from data, the result is called the **standard error** of the statistic. The standard error of the sample mean $\overline{x}$ is $s/\sqrt{n}$.

APPLY YOUR KNOWLEDGE

Tony Freeman/PhotoEdit

18.1   **Travel time to work.**   A study of commuting times reports the travel times to work of a random sample of 20 employed adults in New York State. The mean is $\overline{x} = 31.25$ minutes and the standard deviation is $s = 21.88$ minutes. What is the standard error of the mean?

18.2   **Rats eating oat bran.**   In a study of the effect of diet on cholesterol, rats were fed several different diets.[2] One diet had 5% added fiber from oat bran. The study report gives results in the form "mean plus or minus the standard error of the mean." This form is very common in scientific publications. For the 6 rats fed this diet, blood cholesterol levels (in milligrams per deciliter of blood) were 89.01 ± 5.36. What are $\overline{x}$ and s for these 6 rats?

The t distributions

If we knew the value of σ, we would base confidence intervals and tests for μ on the one-sample z statistic

$$z = \frac{\overline{x} - \mu}{\sigma/\sqrt{n}}$$

This z statistic has the standard Normal distribution $N(0, 1)$. In practice, we don't know σ, so we substitute the standard error $s/\sqrt{n}$ of $\overline{x}$ for its standard deviation $\sigma/\sqrt{n}$. The statistic that results does not have a Normal distribution. It has a distribution that is new to us, called a t *distribution*.

THE ONE-SAMPLE t STATISTIC AND THE t DISTRIBUTIONS

Draw an SRS of size n from a large population that has the Normal distribution with mean μ and standard deviation σ. The **one-sample t statistic**

$$t = \frac{\overline{x} - \mu}{s/\sqrt{n}}$$

has the **t distribution** with $n - 1$ degrees of freedom.

The t statistic has the same interpretation as any standardized statistic: it says how far $\overline{x}$ is from its mean μ in standard deviation units. There is a different t distribution for each sample size. We specify a particular t distribution by giving its **degrees of freedom.** The degrees of freedom for the one-sample t statistic come from the sample standard deviation s in the denominator of t. We saw in Chapter 2 (page 49) that s has $n - 1$ degrees of freedom. There are other t statistics with different degrees of freedom, some of which we will meet later. We will write the t distribution with $n - 1$ degrees of freedom as $t(n - 1)$ for short.

degrees of freedom

Figure 18.1 compares the density curves of the standard Normal distribution and the t distributions with 2 and 9 degrees of freedom. The figure illustrates these facts about the t distributions:

- The density curves of the t distributions are similar in shape to the standard Normal curve. They are symmetric about 0, single-peaked, and bell-shaped.

- The spread of the t distributions is a bit greater than that of the standard Normal distribution. The t distributions in Figure 18.1 have more probability in the tails and less in the center than does the standard Normal. This is true because substituting the estimate s for the fixed parameter σ introduces more variation into the statistic.

- As the degrees of freedom increase, the t density curve approaches the $N(0, 1)$ curve ever more closely. This happens because s estimates σ more accurately as the sample size increases. So using s in place of σ causes little extra variation when the sample is large.

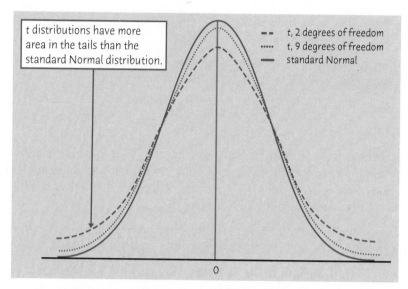

FIGURE 18.1 Density curves for the *t* distributions with 2 and 9 degrees of freedom and the standard Normal distribution. All are symmetric with center 0. The *t* distributions are somewhat more spread out.

Table C in the back of the book gives critical values for the *t* distributions. Each row in the table contains critical values for the *t* distribution whose degrees of freedom appear at the left of the row. For convenience, we label the table entries both by the confidence level C (in percent) required for confidence intervals and by the one-sided and two-sided *P*-values for each critical value. You have already used the standard Normal critical values *z** in the bottom row of Table C. By looking down any column, you can check that the *t* critical values approach the Normal values as the degrees of freedom increase. As in the case of the Normal table, statistical software makes Table C unnecessary.

EXAMPLE 18.1   *t* critical values

Figure 18.1 shows the density curve for the *t* distribution with 9 degrees of freedom. What point on this distribution has probability 0.05 to its right? In Table C, look in the df = 9 row above one-sided *P*-value .05 and you will find that this critical value is $t^* = 1.833$. To use software, enter the degrees of freedom and the probability you want to the *left*, 0.95 in this case. Here is Minitab's output:

```
Student's t distribution with 9 DF
P(X<=x)          x
   0.95   1.83311
```

APPLY YOUR KNOWLEDGE ————————————

18.3   **Critical values.**   Use Table C or software to find

(a) the critical value for a one-sided test with level $\alpha = 0.05$ based on the $t(5)$ distribution.

(b) the critical value for a 98% confidence interval based on the $t(21)$ distribution.

Better statistics, better beer

The *t* distribution and the *t* inference procedures were invented by William S. Gosset (1876–1937). Gosset worked for the Guinness brewery, and his goal in life was to make better beer. He used his new *t* procedures to find the best varieties of barley and hops. Gosset's statistical work helped him become head brewer, a more interesting title than professor of statistics. Because Gosset published under the pen name "Student," you will often see the *t* distribution called "Student's *t*" in his honor.

18.4 More critical values. You have an SRS of size 25 and calculate the one-sample *t* statistic. What is the critical value t^* such that

(a) *t* has probability 0.025 to the right of t^*?

(b) *t* has probability 0.75 to the left of t^*?

The one-sample *t* confidence interval

To analyze samples from Normal populations with unknown σ, just replace the standard deviation $\sigma/\sqrt{n}$ of $\overline{x}$ by its standard error $s/\sqrt{n}$ in the z procedures of Chapters 14 and 15. The confidence interval and test that result are *one-sample t procedures*. Critical values and *P*-values come from the *t* distribution with $n-1$ degrees of freedom. The one-sample *t* procedures are similar in both reasoning and computational detail to the z procedures.

THE ONE-SAMPLE *t* CONFIDENCE INTERVAL

Draw an SRS of size n from a large population having unknown mean μ. A level C **confidence interval for μ** is

$$\overline{x} \pm t^* \frac{s}{\sqrt{n}}$$

where t^* is the critical value for the $t(n-1)$ density curve with area C between $-t^*$ and t^*. This interval is exact when the population distribution is Normal and is approximately correct for large n in other cases.

EXAMPLE 18.2   Healing of skin wounds

4 STEP

Let's look again at the biological study we met in Example 14.3. We follow the four-step process for a confidence interval, outlined on page 350.

STATE: Biologists studying the healing of skin wounds measured the rate at which new cells closed a razor cut made in the skin of an anesthetized newt. Here are data from 18 newts, measured in micrometers (millionths of a meter) per hour:[3]

David A. Northcott/CORBIS

29	27	34	40	22	28	14	35	26
35	12	30	23	18	11	22	23	33

This is one of several sets of measurements made under different conditions. We want to estimate the mean rate for comparison with rates under other conditions.

FORMULATE: We will estimate the mean rate μ for all newts of this species by giving a 95% confidence interval.

SOLVE: We must first check the conditions for inference.

- As in Chapter 14 (page 351), we are willing to regard these newts as an SRS from their species.
- The stemplot in Figure 18.2 does not suggest any strong departures from Normality.

```
1 | 1 2 4
1 | 8
2 | 2 2 3 3
2 | 6 7 8 9
3 | 0 3 4
3 | 5 5
4 | 0
```

FIGURE 18.2 Stemplot of the healing rates in Example 18.2.

We can proceed to calculation. For these data,

$$\bar{x} = 25.67 \quad \text{and} \quad s = 8.324$$

The degrees of freedom are $n - 1 = 17$. From Table C we find that for 95% confidence $t^* = 2.110$. The confidence interval is

$$\bar{x} \pm t^* \frac{s}{\sqrt{n}} = 25.67 \pm 2.110 \frac{8.324}{\sqrt{18}}$$

$$= 25.67 \pm 4.14$$

$$= 21.53 \text{ to } 29.81 \text{ micrometers per hour}$$

CONCLUDE: We are 95% confident that the mean healing rate for all newts of this species is between 21.53 and 29.81 micrometers per hour.

Our work in Example 18.2 is very similar to what we did in Example 14.3 on page 350. To make the inference realistic we replaced the assumed $\sigma = 8$ by $s = 8.324$ calculated from the data and replaced the standard Normal critical value $z^* = 1.960$ by the t critical value $t^* = 2.110$.

The one-sample t confidence interval has the form

$$\text{estimate} \pm t^* \text{SE}_{\text{estimate}}$$

where "SE" stands for "standard error." We will meet a number of confidence intervals that have this common form. In Example 18.2, the estimate is the sample mean $\bar{x}$, and its standard error is

$$\text{SE}_{\bar{x}} = \frac{s}{\sqrt{n}}$$

$$= \frac{8.324}{\sqrt{18}} = 1.962$$

Software will find $\bar{x}$, s, $\text{SE}_{\bar{x}}$, and the confidence interval from the data. Figure 18.5 (page 442) displays typical software output for Example 18.2.

APPLY YOUR KNOWLEDGE

18.5 **Critical values.** What critical value t^* from Table C would you use for a confidence interval for the mean of the population in each of the following situations?

(a) A 95% confidence interval based on $n = 10$ observations.

(b) A 99% confidence interval from an SRS of 20 observations.

(c) An 80% confidence interval from a sample of size 7.

18.6 **The conductivity of glass.** How well materials conduct heat matters when designing houses, for example. Conductivity is measured in terms of watts of heat power transmitted per square meter of surface per degree Celsius of temperature difference on the two sides of the material. In these units, glass has conductivity about 1. The National Institute of Standards and Technology provides exact data on properties of materials. Here are 11 measurements of the heat conductivity of a particular type of glass:[4]

1.11   1.07   1.11   1.07   1.12   1.08   1.08   1.18   1.18   1.18   1.12

(a) We can consider this an SRS of all specimens of glass of this type. Make a stemplot. Is there any sign of major deviation from Normality?

(b) Give a 95% confidence interval for the mean conductivity.

(c) Use your interval to do a test: is there significant evidence at the 5% level that the mean conductivity of this type of glass is not 1?

18.7 **Ancient air.** The composition of the earth's atmosphere may have changed over time. To try to discover the nature of the atmosphere long ago, we can examine the gas in bubbles inside ancient amber. Amber is tree resin that has hardened and been trapped in rocks. The gas in bubbles within amber should be a sample of the atmosphere at the time the amber was formed. Measurements on specimens of amber from the late Cretaceous era (75 to 95 million years ago) give these percents of nitrogen:[5]

David Sanger Photography/Alamy

> 63.4   65.0   64.4   63.3   54.8   64.5   60.8   49.1   51.0

Assume (this is not yet agreed on by experts) that these observations are an SRS from the late Cretaceous atmosphere. Use a 90% confidence interval to estimate the mean percent of nitrogen in ancient air. Follow the four-step process as illustrated in Example 18.2.

The one-sample *t* test

Like the confidence interval, the *t* test is very similar to the *z* test we met earlier.

THE ONE-SAMPLE *t* TEST

Draw an SRS of size n from a large population having unknown mean μ. To **test the hypothesis** $H_0: \mu = \mu_0$, compute the **one-sample *t* statistic**

$$t = \frac{\bar{x} - \mu_0}{s/\sqrt{n}}$$

In terms of a variable T having the $t(n-1)$ distribution, the *P*-value for a test of H_0 against

$H_a: \mu > \mu_0$ is $P(T \geq t)$
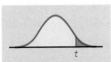

$H_a: \mu < \mu_0$ is $P(T \leq t)$
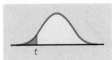

$H_a: \mu \neq \mu_0$ is $2P(T \geq |t|)$
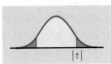

These *P*-values are exact if the population distribution is Normal and are approximately correct for large n in other cases.

STEP

EXAMPLE 18.3 Sweetening colas

Here is a more realistic analysis of the cola-sweetening example from Chapter 15. We follow the four-step process for a significance test, outlined on page 372.

STATE: Cola makers test new recipes for loss of sweetness during storage. Trained tasters rate the sweetness before and after storage. Here are the sweetness losses (sweetness before storage minus sweetness after storage) found by 10 tasters for one new cola recipe:

$$2.0 \quad 0.4 \quad 0.7 \quad 2.0 \quad -0.4 \quad 2.2 \quad -1.3 \quad 1.2 \quad 1.1 \quad 2.3$$

Are these data good evidence that the cola lost sweetness?

FORMULATE: Tasters vary in their perception of sweetness loss. So we ask the question in terms of the mean loss μ for a large population of tasters. The null hypothesis is "no loss," and the alternative hypothesis says "there is a loss."

$$H_0: \mu = 0$$
$$H_a: \mu > 0$$

SOLVE: First check the conditions for inference. As before, we are willing to regard these 10 carefully trained tasters as an SRS from a large population of all trained tasters. Figure 18.3 is a stemplot of the data. We can't judge Normality from just 10 observations; there are no outliers but the data are somewhat skewed. P-values for the t test may be only approximately accurate.

The basic statistics are

$$\overline{x} = 1.02 \quad \text{and} \quad s = 1.196$$

The one-sample t statistic is

$$t = \frac{\overline{x} - \mu_0}{s/\sqrt{n}} = \frac{1.02 - 0}{1.196/\sqrt{10}}$$
$$= 2.697$$

The P-value for $t = 2.697$ is the area to the right of 2.697 under the t distribution curve with degrees of freedom $n - 1 = 9$. Figure 18.4 shows this area. Software (see Figure 18.6) tells us that $P = 0.0123$.

```
-1 | 3
-0 | 4
 0 | 4 7
 1 | 1 2
 2 | 0 0 2 3
```

FIGURE 18.3 Stemplot of the sweetness losses in Example 18.3.

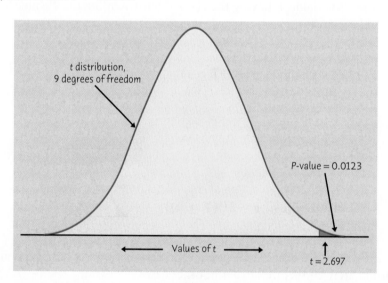

FIGURE 18.4 The P-value for the one-sided t test in Example 18.3.

Without software, we can pin P between two values by using Table C. Search the $df = 9$ row of Table C for entries that bracket $t = 2.697$. The observed t lies between the critical values for one-sided P-values 0.01 and 0.02.

CONCLUDE: There is quite strong evidence ($P < 0.02$) for a loss of sweetness.

df = 9

t^*	2.398	2.821
P	.02	.01

APPLY YOUR KNOWLEDGE

18.8 Is it significant? The one-sample t statistic for testing

$$H_0: \mu = 0$$
$$H_a: \mu > 0$$

from a sample of $n = 15$ observations has the value $t = 1.82$.

(a) What are the degrees of freedom for this statistic?

(b) Give the two critical values t^* from Table C that bracket t. What are the one-sided P-values for these two entries?

(c) Is the value $t = 1.82$ significant at the 5% level? Is it significant at the 1% level?

18.9 Is it significant? The one-sample t statistic from a sample of $n = 25$ observations for the two-sided test of

$$H_0: \mu = 64$$
$$H_a: \mu \neq 64$$

has the value $t = 1.12$.

(a) What are the degrees of freedom for t?

(b) Locate the two critical values t^* from Table C that bracket t. What are the two-sided P-values for these two entries?

(c) Is the value $t = 1.12$ statistically significant at the 10% level? At the 5% level?

18.10 Ancient air, continued. Do the data of Exercise 18.7 give good reason to think that the percent of nitrogen in the air during the Cretaceous era was quite different from the present 78.1%? Carry out a test of significance, following the four-step process as illustrated in Example 18.3.

4
STEP

Using technology

Any technology suitable for statistics will implement the one-sample t procedures. As usual, you can read and use almost any output now that you know what to look for. Figure 18.5 displays output for the 95% confidence interval of Example 18.2

Texas Instruments TI-83 Plus

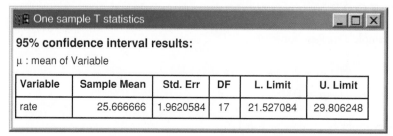

```
TInterval
 (21.527,29.806)
 x=25.6667
 Sx=8.3243
 n=18.0000
```

CrunchIt!

One sample T statistics

95% confidence interval results:

μ : mean of Variable

Variable	Sample Mean	Std. Err	DF	L. Limit	U. Limit
rate	25.666666	1.9620584	17	21.527084	29.806248

Minitab

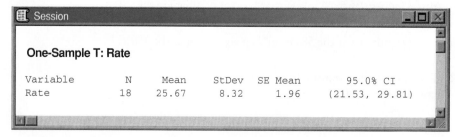

Session

One-Sample T: Rate

```
Variable       N     Mean    StDev   SE Mean      95.0% CI
Rate          18    25.67     8.32      1.96   (21.53, 29.81)
```

Excel

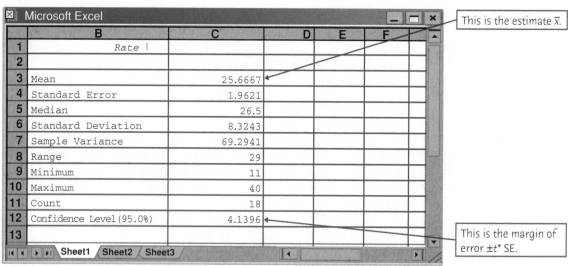

Microsoft Excel

	B	C	D	E	F
1	*Rate*				
2					
3	Mean	25.6667			
4	Standard Error	1.9621			
5	Median	26.5			
6	Standard Deviation	8.3243			
7	Sample Variance	69.2941			
8	Range	29			
9	Minimum	11			
10	Maximum	40			
11	Count	18			
12	Confidence Level(95.0%)	4.1396			
13					

This is the estimate $\bar{x}$.

This is the margin of error $\pm t^*$ SE.

FIGURE 18.5 The t confidence interval of Example 18.2: output from a graphing calculator, two statistical programs, and a spreadsheet program.

Texas Instruments TI-83 Plus

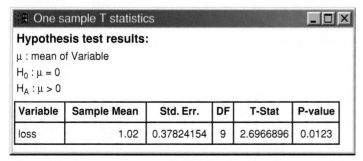

```
T-Test
 μ>0.0000
 t=2.6967
 P=.0123
 x̄=1.0200
 Sx=1.1961
 n=10.0000
```

CrunchIt!

One sample T statistics   _ □ ✕

Hypothesis test results:

μ : mean of Variable

$H_0 : \mu = 0$

$H_A : \mu > 0$

Variable	Sample Mean	Std. Err.	DF	T-Stat	P-value
loss	1.02	0.37824154	9	2.6966896	0.0123

Minitab

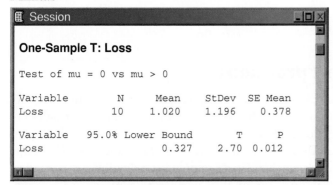

Session   _ □ ✕

One-Sample T: Loss

```
Test of mu = 0 vs mu > 0

Variable        N      Mean    StDev  SE Mean
Loss           10     1.020    1.196    0.378

Variable   95.0% Lower Bound       T       P
Loss                     0.327    2.70   0.012
```

Excel

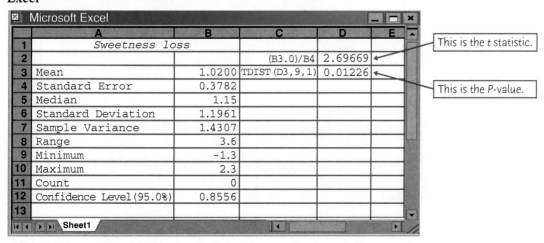

	A	B	C	D	E
1	*Sweetness loss*				
2			(B3.0)/B4	2.69669		← This is the *t* statistic.
3	Mean	1.0200	TDIST(D3,9,1)	0.01226		← This is the *P*-value.
4	Standard Error	0.3782			
5	Median	1.15			
6	Standard Deviation	1.1961			
7	Sample Variance	1.4307			
8	Range	3.6			
9	Minimum	-1.3			
10	Maximum	2.3			
11	Count	0			
12	Confidence Level(95.0%)	0.8556			
13					

FIGURE 18.6 The *t* test of Example 18.3: output from a graphing calculator, two statistical programs, and a spreadsheet program.

from a graphing calculator, two statistical programs, and a spreadsheet program. The TI-83, CrunchIt!, and Minitab outputs are straightforward. All three give the estimate $\overline{x}$ and the confidence interval plus a clearly labeled selection of other information. The confidence interval agrees with our hand calculation in Example 18.2. In general, software results are more accurate because of the rounding in hand calculations. Excel gives several descriptive measures but does not give the confidence interval. The entry labeled "Confidence Level (95.0%)" is the margin of error. You can use this together with $\overline{x}$ to get the interval using either a calculator or the spreadsheet's formula capability.

Figure 18.6 displays output for the t test in Example 18.3. The TI-83, CrunchIt!, and Minitab all give the sample mean $\overline{x}$, the t statistic, and its P-value. Accurate P-values are the biggest advantage of software for the t procedures. Excel is as usual more awkward than software designed for statistics. It lacks a one-sample t test menu selection but does have a function named TDIST for tail areas under t density curves. The Excel output shows functions for the t statistic and its P-value to the right of the main display, along with their values $t = 2.69669$ and $P = 0.01226$.

Matched pairs t procedures

matched pairs design

The study of healing in Example 18.2 estimated the mean healing rate for newts under natural conditions, but the researchers then compared results under several conditions. The taste test in Example 18.3 was a matched pairs study in which the same 10 tasters rated before-and-after sweetness. Comparative studies are more convincing than single-sample investigations. For that reason, one-sample inference is less common than comparative inference. One common design to compare two treatments makes use of one-sample procedures. In a **matched pairs design,** subjects are matched in pairs and each treatment is given to one subject in each pair. Another situation calling for matched pairs is before-and-after observations on the same subjects, as in the taste test of Example 18.3.

> ### MATCHED PAIRS t PROCEDURES
>
> To compare the responses to the two treatments in a matched pairs design, find the difference between the responses within each pair. Then apply the one-sample t procedures to these differences.

The parameter μ in a matched pairs t procedure is the mean difference in the responses to the two treatments within matched pairs of subjects in the entire population.

TABLE 18.1   Average time (seconds) to complete a maze

Subject	Unscented	Scented	Difference	Subject	Unscented	Scented	Difference
1	30.60	37.97	−7.37	12	58.93	83.50	−24.57
2	48.43	51.57	−3.14	13	54.47	38.30	16.17
3	60.77	56.67	4.10	14	43.53	51.37	−7.84
4	36.07	40.47	−4.40	15	37.93	29.33	8.60
5	68.47	49.00	19.47	16	43.50	54.27	−10.77
6	32.43	43.23	−10.80	17	87.70	62.73	24.97
7	43.70	44.57	−0.87	18	53.53	58.00	−4.47
8	37.10	28.40	8.70	19	64.30	52.40	11.90
9	31.17	28.23	2.94	20	47.37	53.63	−6.26
10	51.23	68.47	−17.24	21	53.67	47.00	6.67
11	65.40	51.10	14.30				

EXAMPLE 18.4 *Floral scents and learning*

STATE: We hear that listening to Mozart improves students' performance on tests. In the EESEE case study "Floral Scents and Learning," investigators asked whether pleasant odors have a similar effect. Twenty-one subjects worked a paper-and-pencil maze while wearing a mask. The mask was either unscented or carried a floral scent. The response variable is their average time on three trials. Each subject worked the maze with both masks, in a random order. The randomization is important because subjects tend to improve their times as they work a maze repeatedly. Table 18.1 gives the subjects' average times with both masks. Is there evidence that subjects worked the maze faster wearing the scented mask?

FORMULATE: Take μ to be the mean difference (time unscented minus time scented) in the population of healthy adults. The null hypothesis says that the scents have no effect, and H_a says that unscented times are longer than scented times on the average. So we test the hypotheses

$$H_0: \mu = 0$$

$$H_a: \mu > 0$$

Image State Royalty Free/Alamy

SOLVE: The subjects are not an actual SRS from the population of all healthy adults. But we are willing to regard them as an SRS in their performance on a maze. To analyze the data, subtract the scented time from the unscented time for each subject. The 21 differences form a single sample from the population with unknown mean μ. They appear in the "Difference" column in Table 18.1. Positive differences show that a subject's scented time was shorter than the unscented time. Figure 18.7 is a stemplot of the differences, rounded to the nearest whole second. The distribution is symmetric and reasonably Normal in shape.

The 21 differences have

$$\bar{x} = 0.9567 \quad \text{and} \quad s = 12.5479$$

```
−2 | 5
−1 | 7 1 1
−0 | 8 7 6 4 4 3 1
 0 | 3 4 7 9 9
 1 | 2 4 6 9
 2 | 5
```

FIGURE 18.7 Stemplot of the time differences in Example 18.4.

The one-sample t statistic is therefore

$$t = \frac{\bar{x} - 0}{s/\sqrt{n}} = \frac{0.9567 - 0}{12.5479/\sqrt{21}}$$

$$= 0.349$$

df = 20		
t^*	0.687	0.860
P	.25	.20

Find the P-value from the $t(20)$ distribution. (Remember that the degrees of freedom are 1 less than the sample size.) Table C shows that 0.349 is less than critical value for one-sided $P = 0.25$. The P-value is therefore greater than 0.25. Software gives the value $P = 0.3652$.

CONCLUDE: The data do not support the claim that floral scents improve performance. The average improvement is small, just 0.96 seconds over the 50 seconds that the average subject took when wearing the unscented mask. This small improvement is not statistically significant at even the 25% level.

Example 18.4 illustrates how to turn matched pairs data into single-sample data by taking differences within each pair. We are making inferences about a single population, the population of all differences within matched pairs. *It is incorrect to ignore the matching and analyze the data as if we had two samples, one from subjects who wore unscented masks and a second from subjects who wore scented masks.* Inference procedures for comparing two samples assume that the samples are selected independently of each other. This condition does not hold when the same subjects are measured twice. The proper analysis depends on the design used to produce the data.

APPLY YOUR KNOWLEDGE

Many exercises from this point on ask you to give the P-value of a t test. If you have suitable technology, give the exact P-value. Otherwise, use Table C to give two values between which P lies.

18.11 Does nature heal better? Our bodies have a natural electrical field that is known to help wounds heal. Might higher or lower levels speed healing? A series of experiments with newts investigated this question. In one experiment, the two hind limbs of 14 newts were assigned at random to either experimental or control groups. This is a matched pairs design. The electrical field in the experimental limbs was reduced to half its natural value by applying a voltage. The control limbs were not manipulated. Table 18.2 gives the rates at which new cells closed a razor cut in each limb.[6] Is there good evidence that changing the electrical field from its natural level slows healing?

(a) State hypotheses to be tested. Explain what the parameter μ in your hypotheses stands for.

(b) We are willing to regard these 14 newts, which were randomly assigned from a larger group, as an SRS of all newts of this species. Because the t test uses the differences within matched pairs, these differences must be at least roughly Normal. Make a stemplot of the 14 differences and comment on its shape.

(c) Complete the *Solve* and *Conclude* steps by carrying out the matched pairs t test.

TABLE 18.2 Healing rates (micrometers per hour) for newts

Newt	Experimental limb	Control limb	Newt	Experimental limb	Control limb
1	24	25	8	33	36
2	23	13	9	28	35
3	47	44	10	28	38
4	42	45	11	21	43
5	26	57	12	27	31
6	46	42	13	25	26
7	38	50	14	45	48

18.12 How much better does nature heal? Give a 90% confidence interval for the difference in healing rates (control minus experimental) in Table 18.2.

Robustness of t procedures

The t confidence interval and test are exactly correct when the distribution of the population is exactly Normal. No real data are exactly Normal. The usefulness of the t procedures in practice therefore depends on how strongly they are affected by lack of Normality.

> **ROBUST PROCEDURES**
>
> A confidence interval or significance test is called **robust** if the confidence level or P-value does not change very much when the conditions for use of the procedure are violated.

The condition that the population be Normal rules out outliers, so the presence of outliers shows that this condition is not fulfilled. The t procedures are not robust against outliers unless the sample is very large, because $\bar{x}$ and s are not resistant to outliers.

Fortunately, the t procedures are quite robust against non-Normality of the population except when outliers or strong skewness are present. (Skewness is more serious than other kinds of non-Normality.) As the size of the sample increases, the central limit theorem ensures that the distribution of the sample mean $\bar{x}$ becomes more nearly Normal and that the t distribution becomes more accurate for critical values and P-values of the t procedures.

Always make a plot to check for skewness and outliers before you use the t procedures for small samples. For most purposes, you can safely use the one-sample

Catching cheaters

A certification test for surgeons asks 277 multiple-choice questions. Smith and Jones have 193 common right answers and 53 identical wrong choices. The computer flags their 246 identical answers as evidence of possible cheating. They sue. The court wants to know how unlikely it is that exams this similar would occur just by chance. That is, the court wants a P-value. Statisticians offer several P-values based on different models for the exam-taking process. They all say that results this similar would almost never happen just by chance. Smith and Jones fail the exam.

t procedures when $n \geq 15$ unless an outlier or quite strong skewness is present. Here are practical guidelines for inference on a single mean.[7]

USING THE t PROCEDURES

- Except in the case of small samples, the condition that the data are an SRS from the population of interest is more important than the condition that the population distribution is Normal.

- *Sample size less than 15:* Use t procedures if the data appear close to Normal (roughly symmetric, single peak, no outliers). If the data are skewed or if outliers are present, do not use t.

- *Sample size at least 15:* The t procedures can be used except in the presence of outliers or strong skewness.

- *Large samples:* The t procedures can be used even for clearly skewed distributions when the sample is large, roughly $n \geq 40$.

EXAMPLE 18.5   Can we use t?

Figure 18.8 shows plots of several data sets. For which of these can we safely use the t procedures?[8]

- Figure 18.8(a) is a histogram of the percent of each state's adult residents who are college graduates. *We have data on the entire population of 50 states, so inference is not needed. We can calculate the exact mean for the population. There is no uncertainty due to having only a sample from the population, and no need for a confidence interval or test. If these data were an SRS from a larger population, t inference would be safe despite the mild skewness because* $n = 50$.

- Figure 18.8(b) is a stemplot of the force required to pull apart 20 pieces of Douglas fir. *The data are strongly skewed to the left with possible low outliers, so we cannot trust the t procedures for n = 20.*

- Figure 18.8(c) is a stemplot of the lengths of 23 specimens of the red variety of the tropical flower *Heliconia*. *The histogram is mildly skewed to the right and there are no outliers. We can use the t distributions for such data.*

- Figure 18.8(d) is a histogram of the heights of the students in a college class. *This distribution is quite symmetric and appears close to Normal. We can use the t procedures for any sample size.*

APPLY YOUR KNOWLEDGE

18.13 **An outlier strikes.** Table 18.3 (page 450) gives data for another experiment from the study of healing rates in newts. The setup is exactly as in Exercise 18.11, except that the electrical field in the experimental limbs was reduced to zero by applying a voltage.

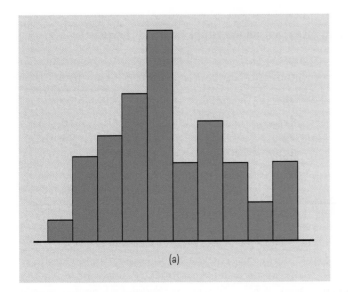

(a)

```
23 | 0
24 | 0
25 |
26 | 5
27 |
28 | 7
29 |
30 | 2 5 9
31 | 3 9 9
32 | 0 3 3 6 7 7
33 | 0 2 3 6
```
(b)

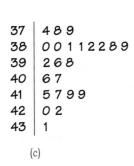

```
37 | 4 8 9
38 | 0 0 1 1 2 2 8 9
39 | 2 6 8
40 | 6 7
41 | 5 7 9 9
42 | 0 2
43 | 1
```
(c)

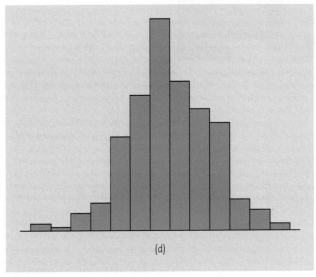

(d)

FIGURE 18.8 Can we use *t* procedures for these data? **(a)** Percent of adult college graduates in the 50 states. *No,* this is an entire population, not a sample. **(b)** Force required to pull apart 20 pieces of Douglas fir. *No,* there are just 20 observations and strong skewness. **(c)** Lengths of 23 tropical flowers of the same variety. *Yes,* the sample is large enough to overcome the mild skewness. **(d)** Heights of college students. *Yes, for any size sample,* because the distribution is close to Normal.

(a) Make a stemplot of the differences between limbs of the same newt (control limb minus experimental limb). There is a high outlier.

(b) Carry out two *t* tests to see if the mean healing rate is significantly higher in the control limbs, one including all 12 newts and another that omits the outlier. What are the test statistics and their *P*-values? Does the outlier have a strong influence on your conclusion?

TABLE 18.3   Healing rates (micrometers per hour) for newts

Newt	Experimental limb	Control limb	Newt	Experimental limb	Control limb
1	28	36	7	45	39
2	31	41	8	25	56
3	27	39	9	28	33
4	33	42	10	33	20
5	33	44	11	47	49
6	38	39	12	23	30

David Grossman/The Image Works

18.14 Reading scores in Atlanta. The Trial Urban District Assessment (TUDA) is a government-sponsored study of student achievement in large urban school districts. TUDA gives a reading test scored from 0 to 500. A score of 243 is a "basic" reading level and a score of 281 is "proficient." Scores for a random sample of 1470 eighth-graders in Atlanta had $\bar{x} = 240$ with standard error 1.1.[9]

(a) We don't have the 1470 individual scores, but use of the t procedures is surely safe. Why?

(b) Give a 99% confidence interval for the mean score of all Atlanta eighth-graders. (Be careful: the report gives the standard error of $\bar{x}$, not the standard deviation s.)

(c) Urban children often perform below the basic level. Is there good evidence that the mean for all Atlanta eighth-graders is less than the basic level?

CHAPTER 18 SUMMARY

Tests and confidence intervals for the mean μ of a Normal population are based on the sample mean $\bar{x}$ of an SRS. Because of the central limit theorem, the resulting procedures are approximately correct for other population distributions when the sample is large.

The standardized sample mean is the **one-sample z statistic**

$$z = \frac{\bar{x} - \mu}{\sigma/\sqrt{n}}$$

If we knew σ, we would use the z statistic and the standard Normal distribution. In practice, we do not know σ. Replace the standard deviation $\sigma/\sqrt{n}$ of $\bar{x}$ by the **standard error** $s/\sqrt{n}$ to get the **one-sample t statistic**

$$t = \frac{\bar{x} - \mu}{s/\sqrt{n}}$$

The t statistic has the **t distribution** with $n - 1$ degrees of freedom.

There is a t distribution for every positive **degrees of freedom.** All are symmetric distributions similar in shape to the standard Normal distribution. The

t distribution approaches the $N(0, 1)$ distribution as the degrees of freedom increase.

A level C **confidence interval for the mean** μ of a Normal population is

$$\bar{x} \pm t^* \frac{s}{\sqrt{n}}$$

The **critical value** t^* is chosen so that the t curve with $n - 1$ degrees of freedom has area C between $-t^*$ and t^*.

Significance tests for H_0: $\mu = \mu_0$ are based on the t statistic. Use P-values or fixed significance levels from the $t(n - 1)$ distribution.

Use these one-sample procedures to analyze **matched pairs** data by first taking the difference within each matched pair to produce a single sample.

The t procedures are quite **robust** when the population is non-Normal, especially for larger sample sizes. The t procedures are useful for non-Normal data when $n \geq 15$ unless the data show outliers or strong skewness.

CHECK YOUR SKILLS

18.15 We prefer the t procedures to the z procedures for inference about a population mean because

(a) z can be used only for large samples.

(b) z requires that you know the population standard deviation σ.

(c) z requires that you can regard your data as an SRS from the population.

18.16 You are testing H_0: $\mu = 10$ against H_a: $\mu < 10$ based on an SRS of 20 observations from a Normal population. The data give $\bar{x} = 8$ and $s = 4$. The value of the t statistic is

(a) -0.5.   (b) -10.   (c) -2.24.

18.17 You are testing H_0: $\mu = 10$ against H_a: $\mu < 10$ based on an SRS of 20 observations from a Normal population. The t statistic is $t = -2.25$. The degrees of freedom for this statistic are

(a) 19.   (b) 20.   (c) 21.

18.18 The P-value for the statistic in the previous exercise

(a) falls between 0.01 and 0.02.

(b) falls between 0.02 and 0.04.

(c) is greater than 0.25.

18.19 You have an SRS of 15 observations from a Normally distributed population. What critical value would you use to obtain a 98% confidence interval for the mean μ of the population?

(a) 2.326   (b) 2.602   (c) 2.624

18.20 You are testing H_0: $\mu = 0$ against H_a: $\mu \neq 0$ based on an SRS of 15 observations from a Normal population. What values of the t statistic are statistically significant at the $\alpha = 0.005$ level?

(a) $t < -3.326$ or $t > 3.326$ (b) $t < -3.286$ or $t > 3.286$ (c) $t > 2.977$

18.21 You are testing H_0: $\mu = 0$ against H_a: $\mu > 0$ based on an SRS of 15 observations from a Normal population. What values of the t statistic are statistically significant at the $\alpha = 0.005$ level?

(a) $t < -3.326$ or $t > 3.326$ (b) $t > 2.947$ (c) $t > 2.977$

18.22 Data on the blood cholesterol levels of 6 rats (milligrams per deciliter of blood) give $\bar{x} = 85$ and $s = 12$. A 95% confidence interval for the mean blood cholesterol of rats under this condition is

(a) 72.4 to 97.6.   (b) 73.0 to 97.0.   (c) 75.4 to 94.6.

18.23 Which of these settings does *not* allow use of a matched pairs t procedure?

(a) You interview both the husband and the wife in 64 married couples and ask each about their ideal number of children.

(b) You interview a sample of 64 unmarried male students and another sample of 64 unmarried female students and ask each about their ideal number of children.

(c) You interview 64 female students in their freshman year and again in their senior year and ask each about their ideal number of children.

18.24 Because the t procedures are robust, the most important condition for their safe use is that

(a) the population standard deviation σ is known.

(b) the population distribution is exactly Normal.

(c) the data can be regarded as an SRS from the population.

CHAPTER 18 EXERCISES

18.25 Read carefully. You read in the report of a psychology experiment that, "Separate analyses for our two groups of 12 participants revealed no overall placebo effect for our student group (mean = 0.08, SD = 0.37, $t(11) = 0.49$) and a significant effect for our non-student group (mean = 0.35, SD = 0.37, $t(11) = 3.25$, $p < 0.01$)."[10] What are the correct values of the two t statistics based on the means and standard deviations? (The null hypothesis is that the mean effect is zero.) Compare each correct t-value with the critical values in Table C. What can you say about the two-sided P-value in each case?

18.26 Alcohol in wine. The alcohol content of wine depends on the grape variety, the way in which the wine is produced from the grapes, the weather, and other influences. Here are data on the percent of alcohol in wine produced from the same grape variety in the same year by 48 winemakers in the same region of Italy:[11]

12.86	12.88	12.81	12.70	12.51	12.60	12.25	12.53	13.49	12.84
12.93	13.36	13.52	13.62	12.25	13.16	13.88	12.87	13.32	13.08
13.50	12.79	13.11	13.23	12.58	13.17	13.84	12.45	14.34	13.48
12.36	13.69	12.85	12.96	13.78	13.73	13.45	12.82	13.58	13.40
12.20	12.77	14.16	13.71	13.40	13.27	13.17	14.13		

(a) Make a histogram of the data, using class width 0.25. The shape of the distribution is a bit irregular, but there are no outliers or strong skewness. There is no reason to avoid use of t procedures for $n = 48$.

(b) Give a 95% confidence interval for the mean alcohol content of wine of this type.

(c) Based on your confidence interval, is the mean alcohol content significantly different at the $\alpha = 0.05$ level from 12%? From 13%?

18.27 Sharks. Great white sharks are big and hungry. Here are the lengths in feet of 44 great whites:[12]

18.7	12.3	18.6	16.4	15.7	18.3	14.6	15.8	14.9	17.6	12.1
16.4	16.7	17.8	16.2	12.6	17.8	13.8	12.2	15.2	14.7	12.4
13.2	15.8	14.3	16.6	9.4	18.2	13.2	13.6	15.3	16.1	13.5
19.1	16.2	22.8	16.8	13.6	13.2	15.7	19.7	18.7	13.2	16.8

David Fleetham/Taxi/Getty Images

(a) Examine these data for shape, center, spread, and outliers. The distribution is reasonably Normal except for one outlier in each direction. Because these are not extreme and preserve the symmetry of the distribution, use of the t procedures is safe with 44 observations.

(b) Give a 95% confidence interval for the mean length of great white sharks. Based on this interval, is there significant evidence at the 5% level to reject the claim "Great white sharks average 20 feet in length"?

(c) Before accepting the conclusions of (b), you need more information about the data. What would you like to know?

18.28 Learning Blissymbols. Blissymbols are pictographs (think of Egyptian hieroglyphics) sometimes used to help learning-disabled children. In a study of computer-assisted learning, 12 normal-ability schoolchildren were assigned at random to each of four computer learning programs. After they used the program, they attempted to recognize 24 Blissymbols. Here are the counts correct for one of the programs:[13]

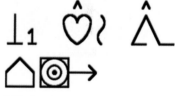

Public Domain

$$12 \quad 22 \quad 9 \quad 14 \quad 20 \quad 15 \quad 9 \quad 10 \quad 11 \quad 11 \quad 15 \quad 6$$

(a) Make a stemplot (split the stems). Are there outliers or strong skewness that would forbid use of the t procedures?

(b) Give a 90% confidence interval for the mean count correct among all children of this age who use the program.

18.29 Worker absenteeism. A study of unexcused absenteeism among factory workers looked at a year's records for 668 workers in an English factory. The mean number of days absent was 9.88 and the standard deviation was 17.847 days.[14] Regard these workers in this year as a random sample of all workers in all years as long as this factory does not change work conditions or worker benefits. What can you say with 99% confidence about the mean number of unexcused absences for all workers?

18.30 A big toe problem. Hallux abducto valgus (call it HAV) is a deformation of the big toe that often requires surgery. Doctors used X-rays to measure the angle (in degrees) of deformity in 38 consecutive patients under the age of 21 who came to a medical center for surgery to correct HAV. The angle is a measure of the seriousness of the deformity. Here are the data:[15]

STEP

28	32	25	34	38	26	25	18	30	26	28	13	20
21	17	16	21	23	14	32	25	21	22	20	18	26
16	30	30	20	50	25	26	28	31	38	32	21	

It is reasonable to regard these patients as a random sample of young patients who require HAV surgery. Carry out the *Solve* and *Conclude* steps of a 95% confidence interval for the mean HAV angle in the population of all such patients.

18.31 Conditions for inference. The number of days absent for a worker in a year cannot be less than 0. The data in Exercise 18.29 have standard deviation much greater than the mean days absent. What does this say about the shape of the distribution of days absent? Why can we nonetheless use a *t* confidence interval for the population mean?

18.32 An outlier's effect. The data in Exercise 18.30 follow a Normal distribution quite closely except for one patient with HAV angle 50 degrees, a high outlier.

(a) Find the 95% confidence interval for the population mean based on the 37 patients who remain after you drop the outlier.

(b) Compare your interval in (a) with your interval from Exercise 18.30. What is the most important effect of removing the outlier?

18.33 Cockroach metabolism. To study the metabolism of insects, researchers fed cockroaches measured amounts of a sugar solution. After 2, 5, and 10 hours, they dissected some of the cockroaches and measured the amount of sugar in various tissues.[16] Five roaches fed the sugar D-glucose and dissected after 10 hours had the following amounts (in micrograms) of D-glucose in their hindguts:

55.95   68.24   52.73   21.50   23.78

Martin Dohrn/Photo Researchers

The researchers gave a 95% confidence interval for the mean amount of D-glucose in cockroach hindguts under these conditions. The insects are a random sample from a uniform population grown in the laboratory. We therefore expect responses to be Normal. What confidence interval did the researchers give?

18.34 Growing trees faster. The concentration of carbon dioxide (CO_2) in the atmosphere is increasing rapidly due to our use of fossil fuels. Because plants use CO_2 to fuel photosynthesis, more CO_2 may cause trees and other plants to grow faster. An elaborate apparatus allows researchers to pipe extra CO_2 to a 30-meter circle of forest. They selected two nearby circles in each of three parts of a pine forest and randomly chose one of each pair to receive extra CO_2. The response variable is the mean increase in base area for 30 to 40 trees in a circle during a growing season. We measure this in percent increase per year. Here are one year's data:[17]

Pair	Control plot	Treated plot
1	9.752	10.587
2	7.263	9.244
3	5.742	8.675

(a) State the null and alternative hypotheses. Explain clearly why the investigators used a one-sided alternative.

(b) Carry out a test and report your conclusion in simple language.

(c) The investigators used the test you just carried out. Any use of the *t* procedures with samples this size is risky. Why?

18.35 Fungus in the air. The air in poultry-processing plants often contains fungus spores. Inadequate ventilation can affect the health of the workers. The problem is most serious during the summer. To measure the presence of spores, air samples are pumped to an agar plate and "colony forming units (CFUs)" are counted after an incubation period. Here are data from two locations in a plant that processes 37,000 turkeys per day, taken on four days in the summer. The units are CFUs per cubic meter of air.[18]

	Day 1	Day 2	Day 3	Day 4
Kill room	3175	2526	1763	1090
Processing	529	141	362	224

(a) Explain carefully why these are matched pairs data.

(b) The spore count is clearly higher in the kill room. Give sample means and a 90% confidence interval to estimate how much higher. Be sure to state your conclusion in plain English.

(c) You will often see the t procedures used for data like these. You should regard the results as only rough approximations. Why?

18.36 Calcium and blood pressure. In a randomized comparative experiment on the effect of calcium in the diet on blood pressure, researchers divided 54 healthy white males at random into two groups. One group received calcium; the other, a placebo. At the beginning of the study, the researchers measured many variables on the subjects. The paper reporting the study gives $\bar{x} = 114.9$ and $s = 9.3$ for the seated systolic blood pressure of the 27 members of the placebo group.

(a) Give a 95% confidence interval for the mean blood pressure in the population from which the subjects were recruited.

(b) What conditions for the population and the study design are required by the procedure you used in (a)? Which of these conditions are important for the validity of the procedure in this case?

18.37 The placebo effect. The placebo effect is particularly strong in patients with Parkinson's disease. To understand the workings of the placebo effect, scientists measure activity at a key point in the brain when patients receive a placebo that they think is an active drug and also when no treatment is given.[19] The same six patients are measured both with and without the placebo, at different times.

(a) Explain why the proper procedure to compare the mean response to placebo with control (no treatment) is a matched pairs t test.

(b) The six differences (treatment minus control) had $\bar{x} = -0.326$ and $s = 0.181$. Is there significant evidence of a difference between treatment and control?

18.38 How much oil? How much oil wells in a given field will ultimately produce is key information in deciding whether to drill more wells. Following are the estimated total amounts of oil recovered from 64 wells in the Devonian Richmond Dolomite area of the Michigan basin, in thousands of barrels.[20]

21.71	53.2	46.4	42.7	50.4	97.7	103.1	51.9
43.4	69.5	156.5	34.6	37.9	12.9	2.5	31.4
79.5	26.9	18.5	14.7	32.9	196	24.9	118.2
82.2	35.1	47.6	54.2	63.1	69.8	57.4	65.6
56.4	49.4	44.9	34.6	92.2	37.0	58.8	21.3
36.6	64.9	14.8	17.6	29.1	61.4	38.6	32.5
12.0	28.3	204.9	44.5	10.3	37.7	33.7	81.1
12.1	20.1	30.5	7.1	10.1	18.0	3.0	2.0

Take these wells to be an SRS of wells in this area.

(a) Give a 95% t confidence interval for the mean amount of oil recovered from all wells in this area.

(b) Make a graph of the data. The distribution is very skewed, with several high outliers. A computer-intensive method that gives accurate confidence intervals without assuming any specific shape for the distribution gives a 95% confidence interval of 40.28 to 60.32. How does the t interval compare with this? Should the t procedures be used with these data?

Cuboimages srl/Alamy

18.39 **Weeds among the corn.** Velvetleaf is a particularly annoying weed in corn fields. It produces lots of seeds, and the seeds wait in the soil for years until conditions are right. How many seeds do velvetleaf plants produce? Here are counts from 28 plants that came up in a corn field when no herbicide was used:[21]

2450	2504	2114	1110	2137	8015	1623	1531	2008	1716
721	863	1136	2819	1911	2101	1051	218	1711	164
2228	363	5973	1050	1961	1809	130	880		

We would like to give a confidence interval for the mean number of seeds produced by velvetleaf plants. Alas, the t interval can't be safely used for these data. Why not?

*The following exercises ask you to answer questions from data without having the steps outlined as part of the exercise. Follow the **Formulate, Solve,** and **Conclude** steps of the four-step process. The process is illustrated in Examples 18.2, 18.3, and 18.4. It may be helpful to restate in your own words the **State** information given in the exercise.*

18.40 **Natural weed control?** Fortunately, we aren't really interested in the number of seeds velvetleaf plants produce (see Exercise 18.39). The velvetleaf seed beetle feeds on the seeds and might be a natural weed control. Here are the total seeds, seeds infected by the beetle, and percent of seeds infected for 28 velvetleaf plants:

Seeds	2450	2504	2114	1110	2137	8015	1623	1531	2008	1716
Infected	135	101	76	24	121	189	31	44	73	12
Percent	5.5	4.0	3.6	2.2	5.7	2.4	1.9	2.9	3.6	0.7
Seeds	721	863	1136	2819	1911	2101	1051	218	1711	164
Infected	27	40	41	79	82	85	42	0	64	7
Percent	3.7	4.6	3.6	2.8	4.3	4.0	4.0	0.0	3.7	4.3
Seeds	2228	363	5973	1050	1961	1809	130	880		
Infected	156	31	240	91	137	92	5	23		
Percent	7.0	8.5	4.0	8.7	7.0	5.1	3.8	2.6		

Do a complete analysis of the percent of seeds infected by the beetle. Include a 90% confidence interval for the mean percent infected in the population of all velvetleaf plants. Do you think that the beetle is very helpful in controlling the weed? Follow the four-step process as illustrated in Example 18.2.

18.41 Auto crankshafts. Here are measurements (in millimeters) of a critical dimension for 16 auto engine crankshafts:

224.120 224.001 224.017 223.982 223.989 223.961
223.960 224.089 223.987 223.976 223.902 223.980
224.098 224.057 223.913 223.999

The dimension is supposed to be 224 mm and the variability of the manufacturing process is unknown. Is there evidence that the mean dimension is not 224 mm? Do a complete analysis, following the four-step process as illustrated in Example 18.3.

18.42 Mutual-funds performance. Mutual funds often compare their performance with a benchmark provided by an "index" that describes the performance of the class of assets in which the fund invests. For example, the Vanguard International Growth Fund benchmarks its performance against the EAFE (Europe, Australasia, Far East) index. Table 18.4 gives the annual returns (percent) for the fund and the index. Does the fund's performance differ significantly from that of its benchmark?

(a) Explain clearly why the matched pairs t test is the proper choice to answer this question.

(b) Do a complete analysis that answers the question posed. Follow the four-step process as illustrated in Example 18.4.

18.43 Right versus left. The design of controls and instruments affects how easily people can use them. A student project investigated this effect by asking 25 right-handed students to turn a knob (with their right hands) that moved an

TABLE 18.4   A mutual fund versus its benchmark index

Year	Fund return	Index return	Year	Fund return	Index return
1982	5.27	−1.86	1994	0.76	7.78
1983	43.08	23.69	1995	14.89	11.21
1984	−1.02	7.38	1996	14.65	6.05
1985	56.94	56.16	1997	4.12	1.78
1986	56.71	69.44	1998	16.93	20.00
1987	12.48	24.63	1999	26.34	26.96
1988	11.61	28.27	2000	−8.60	−14.17
1989	24.76	10.54	2001	−18.92	−21.44
1990	−12.05	−23.45	2002	−17.79	−15.94
1991	4.74	12.13	2003	34.45	38.59
1992	−5.79	−12.17	2004	18.95	20.25
1993	44.74	32.56	2005	15.00	13.54

TABLE 18.5	Performance times (seconds) using right-hand and left-hand threads				
Subject	Right thread	Left thread	Subject	Right thread	Left thread
1	113	137	14	107	87
2	105	105	15	118	166
3	130	133	16	103	146
4	101	108	17	111	123
5	138	115	18	104	135
6	118	170	19	111	112
7	87	103	20	89	93
8	116	145	21	78	76
9	75	78	22	100	116
10	96	107	23	89	78
11	122	84	24	85	101
12	103	148	25	88	123
13	116	147			

TABLE 18.6	Absorption extent for two versions of a drug	
Subject	Reference drug	Generic drug
15	4108	1755
3	2526	1138
9	2779	1613
13	3852	2254
12	1833	1310
8	2463	2120
18	2059	1851
20	1709	1878
17	1829	1682
2	2594	2613
4	2344	2738
16	1864	2302
6	1022	1284
10	2256	3052
5	938	1287
7	1339	1930
14	1262	1964
11	1438	2549
1	1735	3340
19	1020	3050

indicator by screw action. There were two identical instruments, one with a right-hand thread (the knob turns clockwise) and the other with a left-hand thread (the knob turns counterclockwise). Table 18.5 gives the times in seconds each subject took to move the indicator a fixed distance.[22]

(a) Each of the 25 students used both instruments. Discuss briefly how you would use randomization in arranging the experiment.

(b) The project hoped to show that right-handed people find right-hand threads easier to use. Do an analysis that leads to a conclusion about this issue.

18.44 **Comparing two drugs.** Makers of generic drugs must show that they do not differ significantly from the "reference" drugs that they imitate. One aspect in which drugs might differ is their extent of absorption in the blood. Table 18.6 gives data taken from 20 healthy nonsmoking male subjects for one pair of drugs.[23] This is a matched pairs design. Numbers 1 to 20 were assigned at random to the subjects. Subjects 1 to 10 received the generic drug first, and Subjects 11 to 20 received the reference drug first. In all cases, a washout period separated the two drugs so that the first had disappeared from the blood before the subject took the second. Do the drugs differ significantly in absorption?

18.45 **Practical significance?** Give a 90% confidence interval for the mean time advantage of right-hand over left-hand threads in the setting of Exercise 18.43. Do you think that the time saved would be of practical importance if the task were performed many times—for example, by an assembly-line worker? To help answer this question, find the mean time for right-hand threads as a percent of the mean time for left-hand threads.

Paula Bronstein/Getty Images

Two-Sample Problems

Comparing two populations or two treatments is one of the most common situations encountered in statistical practice. We call such situations *two-sample problems*.

TWO-SAMPLE PROBLEMS

- The goal of inference is to compare the responses to two treatments or to compare the characteristics of two populations.
- We have a separate sample from each treatment or each population.

Two-sample problems

A two-sample problem can arise from a randomized comparative experiment that randomly divides subjects into two groups and exposes each group to a different treatment. Comparing random samples separately selected from two populations is also a two-sample problem. Unlike the matched pairs designs studied earlier, there is no matching of the individuals in the two samples, and the two samples can be of different sizes. Inference procedures for two-sample data differ from those for matched pairs. Here are some typical two-sample problems.

EXAMPLE 19.1 *Two-sample problems*

(a) Does regular physical therapy help lower back pain? A randomized experiment assigned patients with lower back pain to two groups: 142 received an examination and advice from a physical therapist; another 144 received regular physical therapy for up to five weeks. After a year, the change in their level of disability (0% to 100%) was assessed by a doctor who did not know which treatment the patients had received.

(b) A psychologist develops a test that measures social insight. He compares the social insight of female college students with that of male college students by giving the test to a sample of female students and a separate sample of male students.

(c) A bank wants to know which of two incentive plans will most increase the use of its credit cards. It offers each incentive to a random sample of credit card customers and compares the amounts charged during the following six months.

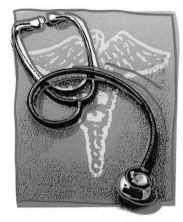

Sounds good—but no comparison

Most women have mammograms to check for breast cancer once they reach middle age. Could a fancier test do a better job of finding cancers early? PET scans are a fancier (and more expensive) test. Doctors used PET scans on 14 women with tumors and got the detailed diagnosis right in 12 cases. That's promising. But there were no controls, and 14 cases are not statistically significant. Medical standards require randomized comparative experiments and statistically significant results. Only then can we be confident that the fancy test really is better.

We may wish to compare either the *centers* or the *spreads* of the two groups in a two-sample setting. This chapter emphasizes the most common inference procedures, those for comparing two population means. We comment briefly on the issue of comparing spreads (standard deviations), where simple inference is much less satisfactory.

APPLY YOUR KNOWLEDGE

Which data design? *Each situation described in Exercises 19.1 to 19.4 requires inference about a mean or means. Identify each as involving (1) a single sample, (2) matched pairs, or (3) two independent samples. The procedures of Chapter 18 apply to designs (1) and (2). We are about to learn procedures for (3).*

19.1 **Looking back on love.** Choose 40 romantically attached couples in their midtwenties. Interview the man and woman separately about a romantic attachment they had at age 15 or 16. Compare the attitudes of men and women.

19.2 **Community service.** Choose a random sample of college students. Use a questionnaire to discover which of the students have ever done volunteer work in the community and which have not. Compare the attitudes of the two groups toward people of other races.

19.3 **Chemical analysis.** To check a new analytical method, a chemist obtains a reference specimen of known concentration from the National Institute of Standards and Technology. She then makes 20 measurements of the concentration of this specimen with the new method and checks for bias by comparing the mean result with the known concentration.

19.4 **Chemical analysis, continued.** Another chemist is checking the same new method. He has no reference specimen, but a familiar analytic method is available. He wants to know if the new and old methods agree. He takes a specimen of unknown concentration and measures the concentration 10 times with the new method and 10 times with the old method.

Comparing two population means

We can examine two-sample data graphically by comparing boxplots, stemplots (for small samples), or histograms (for larger samples). Now we will learn confidence intervals and tests in this setting. When both population distributions are symmetric, and especially when they are at least approximately Normal, a comparison of the mean responses in the two populations is the most common goal of inference. Here are the conditions for inference.

CONDITIONS FOR INFERENCE COMPARING TWO MEANS

- We have **two SRSs,** from two distinct populations. The samples are **independent.** That is, one sample has no influence on the other. Matching violates independence, for example. We measure the same variable for both samples.

- Both populations are **Normally distributed.** The means and standard deviations of the populations are unknown. In practice, it is enough that the distributions have similar shapes and that the data have no strong outliers.

Call the variable we measure x_1 in the first population and x_2 in the second because the variable may have different distributions in the two populations. Here is the notation we will use to describe the two populations:

Population	Variable	Mean	Standard deviation
1	x_1	μ_1	σ_1
2	x_2	μ_2	σ_2

There are four unknown parameters, the two means and the two standard deviations. The subscripts remind us which population a parameter describes. We want to compare the two population means, either by giving a confidence interval for their difference $\mu_1 - \mu_2$ or by testing the hypothesis of no difference, $H_0: \mu_1 = \mu_2$ (the same as $H_0: \mu_1 - \mu_2 = 0$).

We use the sample means and standard deviations to estimate the unknown parameters. Again, subscripts remind us which sample a statistic comes from. Here is the notation that describes the samples:

Population	Sample size	Sample mean	Sample standard deviation
1	n_1	$\overline{x}_1$	s_1
2	n_2	$\overline{x}_2$	s_2

To do inference about the difference $\mu_1 - \mu_2$ between the means of the two populations, we start from the difference $\bar{x}_1 - \bar{x}_2$ between the means of the two samples.

EXAMPLE 19.2 Does polyester decay?

STATE: How quickly do synthetic fabrics such as polyester decay in landfills? A researcher buried polyester strips in the soil for different lengths of time, then dug up the strips and measured the force required to break them. Breaking strength is easy to measure and is a good indicator of decay. Lower strength means the fabric has decayed.

Part of the study buried 10 strips of polyester fabric in well-drained soil in the summer. Five of the strips, chosen at random, were dug up after 2 weeks; the other 5 were dug up after 16 weeks. Here are the breaking strengths in pounds:[1]

Sample 1 (2 weeks)	118	126	126	120	129
Sample 2 (16 weeks)	124	98	110	140	110

We suspect that decay increases over time. Do the data give good evidence that mean breaking strength is less after 16 weeks than after 2 weeks?

FORMULATE: This is a two-sample setting. We want to compare the mean breaking strengths in the entire population of polyester fabric, μ_1 for fabric buried for 2 weeks and μ_2 for fabric buried for 16 weeks. So we will test the hypotheses

$$H_0: \mu_1 = \mu_2$$

$$H_a: \mu_1 > \mu_2$$

SOLVE (FIRST STEPS): Are the conditions for inference met? Because of the randomization, we are willing to regard the two groups of fabric strips as two independent SRSs from large populations of fabric. Although the samples are small, we check for serious non-Normality by examining the data. Figure 19.1 is a back-to-back stemplot of the responses. The 16-week group is much more spread out. As far as we can tell from so few observations, there are no departures from Normality that violate the conditions for comparing two means.

From the data, calculate the summary statistics:

Group	Treatment	n	$\bar{x}$	s
1	2 weeks	5	123.80	4.60
2	16 weeks	5	116.40	16.09

The fabric that was buried longer has somewhat lower mean strength, along with more variation. The observed difference in mean strengths is

$$\bar{x}_1 - \bar{x}_2 = 123.80 - 116.40 = 7.40 \text{ pounds}$$

To complete the *Solve* step, we must learn the details of inference comparing two means.

Stephen Wilkes/Getty Images

2 weeks		16 weeks
	9	8
	10	
8	11	00
9660	12	4
	13	
	14	0

FIGURE 19.1 Back-to-back stemplot of the breaking strength data from Example 19.2.

Two-sample t procedures

To assess the significance of the observed difference between the means of our two samples, we follow a familiar path. Whether an observed difference is surprising depends on the spread of the observations as well as on the two means. Widely different means can arise just by chance if the individual observations vary a great deal. To take variation into account, we would like to standardize the observed difference $\bar{x}_1 - \bar{x}_2$ by dividing by its standard deviation. This standard deviation is

$$\sqrt{\frac{\sigma_1^2}{n_1} + \frac{\sigma_2^2}{n_2}}$$

This standard deviation gets larger as either population gets more variable, that is, as σ_1 or σ_2 increases. It gets smaller as the sample sizes n_1 and n_2 increase.

standard error   Because we don't know the population standard deviations, we estimate them by the sample standard deviations from our two samples. The result is the **standard error,** or estimated standard deviation, of the difference in sample means:

$$\text{SE} = \sqrt{\frac{s_1^2}{n_1} + \frac{s_2^2}{n_2}}$$

two-sample t statistic   When we standardize the estimate by dividing it by its standard error, the result is the **two-sample t statistic:**

$$t = \frac{\bar{x}_1 - \bar{x}_2}{\text{SE}}$$

The statistic t has the same interpretation as any z or t statistic: it says how far $\bar{x}_1 - \bar{x}_2$ is from 0 in standard deviation units.

The two-sample t statistic has approximately a t distribution. It does not have exactly a t distribution even if the populations are both exactly Normal. In practice, however, the approximation is very accurate. There is a catch: the degrees of freedom of the t distribution we want to use are calculated from the data by a somewhat messy formula; moreover, the degrees of freedom need not be a whole number. There are two practical options for using the two-sample t procedures:

Option 1. With software, use the statistic t with accurate critical values from the approximating t distribution.

Option 2. Without software, use the statistic t with critical values from the t distribution with degrees of freedom equal to the smaller of $n_1 - 1$ and $n_2 - 1$. These procedures are always conservative for any two Normal populations.

The two options are exactly the same except for the degrees of freedom used for t critical values and P-values. The Using Technology section (page 470) illustrates how software uses Option 1. Some details of Option 1 appear in the optional section on page 473. We recommend that you use Option 1 unless you are working without software. Here is a description of the Option 2 procedures that includes a statement of just how they are "conservative." The formulas are the same as in Option 1; only the degrees of freedom differ.

THE TWO-SAMPLE *t* PROCEDURES (OPTION 2)

Draw an SRS of size n_1 from a large Normal population with unknown mean μ_1, and draw an independent SRS of size n_2 from another large Normal population with unknown mean μ_2. A level C **confidence interval for $\mu_1 - \mu_2$** is given by

$$(\overline{x}_1 - \overline{x}_2) \pm t^* \sqrt{\frac{s_1^2}{n_1} + \frac{s_2^2}{n_2}}$$

Here t^* is the critical value with area C between $-t^*$ and t^* under the *t* density curve with degrees of freedom equal to the smaller of $n_1 - 1$ and $n_2 - 1$. This critical value gives a conservative margin of error *as large or larger* than is needed for confidence level C, no matter what the population standard deviations may be.

To **test the hypothesis $H_0: \mu_1 = \mu_2$,** calculate the **two-sample *t* statistic**

$$t = \frac{\overline{x}_1 - \overline{x}_2}{\sqrt{\dfrac{s_1^2}{n_1} + \dfrac{s_2^2}{n_2}}}$$

Find *P*-values from the *t* distribution with degrees of freedom equal to the smaller of $n_1 - 1$ and $n_2 - 1$. This distribution gives a conservative *P*-value *equal to or greater than* the true *P*-value, no matter what the population standard deviations may be.

The Option 2 two-sample *t* procedures always err on the safe side. They report *wider* confidence intervals and *higher* *P*-values than the more accurate Option 1 method. As the sample sizes increase, confidence levels and *P*-values from Option 2 become more accurate. The gap between what Option 2 reports and the truth is quite small unless the sample sizes are both small and unequal.[2]

APPLY YOUR KNOWLEDGE ————————

19.5 **Whelks on the Pacific coast.** Published reports of statistical analyses are often very terse. A knowledge of basic statistics helps you decode what you read. In a study of the presence of whelks along the Pacific coast, investigators put down a frame that covers 0.25 square meter and counted the whelks on the sea bottom inside the frame. They did this at 7 locations in California and 6 locations in Oregon. The report says that whelk densities "were twice as high in Oregon as in

Peter Egerton

California (mean $\pm$ SEM, 26.9 ± 1.56 versus 11.9 ± 2.68 whelks per $0.25\ m^2$, Oregon versus California, respectively; Student's t test, $P < 0.001$)."[3]

(a) SEM stands for the standard error of the mean, $s/\sqrt{n}$. Fill in the values in this summary table:

Group	Location	n	$\bar{x}$	s
1	Oregon	?	?	?
2	California	?	?	?

(b) What degrees of freedom would you use in the conservative two-sample t procedures to compare Oregon and California?

19.6 Whom do you trust? Companies often place advertisements to improve the image of their brand rather than to promote specific products. In a randomized comparative experiment, business students read ads that cited either the *Wall Street Journal* or the *National Enquirer* for important facts about a fictitious company. The students then rated the trustworthiness of the source on a 7-point scale. The mean trustworthiness scores were 4.77 for the *Journal* and 2.43 for the *Enquirer*. The two-sample t statistic was $t = 8.37$.[4]

(a) You can draw a conclusion from this t without using a table and even without knowing the sizes of the samples (as long as the samples are not tiny). What is your conclusion? Why don't you need the sample sizes and a table?

(b) In fact, 66 students read the ad citing the *Journal* and 61 read the ad citing the *Enquirer*. What degrees of freedom would you use for the t test if you follow the conservative approach recommended for use without software?

Examples of the two-sample t procedures

STEP

── **EXAMPLE 19.3** Does polyester decay? ──

We can now complete Example 19.2.

SOLVE (INFERENCE): The test statistic for the null hypothesis $H_0: \mu_1 = \mu_2$ is

$$t = \frac{\bar{x}_1 - \bar{x}_2}{\sqrt{\dfrac{s_1^2}{n_1} + \dfrac{s_2^2}{n_2}}}$$

$$= \frac{123.8 - 116.4}{\sqrt{\dfrac{4.60^2}{5} + \dfrac{16.09^2}{5}}}$$

$$= \frac{7.4}{7.484} = 0.9889$$

Software (Option 1) gives one-sided P-value $P = 0.1857$.

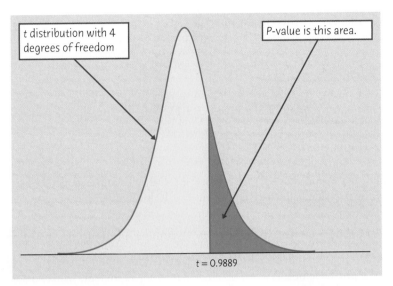

t distribution with 4 degrees of freedom

P-value is this area.

t = 0.9889

FIGURE 19.2 The P-value in Example 19.3. The conservative Option 2 leads to the t distribution with 4 degrees of freedom.

Without software, use the conservative Option 2. Because $n_1 - 1 = 4$ and $n_2 - 1 = 4$, there are 4 degrees of freedom. Because H_a is one-sided on the high side, the P-value is the area to the right of $t = 0.9889$ under the $t(4)$ curve. Figure 19.2 illustrates this P-value. Table C shows that it lies between 0.15 and 0.20.

df = 4

t^*	0.941	1.190
P	.20	.15

CONCLUDE: The experiment did not find convincing evidence that polyester decays more in 16 weeks than in 2 weeks ($P > 0.15$).

Sample size strongly influences the P-value of a test. An effect that fails to be significant at a level α in a small sample may be significant in a larger sample. In the light of the small samples in Example 19.3, we suspect that more data might show that longer burial time does significantly reduce strength. Even if significant, however, the reduction may be quite small. Our data suggest that buried polyester decays slowly, as the mean breaking strength dropped only from 123.8 pounds to 116.4 pounds between 2 and 16 weeks. A confidence interval will add a margin of error to this comparison of means.

EXAMPLE 19.4 How much strength is lost?

STEP

FORMULATE: Give a 90% confidence interval for $\mu_1 - \mu_2$, the decrease in mean breaking strength between 2 weeks and 16 weeks in the ground.

SOLVE AND CONCLUDE: As in Example 19.3, the conservative Option 2 uses 4 degrees of freedom. Table C shows that the $t(4)$ critical value is $t^* = 2.132$. We are 90%

confident that $\mu_1 - \mu_2$ lies in the interval

$$(\overline{x}_1 - \overline{x}_2) \pm t^* \sqrt{\frac{s_1^2}{n_1} + \frac{s_2^2}{n_2}}$$

$$= (123.8 - 116.4) \pm 2.132 \sqrt{\frac{4.60^2}{5} + \frac{16.09^2}{5}}$$

$$= 7.40 \pm 15.96$$

$$= -8.56 \text{ to } 23.36$$

Because 0 lies inside the 90% confidence interval, we cannot reject $H_0: \mu_1 = \mu_2$ in favor of the two-sided alternative at the $\alpha = 0.10$ level of significance.

STEP

EXAMPLE 19.5   Community service and attachment to friends

STATE: Do college students who have volunteered for community service work differ from those who have not? A study obtained data from 57 students who had done service work and 17 who had not. One of the response variables was a measure of attachment to friends (roughly, secure relationships), measured by the Inventory of Parent and Peer Attachment. Here are the results:[5]

Group	Condition	n	$\overline{x}$	s
1	Service	57	105.32	14.68
2	No service	17	96.82	14.26

FORMULATE: The investigator had no specific direction for the difference in mind before looking at the data, so the alternative is two-sided. We will test the hypotheses

$$H_0: \mu_1 = \mu_2$$

$$H_a: \mu_1 \neq \mu_2$$

SOLVE: The investigator says that the individual scores, examined separately in the two samples, appear roughly Normal. There is a serious problem with the more important condition that the two samples can be regarded as SRSs from two student populations. We will discuss that after we illustrate the calculations.

The two-sample t statistic is

$$t = \frac{\overline{x}_1 - \overline{x}_2}{\sqrt{\dfrac{s_1^2}{n_1} + \dfrac{s_2^2}{n_2}}}$$

$$= \frac{105.32 - 96.82}{\sqrt{\dfrac{14.68^2}{57} + \dfrac{14.26^2}{17}}}$$

$$= \frac{8.5}{3.9677} = 2.142$$

Software (Option 1) says that the two-sided P-value is $P = 0.0414$.

Meta-analysis

Small samples have large margins of error. Large samples are expensive. Often we can find several studies of the same issue; if we could combine their results, we would have a large sample with a small margin of error. That is the idea of "meta-analysis." Of course, we can't just lump the studies together, because of differences in design and quality. Statisticians have more sophisticated ways of combining the results. Meta-analysis has been applied to issues ranging from the effect of secondhand smoke to whether coaching improves SAT scores.

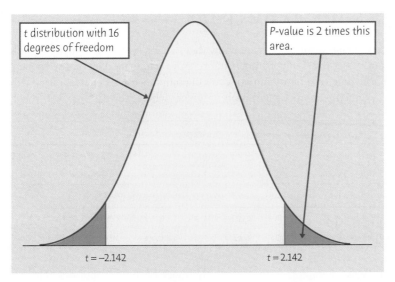

FIGURE 19.3 The *P*-value in Example 19.5. Because the alternative is two-sided, the *P*-value is double the area to the right of $t = 2.142$.

Without software, use Option 2 to find a conservative *P*-value. There are 16 degrees of freedom, the smaller of

$$n_1 - 1 = 57 - 1 = 56 \quad \text{and} \quad n_2 - 1 = 17 - 1 = 16$$

Figure 19.3 illustrates the *P*-value. Find it by comparing 2.142 with the two-sided critical values for the $t(16)$ distribution. Table C shows that the *P*-value is between 0.05 and 0.04.

CONCLUDE: The data give moderately strong evidence ($P < 0.05$) that students who have engaged in community service are on the average more attached to their friends.

df = 16		
t^*	2.120	2.235
P	.025	.02

Is the *t* test in Example 19.5 justified? The student subjects were "enrolled in a course on U.S. Diversity at a large mid-western university." Unless this course is required of all students, the subjects cannot be considered a random sample even from this campus. Students were placed in the two groups on the basis of a questionnaire, 39 in the "no service" group and 71 in the "service" group. The data were gathered from a follow-up survey two years later; 17 of the 39 "no service" students responded (44%), compared with 80% response (57 of 71) in the "service" group. Nonresponse is confounded with group: students who had done community service were much more likely to respond. Finally, 75% of the "service" respondents were women, compared with 47% of the "no service" respondents. Gender, which can strongly affect attachment, is badly confounded with the presence or absence of community service. The data are so far from meeting the SRS condition for inference that the *t* test is meaningless. Difficulties like these are common in social science research, where confounding variables have stronger effects than is usual when biological or physical variables are measured. This researcher honestly disclosed the weaknesses in data production but left it to readers to decide whether to trust her inferences.

APPLY YOUR KNOWLEDGE

19.7 Compressing soil. Farmers know that driving heavy equipment on wet soil compresses the soil and injures future crops. Here are data on the "penetrability" of the same type of soil at two levels of compression.[6] Penetrability is a measure of how much resistance plant roots will meet when they try to grow through the soil.

Compressed soil									
2.86	2.68	2.92	2.82	2.76	2.81	2.78	3.08	2.94	2.86
3.08	2.82	2.78	2.98	3.00	2.78	2.96	2.90	3.18	3.16

Intermediate soil									
3.14	3.38	3.10	3.40	3.38	3.14	3.18	3.26	2.96	3.02
3.54	3.36	3.18	3.12	3.86	2.92	3.46	3.44	3.62	4.26

(a) Make stemplots to investigate the shape of the distributions. The penetrabilities for intermediate soil are skewed to the right and have a high outlier. Returning to the source of the data shows that the outlying sample had unusually low soil density, so that it belongs in the "loose soil" class. We are justified in removing the outlier.

(b) We suspect that the penetrability of compressed soil is less than that of intermediate soil. Do the data (with the outlier removed) support this suspicion?

19.8 Logging in the rain forest. "Conservationists have despaired over destruction of tropical rain forest by logging, clearing, and burning." These words begin a report on a statistical study of the effects of logging in Borneo.[7] Here are data on the number of tree species in 12 unlogged forest plots and 9 similar plots logged 8 years earlier:

Unlogged	22	18	22	20	15	21	13	13	19	13	19	15
Logged	17	4	18	14	18	15	15	10	12			

(a) The study report says, "Loggers were unaware that the effects of logging would be assessed." Why is this important? The study report also explains why the plots can be considered to be randomly assigned.

(b) Does logging significantly reduce the mean number of species in a plot after 8 years? Follow the four-step process as illustrated in Examples 19.2 and 19.3.

19.9 Compressing soil, continued. Use the data in Exercise 19.7, omitting the outlier, to give a 95% confidence interval for the decrease in penetrability of compressed soil relative to intermediate soil.

19.10 Logging in the rain forest, continued. Use the data in Exercise 19.8 to give a 90% confidence interval for the difference in mean number of species between unlogged and logged plots.

Using technology

Software should use Option 1 for the degrees of freedom to give accurate confidence intervals and *P*-values. Unfortunately, there is variation in how well software implements Option 1. Figure 19.4 displays output from a graphing calculator, two statistical programs, and a spreadsheet program for the test and 90% confidence interval of Examples 19.3 and 19.4. All four claim to use Option 1.

Texas Instruments TI-83 Plus

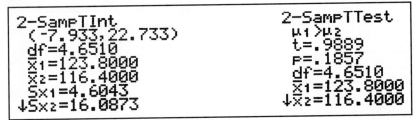

CrunchIt!

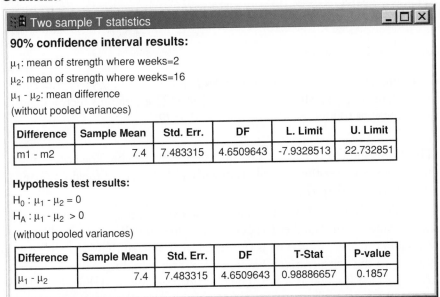

Two sample T statistics

90% confidence interval results:

μ_1: mean of strength where weeks=2
μ_2: mean of strength where weeks=16
$\mu_1 - \mu_2$: mean difference
(without pooled variances)

Difference	Sample Mean	Std. Err.	DF	L. Limit	U. Limit
m1 - m2	7.4	7.483315	4.6509643	-7.9328513	22.732851

Hypothesis test results:

$H_0 : \mu_1 - \mu_2 = 0$
$H_A : \mu_1 - \mu_2 > 0$

(without pooled variances)

Difference	Sample Mean	Std. Err.	DF	T-Stat	P-value
$\mu_1 - \mu_2$	7.4	7.483315	4.6509643	0.98886657	0.1857

Minitab

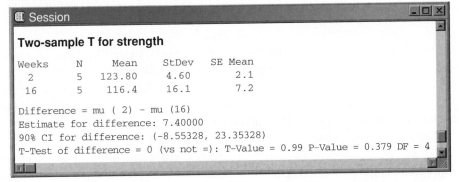

Two-sample T for strength

Weeks	N	Mean	StDev	SE Mean
2	5	123.80	4.60	2.1
16	5	116.4	16.1	7.2

Difference = mu (2) − mu (16)
Estimate for difference: 7.40000
90% CI for difference: (−8.55328, 23.35328)
T-Test of difference = 0 (vs not =): T-Value = 0.99 P-Value = 0.379 DF = 4

FIGURE 19.4 The two-sample t procedures applied to the polyester decay data: output from a graphing calculator, two statistical programs, and a spreadsheet program (*continued*).

Excel

	A	B	C
1	t-Test: Two-Sample Assuming Unequal Variances		
2			
3		*2 weeks*	*16 weeks*
4	Mean	123.8	116.4
5	Variance	21.2	258.8
6	Observations	5	5
7	Hypothesized Mean Difference	0	
8	df	5	
9	t Stat	0.9889	
10	P(T<=t) one-tail	0.1841	
11	t Critical one-tail	2.0150	
12	P(T<=t) Two-tail	0.3681	
13	t Critical two-tail	2.5706	
14			

Sheet1   Sheet2

FIGURE 19.4 (*continued*)

The two-sample t statistic is exactly as in Example 19.3, $t = 0.9889$. You can find this in all four outputs (Minitab rounds to 0.99). The different technologies use different methods to find the P-value for $t = 0.9889$.

- The TI-83 and CrunchIt! get Option 1 completely right. The accurate approximation uses the t distribution with 4.65 degrees of freedom. The P-value is $P = 0.1857$.

- Minitab uses Option 1, but it truncates the exact degrees of freedom to the next smaller whole number to get critical values and P-values. In this example, the exact df $= 4.65$ is truncated to df $= 4$, so that Minitab's results agree with the conservative Option 2 except for rounding. Minitab reports the two-sided P-value as 0.379. The one-sided value is half that, $P = 0.1895$.

- Excel rounds the exact degrees of freedom to the nearest whole number, so that df $= 4.65$ becomes df $= 5$. Excel's P-value $P = 0.1841$ is therefore slightly smaller than is correct. *Because Excel suggests that the evidence against H_0 is stronger than is actually the case, its output is a bit misleading.*

Excel's label for the test, "Two-Sample Assuming Unequal Variances," is seriously misleading. *The two-sample t procedures we have described work whether or not the two populations have the same variance.* There is an old-fashioned special procedure that works only when the two variances are equal. We discuss this method in an optional section on page 476, but you should never use it.

Technology gave us three P-values: 0.1841, 0.1857, and 0.1895. $P = 0.1857$ from df $= 4.65$ is accurate; the other two differ slightly because they are based on whole-number degrees of freedom, df $= 4$ and df $= 5$. In practice, just accept what your technology says. The small differences in P don't affect the conclusion. Even "between 0.15 and 0.20" from Table C is close enough for practical purposes.

Robustness again

The two-sample *t* procedures are more robust than the one-sample *t* methods, particularly when the distributions are not symmetric. When the sizes of the two samples are equal and the two populations being compared have distributions with similar shapes, probability values from the *t* table are quite accurate for a broad range of distributions when the sample sizes are as small as $n_1 = n_2 = 5$.[8] When the two population distributions have different shapes, larger samples are needed.

As a guide to practice, adapt the guidelines given on page 448 for the use of one-sample *t* procedures to two-sample procedures by replacing "sample size" with the "sum of the sample sizes," $n_1 + n_2$. These guidelines err on the side of safety, especially when the two samples are of equal size. *In planning a two-sample study, choose equal sample sizes whenever possible. The two-sample t procedures are most robust against non-Normality in this case, and the conservative probability values are most accurate.*

CAUTION

APPLY YOUR KNOWLEDGE

19.11 Bone loss by nursing mothers. Exercise 2.36 (page 60) gives the percent change in the mineral content of the spine for 47 mothers during three months of nursing a baby and for a control group of 22 women of similar age who were neither pregnant nor lactating.

(a) What two populations did the investigators want to compare? We must be willing to regard the women recruited for this observational study as SRSs from these populations.

(b) Do these data give good evidence that the average bone mineral loss is higher in the population of nursing mothers? Complete the *Formulate, Solve,* and *Conclude* steps of the four-step process as illustrated in Examples 19.2 and 19.3.

19.12 Weeds among the corn. Exercise 7.45 (page 184) gives these corn yields (bushels per acre) for experimental plots controlled to have 1 weed per meter of row and 3 weeds per meter of row:

1 weed/meter	166.2	157.3	166.7	161.1
3 weeds/meter	158.6	176.4	153.1	156.0

Explain carefully why a two-sample *t* confidence interval for the difference in mean yields may not be accurate.

Photo Resource Hawaii/Alamy

Details of the *t* approximation*

The exact distribution of the two-sample *t* statistic is not a *t* distribution. Moreover, the distribution changes as the unknown population standard deviations σ_1

---

*This section can be omitted unless you are using software and wish to understand what the software does.

and σ_2 change. However, an excellent approximation is available. We call this Option 1 for t procedures.

APPROXIMATE DISTRIBUTION OF THE TWO-SAMPLE t STATISTIC

The distribution of the two-sample t statistic is very close to the t distribution with degrees of freedom df given by

$$df = \frac{\left(\dfrac{s_1^2}{n_1} + \dfrac{s_2^2}{n_2} \right)^2}{\dfrac{1}{n_1 - 1}\left(\dfrac{s_1^2}{n_1} \right)^2 + \dfrac{1}{n_2 - 1}\left(\dfrac{s_2^2}{n_2} \right)^2}$$

This approximation is accurate when both sample sizes n_1 and n_2 are 5 or larger.

The t procedures remain exactly as before except that we use the t distribution with df degrees of freedom to give critical values and P-values.

EXAMPLE 19.6   Does polyester decay? ━━━━━━━━

In the experiment of Examples 19.2 and 19.3, the data on buried polyester fabric gave

Group	Treatment	n	$\bar{x}$	s
1	2 weeks	5	123.80	4.60
2	16 weeks	5	116.40	16.09

The two-sample t test statistic calculated from these values is $t = 0.9889$.

The one-sided P-value is the area to the right of 0.9889 under a t density curve, as in Figure 19.2. The conservative Option 2 uses the t distribution with 4 degrees of freedom. Option 1 finds a very accurate P-value by using the t distribution with degrees of freedom df given by

$$df = \frac{\left(\dfrac{4.60^2}{5} + \dfrac{16.09^2}{5} \right)^2}{\dfrac{1}{4}\left(\dfrac{4.60^2}{5} \right)^2 + \dfrac{1}{4}\left(\dfrac{16.09^2}{5} \right)^2}$$

$$= \frac{3137.08}{674.71} = 4.65$$

These degrees of freedom appear in the output from the TI-83 and CrunchIt! in Figure 19.4.

The degrees of freedom df is generally not a whole number. It is always at least as large as the smaller of $n_1 - 1$ and $n_2 - 1$. The larger degrees of freedom that result from Option 1 give slightly shorter confidence intervals and slightly smaller *P*-values than the conservative Option 2 produces. There is a *t* distribution for any positive degrees of freedom, even though Table C contains entries only for whole-number degrees of freedom.

The difference between the *t* procedures using Options 1 and 2 is rarely of practical importance. That is why we recommend the simpler, conservative Option 2 for inference without software. With software, the more accurate Option 1 procedures are painless.

APPLY YOUR KNOWLEDGE

19.13 **DDT poisoning.** In a randomized comparative experiment, researchers compared 6 white rats poisoned with DDT with a control group of 6 unpoisoned rats. Electrical measurements of nerve activity are the main clue to the nature of DDT poisoning. When a nerve is stimulated, its electrical response shows a sharp spike followed by a much smaller second spike. The experiment found that the second spike is larger in rats fed DDT than in normal rats.[9]

The researchers measured the height of the second spike as a percent of the first spike when a nerve in the rat's leg was stimulated. Here are the results:

Poisoned	12.207	16.869	25.050	22.429	8.456	20.589
Unpoisoned	11.074	9.686	12.064	9.351	8.182	6.642

Figure 19.5 shows the CrunchIt! output for the two-sample *t* test. What are $\bar{x}_i$ and s_i for the two samples? Starting from these values, find the *t* test statistic and its degrees of freedom. Your work should agree with Figure 19.5.

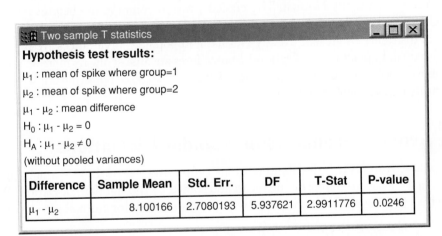

FIGURE 19.5 Two-sample *t* output from CrunchIt! for Exercise 19.13.

19.14 Students' self-concept. A study of the self-concept of seventh-grade students asked if male and female students differ in mean score on the Piers-Harris Children's Self-Concept Scale. Software gave these summary results:[10]

Gender	n	Mean	Std dev	Std err	t	df	P
F	31	55.5161	12.6961	2.2803	-0.8276	62.8	0.4110
M	47	57.9149	12.2649	1.7890			

Starting from the sample means and standard deviations, verify each of these entries: the standard errors of the means; the degrees of freedom for two-sample t; the value of t.

19.15 DDT poisoning, continued. Do poisoned rats differ significantly from unpoisoned rats in the study of Exercise 19.13? Write a summary in a sentence or two, including t, df, P, and a conclusion. Use the output in Figure 19.5.

19.16 Students' self-concept, continued. Write a sentence or two summarizing the comparison of female and male students in Exercise 19.14, as if you were preparing a report for publication. Use the output in Exercise 19.14.

Avoid the pooled two-sample t procedures*

Most software, including all four illustrated in Figure 19.4, offers a choice of two-sample t statistics. One is often labeled for "unequal" variances, the other for "equal" variances. The "unequal" variance procedure is our two-sample t. *This test is valid whether or not the population variances are equal.* The other choice is a special version of the two-sample t statistic that assumes that the two populations have the same variance. This procedure averages (the statistical term is "pools") the two sample variances to estimate the common population variance. The resulting statistic is called the *pooled two-sample t statistic.* It is equal to our t statistic if the two sample sizes are the same, but not otherwise. We could choose to use the pooled t for tests and confidence intervals.

The pooled t statistic has exactly the t distribution with $n_1 + n_2 - 2$ degrees of freedom *if* the two population variances really are equal and the population distributions are exactly Normal. The pooled t was in common use before software made it easy to use Option 1 for our two-sample t statistic. Of course, in the real world distributions are not exactly Normal and population variances are not exactly equal. In practice, the Option 1 t procedures are almost always more accurate than the pooled procedures. Our advice: *Never use the pooled t procedures if you have software that will implement Option 1.*

Avoid inference about standard deviations*

Two basic features of a distribution are its center and spread. In a Normal population, we measure center by the mean and spread by the standard deviation. We use the t procedures for inference about population means for Normal populations,

---

*The remaining sections of this chapter concern optional special topics. They are needed only as background for Chapter 25.

and we know that t procedures are widely useful for non-Normal populations as well. It is natural to turn next to inference about the standard deviations of Normal populations. Our advice here is short and clear: Don't do it without expert advice.

There are methods for inference about the standard deviations of Normal populations. The most common such method is the F test for comparing the spread of two Normal populations. *Unlike the t procedures for means, the F test is extremely sensitive to non-Normal distributions.* This lack of robustness does not improve in large samples. It is difficult in practice to tell whether a significant F-value is evidence of unequal population spreads or simply a sign that the populations are not Normal.

The deeper difficulty underlying the very poor robustness of Normal population procedures for inference about spread already appeared in our work on describing data. The standard deviation is a natural measure of spread for Normal distributions but not for distributions in general. In fact, because skewed distributions have unequally spread tails, no single numerical measure does a good job of describing the spread of a skewed distribution. In summary, the standard deviation is not always a useful parameter, and even when it is (for symmetric distributions), the results of inference are not trustworthy. Consequently, *we do not recommend trying to do inference about population standard deviations in basic statistical practice.*[11]

The F test for comparing two standard deviations*

Because of the limited usefulness of procedures for inference about the standard deviations of Normal distributions, we will describe only one such procedure. Suppose that we have independent SRSs from two Normal populations, a sample of size n_1 from $N(\mu_1, \sigma_1)$ and a sample of size n_2 from $N(\mu_2, \sigma_2)$. The population means and standard deviations are all unknown. The two-sample t test examines whether the means are equal in this setting. To test the hypothesis of equal spread,

$$H_0: \sigma_1 = \sigma_2$$

$$H_a: \sigma_1 \neq \sigma_2$$

we use the ratio of sample variances. This is the F *statistic*.

THE F STATISTIC AND F DISTRIBUTIONS

When s_1^2 and s_2^2 are sample variances from independent SRSs of sizes n_1 and n_2 drawn from large Normal populations, the **F statistic**

$$F = \frac{s_1^2}{s_2^2}$$

has the **F distribution** with $n_1 - 1$ and $n_2 - 1$ degrees of freedom when $H_0: \sigma_1 = \sigma_2$ is true.

CAUTION

The F distributions are a family of distributions with two parameters. The parameters are the degrees of freedom of the sample variances in the numerator and denominator of the F statistic. The numerator degrees of freedom are always mentioned first. *Interchanging the degrees of freedom changes the distribution, so the order is important.* Our brief notation will be $F(\text{df1}, \text{df2})$ for the F distribution with df1 degrees of freedom in the numerator and df2 in the denominator. The F distributions are right-skewed. The density curve in Figure 19.6 illustrates the shape. Because sample variances cannot be negative, the F statistic takes only positive values, and the F distribution has no probability below 0. The peak of the F density curve is near 1. When the two populations have the same standard deviation, we expect the two sample variances to be close in size, so that F takes a value near 1. Values of F far from 1 in either direction provide evidence against the hypothesis of equal standard deviations.

Tables of F critical points are awkward, because we need a separate table for every pair of degrees of freedom df1 and df2. Table D in the back of the book gives upper p critical points of the F distributions for $p = 0.10, 0.05, 0.025, 0.01$, and 0.001. For example, these critical values for the $F(9, 10)$ distribution shown in Figure 19.6 are

p	.10	.05	.025	.01	.001
F^*	2.35	3.02	3.78	4.94	8.96

The skewness of the F distributions causes additional complications. In the symmetric Normal and t distributions, the point with probability 0.05 below it is just the negative of the point with probability 0.05 above it. This is not true for F distributions. We therefore need either tables of both the upper and lower tails or some way to eliminate the need for lower-tail critical values. Software that

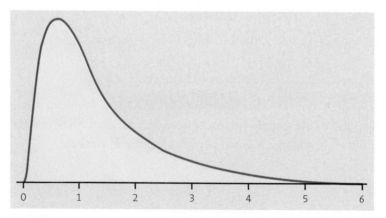

FIGURE 19.6 The density curve for the $F(9, 10)$ distribution. The F distributions are skewed to the right.

does away with the need for tables is very convenient. If you do not use software, arrange the two-sided F test as follows.

CARRYING OUT THE F TEST

Step 1. Take the test statistic to be

$$F = \frac{\text{larger } s^2}{\text{smaller } s^2}$$

This amounts to naming the populations so that Population 1 has the larger of the observed sample variances. The resulting F is always 1 or greater.

Step 2. Compare the value of F with critical values from Table D. Then *double* the significance levels from the table to obtain the significance level for the two-sided F test.

The idea is that we calculate the probability in the upper tail and double it to obtain the probability of all ratios on either side of 1 that are at least as improbable as that observed. Remember that the order of the degrees of freedom is important in using Table D.

EXAMPLE 19.7 *Comparing variability*

STEP

STATE: Example 19.2 describes an experiment to compare the breaking strengths of polyester fabric after being buried for 2 weeks and for 16 weeks. Here are the data summaries:

Group	Treatment	n	$\bar{x}$	s
2	2 weeks	5	123.80	4.60
1	16 weeks	5	116.40	16.09

Does the variability of breaking strengths change when strips are buried for different lengths of time?

FORMULATE: We want to test

$$H_0\text{: } \sigma_1 = \sigma_2$$

$$H_a\text{: } \sigma_1 \neq \sigma_2$$

Note that we relabeled the groups so that Group 1 (16 weeks) has the larger standard deviation.

SOLVE: The F test statistic is

$$F = \frac{\text{larger } s^2}{\text{smaller } s^2} = \frac{16.09^2}{4.60^2} = 12.23$$

Compare the calculated value $F = 12.23$ with critical values for the $F(4, 4)$ distribution. Table D shows that 12.23 lies between the 0.025 and 0.01 critical values of the

$F(4, 4)$ distribution. So the two-sided P-value lies between 0.05 and 0.02. Software gives $P = 0.0326$.

CONCLUDE: The data show significantly unequal spreads ($P < 0.05$). Variation in breaking strength is higher among strips of fabric that have been buried longer. (This conclusion can't be trusted because the F test depends heavily on Normality and we can't assess Normality from such small samples.)

APPLY YOUR KNOWLEDGE

In all exercises calling for use of the F test, assume that both population distributions are very close to Normal. The actual data are sometimes not sufficiently Normal to justify use of the F test.

19.17 F distributions. The F statistic $F = s_1^2/s_2^2$ is calculated from samples of sizes $n_1 = 10$ and $n_2 = 8$. (Remember that n_1 is the numerator sample size.)

(a) What is the upper 5% critical value for this F?

(b) In a test of equality of standard deviations against the two-sided alternative, this statistic has the value $F = 3.45$. Is this value significant at the 10% level? Is it significant at the 5% level?

19.18 F distributions. The F statistic for equality of standard deviations based on samples of sizes $n_1 = 21$ and $n_2 = 16$ takes the value $F = 2.78$.

(a) Is this significant evidence of unequal population standard deviations at the 5% level? At the 1% level?

(b) Between which two values obtained from Table D does the P-value of the test fall?

19.19 Compressing soil. Is there a statistically significant difference between the standard deviations of soil penetrability for compressed and intermediate soils? Use the data in Exercise 19.7, omitting the outlier. Follow the four-step process as illustrated in Example 19.7.

19.20 Logging in the rain forest. Variation in species counts as well as mean counts may be of interest to ecologists. Do the data in Exercise 19.8 give evidence that logging affects the variation in species counts among plots? Follow the four-step process as illustrated in Example 19.7.

19.21 DDT poisoning. The sample variance for the treatment group in the DDT experiment of Exercise 19.13 is more than 10 times as large as the sample variance for the control group. Calculate the F statistic. Can you reject the hypothesis of equal population standard deviations at the 5% significance level? At the 1% level?

CHAPTER 19 SUMMARY

The data in a **two-sample problem** are two independent SRSs, each drawn from a separate population.

Tests and confidence intervals for the difference between the means μ_1 and μ_2 of two Normal populations start from the difference $\overline{x}_1 - \overline{x}_2$ between the two sample means. Because of the central limit theorem, the resulting procedures are approximately correct for other population distributions when the sample sizes are large.

Draw independent SRSs of sizes n_1 and n_2 from two Normal populations with parameters μ_1, σ_1 and μ_2, σ_2. The **two-sample t statistic** is

$$t = \frac{(\bar{x}_1 - \bar{x}_2) - (\mu_1 - \mu_2)}{\sqrt{\dfrac{s_1^2}{n_1} + \dfrac{s_2^2}{n_2}}}$$

The statistic t has approximately a t distribution.

There are two choices for the **degrees of freedom** of the two-sample t statistic. Option 1: software produces accurate probability values using degrees of freedom calculated from the data. Option 2: for conservative inference procedures, use degrees of freedom equal to the smaller of $n_1 - 1$ and $n_2 - 1$.

The **confidence interval for $\mu_1 - \mu_2$** is

$$(\bar{x}_1 - \bar{x}_2) \pm t^* \sqrt{\frac{s_1^2}{n_1} + \frac{s_2^2}{n_2}}$$

The critical value t^* from Option 1 gives a confidence level very close to the desired level C. Option 2 produces a margin of error at least as wide as is needed for the desired level C.

Significance tests for H_0: $\mu_1 = \mu_2$ are based on

$$t = \frac{\bar{x}_1 - \bar{x}_2}{\sqrt{\dfrac{s_1^2}{n_1} + \dfrac{s_2^2}{n_2}}}$$

P-values calculated from Option 1 are very accurate. Option 2 P-values are always at least as large as the true P.

The guidelines for practical use of two-sample t procedures are similar to those for one-sample t procedures. Equal sample sizes are recommended.

Inference procedures for comparing the standard deviations of two Normal populations are based on the **F statistic,** which is the ratio of sample variances

$$F = \frac{s_1^2}{s_2^2}$$

If an SRS of size n_1 is drawn from Population 1 and an independent SRS of size n_2 is drawn from Population 2, the F statistic has the **F distribution** $F(n_1 - 1, n_2 - 1)$ if the two population standard deviations σ_1 and σ_2 are in fact equal.

The F test for $H_0: \sigma_1 = \sigma_2$ and other procedures for inference on the spread of one or more Normal distributions are so strongly affected by lack of Normality that we do not recommend them for regular use.

CHECK YOUR SKILLS

19.22 In 2003, the National Assessment of Educational Progress gave a mathematics test to 4398 eighth-graders in Texas. The mean score was 277 out of 500, with standard error 1.1. To give a confidence interval for the mean score of all Texas eighth-graders, you would use

(a) the one-sample t interval.

(b) the matched pairs t interval.

(c) the two-sample t interval.

19.23 In 2003, the National Assessment of Educational Progress gave a mathematics test to 4398 eighth-graders in Texas. To test whether there is a difference in the mean scores of all female and male eighth-grade students in Texas, you would use

(a) the one-sample t test.

(b) the matched pairs t test.

(c) the two-sample t test.

19.24 There are two common methods for measuring the concentration of a pollutant in fish tissue. Do the two methods differ on the average? You apply both methods to a sample of 18 carp and use

(a) the one-sample t test.

(b) the matched pairs t test.

(c) the two-sample t test.

19.25 A study of the effects of exercise used rats bred to have high or low capacity for exercise. There were 8 high-capacity and 8 low-capacity rats. To compare the mean blood pressure of the two types of rats using the conservative Option 2 t procedures, the correct degrees of freedom is

(a) 7.   (b) 14.   (c) 15.

19.26 The 8 high-capacity rats had mean blood pressure 89 with standard deviation 9; the 8 low-capacity rats had mean blood pressure 105 with standard deviation 13. (Blood pressure is measured in millimeters of mercury.) The two-sample t statistic for comparing the population means has value

(a) 0.5.   (b) 2.86.   (c) 9.65.

19.27 A study of road rage asked samples of 596 men and 523 women about their behavior while driving. Based on their answers, each subject was assigned a road rage score on a scale of 0 to 20. The subjects were chosen by random digit dialing of telephone numbers. Are the conditions for two-sample t inference satisfied?

(a) Maybe: the SRS condition is OK but we need to look at the data to check Normality.

(b) No: scores in a range between 0 and 20 can't be Normal.

(c) Yes: the SRS condition is OK and large sample sizes make the Normality condition unnecessary.

19.28 We suspect that men are more prone to road rage than women. To see if this is true, test these hypotheses for the mean road rage scores of all male and female drivers:

(a) $H_0: \mu_M = \mu_F$ versus $H_a: \mu_M > \mu_F$.

(b) $H_0: \mu_M = \mu_F$ versus $H_a: \mu_M \neq \mu_F$.

(c) $H_0: \mu_M = \mu_F$ versus $H_a: \mu_M < \mu_F$.

19.29 The two-sample t statistic for the road rage study (male mean minus female mean) is $t = 3.18$. The P-value for testing the hypotheses from the previous exercise satisfies

(a) $0.001 < P < 0.005$.   (b) $0.0005 < P < 0.001$.   (c) $0.001 < P < 0.002$.

CHAPTER 19 EXERCISES

In exercises that call for two-sample t procedures, use Option 1 if you have technology that implements that method. Otherwise, use Option 2 (degrees of freedom the smaller of n_1-1 and n_2-1). Many of these exercises ask you to think about issues of statistical practice as well as to carry out procedures.

19.30 Active versus passive learning. A study of computer-assisted learning examined the learning of "Blissymbols" by children. Blissymbols are pictographs (think of Egyptian hieroglyphs) that are sometimes used to help learning-impaired children communicate. The researcher designed two computer lessons that taught the same content using the same examples. One lesson required the children to interact with the material, while in the other the children controlled only the pace of the lesson. Call these two styles "Active" and "Passive." Children were assigned at random to Active and Passive groups. After the lesson, the computer presented a quiz that asked the children to identify 56 Blissymbols. Here are the numbers of correct identifications by the 24 children in the Active group:[12]

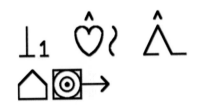

```
29   28   24   31   15   24   27   23   20   22   23   21
24   35   21   24   44   28   17   21   21   20   28   16
```

The 24 children in the Passive group had these counts of correct identifications:

```
16   14   17   15   26   17   12   25   21   20   18   21
20   16   18   15   26   15   13   17   21   19   15   12
```

Is there good evidence that active learning is superior to passive learning? Follow the four-step process as illustrated in Examples 19.2 and 19.3. That is, state hypotheses, make graphs to examine the data, discuss the conditions for inference, carry out a test, and state your conclusion.

19.31 IQ scores for boys and girls. Here are the IQ test scores of 31 seventh-grade girls in a Midwest school district:[13]

```
114   100   104    89   102    91   114   114   103   105
108   130   120   132   111   128   118   119    86    72
111   103    74   112   107   103    98    96   112   112   93
```

The IQ test scores of 47 seventh-grade boys in the same district are

111	107	100	107	115	111	97	112	104	106	113
109	113	128	128	118	113	124	127	136	106	123
124	126	116	127	119	97	102	110	120	103	115
93	123	79	119	110	110	107	105	105	110	77
90	114	106								

(a) Make stemplots or histograms of both sets of data. Because the distributions are reasonably symmetric with no extreme outliers, the *t* procedures will work well.

(b) Treat these data as SRSs from all seventh-grade students in the district. Is there good evidence that girls and boys differ in their mean IQ scores?

19.32 Active versus passive learning, continued.

(a) Use the data in Exercise 19.30 to give a 90% confidence interval for the difference in mean number of Blissymbols identified correctly by children after active and passive lessons.

(b) Give a 90% confidence interval for the mean number of Blissymbols identified correctly by children after the active lesson.

19.33 IQ scores for boys and girls, continued. Use the data in Exercise 19.31 to give a 95% confidence interval for the difference between the mean IQ scores of all boys and girls in the district.

19.34 Students' attitudes. The Survey of Study Habits and Attitudes (SSHA) is a psychological test that measures the motivation, attitude toward school, and study habits of students. Scores range from 0 to 200. A selective private college gives the SSHA to an SRS of both male and female first-year students. The data for the women are as follows:

| 154 | 109 | 137 | 115 | 152 | 140 | 154 | 178 | 101 |
| 103 | 126 | 126 | 137 | 165 | 165 | 129 | 200 | 148 |

Here are the scores of the men:

| 108 | 140 | 114 | 91 | 180 | 115 | 126 | 92 | 169 | 146 |
| 109 | 132 | 75 | 88 | 113 | 151 | 70 | 115 | 187 | 104 |

Most studies have found that the mean SSHA score for men is lower than the mean score in a comparable group of women. Is this true for first-year students at this college? Follow the four-step process as illustrated in Examples 19.2 and 19.3. That is, state hypotheses, make graphs to examine the data, discuss the conditions for inference, carry out a test, and state your conclusion.

19.35 Fungus in the air. The air in poultry-processing plants often contains fungus spores. Inadequate ventilation can affect the health of the workers. The problem is most serious during the summer and least serious during the winter. To measure the presence of spores, air samples are pumped to an agar plate and "colony forming units (CFUs)" are counted after an incubation period. Here are data from the "kill room" of a plant that processes 37,000 turkeys per day, taken on four separate days in the summer and in the winter. The units are CFUs per cubic meter of air.[14]

Summer	3175	2526	1763	1090
Winter	384	104	251	97

Paula Bronstein/Getty Images

The counts are clearly much higher in the summer. Give a 90% confidence interval to estimate how much higher the mean count is during the summer. Follow the four-step process as illustrated in Example 19.4.

Do birds learn to time their breeding? *Blue titmice eat caterpillars. The birds would like lots of caterpillars around when they have young to feed, but they breed earlier than peak caterpillar season. Do the birds learn from one year's experience when they time breeding the next year? Researchers randomly assigned 7 pairs of birds to have the natural caterpillar supply supplemented while feeding their young and another 6 pairs to serve as a control group relying on natural food supply. The next year, they measured how many days after the caterpillar peak the birds produced their nestlings.[15] Exercises 19.36 to 19.38 are based on this experiment.*

Hugh Clark/Frank Lane Picture Agency/ CORBIS

19.36 Did the randomization produce similar groups?   First, compare the two groups in the first year. The only difference should be the chance effect of the random assignment. The study report says: "In the experimental year, the degree of synchronization did not differ between food-supplemented and control females." For this comparison, the report gives $t = -1.05$. What type of t statistic (paired or two-sample) is this? Show that this t leads to the quoted conclusion.

19.37 Did the treatment have an effect?   The investigators expected the control group to adjust their breeding date the next year, whereas the well-fed supplemented group had no reason to change. The report continues: "but in the following year food-supplemented females were more out of synchrony with the caterpillar peak than the controls." Here are the data (days behind the caterpillar peak):

Control	4.6	2.3	7.7	6.0	4.6	−1.2	
Supplemented	15.5	11.3	5.4	16.5	11.3	11.4	7.7

Carry out a t test and show that it leads to the quoted conclusion.

19.38 Year-to-year comparison.   Rather than comparing the two groups in each year, we could compare the behavior of each group in the first and second years. The study report says: "Our main prediction was that females receiving additional food in the nestling period should not change laying date the next year, whereas controls, which (in our area) breed too late in their first year, were expected to advance their laying date in the second year."

Comparing days behind the caterpillar peak in Years 1 and 2 gave $t = 0.63$ for the control group and $t = -2.63$ for the supplemented group. Are these paired or two-sample t statistics? What are the degrees of freedom for each t? Show that these t-values do *not* agree with the prediction.

Exercises 19.39 to 19.44 are based on summary statistics rather than raw data. This information is typically all that is presented in published reports. Inference procedures can be calculated by hand from the summaries. You must trust that the authors understood the conditions for inference and verified that they apply. This isn't always true.

CAUTION

19.39 Eating potato chips. Healthy women aged 18 to 40 participated in a study of eating habits. Subjects were given bags of potato chips and bottled water and invited to snack freely. Interviews showed that some women were trying to restrain their diet out of concern about their weight. How much effect did these good intentions have on their eating habits? Here are the data on grams of potato chips consumed (note that the study report gave the standard error of the mean rather than the standard deviation):[16]

Group	n	$\bar{x}$	SEM
Unrestrained	9	59	7
Restrained	11	32	10

Give a 90% confidence interval that describes the effect of restraint. Based on this interval, is there a significant difference between the two groups? At what significance level does the interval allow this conclusion?

19.40 Hispanic customers and Anglo customers. As the presence of Hispanics in the United States grows, businesses are trying to understand what Hispanics like. One study sampled customers leaving a bank. Customers were classified as Hispanic if they preferred to be interviewed in Spanish and as Anglo if they preferred English. Each customer rated the importance of several aspects of bank service on a 10-point scale.[17] Here are summary results for the importance of "reliability" (the accuracy of account records and so on):

Group	n	$\bar{x}$	s
Anglo	92	6.37	0.60
Hispanic	86	5.91	0.93

Another aspect of service quality is "empathy," the relationship that bank employees have with customers. The summary data are

Group	n	$\bar{x}$	s
Anglo	92	6.00	0.89
Hispanic	86	6.43	0.70

Do Hispanic and Anglo bank customers differ in the importance they place on either or both of these qualities? Write a one-sentence description of the differences in what the two groups find important.

19.41 Extraterrestrial handedness? Molecules often have "left-handed" and "right-handed" versions. Some classes of molecules found in life on earth are almost entirely left-handed. Did this left-handedness precede the origin of life? To find out, scientists analyzed meteorites from space. To correct for bias in the delicate analysis, they also analyzed standard compounds known to have equal proportions of left-handed and right-handed forms. Here are the results for the percents of left-handed forms of one molecule in two analyses:[18]

Analysis	Meteorite			Standard		
	n	$\bar{x}$	s	n	$\bar{x}$	s
1	5	52.6	0.5	14	48.8	1.9
2	10	51.7	0.4	13	49.0	1.3

The researchers used the t test to see if the meteorite had a significantly higher percent than the standard. Carry out the tests for both analyses and report the results. The researchers concluded: "The observations suggest that organic matter of extraterrestrial origin could have played an essential role in the origin of terrestrial life."

19.42 **Coaching and SAT scores.**   Coaching companies claim that their courses can raise the SAT scores of high school students. Of course, students who retake the SAT without paying for coaching generally raise their scores. A random sample of students who took the SAT twice found 427 who were coached and 2733 who were uncoached.[19] Starting with their verbal scores on the first and second tries, we have these summary statistics:

	Try 1		Try 2		Gain	
	$\bar{x}$	s	$\bar{x}$	s	$\bar{x}$	s
Coached	500	92	529	97	29	59
Uncoached	506	101	527	101	21	52

Let's first ask if students who are coached significantly increased their scores.

(a) You could use the information given to carry out either a two-sample t test comparing Try 1 with Try 2 for coached students or a matched pairs t test using Gain. Which is the correct test? Why?

(b) Carry out the proper test. What do you conclude?

(c) Give a 99% confidence interval for the mean gain of all students who are coached.

19.43 **Coaching and SAT scores, continued.**   What we really want to know is whether coached students improve more than uncoached students, and whether any advantage is large enough to be worth paying for. Use the information in the previous exercise to answer these questions:

(a) Is there good evidence that coached students gained more on the average than uncoached students?

(b) How much more do coached students gain on the average? Give a 99% confidence interval.

(c) Based on your work, what is your opinion: do you think coaching courses are worth paying for?

19.44 **Coaching and SAT scores: critique.**   The data you used in the previous two problems came from a random sample of students who took the SAT twice. The response rate was 63%, which is pretty good for nongovernment surveys, so let's accept that the respondents do represent all students who took the exam twice.

Nonetheless, we can't be sure that coaching actually *caused* the coached students to gain more than the uncoached students. Explain briefly but clearly why this is so.

The following exercises ask you to answer real questions from real data without having your work outlined in the exercise statement. Follow the **Formulate, Solve,** *and* **Conclude** *steps of the four-step process. It may be helpful to restate in your own words the* **State** *information given in the exercise.*

19.45 Each day I am getting better in math. A "subliminal" message is below our threshold of awareness but may nonetheless influence us. Can subliminal messages help students learn math? A group of students who had failed the mathematics part of the City University of New York Skills Assessment Test agreed to participate in a study to find out.

TABLE 19.1	Mathematics skills scores before and after a subliminal message		
Treatment Group		Control Group	
Before	After	Before	After
18	24	18	29
18	25	24	29
21	33	20	24
18	29	18	26
18	33	24	38
20	36	22	27
23	34	15	22
23	36	19	31
21	34		
17	27		

All received a daily subliminal message, flashed on a screen too rapidly to be consciously read. The treatment group of 10 students (chosen at random) was exposed to "Each day I am getting better in math." The control group of 8 students was exposed to a neutral message, "People are walking on the street." All students participated in a summer program designed to raise their math skills, and all took the assessment test again at the end of the program. Table 19.1 gives data on the subjects' scores before and after the program.[20] Is there good evidence that the treatment brought about a greater improvement in math scores than the neutral message? How large is the mean difference in gains between treatment and control? (Use 90% confidence.)

19.46 Tropical flowers. Different varieties of the tropical flower *Heliconia* are fertilized by different species of hummingbirds. Over time, the lengths of the flowers and the form of the hummingbirds' beaks have evolved to match each other. Here are data on the lengths in millimeters of two color varieties of the same species of flower on the island of Dominica:[21]

Art Wolfe/Getty Images

			H. caribaea red				
41.90	42.01	41.93	43.09	41.47	41.69	39.78	40.57
39.63	42.18	40.66	37.87	39.16	37.40	38.20	38.07
38.10	37.97	38.79	38.23	38.87	37.78	38.01	

			H. caribaea yellow				
36.78	37.02	36.52	36.11	36.03	35.45	38.13	37.1
35.17	36.82	36.66	35.68	36.03	34.57	34.63	

Is there good evidence that the mean lengths of the two varieties differ? Estimate the difference between the population means. (Use 95% confidence.)

19.47 **How strong are durable press fabrics?** "Durable press" cotton fabrics are treated to improve their recovery from wrinkles after washing. Unfortunately, the treatment also reduces the strength of the fabric. A study compared the breaking strength of fabrics treated by two commercial durable press processes. Five specimens of the same fabric were assigned at random to each process. Here are the data, in pounds of pull needed to tear the fabric:[22]

Permafresh	29.9	30.7	30.0	29.5	27.6
Hylite	28.8	23.9	27.0	22.1	24.2

Is there good evidence that the two processes result in different mean breaking strengths?

19.48 **Reducing wrinkles.** Of course, the reason for durable press treatment is to reduce wrinkling. "Wrinkle recovery angle" measures how well a fabric recovers from wrinkles. Higher is better. Here are data on the wrinkle recovery angle (in degrees) for the same fabric specimens discussed in the previous exercise:

Permafresh	136	135	132	137	134
Hylite	143	141	146	141	145

Is there a significant difference in wrinkle resistance? Which process does better?

19.49 **How much stronger?** Continue your work from Exercise 19.47. A fabric manufacturer wants to know how large an advantage in strength fabrics treated by the Permafresh method have over fabrics treated by the Hylite process. Give a 95% confidence interval for the difference in mean breaking strengths.

19.50 **How much less wrinkling?** In Exercise 19.48, you found that the Hylite process results in significantly greater wrinkle resistance than the Permafresh process. How large is the difference in mean wrinkle recovery angle? Give a 95% confidence interval.

19.51 **Student drinking.** A professor asked her sophomore students, "How many drinks do you typically have per session? (A drink is defined as one 12 oz beer, one 4 oz glass of wine, or one 1 oz shot of liquor.)" Some of the students didn't drink.

TABLE 19.2		Drinks per session claimed by female and male students										
					Female students							
2.5	9	1	3.5	2.5	3	1	3	3	3	3	2.5	2.5
5	3.5	5	1	2	1	7	3	7	4	4	6.5	4
3	6	5	3	8	6	6	3	6	8	3	4	7
4	5	3.5	4	2	1	5	5	3	3	6	4	2
7	7	7	3.5	3	2.5	10	5	4	9	8	1	6
2	5	2.5	3	4.5	9	5	4	4	3	4	6	7
4	5	1	5	3	4	10	7	3	4	4	4	4
2	1	2.5	2.5									
					Male students							
7	7.5	8	15	3	4	1	5	11	4.5	6	4	10
16	4	8	5	9	7	7	3	5	6.5	1	12	4
6	8	8	4.5	10.5	8	6	10	1	9	8	7	8
15	3	10	7	4	6	5	2	10	7	9	5	8
7	3	7	6	4	5	2	5	5.5	9	10	10	4
8	4	2	4	12.5	3	15	2	6	3	4	3	10
6	4.5	5										

Table 19.2 gives the responses of the female and male students who did drink.[23] It is likely that some of the students exaggerated a bit. The sample is all students in one large sophomore-level class. The class is popular, so we are tentatively willing to regard its members as an SRS of sophomore students at this college. Do a complete analysis that reports on

(a) the drinking behavior claimed by sophomore women.

(b) the drinking behavior claimed by sophomore men.

(c) a comparison of the behavior of women and men.

Blaine Harrington III/CORBIS

Inference about a Population Proportion

Our discussion of statistical inference to this point has concerned making inferences about population *means*. Now we turn to questions about the *proportion* of some outcome in a population. Here are some examples that call for inference about population proportions.

┌─ **EXAMPLE 20.1**   Risky behavior in the age of AIDS ─────

How common is behavior that puts people at risk of AIDS? The National AIDS Behavioral Surveys interviewed a random sample of 2673 adult heterosexuals. Of these, 170 had more than one sexual partner in the past year. That's 6.36% of the sample.[1] Based on these data, what can we say about the percent of all adult heterosexuals who have multiple partners? We want to *estimate a single population proportion*. This chapter concerns inference about one proportion.

┌─ **EXAMPLE 20.2**   Young adults living at home ─────

A surprising number of young adults (ages 19 to 25) still live at home with their parents. A random sample of 2253 men and 2629 women in this age group found that 44% of the men but only 35% of the women lived at home. Is this significant evidence that the proportions living at home differ in the populations of all young men and all young women? We want to *compare two population proportions*. This is the topic of Chapter 21.

To do inference about a population mean μ, we use the mean $\bar{x}$ of a random sample from the population. The reasoning of inference starts with the sampling distribution of $\bar{x}$. Now we follow the same pattern, replacing means by proportions.

The sample proportion $\hat{p}$

We are interested in the unknown proportion p of a population that has some outcome. For convenience, call the outcome we are looking for a "success." In Example 20.1, the population is adult heterosexuals, and the parameter p is the proportion who have had more than one sexual partner in the past year. To estimate p, the National AIDS Behavioral Surveys used random dialing of telephone numbers to contact a sample of 2673 people. Of these, 170 said they had multiple sexual partners. The statistic that estimates the parameter p is the **sample proportion**

sample proportion

$$\hat{p} = \frac{\text{number of successes in the sample}}{\text{total number of individuals in the sample}}$$
$$= \frac{170}{2673} = 0.0636$$

Read the sample proportion $\hat{p}$ as "p-hat."

APPLY YOUR KNOWLEDGE

In each of the following settings: (a) Describe the population and explain in words what the parameter p is. (b) Give the numerical value of the statistic $\hat{p}$ that estimates p.

20.1   **Do college students pray?**   A study of religious practices among college students interviewed a sample of 127 students; 107 of the students said that they prayed at least once in a while.

20.2   **Playing games online.**   A random sample of 1100 teenagers (ages 12 to 17) were asked whether they played games online; 775 said that they did.

The sampling distribution of $\hat{p}$

How good is the statistic $\hat{p}$ as an estimate of the parameter p? To find out, we ask, "What would happen if we took many samples?" The sampling distribution of $\hat{p}$ answers this question. Here are the facts.

SAMPLING DISTRIBUTION OF A SAMPLE PROPORTION

Draw an SRS of size n from a large population that contains proportion p of successes. Let $\hat{p}$ be the **sample proportion** of successes,

$$\hat{p} = \frac{\text{number of successes in the sample}}{n}$$

Then:

- As the sample size increases, the sampling distribution of $\hat{p}$ becomes **approximately Normal.**
- The **mean** of the sampling distribution is p.
- The **standard deviation** of the sampling distribution is

$$\sqrt{\frac{p(1-p)}{n}}$$

Figure 20.1 summarizes these facts in a form that helps you recall the big idea of a sampling distribution. The behavior of sample proportions $\hat{p}$ is similar to the behavior of sample means $\overline{x}$. When the sample size n is large, the sampling distribution is approximately Normal. The larger the sample, the more nearly Normal the distribution is. *Don't use the Normal approximation to the distribution of $\hat{p}$ when the sample size n is small.*

The mean of the sampling distribution of $\hat{p}$ is the true value of the population proportion p. That is, $\hat{p}$ is an unbiased estimator of p. The standard deviation of $\hat{p}$ gets smaller as the sample size n gets larger, so that estimation is likely to be more

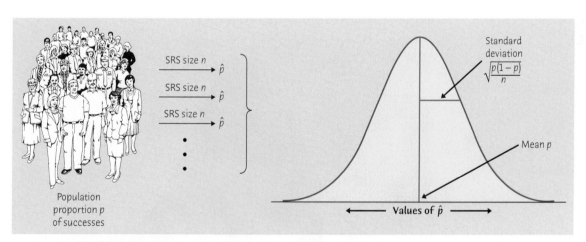

FIGURE 20.1 Select a large SRS from a population of which the proportion p are successes. The sampling distribution of the proportion $\hat{p}$ of successes in the sample is approximately Normal. The mean is p and the standard deviation is $\sqrt{p(1-p)/n}$.

accurate when the sample is larger. As is the case for $\bar{x}$, the standard deviation gets smaller only at the rate $\sqrt{n}$. We need four times as many observations to cut the standard deviation in half.

STEP

EXAMPLE 20.3 *Asking about risky behavior*

STATE: Suppose that in fact 6% of all adult heterosexuals had more than one sexual partner in the past year (and would admit it when asked). The National AIDS Behavioral Surveys interviewed a random sample of 2673 people from this population. What is the probability that at least 5% of such a sample admit to having more than one partner?

FORMULATE: Take $\hat{p}$ to be the proportion of individuals among the 2673 in the sample who had more than one partner. We want to find $P(\hat{p} \geq 0.05)$.

SOLVE: The sample size is $n = 2673$ and the population proportion is $p = 0.06$. So the sample proportion $\hat{p}$ is approximately Normal with mean 0.06 and standard deviation

$$\sqrt{\frac{p(1-p)}{n}} = \sqrt{\frac{(0.06)(0.94)}{2673}}$$
$$= \sqrt{0.0000211} = 0.00459$$

Standardize $\hat{p}$ by subtracting the mean 0.06 and dividing by the standard deviation 0.00459. The standardized statistic has approximately the standard Normal distribution. In terms of a standard Normal variable Z,

$$P(\hat{p} \geq 0.05) = P\left(\frac{\hat{p} - 0.06}{0.00459} \geq \frac{0.05 - 0.06}{0.00459}\right)$$
$$= P(Z \geq -2.18)$$
$$= 1 - 0.0146 = 0.9854$$

Figure 20.2 shows this probability as an area under the standard Normal curve.

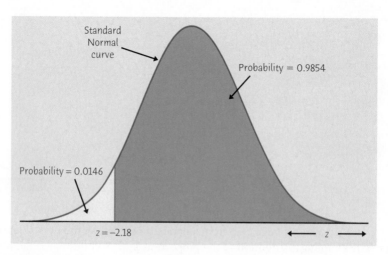

FIGURE 20.2 Probabilities in Example 20.3 as areas under the standard Normal curve.

CONCLUDE: If we repeat the National AIDS Behavioral Surveys many times, more than 98% of all the samples will contain at least 5% of respondents who admit to more than one sexual partner.

The Normal approximation for the sampling distribution of $\hat{p}$ is least accurate when p is close to 0 or 1. If $p = 0$, successes are impossible. Every sample has $\hat{p} = 0$ and there is no Normal distribution in sight. In the same way, the approximation works poorly when p is close to 1. In practice, this means that we need larger n for values of p near 0 or 1. In Example 20.3, p is small but n is large. The exact probability is $P(\hat{p} \geq 0.05) = 0.9843$, so the Normal approximation is quite accurate.

Inference about a population proportion p starts by using the sample proportion $\hat{p}$ to estimate p. Confidence levels and P-values are probabilities calculated from the sampling distribution of $\hat{p}$. We will consider only situations that allow us to use the Normal approximation to this sampling distribution. Here is a summary of the conditions we need.

CONDITIONS FOR INFERENCE ABOUT A PROPORTION

- We can regard our data as a **simple random sample** (SRS) from the population. This is, as usual, the most important condition.

- The **sample size n is large enough** to ensure that the distribution of $\hat{p}$ is close to Normal. We will see that different inference procedures require different answers to the question "how large is large enough?"

Remember also that *all of our inference procedures require that the population be much larger than the sample.*[2] This condition is usually satisfied in practice and is satisfied in all of our examples and exercises.

APPLY YOUR KNOWLEDGE

20.3 Student drinking. The College Alcohol Study interviewed an SRS of 14,941 college students about their drinking habits. Suppose that half of all college students "drink to get drunk" at least once in a while. That is, $p = 0.5$.

(a) What are the mean and standard deviation of the proportion $\hat{p}$ of the sample who drink to get drunk?

(b) Use the Normal approximation to find the probability that $\hat{p}$ is between 0.49 and 0.51.

20.4 Students on diets. A sample survey interviews an SRS of 267 college women. Suppose (as is roughly true) that 70% of all college women have been on a diet within the past 12 months. What is the probability that 75% or more of the women in the sample have been on a diet?

20.5 Student drinking, continued. Suppose that half of all college students drink to get drunk at least once in a while. Exercise 20.3 asks for the probability that the sample proportion $\hat{p}$ estimates $p = 0.5$ within ±1 percentage point. Find this probability for SRSs of sizes 1000, 4000, and 16,000. What general fact do your results illustrate?

20.6 **No inference.** A local television station conducts a call-in poll about a proposed city tax increase to buy natural areas and protect them from development. Of the 2372 calls, 1921 support the proposal. We can't use these data as the basis for inference about the proportion of all citizens who support the tax increase. Why not?

Large-sample confidence intervals for a proportion

To estimate a population proportion p, use the sample proportion $\hat{p}$. If our conditions for inference apply, the sampling distribution of $\hat{p}$ is close to Normal with mean p and standard deviation $\sqrt{p(1-p)/n}$. To obtain a level C confidence interval for p, we would like to use

$$\hat{p} \pm z^* \sqrt{\frac{p(1-p)}{n}}$$

with the critical value z^* chosen to cover the central area C under the standard Normal curve. Figure 20.3 shows why.

Because we don't know the value of p, we replace the standard deviation by the **standard error of $\hat{p}$**

standard error of $\hat{p}$

$$SE = \sqrt{\frac{\hat{p}(1-\hat{p})}{n}}$$

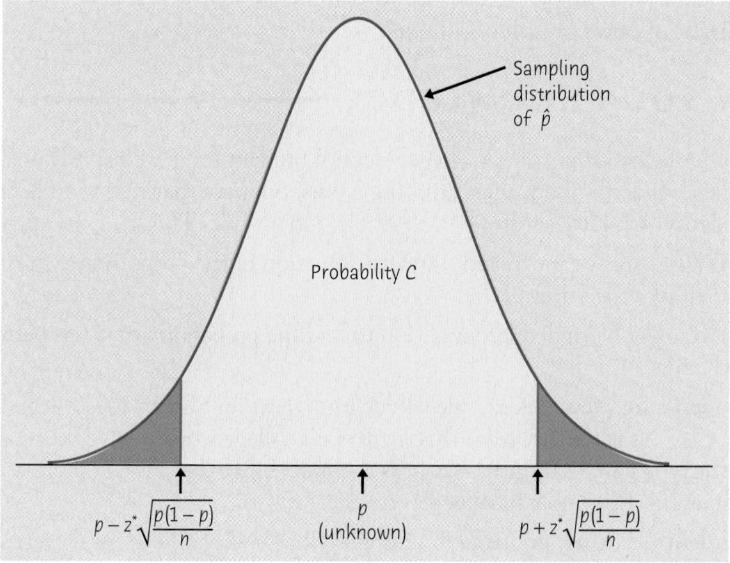

FIGURE 20.3 With probability C, $\hat{p}$ lies within $\pm z^* \sqrt{p(1-p)/n}$ of the unknown population proportion p. That is to say that in these samples p lies within $\pm z^* \sqrt{p(1-p)/n}$ of $\hat{p}$.

to get the confidence interval

$$\hat{p} \pm z^* \sqrt{\frac{\hat{p}(1 - \hat{p})}{n}}$$

This interval has the form

$$\text{estimate} \pm z^* \text{SE}_{\text{estimate}}$$

Notice that we *don't* change z^* to t^* when we replace the standard deviation by the standard error. When the sample mean $\bar{x}$ estimates the population mean μ, a separate parameter σ describes the spread of the distribution of $\bar{x}$. We separately estimate σ, and this leads to a t distribution. When the sample proportion $\hat{p}$ estimates the population proportion p, the spread depends on p, not on a separate parameter. There is no t distribution—we just make the Normal approximation slightly less accurate when we replace p in the standard deviation by $\hat{p}$.

We now have a confidence interval for a proportion. *This interval can be trusted only for quite large samples.* A rule of thumb for "how large" must take into account the fact that n must be larger if the sample proportion $\hat{p}$ suggests that p may be close to 0 or 1. Because $n\hat{p}$ is just the number of successes in the sample and $n(1 - \hat{p})$ is the number of failures, we can count successes and failures to get a simple guideline for "n is large and $\hat{p}$ is not too close to 0 or 1."

LARGE-SAMPLE CONFIDENCE INTERVAL FOR A POPULATION PROPORTION

Draw an SRS of size n from a large population that contains an unknown proportion p of successes. An approximate level C **confidence interval for p** is

$$\hat{p} \pm z^* \sqrt{\frac{\hat{p}(1 - \hat{p})}{n}}$$

where z^* is the critical value for the standard Normal density curve with area C between $-z^*$ and z^*.

Use this interval only when the numbers of successes and failures in the sample are both at least 15.[3]

EXAMPLE 20.4 *Estimating risky behavior*

4 STEP

The four-step process for any confidence interval is outlined on page 350.

STATE: The National AIDS Behavioral Surveys found that 170 of a sample of 2673 adult heterosexuals had multiple partners. That is, $\hat{p} = 0.0636$. What can we say about the population of all adult heterosexuals?

FORMULATE: We will give a 99% confidence interval to estimate the proportion p of all adult heterosexuals who have multiple partners.

SOLVE: First verify the conditions for inference:

- The sampling design was a complex stratified sample, and the survey used inference procedures for that design. The overall effect is close to an SRS, however.

- The sample is large enough: the numbers of successes (170) and failures (2503) in the sample are both much larger than 15.

The sample size condition is easily satisfied. The condition that the sample be an SRS is only approximately met.

A 99% confidence interval for the proportion p of all adult heterosexuals with multiple partners uses the standard Normal critical value $z^* = 2.576$. The confidence interval is

$$\hat{p} \pm z^* \sqrt{\frac{\hat{p}(1 - \hat{p})}{n}} = 0.0636 \pm 2.576 \sqrt{\frac{(0.0636)(0.9364)}{2673}}$$

$$= 0.0636 \pm 0.0122$$

$$= 0.0514 \text{ to } 0.0758$$

CONCLUDE: We are 99% confident that the percent of adult heterosexuals who have had more than one sexual partner in the past year lies between about 5% and 7.6%.

As usual, the practical problems of a large sample survey weaken our confidence in the AIDS survey's conclusions. Only people in households with telephones could be reached. This is acceptable for surveys of the general population, because about 95% of American households have telephones. However, some groups at high risk for AIDS, like intravenous drug users, often don't live in settled households and therefore are underrepresented in the sample. About 30% of the people reached refused to cooperate. A nonresponse rate of 30% is not unusual in large sample surveys, but it may cause some bias if those who refuse differ systematically from those who cooperate. The survey used statistical methods that adjust for unequal response rates in different groups. Finally, some respondents may not have told the truth when asked about their sexual behavior. The survey team tried hard to make respondents feel comfortable. For example, Hispanic women were interviewed only by Hispanic women, and Spanish speakers were interviewed by Spanish speakers with the same regional accent (Cuban, Mexican, or Puerto Rican). Nonetheless, the survey report says that some bias is probably present:

> *It is more likely that the present figures are underestimates; some respondents may underreport their numbers of sexual partners and intravenous drug use because of embarrassment and fear of reprisal, or they may forget or not know details of their own or of their partner's HIV risk and their antibody testing history.*[4]

Reading the report of a large study like the National AIDS Behavioral Surveys reminds us that statistics in practice involves much more than formulas for inference.

APPLY YOUR KNOWLEDGE

20.7 **No confidence interval.** In the National AIDS Behavioral Surveys sample of 2673 adult heterosexuals, 0.2% (that's 0.002 as a decimal fraction) had both received a blood transfusion and had a sexual partner from a group at high risk of AIDS. Explain why we can't use the large-sample confidence interval to estimate the proportion p in the population who share these two risk factors.

20.8 **How common is SAT coaching?** A random sample of students who took the SAT college entrance examination twice found that 427 of the respondents had paid for coaching courses and that the remaining 2733 had not.[5] Give a 99% confidence interval for the proportion of coaching among students who retake the SAT. Follow the four-step process as illustrated in Example 20.4.

4
STEP

20.9 **Deaths from guns.** The Harris Poll asked a random sample of 1009 adults which causes of death they thought would become more common in the future. Topping the list was gun violence: 70% of the sample thought deaths from guns would increase.

(a) How many of the 1009 people interviewed thought deaths from gun violence would increase?

(b) Harris says that the margin of error for this poll is plus or minus 3 percentage points. Explain to someone who knows no statistics what "margin of error plus or minus 3 percentage points" means.

(c) Give a 95% confidence interval for this survey. Does your margin of error agree with the 3 percentage points announced by Harris?

Accurate confidence intervals for a proportion

The confidence interval $\hat{p} \pm z^*\sqrt{\hat{p}(1-\hat{p})/n}$ for a sample proportion p is easy to calculate. It is also easy to understand because it rests directly on the approximately Normal distribution of $\hat{p}$. Unfortunately, confidence levels from this interval are often quite inaccurate unless the sample is very large. The actual confidence level is usually *less* than the confidence level you asked for in choosing the critical value z^*. That's bad. What is worse, accuracy does not consistently get better as the sample size n increases. There are "lucky" and "unlucky" combinations of the sample size n and the true population proportion p.

Fortunately, there is a simple modification that is almost magically effective in improving the accuracy of the confidence interval. We call it the "plus four" method because all you need to do is *add four imaginary observations, two successes and two failures*. With the added observations, the **plus four estimate** of p is

plus four estimate

$$\tilde{p} = \frac{\text{number of successes in the sample} + 2}{n + 4}$$

The formula for the confidence interval is exactly as before, with the new sample size and number of successes.[6] You do not need software that offers the plus four interval—just enter the new sample size (actual size + 4) and number of successes (actual number + 2) into the large-sample procedure.

PLUS FOUR CONFIDENCE INTERVAL FOR A PROPORTION

Draw an SRS of size n from a large population that contains an unknown proportion p of successes. To get the **plus four confidence interval for p**, add four imaginary observations, two successes and two failures. Then use the large-sample confidence interval with the new sample size ($n + 4$) and count of successes (actual count $+ 2$).

Use this interval when the confidence level is at least 90% and the sample size n is at least 10.

4
STEP

EXAMPLE 20.5 Blinding in medical trials

STATE: Many medical trials randomly assign patients to either an active treatment or a placebo. These trials are always double-blind. Sometimes the patients can tell whether or not they are getting the active treatment. This defeats the purpose of blinding. Reports of medical research usually ignore this problem. Investigators looked at a random sample of 97 articles reporting on placebo-controlled randomized trials in the top five general medical journals. Only 7 of the 97 discussed the success of blinding—and in 5 of these the blinding was imperfect.[7] What proportion of all such studies discuss the success of blinding?

FORMULATE: Take p to be the proportion of articles that discuss the success of blinding. Give a 95% confidence interval for p.

SOLVE: The conditions for use of the large-sample interval are not met because there are fewer than 15 successes in the sample. Add two successes and two failures to the original data. The plus four estimate of p is

$$\tilde{p} = \frac{7+2}{97+4} = \frac{9}{101} = 0.0891$$

The plus four confidence interval is the same as the large-sample interval based on 9 successes in 101 observations. Here it is:

$$\tilde{p} \pm z^* \sqrt{\frac{\tilde{p}(1-\tilde{p})}{n+4}} = 0.0891 \pm 1.960 \sqrt{\frac{(0.0891)(0.9109)}{101}}$$
$$= 0.0891 \pm 0.0556$$
$$= 0.0335 \text{ to } 0.1447$$

CONCLUDE: We estimate with 95% confidence that between about 3.4% and 14.5% of all such articles discuss whether the blinding succeeded.

For comparison, the ordinary sample proportion is

$$\hat{p} = \frac{7}{97} = 0.0722$$

The plus four estimate $\tilde{p} = 0.0891$ in Example 20.5 is farther away from zero than $\hat{p} = 0.0722$. The plus four estimate gains its added accuracy by always moving toward 0.5 and away from 0 or 1, whichever is closer. This is particularly helpful

Who is a smoker?

When estimating a proportion p, be sure you know what counts as a "success." The news says that 20% of adolescents smoke. Shocking. It turns out that this is the percent who smoked at least once in the past month. If we say that a smoker is someone who smoked on at least 20 of the past 30 days and smoked at least half a pack on those days, fewer than 4% of adolescents qualify.

when the sample contains only a few successes or a few failures. The numerical difference between a large-sample interval and the corresponding plus four interval is often small. Remember that the confidence level is the probability that the interval will catch the true population proportion *in very many uses*. Small differences every time add up to accurate confidence levels from plus four versus inaccurate levels from the large-sample interval.

How much more accurate is the plus four interval? Computer studies have asked how large n must be to guarantee that the actual probability that a 95% confidence interval covers the true parameter value is at least 0.94 for all samples of size n or larger. If $p = 0.1$, for example, the answer is $n = 646$ for the large-sample interval and $n = 11$ for the plus four interval.[8] The consensus of computational and theoretical studies is that plus four is very much better than the large-sample interval for many combinations of n and p. **We recommend that you always use the plus four interval.**

APPLY YOUR KNOWLEDGE

20.10 Drug-detecting rats? Dogs are big and expensive. Rats are small and cheap. Might rats be trained to replace dogs in sniffing out illegal drugs? A first study of this idea trained rats to rear up on their hind legs when they smelled simulated cocaine. To see how well rats performed after training, they were let loose on a surface with many cups sunk in it, one of which contained simulated cocaine. Four out of six trained rats succeeded in 80 out of 80 trials.[9] How should we estimate the long-term success rate p of a rat that succeeds in every one of 80 trials?

Holt Studios International/Alamy

(a) What is the rat's sample proportion $\hat{p}$? What is the large-sample 95% confidence interval for p? It's not plausible that the rat will *always* be successful, as this interval says.

(b) Find the plus four estimate $\tilde{p}$ and the plus four 95% confidence interval for p. These results are more reasonable. This example illustrates how $\tilde{p}$ improves on $\hat{p}$ when a sample has almost all successes or almost all failures.

20.11 Whelks and mussels. Sample surveys usually contact large samples, so we can use the large-sample confidence interval if the sample design is close to an SRS. Scientific studies often use small samples that require the plus four method. For example, the small round holes you often see in sea shells were drilled by other sea creatures, who ate the former owners of the shells. Whelks often drill into mussels, but this behavior appears to be more or less common in different locations. Investigators collected whelk eggs from the coast of Oregon, raised the whelks in the laboratory, then put each whelk in a container with some delicious mussels. Only 9 of 98 whelks drilled into a mussel.[10]

(a) Why can't we use the large-sample confidence interval?

(b) Give the plus four 90% confidence interval for the proportion of Oregon whelks that will spontaneously drill mussels.

20.12 High-risk behavior. In the National AIDS Behavioral Surveys sample of 2673 adult heterosexuals, 5 respondents had both received a blood transfusion and had a sexual partner from a group at high risk of AIDS.

(a) You should not use the large-sample confidence interval for the proportion p in the population who share these two risk factors. Why not?

(b) The plus four method adds four observations, two successes and two failures. What are the sample size and the count of successes after you do this? What is the plus four estimate $\tilde{p}$ of p?

(c) Give the plus four 95% confidence interval for p.

Choosing the sample size

In planning a study, we may want to choose a sample size that will allow us to estimate the parameter within a given margin of error. We saw earlier (page 355) how to do this for a population mean. The method is similar for estimating a population proportion.

The margin of error in the large-sample confidence interval for p is

$$m = z^* \sqrt{\frac{\hat{p}(1 - \hat{p})}{n}}$$

Here z^* is the standard Normal critical value for the level of confidence we want. Because the margin of error involves the sample proportion of successes $\hat{p}$, we need to guess this value when choosing n. Call our guess p^*. Here are two ways to get p^*:

1. Use a guess p^* based on a pilot study or on past experience with similar studies. You can do several calculations to cover the range of values of $\hat{p}$ you might get.

2. Use $p^* = 0.5$ as the guess. The margin of error m is largest when $\hat{p} = 0.5$, so this guess is conservative in the sense that if we get any other $\hat{p}$ when we do our study, we will get a margin of error smaller than planned.

Once you have a guess p^*, the recipe for the margin of error can be solved to give the sample size n needed. Here is the result for the large-sample confidence interval. For simplicity, use this result even if you plan to use the plus four interval.

New York, New York

New York City, they say, is bigger, richer, faster, ruder. Maybe there's something to that. The sample survey firm Zogby International says that as a national average it takes 5 telephone calls to reach a live person. When calling to New York, it takes 12 calls. Survey firms assign their best interviewers to make calls to New York and often pay them bonuses to cope with the stress.

SAMPLE SIZE FOR DESIRED MARGIN OF ERROR

The level C confidence interval for a population proportion p will have margin of error approximately equal to a specified value m when the sample size is

$$n = \left(\frac{z^*}{m}\right)^2 p^*(1 - p^*)$$

where p^* is a guessed value for the sample proportion. The margin of error will be less than or equal to m if you take the guess p^* to be 0.5.

Which method for finding the guess p^* should you use? The n you get doesn't change much when you change p^* as long as p^* is not too far from 0.5. You can use the conservative guess $p^* = 0.5$ if you expect the true $\hat{p}$ to be roughly between 0.3 and 0.7. If the true $\hat{p}$ is close to 0 or 1, using $p^* = 0.5$ as your guess will give a sample much larger than you need. Try to use a better guess from a pilot study when you suspect that $\hat{p}$ will be less than 0.3 or greater than 0.7.

EXAMPLE 20.6 Planning a poll

STEP 4

STATE: Gloria Chavez and Ronald Flynn are the candidates for mayor in a large city. You are planning a sample survey to determine what percent of the voters plan to vote for Chavez. You will contact an SRS of registered voters in the city. You want to estimate the proportion p of Chavez voters with 95% confidence and a margin of error no greater than 3%, or 0.03. How large a sample do you need?

FORMULATE: Find the sample size n needed for margin of error $m = 0.03$ and 95% confidence. The winner's share in all but the most lopsided elections is between 30% and 70% of the vote. You can use the guess $p^* = 0.5$.

SOLVE: The sample size you need is

$$n = \left(\frac{1.96}{0.03}\right)^2 (0.5)(1 - 0.5) = 1067.1$$

Round the result up to $n = 1068$. (Rounding down would give a margin of error slightly greater than 0.03.)

CONCLUDE: An SRS of 1068 registered voters is adequate for margin of error $\pm 3\%$.

Colin Anderson/BrandX/Agefotostock

If you want a 2.5% margin of error rather than 3%, then (after rounding up)

$$n = \left(\frac{1.96}{0.025}\right)^2 (0.5)(1 - 0.5) = 1537$$

For a 2% margin of error the sample size you need is

$$n = \left(\frac{1.96}{0.02}\right)^2 (0.5)(1 - 0.5) = 2401$$

As usual, smaller margins of error call for larger samples.

APPLY YOUR KNOWLEDGE

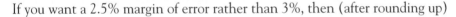

20.13 Canadians and doctor-assisted suicide. A Gallup Poll asked a sample of Canadian adults if they thought the law should allow doctors to end the life of a patient who is in great pain and near death if the patient makes a request in writing. The poll included 270 people in Québec, 221 of whom agreed that doctor-assisted suicide should be allowed.[11]

(a) What is the margin of error of the large-sample 95% confidence interval for the proportion of all Québec adults who would allow doctor-assisted suicide?

(b) How large a sample is needed to get the common ± 3 percentage point margin of error? Use the previous sample as a pilot study to get p^*.

20.14 Can you taste PTC? PTC is a substance that has a strong bitter taste for some people and is tasteless for others. The ability to taste PTC is inherited. About

75% of Italians can taste PTC, for example. You want to estimate the proportion of Americans with at least one Italian grandparent who can taste PTC. Starting with the 75% estimate for Italians, how large a sample must you collect in order to estimate the proportion of PTC tasters within ±0.04 with 90% confidence?

Significance tests for a proportion

The test statistic for the null hypothesis H_0: $p = p_0$ is the sample proportion $\hat{p}$ standardized using the value p_0 specified by H_0,

$$z = \frac{\hat{p} - p_0}{\sqrt{\dfrac{p_0(1 - p_0)}{n}}}$$

This z statistic has approximately the standard Normal distribution when H_0 is true. P-values therefore come from the standard Normal distribution. Because H_0 fixes a value of p, the inaccuracy that plagues the large-sample confidence interval does not affect tests. Here is the procedure for tests.

SIGNIFICANCE TESTS FOR A PROPORTION

Draw an SRS of size n from a large population that contains an unknown proportion p of successes. To **test the hypothesis H_0: $p = p_0$**, compute the z statistic

$$z = \frac{\hat{p} - p_0}{\sqrt{\dfrac{p_0(1 - p_0)}{n}}}$$

In terms of a variable Z having the standard Normal distribution, the approximate P-value for a test of H_0 against

H_a: $p > p_0$ is $P(Z \geq z)$
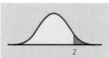

H_a: $p < p_0$ is $P(Z \leq z)$
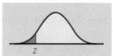

H_a: $p \neq p_0$ is $2P(Z \geq |z|)$
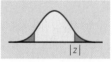

Use this test when the sample size n is so large that both np_0 and $n(1 - p_0)$ are 10 or more.[12]

EXAMPLE 20.7 *Are boys more likely?*

The four-step process for any significance test is outlined on page 372.

STATE: We hear that newborn babies are more likely to be boys than girls, presumably to compensate for higher mortality among boys in early life. Is this true? A random sample found 13,173 boys among 25,468 firstborn children.[13] The sample proportion of boys was

$$\hat{p} = \frac{13,173}{25,468} = 0.5172$$

Blaine Harrington III/CORBIS

Boys do make up more than half of the sample, but of course we don't expect a perfect 50-50 split in a random sample. Is this sample evidence that boys are more common than girls in the entire population?

FORMULATE: Take p to be the proportion of boys among all firstborn children of American mothers. (Biology says that this should be the same as the proportion among all children, but the survey data concern first births.) We want to test the hypotheses

$$H_0: p = 0.5$$
$$H_a: p > 0.5$$

SOLVE: The conditions for inference are met, so we can go on to the z test statistic:

$$z = \frac{\hat{p} - p_0}{\sqrt{\dfrac{p_0(1 - p_0)}{n}}}$$

$$= \frac{0.5172 - 0.5}{\sqrt{\dfrac{(0.5)(0.5)}{25,468}}} = 5.49$$

The *P*-value is the area under the standard Normal curve to the right of $z = 5.49$. We know that this is very small; Table C shows that $P < 0.0005$. Software (see Figure 20.4) tells us that in fact $P < 0.0001$.

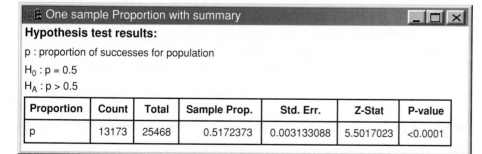

One sample Proportion with summary

Hypothesis test results:

p : proportion of successes for population
$H_0 : p = 0.5$
$H_A : p > 0.5$

Proportion	Count	Total	Sample Prop.	Std. Err.	Z-Stat	P-value
p	13173	25468	0.5172373	0.003133088	5.5017023	<0.0001

FIGURE 20.4 CrunchIt! output for the significance test of Example 20.7. Roundoff error in Example 20.7 explains the small difference (5.49 versus 5.50) in the values of the z statistic.

CONCLUDE: There is very strong evidence that more than half of newborns are boys ($P < 0.0001$).

EXAMPLE 20.8 *Estimating the chance of a boy*

With 13,173 successes in 25,468 trials, the large-sample and plus four estimates of p are almost identical. Both are 0.5172 to four decimal places. So both methods give the 99% confidence interval

$$\hat{p} \pm z^* \sqrt{\frac{\hat{p}(1-\hat{p})}{n}} = 0.5172 \pm 2.576 \sqrt{\frac{(0.5172)(0.4828)}{25,468}}$$

$$= 0.5172 \pm 0.0081$$

$$= 0.5091 \text{ to } 0.5253$$

We are 99% confident that between about 51% and 52.5% of first children are boys.

The confidence interval is more informative than the test in Example 20.7, which tells us only that more than half are boys.

APPLY YOUR KNOWLEDGE

20.15 **Spinning pennies.** Spinning a coin, unlike tossing it, may not give heads and tails equal probabilities. I spun a penny 200 times and got 83 heads. How significant is this evidence against equal probabilities? Follow the four-step process as illustrated in Example 20.7.

20.16 **Vote for the best face?** We often judge other people by their faces. It appears that some people judge candidates for elected office by their faces. Psychologists showed head-and-shoulders photos of the two main candidates in 32 races for the U.S. Senate to many subjects (dropping subjects who recognized one of the candidates) to see which candidate was rated "more competent" based on nothing but the photos. On election day, the candidates whose faces looked more competent won 22 of the 32 contests.[14] If faces don't influence voting, half of all races in the long run should be won by the candidate with the better face. Is there evidence that the candidate with the better face wins more than half the time? Follow the four-step process as illustrated in Example 20.7.

20.17 **No test.** Explain why we can't use the z test for a proportion in these situations:

(a) You toss a coin 10 times in order to test the hypothesis H_0: $p = 0.5$ that the coin is balanced.

(b) A college president says, "99% of the alumni support my firing of Coach Boggs." You contact an SRS of 200 of the college's 15,000 living alumni to test the hypothesis H_0: $p = 0.99$.

CHAPTER 20 SUMMARY

Tests and confidence intervals for a population proportion p when the data are an SRS of size n are based on the **sample proportion $\hat{p}$.**

When n is large, $\hat{p}$ has approximately the Normal distribution with mean p and standard deviation $\sqrt{p(1-p)/n}$.

The level C **large-sample confidence interval for p** is

$$\hat{p} \pm z^* \sqrt{\frac{\hat{p}(1 - \hat{p})}{n}}$$

where z^* is the critical value for the standard Normal curve with area C between $-z^*$ and z^*.

The true confidence level of the large-sample interval can be substantially less than the planned level C unless the sample is very large. We recommend using the plus four interval instead.

To get a more accurate confidence interval, add four imaginary observations, two successes and two failures, to your sample. Then use the same formula for the confidence interval. This is the **plus four confidence interval.** Use this interval in practice for confidence level 90% or higher and sample size n at least 10.

The **sample size** needed to obtain a confidence interval with approximate margin of error m for a population proportion is

$$n = \left(\frac{z^*}{m}\right)^2 p^*(1 - p^*)$$

where p^* is a guessed value for the sample proportion $\hat{p}$, and z^* is the standard Normal critical point for the level of confidence you want. If you use $p^* = 0.5$ in this formula, the margin of error of the interval will be less than or equal to m no matter what the value of $\hat{p}$ is.

Significance tests for H_0: $p = p_0$ are based on the z statistic

$$z = \frac{\hat{p} - p_0}{\sqrt{\dfrac{p_0(1 - p_0)}{n}}}$$

with P-values calculated from the standard Normal distribution. Use this test in practice when $np_0 \geq 10$ and $n(1 - p_0) \geq 10$.

Kids on bikes

In the most recent year for which data are available, 77% of children killed in bicycle accidents were boys. You might take these data as a sample and start from $\hat{p} = 0.77$ to do inference about bicycle deaths in the near future. What you should not do is conclude that boys on bikes are in greater danger than girls. We don't know how many boys and girls ride bikes—it may be that most fatalities are boys because most riders are boys.

CHECK YOUR SKILLS

20.18 *Sports Illustrated* asked a random sample of 757 Division I college athletes, "Do you believe performance-enhancing drugs are a problem in college sports?" Suppose that in fact 30% of all Division I athletes think that drugs are a problem. In repeated samples, the sample proportion $\hat{p}$ would follow a Normal distribution with mean

(a) 227.   (b) 0.3.   (c) 0.017.

20.19 The standard deviation of the distribution of $\hat{p}$ in the previous exercise is about

(a) 0.00028.   (b) 0.033.   (c) 0.017.

20.20 In fact, 273 of the 757 athletes in the *Sports Illustrated* sample said "Yes." The sample proportion $\hat{p}$ who said "Yes" is

(a) 36.   (b) 2.77.   (c) 0.36.

20.21 Based on the *Sports Illustrated* sample, the 95% large-sample confidence interval for the proportion of all Division I athletes who think performance-enhancing drugs are a problem is

(a) 0.36 ± 0.017.   (b) 0.36 ± 0.034.   (c) 0.36 ± 0.00030.

20.22 How many athletes must be interviewed to estimate the proportion concerned about use of drugs within ± 0.02 with 95% confidence? Use 0.5 as the conservative guess for p.

(a) $n = 25$ (b) $n = 1225$ (c) $n = 2401$

20.23 An opinion poll asks an SRS of 100 college seniors how they view their job prospects. In all, 53 say "Good." The plus four 95% confidence interval for estimating the proportion of all college seniors who think their job prospects are good is

(a) 0.529 ± 0.096.   (b) 0.059 ± 0.098.   (c) 0.059 ± 0.049.

20.24 The sample survey in Exercise 20.23 actually called 130 seniors, but 30 of the seniors refused to answer. This nonresponse could cause the survey result to be in error. The error due to nonresponse

(a) is in addition to the margin of error found in Exercise 20.23.

(b) is included in the margin of error found in Exercise 20.23.

(c) can be ignored because it isn't random.

20.25 Does the poll in Exercise 20.23 give reason to conclude that more than half of all seniors think their job prospects are good? The hypotheses for a test to answer this question are

(a) $H_0: p = 0.5$, $H_a: p > 0.5$.

(b) $H_0: p > 0.5$, $H_a: p = 0.5$.

(c) $H_0: p = 0.5$, $H_a: p \neq 0.5$.

20.26 The value of the z statistic for the test of the previous exercise is about

(a) $z = 12$.   (b) $z = 6$.   (c) $z = 0.6$.

20.27 A Harris Poll found that 54% of American adults do not think that human beings developed from earlier species. The poll's margin of error was 3%. This means that

(a) the poll used a method that gets an answer within 3% of the truth about the population 95% of the time.

(b) we can be sure that the percent of all adults who feel this way is between 51% and 57%.

(c) if Harris takes another poll using the same method, the results of the second poll will lie between 51% and 57%.

CHAPTER 20 EXERCISES

We recommend using the plus four method for all confidence intervals for a proportion. However, the large-sample method is acceptable when the guidelines for its use are met.

20.28 **Reporting cheating.** Students are reluctant to report cheating by other students. A student project put this question to an SRS of 172 undergraduates at a large university: "You witness two students cheating on a quiz. Do you go to the professor?" Only 19 answered "Yes."[15] Give a 95% confidence interval for the proportion of all undergraduates at this university who would report cheating.

20.29 Do college students pray?   Social scientists asked 127 undergraduate students "from courses in psychology and communications" about prayer and found that 107 prayed at least a few times a year.[16]

(a) Give the plus four 99% confidence interval for the proportion p of all students who pray.

(b) To use any inference procedure, we must be willing to regard these 127 students, as far as their religious behavior goes, as an SRS from the population of all undergraduate students. Do you think it is reasonable to do this? Why or why not?

20.30 Which font?   Plain type fonts such as Times New Roman are easier to read than fancy fonts such as Gigi. A group of 25 volunteer subjects read the same text in both fonts. (This is a matched pairs design. One-sample procedures for proportions, like those for means, are used to analyze data from matched pairs designs.) Of the 25 subjects, 17 said that they preferred Times New Roman for Web use. But 20 said that Gigi was more attractive.[17]

(a) Because the subjects were volunteers, conclusions from this sample can be challenged. Show that the sample size condition for the large-sample confidence interval is not met, but that the condition for the plus four interval is met.

(b) Give a 95% confidence interval for the proportion of all adults who prefer Times New Roman for Web use. Give a 90% confidence interval for the proportion of all adults who think Gigi is more attractive.

20.31 Seat belt use.   The proportion of drivers who use seat belts depends on things like age, gender, ethnicity, and local law. As part of a broader study, investigators observed a random sample of 117 female Hispanic drivers in Boston; 68 of these drivers were wearing seat belts.[18] Give a 95% confidence interval for the proportion of all female Hispanic drivers in Boston who wear seat belts. Follow the four-step process as illustrated in Example 20.5.

20.32 Running red lights.   A random digit dialing telephone survey of 880 drivers asked, "Recalling the last ten traffic lights you drove through, how many of them were red when you entered the intersections?" Of the 880 respondents, 171 admitted that at least one light had been red.[19]

(a) Give a 95% confidence interval for the proportion of all drivers who ran one or more of the last ten red lights they met.

(b) Nonresponse is a practical problem for this survey—only 21.6% of calls that reached a live person were completed. Another practical problem is that people may not give truthful answers. What is the likely direction of the bias: do you think more or fewer than 171 of the 880 respondents really ran a red light? Why?

Ted Horowitz/CORBIS

20.33 Seat belt use, continued.   Do the data in Exercise 20.31 give good reason to conclude that more than half of Hispanic female drivers in Boston wear seat belts? Follow the four-step process as illustrated in Example 20.7.

20.34 Seat belt use: planning a study.   How large a sample would be needed to obtain margin of error ±0.05 in the study of seat belt use among Hispanic females? Use the $\hat{p}$ from Exercise 20.31 as your guess for the unknown p.

20.35 Detecting genetically modified soybeans.   Most soybeans grown in the United States are genetically modified to, for example, resist pests and so reduce use of pesticides. Because some nations do not accept genetically modified (GM) foods,

grain-handling facilities routinely test soybean shipments for the presence of GM beans. In a study of the accuracy of these tests, researchers submitted lots of soybeans containing 1% of GM beans to 23 randomly selected facilities. Eighteen detected the GM beans.[20]

(a) Show that the conditions for the large-sample confidence interval are not met. Show that the conditions for the plus four interval are met.

(b) Use the plus four method to give a 90% confidence interval for the percent of all grain-handling facilities that will correctly detect 1% of GM beans in a shipment.

20.36 The IRS plans an SRS. The Internal Revenue Service plans to examine an SRS of individual federal income tax returns from each state. One variable of interest is the proportion of returns claiming itemized deductions. The total number of tax returns in a state varies from more than 15 million in California to about 240,000 in Wyoming.

(a) Will the margin of error for estimating the population proportion change from state to state if an SRS of 2000 tax returns is selected in each state? Explain your answer.

(b) Will the margin of error change from state to state if an SRS of 1% of all tax returns is selected in each state? Explain your answer.

20.37 Small-business failures. A study of the survival of small businesses chose an SRS from the telephone directory's Yellow Pages listings of food-and-drink businesses in 12 counties in central Indiana. For various reasons, the study got no response from 45% of the businesses chosen. Interviews were completed with 148 businesses. Three years later, 22 of these businesses had failed.[21]

(a) Give a 95% confidence interval for the percent of all small businesses in this class that fail within three years.

(b) Based on the results of this study, how large a sample would you need to reduce the margin of error to 0.04?

(c) The authors hope that their findings describe the population of all small businesses. What about the study makes this unlikely? What population do you think the study findings describe?

20.38 Customer satisfaction. An automobile manufacturer would like to know what proportion of its customers are not satisfied with the service provided by the local dealer. The customer relations department will survey a random sample of customers and compute a 99% confidence interval for the proportion who are not satisfied.

(a) Past studies suggest that this proportion will be about 0.2. Find the sample size needed if the margin of error of the confidence interval is to be about 0.015.

(b) When the sample is actually contacted, 10% of the sample say they are not satisfied. What is the margin of error of the 99% confidence interval?

20.39 Surveying students. You are planning a survey of students at a large university to determine what proportion favor an increase in student fees to support an expansion of the student newspaper. Using records provided by the registrar, you can select a random sample of students. You will ask each student in the sample whether he or she is in favor of the proposed increase. Your budget will allow a sample of 100 students.

(a) For a sample of size 100, construct a table of the margins of error for 95% confidence intervals when $\hat{p}$ takes the values 0.1, 0.2, 0.3, 0.4, 0.5, 0.6, 0.7, 0.8, and 0.9.

(b) A former editor of the student newspaper offers to provide funds for a sample of size 500. Repeat the margin of error calculations in (a) for the larger sample size. Then write a short thank-you note to the former editor describing how the larger sample size will improve the results of the survey.

*In responding to Exercises 20.40 to 20.43, follow the **Formulate, Solve,** and **Conclude** steps of the four-step process. It may be helpful to restate in your own words the **State** information given in the exercise.*

4 STEP

20.40 **Student drinking.** The College Alcohol Study interviewed a sample of 14,941 college students about their drinking habits. The sample was stratified using 140 colleges as strata, but the overall effect is close to an SRS of students. The response rate was between 60% and 70% at most colleges. This is quite good for a national sample, though nonresponse is as usual the biggest weakness of this survey. Of the students in the sample, 10,010 supported cracking down on underage drinking.[22] Estimate with 99% confidence the proportion of all college students who feel this way.

20.41 **Condom usage.** The National AIDS Behavioral Surveys (Example 20.1) also interviewed a sample of adults in the cities where AIDS is most common. This sample included 803 heterosexuals who reported having more than one sexual partner in the past year. We can consider this an SRS of size 803 from the population of all heterosexuals in high-risk cities who have multiple partners. These people risk infection with the AIDS virus. Yet 304 of the respondents said they never use condoms. Is this strong evidence that more than one-third of this population never use condoms?

20.42 **Online publishing.** Publishing scientific papers online is fast, and the papers can be long. Publishing in a paper journal means that the paper will live forever in libraries. The *British Medical Journal* combines the two: it prints short and readable versions, with longer versions available online. Is this OK with authors? The journal asked a random sample of 104 of its recent authors several questions.[23] One question was "Should the journal continue using this system?" In the sample, 72 said "Yes." What proportion of all authors would say "Yes" if asked? (Estimate with 95% confidence.) Do the data give good evidence that more than two-thirds (67%) of authors support continuing this system? Answer both questions with appropriate inference methods.

20.43 **More online publishing.** The previous exercise describes a survey of authors of papers in a medical journal. Another question in the survey asked whether authors would accept a stronger move toward online publishing: "As an author, how acceptable would it be for us to publish only the abstract of papers in the paper journal and continue to put the full long version on our website?" Of the 104 authors in the sample, 65 said "Not at all acceptable." What proportion of all authors feel that abstract-only publishing is not acceptable? (Estimate with 95% confidence.) Do the data provide good evidence that more than half of all authors feel that abstract-only publishing is not acceptable? Answer both questions with appropriate inference methods.

Michael S. Lewis/CORBIS

Comparing Two Proportions

In a **two-sample problem,** we want to compare two populations or the responses to two treatments based on two independent samples. When the comparison involves the *means* of two populations, we use the two-sample t methods of Chapter 19. Now we turn to methods to compare the *proportions* of successes in two populations.

Two

Two-sample problems: proportions

We will use notation similar to that used in our study of two-sample t statistics. The groups we want to compare are Population 1 and Population 2. We have a separate SRS from each population or responses from two treatments in a randomized comparative experiment. A subscript shows which group a parameter or statistic describes. Here is our notation:

Population	Population proportion	Sample size	Sample proportion
1	p_1	n_1	$\hat{p}_1$
2	p_2	n_2	$\hat{p}_2$

We compare the populations by doing inference about the difference $p_1 - p_2$ between the population proportions. The statistic that estimates this difference is the difference between the two sample proportions, $\hat{p}_1 - \hat{p}_2$.

EXAMPLE 21.1   Young adults living with their parents   **STEP**

STATE: A surprising number of young adults (ages 19 to 25) still live in their parents' home. A random sample by the National Institutes of Health included 2253 men and 2629 women in this age group.[1] The survey found that 986 of the men and 923 of the women lived with their parents. Is this good evidence that different proportions of young men and young women live with their parents? How large is the difference between the proportions of young men and young women who live with their parents?

FORMULATE: Take young men to be Population 1 and young women to be Population 2. The population proportions who live in their parents' home are p_1 for men and p_2 for women. We want to test the hypotheses

$$H_0\colon p_1 = p_2 \quad \text{(the same as } H_0\colon p_1 - p_2 = 0)$$

$$H_a\colon p_1 \neq p_2 \quad \text{(the same as } H_a\colon p_1 - p_2 \neq 0)$$

We also want to give a confidence interval for the difference $p_1 - p_2$.

SOLVE: Inference about population proportions is based on the sample proportions

$$\hat{p}_1 = \frac{986}{2253} = 0.4376 \quad \text{(men)}$$

$$\hat{p}_2 = \frac{923}{2629} = 0.3511 \quad \text{(women)}$$

We see that about 44% of the men but only about 35% of the women lived with their parents. Because the samples are large and the sample proportions are quite different, we expect that a test will be highly significant (in fact, $P < 0.0001$). So we concentrate on the confidence interval. To estimate $p_1 - p_2$, start from the difference of sample proportions

$$\hat{p}_1 - \hat{p}_2 = 0.4376 - 0.3511 = 0.0865$$

To complete the *Solve* step, we must know how this difference behaves.

The sampling distribution of a difference between proportions

To use $\hat{p}_1 - \hat{p}_2$ for inference, we must know its sampling distribution. Here are the facts we need:

- When the samples are large, the distribution of $\hat{p}_1 - \hat{p}_2$ is **approximately Normal.**
- The **mean** of the sampling distribution is $p_1 - p_2$. That is, the difference between sample proportions is an unbiased estimator of the difference between population proportions.

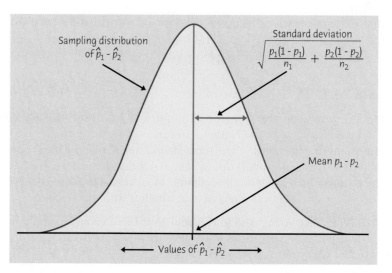

FIGURE 21.1 Select independent SRSs from two populations having proportions of successes p_1 and p_2. The proportions of successes in the two samples are $\hat{p}_1$ and $\hat{p}_2$. When the samples are large, the sampling distribution of the difference $\hat{p}_1 - \hat{p}_2$ is approximately Normal.

- The **standard deviation** of the distribution is

$$\sqrt{\frac{p_1(1-p_1)}{n_1} + \frac{p_2(1-p_2)}{n_2}}$$

Figure 21.1 displays the distribution of $\hat{p}_1 - \hat{p}_2$. The standard deviation of $\hat{p}_1 - \hat{p}_2$ involves the unknown parameters p_1 and p_2. Just as in the previous chapter, we must replace these by estimates in order to do inference. And just as in the previous chapter, we do this a bit differently for confidence intervals and for tests.

Large-sample confidence intervals for comparing proportions

standard error   To obtain a confidence interval, replace the population proportions p_1 and p_2 in the standard deviation by the sample proportions. The result is the **standard error** of the statistic $\hat{p}_1 - \hat{p}_2$:

$$\text{SE} = \sqrt{\frac{\hat{p}_1(1-\hat{p}_1)}{n_1} + \frac{\hat{p}_2(1-\hat{p}_2)}{n_2}}$$

The confidence interval has the same form we met in the previous chapter

$$\text{estimate} \pm z^* \text{SE}_{\text{estimate}}$$

LARGE-SAMPLE CONFIDENCE INTERVAL FOR COMPARING TWO PROPORTIONS

Draw an SRS of size n_1 from a large population having proportion p_1 of successes and draw an independent SRS of size n_2 from another large population having proportion p_2 of successes. When n_1 and n_2 are large, an approximate level C **confidence interval for $p_1 - p_2$** is

$$(\hat{p}_1 - \hat{p}_2) \pm z^*\text{SE}$$

In this formula the standard error SE of $\hat{p}_1 - \hat{p}_2$ is

$$\text{SE} = \sqrt{\frac{\hat{p}_1(1 - \hat{p}_1)}{n_1} + \frac{\hat{p}_2(1 - \hat{p}_2)}{n_2}}$$

and z^* is the critical value for the standard Normal density curve with area C between $-z^*$ and z^*.

Use this interval only when the numbers of successes and failures are each 10 or more in both samples.

EXAMPLE 21.2   Men versus women living with their parents
STEP

We can now complete Example 21.1. Here is a summary of the basic information:

Population	Population description	Sample size	Number of successes	Sample proportion
1	men	$n_1 = 2253$	986	$\hat{p}_1 = 986/2253 = 0.4376$
2	women	$n_2 = 2629$	923	$\hat{p}_2 = 923/2629 = 0.3511$

SOLVE: We will give a 95% confidence interval for $p_1 - p_2$, the difference between the proportions of young men and young women who live with their parents. To check that the large-sample confidence interval is safe, look at the counts of successes and failures in the two samples. All of these four counts are much larger than 10, so the large-sample method will be accurate. The standard error is

$$\begin{aligned}
\text{SE} &= \sqrt{\frac{\hat{p}_1(1 - \hat{p}_1)}{n_1} + \frac{\hat{p}_2(1 - \hat{p}_2)}{n_2}} \\[2mm]
&= \sqrt{\frac{(0.4376)(0.5624)}{2253} + \frac{(0.3511)(0.6489)}{2629}} \\[2mm]
&= \sqrt{0.0001959} = 0.01400
\end{aligned}$$

The 95% confidence interval is

$$(\hat{p}_1 - \hat{p}_2) \pm z^*\text{SE} = (0.4376 - 0.3511) \pm (1.960)(0.01400)$$
$$= 0.0865 \pm 0.0274$$
$$= 0.059 \text{ to } 0.114$$

CONCLUDE: We are 95% confident that the percent of young men living with their parents is between 5.9 and 11.4 percentage points higher than the percent of young women who live with their parents.

The sample survey in this example selected a single random sample of young adults, not two separate random samples of young men and young women. To get two samples, we divided the single sample by sex. This means that we did not know the two sample sizes n_1 and n_2 until after the data were in hand. The two-sample z procedures for comparing proportions are valid in such situations. This is an important fact about these methods.

Using technology

Figure 21.2 displays software output for Example 21.2 from a graphing calculator and two statistical software programs. As usual, you can understand the output even without knowledge of the program that produced it. Minitab gives the test as well as the confidence interval, confirming that the difference between men and women is highly significant. Excel spreadsheet output is not shown because Excel lacks menu items for inference about proportions. You must use the spreadsheet's

Computer-assisted interviewing.

The days of the interviewer with a clipboard are past. Interviewers now read questions from a computer screen and use the keyboard to enter responses. The computer skips irrelevant items—once a woman says that she has no children, further questions about her children never appear. The computer can even present questions in random order to avoid bias due to always following the same order. Software keeps records of who has responded and prepares a file of data from the responses. The tedious process of transferring responses from paper to computer, once a source of errors, has disappeared.

Texas Instruments TI-83 or TI-84

```
2-PropZInt
 (.05912,.11399)
 p̂₁=.437638704
 p̂₂=.3510840624
 n₁=2253
 n₂=2629
```

CrunchIt!

| Two sample Proportion with summary | | | | | | | | |

95% confidence interval results:
p_1 : proportion of successes for population 1
p_2 : proportion of successes for population 2
$p_1 - p_2$: difference in proportions

Difference	Count1	Total1	count2	Total2	Sample Diff.	Std. Err.	L. Limit	U. Limit
p1 - p2	986	2253	923	2629	0.08655464	0.013996254	0.059122488	0.1139868

FIGURE 21.2 Output from the TI-83 graphing calculator, CrunchIt!, and Minitab for the 95% confidence interval of Example 21.2 (*continued*).

Minitab

```
Session                                              _ □ ×

Test and CI for Two Proportions

Sample    X      N   Sample p
1        986   2253  0.437639
2        923   2629  0.351084

Difference = p (1) - p (2)
Estimate for difference: 0.0865546
95% CI for difference: (0.0591225, 0.113987)
Test for difference = 0 (vs not = 0): Z = 6.18   P-Value = 0.000
```

FIGURE 21.2 (*continued*).

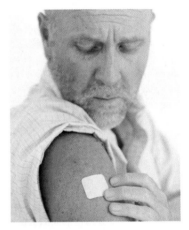

Stockbyte Platinum/Alamy

formula capability to program the confidence interval or test statistic and then to find the *P*-value of a test.

APPLY YOUR KNOWLEDGE

21.1   **Who uses instant messaging?**   Teenagers (ages 12 to 17) are much more likely to use instant messaging online than are adults (ages 18 and older). How much more likely? A random sample of Internet users found that 736 out of 981 teens and 511 out of 1217 adults use instant messaging.[2] Give a 95% confidence interval for the difference between the proportions of teenage and adult Internet users who use instant messaging. Follow the four-step process as illustrated in Examples 21.1 and 21.2.

21.2   **How to quit smoking.**   Nicotine patches are often used to help smokers quit. Does giving medicine to fight depression help? A randomized double-blind experiment assigned 244 smokers who wanted to stop to receive nicotine patches and another 245 to receive both a patch and the antidepression drug bupropion. After a year, 40 subjects in the nicotine patch group and 87 in the patch-plus-drug group had abstained from smoking.[3] Give a 99% confidence interval for the difference (treatment minus control) in the proportion of smokers who quit. Follow the four-step process as illustrated in Examples 21.1 and 21.2.

Accurate confidence intervals for comparing proportions

Like the large-sample confidence interval for a single proportion p, the large-sample interval for $p_1 - p_2$ generally has true confidence level less than the level you asked for. The inaccuracy is not as serious as in the one-sample case, at least if our guidelines for use are followed. Once again, adding imaginary observations greatly improves the accuracy.[4]

CAUTION

> ## PLUS FOUR CONFIDENCE INTERVAL FOR COMPARING TWO PROPORTIONS
>
> Draw independent SRSs from two populations with population proportions of successes p_1 and p_2. To get the **plus four confidence interval for the difference $p_1 - p_2$,** add four imaginary observations, one success and one failure in each of the two samples. Then use the large-sample confidence interval with the new sample sizes (actual sample sizes + 2) and counts of successes (actual counts + 1).
>
> Use this interval when the sample size is at least 5 in each group, with any counts of successes and failures.

If your software does not offer the plus four method, just enter the new plus four sample sizes and success counts into the large-sample procedure.

EXAMPLE 21.3   Shrubs that withstand fire

STATE: Some shrubs can resprout from their roots after their tops are destroyed. Fire is a serious threat to shrubs in dry climates, as it can injure the roots as well as destroy the tops. One study of resprouting took place in a dry area of Mexico.[5] The investigators randomly assigned shrubs to treatment and control groups. They clipped the tops of all the shrubs. They then applied a propane torch to the stumps of the treatment group to simulate a fire. A shrub is a success if it resprouts. Here are the data for the shrub *Xerospirea hartwegiana:*

Population	Population description	Sample size	Number of successes	Sample proportion
1	control	$n_1 = 12$	12	$\hat{p}_1 = 12/12 = 1.000$
2	treatment	$n_2 = 12$	8	$\hat{p}_2 = 8/12 = 0.667$

How much does burning reduce the proportion of shrubs of this species that resprout?

FORMULATE: Give a 90% confidence interval for the difference of population proportions, $p_1 - p_2$.

SOLVE: The conditions for the large-sample interval are not met. In fact, there are *no* failures in the control group. We will use the plus four method. Add four imaginary observations. The new data summary is

Population	Population description	Sample size	Number of successes	Plus four sample proportion
1	control	$n_1 + 2 = 14$	$12 + 1 = 13$	$\tilde{p}_1 = 13/14 = 0.9286$
2	treatment	$n_2 + 2 = 14$	$8 + 1 = 9$	$\tilde{p}_2 = 9/14 = 0.6429$

The standard error based on the new facts is

$$SE = \sqrt{\frac{\tilde{p}_1(1 - \tilde{p}_1)}{n_1 + 2} + \frac{\tilde{p}_2(1 - \tilde{p}_2)}{n_2 + 2}}$$

$$= \sqrt{\frac{(0.9286)(0.0714)}{14} + \frac{(0.6429)(0.3571)}{14}}$$

$$= \sqrt{0.02113} = 0.1454$$

The plus four 90% confidence interval is

$$(\tilde{p}_1 - \tilde{p}_2) \pm z^*SE = (0.9286 - 0.6429) \pm (1.645)(0.1454)$$

$$= 0.2857 \pm 0.2392$$

$$= 0.047 \text{ to } 0.525$$

CONCLUDE: We are 90% confident that burning reduces the percent of these shrubs that resprout by between 4.7% and 52.5%.

The plus four interval may be conservative (that is, the true confidence level may be *higher* than you asked for) for very small samples and population p's close to 0 or 1, as in this example. It is generally much more accurate than the large-sample interval when the samples are small. Nevertheless, the plus four interval in Example 21.3 cannot save us from the fact that small samples produce wide confidence intervals.

APPLY YOUR KNOWLEDGE

21.3 **Broken crackers.** We don't like to find broken crackers when we open the package. How can makers reduce breaking? One idea is to microwave the crackers for 30 seconds right after baking them. Breaks start as hairline cracks called "checking." Assign 65 newly baked crackers to the microwave and another 65 to a control group that is not microwaved. After one day, none of the microwave group and 16 of the control group show checking.[6] Give the 95% plus four confidence interval for the amount by which microwaving reduces the proportion of checking. The plus four method is particularly helpful when, as here, a count of successes is zero. Follow the four-step process as illustrated in Example 21.3.

21.4 **In-line skaters.** A study of injuries to in-line skaters used data from the National Electronic Injury Surveillance System, which collects data from a random sample of hospital emergency rooms. The researchers interviewed 161 people who came to emergency rooms with injuries from in-line skating. Wrist injuries (mostly fractures) were the most common.[7]

(a) The interviews found that 53 people were wearing wrist guards and 6 of these had wrist injuries. Of the 108 who did not wear wrist guards, 45 had wrist injuries. Why should we not use the large-sample confidence interval for these data?

(b) Give the plus four 95% confidence interval for the difference between the two population proportions of wrist injuries. State carefully what populations your inference compares. We would like to draw conclusions about all in-line skaters, but we have data only for injured skaters.

Jim Cummins/Getty Images

Significance tests for comparing proportions

An observed difference between two sample proportions can reflect an actual difference between the populations, or it may just be due to chance variation in random sampling. Significance tests help us decide if the effect we see in the samples is really there in the populations. The null hypothesis says that there is no difference between the two populations:

$$H_0: p_1 = p_2$$

The alternative hypothesis says what kind of difference we expect.

EXAMPLE 21.4   *Choosing a mate*

STATE: "Would you marry a person from a lower social class than your own?" Researchers asked this question of a sample of 385 black, never-married students at two historically black colleges in the South. We will consider this to be an SRS of black students at historically black colleges. Of the 149 men in the sample, 91 said "Yes." Among the 236 women, 117 said "Yes."[8] Is there reason to think that different proportions of men and women in this student population would be willing to marry beneath their class?

FORMULATE: Take men to be Population 1 and women to be Population 2. We had no direction for the difference in mind before looking at the data, so we have a two-sided alternative:

$$H_0: p_1 = p_2$$
$$H_a: p_1 \neq p_2$$

SOLVE: The men and women in a single SRS can be treated as if they were separate SRSs of men and women students. The sample proportions who would marry someone from a lower social class are

$$\hat{p}_1 = \frac{91}{149} = 0.611 \quad \text{(men)}$$

$$\hat{p}_2 = \frac{117}{236} = 0.496 \quad \text{(women)}$$

That is, about 61% of the men but only about 50% of the women would marry beneath their class. Is this apparent difference statistically significant? To continue the solution, we must learn the proper test.

To do a test, standardize $\hat{p}_1 - \hat{p}_2$ to get a z statistic. If H_0 is true, all the observations in both samples come from a single population of students of whom a single unknown proportion p would marry someone from a lower social class. So instead of estimating p_1 and p_2 separately, we pool the two samples and use the overall sample proportion to estimate the single population parameter p. Call this the **pooled sample proportion.** It is

pooled sample proportion

$$\hat{p} = \frac{\text{number of successes in both samples combined}}{\text{number of individuals in both samples combined}}$$

Use $\hat{p}$ in place of both $\hat{p}_1$ and $\hat{p}_2$ in the expression for the standard error SE of $\hat{p}_1 - \hat{p}_2$ to get a z statistic that has the standard Normal distribution when H_0 is true. Here is the test.

SIGNIFICANCE TEST FOR COMPARING TWO PROPORTIONS

Draw an SRS of size n_1 from a large population having proportion p_1 of successes and draw an independent SRS of size n_2 from another large population having proportion p_2 of successes. To **test the hypothesis** H_0: $p_1 = p_2$, first find the pooled proportion $\hat{p}$ of successes in both samples combined. Then compute the z statistic

$$z = \frac{\hat{p}_1 - \hat{p}_2}{\sqrt{\hat{p}(1 - \hat{p})\left(\dfrac{1}{n_1} + \dfrac{1}{n_2}\right)}}$$

In terms of a variable Z having the standard Normal distribution, the P-value for a test of H_0 against

H_a: $p_1 > p_2$ is $P(Z \geq z)$
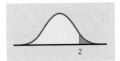

H_a: $p_1 < p_2$ is $P(Z \leq z)$
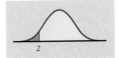

H_a: $p_1 \neq p_2$ is $2P(Z \geq |z|)$
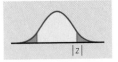

Use this test when the counts of successes and failures are each 5 or more in both samples.

Statisticians honest and dishonest

Government statisticians ought to produce honest data. We trust the monthly unemployment rate and Consumer Price Index to guide both public and private decisions. Honesty can't be taken for granted everywhere, however. In 1998, the Russian government arrested the top statisticians in the State Committee for Statistics. They were accused of taking bribes to fudge data to help companies avoid taxes. "It means that we know nothing about the performance of Russian companies," said one newspaper editor.

┌─ **EXAMPLE 21.5** *Choosing a mate, continued*

STEP

SOLVE: The data come from an SRS and the counts of successes and failures are all much larger than 5. The pooled proportion of students who would marry beneath their own social class is

$$\hat{p} = \frac{\text{number of "Yes" responses among men and women combined}}{\text{number of men and women combined}}$$

$$= \frac{91 + 117}{149 + 236}$$

$$= \frac{208}{385} = 0.5403$$

The z test statistic is

$$z = \frac{\hat{p}_1 - \hat{p}_2}{\sqrt{\hat{p}(1-\hat{p})\left(\dfrac{1}{n_1} + \dfrac{1}{n_2}\right)}}$$

$$= \frac{0.611 - 0.496}{\sqrt{(0.5403)(0.4597)\left(\dfrac{1}{149} + \dfrac{1}{236}\right)}}$$

$$= \frac{0.115}{0.05215} = 2.205$$

The two-sided P-value is the area under the standard Normal curve more than 2.205 distant from 0. Figure 21.3 shows this area. Software tells us that $P = 0.0275$.

Without software, you can use the bottom row of Table C (standard Normal critical values) to approximate P with no calculations: $z = 2.205$ lies between the critical values 2.054 and 2.326 for two-sided P-values 0.04 and 0.02.

CONCLUDE: There is good evidence ($P < 0.04$) that men are more likely than women to say they will marry someone from a lower social class.

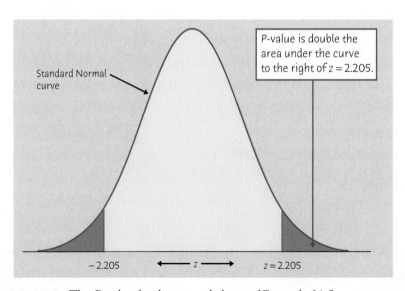

FIGURE 21.3 The P-value for the two-sided test of Example 21.5.

APPLY YOUR KNOWLEDGE

21.5   **The Gold Coast.**   A historian examining British colonial records for the Gold Coast in Africa suspects that the death rate was higher among African miners than among European miners. In the year 1936, there were 223 deaths among 33,809 African miners and 7 deaths among 1541 European miners on the Gold Coast.[9] (The Gold Coast became the independent nation of Ghana in 1957.)

     Consider this year as a random sample from the colonial era in West Africa. Is there good evidence that the proportion of African miners who died was higher than the proportion of European miners who died? Follow the four-step process as illustrated in Example 21.5.

21.6   **How to quit smoking, continued.**   Exercise 21.2 describes a randomized comparative experiment to test whether adding medicine to fight depression increases the effectiveness of nicotine patches in helping smokers to quit. How significant is the evidence that the medicine increases the success rate? Follow the four-step process as illustrated in Example 21.5.

Michael S. Lewis/CORBIS

CHAPTER 21 SUMMARY

The data in a **two-sample problem** are two independent SRSs, each drawn from a separate population.

Tests and confidence intervals to compare the proportions p_1 and p_2 of successes in the two populations are based on the difference $\hat{p}_1 - \hat{p}_2$ between the sample proportions of successes in the two SRSs.

When the sample sizes n_1 and n_2 are large, the sampling distribution of $\hat{p}_1 - \hat{p}_2$ is close to Normal with mean $p_1 - p_2$.

The level C **large-sample confidence interval for $p_1 - p_2$** is

$$(\hat{p}_1 - \hat{p}_2) \pm z^* SE$$

where the standard error of $\hat{p}_1 - \hat{p}_2$ is

$$SE = \sqrt{\frac{\hat{p}_1(1 - \hat{p}_1)}{n_1} + \frac{\hat{p}_2(1 - \hat{p}_2)}{n_2}}$$

and z^* is a standard Normal critical value.

The true confidence level of the large-sample interval can be substantially less than the planned level C. Use this interval only if the counts of successes and failures in both samples are 10 or greater.

To get a more accurate confidence interval, add four imaginary observations: one success and one failure in each sample. Then use the same formula for the confidence interval. This is the **plus four confidence interval.** You can use it whenever both samples have 5 or more observations.

Significance tests for H_0: $p_1 = p_2$ use the **pooled sample proportion**

$$\hat{p} = \frac{\text{number of successes in both samples combined}}{\text{number of individuals in both samples combined}}$$

and the z statistic

$$z = \frac{\hat{p}_1 - \hat{p}_2}{\sqrt{\hat{p}(1 - \hat{p})\left(\dfrac{1}{n_1} + \dfrac{1}{n_2}\right)}}$$

P-values come from the standard Normal distribution. Use this test when there are 5 or more successes and 5 or more failures in both samples.

CHECK YOUR SKILLS ──────────────────────

A sample survey interviews SRSs of 500 female college students and 550 male college students. Each student is asked if he or she worked for pay last summer. In all, 410 of the women and 484 of the men say "Yes." Exercises 21.7 to 21.11 are based on this survey.

21.7 Take p_M and p_F to be the proportions of all college males and females who worked last summer. We conjectured before seeing the data that men are more likely to work. The hypotheses to be tested are

(a) $H_0: p_M = p_F$ versus $H_a: p_M \neq p_F$.

(b) $H_0: p_M = p_F$ versus $H_a: p_M > p_F$.

(c) $H_0: p_M = p_F$ versus $H_a: p_M < p_F$.

21.8 The sample proportions of college males and females who worked last summer are about

(a) $\hat{p}_M = 0.88$ and $\hat{p}_F = 0.82$.

(b) $\hat{p}_M = 0.82$ and $\hat{p}_F = 0.88$.

(c) $\hat{p}_M = 0.75$ and $\hat{p}_F = 0.97$.

21.9 The pooled sample proportion who worked last summer is about

(a) $\hat{p} = 1.70$.   (b) $\hat{p} = 0.89$.   (c) $\hat{p} = 0.85$.

21.10 The z statistic for a test comparing the proportions of college men and women who worked last summer is about

(a) $z = 2.66$.   (b) $z = 2.72$.   (c) $z = 3.10$.

21.11 The 95% large-sample confidence interval for the difference $p_M - p_F$ in the proportions of college men and women who worked last summer is about

(a) 0.06 ± 0.00095.   (b) 0.06 ± 0.043.   (c) 0.06 ± 0.036.

21.12 In an experiment to learn if substance M can help restore memory, the brains of 20 rats were treated to damage their memories. The rats were trained to run a maze. After a day, 10 rats were given M and 7 of them succeeded in the maze; only 2 of the 10 control rats were successful. The z test for "no difference" against "a higher proportion of the M group succeeds" has

(a) $z = 2.25$, $P < 0.02$.

(b) $z = 2.60$, $P < 0.005$.

(c) $z = 2.25$, $P < 0.04$ but not < 0.02.

21.13 The z test in the previous exercise

(a) may be inaccurate because the populations are too small.

(b) may be inaccurate because some counts of successes and failures are too small.

(c) is reasonably accurate because the conditions for inference are met.

21.14 The plus four 90% confidence interval for the difference between the proportion of rats that succeed when given M and the proportion that succeed without it is

(a) 0.455 ± 0.312.   (b) 0.417 ± 0.304.   (c) 0.417 ± 0.185.

CHAPTER 21 EXERCISES

We recommend using the plus four method for all confidence intervals for proportions. However, the large-sample method is acceptable when the guidelines for its use are met.

21.15 Genetically altered mice. Genetic influences on cancer can be studied by manipulating the genetic makeup of mice. One of the processes that turn genes on or off (so to speak) in particular locations is called "DNA methylation." Do low levels of this process help cause tumors? Compare mice altered to have low levels with normal mice. Of 33 mice with lowered levels of DNA methylation, 23 developed tumors. None of the control group of 18 normal mice developed tumors in the same time period.[10]

(a) Explain why we cannot safely use either the large-sample confidence interval or the test for comparing the proportions of normal and altered mice that develop tumors.

(b) Give a 99% confidence interval for the difference in the proportions of the two populations that develop tumors.

(c) Based on your confidence interval, is the difference between normal and altered mice significant at the 1% level?

21.16 Drug testing in schools. In 2002 the Supreme Court ruled that schools could require random drug tests of students participating in competitive after-school activities such as athletics. Does drug testing reduce use of illegal drugs? A study compared two similar high schools in Oregon. Wahtonka High School tested athletes at random and Warrenton High School did not. In a confidential survey, 7 of 135 athletes at Wahtonka and 27 of 141 athletes at Warrenton said they were using drugs.[11] Regard these athletes as SRSs from the populations of athletes at similar schools with and without drug testing.

(a) You should not use the large-sample confidence interval. Why not?

(b) The plus four method adds two observations, a success and a failure, to each sample. What are the sample sizes and the numbers of drug users after you do this?

(c) Give the plus four 95% confidence interval for the difference between the proportion of athletes using drugs at schools with and without testing.

21.17 I refuse! Do our emotions influence economic decisions? One way to examine the issue is to have subjects play an "ultimatum game" against other people and against a computer. Your partner (person or computer) gets $10, on the condition that it be shared with you. The partner makes you an offer. If you refuse, neither of you gets anything. So it's to your advantage to accept even the unfair offer of $2 out of the $10. Some people get mad and refuse unfair offers. Here are data on the responses of 76 subjects randomly assigned to receive an offer of $2 from either a person they were introduced to or a computer:[12]

	Accept	Reject
Human offers	20	18
Computer offers	32	6

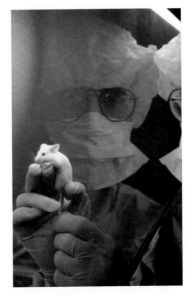

Mark Harmel/Getty Images

We suspect that emotion will lead to offers from another person being rejected more often than offers from an impersonal computer. Do a test to assess the evidence for this conjecture. Follow the four-step process as illustrated in Example 21.5.

21.18 **Drug testing in schools, continued.**   Exercise 21.16 describes a study that compared the proportions of athletes who use illegal drugs in two similar high schools, one that tests for drugs and one that does not. Drug testing is intended to reduce use of drugs. Do the data give good reason to think that drug use among athletes is lower in schools that test for drugs? State hypotheses, find the test statistic, and use either software or the bottom row of Table C for the P-value. Be sure to state your conclusion. (Because the study is not an experiment, the conclusion depends on the condition that athletes in these two schools can be considered SRSs from all similar schools.)

Call a statistician.   *Does involving a statistician to help with statistical methods improve the chance that a medical research paper will be published? A study of papers submitted to two medical journals found that 135 of 190 papers that lacked statistical assistance were rejected without even being reviewed in detail. In contrast, 293 of the 514 papers with statistical help were sent back without review.*[13] *Exercises 21.19 to 21.21 are based on this study.*

21.19 **Does statistical help make a difference?**   Is there a significant difference in the proportions of papers with and without statistical help that are rejected without review? Use software or the bottom row of Table C to get a P-value. (This observational study does not establish causation: studies that include statistical help may also be better in other ways than those that do not.)

21.20 **How often are statisticians involved?**   Give a 95% confidence interval for the proportion of papers submitted to these journals that include help from a statistician.

21.21 **How big a difference?**   Give a 95% confidence interval for the difference between the proportions of papers rejected without review when a statistician is and is not involved in the research.

21.22 **Steroids in high school.**   A study by the National Athletic Trainers Association surveyed 1679 high school freshmen and 1366 high school seniors in Illinois. Results showed that 34 of the freshmen and 24 of the seniors had used anabolic steroids. Steroids, which are dangerous, are sometimes used to improve athletic performance.[14]

(a) In order to draw conclusions about all Illinois freshmen and seniors, how should the study samples be chosen?

(b) Give a 95% confidence interval for the proportion of all high school freshmen in Illinois who have used steroids.

(c) Is there a significant difference between the proportions of freshmen and seniors who have used steroids?

21.23 **Detecting genetically modified soybeans.**   Exercise 20.35 (page 509) describes a study in which batches of soybeans containing some genetically modified (GM) beans were submitted to 23 grain-handling facilities. When batches contained 1% of GM beans, 18 of the facilities detected the presence of GM beans. Only 7 of the facilities detected GM beans when they made up one-tenth of 1% of the beans in the batches. Explain why we *cannot* use the methods of this chapter to compare the proportions of facilities that will detect the two levels of GM soybeans.

21.24 **Significant does not mean important.** Never forget that even small effects can be statistically significant if the samples are large. To illustrate this fact, return to the study of 148 small businesses described in Exercise 20.37 (page 510). Of these, 106 were headed by men and 42 were headed by women. During a three-year period, 15 of the men's businesses and 7 of the women's businesses failed.

(a) Find the proportions of failures for businesses headed by women and businesses headed by men. These sample proportions are quite close to each other. Give the P-value for the z test of the hypothesis that the same proportion of women's and men's businesses fail. (Use the two-sided alternative.) The test is very far from being significant.

(b) Now suppose that the same sample proportions came from a sample 30 times as large. That is, 210 out of 1260 businesses headed by women and 450 out of 3180 businesses headed by men fail. Verify that the proportions of failures are exactly the same as in (a). Repeat the z test for the new data, and show that it is now significant at the $\alpha = 0.05$ level.

(c) It is wise to use a confidence interval to estimate the size of an effect, rather than just giving a P-value. Give 95% confidence intervals for the difference between the proportions of women's and men's businesses that fail for the settings of both (a) and (b). What is the effect of larger samples on the confidence interval?

*In responding to Exercises 21.25 to 21.34, follow the **Formulate, Solve,** and **Conclude** steps of the four-step process. It may be helpful to restate in your own words the **State** information given in the exercise.*

21.25 **Satisfaction with high schools.** A sample survey asked 202 black parents and 201 white parents of high school children, "Are the public high schools in your state doing an excellent, good, fair or poor job, or don't you know enough to say?" The investigators suspected that black parents are generally less satisfied with their public schools than are whites. Among the black parents, 81 thought high schools were doing a "good" or "excellent" job; 103 of the white parents felt this way.[15] Is there good evidence that the proportion of all black parents who think their state's high schools are good or excellent is lower than the proportion of white parents with this opinion?

21.26 **College is important.** The sample survey described in the previous exercise also asked respondents if they agreed with the statement "A college education has become as important as a high school diploma used to be." In the sample, 125 of 201 white parents and 154 of 202 black parents said that they "strongly agreed." Is there good reason to think that different percents of all black and white parents would strongly agree with the statement?

21.27 **Seat belt use.** The proportion of drivers who use seat belts depends on things like age (young people are more likely to go unbelted) and gender (women are more likely to use belts). It also depends on local law. In New York City, police can stop a driver who is not belted. In Boston at the time of the survey, police could cite a driver for not wearing a seat belt only if the driver had been stopped for some other violation. Here are data from observing random samples of female Hispanic drivers in these two cities:[16]

City	Drivers	Belted
New York	220	183
Boston	117	68

(a) Is this an experiment or an observational study? Why?

(b) Comparing local laws suggests the hypothesis that a smaller proportion of drivers wear seat belts in Boston than in New York. Do the data give good evidence that this is true for female Hispanic drivers?

21.28 Ethnicity and seat belt use. Here are data from the study described in the previous exercise for Hispanic and white male drivers in Chicago:

Group	Drivers	Belted
Hispanic	539	286
White	292	164

Is there a significant difference between Hispanic and white drivers? How large is the difference? Do inference to answer both questions. Be sure to explain exactly what inference you choose to do.

21.29 Lyme disease. Lyme disease is spread in the northeastern United States by infected ticks. The ticks are infected mainly by feeding on mice, so more mice result in more infected ticks. The mouse population in turn rises and falls with the abundance of acorns, their favored food. Experimenters studied two similar forest areas in a year when the acorn crop failed. They added hundreds of thousands of acorns to one area to imitate an abundant acorn crop, while leaving the other area untouched. The next spring, 54 of the 72 mice trapped in the first area were in breeding condition, versus 10 of the 17 mice trapped in the second area.[17] Estimate the difference between the proportions of mice ready to breed in good acorn years and bad acorn years. (Use 90% confidence. Be sure to justify your choice of confidence interval.)

21.30 Are urban students more successful? North Carolina State University looked at the factors that affect the success of students in a required chemical engineering course. Students must get a C or better in the course in order to continue as chemical engineering majors, so a "success" is a grade of C or better. There were 65 students from urban or suburban backgrounds, and 52 of these students succeeded. Another 55 students were from rural or small-town backgrounds; 30 of these students succeeded in the course.[18] Is there good evidence that the proportion of students who succeed is different for urban/suburban versus rural/small-town backgrounds? How large is the difference? (Use 90% confidence.)

21.31 Does preschool help? To study the long-term effects of preschool programs for poor children, the High/Scope Educational Research Foundation has followed two groups of Michigan children since early childhood.[19] One group of 62 attended preschool as 3- and 4-year-olds. A control group of 61 children from the

Scott Camazine/Photo Researchers

same area and similar backgrounds did not attend preschool. Over a ten-year period as adults, 38 of the preschool sample and 49 of the control sample needed social services (mainly welfare). Does the study provide significant evidence that children who attend preschool have less need for social services as adults? How large is the difference between the proportions of the preschool and no-preschool populations that require social services? Do inference to answer both questions. Be sure to explain exactly what inference you choose to do.

21.32 **Female and male students.** The North Carolina State University study (Exercise 21.30) also looked at possible differences in the proportions of female and male students who succeeded in the course. They found that 23 of the 34 women and 60 of the 89 men succeeded. Is there evidence of a difference between the proportions of women and men who succeed?

21.33 **Study design.** The study in Exercise 21.31 randomly assigned 123 children to the two groups. The same data could have come from a study that followed children whose parents did or did not enroll them in preschool. Explain carefully how the conclusions we can draw depend on which design was used.

21.34 **Using credit cards.** Are shoppers more or less likely to use credit cards for "impulse purchases" that they decide to make on the spot, as opposed to purchases that they had in mind when they went to the store? Stop every third person leaving a department store with a purchase. (This is in effect a random sample of people who buy at that store.) A few questions allow us to classify the purchase as impulse or not. Here are the data on how the customer paid:[20]

	Credit Card?	
	Yes	No
Impulse purchases	13	18
Planned purchases	35	31

Estimate with 95% confidence the percent of all customers at this store who use a credit card. Give numerical summaries to describe the difference in credit card use between impulse and planned purchases. Is this difference statistically significant?

Lee Snider/CORBIS

Inference about Variables: Part III Review

The procedures of Chapters 18 to 21 are among the most common of all statistical inference methods. The Statistics in Summary flowchart on the next page helps you decide when to use them. It is important to do some of the review exercises because now, for the first time, you must decide which of several inference procedures to use. Learning to recognize problem settings in order to choose the right type of inference is a key step in advancing your mastery of statistics. The flowchart is based on two key questions:

- **What population parameter** does your problem concern? You should be familiar in detail with inference for *means* (Chapters 18 and 19) and for *proportions* (Chapters 20 and 21). This is the first branch point in the flowchart.

- **What type of design** produced the data? You should be familiar with data from a *single sample*, from *matched pairs*, and from *two independent samples*. This is the second branch point in the flowchart. Your choice here is the same for experiments and for observational studies—inference methods are the same for both. But don't forget that experiments give much better evidence that an effect uncovered by inference can be explained by direct causation.

Answering these questions is part of the *Formulate* step in the four-step process. To begin the *Solve* step, follow the flowchart to the correct procedure. Then ask another question:

- **Are the conditions for this procedure met?** Can you act as if the data come from a random sample or randomized comparative experiment? Do the data show extreme outliers or strong skewness that forbid use of inference based on Normality? Do you have enough observations for your intended procedure?

You may ask, as you study the Statistics in Summary flowchart, "What if I have an experiment comparing four treatments, or samples from three populations?" The flowchart allows only one or two, not three or four or more. Be patient: methods for comparing more than two means or proportions, as well as some other settings for inference, appear in Part IV.

There is of course more to doing statistics well than choosing and carrying out the proper procedures. At the end of the book you will find a short outline of "Statistical Thinking Revisited," which will remind you of some of the big ideas that guide statistics in practice, as well as warn of some of the most common pitfalls. Look at that outline now, especially if you are near the end of your study of this book.

STATISTICS IN SUMMARY
Inference about Means and Proportions

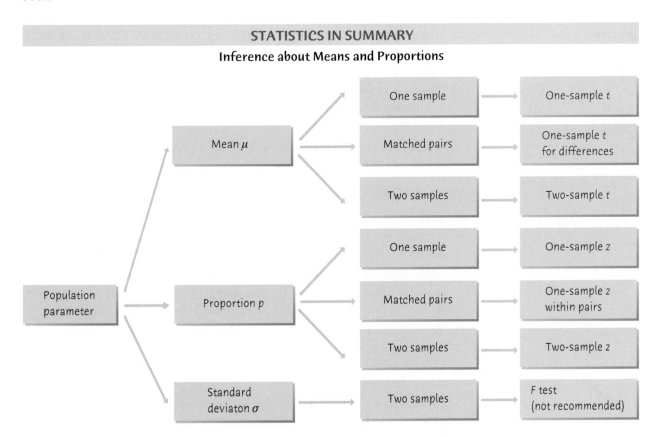

How many was that?

Good causes often breed bad statistics. An advocacy group claims, without much evidence, that 150,000 Americans suffer from the eating disorder anorexia nervosa. Soon someone misunderstands and says that 150,000 people *die* from anorexia nervosa each year. This wild number gets repeated in countless books and articles. It really is a wild number: only about 55,000 women aged 15 to 44 (the main group affected) die of *all causes* each year.

PART III SUMMARY

Here are the most important skills you should have acquired from reading Chapters 18 to 21.

A. RECOGNITION

1. Recognize when a problem requires inference about population means (quantitative response variable) or population proportions (usually categorical response variable).

2. Recognize from the design of a study whether one-sample, matched pairs, or two-sample procedures are needed.

3. Based on recognizing the problem setting, choose among the one- and two-sample t procedures for means and the one- and two-sample z procedures for proportions.

B. INFERENCE ABOUT ONE MEAN

1. Verify that the t procedures are appropriate in a particular setting. Check the study design and the distribution of the data and take advantage of robustness against lack of Normality.

2. Recognize when poor study design, outliers, or a small sample from a skewed distribution make the t procedures risky.

3. Use the one-sample t procedure to obtain a confidence interval at a stated level of confidence for the mean μ of a population.

4. Carry out a one-sample t test for the hypothesis that a population mean μ has a specified value against either a one-sided or a two-sided alternative. Use software to find the P-value or Table C to get an approximate value.

5. Recognize matched pairs data and use the t procedures to obtain confidence intervals and to perform tests of significance for such data.

C. COMPARING TWO MEANS

1. Verify that the two-sample t procedures are appropriate in a particular setting. Check the study design and the distribution of the data and take advantage of robustness against lack of Normality.

2. Give a confidence interval for the difference between two means. Use software if you have it. Use the two-sample t statistic with conservative degrees of freedom and Table C if you do not have statistical software.

3. Test the hypothesis that two populations have equal means against either a one-sided or a two-sided alternative. Use software if you have it. Use the two-sample t test with conservative degrees of freedom and Table C if you do not have statistical software.

4. Know that procedures for comparing the standard deviations of two Normal populations are available, but that these procedures are risky because they are not at all robust against non-Normal distributions.

D. INFERENCE ABOUT ONE PROPORTION

1. Verify that you can safely use either the large-sample or the plus four z procedures in a particular setting. Check the study design and the guidelines for sample size.

2. Use the large-sample z procedure to give a confidence interval for a population proportion p. Understand that the true confidence level may be substantially less than you ask for unless the sample is very large and the true p is not close to 0 or 1.

3. Use the plus four modification of the z procedure to give a confidence interval for p that is accurate even for small samples and for any value of p.

4. Use the z statistic to carry out a test of significance for the hypothesis $H_0: p = p_0$ about a population proportion p against either a one-sided or a two-sided alternative. Use software or Table A to find the P-value, or Table C to get an approximate value.

E. COMPARING TWO PROPORTIONS

1. Verify that you can safely use either the large-sample or the plus four z procedures in a particular setting. Check the study design and the guidelines for sample sizes.

2. Use the large-sample z procedure to give a confidence interval for the difference $p_1 - p_2$ between proportions in two populations based on independent samples from the populations. Understand that the true confidence level may be less than you ask for unless the samples are quite large.

3. Use the plus four modification of the z procedure to give a confidence interval for $p_1 - p_2$ that is accurate even for very small samples and for any values of p_1 and p_2.

4. Use a z statistic to test the hypothesis $H_0: p_1 = p_2$ that proportions in two distinct populations are equal. Use software or Table A to find the P-value, or Table C to get an approximate value.

REVIEW EXERCISES

Review exercises are short and straightforward exercises that help you solidify the basic ideas and skills from Chapters 18 to 21.

*For exercises that call for inference, your answers should include the **Formulate, Solve, and Conclude** steps of the four-step process. It is helpful to also summarize in your own words the **State** information given in the exercise. For tests of significance, use Table C to approximate P-values unless you use software that reports the P-value or the exercise asks you to use Table A for a z test. For confidence intervals for proportions, use the plus four procedures unless the sample sizes are very large.*

22.1   **Comparing universities.**   You have data on a random sample of students from each of two large universities. Which procedure from the Statistics in Summary flowchart would you use to compare

Lee Snider/CORBIS

(a) the percents of foreign students among undergraduates?

(b) the average SAT scores of undergraduates?

22.2   **Acid rain?**   You have data on rainwater collected at 16 locations in the Adirondack Mountains of New York State. One measurement is the acidity of the water, measured by pH on a scale of 0 to 14 (the pH of distilled water is 7.0). Which procedure from the Statistics in Summary flowchart would you use to estimate the average acidity of rainwater in the Adirondacks?

22.3   **Athletes' salaries.**   Looking online, you find the salaries of all 26 players for the Chicago Cubs as of opening day of the 2006 baseball season. The club total was $94.8 million, seventh in the major leagues. Can you use a procedure from the Statistics in Summary flowchart to estimate the average salary of the Cubs players?

22.4   **Looking back on love.**   How do young adults look back on adolescent romance? Investigators interviewed 40 couples in their midtwenties. The female and male partners were interviewed separately. Each was asked about their current relationship and also about a romantic relationship that lasted at least two months when they were aged 15 or 16. One response variable was a measure on a numerical scale of how much the attractiveness of the adolescent partner mattered. Which of the tests in the Statistics in Summary flowchart should you use to compare the men and women on this measure?

(a) t for means or z for proportions?

(b) one-sample, matched pairs, or two-sample?

22.5   **Preventing AIDS through education.**   The Multisite HIV Prevention Trial was a randomized comparative experiment to compare the effects of twice-weekly small-group AIDS discussion sessions (the treatment) with a single one-hour session (the control). Which of the procedures in the Statistics in Summary flowchart should you use to compare the effects of treatment and control on each of the following response variables?

(a) A subject does or does not use condoms 6 months after the education sessions.

(b) The number of unprotected intercourse acts by a subject between 4 and 8 months after the sessions.

(c) A subject is or is not infected with a sexually transmitted disease 6 months after the sessions.

22.6   **Potato chips.**   Here is the description of the design of a study that compared subjects' responses to regular and fat-free potato chips:

During a given 2-wk period, the participants received the same type of chip (regular or fat-free) each day. After the first 2-wk period, there was a 1-wk washout period in which no testing was performed. There was then another 2-wk period in which the participants received the alternate type of potato chip (regular or fat-free) each day under the same protocol. The order in which the chips were presented was determined by random assignment.[1]

One response variable was the weight in grams of potato chips that a subject ate. We want to compare the amounts of regular and fat-free chips eaten.

(a) The subjects were 44 women. Explain how the design should use random assignment. Use the *Simple Random Sample* applet, other software, or Table B to do the randomization. If you use Table B, start at line 101 and assign only the first 5 women.

APPLET

(b) Which test from the Statistics in Summary flowchart should you use to test the null hypothesis of no difference between regular and fat-free chips?

Many low- and middle-income families don't save enough for their future retirement. It would be to their advantage to contribute to an individual retirement account (IRA), which allows money to be invested for retirement without paying taxes on it now. Would more families contribute to an IRA if the money they invest was matched by their employer or other group? In an experiment on this question, the tax firm H&R Block offered to partly match IRA contributions of families with incomes below $40,000. In all, 1681 married taxpayers were assigned at random to the control group (no match), 1780 to a 20% match, and 1831 to a 50% match. All were offered the chance to open an IRA.[2] Exercises 22.7 to 22.11 concern this experiment.

22.7 **The design.** Outline the design of this experiment. (The subjects were taxpayers visiting H&R Block offices in the St. Louis area. It isn't practical to start with an SRS of all taxpayers. So the findings may not apply to, for example, taxpayers in California.)

22.8 **The response.** The study found that 49 married taxpayers in the control group, 240 in the 20% group, and 456 in the 50% group opened IRAs. Give three 95% confidence intervals, for the proportions of all married taxpayers who would open IRAs if given each offer. Does it appear that matching raises the proportion who open an IRA?

22.9 **Is more better?** Does a significantly higher proportion of married taxpayers open an IRA when offered a 50% match than when offered a 20% match?

22.10 **How much was contributed?** Each taxpayer who opened an IRA decided how much to contribute. Here are the summaries of the contributions for the three groups:

Group	n	$\overline{x}$	s
Control	49	$1549	$1652
20% match	240	$1723	$1332
50% match	456	$1742	$1174

The amounts contributed exclude the matching amount. Is the mean contribution by taxpayers offered a 50% match significantly higher than for taxpayers offered a 20% match?

22.11 **How much more?** Give a 95% confidence interval for the mean added contribution (among taxpayers who decide to contribute) due to offering a 20% match versus no match.

The National Assessment of Educational Progress (NAEP) includes a "long-term trend" study that tracks reading and mathematics skills over time in a way that allows comparisons between results from different years. Exercises 22.12 to 22.16 are based on information on 17-year-old students from the report on the latest long-term trend study, carried out in 2004.[3] The NAEP sample used a multistage design, but the overall effect is quite similar to an SRS of 17-year-olds who are still in school.

22.12 **Better-educated parents.** In the 1978 sample of 17,554 students, 5617 had at least one parent who was a college graduate. In the 2004 sample of 2158 students, 1014 had at least one college graduate parent. Give a 99% confidence interval for the increase in the proportion of students with a college graduate parent between 1978 and 2004.

22.13 College-educated parents.   Use the information in the previous exercise to give a 99% confidence interval for the proportion of all students in 2004 who had at least one college-educated parent. (Do notice that the sample excludes 17-year-olds who had dropped out of school.)

22.14 The effect of parents' education.   The mean NAEP mathematics score (on a scale of 0 to 500) for the 1014 students in the 2004 sample with at least one parent who graduated from college was 317, with standard deviation 28.6. The 2004 sample contained 410 students whose parents' highest level of education was high school graduate. The mean score for these students was 295, with standard deviation 22.3. Is there a significant difference in mean score between these two groups of students? Estimate the size of the difference in the entire student population (use 95% confidence).

22.15 Students with college-educated parents.   Use the information in the previous exercise to give a 95% confidence interval for the mean NAEP mathematics score of all 17-year-old students with at least one parent who graduated from college.

22.16 Men versus women.   The 2004 NAEP sample contained 1122 female students and 1036 male students. The women had a mean mathematics score (on a scale of 0 to 500) of 305, with standard error 0.9. The male mean was 308, with standard error 1.0. Is there evidence that the mean mathematics scores of men and women differ in the population of all 17-year-old students?

22.17 Favoritism for college athletes?   *Sports Illustrated* surveyed a random sample of 757 Division I college athletes in 36 sports. One question asked was "Have you ever received preferential treatment from a professor because of your status as an athlete?" Of the athletes polled, 225 said "Yes." Give a 99% confidence interval for the proportion of all Division I college athletes who believe they have received preferential treatment.

22.18 Mouse endurance.   A study of the inheritance of speed and endurance in mice found a trade-off between these two characteristics, both of which help mice survive. To test endurance, mice were made to swim in a bucket with a weight attached to their tails. (The mice were rescued when exhausted.) Here are data on endurance in minutes for female and male mice:[4]

Group	n	Mean	Std. dev.
Female	162	11.4	26.09
Male	135	6.7	6.69

(a) Both sets of endurance data are skewed to the right. Why are t procedures nonetheless reasonably accurate for these data?

(b) Give a 95% confidence interval for the mean endurance of female mice swimming.

(c) Give a 95% confidence interval for the mean difference (female minus male) in endurance times.

22.19 Mouse endurance, continued.   Do the data in the previous exercise show that female mice have significantly higher endurance on the average than male mice?

22.20 Registering handguns. The National Gun Policy Survey has been carried out regularly at intervals of several years by the National Opinion Research Center at the University of Chicago. The sample can be considered an SRS of adult residents of the United States. It is selected by calling randomly chosen telephone numbers in all 50 states. When a household answers the phone, the questions are asked of the adult with the most recent birthday. (This is a form of random selection.) One of the questions asked is "Do you favor or oppose the mandatory registration of handguns and pistols?"[5] Of the 1176 people in the 2001 sample, 904 favored mandatory registration. Give a 95% confidence interval for the proportion of all adults who favor registration.

imagebroker/Alamy

22.21 Registering handguns, continued. There has been a trend toward less support for gun control. The 1998 National Gun Policy Survey asked 1201 people the question quoted in the previous exercise; 1024 favored registration. What were the percents in favor in 1998 and 2001? Did a significantly smaller proportion of the population favor mandatory registration in 2001 than in 1998?

22.22 Genetically modified foods. Europeans have been more skeptical than Americans about the use of genetic engineering to improve foods. A sample survey gathered responses from random samples of 863 Americans and 12,178 Europeans.[6] (The European sample was larger because Europe is divided into many nations.) Subjects were asked to consider the following issue:

Using modern biotechnology in the production of foods, for example to make them higher in protein, keep longer, or change in taste.

They were asked if they considered this "risky for society." In all, 52% of Americans and 64% of Europeans thought the application was risky.

(a) It is clear without a formal test that the proportion of the population who consider this use of technology risky is significantly higher in Europe than in the United States. Why is this?

(b) Give a 99% confidence interval for the percent difference between Europe and the United States.

22.23 Genetically modified foods, continued. Give a 95% confidence interval for the proportion of all European adults who consider the use of biotechnology in food production risky.

22.24 Genetically modified foods, continued. Is there convincing evidence that more than half of all adult Americans consider applying biotechnology to the production of foods risky? If you do not use software, use Table A to find the *P*-value.

22.25 Spinning euros. When the new euro coins were introduced throughout Europe in 2002, curious people tried all sorts of things. Two Polish mathematicians spun a Belgian euro (one side of the coin has a different design for each country) 250 times. They got 140 heads. Newspapers reported this result widely. Is it significant evidence that the coin is not balanced when spun? If you do not use software, use Table A to find the *P*-value.

22.26 Spinning euros, continued. What do the data in Exercise 22.25 allow you to say with 90% confidence about the proportion of heads in spinning Belgian euro coins?

Matthias Kulka/CORBIS

22.27 Butterflies mating. Here's how butterflies mate: a male passes to a female a packet of sperm called a spermatophore. Females may mate several times. Will they remate sooner if the first spermatophore they receive is small? Among

20 females who received a large spermatophore (greater than 25 milligrams), the mean time to the next mating was 5.15 days, with standard deviation 0.18 day. For 21 females who received a small spermatophore (about 7 milligrams), the mean was 4.33 days and the standard deviation was 0.31 day.[7] Is the observed difference in means statistically significant?

22.28 **Very-low-birth-weight babies.** Starting in the 1970s, medical technology allowed babies with very low birth weight (VLBW, less than 1500 grams, about 3.3 pounds) to survive without major handicaps. It was noticed that these children nonetheless had difficulties in school and as adults. A long-term study has followed 242 VLBW babies to age 20 years, along with a control group of 233 babies from the same population who had normal birth weight.[8]

(a) Is this an experiment or an observational study? Why?

(b) At age 20, 179 of the VLBW group and 193 of the control group had graduated from high school. Is the graduation rate among the VLBW group significantly lower than for the normal-birth-weight controls?

22.29 **Very-low-birth-weight babies, continued.** IQ scores were available for 113 men in the VLBW group. The mean IQ was 87.6, and the standard deviation was 15.1. The 106 men in the control group had mean IQ 94.7, with standard deviation 14.9. Is there good evidence that mean IQ is lower among VLBW men than among controls from similar backgrounds?

22.30 **Very-low-birth-weight babies, continued.** Of the 126 women in the VLBW group, 37 said they had used illegal drugs; 52 of the 124 control group women had done so. The IQ scores for these VLBW women had mean 86.2 (standard deviation 13.4), and the normal-birth-weight controls had mean IQ 89.8 (standard deviation 14.0). Are either of these differences between the two groups statistically significant?

22.31 **Do fruit flies sleep?** Mammals and birds sleep. Fruit flies show a daily cycle of rest and activity, but does the rest qualify as sleep? Researchers looking at brain activity and behavior finally concluded that fruit flies do sleep. A small part of the study used an infrared motion sensor to see if flies moved in response to vibrations. Here are results for low levels of vibration:[9]

	Response to Vibration?	
	No	Yes
Fly was walking	10	54
Fly was resting	28	4

Larry F. Jernigan/Index Stock

Analyze these results. Is there good reason to think that resting flies respond differently than flies that are walking? (That's a sign that the resting flies may actually be sleeping.)

22.32 **Cholesterol in dogs.** High levels of cholesterol in the blood are not healthy in either humans or dogs. Because a diet rich in saturated fats raises the cholesterol level, it is plausible that dogs owned as pets have higher cholesterol levels than dogs owned by a veterinary research clinic. "Normal" levels of cholesterol based on the clinic's dogs would then be misleading. A clinic compared healthy dogs it owned with healthy pets brought to the clinic to be neutered. Here are the summary statistics for blood cholesterol levels (milligrams per deciliter of blood):[10]

Group	n	$\overline{x}$	s
Pets	26	193	68
Clinic	23	174	44

Is there strong evidence that pets have a higher mean cholesterol level than clinic dogs?

22.33 Pets versus clinic dogs. Using the information in the previous exercise, give a 95% confidence interval for the difference in mean cholesterol levels between pets and clinic dogs.

22.34 Cholesterol in pets. Continue your work with the information in Exercise 22.32. Give a 95% confidence interval for the mean cholesterol level in pets.

22.35 Conditions for inference. What conditions must be satisfied to justify the procedures you used in Exercise 22.32? In Exercise 22.33? In Exercise 22.34? Assuming that the cholesterol measurements have no outliers and are not strongly skewed, what is the chief threat to the validity of the results of this study?

SUPPLEMENTARY EXERCISES

*Supplementary exercises apply the skills you have learned in ways that require more thought or more use of technology. Many of these exercises, for example, start from the raw data rather than from data summaries. Remember that the **Solve** step for a statistical problem includes checking the conditions for the inference you plan.*

22.36 Starting to talk. At what age do infants speak their first word of English? Here are data on 20 children (ages in months):[11]

15	26	10	9	15	20	18	11	8	20
7	9	10	11	11	10	12	17	11	10

(In fact, the sample contained one more child, who began to speak at 42 months. Child development experts consider this abnormally late, so we dropped the outlier to get a sample of "normal" children. The investigators are willing to treat these data as an SRS.) Is there good evidence that the mean age at first word among all normal children is greater than one year?

22.37 Measurements on meters. The distance between two mounting holes on an electrical meter is important for proper fit of the meter within its housing. Here are measurements (inches) from a random sample of meters, made by workers during production:[12]

0.604	0.603	0.606	0.603	0.604	0.604	0.605	0.606	0.603	0.604
0.603	0.606	0.603	0.605	0.604	0.604	0.602	0.605	0.604	0.603
0.603	0.603	0.604	0.604	0.603	0.603	0.603	0.604	0.603	0.606
0.603	0.605	0.604	0.602	0.605	0.602	0.604	0.602	0.603	0.603

The specifications state that the distance between holes should be 0.604 inch. Is there evidence that the mean distance differs from the specification?

22.38 Starting to talk, continued. Use the data in Exercise 22.36 to give a 90% confidence interval for the mean age at which children speak their first word.

22.39 Dyeing fabrics. Different fabrics respond differently when dyed. This matters to clothing manufacturers, who want the color of the fabric to be just right. A researcher dyed fabrics made of cotton and of ramie with the same "procion blue" dye applied in the same way. Then she used a colorimeter to measure the lightness of the color on a scale in which black is 0 and white is 100. Here are the data for 8 pieces of each fabric:[13]

| Cotton | 48.82 | 48.88 | 48.98 | 49.04 | 48.68 | 49.34 | 48.75 | 49.12 |
| Ramie | 41.72 | 41.83 | 42.05 | 41.44 | 41.27 | 42.27 | 41.12 | 41.49 |

Is there a significant difference between the fabrics? Which fabric is darker when dyed in this way?

22.40 **More on dyeing fabrics.** The color of a fabric depends on the dye used and also on how the dye is applied. This matters to clothing manufacturers, who want the color of the fabric to be just right. The study discussed in the previous exercise went on to dye fabric made of ramie with the same "procion blue" dye applied in two different ways. Here are the lightness scores for 8 pieces of identical fabric dyed in each way:

| Method B | 40.98 | 40.88 | 41.30 | 41.28 | 41.66 | 41.50 | 41.39 | 41.27 |
| Method C | 42.30 | 42.20 | 42.65 | 42.43 | 42.50 | 42.28 | 43.13 | 42.45 |

(a) This is a randomized comparative experiment. Outline the design.

(b) A clothing manufacturer wants to know which method gives the darker color (lower lightness score). Use sample means to answer this question. Is the difference between the two sample means statistically significant? Can you tell from just the P-value whether the difference is large enough to be important in practice?

22.41 **Do parents matter?** A professor asked her sophomore students, "Does either of your parents allow you to drink alcohol around him or her?" and "How many drinks do you typically have per session? (A drink is defined as one 12 oz beer, one 4 oz glass of wine, or one 1 oz shot of liquor.)" Table 22.1 contains the responses of the female students who are not abstainers.[14] The sample is all students in one

TABLE 22.1	Drinks per session by female students												
Parent allows student to drink													
2.5	1	2.5	3	1	3	3	3	2.5	2.5	3.5	5	2
7	7	6.5	4	8	6	6	3	6	3	4	7	5
3.5	2	1	5	3	3	6	4	2	7	5	8	1
6	5	2.5	3	4.5	9	5	4	4	3	4	6	4
5	1	5	3	10	7	4	4	4	4	2	2.5	2.5
Parent does not allow student to drink													
9	3.5	3	5	1	1	3	4	4	3	6	5	3
8	4	4	5	7	7	3.5	3	10	4	9	2	7
4	3	1										

large sophomore-level class. The class is popular, so we are tentatively willing to regard its members as an SRS of sophomore students at this college. Does the behavior of parents make a significant difference in how many drinks students have on the average?

22.42 Parents' behavior. We wonder what proportion of female students have at least one parent who allows the student to drink around him or her. Table 22.1 contains information about a sample of 94 students. Use this sample to give a 95% confidence interval for this proportion.

22.43 Diabetic mice. The body's natural electrical field helps wounds heal. If diabetes changes this field, that might explain why people with diabetes heal slowly. A study of this idea compared normal mice and mice bred to spontaneously develop diabetes. The investigators attached sensors to the right hip and front feet of the mice and measured the difference in electrical potential (millivolts) between these locations. Here are the data:[15]

Diabetic mice						Normal mice				
14.70	13.60	7.40	1.05	10.55	16.40	13.80	9.10	4.95	7.70	9.40
10.00	22.60	15.20	19.60	17.25	18.40	7.20	10.00	14.55	13.30	6.65
9.80	11.70	14.85	14.45	18.25	10.15	9.50	10.40	7.75	8.70	8.85
10.85	10.30	10.45	8.55	8.85	19.20	8.40	8.55	12.60		

(a) Make a stemplot of each sample of potentials. There is a low outlier in the diabetic group. Does it appear that potentials in the two groups differ in a systematic way?

(b) Is there significant evidence of a difference in mean potentials between the two groups?

(c) Repeat your inference without the outlier. Does the outlier affect your conclusion?

22.44 Keeping crackers from breaking. We don't like to find broken crackers when we open the package. How can makers reduce breaking? One idea is to microwave the crackers for 30 seconds right after baking them. Analyze the following results from two experiments intended to examine this idea.[16] Does microwaving significantly improve indicators of future breaking? How large is the improvement? What do you conclude about the idea of microwaving crackers?

(a) The experimenter randomly assigned 65 newly baked crackers to be microwaved and another 65 to a control group that is not microwaved. Fourteen days after baking, 3 of the 65 microwaved crackers and 57 of the 65 crackers in the control group showed visible checking, which is the starting point for breaks.

(b) The experimenter randomly assigned 20 crackers to be microwaved and another 20 to a control group. After 14 days, he broke the crackers. Here are summaries of the pressure needed to break them, in pounds per square inch:

	Microwave	Control
Mean	139.6	77.0
Standard deviation	33.6	22.6

2006 Bill Watkins/AlaskaStock.com

22.45 Falling through the ice. Table 7.4 (page 182) gives the dates on which a wooden tripod fell through the ice of the Tanana River in Alaska, thus deciding the winner of the Nenana Ice Classic contest, for the years 1917 to 2005. Give a 95% confidence interval for the mean date on which the tripod falls through the ice. After calculating the interval in the scale used in the table (days from April 20, which is Day 1), translate your result into calendar dates.

22.46 A case for the Supreme Court. In 1986, a Texas jury found a black man guilty of murder. The prosecutors had used "peremptory challenges" to remove 10 of the 11 blacks and 4 of the 31 whites in the pool from which the jury was chosen. The law says that there must be a plausible reason (that is, a reason other than race) for different treatment of blacks and whites in the jury pool. When the case reached the Supreme Court 17 years later, the Court said that "happenstance is unlikely to produce this disparity." They then went on to examine the state's claim that the disparity was explained not by race but by attitudes toward the death penalty.[17] Explain why the methods we know can't be safely used to do the inference that lies behind the Court's finding that chance is unlikely to produce so large a black-white difference.

22.47 Mouse genes. A study of genetic influences on diabetes compared normal mice with similar mice genetically altered to remove a gene called $aP2$. Mice of both types were allowed to become obese by eating a high-fat diet. The researchers then measured the levels of insulin and glucose in their blood plasma. Here are some excerpts from their findings.[18] The normal mice are called "wild-type" and the altered mice are called "$aP2^{-/-}$."

Each value is the mean ± SEM of measurements on at least 10 mice. Mean values of each plasma component are compared between $aP2^{-/-}$ mice and wild-type controls by Student's t test (*$P < 0.05$ and **$P < 0.005$).

Parameter	Wild type	$aP2^{-/-}$
Insulin (ng/ml)	5.9 ± 0.9	0.75 ± 0.2**
Glucose (mg/dl)	230 ± 25	150 ± 17*

Despite much greater circulating amounts of insulin, the wild-type mice had higher blood glucose than the $aP2^{-/-}$ animals. These results indicate that the absence of aP2 interferes with the development of dietary obesity–induced insulin resistance.

Other biologists are supposed to understand the statistics reported so tersely.

(a) What does "SEM" mean? What is the expression for SEM based on n, $\bar{x}$, and s from a sample?

(b) Which of the tests we have studied did the researchers apply?

(c) Explain to a biologist who knows no statistics what $P < 0.05$ and $P < 0.005$ mean. Which is stronger evidence of a difference between the two types of mice?

22.48 Mouse genes, continued. The report quoted in the previous exercise says only that the sample sizes were "at least 10." Suppose that the results are based on exactly 10 mice of each type. Use the values in the table to find $\bar{x}$ and s for the insulin concentrations in the two types of mice. Carry out a test to assess the significance of the difference in mean insulin concentration. Does your P-value confirm the claim in the report that $P < 0.005$?

22.49 Contributing to IRAs (optional). Is the variability in the amount contributed (as measured by the standard deviation) significantly different in the control group and the 20% match group in Exercise 22.10? Use the F test. Explain why this test can't be trusted when comparing dollar amounts. (*Hint:* What is the usual shape of distributions of financial variables?)

22.50 Cholesterol in dogs (optional). Do the data in Exercise 22.32 provide evidence of different standard deviations for cholesterol levels in pet dogs and clinic dogs? State the hypotheses and carry out the test. (Assume that the data follow a Normal distribution closely.) Software can assess significance exactly, but inspection of the proper table is enough to draw a conclusion.

22.51 The power of a t test (optional). A large bank plans an experiment to learn whether offering cash back on purchases of gasoline will increase use of its credit cards. The bank wants to be quite certain of detecting a mean increase of $\mu = \$100$ in the amount charged per month, at the $\alpha = 0.01$ significance level. It makes the cash back offer to 50 customers and compares their charges for the months before and after the offer. Find the approximate power of the t test with $n = 50$ against the alternative $\mu = \$100$ as follows.

(a) What is the critical value t^* for the one-sided test with $\alpha = 0.01$ and $n = 50$?

(b) Write the rule for rejecting H_0: $\mu = 0$ in terms of the t statistic. Then take $s = 108$ (an estimate based on the bank's past experience) and state the rejection rule in terms of $\bar{x}$.

(c) Assume that $\mu = 100$ (the given alternative) and that $\sigma = 108$. The approximate power is the probability of the event you found in (b), calculated under these conditions. Find the power. Would you recommend that the bank do a test on 50 customers, or should more customers be included?

EESEE CASE STUDIES

The Electronic Encyclopedia of Statistical Examples and Exercises (EESEE) is available on the text CD and Web site. These more elaborate stories, with data, provide settings for longer case studies. Here are some suggestions for EESEE stories that apply the ideas you have learned in Chapters 18 to 21.

22.52 Is Caffeine Dependence Real? Answer Questions 2, 3, 4, and 6 for this case study. (Matched pairs study.)

22.53 Seasonal Weevil Migration. Respond to Question 1. (Proportions.)

22.54 Radar Detectors and Speeding. Read this case study and answer Questions 1, 3, and 5. (Study design, proportions.)

22.55 Leave Survey after the Beep. Carefully answer Question 3; in part (a), use the preferred two-sample t procedure rather than the pooled t. (Two-sample problems, choice of procedure.)

22.56 Passive Smoking and Respiratory Health. Write careful answers to Questions 1, 3, and 4. (Conditions for inference, choice of procedure.)

22.57 Emissions from an Oil Refinery. Answer both questions. (Conditions for inference.)

22.58 Surgery in a Blanket. Read this case study and answer Questions 1, 2, 3, and 4. (Study design, choice of procedure, interpretation of results.)

Inference about Relationships

Statistical inference offers more methods than anyone can know well, as a glance at the offerings of any large statistical software package demonstrates. In a basic text, we must be selective. In Parts I to III we laid a foundation for understanding statistics:

- The nature and purpose of data analysis.
- The central ideas of designs for data production.
- The reasoning behind confidence intervals and significance tests.
- Experience applying these ideas in practice.

Each of the three chapters of Part IV offers a short introduction to a more advanced topic in statistical inference. You may choose to read any or all of them, in any order.

What makes a statistical method "more advanced"? More complex data, for one thing. In Part III, we looked only at methods for inference about a single population parameter and for comparing two parameters. All of the chapters in Part IV present methods for studying relationships between two variables. In Chapter 23, both variables are categorical, with data given as a two-way table of counts of outcomes. Chapter 24 considers inference in the setting of regressing a response variable on an explanatory variable. This is an important type of relationship between two quantitative variables. In Chapter 25 we meet methods for comparing the mean response in more than two groups. Here, the explanatory variable (group) is categorical and the response variable is quantitative. These chapters together bring our knowledge of inference to the same point that our study of data analysis reached in Chapters 1 to 7.

With greater complexity comes greater reliance on technology. In these final three chapters you will more often be interpreting the output of statistical software or using software yourself. You can do the calculations needed in Chapter 23 without software or a specialized calculator. In Chapters 24 and 25, the pain is too great and the contribution to learning too small. Fortunately, you can grasp the ideas without step-by-step arithmetic.

"It was a numbers explosion."

Another aspect of "more advanced" methods is new concepts and ideas. This is where we draw the line in deciding what statistical topics we can master in a first course. Part IV builds elaborate methods on the foundation we have laid without introducing fundamentally new concepts. You can see that statistical practice does need additional big ideas by reading the sections on "the problem of multiple comparisons" in Chapters 23 and 25. But the ideas you already know place you among the world's statistical sophisticates.

INFERENCE ABOUT RELATIONSHIPS

Two Categorical Variables: The Chi-Square Test

The two-sample z procedures of Chapter 21 allow us to compare the proportions of successes in two groups, either two populations or two treatment groups in an experiment. In the first example in Chapter 21 (page 513), we compared young men and young women by looking at whether or not they lived with their parents. That is, we looked at a relationship between two categorical variables, gender (female or male) and "Where do you live?" (with parents or not). In fact, the data include three more outcomes for "Where do you live?": in another person's home, in your own place, and in group quarters such as a dormitory. When there are more than two outcomes, or when we want to compare more than two groups, we need a new statistical test. The new test addresses a general question: *is there a relationship between two categorical variables?*

Two-way tables

We saw in Chapter 6 that we can present data on two categorical variables in a **two-way table** of counts. That's our starting point. Here is an example.

EXAMPLE 23.1 Health care: Canada and the United States

Canada has universal health care. The United States does not, but often offers more elaborate treatment to patients with access. How do the two systems compare in treating heart attacks? A comparison of random samples of 2600 U.S. and 400 Canadian heart attack patients found that "the Canadian patients typically stayed in the hospital one day longer ($P = 0.009$) than the U.S. patients but had a much lower rate of cardiac catheterization (25 percent vs. 72 percent, $P < 0.001$), coronary angioplasty (11 percent vs. 29 percent, $P < 0.001$), and coronary bypass surgery (3 percent vs. 14 percent, $P < 0.001$)."[1]

The study then looked at many outcomes a year after the heart attack. There was no significant difference in the patients' survival rate. Another key outcome was the patients' own assessment of their quality of life relative to what it had been before the heart attack. Here are the data for the patients who survived a year:

Quality of life	Canada	United States
Much better	75	541
Somewhat better	71	498
About the same	96	779
Somewhat worse	50	282
Much worse	19	65
Total	311	2165

The two-way table in Example 23.1 shows the relationship between two categorical variables. The explanatory variable is the patient's country, Canada or the United States. The response variable is quality of life a year after a heart attack, with 5 categories. The two-way table gives the counts for all 10 combinations of values of these variables. Each of the 10 counts occupies a **cell** of the table.

cell

It is hard to compare the counts because the U.S. sample is much larger. Here are the percents of each sample with each outcome:

Quality of life	Canada	United States
Much better	24%	25%
Somewhat better	23%	23%
About the same	31%	36%
Somewhat worse	16%	13%
Much worse	6%	3%
Total	100%	100%

In the language of Chapter 6 (page 153), these are the *conditional distributions* of outcomes, given the patients' nationality. The differences are not large, but slightly higher percents of Canadians thought their quality of life was "somewhat worse" or "much worse." Figure 23.1 compares the two distributions. We want to know if there is a significant difference between the two distributions of outcomes.

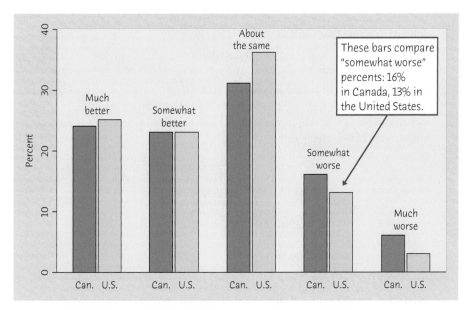

FIGURE 23.1 Bar graph comparing quality of life a year after a heart attack in Canada and the United States, for Example 23.1.

APPLY YOUR KNOWLEDGE

Lisl Dennis/Getty Images

23.1 Smoking among French men. Smoking remains more common in much of Europe than in the United States. In the United States, there is a strong relationship between education and smoking: well-educated people are less likely to smoke. Does a similar relationship hold in France? Here is a two-way table of the level of education and smoking status (nonsmoker, former smoker, moderate smoker, heavy smoker) of a sample of 459 French men aged 20 to 60 years.[2] The subjects are a random sample of men who visited a health center for a routine checkup. We are willing to consider them an SRS of men from their region of France.

	Smoking Status			
Education	Nonsmoker	Former	Moderate	Heavy
Primary school	56	54	41	36
Secondary school	37	43	27	32
University	53	28	36	16

(a) What percent of men with a primary school education are nonsmokers? Former smokers? Moderate smokers? Heavy smokers? These percents should add to 100% (up to roundoff error). They form the conditional distribution of smoking, given a primary education.

(b) In a similar way, find the conditional distributions of smoking among men with a secondary education and among men with a university education. Make a table that presents the three conditional distributions. Be sure to include a "Total" column showing that each row adds to 100%.

(c) Compare the three conditional distributions. Is there any clear relationship between education and smoking?

23.2 **Attitudes toward recycled products.** Recycling is supposed to save resources. Some people think recycled products are lower in quality than other products, a fact that makes recycling less practical. Here are data on attitudes toward coffee filters made of recycled paper.[3]

	Think the quality of the recycled product is		
	Higher	The same	Lower
Buyers	20	7	9
Nonbuyers	29	25	43

(a) It appears that people who have bought the recycled filters have more positive opinions than those who have not. Give percents to back up this claim. Make a bar graph that compares your percents for buyers and nonbuyers.

(b) Association does not prove causation. Explain how buying recycled filters might improve a person's opinion of their quality. Then explain how the opinion a person holds might influence his or her decision to buy or not. You see that the cause-and-effect relationship might go in either direction.

The problem of multiple comparisons

The null hypothesis in Example 23.1 is that there is *no difference* between the distributions of outcomes in Canada and the United States. Put more generally, the null hypothesis is that there is *no relationship* between two categorical variables,

H_0: there is no relationship between nationality and quality of life

The alternative hypothesis says that there *is* a relationship but does not specify any particular kind of relationship,

H_a: there is some relationship between nationality and quality of life

Any difference between the Canadian and American distributions means that the null hypothesis is false and the alternative hypothesis is true. The alternative hypothesis is not one-sided or two-sided. We might call it "many-sided" because it allows any kind of difference.

With only the methods we already know, we might start by comparing the proportions of patients in the two nations with "much better" quality of life, using the two-sample z test for proportions. We could similarly compare the proportions with each of the other outcomes: five tests in all, with five P-values. This is a bad idea. The *P*-values belong to each test separately, not to the collection of five tests together. Think of the distinction between the probability that a basketball player makes a free throw and the probability that she makes all of five free throws. *When we do many individual tests or confidence intervals, the individual P-values and confidence levels don't tell us how confident we can be in all of the inferences taken together.*

Because of this, it's cheating to pick out the largest of the five differences and then test its significance as if it were the only comparison we had in mind. For example, the "much worse" proportions in Example 23.1 are significantly different ($P = 0.0047$) if we compare just this one outcome. But is it surprising that the *most different* proportions among five outcomes differ by this much? That's a different question.

The problem of how to do many comparisons at once with an overall measure of confidence in all our conclusions is common in statistics. This is the problem of **multiple comparisons.** Statistical methods for dealing with multiple comparisons usually have two steps:

multiple comparisons

1. An *overall test* to see if there is good evidence of *any* differences among the parameters that we want to compare.

2. A detailed *follow-up analysis* to decide which of the parameters differ and to estimate how large the differences are.

The overall test, though more complex than the tests we met earlier, is often reasonably straightforward. The follow-up analysis can be quite elaborate. In our basic introduction to statistical practice, we will concentrate on the overall test, along with data analysis that points to the nature of the differences.

APPLY YOUR KNOWLEDGE

23.3 **Nonsmokers and education in France.** In the setting of Exercise 23.1, consider only the proportions of nonsmokers in the three populations of men with primary, secondary, and university education. Do three significance tests of the three null hypotheses

$$H_0: p_{primary} = p_{secondary}$$
$$H_0: p_{primary} = p_{university}$$
$$H_0: p_{secondary} = p_{university}$$

against the two-sided alternatives. Give *P*-values for each test. These three *P*-values don't tell us how often the three proportions for the three education groups will be spread this far apart just by chance.

23.4 **Who's online?** A sample survey by the Pew Internet and American Life Project asked a random sample of adults about use of the Internet and about the type of community they lived in. Following is the two-way table:[4]

| | Community Type | | |
	Rural	Suburban	Urban
Internet users	433	1072	536
Nonusers	463	627	388

(a) Give three 95% confidence intervals, for the percents of adults in rural, suburban, and urban communities who use the Internet.

(b) Explain clearly why we are *not* 95% confident that *all three* of these intervals capture their respective population proportions.

Expected counts in two-way tables

Our general null hypothesis H_0 is that there is *no relationship* between the two categorical variables that label the rows and columns of a two-way table. To test H_0, we compare the observed counts in the table with the *expected counts*, the counts we would expect—except for random variation—if H_0 were true. If the observed counts are far from the expected counts, that is evidence against H_0. It is easy to find the expected counts.

He started it!

A study of deaths in bar fights showed that in 90% of the cases, the person who died started the fight. You shouldn't believe this. If you killed someone in a fight, what would you say when the police ask you who started the fight? After all, dead men tell no tales.

EXPECTED COUNTS

The **expected count** in any cell of a two-way table when H_0 is true is

$$\text{expected count} = \frac{\text{row total} \times \text{column total}}{\text{table total}}$$

EXAMPLE 23.2   *Observed versus expected counts*

Let's find the expected counts for the quality-of-life study. Here is the two-way table with row and column totals:

Quality of life	Canada	United States	Total
Much better	75	541	616
Somewhat better	71	498	569
About the same	96	779	875
Somewhat worse	50	282	332
Much worse	19	65	84
Total	311	2165	2476

The expected count of Canadians with much better quality of life a year after a heart attack is

$$\frac{\text{row 1 total} \times \text{column 1 total}}{\text{table total}} = \frac{(616)(311)}{2476} = 77.37$$

Here is the table of all 10 expected counts:

Quality of life	Canada	United States	Total
Much better	77.37	538.63	616
Somewhat better	71.47	497.53	569
About the same	109.91	765.09	875
Somewhat worse	41.70	290.30	332
Much worse	10.55	73.45	84
Total	311	2165	

As this table shows, *the expected counts have exactly the same row and column totals (up to roundoff error) as the observed counts.* That's a good way to check your work.

To see how the data diverge from the null hypothesis, compare the observed counts with these expected counts. You see, for example, that 19 Canadians reported much worse quality of life, whereas we would expect only 10.55 if the null hypothesis were true.

Why the formula works Where does the formula for an expected cell count come from? Think of a basketball player who makes 70% of her free throws in the long run. If she shoots 10 free throws in a game, we expect her to make 70% of them, or 7 of the 10. Of course, she won't make exactly 7 every time she shoots 10 free throws in a game. There is chance variation from game to game. But in the long run, 7 of 10 is what we expect. In more formal language, if we have n independent tries and the probability of a success on each try is p, we expect np successes.

Now go back to the count of Canadians with much better quality of life a year after a heart attack. The proportion of all 2476 subjects with much better quality of life is

$$\frac{\text{count of successes}}{\text{table total}} = \frac{\text{row 1 total}}{\text{table total}} = \frac{616}{2476}$$

Think of this as p, the overall proportion of successes. If H_0 is true, we expect (except for random variation) this same proportion of successes in both countries. So the expected count of successes among the 311 Canadians is

$$np = (311)\left(\frac{616}{2476}\right) = 77.37$$

That's the formula in the Expected Counts box.

APPLY YOUR KNOWLEDGE

23.5 **Smoking among French men.** The two-way table in Exercise 23.1 displays data on the education and smoking behavior of a sample of French men. The null hypothesis says that there is no relationship between these variables. That is, the distribution of smoking is the same for all three levels of education.

(a) Find the expected counts for each smoking status among men with a university education. This is one row of the two-way table of expected counts. Find the row total and verify that it agrees with the row total for the observed counts.

(b) We conjecture that men with a university education smoke less than the null hypothesis calls for. How does comparing the observed and expected counts in this row confirm this conjecture?

23.6 **Attitudes toward recycled products.** Exercise 23.2 describes a comparison of the attitudes of people who do and don't buy coffee filters made of recycled paper. The null hypothesis "no relationship" says that in the population of all consumers, the proportions who hold each attitude are the same for buyers and nonbuyers.

(a) Find the expected cell counts if this hypothesis is true and display them in a two-way table. Add the row and column totals to your table and check that they agree with the totals for the observed counts.

(b) Are there any large deviations between the observed counts and the expected counts? What kind of relationship between the two variables do these deviations point to?

The chi-square test

The statistical test that tells us whether the observed differences between Canada and the United States are statistically significant compares the observed and expected counts. The test statistic that makes the comparison is the *chi-square statistic*.

CHI-SQUARE STATISTIC

The **chi-square statistic** is a measure of how far the observed counts in a two-way table are from the expected counts. The formula for the statistic is

$$X^2 = \sum \frac{(\text{observed count} - \text{expected count})^2}{\text{expected count}}$$

The sum is over all cells in the table.

The chi-square statistic is a sum of terms, one for each cell in the table. In the quality-of-life example, 75 Canadian patients reported much better quality of life. The expected count for this cell is 77.37. So the term of the chi-square statistic from this cell is

$$\frac{(\text{observed count} - \text{expected count})^2}{\text{expected count}} = \frac{(75 - 77.37)^2}{77.37}$$
$$= \frac{5.617}{77.37} = 0.073$$

Think of the chi-square statistic X^2 as a measure of the distance of the observed counts from the expected counts. Like any distance, it is always zero or positive, and it is zero only when the observed counts are exactly equal to the expected counts. Large values of X^2 are evidence against H_0 because they say that the observed counts are far from what we would expect if H_0 were true. *Although the alternative hypothesis H_a is many-sided, the chi-square test is one-sided* because any violation of H_0 tends to produce a large value of X^2. Small values of X^2 are not evidence against H_0.

Using technology

Calculating the expected counts and then the chi-square statistic by hand is a bit time-consuming. As usual, software saves time and always gets the arithmetic right. Figure 23.2 (pages 556 and 557) shows output for the chi-square test for the quality-of-life data from a graphing calculator, two statistical programs, and a spreadsheet program.

EXAMPLE 23.3   Chi-square from software

The outputs differ in the information they give. All except the Excel spreadsheet tell us that the chi-square statistic is $X^2 = 11.725$, with P-value 0.020. There is quite good evidence that the distributions of outcomes are different in Canada and the United States.

The two statistical programs repeat the two-way table of observed counts and add the row and column totals. Both programs offer additional information on request. We asked CrunchIt! to add the column percents that enable us to compare the Canadian and American distributions. The chi-square statistic is a sum of 10 terms, one for each cell in the table. We asked Minitab to give the expected count and the contribution to chi-square for each cell. The top-left cell has expected count 77.4 and chi-square term 0.073, just as we calculated. Look at the 10 terms. More than half the value of X^2 (6.766 out of 11.725) comes from just one cell. This points to the most important difference between the two countries: a higher proportion of Canadians report much worse quality of life. Most of the rest of X^2 comes from two other cells: more Canadians report somewhat worse quality of life, and fewer report about the same quality.

Excel is as usual more awkward than software designed for statistics. It lacks a menu selection for the chi-square test. You must program the spreadsheet to calculate the expected cell counts and then use the CHITEST worksheet formula. This gives the P-value but not the test statistic itself. You can of course program the spreadsheet to find the value of X^2. The Excel output shows the observed and expected cell counts and the P-value.

The chi-square test is the overall test for detecting relationships between two categorical variables. If the test is significant, it is important to look at the data to learn the nature of the relationship. We have three ways to look at the quality-of-life data:

- **Compare appropriate percents:** which outcomes occur in quite different percents of Canadian and American patients? This is the method we learned in Chapter 6.

TI-83

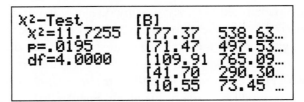

CrunchIt!

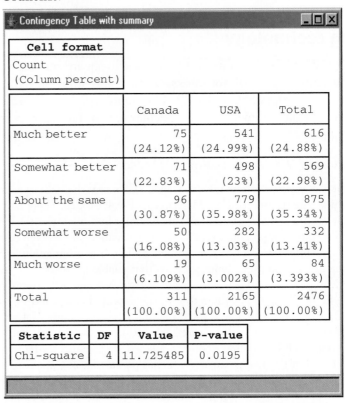

FIGURE 23.2 Output from the TI-83 graphing calculator, CrunchIt!, Minitab, and Excel for the two-way table in the quality-of-life study (*continued*).

- **Compare observed and expected cell counts:** which cells have more or fewer observations than we would expect if H_0 were true?
- **Look at the terms of the chi-square statistic:** which cells contribute the most to the value of X^2?

EXAMPLE 23.4 *Canada and the United States: conclusions*

There is a significant difference between the distributions of quality of life reported by Canadian and American patients a year after a heart attack. All three ways of comparing the distributions agree that the main difference is that a higher proportion of Canadians

Minitab

```
Session                                                        _ □ X
                        Canada          USA          All

Much better               75            541          616
                          77.4          538.6        616.0
                          0.0728        0.0105         *

Somewhat better           71            498          569
                          71.5          497.5        569.0
                          0.0031        0.0004         *

About the same            96            779          875
                          109.9         765.1        875.0
                          1.7593        0.2527         *

Somewhat worse            50            282          332
                          41.7          290.3        332.0
                          1.6515        0.2372         *

Much worse                19            65           84
                          10.6          73.4         84.0
                          6.7660        0.9719         *

All                       311           2165         2476
                          311.0         2165.0       2476.0
                           *             *             *

Cell Contents:       Count
                     Expected count
                     Contribution to Chi-square

Pearson Chi-Square = 11.725, DF = 4, P-Value = 0.020
```

> This key identifies the output for each cell in the table.

Excel

	A	B	C	D
1	Observed	Canada	USA	
2		75	541	
3		71	498	
4		96	779	
5		50	282	
6		19	65	
7				
8	Expected	Canada	USA	
9		77.37	538.63	
10		71.47	497.53	
11		109.91	765.09	
12		41.7	290.3	
13		10.55	73.45	
14				
15				
16	CHITEST(B2:C6,B9:C13)		0.019482	
17				

Microsoft Excel - Book1

Sheet1 / Sheet2 / Sheet3

FIGURE 23.2 (*continued*).

report that their quality of life is worse than before their heart attack. Other response variables measured in the study agree with this conclusion.

The broader conclusion, however, is controversial. Americans are likely to point to the better outcomes produced by their much more intensive treatment. Canadians reply that the differences are small, that there was no significant difference in survival, and that the American advantage comes at high cost. The resources spent on expensive treatment of heart attack victims could instead be spent on providing basic health care to the many Americans who lack it.

There is an important message here: although statistical studies shed light on issues of public policy, statistics alone rarely settles complicated questions such as "Which kind of health care system works better?"

APPLY YOUR KNOWLEDGE

23.7 **Smoking among French men.** In Exercises 23.1 and 23.5, you began to analyze data on the smoking status and education of French men. Figure 23.3 displays the Minitab output for the chi-square test applied to these data.

(a) Starting from the observed and expected counts in the output, calculate the four terms of the chi-square statistic for the bottom row (university education). Verify that your work agrees with Minitab's "Contribution to Chi-square" up to roundoff error.

```
 Session                                                        _ | □ | x

               Nonsmoker    Former   Moderate    Heavy      All

Primary               56        54         41        36      187
                   59.48     50.93      42.37     34.22   187.00
                  0.2038    0.1856     0.0443    0.0924        *

Secondary             37        43         27        32      139
                   44.21     37.85      31.49     25.44   139.00
                  1.1769    0.6996     0.6414    1.6928        *

University            53        28         36        16      133
                   42.31     36.22      30.14     24.34   133.00
                  2.7038    1.8655     1.1414    2.8576        *

All                  146       125        104        84      459
                  146.00    125.00     104.00     84.00   459.00
                       *         *          *         *        *

Cell Contents:     Count
                   Expected count
                   Contribution to Chi-square


Pearson Chi-Square = 13.305, DF = 6, P-Value = 0.038
```

FIGURE 23.3 Minitab output for the two-way table of education level and smoking status among French men, for Exercise 23.7.

(b) According to Minitab, what is the value of the chi-square statistic X^2 and the P-value of the chi-square test?

(c) Look at the "Contribution to Chi-square" entries in Minitab's display. Which terms contribute the most to X^2? Write a brief summary of the nature and significance of the relationship between education and smoking.

23.8 **Attitudes toward recycled products.** In Exercises 23.2 and 23.6 you began to analyze data on consumer attitudes toward recycled products. Figure 23.4 gives CrunchIt! output for these data.

(a) Starting from the observed and expected counts, find the six terms of the chi-square statistic and then the statistic X^2 itself. Check your work against the computer output.

(b) What is the P-value for the test? Explain in simple language what it means to reject H_0 in this setting.

(c) Which cells contribute the most to X^2? What kind of relationship do these terms in combination with the row percents in the table point to?

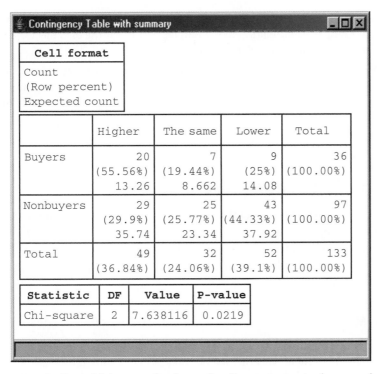

FIGURE 23.4 CrunchIt! output for the study of consumer attitudes toward recycled products, for Exercise 23.8.

Cell counts required for the chi-square test

The chi-square test, like the z procedures for comparing two proportions, is an approximate method that becomes more accurate as the counts in the cells of the table get larger. We must therefore check that the counts are large enough to trust the P-value. Fortunately, the chi-square approximation is accurate for quite modest counts. Here is a practical guideline.[5]

CELL COUNTS REQUIRED FOR THE CHI-SQUARE TEST

You can safely use the chi-square test with critical values from the chi-square distribution when no more than 20% of the expected counts are less than 5 and all individual expected counts are 1 or greater. In particular, all four expected counts in a 2 × 2 table should be 5 or greater.

Note that the guideline uses *expected* cell counts. The expected counts for the quality of life study of Example 23.1 appear in the Minitab output in Figure 23.2. The smallest expected count is 10.6, so the data easily meet the guideline for safe use of chi-square.

APPLY YOUR KNOWLEDGE ———————————————

23.9 Does chi-square apply?   Figure 23.3 displays Minitab output for data on French men. Using the information in the output, verify that the data meet the cell count requirement for use of chi-square.

23.10 Does chi-square apply?   Figure 23.4 displays CrunchIt! output for data on consumer attitudes toward recycled products. Using the information in the output, verify that the data meet the cell count requirement for use of chi-square.

Uses of the chi-square test

Two-way tables can arise in several ways. The study of the quality of life of heart attack patients compared two independent random samples, one in Canada and the other in the United States. The design of the study fixed the sizes of the two samples. The next example illustrates a different setting, in which all the observations come from just one sample.

EXAMPLE 23.5   Extracurricular activities and grades ———

STATE: North Carolina State University studied student performance in a course required by its chemical engineering major. Students must earn at least a C in the course in order to continue in the major. One question of interest was the relationship between time spent in extracurricular activities and success in the course. Students were asked to estimate how many hours per week they spent on extracurricular activities (less than 2, 2 to 12, or greater than 12). The CrunchIt! output in Figure 23.5 shows the two-way table of extracurricular activity time and course grade for the 119 students who answered the question.[6]

FORMULATE: Carry out a chi-square test for

H_0: there is no relationship between extracurricular activity time and course grade

H_a: there is some relationship between these two variables

Compare column percents or observed versus expected cell counts or terms of chi-square to see the nature of the relationship.

SOLVE: First check the guideline for use of chi-square. The expected cell counts appear in the output in Figure 23.5. Two of the expected counts are quite small, 5.513 and 2.487. But all the expected counts are greater than 1, and only 1 out of 6 (17%) is less than 5. We can safely use chi-square. The output shows that there is a significant relationship ($X^2 = 6.926$, $P = 0.0313$). The column percents show an interesting pattern: students who spend low and high amounts of time on extracurricular activities are both less likely to earn a C or better than students who spend a moderate amount of time.

CONCLUDE: We find that 75% of students in the moderate extracurricular activity group succeed in the course, compared with 55% in the low group and only 38% in the high group. These differences in success percents are significant ($P = 0.03$). Because there are few students in the low and (especially) high groups, we now wish that the questionnaire had not lumped 2 to 12 hours together. We should also look at other data that might help explain the pattern. For example, are the "low extracurricular" students more often employed? Or are they students with low GPAs who are struggling despite lots of study time?

Alt-6/Alamy

Contingency Table with summary ▭□✕

Cell format
Count
(Column percent)
Expected count

	Less than 2 hours	2 to 12 hours	More than 12 hours	Total
C or better	11 (55%) 13.78	68 (74.73%) 62.71	3 (37.5%) 5.513	82 (68.91%)
D or F	9 (45%) 6.218	23 (25.27%) 28.29	5 (62.5%) 2.487	37 (31.09%)
Total	20 (100.00%)	91 (100.00%)	8 (100.00%)	119 (100.00%)

Statistic	DF	Value	P-value
Chi-square	2	6.9264054	0.0313

FIGURE 23.5 CrunchIt! output for the two-way table of course grade and extracurricular activities, for Example 23.5.

Pay attention to the nature of the data in Example 23.5:

- We do not have three separate samples of students with low, moderate, and high extracurricular activity. We have a single group of 119 students, each classified in two ways (extracurricular activity and course grade).

- The data (except for small nonresponse) cover *all* of the students enrolled in this course in one semester. We might regard this as a sample of students enrolled in the course over several years. But we might also regard these 119 students as the entire population rather than a sample from a larger population.

One of the most useful properties of chi-square is that it tests the null hypothesis "the row and column variables are not related to each other" whenever this hypothesis makes sense for a two-way table. It makes sense when we are comparing a categorical response in two or more samples, as when we compared quality of life for patients in Canada and the United States. The hypothesis also makes sense when we have data on two categorical variables for the individuals in a single sample, as when we examined grades and extracurricular activities for a sample of college students. The hypothesis "no relationship" makes sense even if the single sample is an entire population. Statistical significance has the same meaning in all these settings: "A relationship this strong is not likely to happen just by chance." This makes sense whether the data are a sample or an entire population.

USES OF THE CHI-SQUARE TEST

Use the chi-square test to test the null hypothesis

H_0: there is no relationship between two categorical variables

when you have a two-way table from one of these situations:

- Independent SRSs from each of two or more populations, with each individual classified according to one categorical variable. (The other variable says which sample the individual comes from.)

- A single SRS, with each individual classified according to both of two categorical variables.

APPLY YOUR KNOWLEDGE

23.11 Majors for men and women in business. A study of the career plans of young women and men sent questionnaires to all 722 members of the senior class in the

College of Business Administration at the University of Illinois. One question asked which major within the business program the student had chosen. Here are the data from the students who responded:[7]

	Female	Male
Accounting	68	56
Administration	91	40
Economics	5	6
Finance	61	59

This is an example of a single sample classified according to two categorical variables (gender and major).

(a) Describe the differences between the distributions of majors for women and men with percents, with a bar graph, and in words.

(b) Verify that the expected cell counts satisfy the requirement for use of chi-square.

(c) Test the null hypothesis that there is no relationship between the gender of students and their choice of major. Give a P-value.

(d) Which two cells have the largest terms of the chi-square statistic? How do the observed and expected counts differ in these cells? (This should strengthen your conclusions in (a).)

(e) What percent of the students did not respond to the questionnaire? Why does this nonresponse weaken conclusions drawn from these data?

The chi-square distributions

Software usually finds P-values for us. The P-value for a chi-square test comes from comparing the value of the chi-square statistic with critical values for a *chi-square distribution*.

THE CHI-SQUARE DISTRIBUTIONS

The **chi-square distributions** are a family of distributions that take only positive values and are skewed to the right. A specific chi-square distribution is specified by giving its **degrees of freedom.**

The chi-square test for a two-way table with r rows and c columns uses critical values from the chi-square distribution with $(r-1)(c-1)$ degrees of freedom. The P-value is the area to the right of X^2 under the density curve of this chi-square distribution.

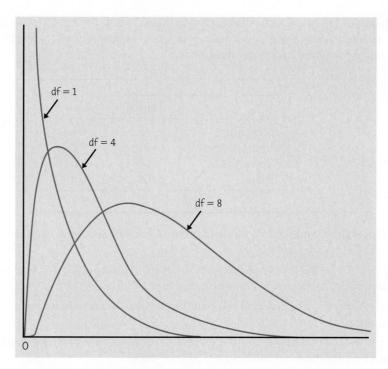

FIGURE 23.6 Density curves for the chi-square distributions with 1, 4, and 8 degrees of freedom. Chi-square distributions take only positive values and are right-skewed.

Figure 23.6 shows the density curves for three members of the chi-square family of distributions. As the degrees of freedom increase, the density curves become less skewed and larger values become more probable. Table E in the back of the book gives critical values for chi-square distributions. You can use Table E if you do not have software that gives you P-values for a chi-square test.

EXAMPLE 23.6   Using the chi-square table

The two-way table of 5 outcomes by 2 countries for the quality-of-life study has 5 rows and 2 columns. That is, $r = 5$ and $c = 2$. The chi-square statistic therefore has degrees of freedom

$$(r - 1)(c - 1) = (5 - 1)(2 - 1) = (4)(1) = 4$$

Three of the outputs in Figure 23.2 give 4 as the degrees of freedom.

The observed value of the chi-square statistic is $X^2 = 11.725$. Look in the df = 4 row of Table E. The value $X^2 = 11.725$ falls between the 0.02 and 0.01 critical values of the chi-square distribution with 4 degrees of freedom. Remember that the chi-square test is always one-sided. So the P-value of $X^2 = 11.725$ is between 0.02 and 0.01. The outputs in Figure 23.2 show that the P-value is 0.0195, close to 0.02.

df = 4

p	.02	.01
x^*	11.67	13.28

We know that all z and t statistics measure the size of an effect in the standard scale centered at zero. We can roughly assess the size of any z or t statistic by the 68–95–99.7 rule, though this is exact only for z. The chi-square statistic does not have any such natural interpretation. But here is a helpful fact: *the mean of any chi-square distribution is equal to its degrees of freedom.* In Example 23.6, X^2 would have mean 4 if the null hypothesis were true. The observed value $X^2 = 11.725$ is so much larger than 4 that we suspect it is significant even before we look at Table E.

APPLY YOUR KNOWLEDGE

23.12 Attitudes toward recycled products. The CrunchIt! output in Figure 23.4 gives 2 degrees of freedom for the table in Exercise 23.2.

(a) Verify that this is correct.

(b) The computer gives the value of the chi-square statistic as $X^2 = 7.638$. Between what two entries in Table E does this value lie? What does the table tell you about the P-value?

(c) What is the mean value of the statistic X^2 if the null hypothesis is true? How does the observed value of X^2 compare with this mean?

23.13 Smoking among French men. The Minitab output in Figure 23.3 gives the degrees of freedom for the table of education and smoking status as DF = 6.

(a) Show that this is correct for a table with 3 rows and 4 columns.

(b) Minitab gives the chi-square statistic as Chi-Square 13.305. Between which two entries in Table E does this value lie? Verify that Minitab's result P-Value = 0.038 lies between the tail areas for these values.

The chi-square test and the z test*

One use of the chi-square test is to compare the proportions of successes in any number of groups. If the r rows of the two-way table are r groups and the columns are "success" and "failure," the counts form an $r \times 2$ table. P-values come from the chi-square distribution with $r - 1$ degrees of freedom. If $r = 2$, we are comparing just two proportions. We now have two ways to do this: the z test from Chapter 21 and the chi-square test with 1 degree of freedom for a 2×2 table. *These two tests always agree.* In fact, the chi-square statistic X^2 is just the square of the z statistic, and the P-value for X^2 is exactly the same as the two-sided P-value for z. We recommend using the z test to compare two proportions because it gives you the choice of a one-sided test and is related to a confidence interval for the difference $p_1 - p_2$.

APPLY YOUR KNOWLEDGE

23.14 Treating ulcers. Gastric freezing was once a recommended treatment for ulcers in the upper intestine. Use of gastric freezing stopped after experiments showed it had no effect. One randomized comparative experiment found that 28 of the 82

---

*The remainder of the material in this chapter is optional.

gastric-freezing patients improved, while 30 of the 78 patients in the placebo group improved.[8] We can test the hypothesis of "no difference" between the two groups in two ways: using the two-sample z statistic or using the chi-square statistic.

(a) Check the conditions required for both tests, given in the boxes on pages 521 and 560. The conditions are very similar, as they ought to be.

(b) State the null hypothesis with a two-sided alternative and carry out the z test. What is the P-value, exactly from software or approximately from the bottom row of Table C?

(c) Present the data in a 2×2 table. Use the chi-square test to test the hypothesis from (a). Verify that the X^2 statistic is the square of the z statistic. Use software or Table E to verify that the chi-square P-value agrees with the z result (up to the accuracy of the tables if you do not use software).

(d) What do you conclude about the effectiveness of gastric freezing as a treatment for ulcers?

More chi-square tests

There are other chi-square tests for hypotheses more specific than "no relationship." A sociologist places people in classes by social status, waits ten years, then classifies the same people again. The row and column variables are the classes at the two times. She might test the hypothesis that there has been no change in the overall distribution of social status in the group. Or she might ask if moves up in status are balanced by matching moves down. These and other null hypotheses can be tested by variations of the chi-square test.

The chi-square test for goodness of fit*

The most common and most important use of the chi-square statistic is to test the hypothesis that there is *no relationship between two categorical variables*. A variation of the statistic can be used to test a different kind of null hypothesis: that *a categorical variable has a specified distribution*. Here is an example that illustrates this use of chi-square.

EXAMPLE 23.7   Never on Sunday?

Births are not evenly distributed across the days of the week. Fewer babies are born on Saturday and Sunday than on other days, probably because doctors find weekend births inconvenient. Exercise 1.4 (page 10) gives national data that demonstrate this fact.

A random sample of 140 births from local records shows this distribution across the days of the week:

Day	Sun.	Mon.	Tue.	Wed.	Thu.	Fri.	Sat.
Births	13	23	24	20	27	18	15

Sure enough, the two smallest counts of births are on Saturday and Sunday. Do these data give significant evidence that local births are not equally likely on all days of the week?

The chi-square test answers the question of Example 23.7 by comparing observed counts with expected counts under the null hypothesis. The null hypothesis for births says that they *are* evenly distributed. To state the hypotheses carefully, write the discrete probability distribution for days of birth:

Day	Sun.	Mon.	Tue.	Wed.	Thu.	Fri.	Sat.
Probability	p_1	p_2	p_3	p_4	p_5	p_6	p_7

The null hypothesis says that the probabilities are the same on all days. In that case, all 7 probabilities must be 1/7. So the null hypothesis is

$$H_0:\ p_1 = p_2 = p_3 = p_4 = p_5 = p_6 = p_7 = \frac{1}{7}$$

The alternative hypothesis says that days are *not* all equally probable:

$$H_a:\ \text{not all } p_i = \frac{1}{7}$$

As usual in chi-square tests, H_a is a "many-sided" hypothesis that simply says that H_0 is not true. The chi-square statistic is also as usual:

$$X^2 = \sum \frac{(\text{observed count} - \text{expected count})^2}{\text{expected count}}$$

The expected count for an outcome with probability p is np, as we saw in the discussion following Example 23.2. Under the null hypothesis, all the probabilities p_i are the same, so all 7 expected counts are equal to

$$np_i = 140 \times \frac{1}{7} = 20$$

These expected counts easily satisfy our guideline for using chi-square. The chi-square statistic is

$$X^2 = \sum \frac{(\text{observed count} - 20)^2}{20}$$
$$= \frac{(13 - 20)^2}{20} + \frac{(23 - 20)^2}{20} + \cdots + \frac{(15 - 20)^2}{20}$$
$$= 7.6$$

This new use of X^2 requires a different degrees of freedom. To find the P-value, compare X^2 with critical values from the chi-square distribution with degrees of freedom one less than the number of values the birth day can take. That's $7 - 1 = 6$ degrees of freedom. From Table E, we see that $X^2 = 7.6$ is smaller than the smallest entry in the df $= 6$ row, which is the critical value for tail area 0.25. The P-value is therefore greater than 0.25 (software gives the more exact value $P = 0.269$). These 140 births don't give convincing evidence that births are not equally likely on all days of the week.

df = 6		
p	.25	.20
x^*	7.84	8.56

The chi-square test applied to the hypothesis that a categorical variable has a specified distribution is called the test for *goodness of fit*. The idea is that the test assesses whether the observed counts "fit" the distribution. The only differences between the test of fit and the test for a two-way table are that the expected counts are based on the distribution specified by the null hypothesis and that the degrees of freedom are one less than the number of possible outcomes in this distribution. Here are the details.

THE CHI-SQUARE TEST FOR GOODNESS OF FIT

A categorical variable has k possible outcomes, with probabilities p_1, p_2, p_3, ..., p_k. That is, p_i is the probability of the ith outcome. We have n independent observations from this categorical variable.

To test the null hypothesis that the probabilities have specified values

$$H_0: p_1 = p_{10}, \quad p_2 = p_{20}, \quad \ldots, \quad p_k = p_{k0}$$

use the **chi-square statistic**

$$X^2 = \sum \frac{(\text{count of outcome } i - np_{i0})^2}{np_{i0}}$$

The P-value is the area to the right of X^2 under the density curve of the chi-square distribution with $k - 1$ degrees of freedom.

In Example 23.7, the outcomes are days of the week, with $k = 7$. The null hypothesis says that the probability of a birth on the ith day is $p_{i0} = 1/7$ for all days. We observe $n = 140$ births and count how many fall on each day. These are the counts used in the chi-square statistic.

APPLY YOUR KNOWLEDGE

23.15 Saving birds from windows. Many birds are injured or killed by flying into windows. It appears that birds don't see windows. Can tilting windows down so that they reflect earth rather than sky reduce bird strikes? Place six windows at the edge of a woods: two vertical, two tilted 20 degrees, and two tilted 40 degrees. During the next four months, there were 53 bird strikes, 31 on the vertical window, 14 on the 20-degree window, and 8 on the 40-degree window.[9] If the tilt has no effect, we expect strikes on all three windows to have equal probability. Test this null hypothesis. What do you conclude?

23.16 More on birth days. Births really are not evenly distributed across the days of the week. The data in Example 23.7 failed to reject this null hypothesis because of random variation in a quite small number of births. Here are data on 700 births in the same locale:

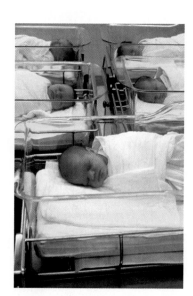

Day	Sun.	Mon.	Tue.	Wed.	Thu.	Fri.	Sat.
Births	84	110	124	104	94	112	72

(a) The null hypothesis is that all days are equally probable. What are the probabilities specified by this null hypothesis? What are the expected counts for each day in 700 births?

(b) Calculate the chi-square statistic for goodness of fit.

(c) What are the degrees of freedom for this statistic? Do these 700 births give significant evidence that births are not equally probable on all days of the week?

23.17 Course grades. Most students in a large statistics course are taught by teaching assistants (TAs). One section is taught by the course supervisor, a senior professor. The distribution of grades for the hundreds of students taught by TAs this semester was

Grade	A	B	C	D/F
Probability	0.32	0.41	0.20	0.07

The grades assigned by the professor to students in his section were

Grade	A	B	C	D/F
Count	22	38	20	11

(These data are real. We won't say when and where, but the professor was not the author of this book.)

(a) What percents of each grade did students in the professor's section earn? In what ways does this distribution of grades differ from the TA distribution?

(b) Because the TA distribution is based on hundreds of students, we are willing to regard it as a fixed probability distribution. If the professor's grading follows this distribution, what are the expected counts of each grade in his section?

(c) Does the chi-square test for goodness of fit give good evidence that the professor's grades follow a different distribution? (State hypotheses, check the guideline for using chi-square, give the test statistic and its P-value, and state your conclusion.)

23.18 What's your sign? The University of Chicago's General Social Survey (GSS) is the nation's most important social science sample survey. For reasons known only to social scientists, the GSS regularly asks its subjects their astrological sign. Here are the counts of responses in the most recent year this question was asked:[10]

Sign	Aries	Taurus	Gemini	Cancer	Leo	Virgo
Count	225	222	241	240	260	250

Sign	Libra	Scorpio	Sagittarius	Capricorn	Aquarius	Pisces
Count	243	214	200	216	224	244

If births are spread uniformly across the year, we expect all 12 signs to be equally likely. Are they? Follow the four-step process in your answer.

CHAPTER 23 SUMMARY

The **chi-square test** for a two-way table tests the null hypothesis H_0 that there is no relationship between the row variable and the column variable. The alternative hypothesis H_a says that there is some relationship but does not say what kind.

The test compares the observed counts of observations in the cells of the table with the counts that would be expected if H_0 were true. The **expected count** in any cell is

$$\text{expected count} = \frac{\text{row total} \times \text{column total}}{\text{table total}}$$

The **chi-square statistic** is

$$X^2 = \sum \frac{(\text{observed count} - \text{expected count})^2}{\text{expected count}}$$

The chi-square test compares the value of the statistic X^2 with critical values from the **chi-square distribution** with $(r - 1)(c - 1)$ **degrees of freedom.** Large values of X^2 are evidence against H_0, so the P-value is the area under the chi-square density curve to the right of X^2.

The chi-square distribution is an approximation to the distribution of the statistic X^2. You can safely use this approximation when all expected cell counts are at least 1 and no more than 20% are less than 5.

If the chi-square test finds a statistically significant relationship between the row and column variables in a two-way table, do data analysis to describe the nature of the relationship. You can do this by comparing well-chosen percents, comparing the observed counts with the expected counts, and looking for the largest **terms of the chi-square statistic.**

STATISTICS IN SUMMARY

Here are the most important skills you should have acquired from reading this chapter.

A. TWO-WAY TABLES

1. Understand that the data for a chi-square test must be presented as a two-way table of counts of outcomes.

2. Use percents to describe the relationship between any two categorical variables, starting from the counts in a two-way table.

B. INTERPRETING CHI-SQUARE TESTS

1. Locate the chi-square statistic, its P-value, and other useful facts (row or column percents, expected counts, terms of chi-square) in output from your software or calculator.

2. Use the expected counts to check whether you can safely use the chi-square test.

3. Explain what null hypothesis the chi-square statistic tests in a specific two-way table.

4. If the test is significant, compare percents, compare observed with expected cell counts, or look for the largest terms of the chi-square statistic to see what deviations from the null hypothesis are most important.

C. DOING CHI-SQUARE TESTS BY HAND

1. Calculate the expected count for any cell from the observed counts in a two-way table. Check whether you can safely use the chi-square test.

2. Calculate the term of the chi-square statistic for any cell, as well as the overall statistic.

3. Give the degrees of freedom of a chi-square statistic. Make a quick assessment of the significance of the statistic by comparing the observed value with the degrees of freedom.

4. Use the chi-square critical values in Table E to approximate the P-value of a chi-square test.

CHECK YOUR SKILLS

The National Survey of Adolescent Health interviewed several thousand teens (grades 7 to 12). One question asked was "What do you think are the chances you will be married in the next ten years?" Here is a two-way table of the responses by sex:[11]

	Female	Male
Almost no chance	119	103
Some chance, but probably not	150	171
A 50-50 chance	447	512
A good chance	735	710
Almost certain	1174	756

23.19 The number of female teenagers in the sample is
   (a) 4877.   (b) 2625.   (c) 2252.

23.20 The percent of the females in the sample who responded "almost certain" is about
   (a) 44.7%.   (b) 39.6%.   (c) 33.6%.

23.21 The percent of the females in the sample who responded "almost certain" is
   (a) higher than the percent of males who felt this way.
   (b) about the same as the percent of males who felt this way.
   (c) lower than the percent of males who felt this way.

23.22 The expected count of females who respond "almost certain" is about
   (a) 464.6.   (b) 891.2.   (c) 1038.8.

23.23 The term in the chi-square statistic for the cell of females who respond "almost certain" is about

(a) 17.6. (b) 15.6. (c) 0.1.

23.24 The degrees of freedom for the chi-square test for this two-way table are

(a) 4. (b) 8. (c) 20.

23.25 The null hypothesis for the chi-square test for this two-way table is

(a) Equal proportions of female and male teenagers are almost certain they will be married in ten years.

(b) There is no difference between female and male teenagers in their distributions of opinions about marriage.

(c) There are equal numbers of female and male teenagers.

23.26 The alternative hypothesis for the chi-square test for this two-way table is

(a) Female and male teenagers do not have the same distribution of opinions about marriage.

(b) Female teenagers are more likely than male teenagers to think it is almost certain they will be married in ten years.

(c) Female teenagers are less likely than male teenagers to think it is almost certain they will be married in ten years.

23.27 Software gives chi-square statistic $X^2 = 69.8$ for this table. From the table of critical values, we can say that the P-value is

(a) between 0.0025 and 0.001.

(b) between 0.001 and 0.0005.

(c) less than 0.0005.

23.28 The most important fact that allows us to trust the results of the chi-square test is that

(a) the sample is large, 4877 teenagers in all.

(b) the sample is close to an SRS of all teenagers.

(c) all of the cell counts are greater than 100.

CHAPTER 23 EXERCISES

If you have access to software or a graphing calculator, use it to speed your analysis of the data in these exercises. Exercises 23.29 to 23.38 are suitable for hand calculation if necessary.

23.29 **Who's online?** A sample survey by the Pew Internet and American Life Project asked a random sample of adults about use of the Internet and about the type of community they lived in. Here, repeated from Exercise 23.4, is the two-way table:

	Community Type		
	Rural	Suburban	Urban
Internet users	433	1072	536
Nonusers	463	627	388

(a) Give a 95% confidence interval for the difference between the proportions of rural and suburban adults who use the Internet.

(b) What is the overall pattern of the relationship between Internet use and community type? Is the relationship statistically significant?

23.30 **Child care workers.** A large study of child care used samples from the data tapes of the Current Population Survey over a period of several years. The result is close to an SRS of child care workers. The Current Population Survey has three classes of child care workers: private household, nonhousehold, and preschool teacher. Here are data on the number of blacks among women workers in these three classes:[12]

First Light/Getty Images

	Total	Black
Household	2455	172
Nonhousehold	1191	167
Teachers	659	86

(a) What percent of each class of child care workers is black?

(b) Make a two-way table of class of worker by race (black or other).

(c) Can we safely use the chi-square test? What null and alternative hypotheses does X^2 test?

(d) The chi-square statistic for this table is $X^2 = 53.194$. What are its degrees of freedom? What is the mean of X^2 if the null hypothesis is true? Use Table E to approximate the P-value of the test.

(e) What do you conclude from these data?

23.31 **Free speech for racists?** The General Social Survey (GSS) for 2002 asked this question: "Consider a person who believes that Blacks are genetically inferior. If such a person wanted to make a speech in your community claiming that Blacks are inferior, should he be allowed to speak, or not?" Here are the responses, broken down by the race of the respondent:[13]

	Black	White	Other
Allowed	67	476	35
Not allowed	53	252	17

(a) Because the GSS is essentially an SRS of all adults, we can combine the races in these data and give a 99% confidence interval for the proportion of all adults who would allow a racist to speak. Do this.

(b) Find the column percents and use them to compare the attitudes of the three racial groups. How significant are the differences found in the sample?

23.32 **Do you use cocaine?** Sample surveys on sensitive issues can give different results depending on how the question is asked. A University of Wisconsin study divided 2400 respondents into 3 groups at random. All were asked if they had ever used cocaine. One group of 800 was interviewed by phone; 21% said they had used cocaine. Another 800 people were asked the question in a one-on-one personal interview; 25% said "Yes." The remaining 800 were allowed to make an anonymous written response; 28% said "Yes."[14] Are there statistically significant differences among these proportions? State the hypotheses, convert the information given into a two-way table of counts, give the test statistic and its *P*-value, and state your conclusions.

23.33 **Ethnicity and seat belt use.** How does seat belt use vary with drivers' race or ethnic group? The answer depends on gender (males are less likely to buckle up) and also on location. Here are data on a random sample of male drivers observed in Houston:[15]

	Drivers	Belted
Black	369	273
Hispanic	540	372
White	257	193

(a) The table gives the number of drivers in each group and the number of these who were wearing seat belts. Make a two-way table of group by belted or not.

(b) Are there statistically significant differences in seat belt use among men in these three groups? If there are, describe the differences.

23.34 **Did the randomization work?** After randomly assigning subjects to treatments in a randomized comparative experiment, we can compare the treatment groups to see how well the randomization worked. We hope to find no significant differences among the groups. A study of how to provide premature infants with a substance essential to their development assigned infants at random to receive one of four types of supplement, called PBM, NLCP, PL-LCP, and TG-LCP.[16]

(a) The subjects were 77 premature infants. Outline the design of the experiment if 20 are assigned to the PBM group and 19 to each of the other treatments.

(b) The random assignment resulted in 9 females in the TG-LCP group and 11 females in each of the other groups. Make a two-way table of group by gender and do a chi-square test to see if there are significant differences among the groups. What do you find?

23.35 **Opinions about the death penalty.** "Do you favor or oppose the death penalty for persons convicted of murder?" When the General Social Survey asked this question in its 2002 survey, the responses of people whose highest education was a bachelor's degree and of people with a graduate degree were as follows:[17]

	Favor	Oppose
Bachelor	135	71
Graduate	64	50

(a) Is there evidence that the proportions of all people at these levels of education who favor the death penalty differ? Find the two sample proportions, the *z* statistic, and its *P*-value.

(b) Is there evidence that the opinions of all people at these levels of education differ? Find the chi-square statistic X^2 and its P-value. If your work is correct, X^2 should be the same as z^2 and the two P-values should be identical.

23.36 Unhappy rats and tumors. Some people think that the attitude of cancer patients can influence the progress of their disease. We can't experiment with humans, but here is a rat experiment on this theme. Inject 60 rats with tumor cells and then divide them at random into two groups of 30. All the rats receive electric shocks, but rats in Group 1 can end the shock by pressing a lever. (Rats learn this sort of thing quickly.) The rats in Group 2 cannot control the shocks, which presumably makes them feel helpless and unhappy. We suspect that the rats in Group 1 will develop fewer tumors. The results: 11 of the Group 1 rats and 22 of the Group 2 rats developed tumors.[18]

(a) State the null and alternative hypotheses for this investigation. Explain why the z test rather than the chi-square test for a 2×2 table is the proper test.

(b) Carry out the test and report your conclusion.

23.37 Regulating guns. The National Gun Policy Survey, conducted by the National Opinion Research Center at the University of Chicago, asked a random sample of adults many questions about regulation of guns in the United States. One of the questions was "Do you think there should be a law that would ban possession of handguns except for the police and other authorized persons?" Figure 23.7

```
Session                                                              _|□|×

           Less
           than      High
           high     school     Some    College  Postgraduate
          school   Graduate   college  Graduate     degree      All

  Yes        58        84       169        98          77        486
           50.00     39.44     36.50     42.06       43.75      40.47
          2.6055    0.0558    1.7989    0.1463      0.4690        *


  No         58       129       294       135          99        715
           50.00     60.56     63.50     57.94       56.25      59.53
          1.7710    0.0379    1.2228    0.0994      0.3188        *


  All       116       213       463       233         176       1201
          100.00    100.00    100.00    100.00      100.00    100.00
             *         *         *         *           *          *



  Cell Contents:      Count
                      % of Column
                      Contribution to Chi-square

  Pearson Chi-Square = 8.525, DF = 4, P-Value = 0.074
```

FIGURE 23.7 Minitab output for the sample survey responses of Exercise 23.37.

displays Minitab output that includes the two-way table of response versus the respondents' highest level of education.[19]

(a) The column percents show the breakdown of responses separately for each level of education. Which education groups show particularly high and low support for the proposed law? Which education group's responses contribute the most to the size of the chi-square statistic? Is there a consistent direction in the relationship, such as "people with more education are more likely to support strong gun laws"?

(b) Verify the degrees of freedom given by Minitab. How does the value of the chi-square statistic compare with its mean under the null hypothesis? What do you conclude from the chi-square test?

23.38 **I think I'll be rich by age 30.** A sample survey of young adults (aged 19 to 25) asked, "What do you think are the chances you will have much more than a middle-class income at age 30?" The CrunchIt! output in Figure 23.8 shows the two-way table and related information, omitting a few subjects who refused to respond or who said they were already rich.[20]

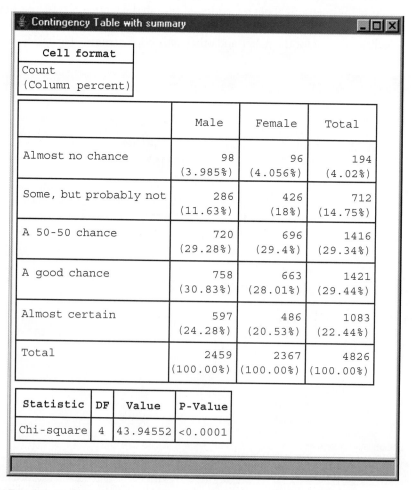

FIGURE 23.8 CrunchIt! output for the sample survey responses of Exercise 23.38.

Use the output as the basis for a discussion of the differences between young men and young women in assessing their chances of being rich by age 30.

The remaining exercises concern larger tables that require software for easy analysis. Follow the **Formulate, Solve,** *and* **Conclude** *steps of the four-part process in your answers to these exercises. It may be helpful to restate in your own words the* **State** *information given in the exercise.*

23.39 Students and catalog shopping. What is the most important reason that students buy from catalogs? The answer may differ for different groups of students. Here are results for samples of American and East Asian students at a large midwestern university:[21]

	American	Asian
Save time	29	10
Easy	28	11
Low price	17	34
Live far from stores	11	4
No pressure to buy	10	3
Other reason	20	7
Total	115	69

Describe the most important differences between American and Asian students. Is there a significant overall difference between the two distributions of responses?

23.40 Where do young adults live? A survey by the National Institutes of Health asked a random sample of young adults (aged 19 to 25), "Where do you live now? That is, where do you stay most often?" We earlier (page 513) compared the proportions of men and women who lived with their parents. Here now is the full two-way table (omitting a few who refused to answer and one who claimed to be homeless):[22]

	Female	Male
Parents' home	923	986
Another person's home	144	132
Own place	1294	1129
Group quarters	127	119

What are the most important differences between young men and women? Are their choices of living places significantly different?

23.41 How are schools doing? The nonprofit group Public Agenda conducted telephone interviews with a stratified sample of parents of high school children. There were 202 black parents, 202 Hispanic parents, and 201 white parents.

One question asked was "Are the high schools in your state doing an excellent, good, fair or poor job, or don't you know enough to say?" Here are the survey results:[23]

	Black parents	Hispanic parents	White parents
Excellent	12	34	22
Good	69	55	81
Fair	75	61	60
Poor	24	24	24
Don't know	22	28	14
Total	202	202	201

Are the differences in the distributions of responses for the three groups of parents statistically significant? What departures from the null hypothesis "no relationship between group and response" contribute most to the value of the chi-square statistic? Write a brief conclusion based on your analysis.

23.42 The Mediterranean diet. Cancer of the colon and rectum is less common in the Mediterranean region than in other Western countries. The Mediterranean diet contains little animal fat and lots of olive oil. Italian researchers compared 1953 patients with colon or rectal cancer with a control group of 4154 patients admitted to the same hospitals for unrelated reasons. They estimated consumption of various foods from a detailed interview, then divided the patients into three groups according to their consumption of olive oil. Here are some of the data:[24]

Hugh Burden/SuperStock

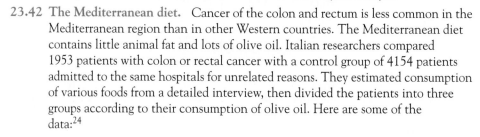

	Olive Oil			
	Low	Medium	High	Total
Colon cancer	398	397	430	1225
Rectal cancer	250	241	237	728
Controls	1368	1377	1409	4154

(a) Is this study an experiment? Explain your answer.

(b) The investigators report that "less than 4% of cases or controls refused to participate." Why does this fact strengthen our confidence in the results?

(c) The researchers conjectured that high olive oil consumption would be more common among patients without cancer than among patients with colon cancer or rectal cancer. What do the data say?

23.43 Market research. Before bringing a new product to market, firms carry out extensive studies to learn how consumers react to the product and how best to advertise its advantages. Here are data from a study of a new laundry detergent.[25] The subjects are people who don't currently use the established brand that the new product will compete with. Give subjects free samples of both detergents.

After they have tried both for a while, ask which they prefer. The answers may depend on other facts about how people do laundry.

	Laundry Practices			
	Soft water, warm wash	Soft water, hot wash	Hard water, warm wash	Hard water, hot wash
Prefer standard product	53	27	42	30
Prefer new product	63	29	68	42

How do laundry practices (water hardness and wash temperature) influence the choice of detergent? In which settings does the new detergent do best? Are the differences between the detergents statistically significant?

Support for political parties.   *Political parties anxiously ask what groups of people support them. The General Social Survey (GSS) asked its 2002 sample, "Generally speaking, do you usually think of yourself as a Republican, Democrat, Independent, or what?" Here is a large two-way table breaking down the responses by age group:*[26]

	Age Group			
	18–30	31–40	41–55	56–89
Strong Democrat	60	83	113	151
Not strong Democrat	99	126	138	148
Independent, near Democrat	72	56	77	62
Independent	152	124	149	102
Independent, near Republican	53	41	50	54
Not strong Republican	90	85	133	138
Strong Republican	42	56	89	127
Other party	9	12	14	13

Exercises 23.44 to 23.46 are based on this table.

23.44 Other parties.   The GSS is essentially an SRS of American adults. Give a 95% confidence interval for the proportion of adults who support "other parties."

23.45 Party support.   Make a 2 × 4 table by combining the counts in the three rows that mention Democrat and in the three rows that mention Republican and ignoring strict independents and supporters of other parties. We might think of this table as comparing all adults who lean Democrat and all adults who lean Republican. How does support of the two major parties differ among age groups?

23.46 Politics and age.   Use the full table to analyze the differences in political party support among age groups. The sample is so large that the differences are bound to be highly significant, but give the chi-square statistic and its *P*-value nonetheless. The main challenge is in seeing what the data say. Does the full table yield any insights not found in the compressed table you analyzed in the previous exercise?

EESEE CASE STUDIES

The Electronic Encyclopedia of Statistical Examples and Exercises (EESEE) is available on the text CD and Web site. These more elaborate stories, with data, provide settings for longer case studies. Here are some suggestions for EESEE stories that apply the chi-square test.

23.47 Read the EESEE story "Surgery in a Blanket." Write a report that answers Questions 1, 3, 5, 6, and 7 for this case study.

23.48 Read the EESEE story "Trilobite Bites." Write a report that answers Questions 1, 2, 4, and 5 for this case study.

Monika Graff/The Image Works

Inference for Regression

When a scatterplot shows a linear relationship between a quantitative explanatory variable x and a quantitative response variable y, we can use the least-squares line fitted to the data to predict y for a given value of x. When the data are a sample from a larger population, we need statistical inference to answer questions like these about the population:

- Is there really a linear relationship between x and y in the population, or might the pattern we see in the scatterplot plausibly arise just by chance?
- How large is the slope (rate of change) that relates y to x in the population, including a margin of error for our estimate of the slope?
- If we use the least-squares line to predict y for a given value of x, how accurate is our prediction (again, with a margin of error)?

This chapter shows you how to answer these questions. Here is an example we will explore.

┌─ **EXAMPLE 24.1** Crying and IQ ───────────────

STATE: Infants who cry easily may be more easily stimulated than others. This may be a sign of higher IQ. Child development researchers explored the relationship between the crying of infants four to ten days old and their later IQ test scores. A snap of a rubber band on the sole of the foot caused the infants to cry. The researchers recorded the crying and measured its intensity by the number of peaks in the most active 20 seconds. They later measured the children's IQ at age three years using the Stanford-Binet IQ test.

Benelux Press/Index Stock Imagery/
PictureQuest

TABLE 24.1		Infants' crying and IQ scores					
Crying	IQ	Crying	IQ	Crying	IQ	Crying	IQ
10	87	20	90	17	94	12	94
12	97	16	100	19	103	12	103
9	103	23	103	13	104	14	106
16	106	27	108	18	109	10	109
18	109	15	112	18	112	23	113
15	114	21	114	16	118	9	119
12	119	12	120	19	120	16	124
20	132	15	133	22	135	31	135
16	136	17	141	30	155	22	157
33	159	13	162				

Table 24.1 contains data on 38 infants.[1] Do children with higher crying counts tend to have higher IQ?

FORMULATE: Make a scatterplot. If the relationship appears linear, use correlation and regression to describe it. Finally, ask whether there is a *statistically significant* relationship between crying and IQ.

SOLVE (first steps): Chapters 4 and 5 introduced the data analysis that must come before inference. The first steps we take are a review of this data analysis. Figure 24.1 is a *scatterplot*

scatterplot   **scatterplot** of the crying data. Plot the explanatory variable (count of crying peaks)

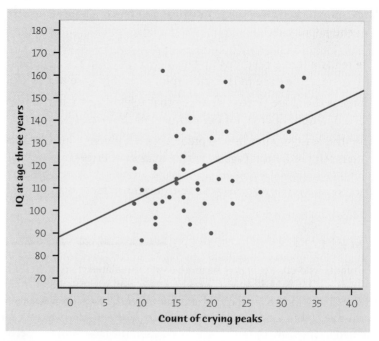

FIGURE 24.1 Scatterplot of the IQ score of infants at age three years against the intensity of their crying soon after birth, with the least-squares regression line.

horizontally and the response variable (IQ) vertically. Look for the form, direction, and strength of the relationship as well as for outliers or other deviations. There is a moderate positive linear relationship, with no extreme outliers or potentially influential observations.

Because the scatterplot shows a roughly linear (straight-line) pattern, the **correlation** describes the direction and strength of the relationship. The correlation between crying and IQ is $r = 0.455$. We are interested in predicting the response from information about the explanatory variable. So we find the **least-squares regression line** for predicting IQ from crying. The equation of the regression line is

$$\hat{y} = a + bx$$
$$= 91.27 + 1.493x$$

correlation

least-squares line

CONCLUDE (first steps): Children who cry more vigorously do tend to have higher IQs. Because $r^2 = 0.207$, only about 21% of the variation in IQ scores is explained by crying intensity. Prediction of IQ will not be very accurate. It is nonetheless impressive that behavior soon after birth can even partly predict IQ three years later. Is this observed relationship statistically significant? We must now develop tools for inference in the regression setting.

Conditions for regression inference

We can fit a regression line to *any* data relating two quantitative variables, though the results are useful only if the scatterplot shows a linear pattern. Statistical inference requires more detailed conditions. Because the conclusions of inference always concern some *population*, the conditions describe the population and how the data are produced from it. The slope b and intercept a of the least-squares line are *statistics*. That is, we calculated them from the sample data. These statistics would take somewhat different values if we repeated the study with different infants. To do inference, think of a and b as estimates of unknown *parameters* that describe the population of all infants.

CONDITIONS FOR REGRESSION INFERENCE

We have n observations on an explanatory variable x and a response variable y. Our goal is to study or predict the behavior of y for given values of x.

- For any fixed value of x, the response y varies according to a **Normal distribution.** Repeated responses y are **independent** of each other.

- The mean response μ_y has a **straight-line relationship** with x given by a **population regression line**

$$\mu_y = \alpha + \beta x$$

The slope β and intercept α are unknown parameters.

- The **standard deviation** of y (call it σ) is the same for all values of x. The value of σ is unknown.

There are thus three population parameters that we must estimate from the data: α, β, and σ.

FIGURE 24.2 The nature of regression data when the conditions for inference are met. The line is the population regression line, which shows how the mean response μ_y changes as the explanatory variable x changes. For any fixed value of x, the observed response y varies according to a Normal distribution having mean μ_y and standard deviation σ.

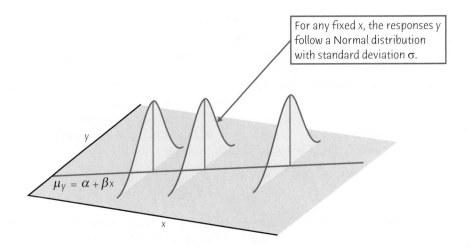

For any fixed x, the responses y follow a Normal distribution with standard deviation σ.

$\mu_y = \alpha + \beta x$

These conditions say that in the population there is an "on the average" straight-line relationship between y and x. The population regression line $\mu_y = \alpha + \beta x$ says that the *mean* response μ_y moves along a straight line as the explanatory variable x changes. We can't observe the population regression line. The values of y that we do observe vary about their means according to a Normal distribution. If we hold x fixed and take many observations on y, the Normal pattern will eventually appear in a stemplot or histogram. In practice, we observe y for many different values of x, so that we see an overall linear pattern formed by points scattered about the population line. The standard deviation σ determines whether the points fall close to the population regression line (small σ) or are widely scattered (large σ).

Figure 24.2 shows the nature of regression data in picture form. The line in the figure is the population regression line. The mean of the response y moves along this line as the explanatory variable x takes different values. The Normal curves show how y will vary when x is held fixed at different values. All of the curves have the same σ, so the variability of y is the same for all values of x. You should check the conditions for inference when you do inference about regression. We will see later how to do that.

Estimating the parameters

The first step in inference is to estimate the unknown parameters α, β, and σ.

ESTIMATING THE POPULATION REGRESSION LINE

When the conditions for regression are met and we calculate the least-squares line $\hat{y} = a + bx$, the slope b of the least-squares line is an unbiased estimator of the population slope β, and the intercept a of the least-squares line is an unbiased estimator of the population intercept α.

EXAMPLE 24.2   Crying and IQ: slope and intercept

The data in Figure 24.1 satisfy the condition of scatter about an invisible population regression line reasonably well. The least-squares line is $\hat{y} = 91.27 + 1.493x$. The slope is particularly important. *A slope is a rate of change.* The population slope β says how much higher average IQ is for children with one more peak in their crying measurement. Because $b = 1.493$ estimates the unknown β, we estimate that, on the average, IQ is about 1.5 points higher for each added crying peak.

We need the intercept $a = 91.27$ to draw the line, but it has no statistical meaning in this example. No child had fewer than 9 crying peaks, so we have no data near $x = 0$. We suspect that all normal children would cry when snapped with a rubber band, so that we will never observe $x = 0$.

The remaining parameter is the standard deviation σ, which describes the variability of the response y about the population regression line. The least-squares line estimates the population regression line. So the **residuals** estimate how much *residuals* y varies about the population line. Recall that the residuals are the vertical deviations of the data points from the least-squares line:

$$\text{residual} = \text{observed } y - \text{predicted } y$$
$$= y - \hat{y}$$

There are n residuals, one for each data point. Because σ is the standard deviation of responses about the population regression line, we estimate it by a sample standard deviation of the residuals. We call this sample standard deviation the *regression standard error* to emphasize that it is estimated from data. The residuals from a least-squares line always have mean zero. That simplifies their standard error.

REGRESSION STANDARD ERROR

The **regression standard error** is

$$s = \sqrt{\frac{1}{n-2}\sum \text{residual}^2}$$

$$= \sqrt{\frac{1}{n-2}\sum(y - \hat{y})^2}$$

Use s to estimate the standard deviation σ of responses about the mean given by the population regression line.

Because we use the regression standard error so often, we just call it s. Notice that s^2 is an average of the squared deviations of the data points from the line, so it qualifies as a variance. We average the squared deviations by dividing by $n - 2$, the number of data points less 2. It turns out that if we know $n - 2$ of the n residuals, the other two are determined. That is, $n - 2$ are the **degrees of freedom** of s. We   *degrees of freedom*

The jinx!

Athletes are often jinxed. We read of "the rookie of the year jinx," the "cover of *Sports Illustrated* jinx," and many others. That is, athletes who are recognized for an outstanding performance often fail to do as well in the future. No, nature isn't retaliating against them. It's just random variation about their long-term mean performance. They were recognized because they randomly varied above their typical performance, and in the future they return to the mean or randomly vary down from it. If they randomly vary down, they can hope for a "comeback" award the next year.

first met the idea of degrees of freedom in the case of the ordinary sample standard deviation of n observations, which has $n - 1$ degrees of freedom. Now we observe two variables rather than one, and the proper degrees of freedom are $n - 2$ rather than $n - 1$.

Calculating s is unpleasant. You must find the predicted response for each x in your data set, then the residuals, and then s. In practice you will use software that does this arithmetic instantly. Nonetheless, here is an example to help you understand the standard error s.

EXAMPLE 24.3 Crying and IQ: residuals and standard error ——

Table 24.1 shows that the first infant studied had 10 crying peaks and a later IQ of 87. The predicted IQ for $x = 10$ is

$$\hat{y} = 91.27 + 1.493x$$
$$= 91.27 + 1.493(10) = 106.2$$

The residual for this observation is

$$\text{residual} = y - \hat{y}$$
$$= 87 - 106.2 = -19.2$$

That is, the observed IQ for this infant lies 19.2 points below the least-squares line on the scatterplot.

Repeat this calculation 37 more times, once for each subject. The 38 residuals are

−19.20	−31.13	−22.65	−15.18	−12.18	−15.15	−16.63	−6.18
−1.70	−22.60	−6.68	−6.17	−9.15	−23.58	−9.14	2.80
−9.14	−1.66	−6.14	−12.60	0.34	−8.62	2.85	14.30
9.82	10.82	0.37	8.85	10.87	19.34	10.89	−2.55
20.85	24.35	18.94	32.89	18.47	51.32		

Check the calculations by verifying that the sum of the residuals is zero. It is 0.04, not quite zero, because of roundoff error. Another reason to use software in regression is that roundoff errors in hand calculation can accumulate to make the results inaccurate.

The variance about the line is

$$s^2 = \frac{1}{n-2} \sum \text{residual}^2$$
$$= \frac{1}{38-2}[(-19.20)^2 + (-31.13)^2 + \cdots + (51.32)^2]$$
$$= \frac{1}{36}(11023.3) = 306.20$$

Finally, the regression standard error is

$$s = \sqrt{306.20} = 17.50$$

We will study several kinds of inference in the regression setting. The regression standard error s is the key measure of the variability of the responses in regression. It is part of the standard error of all the statistics we will use for inference.

APPLY YOUR KNOWLEDGE

24.1   **Coffee and deforestation.**   Coffee is a leading export from several developing countries. When coffee prices are high, farmers often clear forest to plant more coffee trees. Here are five years' data on prices paid to coffee growers in Indonesia and the percent of forest area lost in a national park that lies in a coffee-producing region:[2]

Price (cents per pound)	29	40	54	55	72
Forest lost (percent)	0.49	1.59	1.69	1.82	3.10

(a) Examine the data. Make a scatterplot with coffee price as the explanatory variable. What are the correlation r and the equation of the least-squares regression line? Do you think that coffee price will allow good prediction of forest lost?

(b) Explain in words what the slope β of the population regression line would tell us if we knew it. Based on the data, what are the estimates of β and the intercept α of the population regression line?

(c) Calculate by hand the residuals for the five data points. Check that their sum is 0 (up to roundoff error). Use the residuals to estimate the standard deviation σ of percents of forest lost about the means given by the population regression line. You have now estimated all three parameters.

Using technology

Basic "two-variable statistics" calculators will find the slope b and intercept a of the least-squares line from keyed-in data. Inference about regression requires in addition the regression standard error s. At this point, software or a graphing calculator that includes procedures for regression inference becomes almost essential for practical work.

Figure 24.3 shows regression output for the data of Table 24.1 from a graphing calculator, two statistical programs, and a spreadsheet program. When we entered the data into the programs, we called the explanatory variable "Crycount." The outputs use that label. The TI-83 just uses "x" and "y" to label the explanatory and response variables. You can locate the basic information in all of the outputs. The regression slope is $b = 1.4929$ and the regression intercept is $a = 91.268$. The equation of the least-squares line is therefore (after rounding) just as given in Example 24.1. The regression standard error is $s = 17.4987$ and the squared correlation is $r^2 = 0.207$. Both of these results reflect the rather wide scatter of the points in Figure 24.1 about the least-squares line.

Each output contains other information, some of which we will need shortly and some of which we don't need. In fact, we left out some output to save space. Once you know what to look for, you can find what you want in almost any output and ignore what doesn't interest you.

TI-83

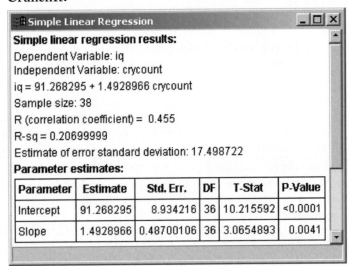

CrunchIt!

Simple Linear Regression

Simple linear regression results:

Dependent Variable: iq
Independent Variable: crycount

iq = 91.268295 + 1.4928966 crycount

Sample size: 38

R (correlation coefficient) = 0.455

R-sq = 0.20699999

Estimate of error standard deviation: 17.498722

Parameter estimates:

Parameter	Estimate	Std. Err.	DF	T-Stat	P-Value
Intercept	91.268295	8.934216	36	10.215592	<0.0001
Slope	1.4928966	0.48700106	36	3.0654893	0.0041

Minitab

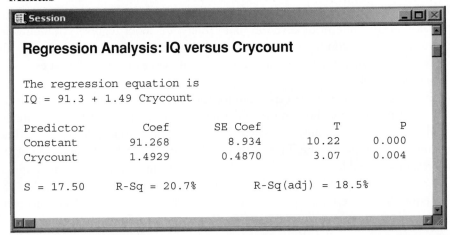

Regression Analysis: IQ versus Crycount

```
The regression equation is
IQ = 91.3 + 1.49 Crycount

Predictor        Coef      SE Coef         T         P
Constant       91.268        8.934     10.22     0.000
Crycount       1.4929       0.4870      3.07     0.004

S = 17.50    R-Sq = 20.7%       R-Sq(adj) = 18.5%
```

FIGURE 24.3 Regression of IQ on crying peaks: output from a graphing calculator, two statistical programs, and a spreadsheet program (*continued*).

Excel

	A	B	C	D	E	F	G
1	SUMMARY OUTPUT						
2							
3	*Regression statistics*						
4	Multiple R	0.4550					
5	R Square	0.2070					
6	Adjusted R Square	0.1850					
7	Standard Error	17.4987					
8	Observations	38					
9							
10		Coefficients	Standard Error	t Stat	P-value	Lower 95%	Upper 95%
11	Intercept	91.2683	8.9342	10.2156	3.5E-12	73.1489	109.3877
12	Crycount	1.4929	0.4870	3.0655	0.004105	0.5052	2.4806
13							

Sheet4 / Sheet1 / Sheet2 / Sheet3

FIGURE 24.3 (*continued*)

APPLY YOUR KNOWLEDGE

24.2 **How fast do icicles grow?** The rate at which an icicle grows depends on temperature, water flow, and wind. The data below are for an icicle grown in a cold chamber at $-11°C$ with no wind and a water flow of 11.9 milligrams per second.[3]

Time (min)	10	20	30	40	50	60	70	80	90
Length (cm)	0.6	1.8	2.9	4.0	5.0	6.1	7.9	10.1	10.9

Time (min)	100	110	120	130	140	150	160	170	180
Length (cm)	12.7	14.4	16.6	18.1	19.9	21.0	23.4	24.7	27.8

Kristjan Fridriksson/Getty Images

We want to predict length from time. Figure 24.4 shows Minitab regression output for these data.

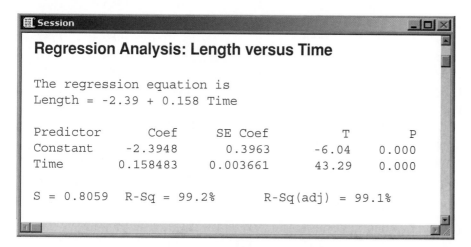

Regression Analysis: Length versus Time

```
The regression equation is
Length = -2.39 + 0.158 Time

Predictor       Coef       SE Coef          T          P
Constant      -2.3948       0.3963       -6.04      0.000
Time         0.158483      0.003661       43.29      0.000

S = 0.8059   R-Sq = 99.2%      R-Sq(adj) = 99.1%
```

FIGURE 24.4 Minitab output for the icicle growth data, for Exercise 24.2.

(a) Make a scatterplot suitable for predicting length from time. The pattern is very linear. What is the squared correlation r^2? Time explains almost all of the change in length.

(b) For regression inference, we must estimate the three parameters α, β, and σ. From the output, what are the estimates of these parameters?

(c) What is the equation of the least-squares regression line of length on time? Add this line to your plot. We will continue the analysis of these data in later exercises.

24.3   **Great Arctic rivers.**   One effect of global warming is to increase the flow of water into the Arctic Ocean from rivers. Such an increase may have major effects on the world's climate. Six rivers (Yenisey, Lena, Ob, Pechora, Kolyma, and Severnaya Dvina) drain two-thirds of the Arctic in Europe and Asia. Several of these are among the largest rivers on earth. Table 24.2 presents the total discharge from these rivers each year from 1936 to 1999.[4] Discharge is measured in cubic kilometers of water. Use software to analyze these data.

(a) Make a scatterplot of river discharge against time. Is there a clear increasing trend? Calculate r^2 and briefly interpret its value. There is considerable year-to-year variation, so we wonder if the trend is statistically significant.

(b) As a first step, find the least-squares line and draw it on your plot. Then find the regression standard error s, which measures scatter about this line. We will continue the analysis in later exercises.

TABLE 24.2   Arctic river discharge (cubic kilometers), 1936 to 1999

Year	Discharge	Year	Discharge	Year	Discharge	Year	Discharge
1936	1721	1952	1829	1968	1713	1984	1823
1937	1713	1953	1652	1969	1742	1985	1822
1938	1860	1954	1589	1970	1751	1986	1860
1939	1739	1955	1656	1971	1879	1987	1732
1940	1615	1956	1721	1972	1736	1988	1906
1941	1838	1957	1762	1973	1861	1989	1932
1942	1762	1958	1936	1974	2000	1990	1861
1943	1709	1959	1906	1975	1928	1991	1801
1944	1921	1960	1736	1976	1653	1992	1793
1945	1581	1961	1970	1977	1698	1993	1845
1946	1834	1962	1849	1978	2008	1994	1902
1947	1890	1963	1774	1979	1970	1995	1842
1948	1898	1964	1606	1980	1758	1996	1849
1949	1958	1965	1735	1981	1774	1997	2007
1950	1830	1966	1883	1982	1728	1998	1903
1951	1864	1967	1642	1983	1920	1999	1970

Testing the hypothesis of no linear relationship

Example 24.1 asked, "Do children with higher crying counts tend to have higher IQ?" Data analysis supports this conjecture. But is the positive association statistically significant? That is, is it too strong to often occur just by chance? To answer this question, test hypotheses about the slope β of the population regression line:

$$H_0: \beta = 0$$
$$H_a: \beta > 0$$

A regression line with slope 0 is horizontal. That is, the mean of y does not change at all when x changes. So H_0 says that there is *no linear relationship* between x and y in the population. Put another way, H_0 says that *linear regression of y on x is of no value for predicting y*.

The test statistic is just the standardized version of the least-squares slope b, using the hypothesized value $\beta = 0$ for the mean of b. It is another t statistic. Here are the details.

SIGNIFICANCE TEST FOR REGRESSION SLOPE

To **test the hypothesis $H_0: \beta = 0$,** compute the t statistic

$$t = \frac{b}{\mathrm{SE}_b}$$

In this formula, the standard error of the least-squares slope b is

$$\mathrm{SE}_b = \frac{s}{\sqrt{\sum (x - \bar{x})^2}}$$

The sum runs over all observations on the explanatory variable x. In terms of a random variable T having the $t(n - 2)$ distribution, the P-value for a test of H_0 against

$H_a: \beta > 0$	is	$P(T \ge t)$

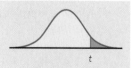

$H_a: \beta < 0$	is	$P(T \le t)$

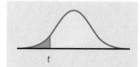

$H_a: \beta \ne 0$	is	$2P(T \ge |t|)$

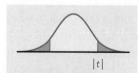

Is regression garbage?

No—but garbage can be the setting for regression. The Census Bureau once asked if weighing a neighborhood's garbage would help count its people. So 63 households had their garbage sorted and weighed. It turned out that pounds of plastic in the trash gave the best garbage prediction of the number of people in a neighborhood. The margin of error for a 95% prediction interval in a neighborhood of about 100 households, based on five weeks' worth of garbage, was about ±2.5 people. Alas, that is not accurate enough to help the Census Bureau.

As advertised, the standard error of b is a multiple of the regression standard error s. The degrees of freedom $n - 2$ are the degrees of freedom of s. Although we give the formula for this standard error, you should not try to calculate it by hand. Regression software gives the standard error SE_b along with b itself.

> **EXAMPLE 24.4**   Crying and IQ: is the relationship significant?
>
> The hypothesis $H_0: \beta = 0$ says that crying has no straight-line relationship with IQ. We conjecture that there is a positive relationship, so we use the one-sided alternative $H_a: \beta > 0$.
>   Figure 24.1 shows that there is a positive relationship, so it is not surprising that all of the outputs in Figure 24.3 give $t = 3.07$ with two-sided P-value 0.004. The P-value for the one-sided test is half of this, $P = 0.002$. There is very strong evidence that IQ increases as the intensity of crying increases.

APPLY YOUR KNOWLEDGE

24.4   **Coffee and deforestation: testing.**   Exercise 24.1 presents data on coffee prices and loss of forest in Indonesia. In that exercise, you estimated the parameters using only a two-variable statistics calculator. Software tells us that the least-squares slope is $b = 0.0543$ with standard error $SE_b = 0.0097$.

   (a) What is the t statistic for testing $H_0: \beta = 0$?

   (b) How many degrees of freedom does t have? Use Table C to approximate the P-value of t against the one-sided alternative $H_a: \beta > 0$. What do you conclude?

24.5   **Great Arctic rivers: testing.**   The most important question we ask of the data in Table 24.2 is this: is the increasing trend visible in your plot (Exercise 24.3) statistically significant? If so, changes in the Arctic may already be affecting the earth's climate. Use software to answer this question. Give a test statistic, its P-value, and the conclusion you draw from the test.

24.6   **Does fast driving waste fuel?**   Exercise 4.6 (page 96) gives data on the fuel consumption of a small car at various speeds from 10 to 150 kilometers per hour. Is there significant evidence of straight-line dependence between speed and fuel use? Make a scatterplot and use it to explain the result of your test.

Testing lack of correlation

The least-squares slope b is closely related to the correlation r between the explanatory and response variables x and y. In the same way, the slope β of the population regression line is closely related to the correlation between x and y in the population. In particular, the slope is 0 exactly when the correlation is 0.

   Testing the null hypothesis $H_0: \beta = 0$ is therefore exactly the same as testing that there is *no correlation* between x and y in the population from which we drew our data. You can use the test for zero slope to test the hypothesis of zero correlation between any two quantitative variables. That's a useful trick.

   Because correlation also makes sense when there is no explanatory-response distinction, it is handy to be able to test correlation without doing regression.

Table F in the back of the book gives critical values of the sample correlation r under the null hypothesis that the correlation is 0 in the population. Use this table when both variables have at least approximately Normal distributions or when the sample size is large.

EXAMPLE 24.5   Stocks and Treasury bills

Monika Graff/The Image Works

STATE: Figure 24.5 displays the returns on common stocks and Treasury bills over a period of 54 years, from 1950 to 2003. The relationship, if any, appears quite weak. Is there a statistically significant linear relationship between the annual returns on stocks and T-bills? If there is, the return on T-bills (a measure of short-term interest rates) can help predict the return on stocks.

FORMULATE: Test the hypotheses

$$H_0: \text{population correlation} = 0$$
$$H_a: \text{population correlation} \neq 0$$

SOLVE: The data are in the file *eg24-05.dat* on the text CD and Web site. Stemplots (we don't display them) show that stock returns are quite Normal and that T-bill returns are somewhat right-skewed. With 54 observations, the t test is safe. Software tells us that the correlation is $r = -0.113$ and that the t statistic for the test of $H_0: \beta = 0$ is $t = -0.8197$ with two-sided P-value 0.4161. **This is also the P-value for testing correlation 0.**

Without software, compare the correlation $r = -0.113$ (ignoring the minus sign) with the critical values in the $n = 50$ row of Table F. (Because there is no table entry for the exact sample size $n = 54$, use the next lower sample size.) The smallest critical

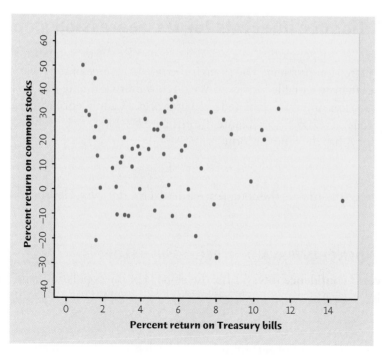

FIGURE 24.5 Scatterplot of the yearly return on common stocks against return on Treasury bills, for Example 24.5.

value in that row is 0.1217, for tail area 0.20. Because r is smaller than 0.1217, the one-sided P-value is greater than 0.20 and the two-sided P-value is greater than twice this, or $P > 0.40$.

CONCLUDE: There is no evidence of a linear relationship between returns on stocks and returns on T-bills.

APPLY YOUR KNOWLEDGE

24.7 **Coffee and deforestation: testing correlation.** Exercise 24.1 gives data showing that deforestation in a national park in Indonesia goes up when high prices for coffee encourage farmers to clear forest in order to plant more coffee. There are only 5 observations, so we worry that the apparent relationship may be just chance. Is the correlation significantly greater than 0? Use Table F to approximate the P-value.

24.8 **Does social rejection hurt?** Exercise 4.40 (page 114) gives data from a study of whether social rejection causes activity in areas of the brain that are known to be activated by physical pain. The explanatory variable is a subject's score on a test of "social distress" after being excluded from an activity. The response variable is activity in an area of the brain that responds to physical pain. Your scatterplot (Exercise 4.40) shows a positive linear relationship. The research report gives the correlation r and the P-value for a test that r is greater than 0. What are r and the P-value? (You can use Table F or you can get more accurate P-values for the correlation from regression software.) What do you conclude about the relationship?

Confidence intervals for the regression slope

The slope β of the population regression line is usually the most important parameter in a regression problem. The slope is the rate of change of the mean response as the explanatory variable increases. We often want to estimate β. The slope b of the least-squares line is an unbiased estimator of β. A confidence interval is more useful because it shows how accurate the estimate b is likely to be. The confidence interval for β has the familiar form

$$\text{estimate} \pm t^* \text{SE}_{\text{estimate}}$$

Because b is our estimate, the confidence interval is $b \pm t^* \text{SE}_b$. Here are the details.

CONFIDENCE INTERVAL FOR REGRESSION SLOPE

A level C **confidence interval for the slope β** of the population regression line is

$$b \pm t^* \text{SE}_b$$

Here t^* is the critical value for the $t(n-2)$ density curve with area C between $-t^*$ and t^*.

EXAMPLE 24.6 Crying and IQ: estimating the slope

The three software outputs in Figure 24.3 give the slope $b = 1.4929$ and also the standard error $SE_b = 0.4870$. The outputs use a similar arrangement, a table in which each regression coefficient is followed by its standard error. Excel also gives the lower and upper endpoints of the 95% confidence interval for the population slope β, 0.505 and 2.481.

Once we know b and SE_b, it is easy to find the confidence interval. There are 38 data points, so the degrees of freedom are $n - 2 = 36$. Because Table C does not have a row for df = 36, we must use either software or the next smaller degrees of freedom in the table, df = 30. To use software, enter 36 degrees of freedom and, for 95% confidence, the cumulative proportion 0.975 that corresponds to tail area 0.025. Minitab gives

```
Student's t distribution with 36 DF
P(X<=x)             x
  0.975    2.02809
```

The 95% confidence interval for the population slope β is

$$b \pm t^* SE_b = 1.4929 \pm (2.02809)(0.4870)$$
$$= 1.4929 \pm 0.9877$$
$$= 0.505 \text{ to } 2.481$$

This agrees with Excel's result. We are 95% confident that mean IQ increases by between about 0.5 and 2.5 points for each additional peak in crying.

You can find a confidence interval for the intercept α of the population regression line in the same way, using a and SE_a from the "Constant" line of the Minitab output or the "Intercept" line in CrunchIt! or Excel. We rarely need to estimate α.

APPLY YOUR KNOWLEDGE

24.9 Coffee and deforestation: estimating slope. Exercise 24.1 presents data on coffee prices and loss of forest in Indonesia. Software tells us that the least-squares slope is $b = 0.0543$ with standard error $SE_b = 0.0097$. Because there are only 5 observations, the observed slope b may not be an accurate estimate of the population slope β. Give a 95% confidence interval for β.

24.10 Growth of icicles: estimating slope. Exercise 24.2 gives data on the growth of an icicle. We want a 95% confidence interval for the slope of the population regression line. Starting from the information in the Minitab output in Figure 24.4, find this interval. Say in words what the slope of the population regression line tells us about the growth of icicles under the conditions of this experiment.

24.11 Great Arctic rivers: estimating slope. Use the data in Table 24.2 to give a 90% confidence interval for the slope of the population regression of Arctic river discharge on year. Does this interval convince you that discharge is actually increasing over time? Explain your answer.

Inference about prediction

One of the most common reasons to fit a line to data is to predict the response to a particular value of the explanatory variable. This is another setting for regression inference: we want, not simply a prediction, but a prediction with a margin of error that describes how accurate the prediction is likely to be.

— **EXAMPLE 24.7** Beer and blood alcohol ——————————

STATE: The EESEE story "Blood Alcohol Content" describes a study in which 16 student volunteers at the Ohio State University drank a randomly assigned number of cans of beer. Thirty minutes later, a police officer measured their blood alcohol content (BAC) in grams of alcohol per deciliter of blood. Here are the data:

Student	1	2	3	4	5	6	7	8
Beers	5	2	9	8	3	7	3	5
BAC	0.10	0.03	0.19	0.12	0.04	0.095	0.07	0.06
Student	9	10	11	12	13	14	15	16
Beers	3	5	4	6	5	7	1	4
BAC	0.02	0.05	0.07	0.10	0.085	0.09	0.01	0.05

Jame Shaffer/The Image Works

The students were equally divided between men and women and differed in weight and usual drinking habits. Because of this variation, many students don't believe that number of drinks predicts blood alcohol well. Steve thinks he can drive legally 30 minutes after he finishes drinking 5 beers. The legal limit for driving is BAC 0.08 in all states. We want to predict Steve's blood alcohol content, using no information except that he drinks 5 beers.

FORMULATE: Regress BAC on number of beers. Use the regression line to predict Steve's BAC. Give a margin of error that allows us to have 95% confidence in our prediction.

SOLVE: The scatterplot in Figure 24.6 and the regression output in Figure 24.7 show that student opinion is wrong: number of beers predicts blood alcohol content quite well. In fact, $r^2 = 0.80$, so that number of beers explains 80% of the observed variation in BAC. To predict Steve's BAC after 5 beers, use the equation of the regression line:

$$\hat{y} = -0.0127 + 0.0180x$$
$$= -0.0127 + 0.0180(5) = 0.077$$

That's dangerously close to the legal limit 0.08. What about 95% confidence? The "Predicted values" part of the output in Figure 24.7 shows *two* 95% intervals. Which should we use?

To decide which interval to use, you must answer this question: do you want to predict the *mean* BAC for *all students* who drink 5 beers, or do you want to predict the BAC of *one individual student* who drinks 5 beers? *Both of these predictions may be interesting, but they are two different problems.* The actual prediction is the same,

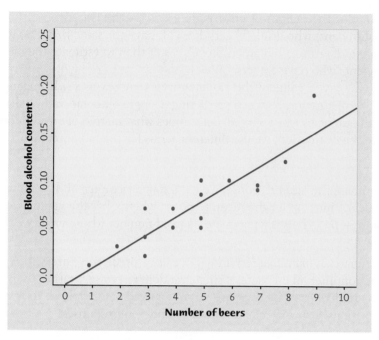

FIGURE 24.6 Scatterplot of students' blood alcohol content against the number of cans of beer consumed, with the least-squares regression line.

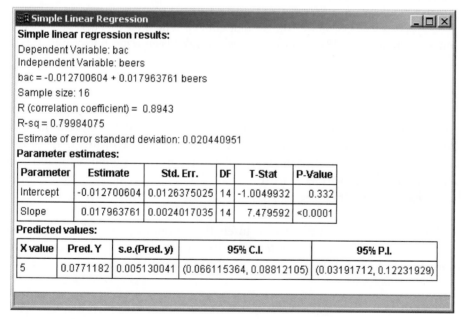

FIGURE 24.7 CrunchIt! regression output for the blood alcohol content data, for Example 24.7.

$\hat{y} = 0.077$. But the margin of error is different for the two kinds of prediction. Individual students who drink 5 beers don't all have the same BAC. So we need a larger margin of error to pin down Steve's result than to estimate the mean BAC for all students who have 5 beers.

Write the given value of the explanatory variable x as x^*. In Example 24.7, $x^* = 5$. The distinction between predicting a single outcome and predicting the mean of all outcomes when $x = x^*$ determines what margin of error is correct. To emphasize the distinction, we use different terms for the two intervals.

- To estimate the *mean* response, we use a *confidence interval*. It is an ordinary confidence interval for the mean response when x has the value x^*, which is $\mu_y = \alpha + \beta x^*$. This is a parameter, a fixed number whose value we don't know.

prediction interval
- To estimate an *individual* response y, we use a **prediction interval.** A prediction interval estimates a single random response y rather than a parameter like μ_y. The response y is not a fixed number. If we took more observations with $x = x^*$, we would get different responses.

EXAMPLE 24.8 *Beer and blood alcohol: conclusion*

Steve is one individual, so we must use the prediction interval. The output in Figure 24.7 helpfully labels the confidence interval as "C.I." and the prediction interval as "P.I." We are 95% confident that Steve's BAC after 5 beers will lie between 0.032 and 0.122. The upper part of that range will get him arrested if he drives. The 95% confidence interval for the mean BAC of all students who drink 5 beers is much narrower, 0.066 to 0.088.

May the longer name win!

Regression is far from perfect, but it beats most other ways of predicting. A writer in the early 1960s noted a simple method for predicting presidential elections: just choose the candidate with the longer name. In the 22 elections from 1876 to 1960, this method failed only once. Let's hope that the writer didn't bet the family silver on this idea. The 11 elections from 1964 to 2004 presented 9 tests of the "long name wins" method (the 1980 candidates and 2000 candidates had names of the same length). The longer name lost 6 of the 9.

The meaning of a prediction interval is very much like the meaning of a confidence interval. A 95% prediction interval, like a 95% confidence interval, is right 95% of the time in repeated use. "Repeated use" now means that we take an observation on y for each of the n values of x in the original data, and then take one more observation y with $x = x^*$. Form the prediction interval from the n observations, then see if it covers the one more y. It will in 95% of all repetitions.

The interpretation of prediction intervals is a minor point. The main point is that it is harder to predict one response than to predict a mean response. Both intervals have the usual form

$$\hat{y} \pm t^* \text{SE}$$

but the prediction interval is wider than the confidence interval because individuals are more variable than averages. You will rarely need to know the details, because software automates the calculation, but here they are.

CONFIDENCE AND PREDICTION INTERVALS FOR REGRESSION RESPONSE

A level C **confidence interval for the mean response** μ_y when x takes the value x^* is

$$\hat{y} \pm t^* SE_{\hat{\mu}}$$

The standard error $SE_{\hat{\mu}}$ is

$$SE_{\hat{\mu}} = s\sqrt{\frac{1}{n} + \frac{(x^* - \overline{x})^2}{\sum(x - \overline{x})^2}}$$

A level C **prediction interval for a single observation** y when x takes the value x^* is

$$\hat{y} \pm t^* SE_{\hat{y}}$$

The standard error for prediction $SE_{\hat{y}}$ is

$$SE_{\hat{y}} = s\sqrt{1 + \frac{1}{n} + \frac{(x^* - \overline{x})^2}{\sum(x - \overline{x})^2}}$$

In both intervals, t^* is the critical value for the $t(n-2)$ density curve with area C between $-t^*$ and t^*.

There are two standard errors: $SE_{\hat{\mu}}$ for estimating the mean response μ_y and $SE_{\hat{y}}$ for predicting an individual response y. The only difference between the two standard errors is the extra 1 under the square root sign in the standard error for prediction. The extra 1 makes the prediction interval wider. Both standard errors are multiples of the regression standard error s. The degrees of freedom are again $n - 2$, the degrees of freedom of s.

APPLY YOUR KNOWLEDGE

24.12 **Coffee and deforestation: prediction.** Exercise 24.1 presents data on coffee prices and loss of forest in Indonesia. If the world coffee price next year is 60 cents per pound, what percent of the national park forest do you predict will be cleared? Figure 24.8 is part of the output from CrunchIt! for prediction when $x^* = 60$.

(a) Which interval in the output is the proper 95% interval for predicting next year's loss of forest?

(b) CrunchIt! gives only one of the two standard errors used in prediction. It is $SE_{\hat{\mu}}$, the standard error for estimating the mean response. Use this fact along with the CrunchIt! output to give a 90% confidence interval for the mean percent of forest lost in years when the coffee price is 60 cents per pound.

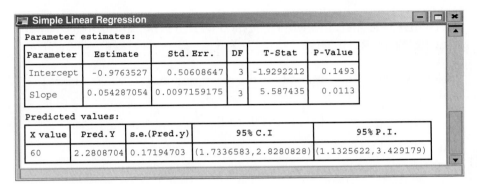

FIGURE 24.8 Partial CrunchIt! output for the regression of percent of forest lost on coffee price, for Exercise 24.12.

24.13 **Growth of icicles: prediction.** Analysis of the data in Exercise 24.2 shows that growth of icicles is very linear. We might want to predict the mean length of icicles after 200 minutes under the same conditions of temperature, wind, and water flow. Here is the Minitab output for prediction when $x^* = 200$ minutes:

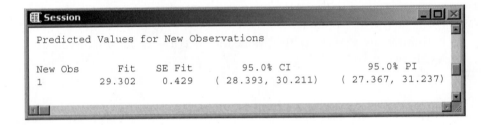

(a) Use the regression line from Figure 24.4 to verify that "Fit" is the predicted value for $x^* = 200$. (Start with the results in the "Coef" column of Figure 24.4 to reduce roundoff error.)

(b) What is the 95% interval we want?

Checking the conditions for inference

You can fit a least-squares line to any set of explanatory-response data when both variables are quantitative. If the scatterplot doesn't show a roughly linear pattern, the fitted line may be almost useless. But it is still the line that fits the data best in the least-squares sense. To use regression inference, however, the data must satisfy additional conditions. *Before we can trust the results of inference, we must check the conditions for inference one by one.* There are ways to deal with violations of any of the conditions. If you see a clear violation, get expert advice.

Although the conditions for regression inference are a bit elaborate, it is not hard to check for gross violations. The residuals are a great help. Most regression software will calculate and save the residuals for you. Let's look at each condition in turn.

The observations are independent. In particular, repeated observations on the same individual are not allowed. We should not use ordinary regression to make inferences about the growth of a single child over time, for example.

The relationship is linear in the population. We can't observe the population regression line, so we will almost never see a perfect straight-line relationship in our data. Look at the scatterplot to check that the overall pattern is roughly linear. A plot of the residuals against x magnifies any unusual pattern. Draw a horizontal line at zero on the residual plot to orient your eye. Because the sum of the residuals is always zero, zero is also the mean of the residuals.

The standard deviation of the response about the population line is the same everywhere. Look at the scatterplot again. The scatter of the data points above and below the line should be roughly the same over the entire range of the data. A plot of the residuals against x, with a horizontal line at zero, makes this easier to check. You will sometimes find that, as the response y gets larger, so does the scatter of the points about the fitted line. Rather than remaining fixed, the standard deviation σ about the line is changing with x as the mean response changes with x. There is no fixed σ for s to estimate. You cannot trust the results of inference when this happens.

The response varies Normally about the population regression line. We can't observe the population regression line. We can observe the least-squares line and the residuals, which show the variation of the response about the fitted line. The residuals estimate the deviations of the response from the population regression line, so they should follow a Normal distribution. Make a histogram or stemplot of the residuals and check for clear skewness or other major departures from Normality. Like other t procedures, inference for regression is (with one exception) not very sensitive to minor lack of Normality, especially when we have many observations. Do beware of influential observations, which move the regression line and can greatly affect the results of inference.

The exception is the prediction interval for a single response y. This interval relies on Normality of individual observations, not just on the approximate Normality of statistics like the slope a and intercept b of the least-squares line. The statistics a and b become more Normal as we take more observations. This contributes to the robustness of regression inference, but it isn't enough for the prediction interval. We will not study methods that carefully check Normality of the residuals, so *you should regard prediction intervals as rough approximations*.

EXAMPLE 24.9 *Climate change chases fish north*

STATE: As the climate grows warmer, we expect many animal species to move toward the poles in an attempt to maintain their preferred temperature range. Do data on fish in the North Sea confirm this expectation? Following are data for 25 years, 1977 to 2001, on mean winter temperatures at the bottom of the North Sea (degrees centigrade) and the center of the distribution of anglerfish in degrees of north latitude.[5]

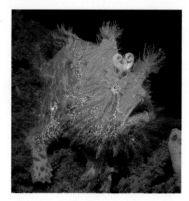

Dave Harasti

Temperature	6.26	6.26	6.27	6.31	6.34	6.32	6.37	6.39	6.42
Latitude	57.20	57.96	57.65	57.59	58.01	59.06	56.85	56.87	57.43
Temperature	6.52	6.68	6.76	6.78	6.89	6.90	6.93	6.98	7.02
Latitude	57.72	57.83	57.87	57.48	58.13	58.52	58.48	57.89	58.71
Temperature	7.09	7.13	7.15	7.29	7.34	7.57	7.65		
Latitude	58.07	58.49	58.28	58.49	58.01	58.57	58.90		

FORMULATE: Regress latitude on temperature. Look for a positive linear relationship and assess its significance. Be sure to check the conditions for regression inference.

SOLVE: The scatterplot in Figure 24.9 shows a clear positive linear relationship. The solid line in the plot is the least-squares regression line of the center of the fish distribution (north latitude) on winter ocean temperature. Software shows that the slope is $b = 0.818$. That is, each degree of ocean warming moves the fish about 0.8 degree of latitude farther north. The t statistic for testing H_0: $\beta = 0$ is $t = 3.6287$ with one-sided P-value $P = 0.0007$ and $r^2 = 0.364$. There is very strong evidence that the population slope is positive, $\beta > 0$.

CONCLUDE: The data give highly significant evidence that anglerfish have moved north as the ocean has grown warmer. Before relying on this conclusion, we must check the conditions for inference.

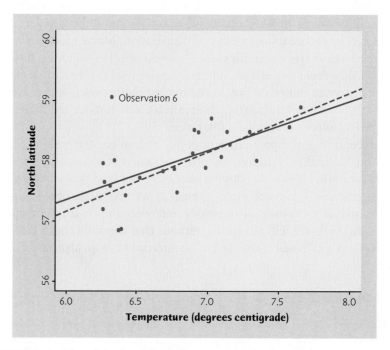

FIGURE 24.9 Plot of the latitude of the center of the distribution of anglerfish in the North Sea against mean winter temperature at the bottom of the sea, for Example 24.9. The two regression lines are for the data with (solid) and without (dashed) Observation 6.

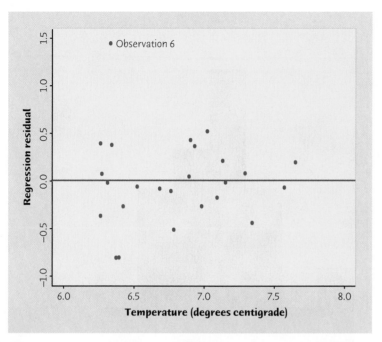

FIGURE 24.10 Residual plot for the regression of latitude on temperature in Example 24.9.

The software that did the regression calculations also finds the 25 residuals. In the same order as the observations in Example 24.9, they are

```
-0.3731   0.3869   0.0687  -0.0240   0.3714   1.4378  -0.8131
-0.8095  -0.2740  -0.0658  -0.0867  -0.1121  -0.5185   0.0415
 0.4234   0.3588  -0.2721   0.5152  -0.1821   0.2052  -0.0211
 0.0743  -0.4466  -0.0747   0.1899
```

Graphs play a central role in checking the conditions for inference. Figure 24.10 plots the residuals against the explanatory variable, sea-bottom temperature. The horizontal line at 0 residual marks the position of the regression line. Both the scatterplot in Figure 24.9 and the residual plot in Figure 24.10 show that Observation 6 is a high outlier.

The observations were taken a year apart, so we are willing to regard them as close to **independent observations.** Except for the outlier, the plots do show **a linear relationship** with roughly **equal variation about the line** for all values of the explanatory variable. A histogram of the residuals (Figure 24.11) shows no strong deviations from a **Normal distribution** except for the high outlier. We conclude that the conditions for regression inference are met except for the presence of the outlier.

How influential is the outlier? The dotted line in Figure 24.9 is the regression line without Observation 6. Because there are several other observations with similar values of temperature, dropping Observation 6 does not move the regression line very much. So the outlier is not influential for regression. It *is* influential for

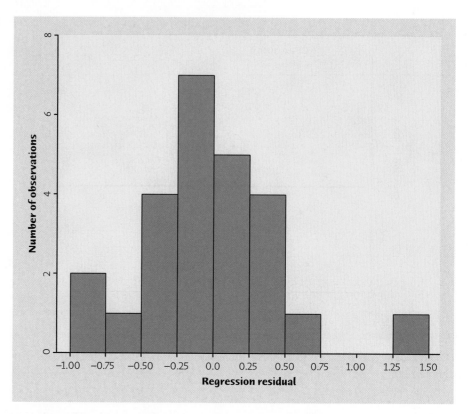

FIGURE 24.11 Histogram of the residuals from the regression of latitude on temperature in Example 24.9.

correlation: r^2 increases from 0.364 to 0.584 when we drop Observation 6. *Even though the outlier is not highly influential for the regression line, it strongly influences inference because of its effect on the regression standard error.* The standard error is $s = 0.4734$ with Observation 6 and $s = 0.3622$ without it. When we omit the outlier, the t statistic changes from $t = 3.6287$ to $t = 5.5599$, and the one-sided P-value changes from $P = 0.0007$ to $P < 0.00001$.

Fortunately, the outlier does not affect the conclusion we drew from the data. Dropping Observation 6 makes the test for the population slope *more* significant and *increases* the percent of variation in fish location explained by ocean temperature.

APPLY YOUR KNOWLEDGE

24.14 **Crying and IQ: residuals.** The residuals for the study of crying and IQ appear in Example 24.3.

(a) Make a stemplot to display the distribution of the residuals. (Round to the nearest whole number first.) Are there outliers or signs of strong departures from Normality?

(b) Make a plot of the residuals against the explanatory variable. Draw a horizontal line at height 0 on your plot. Does the plot show a nonrandom pattern?

TABLE 24.3   Growth of icicles: predictions and residuals

Obs.	Time x	Length y	Prediction $\hat{y}$	Residual $y - \hat{y}$
1	10	0.600	−0.810	1.410
2	20	1.800	0.775	1.025
3	30	2.900	2.360	0.540
4	40	4.000	3.945	0.055
5	50	5.000	5.529	−0.529
6	60	6.100	7.114	−1.014
7	70	7.900	8.699	−0.799
8	80	10.100	10.284	−0.184
9	90	10.900	11.869	−0.969
10	100	12.700	13.454	−0.754
11	110	14.400	15.038	−0.638
12	120	16.600	16.623	−0.023
13	130	18.100	18.208	−0.108
14	140	19.900	19.793	0.107
15	150	21.000	21.378	−0.378
16	160	23.400	22.963	0.437
17	170	24.700	24.547	0.153
18	180	27.800	26.132	1.668

24.15 **Growth of icicles: residuals.**   Figure 24.4 gives part of the Minitab output for the data on growth of icicles in Exercise 24.2. Table 24.3 comes from another part of the output. It gives the predicted response $\hat{y}$ and the residual $y - \hat{y}$ for each of the 18 observations. Most statistical software provides similar output. Examine the conditions for regression inference one by one. This example illustrates mild violations of the conditions that did not prevent the researchers from doing inference.

(a) **Independent observations.** The data come from the growth of a single icicle, not from a different icicle at each time. Explain why this would violate the independence condition if we had data on the growth of a child rather than of an icicle. (The researchers decided that all icicles, unlike all children, grow at the same rate if the conditions are held fixed. So one icicle can stand in for a separate icicle at each time.)

(b) **Linear relationship.** Your plot and r^2 from Exercise 24.2 show that the relationship is very linear. Residual plots magnify effects. Plot the residuals against time. What kind of deviation from a straight line is now visible? (The deviation is clear in the residual plot, but it is very small in the original scale.)

(c) **Spread about the line stays the same.** Your plot in (b) shows that it does not. (Once again, the plot greatly magnifies small deviations.)

(d) **Normal variation about the line.** Make a histogram of the residuals. With only 18 observations, no clear shape emerges. Do strong skewness or outliers suggest lack of Normality?

CHAPTER 24 SUMMARY

Least-squares regression fits a straight line to data in order to predict a response variable y from an explanatory variable x. Inference about regression requires more conditions.

The **conditions for regression inference** say that there is a **population regression line** $\mu_y = \alpha + \beta x$ that describes how the mean response varies as x changes. The observed response y for any x has a Normal distribution with mean given by the population regression line and with the same standard deviation σ for any value of x. Observations on y are independent.

The **parameters to be estimated** are the intercept α and the slope β of the population regression line, and also the standard deviation σ. The slope a and intercept b of the least-squares line estimate α and β. Use the **regression standard error** s to estimate σ.

The regression standard error s has $n - 2$ **degrees of freedom.** All t procedures in regression inference have $n - 2$ degrees of freedom.

To test **the hypothesis that the slope is zero in the population,** use the t statistic $t = b/SE_b$. This null hypothesis says that straight-line dependence on x has no value for predicting y. In practice, use software to find the slope b of the least-squares line, its standard error SE_b, and the t statistic.

The t test for regression slope is also a test for **the hypothesis that the population correlation between x and y is zero.** To do this test without software, use the sample correlation r and Table F.

Confidence intervals for the slope of the population regression line have the form $b \pm t^* SE_b$.

Confidence intervals for the mean response when x has value x^* have the form $\hat{y} \pm t^* SE_{\hat{\mu}}$. **Prediction intervals** for an individual future response y have a similar form with a larger standard error, $\hat{y} \pm t^* SE_{\hat{y}}$. Software often gives these intervals.

STATISTICS IN SUMMARY

Here are the most important skills you should have acquired from reading this chapter.

A. PRELIMINARIES

1. Make a scatterplot to show the relationship between an explanatory and a response variable.

2. Use a calculator or software to find the correlation and the equation of the least-squares regression line.

B. RECOGNITION

1. Recognize the regression setting: a straight-line relationship between an explanatory variable x and a response variable y.

2. Recognize which type of inference you need in a particular regression setting.

3. Inspect the data to recognize situations in which inference isn't safe: a nonlinear relationship, influential observations, strongly skewed residuals in a small sample, or nonconstant variation of the data points about the regression line.

C. INFERENCE USING SOFTWARE OUTPUT

1. Explain in any specific regression setting the meaning of the slope β of the population regression line.

2. Understand software output for regression. Find in the output the slope and intercept of the least-squares line, their standard errors, and the regression standard error.

3. Use that information to carry out tests of $H_0: \beta = 0$ and calculate confidence intervals for β.

4. Explain the distinction between a confidence interval for the mean response and a prediction interval for an individual response.

5. If software gives output for prediction, use that output to give either confidence or prediction intervals.

CHECK YOUR SKILLS

Florida reappraises real estate every year, so the county appraiser's Web site lists the current "fair market value" of each piece of property. Property usually sells for somewhat more than the appraised market value. Here are the appraised market values and actual selling prices (in thousands of dollars) of condominium units sold in a beachfront building over a 19-month period.[6]

Franz Marc Frei/CORBIS

Selling price	Appraised value	Month	Selling price	Appraised value	Month
850	758.0	0	790	605.9	13
900	812.7	1	700	483.8	14
625	504.0	2	715	585.8	14
1075	956.7	2	825	707.6	14
890	747.9	8	675	493.9	17
810	717.7	8	1050	802.6	17
650	576.6	9	1325	1031.8	18
845	648.3	12	845	586.7	19

Here is part of the Minitab output for regressing selling price on appraised value, along with prediction for a unit with appraised value $802,600:

```
Predictor    Coef   SE Coef     T       P
Constant    127.27    79.49   1.60   0.132
appraisal   1.0466   0.1126   9.29   0.000


S = 69.7299    R-Sq = 86.1%    R-Sq(adj) = 85.1%


Predicted Values for New Observations


New
Obs    Fit   SE Fit        95% CI              95% PI
  1   967.3    21.6   (920.9, 1013.7)   (810.7, 1123.9)
```

Exercises 24.16 to 24.24 are based on this information.

24.16 The equation of the least-squares regression line for predicting selling price from appraised value is

(a) price $= 79.49 + 0.1126 \times$ appraised value.

(b) price $= 127.27 + 1.0466 \times$ appraised value.

(c) price $= 1.0466 + 127.27 \times$ appraised value.

24.17 What is the correlation between selling price and appraised value?

(a) 0.1126   (b) 0.861   (c) 0.928

24.18 The slope β of the population regression line describes

(a) the exact increase in the selling price of an individual unit when its appraised value increases by $1000.

(b) the average increase in selling price in a population of units when appraised value increases by $1000.

(c) the average selling price in a population of units when a unit's appraised value is 0.

24.19 Is there significant evidence that selling price increases as appraised value increases? To answer this question, test the hypotheses

(a) $H_0: \beta = 0$ versus $H_a: \beta > 0$.

(b) $H_0: \beta = 0$ versus $H_a: \beta \neq 0$.

(c) $H_0: \alpha = 0$ versus $H_a: \alpha > 0$.

24.20 Minitab shows that the P-value for this test is

(a) 0.132.   (b) less than 0.001.   (c) 0.861.

24.21 The regression standard error for these data is

(a) 0.1126.   (b) 69.7299.   (c) 79.49.

24.22 Confidence intervals and tests for these data use the t distribution with degrees of freedom

(a) 14.   (b) 15.   (c) 16.

24.23 A 95% confidence interval for the population slope β is

(a) 1.0466 ± 0.2415.   (b) 1.0466 ± 149.5706.   (c) 1.0466 ± 0.2387.

24.24 Hamada owns a unit in this building appraised at $802,600. The Minitab output includes prediction for this appraised value. She can be 95% confident that her unit would sell for between

(a) $920,900 and $1,013,700.

(b) $810,700 and $1,123,900.

(c) $945,700 and $988,900.

CHAPTER 24 EXERCISES

24.25 Too much nitrogen? Intensive agriculture and burning of fossil fuels increase the amount of nitrogen deposited on the land. Too much nitrogen can reduce the variety of plants by favoring rapid growth of some species—think of putting fertilizer on your lawn to help grass choke out weeds. A study of 68 grassland sites in Britain measured nitrogen deposited (kilograms of nitrogen per hectare of land area per year) and also the "richness" of plant species (based on number of species and how abundant each species is). The authors reported a regression analysis as follows:[7]

$$\text{plant species richness} = 23.3 - 0.408 \times \text{nitrogen deposited}$$
$$r^2 = 0.55 \quad P < 0.0001$$

(a) What does the slope $b = -0.408$ say about the effect of increased nitrogen deposits on species richness?

(b) What does $r^2 = 0.55$ add to the information given by the equation of the least-squares line?

(c) What null and alternative hypotheses do you think the P-value refers to? What does this P-value tell you?

24.26 Beavers and beetles. Ecologists sometimes find rather strange relationships in our environment. One study seems to show that beavers benefit beetles. The researchers laid out 23 circular plots, each 4 meters in diameter, in an area where beavers were cutting down cottonwood trees. In each plot, they measured the number of stumps from trees cut by beavers and the number of clusters of beetle larvae. Here are the data:[8]

Stumps	2	2	1	3	3	4	3	1	2	5	1	3
Beetle larvae	10	30	12	24	36	40	43	11	27	56	18	40

Stumps	2	1	2	2	1	1	4	1	2	1	4
Beetle larvae	25	8	21	14	16	6	54	9	13	14	50

(a) Make a scatterplot that shows how the number of beaver-caused stumps influences the number of beetle larvae clusters. What does your plot show?

(b) Here is part of the Minitab regression output for these data:

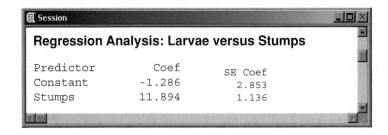

Find the least-squares regression line and draw it on your plot.

(c) Is there strong evidence that beaver stumps help explain beetle larvae counts? State hypotheses, give a test statistic and its P-value, and state your conclusion.

24.27 **Prey attract predators.** Exercise 7.37 (page 181) describes an experiment to test the theory that a higher density of prey attracts more predators. Because the predators remove a higher percent of the prey, this is one way in which nature keeps populations stable. The explanatory variable is the number of perch (the prey) in a confined area. The response variable is the proportion of perch killed by bass (the predator) in 2 hours when the bass are allowed access to the perch.

Perch	Proportion killed			
10	0.0	0.1	0.3	0.3
20	0.2	0.3	0.3	0.6
40	0.075	0.3	0.6	0.725
60	0.517	0.55	0.7	0.817

A scatterplot (Exercise 7.37) shows a linear relationship. Figure 24.12 contains Excel output for the regression.

	A	B	C	D	E	F	G
1	SUMMARY OUTPUT						
2							
3	*Regression statistics*						
4	Multiple R	0.6821					
5	R Square	0.4652					
6	Adjusted R Square	0.4270					
7	Standard Error	0.1886					
8	Observations	16.0000					
9							
10		*Coefficients*	*Standard Error*	*t Stat*	*P-value*	*Lower 95%*	*Upper 95%*
11	Intercept	0.1205	0.0927	1.2999	0.2146	-0.0783	0.3193
12	Perch	0.0086	0.0025	3.4899	0.0036	0.0033	0.0138
13							

FIGURE 24.12 Excel output for the regression of proportion of perch killed by bass on count of perch in a pen, for Exercises 24.27, 24.29, and 24.31.

(a) What is the equation of the least-squares line for predicting proportion killed from count of perch? What part of this equation shows that more perch do result in a higher proportion being killed by bass?

(b) What is the regression standard error s?

24.28 Casting aluminum. Exercise 7.44 (page 183) describes a study aimed at predicting the "gate velocity" of molten metal from the thickness of the aluminum piston being cast. The data come from observing skilled workers and will be used to guide less experienced workers.

Thickness	Velocity	Thickness	Velocity	Thickness	Velocity
0.248	123.8	0.524	228.6	0.697	145.2
0.359	223.9	0.552	223.8	0.752	263.1
0.366	180.9	0.628	326.2	0.806	302.4
0.400	104.8	0.697	302.4	0.821	302.4

Figure 24.13 displays part of the CrunchIt! regression output. We left out the t statistics and their P-values.

(a) Make a scatterplot suitable for predicting gate velocity from thickness. Give the value of r^2 and the equation of the least-squares line. Draw the line on your plot.

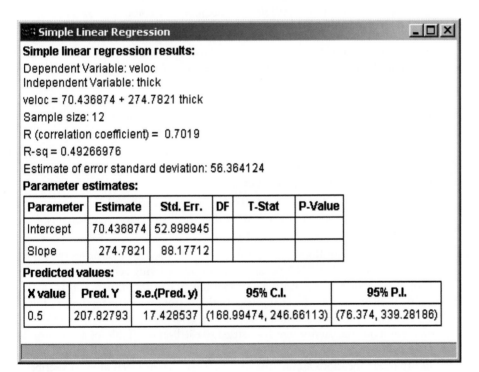

FIGURE 24.13 Partial CrunchIt! output for the regression of gate velocity on piston thickness in casting aluminum parts, for Exercises 24.28 and 24.30.

(b) Based on the information given, test the hypothesis that there is no straight-line relationship between thickness and gate velocity. Give a test statistic, its approximate *P*-value, and your conclusion.

24.29 Prey attract predators: estimating the slope.

(a) The Excel output in Figure 24.12 includes a 95% confidence interval for the slope of the population regression line. What is it? Starting from Excel's values of the least-squares slope *b* and its standard error, verify this confidence interval.

(b) Give a 90% confidence interval for the population slope. As usual, this interval is shorter than the 95% interval.

24.30 Casting aluminum: intervals. The output in Figure 24.13 includes prediction for $x^* = 0.5$ inch. Use the output to give 90% intervals for

(a) the slope of the population regression line of gate velocity on piston thickness.

(b) the average gate velocity for a type of piston with thickness 0.5 inch.

24.31 Prey attract predators: correlation. The Excel output in Figure 24.12 includes the correlation between proportion of perch killed by bass and initial count of perch as $r = 0.6821$. Use Table F to say how significant this correlation is for testing zero correlation against positive correlation in the population. Verify that your result is consistent with Excel's two-sided *P*-value.

24.32 Casting aluminum: residuals. Here are the residuals (rounded to one decimal place) for the regression of gate velocity on piston thickness:

Thickness	0.248	0.359	0.366	0.400	0.524	0.552
Residual	−14.8	54.8	9.9	−75.5	14.2	1.7
Thickness	0.628	0.697	0.697	0.752	0.806	0.821
Residual	83.2	40.4	−116.8	−14.0	10.5	6.4

(a) Check the calculation of residuals by finding their sum. What should the sum be? Does the sum have that value (up to roundoff error)?

(b) Plot the residuals against thickness (the explanatory variable). Does your plot show a systematically nonlinear relationship? Does it show systematic change in the spread about the regression line?

(c) Make a histogram of the residuals. The pattern, with just 12 observations, is irregular. More advanced methods show that the distribution is reasonably Normal.

24.33 DNA on the ocean floor. We think of DNA as the stuff that stores the genetic code. It turns out that DNA occurs, mainly outside living cells, on the ocean floor. It is important in nourishing seafloor life. Scientists think that this DNA comes from organic matter that settles to the bottom from the top layers of the ocean. "Phytopigments," which come mainly from algae, are a measure of the amount of organic matter that has settled to the bottom. Table 24.4 contains data on concentrations of DNA and phytopigments (both in grams per square meter) in 116 ocean locations around the world.[9] Look first at DNA alone. Describe the distribution of DNA concentration and give a confidence interval for the mean concentration. Be sure to explain why your confidence interval is trustworthy in

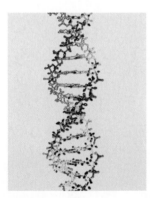

TABLE 24.4　DNA and phytopigment concentrations (g/m^2) on the ocean floor

DNA	Phyto	DNA	Phyto	DNA	Phyto	DNA	Phyto
0.148	0.010	0.276	0.056	0.156	0.032	0.300	0.022
0.108	0.009	0.214	0.023	0.112	0.016	0.116	0.008
0.180	0.008	0.330	0.016	0.280	0.005	0.120	0.004
0.218	0.006	0.240	0.007	0.308	0.005	0.064	0.006
0.152	0.006	0.100	0.006	0.238	0.011	0.228	0.010
0.589	0.050	0.463	0.038	0.461	0.034	0.333	0.020
0.357	0.023	0.382	0.032	0.414	0.034	0.241	0.012
0.458	0.036	0.396	0.033	0.307	0.018	0.236	0.002
0.076	0.001	0.001	0.002	0.009	0	0.099	0
0.187	0.001	0.104	0.004	0.088	0.009	0.072	0.002
0.192	0.005	0.152	0.028	0.152	0.006	0.272	0.004
0.288	0.046	0.232	0.006	0.368	0.003	0.216	0.011
0.248	0.006	0.280	0.002	0.336	0.062	0.320	0.006
0.896	0.055	0.200	0.017	0.408	0.018	0.472	0.017
0.648	0.034	0.384	0.008	0.440	0.042	0.592	0.032
0.392	0.036	0.312	0.002	0.312	0.003	0.208	0.001
0.128	0.001	0.264	0.001	0.264	0.008	0.328	0.010
0.264	0.002	0.376	0.003	0.288	0.001	0.208	0.024
0.224	0.017	0.376	0.010	0.600	0.024	0.168	0.014
0.264	0.018	0.152	0.010	0.184	0.016	0.312	0.017
0.344	0.009	0.184	0.010	0.360	0.010	0.264	0.026
0.464	0.030	0.328	0.028	0.296	0.010	1.056	0.082
0.538	0.055	0.090	0.003	0.130	0.001	0.207	0.001
0.153	0.001	0.206	0.001	0.172	0.001	0.131	0.001
0.095	0	0.307	0.001	0.171	0.001	0.822	0.058
0.901	0.075	0.552	0.040	0.391	0.026	0.172	0.006
0.116	0.003	0.168	0.005	0.074	0	0.100	0.001
0.132	0.005	0.112	0.003	0.121	0.004	0.162	0.001
0.302	0.014	0.179	0.002	0.369	0.023	0.213	0.007

the light of the shape of the distribution. The data show surprisingly high DNA concentration, and this by itself was an important finding.

24.34 Fidgeting keeps you slim: inference. Our first example of regression (Example 5.1, page 116) presented data showing that people who increased their nonexercise activity (NEA) when they were deliberately overfed gained less fat than other people. Use software to add formal inference to the data analysis for these data.

(a) Based on 16 subjects, the correlation between NEA increase and fat gain was $r = -0.7786$. Is this significant evidence that people with higher NEA increase gain less fat?

(b) The slope of the least-squares regression line was $b = -0.00344$, so that fat gain decreased by 0.00344 kilogram for each added calorie of NEA. Give a 90% confidence interval for the slope of the population regression line. This rate of change is the most important parameter to be estimated.

(c) Sam's NEA increases by 400 calories. His predicted fat gain is 2.13 kilograms. Give a 95% interval for predicting Sam's fat gain.

24.35 DNA on the ocean floor, continued. Another conclusion of the study introduced in Exercise 24.33 was that organic matter settling down from the top layers of the ocean is the main source of DNA on the seafloor. An important piece of evidence is the relationship between DNA and phytopigments. Do the data in Table 24.4 give good reason to think that phytopigment concentration helps explain DNA concentration? Describe the data and follow the four-step process in answering this question.

24.36 Sparrowhawk colonies. One of nature's patterns connects the percent of adult birds in a colony that return from the previous year and the number of new adults that join the colony. Here are data for 13 colonies of sparrowhawks:[10]

Percent return x	74	66	81	52	73	62	52	45	62	46	60	46	38
New adults y	5	6	8	11	12	15	16	17	18	18	19	20	20

Earlier (Exercises 4.4, page 93, and 5.4, page 122) you showed that there is a moderately strong linear relationship. Figure 24.14 shows part of the Minitab regression output, including prediction when 60% of the previous year's adult birds return.

(a) Write the equation of the least-squares line and use it to check that the "Fit" in the output is the predicted response for $x^* = 60\%$.

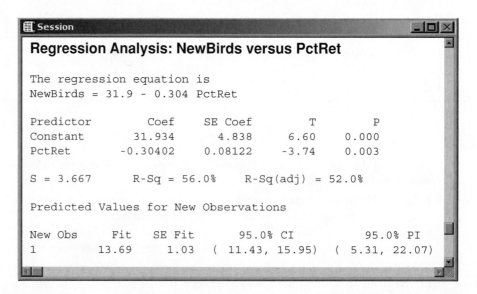

FIGURE 24.14 Partial Minitab output for predicting number of new birds in a sparrowhawk colony from percent of birds returning, for Exercise 24.36.

(b) Which 95% interval in the output gives us a margin of error for predicting the average number of new birds in colonies to which 60% of the past year's adults return?

24.37 **DNA on the ocean floor: residuals.** Save the residuals from the regression of DNA concentration on phytopigment concentration (Exercise 24.33). Examine the residuals to see how well the conditions for regression inference are met.

(a) Plot the residuals against phytopigment concentration (the explanatory variable), using vertical limits -1 to 1 to make the pattern clearer. Add a horizontal line at height 0 to represent the regression line. What do you conclude about the conditions of linear relationship and constant standard deviation?

(b) Make a histogram of the residuals. What do you conclude about Normality?

24.38 **Sparrowhawk residuals.** The regression of number of new birds that join a sparrowhawk colony on the percent of adult birds in the colony that return from the previous year is an example of data that satisfy the conditions for regression inference well. Here are the residuals for the 13 colonies in Exercise 24.36:

Percent return	74	66	81	52	73	62	52
Residual	−4.44	−5.87	0.69	−5.13	2.26	1.92	−0.13

Percent return	45	62	46	60	46	38	
Residual	−1.25	4.92	0.05	5.31	2.05	−0.38	

(a) **Independent observations.** Why are the 13 observations independent?

(b) **Linear relationship.** A plot of the residuals against the explanatory variable x magnifies the deviations from the least-squares line. Does the plot show any systematic deviation from a roughly linear pattern?

(c) **Spread about the line stays the same.** Does your plot in (b) show any systematic change in spread as x changes?

(d) **Normal variation about the line.** Make a histogram of the residuals. With only 13 observations, no clear shape emerges. Do strong skewness or outliers suggest lack of Normality?

24.39 **Residuals on the beach.** Return to the data on selling price versus appraised value for beachfront condominiums that are the basis for the Check Your Skills Exercises 24.16 to 24.24. Prices for beachfront property were rising rapidly during this period. Because property is reassessed just once a year, selling prices might pull away from appraised values over time. The data are in order by date of the sale, and the data table includes the number of months from the start of the data period. The residuals from the regression of selling price on appraised value are (rounded):

−70.60	−77.85	−29.76	−53.56	−20.03	−68.42	−80.75	39.21
28.59	66.38	−25.38	−42.85	30.81	82.72	117.83	103.68

(a) Plot the residuals against the explanatory variable (appraised value). To make the pattern clearer, use vertical limits −200 to 200. Explain why the pattern you see agrees with the conditions of linear relationship and constant standard deviation needed for regression inference.

(b) Make a stemplot of the residuals. The distribution has a bit of a cluster at the left, but there are no outliers or other strong deviations from Normality that would prevent regression inference.

(c) Next, plot the residuals against month. Explain why the pattern fits the fact that selling prices were rising rapidly. Is your prediction in Exercise 24.24 likely to be too low or too high? (*Comment:* The margin of error for prediction includes the effect of rising prices. Your residual plot shows that the prediction could be improved by using month as a second explanatory variable. This is *multiple regression*, using more than one explanatory variable to predict a response.)

24.40 Foot problems. Exercises 7.19 to 7.22 and Table 7.2 (page 177) describe the relationship between two deformities of the feet in young patients. Metatarsus adductus may help predict the severity of hallux abducto valgus. The paper that reports this study says, "Linear regression analysis, using the hallux abductus angle as the response variable, demonstrated a significant correlation between the metatarsus adductus and hallux abductus angles."[11] Do a suitable analysis to verify this finding, following the four-step process. (Be sure to check the conditions for inference as part of the *Solve* step. Parts (a) to (d) of Exercise 24.38 provide a handy outline. The study authors note that the scatterplot suggests that the variation in *y* may change as *x* changes, so they offer a more elaborate analysis as well.)

24.41 Time at the table.   Does how long young children remain at the lunch table help predict how much they eat? Here are data on 20 toddlers observed over several months at a nursery school.[12] "Time" is the average number of minutes a child spent at the table when lunch was served. "Calories" is the average number of calories the child consumed during lunch, calculated from careful observation of what the child ate each day.

Time	21.4	30.8	37.7	33.5	32.8	39.5	22.8	34.1	33.9	43.8
Calories	472	498	465	456	423	437	508	431	479	454
Time	42.4	43.1	29.2	31.3	28.6	32.9	30.6	35.1	33.0	43.7
Calories	450	410	504	437	489	436	480	439	444	408

Bill Aron/PhotoEdit

Follow the four-step process in the following analysis.

(a) Describe the relationship in a graph and by a regression line. Be sure to save the regression residuals.

(b) Check the conditions for inference. Parts (a) to (d) of Exercise 24.38 provide a handy outline. Use vertical limits −100 to 100 in your plot of the residuals against time to help you see the pattern.

(c) Give a 95% confidence interval to estimate how rapidly calories consumed changes as time at the table increases.

24.42 Weeds among the corn. Lamb's-quarter is a common weed that interferes with the growth of corn. An agriculture researcher planted corn at the same rate in 16 small plots of ground, then weeded the plots by hand to allow a fixed number of lamb's-quarter plants to grow in each meter of corn row. No other weeds were allowed to grow. Here are the yields of corn (bushels per acre) in each of the plots:[13]

Weeds per meter	Corn yield	Weeds per meter	Corn yield	Weeds per meter	Corn yield	Weeds per meter	Corn yield
0	166.7	1	166.2	3	158.6	9	162.8
0	172.2	1	157.3	3	176.4	9	142.4
0	165.0	1	166.7	3	153.1	9	162.8
0	176.9	1	161.1	3	156.0	9	162.4

Use software to analyze these data.

(a) Make a scatterplot and find the least-squares line. What percent of the observed variation in corn yield can be explained by a linear relationship between yield and weeds per meter?

(b) Is there good evidence that more weeds reduce corn yield?

(c) Explain from your findings in (a) and (b) why you expect predictions based on this regression to be quite imprecise. Predict the mean corn yield under these experimental conditions when there are 6 weeds per meter of row. If your software allows, give a 95% confidence interval for this mean.

24.43 Time at the table: prediction. Rachel is another child at the nursery school of Exercise 24.41. Over several months, Rachel averages 40 minutes at the lunch table. Give a 95% interval to predict Rachel's average calorie consumption at lunch.

24.44 Revenge! Does revenge feel good? Or do people take revenge just because they are mad about being harmed? Different areas in the brain are active in the two cases, so brain scans can help decide which explanation is correct. Here's a game that supports the first explanation.

Player A is given $10. If he gives it to Player B, it turns into $40. B can keep all of the money or give half to A, who naturally feels that B owes him half. If B keeps all $40, A can take revenge by removing up to $20 of B's ill-gotten gain, at no cost or gain to himself. Scan A's brain at that point, recording activity in the caudate, a region involved in "making decisions or taking actions that are motivated by anticipated rewards." Only the A players who took $20 from B play again, with different partners B. So all the A players have shown the same level of revenge when cheated by B.

The new B also keeps all the money—but punishing B now costs A $1 for every $2 he takes from B. The researchers predicted that A players who get more kicks from revenge, as measured by caudate activity, will punish B more severely even when it costs them money to do it. Here are data for 11 players:[14]

Caudate activity	−0.057	−0.011	−0.032	−0.025	−0.012	0.028
A takes from B	$0	$0	$5	$5	$10	$10
Caudate activity	−0.002	0.008	0.029	0.037	0.043	
A takes from B	$10	$20	$20	$20	$20	

(a) Make a scatterplot with caudate activity as the explanatory variable. Add the least-squares regression line to your plot to show the overall pattern.

(b) The research report mentions positive correlation and its significance. What is the correlation r? Is it significantly greater than zero?

(c) The nature of the data gives some reason to doubt the accuracy of the significance level. Why?

standardized residuals   **24.45 Standardized residuals (optional).** Software often calculates **standardized residuals** as well as the actual residuals from regression. Because the standardized residuals have the standard z-score scale, it is easier to judge whether any are extreme. Here are the standardized residuals from Exercise 24.26 (beavers and beetles), rounded to two decimal places:

$$-1.99 \quad 1.20 \quad 0.23 \quad -1.67 \quad 0.26 \quad -1.06 \quad 1.38 \quad 0.06 \quad 0.72 \quad -0.40 \quad 1.21 \quad 0.90$$
$$0.40 \quad -0.43 \quad -0.24 \quad -1.36 \quad 0.88 \quad -0.75 \quad 1.30 \quad -0.26 \quad -1.51 \quad 0.55 \quad 0.62$$

(a) Find the mean and standard deviation of the standardized residuals. Why do you expect values close to those you obtain?

(b) Make a stemplot of the standardized residuals. Are there any striking deviations from Normality? The most extreme residual is $z = -1.99$. Would this be surprisingly large if the 23 observations had a Normal distribution? Explain your answer.

(c) Plot the standardized residuals against the explanatory variable. Are there any suspicious patterns?

24.46 Tests for the intercept (optional). Figure 24.7 (page 597) gives CrunchIt! output for the regression of blood alcohol content (BAC) on number of beers consumed. The t test for the hypothesis that the population regression line has slope $\beta = 0$ has $P < 0.0001$. The data show a positive linear relationship between BAC and beers. We might expect the *intercept* α of the population regression line to be 0, because no beers ($x = 0$) should produce no alcohol in the blood ($y = 0$). To test

$$H_0: \alpha = 0$$
$$H_a: \alpha \neq 0$$

we use a t statistic formed by dividing the least-squares intercept a by its standard error SE_a. Locate this statistic in the output of Figure 24.7 and verify that it is in fact a divided by its standard error. What is the P-value? Do the data suggest that the intercept is not 0?

24.47 Confidence intervals for the intercept (optional). The output in Figure 24.7 allows you to calculate confidence intervals for both the slope β and the intercept α of the population regression line of BAC on beers in the population of all students. Confidence intervals for the intercept α have the familiar form $a \pm t^* SE_a$ with degrees of freedom $n - 2$. What is the 95% confidence interval for the intercept? Does it contain 0, the value we might guess for α?

EESEE CASE STUDIES

The Electronic Encyclopedia of Statistical Examples and Exercises (EESEE) is available on the text CD and Web site. These more elaborate stories, with data, provide settings for longer case studies. Here are some suggestions for EESEE stories that involve inference for regression.

24.48 Read the EESEE story "Blood Alcohol Content." Write a report that answers all questions for this case study.

24.49 Read the EESEE story "Weighing Trucks in Motion." Write a report that answers all questions for this case study.

24.50 Read the EESEE story "What's Driving Car Sales?" Write a report that answers all questions for this case study.

Photo Resource Hawaii/Alamy

One-Way Analysis of Variance: Comparing Several Means

The two-sample t procedures of Chapter 19 compare the means of two populations or the mean responses to two treatments in an experiment. Of course, studies don't always compare just two groups. We need a method for comparing any number of means.

EXAMPLE 25.1 Comparing tropical flowers

STATE: Ethan Temeles of Amherst College, with his colleague W. John Kress, studied the relationship between varieties of the tropical flower *Heliconia* on the island of Dominica and the different species of hummingbirds that fertilize the flowers.[1] Over time, the researchers believe, the lengths of the flowers and the form of the hummingbirds' beaks have evolved to match each other. If that is true, flower varieties fertilized by different hummingbird species should have distinct distributions of length.

Table 25.1 gives length measurements (in millimeters) for samples of three varieties of *Heliconia*, each fertilized by a different species of hummingbird. Do the three varieties display distinct distributions of length? In particular, are the average lengths of their flowers different?

FORMULATE: Use graphs and numerical descriptions to describe and compare the three distributions of flower length. Finally, ask whether the differences among the mean lengths of the three varieties are *statistically significant*.

TABLE 25.1	Flower lengths (millimeters) for three *Heliconia* varieties						
H. bihai							
47.12	46.75	46.81	47.12	46.67	47.43	46.44	46.64
48.07	48.34	48.15	50.26	50.12	46.34	46.94	48.36
H. caribaea red							
41.90	42.01	41.93	43.09	41.47	41.69	39.78	40.57
39.63	42.18	40.66	37.87	39.16	37.40	38.20	38.07
38.10	37.97	38.79	38.23	38.87	37.78	38.01	
H. caribaea yellow							
36.78	37.02	36.52	36.11	36.03	35.45	38.13	37.10
35.17	36.82	36.66	35.68	36.03	34.57	34.63	

Photo Resource Hawaii/Alamy

SOLVE (first steps): Perhaps these data seem familiar. We first met them in Chapter 2 (page 54), where we compared the distributions. Figure 25.1 repeats a stemplot display from Chapter 2. The lengths have been rounded to the nearest tenth of a millimeter. Here are the summary measures we will use in further analysis:

Sample	Variety	Sample size	Mean length	Standard deviation
1	*bihai*	16	47.60	1.213
2	red	23	39.71	1.799
3	yellow	15	36.18	0.975

```
    bihai              red                yellow
34 |              34 |              34 | 6 6
35 |              35 |              35 | 2 5 7
36 |              36 |              36 | 0 0 1 5 7 8 8
37 |              37 | 4 8 9        37 | 0 1
38 |              38 | 0 0 1 1 2 2 8 9   38 | 1
39 |              39 | 2 6 8        39 |
40 |              40 | 6 7          40 |
41 |              41 | 5 7 9 9      41 |
42 |              42 | 0 2          42 |
43 |              43 | 1            43 |
44 |              44 |              44 |
45 |              45 |              45 |
46 | 3 4 6 7 8 8 9   46 |           46 |
47 | 1 1 4        47 |              47 |
48 | 1 2 3 4      48 |              48 |
49 |              49 |              49 |
50 | 1 3          50 |              50 |
```

FIGURE 25.1 Side-by-side stemplots comparing the lengths in millimeters of samples of flowers from three varieties of *Heliconia*, from Table 25.1.

CONCLUDE (first steps): The three varieties differ so much in flower length that there is little overlap among them. In particular, the flowers of *bihai* are longer than either red or yellow. The mean lengths are 47.6 mm for *H. bihai,* 39.7 mm for *H. caribaea* red, and 36.2 mm for *H. caribaea* yellow. Are these observed differences in sample means statistically significant? We must develop a test for comparing more than two population means.

Comparing several means

Call the mean lengths for the three populations of flowers μ_1 for *bihai,* μ_2 for red, and μ_3 for yellow. The subscript reminds us which group a parameter or statistic describes. To compare these three population means, we might use the two-sample t test several times:

- Test H_0: $\mu_1 = \mu_2$ to see if the mean length for *bihai* differs from the mean for red.
- Test H_0: $\mu_1 = \mu_3$ to see if *bihai* differs from yellow.
- Test H_0: $\mu_2 = \mu_3$ to see if red differs from yellow.

The weakness of doing three tests is that we get three P-values, one for each test alone. That doesn't tell us how likely it is that *three* sample means are spread apart as far as these are. It may be that $\overline{x}_1 = 47.60$ and $\overline{x}_3 = 36.18$ are significantly different if we look at just two groups but not significantly different if we know that they are the largest and the smallest means in three groups. As we look at more groups, we expect the gap between the largest and smallest sample mean to get larger. (Think of comparing the tallest and shortest person in larger and larger groups of people.) *We can't safely compare many parameters by doing tests or confidence intervals for two parameters at a time.*

multiple comparisons

The problem of how to do many comparisons at once with an overall measure of confidence in all our conclusions is common in statistics. This is the problem of **multiple comparisons.** Statistical methods for dealing with multiple comparisons usually have two steps:

1. An *overall test* to see if there is good evidence of *any* differences among the parameters that we want to compare.
2. A detailed *follow-up analysis* to decide which of the parameters differ and to estimate how large the differences are.

The overall test, though more complex than the tests we met earlier, is often reasonably straightforward. The follow-up analysis can be quite elaborate. In our basic introduction to statistical practice, we will concentrate on the overall test, along with data analysis that points to the nature of the differences.

The analysis of variance F test

We want to test the null hypothesis that there are *no differences* among the mean lengths for the three populations of flowers:

$$H_0: \mu_1 = \mu_2 = \mu_3$$

The alternative hypothesis is that there is *some difference*. That is, not all three population means are equal:

$$H_a: \text{not all of } \mu_1, \ \mu_2, \text{ and } \mu_3 \text{ are equal}$$

The alternative hypothesis is no longer one-sided or two-sided. It is "many-sided," because it allows any relationship other than "all three equal." For example, H_a includes the case in which $\mu_2 = \mu_3$ but μ_1 has a different value. The test of H_0 against H_a is called the **analysis of variance F test.** Analysis of variance is usually abbreviated as ANOVA. The ANOVA F test is almost always carried out by software that reports the test statistic and its P-value.

analysis of variance F test

┌─ **EXAMPLE 25.2** Comparing tropical flowers: ANOVA ──── STEP

SOLVE (inference): Software tells us that for the flower length data in Table 25.1, the test statistic is $F = 259.12$ with P-value $P < 0.0001$. There is very strong evidence that the three varieties of flowers do not all have the same mean length.

The F test does not say *which* of the three means are significantly different. It appears from our preliminary data analysis that *bihai* flowers are distinctly longer than either red or yellow. Red and yellow are closer together, but the red flowers tend to be longer.

CONCLUDE: There is strong evidence ($P < 0.0001$) that the population means are not all equal. The most important difference among the means is that the *bihai* variety has longer flowers than the red and yellow varieties.

Example 25.2 illustrates our approach to comparing means. The ANOVA F test (done by software) assesses the evidence for *some* difference among the population means. In most cases, we expect the F test to be significant. We would not undertake a study if we did not expect to find some effect. The formal test is nonetheless important to guard against being misled by chance variation. We will not do the formal follow-up analysis that is often the most useful part of an ANOVA study. Follow-up analysis would allow us to say which means differ and by how much, with (say) 95% confidence that *all* our conclusions are correct. We rely instead on examination of the data to show what differences are present and whether they are large enough to be interesting.

APPLY YOUR KNOWLEDGE ─────────

25.1 **Do fruit flies sleep?** Mammals and birds sleep. Insects such as fruit flies rest, but is this rest sleep? Biologists now think that insects do sleep. One experiment gave caffeine to fruit flies to see if it affected their rest. We know that caffeine reduces sleep in mammals, so if it reduces rest in fruit flies that's another hint that the rest

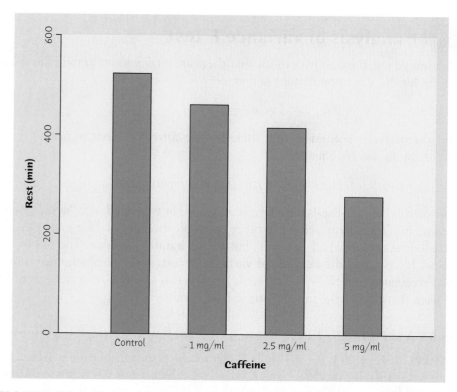

FIGURE 25.2 Bar graph comparing the mean rest of fruit flies given different amounts of caffeine, for Exercise 25.1.

Larry F. Jernigan/Index Stock

is really sleep. The paper reporting the study contains a graph similar to Figure 25.2 and states, "Flies given caffeine obtained less rest during the dark period in a dose-dependent fashion ($n = 36$ per group, $P < 0.0001$)."[2]

(a) The explanatory variable is amount of caffeine, in milligrams per milliliter of blood. The response variable is minutes of rest (measured by an infrared motion sensor) during a 12-hour dark period. Outline the design of this experiment.

(b) The P-value in the report comes from the ANOVA F test. What means does this test compare? State in words the null and alternative hypotheses for the test in this setting. What do the graph and the statistical test together lead you to conclude?

25.2 **Road rage.** "The phenomenon of road rage has been frequently discussed but infrequently examined." So begins a report based on interviews with 1382 randomly selected drivers.[3] The respondents' answers to interview questions produced scores on an "angry/threatening driving scale" with values between 0 and 19. What driver characteristics go with road rage? There were no significant differences among races or levels of education. What about the effect of the driver's age? Here are the mean responses for three age groups:

< 30 yr	30–55 yr	> 55 yr
2.22	1.33	0.66

The report says that $F = 34.96$, with $P < 0.01$.

(a) What are the null and alternative hypotheses for the ANOVA F test? Be sure to explain what means the test compares.

(b) Based on the sample means and the F test, what do you conclude?

Using technology

Any technology used for statistics should perform analysis of variance. Figure 25.3 displays ANOVA output for the data of Table 25.1 from a graphing calculator, two statistical programs, and a spreadsheet program.

TI-83

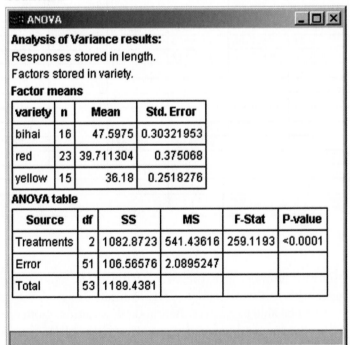

```
One-way ANOVA
 F=259.1192995
 P=1.918818E-27
 Factor
  df=2
  SS=1082.87237
↓ MS=541.436183
```

```
One-way ANOVA
↑ MS=541.436183
 Error
  df=51
  SS=106.565761
  MS=2.08952472
 Sxp=1.44551884
```

CrunchIt!

ANOVA

Analysis of Variance results:

Responses stored in length.

Factors stored in variety.

Factor means

variety	n	Mean	Std. Error
bihai	16	47.5975	0.30321953
red	23	39.711304	0.375068
yellow	15	36.18	0.2518276

ANOVA table

Source	df	SS	MS	F-Stat	P-value
Treatments	2	1082.8723	541.43616	259.1193	<0.0001
Error	51	106.56576	2.0895247		
Total	53	1189.4381			

FIGURE 25.3 ANOVA for the flower length data: output from a graphing calculator, two statistical programs, and a spreadsheet program (*continued*).

Minitab

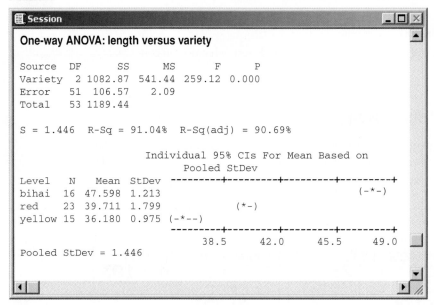

Excel

FIGURE 25.3 (*continued*)

The three software outputs give the sizes of the three samples and their means. These agree with those in Example 25.1. Minitab also gives the standard deviations. You should be able to recover the standard deviations from either the variances (Excel) or the standard errors of the means (CrunchIt!). The most important part of all four outputs reports the F test statistic, $F = 259.12$, and its P-value. CrunchIt! and Minitab sensibly report the P-value as 0 to three decimal places, which is all we need to know in practice. Excel and the TI-83 compute a more specific value. The E – 27 in these displays means move the decimal point 27 digits to the left. There is very strong evidence that the three varieties of flowers do not all have the same mean length.

All four outputs also report degrees of freedom (df), sums of squares (SS), and mean squares (MS). We don't need this information now.

Minitab also gives confidence intervals for all three means that help us see which means differ and by how much. None of the intervals overlap, and *bihai* is much above the other two. These are 95% confidence intervals for each mean separately. We are *not* 95% confident that *all three* intervals cover the three means. This is another example of the peril of multiple comparisons.

APPLY YOUR KNOWLEDGE

25.3 **Logging in the rain forest.** How does logging in a tropical rain forest affect the forest several years later? Researchers compared forest plots in Borneo that had never been logged (Group 1) with similar plots nearby that had been logged 1 year earlier (Group 2) and 8 years earlier (Group 3). Although the study was not an experiment, the authors explain why we can consider the plots to be randomly selected. The data appear in Table 25.2. The variable Trees is the count of trees in a plot; Species is the count of tree species in a plot. The variable Richness is the number of species divided by the number of individual trees, Species/Trees.[4]

(a) Make side-by-side stemplots of Trees for the three groups. Use stems 0, 1, 2, and 3 and split the stems (see page 21). What effects of logging are visible?

(b) Figure 25.4 shows Excel ANOVA output for Trees. What do the group means show about the effects of logging?

(c) What are the values of the ANOVA F statistic and its P-value? What hypotheses does F test? What conclusions about the effects of logging on number of trees do the data lead to?

Microsoft Excel Book 1

Anova: Single Factor

SUMMARY

Groups	Count	Sum	Average	Variance
Group 1	12	285	23.75	25.6591
Group 2	12	169	14.0833	24.8106
Group 3	9	142	15.7778	33.1944

ANOVA

Source of variation	SS	df	MS	F	P-value	F crit
Between Groups	625.1566	2	312.57828	11.4257	0.000205	3.31583
Within Groups	820.7222	30	27.3574			
Total	1445.879	32				

FIGURE 25.4 Excel output for analysis of variance on the number of trees in forest plots, for Exercise 25.3.

TABLE 25.2	Data from a study of logging in Borneo			
Observation	Group	Trees	Species	Richness
1	1	27	22	0.81481
2	1	22	18	0.81818
3	1	29	22	0.75862
4	1	21	20	0.95238
5	1	19	15	0.78947
6	1	33	21	0.63636
7	1	16	13	0.81250
8	1	20	13	0.65000
9	1	24	19	0.79167
10	1	27	13	0.48148
11	1	28	19	0.67857
12	1	19	15	0.78947
13	2	12	11	0.91667
14	2	12	11	0.91667
15	2	15	14	0.93333
16	2	9	7	0.77778
17	2	20	18	0.90000
18	2	18	15	0.83333
19	2	17	15	0.88235
20	2	14	12	0.85714
21	2	14	13	0.92857
22	2	2	2	1.00000
23	2	17	15	0.88235
24	2	19	8	0.42105
25	3	18	17	0.94444
26	3	4	4	1.00000
27	3	22	18	0.81818
28	3	15	14	0.93333
29	3	18	18	1.00000
30	3	19	15	0.78947
31	3	22	15	0.68182
32	3	12	10	0.83333
33	3	12	12	1.00000

Jeff Greenberg/The Image Works

25.4　**Dogs, friends, and stress.**　If you are a dog lover, perhaps having your dog along reduces the effect of stress. To examine the effect of pets in stressful situations, researchers recruited 45 women who said they were dog lovers. The EESEE story "Stress among Pets and Friends" describes the results. Fifteen of the subjects were randomly assigned to each of three groups to do a stressful task alone (the control group), with a good friend present, or with their dog present. The subject's mean heart rate during the task is one measure of the effect of stress. Table 25.3 contains the data.

Group	Rate	Group	Rate	Group	Rate
TABLE 25.3		**Mean heart rates during stress with a pet (P), with a friend (F), and for the control group (C)**			
P	69.169	P	68.862	C	84.738
F	99.692	C	87.231	C	84.877
P	70.169	P	64.169	P	58.692
C	80.369	C	91.754	P	79.662
C	87.446	C	87.785	P	69.231
P	75.985	F	91.354	C	73.277
F	83.400	F	100.877	C	84.523
F	102.154	C	77.800	C	70.877
P	86.446	P	97.538	F	89.815
F	80.277	P	85.000	F	98.200
C	90.015	F	101.062	F	76.908
C	99.046	F	97.046	P	69.538
C	75.477	C	62.646	P	70.077
F	88.015	F	81.600	F	86.985
F	92.492	P	72.262	P	65.446

(a) Make stemplots of the heart rates for the three groups (round to the nearest whole number of beats). Do any of the groups show outliers or extreme skewness?

(b) Figure 25.5 gives the Minitab ANOVA output for these data. Do the mean heart rates for the groups appear to show that the presence of a pet or a friend reduces heart rate during a stressful task?

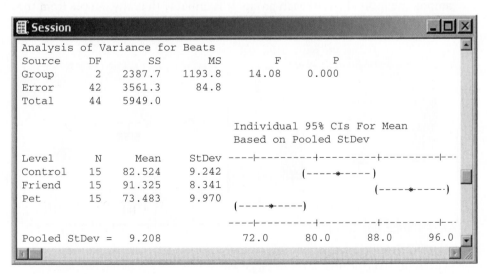

FIGURE 25.5 Minitab output for the data in Table 25.3 on heart rates (beats per minute) during stress, for Exercise 25.4. The "Control" group worked alone, the "Friend" group had a friend present, and the "Pet" group had a pet dog present.

(c) What are the values of the ANOVA F statistic and its P-value? What hypotheses does F test? Briefly describe the conclusions you draw from these data. Did you find anything surprising?

The idea of analysis of variance

The details of ANOVA are a bit daunting (they appear in an optional section at the end of this chapter). The main idea of ANOVA is both more accessible and much more important. Here it is: when we ask if a set of sample means gives evidence for differences among the population means, what matters is not how far apart the sample means are but how far apart they are *relative to the variability of individual observations*.

Look at the two sets of boxplots in Figure 25.6. For simplicity, these distributions are all symmetric, so that the mean and median are the same. The centerline in each boxplot is therefore the sample mean. Both sets of boxplots compare three samples with the same three means. Could differences this large easily arise just due to chance, or are they statistically significant?

- The boxplots in Figure 25.6(a) have tall boxes, which show lots of variation among the individuals in each group. With this much variation among individuals, we would not be surprised if another set of samples gave quite different sample means. The observed differences among the sample means could easily happen just by chance.

- The boxplots in Figure 25.6(b) have the same centers as those in Figure 25.6(a), but the boxes are much shorter. That is, there is much less variation among the individuals in each group. It is unlikely that any sample from the first group would have a mean as small as the mean of the second group.

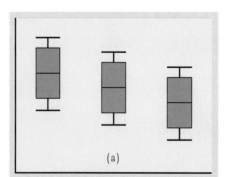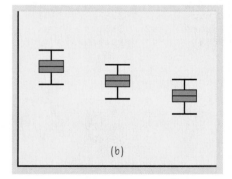

FIGURE 25.6 Boxplots for two sets of three samples each. The sample means are the same in (a) and (b). Analysis of variance will find a more significant difference among the means in (b) because there is less variation among the individuals within those samples.

Because means as far apart as those observed would rarely arise just by chance in repeated sampling, they are good evidence of real differences among the means of the three populations we are sampling from.

You can use the *One-Way ANOVA* applet to demonstrate the analysis of variance idea for yourself. The applet allows you to change both the group means and the spread within groups. You can watch the ANOVA F statistic and its P-value change as you work.

This comparison of the two parts of Figure 25.6 is too simple in one way. It ignores the effect of the sample sizes, an effect that boxplots do not show. *Small differences among sample means can be significant if the samples are large. Large differences among sample means can fail to be significant if the samples are small.* All we can be sure of is that for the same sample size, Figure 25.6(b) will give a much smaller P-value than Figure 25.6(a). Despite this qualification, the big idea remains: if sample means are far apart relative to the variation among individuals in the same groups, that's evidence that something other than chance is at work.

THE ANALYSIS OF VARIANCE IDEA

Analysis of variance compares the variation due to specific sources with the variation among individuals who should be similar. In particular, ANOVA tests whether several populations have the same mean by comparing how far apart the sample means are with how much variation there is within the samples.

It is one of the oddities of statistical language that methods for comparing means are named after the variance. The reason is that the test works by comparing two kinds of variation. Analysis of variance is a general method for studying sources of variation in responses. Comparing several means is the simplest form of ANOVA, called **one-way ANOVA.** One-way ANOVA is the only form of ANOVA that we will study.

one-way ANOVA

THE ANOVA F STATISTIC

The **analysis of variance F statistic** for testing the equality of several means has this form:

$$F = \frac{\text{variation among the sample means}}{\text{variation among individuals in the same sample}}$$

If you want more detail, read the optional section at the end of this chapter. The F statistic can take only values that are zero or positive. It is zero only when all the sample means are identical and gets larger as they move farther apart. Large values of F are evidence against the null hypothesis H_0 that all population means are the same. Although the alternative hypothesis H_a is many-sided, the ANOVA F test is one-sided because any violation of H_0 tends to produce a large value of F.

APPLY YOUR KNOWLEDGE

25.5 ANOVA compares several means. The *One-Way ANOVA* applet displays the observations in three groups, with the group means highlighted by black dots. When you open or reset the applet, the scale at the bottom of the display shows that for these groups the ANOVA F statistic is $F = 31.74$, with $P < 0.001$. (The P-value is marked by a red dot that moves along the scale.)

(a) The middle group has larger mean than the other two. Grab its mean point with the mouse. How small can you make F? What did you do to the mean to make F small? Roughly how significant is your small F?

(b) Starting with the three means aligned from your configuration at the end of (a), drag any one of the group means either up or down. What happens to F? What happens to the P-value? Convince yourself that the same thing happens if you move any one of the means, or if you move one slightly and then another slightly in the opposite direction.

25.6 ANOVA uses within-group variation. Reset the *One-Way ANOVA* applet to its original state. As in Figure 25.6(b), the differences among the three means are highly significant (large F, small P-value) because the observations in each group cluster tightly about the group mean.

(a) Use the mouse to slide the Pooled Standard Error at the top of the display to the right. You see that the group means do not change, but the spread of the observations in each group increases. What happens to F and P as the spread among the observations in each group increases? What are the values of F and P when the slider is all the way to the right? This is similar to Figure 25.6(a): variation within groups hides the differences among the group means.

(b) Leave the Pooled Standard Error slider at the extreme right of its scale, so that spread within groups stays fixed. Use the mouse to move the group means apart. What happens to F and P as you do this?

Conditions for ANOVA

Like all inference procedures, ANOVA is valid only in some circumstances. Here are the conditions under which we can use ANOVA to compare population means.

CONDITIONS FOR APPLYING ANOVA

- We have I **independent SRSs,** one from each of I populations.

- The ith population has a **Normal distribution** with unknown mean μ_i. The means may be different in the different populations. The ANOVA F statistic tests the null hypothesis that all of the populations have the same mean:

$$H_0: \mu_1 = \mu_2 = \cdots = \mu_I$$
$$H_a: \text{not all of the } \mu_i \text{ are equal}$$

- All of the populations have the **same standard deviation** σ, whose value is unknown.

There are $I + 1$ population parameters that we must estimate from the data: the I population means and the standard deviation σ.

The first two requirements are familiar from our study of the two-sample t procedures for comparing two means. As usual, the design of the data production is the most important condition for inference. Biased sampling or confounding can make any inference meaningless. *If we do not actually draw separate SRSs from each population or carry out a randomized comparative experiment, it may be unclear to what population the conclusions of inference apply.* ANOVA, like other inference procedures, is often used when random samples are not available. You must judge each use on its merits, a judgment that usually requires some knowledge of the subject of the study in addition to some knowledge of statistics.

CAUTION

Because no real population has exactly a Normal distribution, the usefulness of inference procedures that assume Normality depends on how sensitive they are to departures from Normality. Fortunately, procedures for comparing means are not very sensitive to lack of Normality. The ANOVA F test, like the t procedures, is **robust.** What matters is Normality of the sample means, so ANOVA becomes *robustness* safer as the sample sizes get larger, because of the central limit theorem effect. Remember to check for outliers that change the value of sample means and for extreme skewness. When there are no outliers and the distributions are roughly symmetric, you can safely use ANOVA for sample sizes as small as 4 or 5. (Don't confuse the ANOVA F, which compares several means, with the F statistic discussed in Chapter 19, which compares two standard deviations and is not robust against non-Normality.)

The third condition is annoying: ANOVA assumes that the variability of observations, measured by the standard deviation, is the same in all populations. You may recall from Chapter 19 (page 476) that there is a special version of the two-sample t test that assumes equal standard deviations in both populations. The ANOVA F for comparing two means is exactly the square of this special

t statistic. We prefer the t test that does not assume equal standard deviations, but for comparing more than two means there is no general alternative to the ANOVA F. It is not easy to check the condition that the populations have equal standard deviations. Statistical tests for equality of standard deviations are very sensitive to lack of Normality, so much so that they are of little practical value. You must either seek expert advice or rely on the robustness of ANOVA.

How serious are unequal standard deviations? ANOVA is not too sensitive to violations of the condition, especially when all samples have the same or similar sizes and no sample is very small. When designing a study, try to take samples of about the same size from all the groups you want to compare. The sample standard deviations estimate the population standard deviations, so check before doing ANOVA that the sample standard deviations are similar to each other. We expect some variation among them due to chance. Here is a rule of thumb that is safe in almost all situations.

CHECKING STANDARD DEVIATIONS IN ANOVA

The results of the ANOVA F test are approximately correct when the largest sample standard deviation is no more than twice as large as the smallest sample standard deviation.

EXAMPLE 25.3   Comparing tropical flowers: conditions for ANOVA

The study of *Heliconia* blossoms is based on three independent samples that the researchers consider to be random samples from all flowers of these varieties in Dominica. The stemplots in Figure 25.1 show that the *bihai* and red varieties have slightly skewed distributions, but the sample means of samples of sizes 16 and 23 will have distributions that are close to Normal. The sample standard deviations for the three varieties are

$$s_1 = 1.213 \quad s_2 = 1.799 \quad s_3 = 0.975$$

These standard deviations satisfy our rule of thumb:

$$\frac{\text{largest } s}{\text{smallest } s} = \frac{1.799}{0.975} = 1.85$$

We can safely use ANOVA to compare the mean lengths for the three populations.

EXAMPLE 25.4   Which color attracts beetles best?

STATE: To detect the presence of harmful insects in farm fields, we can put up boards covered with a sticky material and examine the insects trapped on the boards. Which colors attract insects best? Experimenters placed six boards of each of four colors at random locations in a field of oats and measured the number of cereal leaf beetles trapped. Here are the data:[5]

Board color	Beetles trapped					
Blue	16	11	20	21	14	7
Green	37	32	20	29	37	32
White	21	12	14	17	13	20
Yellow	45	59	48	46	38	47

Holt Studios International/Alamy

FORMULATE: Examine the data to determine the effect of board color on beetles trapped and check that we can safely use ANOVA. If the data allow ANOVA, assess the significance of the observed differences in mean counts of beetles trapped.

SOLVE: Because the samples are small, we plot the data in side-by-side stemplots in Figure 25.7. CrunchIt! output for ANOVA appears in Figure 25.8. The yellow boards attract by far the most beetles ($\bar{x}_4 = 47.2$), with green next ($\bar{x}_2 = 31.2$) and blue and white far behind.

Check that we can safely use ANOVA to test equality of the four means. Because the standard error of $\bar{x}$ is $s/\sqrt{n}$, each sample standard deviation is $\sqrt{6}$ times the standard error given by CrunchIt!. The largest of the four standard deviations is 6.795 and the smallest is 3.764. The ratio

$$\frac{\text{largest } s}{\text{smallest } s} = \frac{6.795}{3.764} = 1.8$$

is less than 2, so these data satisfy our rule of thumb. The shapes of the four distributions are irregular, as we expect with only 6 observations in each group, but there are no outliers. The ANOVA results will be approximately correct. The F statistic is $F = 42.84$, a large F with $P < 0.0001$.

CONCLUDE: Despite the small samples, the experiment gives very strong evidence of differences among the colors. Yellow boards appear best at attracting leaf beetles.

```
    Blue        Green        White        Yellow

  0 | 7       0 |          0 |          0 |
  1 | 146     1 |          1 | 2347     1 |
  2 | 01      2 | 09       2 | 01       2 |
  3 |         3 | 2277     3 |          3 | 8
  4 |         4 |          4 |          4 | 5678
  5 |         5 |          5 |          5 | 9
```

FIGURE 25.7 Side-by-side stemplots comparing the counts of insects attracted by six boards of each of four board colors, for Example 25.4.

APPLY YOUR KNOWLEDGE

25.7 **Checking standard deviations.** Verify that the sample standard deviations for these sets of data do allow use of ANOVA to compare the population means.

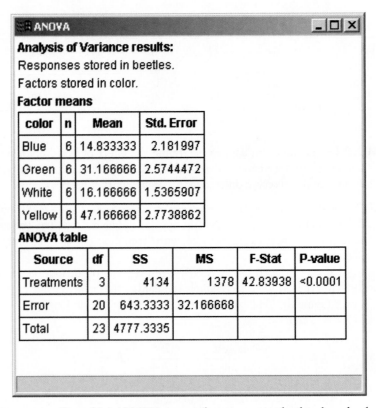

FIGURE 25.8 CrunchIt! ANOVA output for comparing the four board colors in Example 25.4.

(a) The counts of trees in Exercise 25.3 and Figure 25.4.

(b) The heart rates of Exercise 25.4 and Figure 25.5.

25.8   Species richness after logging.   Table 25.2 gives data on the species richness in rain forest plots, defined as the number of tree species in a plot divided by the number of trees in the plot. ANOVA may not be trustworthy for the richness data. Do data analysis: make side-by-side stemplots to examine the distributions of the response variable in the three groups, and also compare the standard deviations. What characteristic of the data makes ANOVA risky?

25.9   Compressing soil.   Farmers know that driving heavy equipment on wet soil compresses the soil and injures future crops. Table 2.3 (page 61) gives data on the "penetrability" of the same soil at three levels of compression.[6] Penetrability is a measure of how much resistance plant roots will meet when they try to grow through the soil.

(a) Do the sample means suggest that penetrability decreases as soil is more compressed? We would like to use ANOVA to assess the significance of the differences among the means.

(b) Examine each of the three samples. Do the standard deviations satisfy our rule of thumb? What are the overall shapes of the distributions? Are there outliers? Can we safely use ANOVA on these data?

(c) Suppose that the outliers you found in part (b) were absent. Could we safely use ANOVA on the remaining data? Explain your answer.

 ## *F* distributions and degrees of freedom

To find the *P*-value for the ANOVA *F* statistic, we must know the sampling distribution of *F* when the null hypothesis (all population means equal) is true. This sampling distribution is an **F distribution.** The *F* distributions are described on page 478 in Chapter 19. A specific *F* distribution is specified by two parameters: a numerator degrees of freedom and a denominator degrees of freedom. Table D in the back of the book contains critical values for *F* distributions with various degrees of freedom. You will rarely need Table D because software gives *P*-values directly.

F distribution

EXAMPLE 25.5 Comparing tropical flowers: the *F* distribution

Look again at the software output for the flower length data in Figure 25.3. All four outputs give the degrees of freedom for the *F* test, labeled "df" or "DF." There are 2 degrees of freedom in the numerator and 51 in the denominator. *P*-values for the *F* test therefore come from the *F* distribution with 2 and 51 degrees of freedom. Figure 25.9 shows the density curve of this distribution. The 5% critical value is 3.179 and the 1% critical value is 5.047. The observed value $F = 259.12$ of the ANOVA *F* statistic lies far to the right of these values, so the *P*-value is extremely small.

The degrees of freedom of the ANOVA *F* statistic depend on the number of means we are comparing and the number of observations in each sample. That

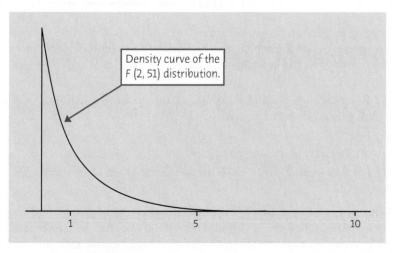

Density curve of the F (2, 51) distribution.

FIGURE 25.9 The density curve of the *F* distribution with 2 degrees of freedom in the numerator and 51 degrees of freedom in the denominator, for Example 25.3.

is, the F test takes into account the number of observations. Here are the details.

DEGREES OF FREEDOM FOR THE F TEST

We want to compare the means of I populations. We have an SRS of size n_i from the ith population, so that the total number of observations in all samples combined is

$$N = n_1 + n_2 + \cdots + n_I$$

If the null hypothesis that all population means are equal is true, the ANOVA F statistic has the F distribution with $I - 1$ degrees of freedom in the numerator and $N - I$ degrees of freedom in the denominator.

EXAMPLE 25.6 Degrees of freedom for F ─────────

In Examples 25.1 and 25.2, we compared the mean lengths for three varieties of flowers, so $I = 3$. The three sample sizes are

$$n_1 = 16 \quad n_2 = 23 \quad n_3 = 15$$

The total number of observations is therefore

$$N = 16 + 23 + 15 = 54$$

The ANOVA F test has numerator degrees of freedom

$$I - 1 = 3 - 1 = 2$$

and denominator degrees of freedom

$$N - I = 54 - 3 = 51$$

These are the degrees of freedom given in the outputs in Figure 25.3.

APPLY YOUR KNOWLEDGE ─────────────────

25.10 Logging in the rain forest, continued. Exercise 25.3 compares the number of tree species in rain forest plots that had never been logged (Group 1) with similar plots nearby that had been logged 1 year earlier (Group 2) and 8 years earlier (Group 3).

(a) What are I, the n_i, and N for these data? Identify these quantities in words and give their numerical values.

(b) Find the degrees of freedom for the ANOVA F statistic. Check your work against the Excel output in Figure 25.4.

(c) For these data, $F = 11.43$. What does Table D tell you about the P-value of this statistic?

25.11 What music will you play? People often match their behavior to their social environment. One study of this idea first established that the type of music most preferred by black college students is R&B and that whites' most preferred music is rock. Will students hosting a small group of other students choose music that matches the makeup of the people attending? Assign 90 black business students at

random to three equal-sized groups. Do the same for 96 white students. Each student sees a picture of the people he or she will host. Group 1 sees 6 blacks, Group 2 sees 3 whites and 3 blacks, and Group 3 sees 6 whites. Ask how likely the host is to play the type of music preferred by the other race. Use ANOVA to compare the three groups to see whether the racial mix of the gathering affects the choice of music.[7]

(a) For the white subjects, $F = 16.48$. What are the degrees of freedom? Use Table D to give the approximate P-value. What do you conclude?

(b) For the black subjects, $F = 2.47$. What are the degrees of freedom? Use Table D to give the approximate P-value. What do you conclude?

Some details of ANOVA: the two-sample case*

One-way ANOVA tests the hypotheses that all of I populations have the same mean,

$$H_0: \mu_1 = \mu_2 = \cdots = \mu_I$$
$$H_a: \text{not all of the } \mu_i \text{ are equal}$$

When there are just two populations, the hypotheses become

$$H_0: \mu_1 = \mu_2$$
$$H_a: \mu_1 \neq \mu_2$$

If the data suggest that the population distributions are at least roughly Normal (see the conditions in Chapter 19, page 462), we know what to do: use the two-sample t test. The idea of the t statistic is to standardize $\overline{x}_1 - \overline{x}_2$, that is,

$$t = \frac{\overline{x}_1 - \overline{x}_2}{\text{SE}}$$

The standard error SE estimates the standard deviation of $\overline{x}_1 - \overline{x}_2$, which is

$$\sqrt{\frac{\sigma_1^2}{n_1} + \frac{\sigma_2^2}{n_2}}$$

The conditions for ANOVA say that two population standard deviations σ_1 and σ_2 have a common value (call it just σ). If we know that this is true, we should use this knowledge in forming the standard error. The key idea is to combine (the statistical term is "pool") information from both samples to get a single estimate s_p of the single standard deviation σ. When we do so, the standard error becomes

$$\text{SE} = \sqrt{\frac{s_p^2}{n_1} + \frac{s_p^2}{n_2}}$$

$$= s_p \sqrt{\frac{1}{n_1} + \frac{1}{n_2}}$$

*This more advanced section is optional if you are using software to find the F statistic.

so that the pooled two-sample t statistic is

$$t = \frac{\overline{x}_1 - \overline{x}_2}{s_p\sqrt{\dfrac{1}{n_1} + \dfrac{1}{n_2}}}$$

What should we use for the estimate s_p of σ? We should give more weight to the larger sample because larger samples contain more information than smaller samples. Theory that we won't go into tells us the right way to do this: take a weighted average of the two sample variances s_1^2 and s_2^2, using their degrees of freedom as the weights. The pooled estimate of the variance σ^2 is then

$$s_p^2 = \frac{(n_1 - 1)s_1^2 + (n_2 - 1)s_2^2}{n_1 + n_2 - 2}$$

The advantage of the pooled t statistic is that when the null hypothesis is true it has exactly a t distribution, with $n_1 + n_2 - 2$ degrees of freedom. The larger degrees of freedom give slightly greater power than the conservative Option 2 method discussed in Chapter 19 (page 464). The disadvantage of pooled t is that the condition that the population standard deviations are the same is hard to verify because tests for equal standard deviations are extremely sensitive to lack of Normality. The Option 1 method, with degrees of freedom provided by software, avoids this disadvantage. Extensive studies show that Option 1 t performs essentially as well as pooled t when the standard deviations really are equal and provides notably more accurate P-values when they are not.

When we want to compare more than two means, however, there is no simple way to avoid the equal standard deviations condition. The ANOVA F statistic extends the idea behind any of the t statistics. You can think of any t statistic as comparing an average overall effect ($\overline{x}_1 - \overline{x}_2$ in the two-sample setting) with a measure of variation among individual observations (s_p, for example). This is the ANOVA idea, though the details are messier when we must compare more than two populations.

Because ANOVA requires equal population standard deviations, it is most closely related to the pooled two-sample t statistic. In fact, in the two-sample case the F statistic is exactly the square of the pooled t,

$$F = \frac{\text{variation among the sample means}}{\text{variation among individuals within samples}}$$

$$= \frac{(\overline{x}_1 - \overline{x}_2)^2}{s_p^2\left(\dfrac{1}{n_1} + \dfrac{1}{n_2}\right)}$$

$$= \frac{(\overline{x}_1 - \overline{x}_2)^2}{s_p^2} \times \frac{n_1 n_2}{n_1 + n_2}$$

(The first term in this expression displays the comparison-of variation idea. The second term plays the role of the various constants in the t statistics, arranging that we get exactly an F distribution when the null hypothesis is true.)

The general ANOVA F for more than two samples extends this idea in a straightforward way. In fact, the denominator of F is exactly the weighted average of all the sample variances with degrees of freedom as weights. The numerator must compare I sample means rather than just 2, so it becomes a bit more complicated.

Some details of ANOVA*

Now we will give the actual formula for the ANOVA F statistic. We have SRSs from each of I populations. Subscripts from 1 to I tell us which sample a statistic refers to:

Population	Sample size	Sample mean	Sample std. dev.
1	n_1	$\overline{x}_1$	s_1
2	n_2	$\overline{x}_2$	s_2
.	.	.	.
.	.	.	.
.	.	.	.
I	n_I	$\overline{x}_I$	s_I

You can find the F statistic from just the sample sizes n_i, the sample means $\overline{x}_i$, and the sample standard deviations s_i. You don't need to go back to the individual observations.

The ANOVA F statistic has the form

$$F = \frac{\text{variation among the sample means}}{\text{variation among individuals in the same sample}}$$

The measures of variation in the numerator and denominator of F are called **mean squares.** A mean square is a more general form of a sample variance. An ordinary sample variance s^2 is an average (or mean) of the squared deviations of observations from their mean, so it qualifies as a "mean square."

mean squares

The numerator of F is a mean square that measures variation among the I sample means $\overline{x}_1, \overline{x}_2, \ldots, \overline{x}_I$. Call the overall mean response (the mean of all N observations together) $\overline{x}$. You can find $\overline{x}$ from the I sample means by

$$\overline{x} = \frac{n_1\overline{x}_1 + n_2\overline{x}_2 + \cdots + n_I\overline{x}_I}{N}$$

The sum of each mean multiplied by the number of observations it represents is the sum of all the individual observations. Dividing this sum by N, the total number of observations, gives the overall mean $\overline{x}$. The numerator mean square in F is an

*This more advanced section is optional if you are using software to find the F statistic.

MSG

average of the I squared deviations of the means of the samples from $\bar{x}$. We call it the **mean square for groups,** abbreviated as MSG.

$$MSG = \frac{n_1(\bar{x}_1 - \bar{x})^2 + n_2(\bar{x}_2 - \bar{x})^2 + \cdots + n_I(\bar{x}_I - \bar{x})^2}{I - 1}$$

Each squared deviation is weighted by n_i, the number of observations it represents.

The mean square in the denominator of F measures variation among individual observations in the same sample. For any one sample, the sample variance s_i^2 does this job. For all I samples together, we use an average of the individual sample variances. It is again a weighted average in which each s_i^2 is weighted by one fewer than the number of observations it represents, $n_i - 1$. Another way to put this is that each s_i^2 is weighted by its degrees of freedom $n_i - 1$. The resulting mean square is called the **mean square for error,** MSE.

MSE

$$MSE = \frac{(n_1 - 1)s_1^2 + (n_2 - 1)s_2^2 + \cdots + (n_I - 1)s_I^2}{N - I}$$

"Error" doesn't mean a mistake has been made. It's a traditional term for chance variation. Here is a summary of the ANOVA test.

THE ANOVA F TEST

Draw an independent SRS from each of I populations. The ith population has the $N(\mu_i, \sigma)$ distribution, where σ is the common standard deviation in all the populations. The ith sample has size n_i, sample mean $\bar{x}_i$, and sample standard deviation s_i.

The **ANOVA F statistic** tests the null hypothesis that all I populations have the same mean:

$$H_0: \mu_1 = \mu_2 = \cdots = \mu_I$$
$$H_a: \text{not all of the } \mu_i \text{ are equal}$$

The statistic is

$$F = \frac{MSG}{MSE}$$

The numerator of F is the **mean square for groups**

$$MSG = \frac{n_1(\bar{x}_1 - \bar{x})^2 + n_2(\bar{x}_2 - \bar{x})^2 + \cdots + n_I(\bar{x}_I - \bar{x})^2}{I - 1}$$

The denominator of F is the **mean square for error**

$$MSE = \frac{(n_1 - 1)s_1^2 + (n_2 - 1)s_2^2 + \cdots + (n_I - 1)s_I^2}{N - I}$$

When H_0 is true, F has the **F distribution** with $I - 1$ and $N - I$ degrees of freedom.

The denominators in the formulas for MSG and MSE are the two degrees of freedom $I - 1$ and $N - I$ of the F test. The numerators are called **sums of squares,** from their algebraic form. It is usual to present the results of ANOVA in an **ANOVA table.** Output from software usually includes an ANOVA table.

sums of squares

ANOVA table

EXAMPLE 25.7 ANOVA calculations: software

Look again at the four outputs in Figure 25.3. The three software outputs give the ANOVA table. The TI-83, with its small screen, gives the degrees of freedom, sums of squares, and mean squares separately. Each output uses slightly different language to identify the two sources of variation. The basic ANOVA table is

Source of variation	df	SS	MS	F statistic
Variation among samples	2	1082.87	MSG = 541.44	259.12
Variation within samples	51	106.57	MSE = 2.09	

You can check that each mean square MS is the corresponding sum of squares SS divided by its degrees of freedom df. The F statistic is MSG divided by MSE.

Because MSE is an average of the individual sample variances, it is also called the *pooled sample variance,* written as s_p^2. When all I populations have the same population variance σ^2, as ANOVA assumes that they do, s_p^2 estimates the common variance σ^2. The square root of MSE is the **pooled standard deviation** s_p. It estimates the common standard deviation σ of observations in each group. The Minitab and TI-83 outputs in Figure 25.3 give the value $s_p = 1.446$.

pooled standard deviation

The pooled standard deviation s_p is a better estimator of the common σ than any individual sample standard deviation s_i because it combines (pools) the information in all I samples. We can get a confidence interval for any of the means μ_i from the usual form

$$\text{estimate} \pm t^* \text{SE}_{\text{estimate}}$$

using s_p to estimate σ. The confidence interval for μ_i is

$$\overline{x}_i \pm t^* \frac{s_p}{\sqrt{n_i}}$$

Use the critical value t^* from the t distribution with $N - I$ degrees of freedom because s_p has $N - I$ degrees of freedom. These are the confidence intervals that appear in Minitab ANOVA output.

EXAMPLE 25.8 ANOVA calculations: without software

We can do the ANOVA test comparing the mean lengths of *bihai*, red, and yellow flower varieties using only the sample sizes, sample means, and sample standard deviations. These appear in Example 25.1, but it is easy to find them with a calculator. There are $I = 3$ groups with a total of $N = 54$ flowers.

The overall mean of the 54 lengths in Table 25.1 is

$$\bar{x} = \frac{n_1\bar{x}_1 + n_2\bar{x}_2 + n_3\bar{x}_3}{N}$$

$$= \frac{(16)(47.598) + (23)(39.711) + (15)(36.180)}{54}$$

$$= \frac{2217.621}{54} = 41.067$$

The mean square for groups is

$$MSG = \frac{n_1(\bar{x}_1 - \bar{x})^2 + n_2(\bar{x}_2 - \bar{x})^2 + n_3(\bar{x}_3 - \bar{x})^2}{I - 1}$$

$$= \frac{1}{3 - 1}[(16)(47.598 - 41.067)^2 + (23)(39.711 - 41.067)^2$$

$$+ (15)(36.180 - 41.067)^2]$$

$$= \frac{1082.996}{2} = 541.50$$

The mean square for error is

$$MSE = \frac{(n_1 - 1)s_1^2 + (n_2 - 1)s_2^2 + (n_3 - 1)s_3^2}{N - I}$$

$$= \frac{(15)(1.213^2) + (22)(1.799^2) + (14)(0.975^2)}{51}$$

$$= \frac{106.580}{51} = 2.09$$

Finally, the ANOVA test statistic is

$$F = \frac{MSG}{MSE} = \frac{541.50}{2.09} = 259.09$$

Our work differs slightly from the output in Figure 25.3 because of roundoff error. We don't recommend doing these calculations, because tedium and roundoff errors cause frequent mistakes.

APPLY YOUR KNOWLEDGE

The calculations of ANOVA use only the sample sizes n_i, the sample means $\bar{x}_i$, and the sample standard deviations s_i. You can therefore re-create the ANOVA calculations when a report gives these summaries but does not give the actual data. These optional exercises ask you to do the ANOVA calculations starting with the summary statistics.

25.12 **Road rage.** Exercise 25.2 describes a study of road rage. Here are the means and standard deviations for a measure of "angry/threatening driving" for random samples of drivers in three age groups:

Age group	n	$\bar{x}$	s
Less than 30 years	244	2.22	3.11
30 to 55 years	734	1.33	2.21
Over 55 years	364	0.66	1.60

(a) The distributions of responses are somewhat right-skewed. ANOVA is nonetheless safe for these data. Why?

(b) Check that the standard deviations satisfy the guideline for ANOVA inference.

(c) Calculate the overall mean response $\bar{x}$, the mean squares MSG and MSE, and the ANOVA F statistic.

(d) What are the degrees of freedom for F? How significant are the differences among the three mean responses?

25.13 Exercise and weight loss. What conditions help overweight people exercise regularly? Subjects were randomly assigned to three treatments: a single long exercise period 5 days per week; several 10-minute exercise periods 5 days per week; and several 10-minute periods 5 days per week on a home treadmill that was provided to the subjects. The study report contains the following information about weight loss (in kilograms) after six months of treatment:[8]

Treatment	n	$\bar{x}$	s
Long exercise periods	37	10.2	4.2
Short exercise periods	36	9.3	4.5
Short periods with equipment	42	10.2	5.2

Purestock/SuperStock

(a) Do the standard deviations satisfy the rule of thumb for safe use of ANOVA?

(b) Calculate the overall mean response $\bar{x}$ and the mean square for groups MSG.

(c) Calculate the mean square for error MSE.

(d) Find the ANOVA F statistic and its approximate P-value. Is there evidence that the mean weight losses of people who follow the three exercise programs differ?

25.14 Attitudes toward math. Do high school students from different racial/ethnic groups have different attitudes toward mathematics? Measure the level of interest in mathematics on a 5-point scale for a national random sample of students. Here are summaries for students who were taking math at the time of the survey:[9]

Racial/ethnic group	n	$\bar{x}$	s
African American	809	2.57	1.40
White	1860	2.32	1.36
Asian/Pacific Islander	654	2.63	1.32
Hispanic	883	2.51	1.31
Native American	207	2.51	1.28

Calculate the ANOVA table and the F statistic. Show that there are significant differences among the mean attitudes of the five groups. What explains the small P-value? Do you think the differences are large enough to be important?

CHAPTER 25 SUMMARY

One-way analysis of variance (ANOVA) compares the means of several populations. The **ANOVA F test** tests the overall H_0 that all the populations have the same mean. If the F test shows significant differences, examine the data to see where the differences lie and whether they are large enough to be important.

The **conditions for ANOVA** state that we have an **independent SRS** from each population; that each population has a **Normal distribution;** and that all populations have the **same standard deviation.**

In practice, ANOVA inference is relatively **robust** when the populations are non-Normal, especially when the samples are large. Before doing the F test, check the observations in each sample for outliers or strong skewness. Also verify that the largest sample standard deviation is no more than twice as large as the smallest standard deviation.

When the null hypothesis is true, the **ANOVA F statistic** for comparing I means from a total of N observations in all samples combined has the **F distribution** with $I - 1$ and $N - I$ degrees of freedom.

ANOVA calculations are reported in an **ANOVA table** that gives sums of squares, mean squares, and degrees of freedom for variation among groups and for variation within groups. In practice, we use software to do the calculations.

STATISTICS IN SUMMARY

Here are the most important skills you should have acquired from reading this chapter.

A. RECOGNITION

1. Recognize when testing the equality of several means is helpful in understanding data.
2. Recognize that the statistical significance of differences among sample means depends on the sizes of the samples and on how much variation there is within the samples.
3. Recognize when you can safely use ANOVA to compare means. Check the data production, the presence of outliers, and the sample standard deviations for the groups you want to compare.

B. INTERPRETING ANOVA

1. Explain what null hypothesis F tests in a specific setting.
2. Locate the F statistic and its P-value on the output of analysis of variance software.
3. Find the degrees of freedom for the F statistic from the number and sizes of the samples. Use Table D of the F distributions to approximate the P-value when software does not give it.
4. If the test is significant, use graphs and descriptive statistics to see what differences among the means are most important.

CHECK YOUR SKILLS

25.15 The purpose of analysis of variance is to compare

(a) the variances of several populations.

(b) the proportions of successes in several populations.

(c) the means of several populations.

25.16 A study of the effects of smoking classifies subjects as nonsmokers, moderate smokers, or heavy smokers. The investigators interview a sample of 200 people in each group. Among the questions is "How many hours do you sleep on a typical night?" The degrees of freedom for the ANOVA F statistic comparing mean hours of sleep are

(a) 2 and 197.   (b) 2 and 597.   (c) 3 and 597.

25.17 The alternative hypothesis for the ANOVA F test in the previous exercise is

(a) the mean hours of sleep in the groups are all the same.

(b) the mean hours of sleep in the groups are all different.

(c) the mean hours of sleep in the groups are not all the same.

The air in poultry processing plants often contains fungus spores. Large spore concentrations can affect the health of the workers. To measure the presence of spores, air samples are pumped to an agar plate and "colony forming units (CFUs)" are counted after an incubation period. Here are data from the "kill room" of a plant that slaughters 37,000 turkeys per day, taken at four seasons of the year. Each observation was made on a different day. The units are CFUs per cubic meter of air.[10]

Fall	Winter	Spring	Summer
1231	384	2105	3175
1254	104	701	2526
752	251	2947	1763
1088	97	842	1090

Here is Minitab output for ANOVA to compare mean CFUs in the four seasons:

```
Source   DF        SS        MS      F      P
Season    3   8236359   2745453   5.38   0.014
Error    12   6124211    510351
Total    15  14360570

                         Individual 95% CIs For Mean Based on
                         Pooled StDev
Level    N    Mean    StDev  ------+---------+---------+---------+---
Fall     4   1081.3   231.5              (-------*-------)
Spring   4   1648.8  1071.2                 (------*-------)
Summer   4   2138.5   906.4                     (------*-------)
Winter   4    209.0   136.6  (-------*-------)
                            ------+---------+---------+---------+---
                                  0      1000      2000      3000
```

Exercises 25.18 to 25.23 are based on this study.

25.18 The most striking conclusion from the numerical summaries for the turkey-processing plant is that

(a) there appears to be little difference among the seasons.

(b) on the average, CFUs are much lower in winter than in other seasons.

(c) the air in the plant is clearly unhealthy.

25.19 We might use the two-sample t procedures to compare summer and winter. The conservative 90% confidence interval for the difference in the two population means is

(a) 1929.5 ± 458.3.   (b) 1929.5 ± 1078.4.   (c) 1929.5 ± 1458.4.

25.20 In all, we would have to give 6 two-sample confidence intervals to compare all pairs of seasons. The weakness of doing this is that

(a) we don't know how confident we can be that all 6 intervals cover the true differences in means.

(b) 90% confidence is OK for one comparison, but it isn't high enough for 6 comparisons done at once.

(c) the conditions for two-sample t inference are not met for all 6 pairs of seasons.

25.21 The conclusion of the ANOVA test is that

(a) there is quite strong evidence ($P = 0.014$) that the mean CFUs are not the same in all four seasons.

(b) there is quite strong evidence ($P = 0.014$) that the mean CFUs are much lower in winter than in any other season.

(c) the data give no evidence ($P = 0.014$) to suggest that mean CFUs differ from season to season.

25.22 Without software, we would compare $F = 5.38$ with critical values from Table D. This comparison shows that

(a) the P-value is greater than 0.1.

(b) the P-value is between 0.01 and 0.025.

(c) the P-value is between 0.001 and 0.01.

25.23 The P-value 0.014 in the output may not be accurate because the conditions for ANOVA are not satisfied. The most serious violation of the conditions is that

(a) the sample standard deviations are too different.

(b) there is an extreme outlier in the data.

(c) the data can't be regarded as random samples.

CHAPTER 25 EXERCISES

Exercises 25.24 to 25.27 describe situations in which we want to compare the mean responses in several populations. For each setting, identify the populations and the response variable. Then give I, the n_i, and N. Finally, give the degrees of freedom of the ANOVA F test.

25.24 **How much do students borrow?** A sample survey of students who had just received their bachelor's degree found that about half had borrowed money to pay for college. Does the type of college attended influence the amount borrowed? Here is information about the students in the sample who did borrow:

	Public nondoctorate	Public doctorate	Private nondoctorate	Private doctorate
Number of students	137	313	148	95
Mean borrowed	$15,000	$17,500	$20,900	$28,000

25.25 Morning or evening? Are you a morning person, an evening person, or neither? Does this personality trait affect how well you perform? A sample of 100 students took a psychological test that found 16 morning people, 30 evening people, and 54 who were neither. All the students then took a test of their ability to memorize at 8 A.M. and again at 9 P.M. Analyze the score at 8 A.M. minus the score at 9 P.M.

25.26 Writing essays. Do strategies such as preparing a written outline help students write better essays? College students were divided at random into four groups of 20 students each, then asked to write an essay on an assigned topic. Group A (the control group) received no additional instruction. Group B was required to prepare a written outline. Group C was given 15 ideas that might be relevant to the essay topic. Group D was given the ideas and also required to prepare an outline. An expert scored the quality of the essays on a scale of 1 to 7.

25.27 A medical study. The Québec (Canada) Cardiovascular Study recruited men aged 34 to 64 at random from towns in the Québec City metropolitan area. Of these, 1824 met the criteria (no diabetes, free of heart disease, and so on) for a study of the relationship between being overweight and medical risks. The 719 normal-weight men had mean triglyceride level 1.5 millimoles per liter (mmol/l); the 885 overweight men had mean 1.7 mmol/l; and the 220 obese men had mean 1.9 mmol/l.[11]

25.28 Whose little bird is that? The males of many animal species signal their fitness to females by displays of various kinds. For male barn swallows, the signal is the color of their plumage. Does better color really lead to more offspring? A randomized comparative experiment assigned barn swallow pairs who had already produced a clutch of eggs to three groups: 13 males had their color "enhanced" by the investigators, 9 were handled but their color was left alone, and 8 were not touched. DNA testing showed whether the eggs were sired by the male of the pair rather than by another male. The investigators then destroyed the eggs. Barn swallows usually produce a second brood in such circumstances. Sure enough, the males with enhanced color fathered more young in the second brood, and males in the other groups fathered fewer. The investigators used ANOVA to compare the three groups.[12]

age fotostock/SuperStock

(a) What are the degrees of freedom for the F statistic that compares the numbers of the male's own young among the eggs in the first brood? The statistic was $F = 0.07$. What can you say about the P-value? What do you conclude?

(b) Of the 30 original pairs, 27 produced a second brood. What are the degrees of freedom for F to compare differences in the number of the male's own young between the first and second broods produced by these 27 pairs? The statistic was $F = 5.45$. How significant is this F?

25.29 **Plants defend themselves.** When some plants are attacked by leaf-eating insects, they release chemical compounds that attract other insects that prey on the leaf-eaters. A study carried out on plants growing naturally in the Utah desert demonstrated both the release of the compounds and that they not only repel the leaf-eaters but attract predators that act as the plants' bodyguards.[13] The investigators chose 8 plants attacked by each of three leaf-eaters and 8 more that were undamaged, 32 plants of the same species in all. They then measured emissions of several compounds during seven hours. Here are data (mean ± standard error of the mean for eight plants) for one compound. The emission rate is measured in nanograms (ng) per hour.

Group	Emission rate (ng/hr)
Control	9.22 ± 5.93
Hornworm	31.03 ± 8.75
Leaf bug	18.97 ± 6.64
Flea beetle	27.12 ± 8.62

(a) Make a graph that compares the mean emission rates for the four groups. Does it appear that emissions increase when a plant is attacked?

(b) What hypotheses does ANOVA test in this setting?

(c) We do not have the full data. What would you look for in deciding whether you can safely use ANOVA?

(d) What is the relationship between the standard error of the mean (SEM) and the standard deviation for a sample? Do the standard deviations satisfy our rule of thumb for safe use of ANOVA?

25.30 **Can you hear these words?** To test whether a hearing aid is right for a patient, audiologists play a tape on which words are pronounced at low volume. The patient tries to repeat the words. There are several different lists of words that are supposed to be equally difficult. Are the lists equally difficult when there is background noise? To find out, an experimenter had subjects with normal hearing listen to four lists with a noisy background. The response variable was the percent of the 50 words in a list that the subject repeated correctly. The data set contains 96 responses.[14] Here are two study designs that could produce these data:

Design A. The experimenter assigns 96 subjects to 4 groups at random. Each group of 24 subjects listens to one of the lists. All individuals listen and respond separately.

Design B. The experimenter has 24 subjects. Each subject listens to all four lists in random order. All individuals listen and respond separately.

Does Design A allow use of one-way ANOVA to compare the lists? Does Design B allow use of one-way ANOVA to compare the lists? Briefly explain your answers.

25.31 **Nematodes and tomato plants.** How do nematodes (microscopic worms) affect plant growth? A botanist prepares 16 identical planting pots and then introduces

Alix Phanie, Rex Interstock/Stock Connection/PictureQuest

different numbers of nematodes into the pots. He transplants a tomato seedling into each pot. Here are data on the increase in height of the seedlings (in centimeters) 16 days after planting:[15]

Nematodes	Seedling growth			
0	10.8	9.1	13.5	9.2
1,000	11.1	11.1	8.2	11.3
5,000	5.4	4.6	7.4	5.0
10,000	5.8	5.3	3.2	7.5

Figure 25.10 shows output from CrunchIt! for ANOVA comparing the four groups of pots.

(a) Make a table of the means and standard deviations in the groups. Make side-by-side stemplots to compare the treatments. What do the data appear to show about the effect of nematodes on growth? Is use of ANOVA justified?

(b) State H_0 and H_a for the ANOVA test for these data, and explain in words what ANOVA tests in this setting.

(c) Report your overall conclusions about the effect of nematodes on plant growth.

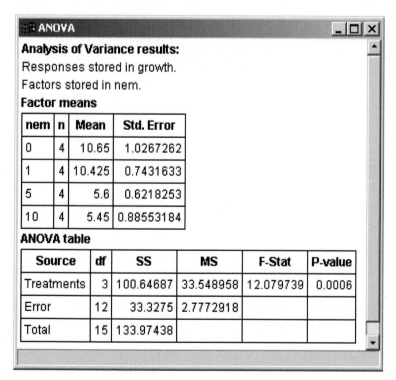

FIGURE 25.10 CrunchIt! ANOVA output for comparing the growth of tomato seedlings with different concentrations of nematodes in the soil, for Exercise 25.31.

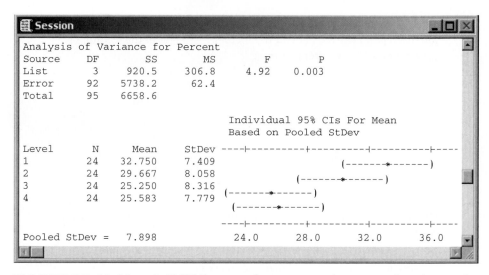

FIGURE 25.11 Minitab ANOVA output for comparing the percents heard correctly in four lists of words, for Exercise 25.32.

25.32 Can you hear these words? Figure 25.11 displays the Minitab output for one-way ANOVA applied to the hearing data described in Exercise 25.30. The response variable is "Percent," and "List" identifies the four lists of words. Based on this analysis, is there good reason to think that the four lists are not all equally difficult? Write a brief summary of the study findings.

25.33 Which blue is most blue? The color of a fabric depends on the dye used and also on how the dye is applied. This matters to clothing manufacturers, who want the color of the fabric to be just right. Dye fabric made of ramie with the same "procion blue" die applied in four different ways. Then use a colorimeter to measure the lightness of the color on a scale in which black is 0 and white is 100. Here are the data for 8 pieces of fabric dyed in each way:[16]

Method A	41.72	41.83	42.05	41.44	41.27	42.27	41.12	41.49
Method B	40.98	40.88	41.30	41.28	41.66	41.50	41.39	41.27
Method C	42.30	42.20	42.65	42.43	42.50	42.28	43.13	42.45
Method D	41.68	41.65	42.30	42.04	42.25	41.99	41.72	41.97

(a) This is a randomized comparative experiment. Outline the design.

(b) A clothing manufacturer wants to know which method gives the darkest color. Follow the four-step process in answering this question.

25.34 Does nature heal best? Our bodies have a natural electrical field that helps wounds heal. Might higher or lower levels speed healing? An experiment with newts investigated this question. Newts were randomly assigned to five groups. In four of the groups, an electrode applied to one hind limb (chosen at random) changed the natural field, while the other hind limb was not manipulated. Both limbs in the fifth (control) group remained in their natural state.[17]

TABLE 25.4 **Effect of electrical field on healing rate in newts**

Group	Diff	Group	Diff	Group	Diff	Group	Diff	Group	Diff
0	−10	0.5	−1	1	−7	1.25	1	1.5	−13
0	−12	0.5	10	1	15	1.25	8	1.5	−49
0	−9	0.5	3	1	−4	1.25	−15	1.5	−16
0	−11	0.5	−3	1	−16	1.25	14	1.5	−8
0	−1	0.5	−31	1	−2	1.25	−7	1.5	−2
0	6	0.5	4	1	−13	1.25	−1	1.5	−35
0	−31	0.5	−12	1	5	1.25	11	1.5	−11
0	−5	0.5	−3	1	−4	1.25	8	1.5	−46
0	13	0.5	−7	1	−2	1.25	11	1.5	−22
0	−2	0.5	−10	1	−14	1.25	−4	1.5	2
0	−7	0.5	−22	1	5	1.25	7	1.5	10
0	−8	0.5	−4	1	11	1.25	−14	1.5	−4
		0.5	−1	1	10	1.25	0	1.5	−10
		0.5	−3	1	3	1.25	5	1.5	2
				1	6	1.25	−2	1.5	−5
				1	−1				
				1	13				
				1	−8				

Table 25.4 gives data from this experiment. The "Group" variable shows the field applied as a multiple of the natural field for each newt. For example, "0.5" is half the natural field, "1" is the natural level (the control group), and "1.5" indicates a field 1.5 times natural. "Diff" is the response variable, the difference in the healing rate (in micrometers per hour) of cuts made in the experimental and control limbs of that newt. Negative values mean that the experimental limb healed more slowly. The investigators conjectured that nature heals best, so that changing the field from the natural state (the "1" group) will slow healing.

Do a complete analysis to see whether the groups differ in the effect of the electrical field level on healing. Follow the four-step process in your work.

25.35 **Does polyester decay?** How quickly do synthetic fabrics such as polyester decay in landfills? A researcher buried polyester strips in the soil for different lengths of time, then dug up the strips and measured the force required to break them. Breaking strength is easy to measure and is a good indicator of decay; lower strength means the fabric has decayed.

Part of the study buried 20 polyester strips in well-drained soil in the summer. Five of the strips, chosen at random, were dug up after each of 2 weeks, 4 weeks, and 8 weeks. Here are the breaking strengths in pounds:[18]

2 weeks	118	126	126	120	129
4 weeks	130	120	114	126	128
8 weeks	122	136	128	146	140

The investigator conjectured that buried polyester loses strength over time. Do the data support this conjecture? Follow the four-step process in data analysis and ANOVA. Be sure to check the conditions for ANOVA.

4
STEP

25.36 Durable press fabrics are weaker. "Durable press" cotton fabrics are treated to improve their recovery from wrinkles after washing. Unfortunately, the treatment also reduces the strength of the fabric. A study compared the breaking strength of untreated fabric with that of fabrics treated by three commercial durable press processes. Five specimens of the same fabric were assigned at random to each group. Here are the data, in pounds of pull needed to tear the fabric:[19]

Untreated	60.1	56.7	61.5	55.1	59.4
Permafresh 55	29.9	30.7	30.0	29.5	27.6
Permafresh 48	24.8	24.6	27.3	28.1	30.3
Hylite LF	28.8	23.9	27.0	22.1	24.2

The untreated fabric is clearly much stronger than any of the treated fabrics. We want to know if there is a significant difference in breaking strength among the three durable press treatments. Analyze the data for the three processes and write a clear summary of your findings. Which process do you recommend if breaking strength is a main concern? Use the four-step process to guide your discussion. (Although the standard deviations do not quite satisfy our rule of thumb, that rule is conservative and many statisticians would use ANOVA for these data.)

25.37 Durable press fabrics wrinkle less. The data in Exercise 25.36 show that durable press treatment greatly reduces the breaking strength of cotton fabric. Of course, durable press treatment also reduces wrinkling. How much? "Wrinkle recovery angle" measures how well a fabric recovers from wrinkles. Higher is better. Here are data on the wrinkle recovery angle (in degrees) for the same fabric specimens discussed in the previous exercise:

Untreated	79	80	78	80	78
Permafresh 55	136	135	132	137	134
Permafresh 48	125	131	125	145	145
Hylite LF	143	141	146	141	145

The untreated fabric once again stands out, this time as inferior to the treated fabrics in wrinkle resistance. Examine the data for the three durable press processes and summarize your findings. How does the ranking of the three processes by wrinkle resistance compare with their ranking by breaking strength in Exercise 25.36? Explain why we can't trust the ANOVA F test.

25.38 Logging in the rain forest: species counts. Table 25.2 gives data on the number of trees per forest plot, the number of species per plot, and species richness. Exercise 25.3 analyzed the effect of logging on number of trees. Exercise 25.8 concludes that it would be risky to use ANOVA to analyze richness. Use software to analyze the effect of logging on the number of species.

(a) Make a table of the group means and standard deviations. Do the standard deviations satisfy our rule of thumb for safe use of ANOVA? What do the means suggest about the effect of logging on the number of species?

(b) Carry out the ANOVA. Report the F statistic and its P-value and state your conclusion.

25.39 Plant defenses (optional). The calculations of ANOVA use only the sample sizes n_i, the sample means $\bar{x}_i$, and the sample standard deviations s_i. You can therefore re-create the ANOVA calculations when a report gives these summaries but does not give the actual data. Use the information in Exercise 25.29 to calculate the ANOVA table (sums of squares, degrees of freedom, mean squares, and the F statistic). Note that the report gives the standard error of the mean (SEM) rather than the standard deviation. Are there significant differences among the mean emission rates for the four populations of plants?

25.40 F versus t (optional). We have two methods to compare the means of two groups: the two-sample t test of Chapter 19 and the ANOVA F test with $I = 2$. We prefer the t test because it allows one-sided alternatives and does not assume that both populations have the same standard deviation. Let us apply both tests to the same data.

There are two types of life insurance companies. "Stock" companies have shareholders, and "mutual" companies are owned by their policyholders. Take an SRS of each type of company from those listed in a directory of the industry. Then ask the annual cost per \$1000 of insurance for a \$50,000 policy insuring the life of a 35-year-old man who does not smoke. Here are the data summaries:[20]

	Stock companies	Mutual companies
n_i	13	17
$\bar{x}_i$	\$2.31	\$2.37
s_i	\$0.38	\$0.58

(a) Calculate the two-sample t statistic for testing $H_0: \mu_1 = \mu_2$ against the two-sided alternative. Use the conservative method to find the P-value.

(b) Calculate MSG, MSE, and the ANOVA F statistic for the same hypotheses. What is the P-value of F?

(c) How close are the two P-values?

25.41 ANOVA or chi-square? (optional). Exercise 25.13 describes a randomized, comparative experiment that assigned subjects to three types of exercise programs intended to help them lose weight. Some of the results of this study were analyzed using the chi-square test for two-way tables, and some others were analyzed using one-way ANOVA. For each of the following excerpts from the study report, say which analysis is appropriate and explain how you made your choice.

(a) "Overall, 115 subjects (78% of 148 subjects randomized) completed 18 months of treatment, with no significant difference in attrition rates between the groups ($P = .12$)."

(b) "In analyses using only the 115 subjects who completed 18 months of treatment, there were no significant differences in weight loss at 6 months among the groups."

(c) "The duration of exercise for weeks 1 through 4 was significantly greater in the SB compared with both LB and SBEQ groups ($P < .05$). ...However, exercise duration was greater in SBEQ compared with both LB and SB groups for months 13 through 18 ($P < .05$)."

EESEE CASE STUDIES

The Electronic Encyclopedia of Statistical Examples and Exercises (EESEE) is available on the text CD and Web site. These more elaborate stories, with data, provide settings for longer case studies. Here are some suggestions for EESEE stories that apply ANOVA.

25.42 Read the EESEE story "Blinded Knee Doctors." Write a report that answers all questions for this case study.

25.43 Read the EESEE story "Stress among Pets and Friends." Write a report that answers all questions for this case study.

25.44 Read the EESEE story "Nutrition and Breakfast Cereals." Write a report that answers all questions for this case study.

![icon] Statistical Thinking Revisited

The Thinking Person's Guide to Basic Statistics

We began our study of statistics with a look at "Statistical Thinking." We end with a review in outline form of the most important ideas of basic statistics, combining statistical thinking with your new knowledge of statistical practice. The outline contains some important warnings: look for the Caution icon.

1. Data Production

- Data basics:

    Individuals (subjects).

    Variables: categorical versus quantitative, units of measurement, explanatory versus response.

    Purpose of study.

- Data production basics:

    Observation versus experiment.

    Simple random samples.

    Completely randomized experiments.

- Beware: really bad data production (voluntary response, confounding) can make interpretation impossible.

- Beware: weaknesses in data production (for example, sampling students at only one campus) can make generalizing conclusions difficult.

2. Data Analysis

- Always plot your data. Look for overall pattern and striking deviations.

- Add numerical descriptions based on what you see.

- Beware: averages and other simple descriptions can miss the real story.

- One quantitative variable:

    Graphs: stemplot, histogram, boxplot.

    Pattern: distribution shape, center, spread. Outliers?

    Density curves (such as Normal curves) to describe overall pattern.

    Numerical descriptions: five-number summary or $\bar{x}$ and s.

- Relationships between two quantitative variables:

    Graph: scatterplot.

    Pattern: relationship form, direction, strength. Outliers? Influential observations?

Numerical description for linear relationships: correlation, regression line.

Beware the lurking variable: correlation does not imply causation.

- Beware the effects of outliers and influential observations.

3. The Reasoning of Inference

- Inference uses data to infer conclusions about a wider population.
- When you do inference, you are acting as if your data come from random samples or randomized comparative experiments. Beware: if they don't, you may have "garbage in, garbage out."
- Always examine your data before doing inference. Inference often requires a regular pattern, such as roughly Normal with no strong outliers.
- Key idea: "What would happen if we did this many times?"
- Confidence intervals: estimate a population parameter.

    95% confidence: I used a method that captures the true parameter 95% of the time in repeated use.

    Beware: the margin of error of a confidence interval does not include the effects of practical errors such as undercoverage and nonresponse.

STATISTICS IN SUMMARY

Overview of basic inference methods

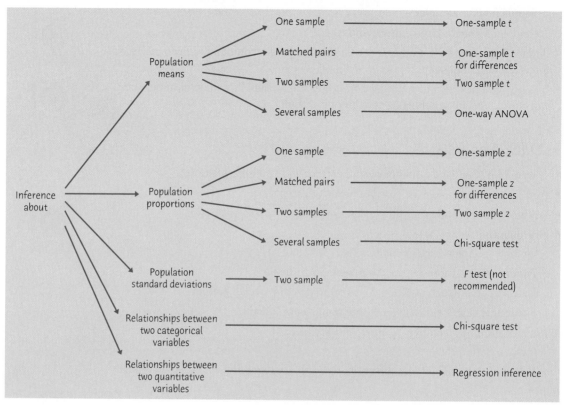

- Significance tests: assess evidence against H_0 in favor of H_a.

    P-value: If H_0 were true, how often would I get an outcome favoring the alternative this strongly? Smaller P = stronger evidence against H_0.

    Statistical significance at the 5% level, $P < 0.05$, means that an outcome this extreme would occur less than 5% of the time if H_0 were true.

    Beware: $P < 0.05$ is not sacred.

    Beware: statistical significance is not the same as practical significance. Large samples can make small effects significant. Small samples can fail to declare large effects significant.

    Always try to estimate the size of an effect (for example, with a confidence interval), not just its significance.

- Choose inference procedures by asking "What parameter?" and "What study design?" See the Statistics in Summary overview.

Notes and Data Sources

"About This Book" Notes

1. D. S. Moore and discussants, "New pedagogy and new content: the case of statistics," *International Statistical Review*, 65 (1997), pp. 123–165. Richard Scheaffer's comment appears on page 156.

2. This summary of the committee's report was unanimously endorsed by the Board of Directors of the American Statistical Association. The full report is George Cobb, "Teaching statistics," in L. A. Steen (ed.), *Heeding the Call for Change: Suggestions for Curricular Action*, Mathematical Association of America, 1990, pp. 3–43.

3. A summary of the GAISE "Introductory College Course Guidelines," which has also been endorsed by the ASA board of directors, appears in *Amstat News*, June 2006, p. 31. See www.amstat.org/education/gaise for details.

4. Lawrence D. Brown, Tony Cai, and Anirban DasGupta, "Interval estimation for a binomial proportion," *Statistical Science*, 16 (2001), pp. 101–133.

"Statistical Thinking" Notes

1. E. W. Campion, "Editorial: power lines, cancer, and fear," *New England Journal of Medicine*, 337, No. 1 (1997). The study report is M. S. Linet et al., "Residential exposure to magnetic fields and acute lymphoblastic leukemia in children," in the same issue. See also G. Taubes, "Magnetic field–cancer link: will it rest in peace?" *Science*, 277 (1997), p. 29.

2. Contributed by Marigene Arnold of Kalamazoo College.

3. See, for example, Martin Enserink, "The vanishing promises of hormone replacement," *Science*, 297 (2002), pp. 325–326; and Brian Vastag, "Hormone replacement therapy falls out of favor with expert committee," *Journal of the American Medical Association*, 287 (2002), pp. 1923–1924. A National Institutes of Health panel's comprehensive report is *International Position Paper on Women's Health and Menopause*, NIH Publication 02-3284, 2002.

4. A. C. Nielsen, Jr., "Statistics in marketing," in *Making Statistics More Effective in Schools of Business*, Graduate School of Business, University of Chicago, 1986.

5. The data in Figure 2 are based on a component of the Consumer Price Index, from the Bureau of Labor Statistics Web site: www.bls.gov. I converted the index number into cents per gallon using retail price information from the Energy Information Agency site: www.eia.doe.gov.

6. H. C. Sox, "Editorial: benefit and harm associated with screening for breast cancer," *New England Journal of Medicine*, 338 (1998), pp. 1145–1146.

Chapter 1 Notes

1. Arbitron, *Radio Today, 2005 Edition*, www.arbitron.com.

2. Arbitron, *Internet and Multimedia 2005*, www.arbitron.com.

3. DuPont Automotive Services, *2005 Automotive Color Popularity Report*, www.automotive.dupont.com.

4. National Center for Health Statistics, *Births: Final Data for 2003*, National Vital Statistics Reports, 54, No. 2, 2005.

5. From the 2003 American Community Survey, at the Bureau of the Census Web site, `www.census.gov`.

6. Our eyes do respond to area, but not quite linearly. It appears that we perceive the ratio of two bars to be about the 0.7 power of the ratio of their actual areas. See W. S. Cleveland, *The Elements of Graphing Data*, Wadsworth, 1985, pp. 278–284.

7. See Note 5.

8. Data from Gary Community School Corporation, courtesy of Celeste Foster, Purdue University.

9. See Note 5.

10. Debora L. Arsenau, "Comparison of diet management instruction for patients with non–insulin dependent diabetes mellitus: learning activity package vs. group instruction," MS thesis, Purdue University, 1993.

11. Raymond W. Schaffranek and Ami L. Riscassi, *Flow Velocity, Water Temperature, and Conductivity at Selected Locations in Shark River Slough, Everglades National Park, Florida; July 1999–July 2003*, Data Series 110, U.S. Geological Survey, 2004, `water.usgs.gov`.

12. College Entrance Examination Board, *Trends in College Pricing*, 2005, `www.collegeboard.com`. The averages are "enrollment weighted," so that they give average tuition over *students* rather than over *colleges*.

13. See Note 3.

14. National Center for Health Statistics, *Deaths: Preliminary Data for 2003*, National Vital Statistics Reports, 53, No. 15, 2005.

15. Bureau of the Census, *Hispanics in the U.S.A.*, public use training module, 2001, `www.census.gov`.

16. *Statistical Abstract of the United States*, 2004–2005, Table 1233.

17. Robyn Greenspan, "The deadly duo: spam and viruses, October 2003," `cyberatlas.internet.com`.

18. Tom Lloyd et al., "Fruit consumption, fitness, and cardiovascular health in female adolescents: the Penn State Young Women's Health Study," *American Journal of Clinical Nutrition*, 67 (1998), pp. 624–630.

19. Monthly stock returns from the Web site of Professor Kenneth French of Dartmouth, `mba.tuck.dartmouth.edu/pages/faculty/ken.french`. A fine point: the data are actually the "excess returns" on stocks, the actual returns less the small monthly returns on Treasury bills.

20. National Climatic Data Center storm events data base, `sciencepolicy.colorado.edu/sourcebook/tornadoes.html`.

21. *Statistical Abstract of the United States*, 2004–2005, Table 150.

22. Found online at `earthtrends.wri.org`.

23. National Oceanic and Atmospheric Administration, `www.noaa.gov`.

24. David M. Fergusson and L. John Horwood, "Cannabis use and traffic accidents in a birth cohort of young adults," *Accident Analysis and Prevention*, 33 (2001), pp. 703–711.

25. From the Web site of the Bureau of Labor Statistics, www.bls.gov/cpi.

26. Florida Fish and Wildlife Conservation Commission, *Alligator Attacks Fact Sheet*, 2005, www.wildflorida.org.

Chapter 2 Notes

1. From 2003 American Community Survey, at the Bureau of the Census Web site, www.census.gov. The data are a subsample of the 13,194 individuals in the ACS North Carolina sample who had travel times greater than zero.

2. This isn't a mathematical theorem. The mean can be less than the median in right-skewed distributions that take only a few values, many of which lie exactly at the median. The rule almost never fails for distributions taking many values, and counterexamples don't appear clearly skewed in graphs even though they may be slightly skewed according to technical measures of skewness. See Paul T. von Hippel, "Mean, median, and skew: correcting a textbook rule," *Journal of Statistics Education*, 13, No. 2 (2005), online journal, www.amstat.org/publications/jse.

3. From the National Association of Realtors, www.realtor.org.

4. Bureau of the Census, *Income, Poverty, and Health Insurance in the United States: 2004*, Current Population Reports P60-229, 2005.

5. Figure 2.2 displays the daily returns for 301 market days starting on March 1, 2004, for the CREF Equity Index Fund and the TIAA Real Estate Fund. Daily price data for these funds are at www.tiaa-cref.org. Returns can be easily calculated because dividends are incorporated in the daily prices rather than given separately.

6. I thank Ethan J. Temeles of Amherst College for providing the data. His work is described in Ethan J. Temeles and W. John Kress, "Adaptation in a plant-hummingbird association," *Science*, 300 (2003), pp. 630–633.

7. I thank Charles Cannon of Duke University for providing the data. The study report is C. H. Cannon, D. R. Peart, and M. Leighton, "Tree species diversity in commercially logged Bornean rainforest," *Science*, 281 (1998), pp. 1366–1367.

8. Douglas Fore, "Do we have a retirement crisis in America?" *TIAA-CREF Institute Research Dialogue*, No. 77, 2003. The data are for the year 2001.

9. National Center for Health Statistics. *Births: Final Data for 2002*, National Vital Statistics Reports, 52, No. 10, 2003. This was the latest final report available as of the end of 2005.

10. From the University of Miami athletics Web site, hurricanesports.collegesports.com.

11. T. Bjerkedal, "Acquisition of resistance in guinea pigs infected with different doses of virulent tubercle bacilli," *American Journal of Hygiene*, 72 (1960), pp. 130–148.

12. Data for 1986 from David Brillinger, University of California, Berkeley. See David R. Brillinger, "Mapping aggregate birth data," in A. C. Singh and P. Whitridge (eds.), *Analysis of Data in Time*, Statistics Canada, 1990, pp. 77–83. A boxplot similar to Figure 2.6 appears in David R. Brillinger, "Some examples of random process environmental data analysis," in P. K. Sen and C. R. Rao (eds.), *Handbook of Statistics*, Vol. 18, *Bioenvironmental and Public Health Statistics*, North Holland, 2000.

13. M. Ann Laskey et al., "Bone changes after 3 mo of lactation: influence of calcium intake, breast-milk output, and vitamin D–receptor genotype," *American Journal of Clinical Nutrition*, 67 (1998), pp. 685–692.

14. Parmeshwar S. Gupta, "Reaction of plants to the density of soil," *Journal of Ecology*, 21 (1933), pp. 452–474.

Chapter 3 Notes

1. See Note 8 for Chapter 1.

2. Based on the National Health and Nutrition Examination Surveys, 1988–1994. From the Web site of the National Center for Health Statistics, `www.cdc.gov/nchs`.

3. Detailed data appear in P. S. Levy et al., *Total Serum Cholesterol Values for Youths 12–17 Years*, Vital and Health Statistics, Series 11, No. 155, National Center for Health Statistics, 1976.

4. Data provided by Darlene Gordon, Purdue University.

5. *ACT High School Profile Report, HS Graduating Class 2004*, 2005, `www.act.org`.

6. National Center for Education Statistics, *Debt Burden: A Comparison of 1992–93 and 1999–2000 Bachelor's Degree Recipients a Year After Graduating*, 2005, `nces.ed.gov`.

Chapter 4 Notes

1. From a graph in Bernt-Erik Saether, Steiner Engen, and Erik Mattysen, "Demographic characteristics and population dynamical patterns of solitary birds," *Science*, 295 (2002), pp. 2070–2073.

2. Chris Carbone and John L. Gittleman, "A common rule for the scaling of carnivore density," *Science*, 295 (2002), pp. 2273–2276.

3. Based on T. N. Lam, "Estimating fuel consumption from engine size," *Journal of Transportation Engineering*, 111 (1985), pp. 339–357. The data for 10 to 50 km/h are measured; those for 60 and higher are calculated from a model given in the paper and are therefore smoothed.

4. N. Maeno et al., "Growth rates of icicles," *Journal of Glaciology*, 40 (1994), pp. 319–326.

5. A careful study of this phenomenon is W. S. Cleveland, P. Diaconis, and R. McGill, "Variables on scatterplots look more highly correlated when the scales are increased," *Science*, 216 (1982), pp. 1138–1141.

6. From a graph in Timothy G. O'Brien and Margaret F. Kinnaird, "Caffeine and conservation," *Science*, 300 (2003), p. 587.

7. James T. Fleming, "The measurement of children's perception of difficulty in reading materials," *Research in the Teaching of English*, 1 (1967), pp. 136–156.

8. Data provided by Robert Dale, Purdue University.

9. Simplified from W. L. Colville and D. P. McGill, "Effect of rate and method of planting on several plant characters and yield of irrigated corn," *Agronomy Journal*, 54 (1962), pp. 235–238.

10. See Note 8.

11. Compiled from Fidelity data by the *Fidelity Insight* newsletter, 20 (2004), No. 1.

12. From a graph in Martin Wild et al., "From dimming to brightening: decadal changes in solar radiation at Earth's surface," *Science*, 308 (2005), pp. 847–850.

13. From a graph in Christer G. Wiklund, "Food as a mechanism of density-dependent regulation of breeding numbers in the merlin *Falco columbarius*," *Ecology*, 82 (2001), pp. 860–867.

14. From a graph in Naomi I. Eisenberger, Matthew D. Lieberman, and Kipling D. Williams, "Does rejection hurt? An fMRI study of social exclusion," *Science*, 302 (2003), pp. 290–292.

Chapter 5 Notes

1. From a graph in James A. Levine, Norman L. Eberhardt, and Michael D. Jensen, "Role of nonexercise activity thermogenesis in resistance to fat gain in humans," *Science*, 283 (1999), pp. 212–214.

2. See Note 1 for Chapter 4.

3. From a graph in Tania Singer et al., "Empathy for pain involves the affective but not sensory components of pain," *Science*, 303 (2004), pp. 1157–1162. Data for other brain regions showed a stronger correlation and no outliers.

4. Contributed by Marigene Arnold, Kalamazoo College.

5. Gannett News Service article appearing in the *Lafayette (Ind.) Journal and Courier*, April 23, 1994.

6. P. Goldblatt (ed.), *Longitudinal Study: Mortality and Social Organization*, Her Majesty's Stationery Office, 1990. At least, so claims Richard Conniff, *The Natural History of the Rich*, Norton, 2002, p. 45. The Goldblatt report is not available to me.

7. Laura L. Calderon et al., "Risk factors for obesity in Mexican-American girls: dietary factors, anthropometric factors, physical activity, and hours of television viewing," *Journal of the American Dietetic Association*, 96 (1996), pp. 1177–1179.

8. *The Health Consequences of Smoking: 1983*, Public Health Service, Washington, D.C., 1983.

9. G. L. Kooyman et al., "Diving behavior and energetics during foraging cycles in king penguins," *Ecological Monographs*, 62 (1992), pp. 143–163.

10. T. Constable and E. McBean, "BOD/TOC correlations and their application to water quality evaluation," *Water, Air, and Soil Pollution*, 11 (1979), pp. 363–375.

11. Karl Pearson and A. Lee, "On the laws of inheritance in man," *Biometrika*, 2 (1902), p. 357. These data also appear in D. J. Hand et al., *A Handbook of Small Data Sets*, Chapman & Hall, 1994. This book offers more than 500 data sets that can be used in statistical exercises.

12. From a presentation by Charles Knauf, Monroe County (New York) Environmental Health Laboratory.

13. Frank J. Anscombe, "Graphs in statistical analysis," *The American Statistician*, 27 (1973), pp. 17–21.

14. From a graph in Feng Sheng Hu et al., "Cyclic variation and solar forcing of Holocene climate in the Alaskan subarctic," *Science*, 301 (2003), pp. 1890–1893.

15. See Note 10 for Chapter 1.

16. From a graph in G. D. Martinsen, E. M. Driebe, and T. G. Whitham, "Indirect interactions mediated by changing plant chemistry: beaver browsing benefits beetles," *Ecology*, 79 (1998), pp. 192–200.

17. From a graph in Joaquim I. Goes et al., "Warming of the Eurasian landmass is making the Arabian Sea more productive," *Science*, 308 (2005), pp. 545–547.

18. P. Velleman, *ActivStats 2.0*, Addison Wesley Interactive, 1997.

19. Gary Smith, "Do statistics test scores regress toward the mean?" *Chance*, 10, No. 4 (1997), pp. 42–45.

Chapter 6 Notes

1. From the October 2003 Current Population Survey, www.census.gov.

2. H. Lindberg, H. Roos, and P. Gardsell, "Prevalence of coxarthritis in former soccer players," *Acta Orthopedica Scandinavica*, 64 (1993), pp. 165–167.

3. National Center for Health Statistics, *Deaths: Preliminary Data for 2003*, National Vital Statistics Reports, 53, No. 15, 2005.

4. Francine D. Blau and Marianne A. Ferber, "Career plans and expectations of young women and men," *Journal of Human Resources*, 26 (1991), pp. 581–607.

5. Siem Oppe and Frank De Charro, "The effect of medical care by a helicopter trauma team on the probability of survival and the quality of life of hospitalized victims," *Accident Analysis and Prevention*, 33 (2001), pp. 129–138. The authors give the data in Example 6.6 as a "theoretical example" to illustrate the need for their more elaborate analysis of actual data using severity scores for each victim.

6. These data, from reports submitted by airlines to the Department of Transportation, appear in A. Barnett, "How numbers can trick you," *Technology Review*, October 1994, pp. 38–45.

7. M. Radelet, "Racial characteristics and imposition of the death penalty," *American Sociological Review*, 46 (1981), pp. 918–927.

8. From the Web site of the Carolina Population Center, www.cpc.unc.edu.

9. Sanders Korenman and David Neumark, "Does marriage really make men more productive?" *Journal of Human Resources*, 26 (1991), pp. 282–307.

10. Lien-Ti Bei, "Consumers' purchase behavior toward recycled products: an acquisition-transaction utility theory perspective," MS thesis, Purdue University, 1993.

11. D. M. Barnes, "Breaking the cycle of addiction," *Science*, 241 (1988), pp. 1029–1030.

12. National Center for Education Statistics, *Digest of Education Statistics, 2003*, Table 249.

13. Janice E. Williams et al., "Anger proneness predicts coronary heart disease risk," *Circulation*, 101 (2000), pp. 2034–2039.

14. R. Shine, T. R. L. Madsen, M. J. Elphick, and P. S. Harlow, "The influence of nest temperatures and maternal brooding on hatchling phenotypes in water pythons," *Ecology*, 78 (1997), pp. 1713–1721.

15. See P. J. Bickel and J. W. O'Connell, "Is there a sex bias in graduate admissions?" *Science*, 187 (1975), pp. 398–404.

Chapter 7 Notes

1. National Center for Education Statistics, nces.ed.gov/das/library.

2. From www.edwardjayepstein.com.

3. J. T. Dwyer et al., "Memory of food intake in the distant past," *American Journal of Epidemiology*, 130 (1989), pp. 1033–1046.

4. Louie H. Yang, "Periodical cicadas as resource pulses in North American forests," *Science*, 306 (2004), pp. 1565–1567. The data are simulated Normal values that match the means and standard deviations reported in this article.

5. *Statistical Abstract of the United States, 2004–2005.*

6. Found online at BevNET, `www.bevnet.com`.

7. From a graph in Peter A. Raymond and Jonathan J. Cole, "Increase in the export of alkalinity from North America's largest river," *Science*, 301 (2003), pp. 88–91.

8. Alan S. Banks et al., "Juvenile hallux abducto valgus association with metatarsus adductus," *Journal of the American Podiatric Medical Association*, 84 (1994), pp. 219–224.

9. Mei-Hui Chen, "An exploratory comparison of American and Asian consumers' catalog patronage behavior," MS thesis, Purdue University, 1994.

10. Data compiled from a table of percents in "Americans view higher education as key to the American dream," press release by the National Center for Public Policy and Higher Education, `www.highereducation.org`, May 3, 2000.

11. Scott DeCarlo with Michael Schubach and Vladimir Naumovski, "A decade of new issues," *Forbes*, March 5, 2001, `www.forbes.com`.

12. "Dancing in step," *Economist*, March 22, 2001.

13. D. E. Powers and D. A. Rock, *Effects of Coaching on SAT I: Reasoning Test Scores*, Educational Testing Service Research Report 98-6, College Entrance Examination Board, 1998.

14. From a graph in Craig Packer et al., "Ecological change, group territoriality, and population dynamics in Serengeti lions," *Science*, 307 (2005), pp. 390–393.

15. Todd W. Anderson, "Predator responses, prey refuges, and density-dependent mortality of a marine fish," *Ecology*, 81 (2001), pp. 245–257.

16. From the Nenana Ice Classic Web page, `www.nenanaakiceclassic.com`. See Raphael Sagarin and Fiorenza Micheli, "Climate change in nontraditional data sets," *Science*, 294 (2001), p. 811, for a careful discussion.

17. James W. Grier, "Ban of DDT and subsequent recovery of reproduction in bald eagles," *Science*, 218 (1982), pp. 1232–1234.

18. From a plot in Jon J. Ramsey et al., "Energy expenditure, body composition, and glucose metabolism in lean and obese rhesus monkeys treated with ephedrine and caffeine," *American Journal of Clinical Nutrition*, 68 (1998), pp. 42–51.

19. Peter H. Chen, Neftali Herrera, and Darren Christiansen, "Relationships between gate velocity and casting features among aluminum round castings," no date. Provided by Darren Christiansen.

20. Data provided by Samuel Phillips, Purdue University.

Chapter 8 Notes

1. See Note 3 for "Statistical Thinking."

2. John C. Barefoot et al., "Alcoholic beverage preference, diet, and health habits in the UNC Alumni Heart Study," *American Journal of Clinical Nutrition*, 76 (2002), pp. 466–472.

3. J. E. Muscat et al., "Handheld cellular telephone use and risk of brain cancer," *Journal of the American Medical Association*, 284 (2000), pp. 3001–3007.

4. Jeffrey G. Johnson et al., "Television viewing and aggressive behavior during adolescence and adulthood," *Science*, 295 (2002), pp. 2468–2471. The authors use statistical adjustments to control for the effects of a number of lurking variables. The association between TV viewing and aggression remains significant. Statistical adjustment had been used in

the observational studies that supported hormone replacement (Example 8.1) as well, a warning not to place too much trust in these methods.

5. From the Web site of the Gallup Organization, www.gallup.com. Press releases remain on this site for only a limited time.

6. Robert C. Parker and Patrick A. Glass, "Preliminary results of double-sample forest inventory of pine and mixed stands with high- and low-density LiDAR," in Kristina F. Connoe (ed.), *Proceedings of the 12th Biennial Southern Silvicultural Research Conference*, U.S. Department of Agriculture, Forest Service, Southern Research Station, 2004. The researchers actually sampled every 10th plot. This is a systematic sample, Exercise 8.45.

7. The regulations that govern seat belt survey design can be found at www.nhtsa.dor.gov. Details on the Hawaii survey are in Karl Kim et al., *Results of the 2002 Highway Seat Belt Use Survey*, at www.state.hi.us/dot.

8. The nonresponse rate for the CPS comes from "Technical notes to household survey data published in *Employment and Earnings*," found on the Bureau of Labor Statistics Web site: stats.bls.gov/cpshome.htm. The GSS reports its response rate on its Web site: www.norc.org/projects/gensoc.asp. The Pew study is described in Gregory Flemming and Kimberly Parker, "Race and reluctant respondents: possible consequences of non-response for pre-election surveys," Pew Research Center for the People and the Press, 1997, found at www.people-press.org.

9. For more detail on the limits of memory in surveys, see N. M. Bradburn, L. J. Rips, and S. K. Shevell, "Answering autobiographical questions: the impact of memory and inference on surveys," *Science*, 236 (1987), pp. 157–161.

10. The responses on welfare are from a *New York Times*/CBS News Poll reported in the *New York Times*, July 5, 1992. Those for Scotland are from "All set for independence?" *Economist*, September 12, 1998. Many other examples appear in T. W. Smith, "That which we call welfare by any other name would smell sweeter," *Public Opinion Quarterly*, 51 (1987), pp. 75–83.

11. Giuliana Coccia, "An overview of non-response in Italian telephone surveys," *Proceedings of the 99th Session of the International Statistical Institute*, 1993, Book 3, pp. 271–272.

12. K. J. Mukamal et al., "Prior alcohol consumption and mortality following acute myocardial infarction," *Journal of the American Medical Association*, 285 (2001), pp. 1965–1970.

13. L. E. Moses and F. Mosteller, "Safety of anesthetics," in J. M. Tanur et al. (eds.), *Statistics: A Guide to the Unknown*, 3rd ed., Wadsworth, 1989, pp. 15–24.

14. From the Web site of the Gallup Organization, www.gallup.com.

15. Mario A. Parada et al., "The validity of self-reported seatbelt use: Hispanic and non-Hispanic drivers in El Paso," *Accident Analysis and Prevention*, 33 (2001), pp. 139–143.

16. Bryan E. Porter and Thomas D. Berry, "A nationwide survey of self-reported red light running: measuring prevalence, predictors, and perceived consequences," *Accident Analysis and Prevention*, 33 (2001), pp. 735–741.

17. Susan B. Sorenson, "Regulating firearms as a consumer product," *Science*, 286 (1999), pp. 1481–1482.

18. Information from Warren McIsaac and Vivek Goel, "Is access to physician services in Ontario equitable?" Institute for Clinical Evaluative Sciences in Ontario, October 18, 1993.

19. Adam Nagourney and Janet Elder, "New York Times CBS Poll: What Hispanics Believe," found at www.Hispanic.cc.

Chapter 9 Notes

1. Details of the Carolina Abecedarian Project, including references to published work, can be found online at www.fpg.unc.edu/~abc.

2. Based loosely on Arno J. Rethans, John L. Swasy, and Lawrence J. Marks, "Effects of television commercial repetition, receiver knowledge, and commercial length: a test of the two-factor model," *Journal of Marketing Research*, 23 (February 1986), pp. 50–61.

3. Paul R. Solomon et al., "Ginkgo for memory enhancement: a randomized controlled trial," *Journal of the American Medical Association*, 288 (2002), pp. 835–840.

4. Geetha Thiagarajan et al., "Antioxidant properties of green and black tea, and their potential ability to retard the progression of eye lens cataract," *Experimental Eye Research*, 73 (2001), pp. 393–401.

5. K. Wang, Y. Li, and J. Erickson, "A new look at the Monday effect," *Journal of Finance*, 52 (1997), pp. 2171–2186.

6. Carol A. Warfield, "Controlled-release morphine tablets in patients with chronic cancer pain," *Cancer*, 82 (1998), pp. 2299–2306.

7. David L. Strayer, Frank A. Drews, and William A. Johnston, "Cell phone-induced failures of visual attention during simulated driving," *Journal of Experimental Psychology: Applied*, 9 (2003), pp. 23–32.

8. Sterling C. Hilton et al., "A randomized controlled experiment to assess technological innovations in the classroom on student outcomes: an overview of a clinical trial in education," manuscript, no date.

9. John H. Kagel, Raymond C. Battalio, and C. G. Miles, "Marijuana and work performance: results from an experiment," *Journal of Human Resources*, 15 (1980), pp. 373–395.

10. Shailja V. Nigdikar et al., "Consumption of red wine polyphenols reduces the susceptibility of low-density lipoproteins to oxidation in vivo," *American Journal of Clinical Nutrition*, 68 (1998), pp. 258–265. (There were in fact only 30 subjects, some of whom received more than one treatment with a four-week period intervening.)

11. Based on Evan H. DeLucia et al., "Net primary production of a forest ecosystem with experimental CO_2 enhancement," *Science*, 284 (1999), pp. 1177–1179. The investigators used the block design.

12. E. M. Peters et al., "Vitamin C supplementation reduces the incidence of postrace symptoms of upper-respiratory tract infection in ultramarathon runners," *American Journal of Clinical Nutrition*, 57 (1993), pp. 170–174.

13. Based on Pierre J. Meunier et al., "The effects of strontium renelate on the risk of vertebral fracture in women with postmenopausal osteoporosis," *New England Journal of Medicine*, 350 (2004), pp. 459–468.

14. The study is described in Gina Kolata, "New study finds vitamins are not cancer preventers," *New York Times*, July 21, 1994. Look in the *Journal of the American Medical Association* of the same date for the details.

15. R. C. Shelton et al., "Effectiveness of St. John's wort in major depression," *Journal of the American Medical Association*, 285 (2001), pp. 1978–1986.

16. Rita F. Redburg, "Vitamin E and cardiovascular health," *Journal of the American Medical Association*, 294 (2005), pp. 107–109.

Data Ethics Notes

1. John C. Bailar III, "The real threats to the integrity of science," *The Chronicle of Higher Education*, April 21, 1995, pp. B1–B2.

2. See the details on the Web site of the Office for Human Research Protections of the Department of Health and Human Services, www.hhs.goc/ohrp.

3. The difficulties of interpreting guidelines for informed consent and for the work of institutional review boards in medical research are a main theme of Beverly Woodward, "Challenges to human subject protections in U.S. medical research," *Journal of the American Medical Association*, 282 (1999), pp. 1947–1952. The references in this paper point to other discussions. Updated regulations and guidelines appear on the OHRP Web site (see Note 2).

4. Quotation from the *Report of the Tuskegee Syphilis Study Legacy Committee*, May 20, 1996. A detailed history is James H. Jones, *Bad Blood: The Tuskegee Syphilis Experiment*, Free Press, 1993.

5. Dr. Hennekens's words are from an interview in the Annenberg/Corporation for Public Broadcasting video series *Against All Odds: Inside Statistics*.

6. R. D. Middlemist, E. S. Knowles, and C. F. Matter, "Personal space invasions in the lavatory: suggestive evidence for arousal," *Journal of Personality and Social Psychology*, 33 (1976), pp. 541–546.

7. For a review of domestic-violence experiments, see C. D. Maxwell et al., *The Effects of Arrest on Intimate Partner Violence: New Evidence from the Spouse Assault Replication Program*, U.S. Department of Justice, NCH188199, 2001. Available online at www.ojp.usdoj.gov/nij/pubs-sum/188199.htm.

Chapter 10 Notes

1. From the Web site of Statistics Canada, www.statcan.ca.

2. You can find a mathematical explanation of Benford's law in Ted Hill, "The first-digit phenomenon," *American Scientist*, 86 (1996), pp. 358–363; and Ted Hill, "The difficulty of faking data," *Chance*, 12, No. 3 (1999), pp. 27–31. Applications in fraud detection are discussed in the second paper by Hill and in Mark A. Nigrini, "I've got your number," *Journal of Accountancy*, May 1999, available online at www.aicpa.org/pubs/jofa/joaiss.htm.

3. Based on interviews in 2000 and 2001 by the National Longitudinal Study of Adolescent Health. Found at the Web site of the Carolina Population Center, www.cpc.unc.edu.

4. Information from www.ncsu.edu/class/grades.

5. See Note 3 for Chapter 1.

6. From the M&M Web site: www.mms.com.

Chapter 11 Notes

1. U. S. Census Bureau, *Income, Poverty, and Health Insurance Coverage in the United States: 2004*, Current Population Reports P60-229, 2005. The median income is of course lower, $44,389.

2. Strictly speaking, the formula $\sigma/\sqrt{n}$ for the standard deviation of $\overline{x}$ assumes that we draw an SRS of size n from an *infinite* population. If the population has finite size N, this standard deviation is multiplied by $\sqrt{1-(n-1)/(N-1)}$. This "finite population correction"

approaches 1 as N increases. When the population is at least 20 times as large as the sample, the correction factor is between about 0.97 and 1. It is reasonable to use the simpler form $\sigma/\sqrt{n}$ in these settings.

3. Sherri A. Buzinski, "The effect of position of methylation on the performance properties of durable press treated fabrics," CSR490 honors paper, Purdue University, 1985.

4. Elroy Dimson, Paul Marsh, and Mike Staunton, *Triumph of the Optimists: 101 Years of Global Investment Returns,* Princeton University Press, 2002. Sophisticates will note that for compounding over several years we want the geometric mean return, which was 6.7%.

Chapter 12 Notes

1. This is one of several tests discussed in Bernard M. Branson, "Rapid HIV testing: 2005 update," a presentation by the Centers for Disease Control and Prevention, at www.cdc.gov. The Malawi clinic result is reported by Bernard M. Branson, "Point-of-care rapid tests for HIV antibody," *Journal of Laboratory Medicine,* 27 (2003), pp. 288–295.

2. Robert P. Dellavalle et al., "Going, going, gone: lost Internet references," *Science,* 302 (2003), pp. 787–788.

3. From the Web site of the Entertainment Software Association, www.theesa.com.

4. Information about Internet users comes from sample surveys carried out by the Pew Internet and American Life Project, www.pewinternet.org.

5. Probabilities from trials with 2897 people known to be free of HIV antibodies and 673 people known to be infected, reported in J. Richard George, "Alternative specimen sources: methods for confirming positives," 1998 Conference on the Laboratory Science of HIV, found online at the Centers for Disease Control and Prevention, www.cdc.gov.

6. Corey Kilgannon, "When New York is on the end of the line," *New York Times,* November 7, 1999.

7. Projections from the 2002 *Digest of Education Statistics,* at nces.ed.gov.

8. The probabilities given are realistic, according to the fundraising firm SCM Associates, scmassoc.com.

Chapter 13 Notes

1. From a Gallup Poll taken in 2002, www.gallup.com.

2. The survey question is reported in Trish Hall, "Shop? Many say 'Only if I must,'" *New York Times,* November 28, 1990. In fact, 66% (1650 of 2500) in the sample said "Agree."

3. John Schwartz, "Leisure pursuits of today's young men," *New York Times,* March 29, 2004. The source cited is comScore Media Matrix.

Chapter 14 Notes

1. Francisco L. Rivera-Batiz, "Quantitative literacy and the likelihood of employment among young adults," *Journal of Human Resources,* 27 (1992), pp. 313–328.

2. This and similar results of Gallup polls are from the Gallup Organization Web site, www.gallup.com.

3. Data provided by Drina Iglesia, Purdue University. The data are part of a larger study reported in D. D. S. Iglesia, E. J. Cragoe, Jr., and J. W. Vanable, "Electric field strength and epithelization in the newt (*Notophthalmus viridescens*)," *Journal of Experimental Zoology,* 274 (1996), pp. 56–62.

4. See Note 4 for Chapter 3.

5. The values $\mu = 22$ and $\sigma = 50$ for the gains of uncoached students on the SAT mathematics exam come from a study of 2733 students reported on the College Board Web site, `www.collegeboard.org`.

6. Ajay Ghei, "An empirical analysis of psychological androgeny in the personality profile of the successful hotel manager," MS thesis, Purdue University, 1992.

7. See Note 13 for Chapter 2.

Chapter 15 Notes

1. Data simulated from a Normal distribution with the mean and standard deviation reported by Sarah Morrison and Jan Noyes, "A comparison of two computer fonts: serif versus ornate sans serif," *Usability News*, 5.2, 2003, `psychology.wichita.edu/surl/usability_news.html`.

2. See Note 6 for Chapter 14.

3. See Note 15 for Chapter 8.

4. Based on Raul de la Fuente-Fernández et al., "Expectation and dopamine release: mechanism of the placebo effect in Parkinson's disease," *Science*, 293 (2001), pp. 1164–1166.

5. Seung-Ok Kim, "Burials, pigs, and political prestige in Neolithic China," *Current Anthropology*, 35 (1994), pp. 119–141.

6. See Note 4 for Chapter 7.

7. Sara L. Webb and Sara E. Scanga, "Windstorm disturbance without patch dynamics: twelve years of change in a Minnesota forest," *Ecology*, 82 (2001), pp. 893–897.

8. Arthur Schatzkin et al., "Lack of effect of a low-fat, high-fiber diet on the recurrence of colorectal adenomas," *New England Journal of Medicine*, 342 (2000), pp. 1149–1155.

Chapter 16 Notes

1. E. M. Barsamian, "The rise and fall of internal mammary artery ligation," in J. P. Bunker, B. A. Barnes, and F. Mosteller (eds.), *Costs, Risks, and Benefits of Surgery*, Oxford University Press, 1977, pp. 212–220.

2. See Note 16 for Chapter 8.

3. For a discussion of statistical significance in the legal setting, see D. H. Kaye, "Is proof of statistical significance relevant?" *Washington Law Review*, 61 (1986), pp. 1333–1365. Kaye argues: "Presenting the P-value without characterizing the evidence by a significance test is a step in the right direction. Interval estimation, in turn, is an improvement over P-values."

4. Warren E. Leary, "Cell phones: questions but no answers," *New York Times*, October 26, 1999.

5. Helen Chmura Kraemer and Sue Thiemann, *How Many Subjects? Statistical Power Analysis in Research*, Sage Publications, 1987.

6. Gabriel Gregoratos et al., "ACC/AHA guidelines for implantation of cardiac pacemakers and antiarrhythmia devices: executive summary," *Circulation*, 97 (1998), pp. 1325–1335.

7. P. H. Lewis, "Technology" column, *New York Times*, May 29, 1995.

8. Tim M. Blackburn et al., "Avian extinction and mammalian introductions on oceanic islands," *Science*, 305 (2004), pp. 1955–1958.

9. Robert J. Schiller, "The volatility of stock market prices," *Science*, 235 (1987), pp. 33–36.

Chapter 17 Notes

1. Based on a news item "Bee off with you," *Economist*, November 2, 2002, p. 78.

2. Pamela J. Goodwin et al., "The effect of group psychological support on survival in metastatic breast cancer," *New England Journal of Medicine*, 345 (2001), pp. 1719–1726.

3. See Note 24 for Chapter 1.

4. K. E. Hobbs et al., "Levels and patterns of persistent organochlorines in minke whale (*Balaenoptera acutorostrata*) stocks from the North Atlantic and European Arctic," *Environmental Pollution*, 121 (2003), pp. 239–252.

5. Maureen Hack et al., "Outcomes in young adulthood for very-low-birth-weight infants," *New England Journal of Medicine*, 346 (2002), pp. 149–157.

6. See Note 17 for Chapter 1.

7. Data simulated from a Normal distribution with $\mu = 98.2$ and $\sigma = 0.7$. These values are based on P. A. Mackowiak, S. S. Wasserman, and M. M. Levine, "A critical appraisal of 98.6 degrees F, the upper limit of the normal body temperature, and other legacies of Carl Reinhold August Wunderlich," *Journal of the American Medical Association*, 268 (1992), pp. 1578–1580.

8. Based on Stephen A. Woodbury and Robert G. Spiegelman, "Bonuses to workers and employers to reduce unemployment: randomized trials in Illinois," *American Economic Review*, 77 (1987), pp. 513–530.

9. Joel Brockner et al., "Layoffs, equity theory, and work performance: further evidence of the impact of survivor guilt," *Academy of Management Journal*, 29 (1986), pp. 373–384.

10. Mikyoung Park et al., "Recycling endosomes supply AMPA receptors for LTP," *Science*, 305 (2004), pp. 1972–1975.

11. Jon E. Keeley, C. J. Fotheringham, and Marco Morais, "Reexamining fire suppression impacts on brushland fire regimes," *Science*, 284 (1999), pp. 1829–1831.

12. Based on a discussion of several polls by David W. Moore on the Gallup Organization Web site, www.gallup.org.

13. Simplified from Sanjay K. Dhar, Claudia González-Vallejo, and Dilip Soman, "Modeling the effects of advertised price claims: tensile versus precise pricing," *Marketing Science*, 18 (1999), pp. 154–177.

14. Charles S. Fuchs et al., "Alcohol consumption and mortality among women," *New England Journal of Medicine*, 332 (1995), pp. 1245–1250.

15. J. F. Swain et al., "Comparison of the effects of oat bran and low-fiber wheat on serum lipoprotein levels and blood pressure," *New England Journal of Medicine*, 322 (1990), pp. 147–152.

16. From the Internal Revenue Service at www.irs.gov/taxstats.

17. Alan Schwarz, "In a game of statistics, some numbers have little meaning," *New York Times*, April 3, 2005.

18. Research by Louis Chan et al., reported by Robert Schiller, *Irrational Exuberance*, Broadway Books, 2001, p. 253.

19. See Note 4 for Chapter 12.

20. Based on a study reported by Alan B. Krueger, "Economic scene" column, *New York Times*, November 14, 2002.

Chapter 18 Notes

1. Note 2 for Chapter 11 explains the reason for this condition in the case of inference about a population mean.

2. Ivette S. Colon, "Effects of cellulose, oat bran, rice bran, and psyllium on serum and liver cholesterol and fecal steroid excretion in rats," MS thesis, Purdue University, 1992.

3. See Note 3 for Chapter 14.

4. From the National Institute of Standards and Technology Web site, `www.nist.gov/srd/online/htm`.

5. R. A. Berner and G. P. Landis, "Gas bubbles in fossil amber as possible indicators of the major gas composition of ancient air," *Science*, 239 (1988), pp. 1406–1409. The 95% t confidence interval is 54.78 to 64.40. A bootstrap BCa interval is 55.03 to 62.63. So t is reasonably accurate despite the skew and the small sample.

6. See Note 3 for Chapter 14.

7. For a qualitative discussion explaining why skewness is the most serious violation of the Normal shape condition, see Dennis D. Boos and Jacqueline M. Hughes-Oliver, "How large does n have to be for the Z and t intervals?" *American Statistician*, 54 (2000), pp. 121–128. Our recommendations are based on extensive computer work. See, for example, Harry O. Posten, "The robustness of the one-sample t-test over the Pearson system," *Journal of Statistical Computation and Simulation*, 9 (1979), pp. 133–149; and E. S. Pearson and N. W. Please, "Relation between the shape of population distribution and the robustness of four simple test statistics," *Biometrika*, 62 (1975), pp. 223–241.

8. For more advanced users, a good way to ascertain if the t procedures are safe is to compare the 95% confidence interval produced by t with the BCa interval from a bootstrap with at least 1000 resamples. For (b) the t interval is 29,428 to 32,254 and a BCa interval is 29,106 to 31,894. For (c), on the other hand, t gives 38.93 to 40.49 and BCa gives 38.97 to 40.44. These results confirm the judgment that t is safe for (c) but not for (b).

9. TUDA results for 2003 from the National Center for Education Statistics, `nces.ed.gov/nationsreportcard`.

10. From the online supplement to Tor D. Wager et al., "Placebo-induced changes in fMRI in the anticipation and experience of pain," *Science*, 303 (2004), pp. 1162–1167.

11. Data from the "wine" data base in the archive of machine learning data bases at the University of California, Irvine, `ftp.ics.uci.edu/pub/machine-learning-databases`.

12. Data provided by Chris Olsen, who found the information in scuba-diving magazines.

13. Orit E. Hetzroni, "The effects of active versus passive computer-assisted instruction on the acquisition, retention, and generalization of Blissymbols while using elements for teaching compounds," PhD thesis, Purdue University, 1995.

14. Tim Barmby and Suzyrman Sibly, "A Markov model of worker absenteeism," manuscript, November 1998.

15. See Note 8 for Chapter 7.

16. This example is based on information in D. L. Shankland et al., "The effect of 5-thio-D-glucose on insect development and its absorption by insects," *Journal of Insect Physiology*, 14 (1968), pp. 63–72.

17. Data provided by Jason Hamilton, University of Illinois. The study is reported in Evan H. DeLucia et al., "Net primary production of a forest ecosystem with experimental CO_2 enhancement," *Science*, 284 (1999), pp. 1177–1179. No method for inference can be trusted with $n = 3$. In this study, each observation is very costly, so the small n is inevitable.

18. Michael W. Peugh, "Field Investigation of ventilation and air quality in duck and turkey slaughter plants," MS thesis, Purdue University, 1996.

19. See Note 4 for Chapter 15.

20. J. Marcus Jobe and Hutch Jobe, "A statistical approach for additional infill development," *Energy Exploration and Exploitation*, 18 (2000), pp. 89–103. The comparison interval is the BCa interval based on 1000 bootstrap resamples.

21. Harry B. Meyers, "Investigations of the life history of the velvetleaf seed beetle, *Althaeus folkertsi* Kingsolver," MS thesis, Purdue University, 1996. The 95% t interval is 1227.9 to 2507.6. A 95% bootstrap BCa interval is 1444 to 2718, confirming that t inference is inaccurate for these data.

22. Data provided by Timothy Sturm.

23. Lianng Yuh, "A biopharmaceutical example for undergraduate students," manuscript, no date.

Chapter 19 Notes

1. Sapna Aneja, "Biodeterioration of textile fibers in soil," MS thesis, Purdue University, 1994.

2. Detailed information about the conservative t procedures can be found in Paul Leaverton and John J. Birch, "Small sample power curves for the two sample location problem," *Technometrics*, 11 (1969), pp. 299–307; in Henry Scheffé, "Practical solutions of the Behrens-Fisher problem," *Journal of the American Statistical Association*, 65 (1970), pp. 1501–1508; and in D. J. Best and J. C. W. Rayner, "Welch's approximate solution for the Behrens-Fisher problem," *Technometrics*, 29 (1987), pp. 205–210.

3. Eric Sanford et al., "Local selection and latitudinal variation in a marine predator-prey interaction," *Science*, 300 (2003), pp. 1135–1137.

4. David Hon-Kuen Chu, "A test of corporate advertising using the elaboration likelihood model," MS thesis, Purdue University, 1993.

5. Kathleen G. McKinney, "Engagement in community service among college students: is it affected by significant attachment relationships?" *Journal of Adolescence*, 25 (2002), pp. 139–154.

6. See Note 14 for Chapter 2.

7. See Note 7 for Chapter 2.

8. See the extensive simulation studies in Harry O. Posten, "The robustness of the two-sample t-test over the Pearson system," *Journal of Statistical Computation and Simulation*, 6 (1978),

pp. 295–311; and in Harry O. Posten, H. Yeh, and Donald B. Owen, "Robustness of the two-sample t-test under violations of the homogeneity assumption," *Communications in Statistics*, 11 (1982), pp. 109–126.

9. D. L. Shankland, "Involvement of spinal cord and peripheral nerves in DDT-poisoning syndrome in albino rats," *Toxicology and Applied Pharmacology*, 6 (1964), pp. 197–213.

10. See Note 4 for Chapter 3.

11. The problem of comparing spreads is difficult even with advanced methods. Common distribution-free procedures do not offer a satisfactory alternative to the F test, because they are sensitive to unequal shapes when comparing two distributions. A recent survey of possible approaches is Dennis D. Boos and Cavell Brownie, "Comparing variances and other measures of dispersion," *Statistical Science*, 19 (2005), pp. 571–578. See also Lewis H. Shoemaker, "Fixing the F test for equal variances," *American Statistician*, 57 (2003), pp. 105–114, for adjustments to F that improve its robustness. The adjustments involve data-dependent degrees of freedom, similar in spirit to the Option 1 two-sample t procedures described in this chapter.

12. See Note 13 for Chapter 18.

13. See Note 4 for Chapter 3.

14. See Note 18 for Chapter 18.

15. From a graph in Fabrizio Grieco, Arie J. van Noordwijk, and Marcel E. Visser, "Evidence for the effect of learning on timing of reproduction in blue tits," *Science*, 296 (2002), pp. 136–138.

16. Debra L. Miller et al., "Effect of fat-free potato chips with and without nutrition labels on fat and energy intakes," *American Journal of Clinical Nutrition*, 68 (1998), pp. 282–290.

17. Gabriela S. Castellani, "The effect of cultural values on Hispanics' expectations about service quality," MS thesis, Purdue University, 2000.

18. John R. Cronin and Sandra Pizzarello, "Enantiometric excesses in meteoritic amino acids," *Science*, 275 (1997), pp. 951–955.

19. Wayne J. Camera and Donald Powers, "Coaching and the SAT I," *TIP* (online journal: www.siop.org/tip), July 1999.

20. Data provided by Warren Page, New York City Technical College, from a study done by John Hudesman.

21. See Note 6 for Chapter 2.

22. See Note 3 for Chapter 11.

23. Data provided by Marigene Arnold of Kalamazoo College.

Chapter 20 Notes

1. Joseph H. Catania et al., "Prevalence of AIDS-related risk factors and condom use in the United States," *Science*, 258 (1992), pp. 1101–1106.

2. Strictly speaking, the formula $\sqrt{p(1-p)/n}$ for the standard deviation of $\hat{p}$ assumes that we draw an SRS of size n from an *infinite* population. If the population has finite size N, this standard deviation is multiplied by $\sqrt{1-(n-1)/(N-1)}$. This "finite population correction" approaches 1 as N increases. When the population is at least 20 times as large as the sample, the correction factor is between about 0.97 and 1. It is reasonable to use the simpler form $\sqrt{p(1-p)/n}$ in these settings. See also Note 2 for Chapter 11.

3. This rule of thumb is based on study of computational results in the papers cited in Note 6 and discussion with Alan Agresti. We strongly recommend using the plus four interval.

4. The quotation is from page 1104 of the article cited in Note 1.

5. See Note 19 for Chapter 19.

6. This interval is proposed by Alan Agresti and Brent A. Coull, "Approximate is better than 'exact' for interval estimation of binomial proportions," *The American Statistician*, 52 (1998), pp. 119–126. There are several even more accurate but considerably more complex intervals for p that might be used in professional practice. See Lawrence D. Brown, Tony Cai, and Anirban DasGupta, "Interval estimation for a binomial proportion," *Statistical Science*, 16 (2001), pp. 101–133. A detailed theoretical study that uncovers the reason the large-sample interval is inaccurate is Lawrence D. Brown, Tony Cai, and Anirban DasGupta, "Confidence intervals for a binomial proportion and asymptotic expansions," *Annals of Statistics*, 30 (2002), pp. 160–201.

7. Dean Fergusson et al., "Turning a blind eye: the success of blinding reported in a random sample of randomised, placebo-controlled trials," *British Medical Journal*, 328 (2004), pp. 432–436.

8. From Alan Agresti and Brian Caffo, "Simple and effective confidence intervals for proportions and differences of proportions result from adding two successes and two failures," *The American Statistician*, 45 (2000), pp. 280–288. When can the plus four interval be safely used? The answer depends on just how much accuracy you insist on. Brown and coauthors (see Note 6) recommend $n \geq 40$. Agresti and Coull demonstrate that performance is almost always satisfactory in their eyes when $n \geq 5$. Our rule of thumb $n \geq 10$ allows for confidence levels C other than 95% and fits our philosophy of not insisting on more exact results than practice requires. The big point is that plus four is very much more accurate than the standard interval for most values of p and all but very large n.

9. James Otto, Michael F. Brown, and William Long III, "Training rats to search and alert on contraband odors," *Applied Animal Behaviour Science*, 77 (2002), pp. 217–232.

10. See Note 3 for Chapter 19.

11. Gary Edwards and Josephine Mazzuca, "Three quarters of Canadians support doctor-assisted suicide," Gallup Poll press release, March 24, 1999, at www.gallup.com.

12. In fact, P-values for two-sided tests are more accurate than those for one-sided tests. Our rule of thumb is a compromise to avoid the confusion of too many rules.

13. Matthew A. Carlton and William D. Stansfield, "Making babies by the flip of a coin?" *American Statistician*, 59 (2005), pp. 180–182.

14. Alexander Todorov et al., "Inferences of competence from faces predict election outcomes," *Science*, 308 (2005), pp. 1623–1626.

15. Michele L. Head, "Examining college students' ethical values," Consumer Science and Retailing honors project, Purdue University, 2003.

16. John Paul McKinney and Kathleen G. McKinney, "Prayer in the lives of late adolescents," *Journal of Adolescence*, 22 (1999), pp. 279–290.

17. See Note 1 for Chapter 15.

18. JoAnn K. Wells, Allan F. Williams, and Charles M. Farmer, "Seat belt use among African Americans, Hispanics, and whites," *Accident Analysis and Prevention*, 34 (2002), pp. 523–529.

19. See Note 16 for Chapter 8.

20. John Fagan et al., "Performance assessment under field conditions of a rapid immunological test for transgenic soybeans," *International Journal of Food Science and Technology*, 36 (2001), pp. 357–367.

21. Arne L. Kalleberg and Kevin T. Leicht, "Gender and organizational performance: determinants of small business survival and success," *The Academy of Management Journal*, 34 (1991), pp. 136–161.

22. Henry Wechsler et al., *Binge Drinking on America's College Campuses*, Harvard School of Public Health, 2001.

23. Sara Schroter, Helen Barratt, and Jane Smith, "Author's perceptions of electronic publishing: two cross sectional surveys," *British Medical Journal*, 328 (2004), pp. 1350–1353.

Chapter 21 Notes

1. The National Longitudinal Study of Adolescent Health interviewed a stratified random sample of 27,000 adolescents, then reinterviewed many of the subjects six years later, when most were aged 19 to 25. These data are from the Wave III reinterviews in 2000 and 2001, found at the Web site of the Carolina Population Center, www.cpc.unc.edu.

2. See Note 4 for Chapter 12.

3. Douglas E. Jorenby et al., "A controlled trial of sustained-release bupropion, a nicotine patch, or both for smoking cessation," *New England Journal of Medicine*, 340 (1999), pp. 685–691.

4. The plus four method is due to Alan Agresti and Brian Caffo. See Note 8 for Chapter 20.

5. Francisco Lloret et al., "Fire and resprouting in Mediterranean ecosystems: insights from an external biogeographical region, the Mexican shrubland," *American Journal of Botany*, 88 (1999), pp. 1655–1661.

6. Saiyad S. Ahmed, "Effects of microwave drying on checking and mechanical strength of low-moisture baked products," MS thesis, Purdue University, 1994.

7. Modified from Richard A. Schieber et al., "Risk factors for injuries from in-line skating and the effectiveness of safety gear," *New England Journal of Medicine*, 335 (1996), Internet summary at content.nejm.org.

8. Louie E. Ross, "Mate selection preferences among African American college students," *Journal of Black Studies*, 27 (1997), pp. 554–569.

9. Data courtesy of Raymond Dumett, Purdue University.

10. François Gaudet et al., "Induction of tumors in mice by genomic hypomethylation," *Science*, 300 (2003), pp. 489–492.

11. From an Associated Press dispatch appearing on December 30, 2002. The study report appeared in the *Journal of Adolescent Health*.

12. Based on Alan G. Sanfey et al., "The neural basis of economic decision-making in the ultimatum game," *Science*, 300 (2003), pp. 1755–1758. The paper reports a chi-square test (equivalent to a two-sided z test). This analysis is incorrect for the paper's data, as there were in fact only 19 participants, each appearing twice in each row of the table given in the exercise. Exercise 21.17 therefore amends the data, assuming 76 participants, so that the elementary analysis is correct.

13. Douglas G. Altman, Steven N. Goodman, and Sara Schroter, "How statistical expertise is used in medical research," *Journal of the American Medical Association*, 287 (2002), pp. 2817–2820.

14. National Athletic Trainers Association, press release dated September 30, 1994.

15. See Note 10 for Chapter 7.

16. See Note 18 for Chapter 20.

17. Clive G. Jones, Richard S. Ostfeld, Michele P. Richard, Eric M. Schauber, and Jerry O. Wolf, "Chain reactions linking acorns to gypsy moth outbreaks and Lyme disease risk," *Science*, 279 (1998), pp. 1023–1026.

18. Richard M. Felder et al., "Who gets it and who doesn't: a study of student performance in an introductory chemical engineering course," *1992 ASEE Annual Conference Proceedings*, American Society for Engineering Education, Washington, D.C., 1992, pp. 1516–1519.

19. The study is reported in William Celis III, "Study suggests Head Start helps beyond school," *New York Times*, April 20, 1993. See www.highscope.org.

20. Karen M. Herbert, "Does impulse buying vary by mode of payment?" MS thesis, Purdue University, 1994.

Chapter 22 Notes

1. See Note 16 for Chapter 19.

2. Esther Duflo et al., "Savings incentives for low- and middle-income families: evidence from a field experiment with H&R Block," The Retirement Security Project, published online at www.retirementsecurityproject.org.

3. Marianne Perle, Rebecca Moran, and Anthony D. Lutkus, *NAEP 2004 Trends in Academic Progress: Three Decades of Student Performance in Reading and Mathematics*, National Center for Education Statistics, 2005, at nces.ed.gov. The data given are approximate due to rounding in the study report.

4. Michael R. Dohm, Jack P. Hayes, and Theodore Garland, Jr., "Quantitative genetics of sprint running speed and swimming endurance in laboratory house mice (*Mus domesticus*)," *Evolution*, 50 (1996), pp. 1688–1701.

5. Tom W. Smith, *2001 National Gun Policy Survey of the National Opinion Research Center: Research Findings*, National Opinion Research Center, 2001.

6. From the online supplement to G. Gaskell et al., "Worlds apart? The reception of genetically modified foods in Europe and the U.S.," *Science*, 285 (1999), pp. 383–387.

7. K. S. Oberhauser, "Fecundity, lifespan and egg mass in butterflies: effects of male-derived nutrients and female size," *Functional Ecology*, 11 (1997), pp. 166–175.

8. See Note 5 for Chapter 17. The exercises are simplified, in that the measures reported in this paper have been statistically adjusted for "sociodemographic status."

9. Based on the online supplement to Paul J. Shaw et al., "Correlates of sleep and waking in *Drosophila melanogaster*," *Science*, 287 (2000), pp. 1834–1837.

10. From V. D. Bass, W. E. Hoffmann, and J. L. Dorner, "Normal canine lipid profiles and effects of experimentally induced pancreatitis and hepatic necrosis on lipids," *American Journal of Veterinary Research*, 37 (1976), pp. 1355–1357.

11. These data were originally collected by L. M. Linde of UCLA but were first published by M. R. Mickey, O. J. Dunn, and V. Clark, "Note on the use of stepwise regression in detecting outliers," *Computers and Biomedical Research*, 1 (1967), pp. 105–111. The data have been used by several authors. I found them in N. R. Draper and J. A. John, "Influential observations and outliers in regression," *Technometrics*, 23 (1981), pp. 21–26.

12. Data provided by Charles Hicks, Purdue University.

13. Yvan R. Germain, "The dyeing of ramie with fiber reactive dyes using the cold pad-batch method," MS thesis, Purdue University, 1988.

14. Data provided by Marigene Arnold, Kalamazoo College.

15. Data provided by Corinne Lim, Purdue University, from a student project supervised by Professor Joseph Vanable.

16. See Note 6 for Chapter 21.

17. Michael O. Finkelstein and Bruce Levin, "Statistical proof of discrimination in peremptory challenges," *Chance*, 17, No. 1 (2004), pp. 35–38.

18. G. S. Hotamisligil, R. S. Johnson, R. J. Distel, R. Ellis, V. E. Papaioannou, and B. M. Spiegelman, "Uncoupling of obesity from insulin resistance through a targeted mutation in *aP2*, the adipocyte fatty acid binding protein," *Science*, 274 (1996), pp. 1377–1379.

Chapter 23 Notes

1. Daniel B. Mark et al., "Use of medical resources and quality of life after acute myocardial infarction in Canada and the United States," *New England Journal of Medicine*, 331 (1994), pp. 1130–1135. See also the discussion in the same journal, 332 (1995), pp. 469–472.

2. Karine Marangon et al., "Diet, antioxidant status, and smoking habits in French men," *American Journal of Clinical Nutrition*, 67 (1998), pp. 231–239.

3. See Note 10 for Chapter 6.

4. Data from www.pewinternet.org. The counts are not exact because the report gave only percents rounded to the nearest whole percent.

5. There are many computer studies of the accuracy of chi-square critical values for X^2. Our guideline goes back to W. G. Cochran (1954). Later work has shown that it is often conservative in the sense that if the expected cell counts are all similar and the degrees of freedom exceed 1, the chi-square approximation works well for an average expected count as small as 1 or 2. Our guideline protects against dissimilar expected counts. It has the added advantage that it is safe in the 2×2 case, where the chi-square approximation is least good. So our guideline is helpful for beginners—there is no single condition that is not conservative and applies to 2×2 and larger tables with similar and dissimilar expected cell counts. There are exact procedures that (with software) should be used for tables that do not satisfy our guideline. For a survey, see Alan Agresti, "A survey of exact inference for contingency tables," *Statistical Science*, 7 (1992), pp. 131–177.

6. See Note 18 for Chapter 21.

7. See Note 4 for Chapter 6.

8. Lillian Lin Miao, "Gastric freezing: an example of the evaluation of medical therapy by randomized clinical trials," in John P. Bunker, Benjamin A. Barnes, and Frederick Mosteller (eds.), *Costs, Risks, and Benefits of Surgery*, Oxford University Press, 1977, pp. 198–211.

9. Based on a news item in *Science*, 305 (2004), p. 1560. The study, by Daniel Klem, appeared in the *Wilson Journal*.

10. From the GSS data base at the University of Michigan, webapp.icpsr.umich.edu/GSS.

11. Public use data available on the Web site of the Carolina Population Center, www.cpc.unc.edu.

12. David M. Blau, "The child care labor market," *Journal of Human Resources*, 27 (1992), pp. 9–39.

13. From the GSS data archive at the Survey Documentation and Analysis site at the University of California, Berkeley, `sda.berkeley.edu`.

14. Modified from Felicity Barringer, "Measuring sexuality through polls can be shaky," *New York Times*, April 25, 1993.

15. See Note 18 for Chapter 20.

16. Virgilio P. Carnielli et al., "Intestinal absorption of long-chain polyunsaturated fatty acids in preterm infants fed breast milk or formula," *American Journal of Clinical Nutrition*, 67 (1998), pp. 97–103.

17. See Note 13.

18. Adapted from M. A. Visintainer, J. R. Volpicelli, and M. E. P. Seligman, "Tumor rejection in rats after inescapable or escapable shock," *Science*, 216 (1982), pp. 437–439.

19. See Note 17 for Chapter 8.

20. See Note 1 for Chapter 21.

21. See Note 9 for Chapter 7.

22. See Note 1 for Chapter 21.

23. See Note 10 for Chapter 7.

24. Claudia Braga et al., "Olive oil, other seasoning fats, and the risk of colorectal carcinoma," *Cancer*, 82 (1998), pp. 448–453.

25. Data produced by Ries and Smith, found in William D. Johnson and Gary G. Koch, "A note on the weighted least squares analysis of the Ries-Smith contingency table data," *Technometrics*, 13 (1971), pp. 438–447.

26. See Note 13.

Chapter 24 Notes

1. Samuel Karelitz et al., "Relation of crying activity in early infancy to speech and intellectual development at age three years," *Child Development*, 35 (1964), pp. 769–777.

2. See Note 6 for Chapter 4.

3. See Note 4 for Chapter 4.

4. From a graph in Bruce J. Peterson et al., "Increasing river discharge to the Arctic Ocean," *Science*, 298 (2002), pp. 2171–2173.

5. From a graph in Allison L. Perry et al., "Climate change and distribution shifts in marine fishes," *Science*, 308 (2005), pp. 1912–1915. The explanatory variable is the five-year running mean of winter (December to March) sea-bottom temperature.

6. Data for the building at 1800 Ben Franklin Drive, Sarasota, Florida, starting in March 2003. From the Web site of the Sarasota County Property Appraiser, `www.sarasotaproperty.net`.

7. Carly J. Stevens et al., "Impact of nitrogen deposition on the species richness of grasslands," *Science*, 303 (2004), pp. 1876–1879.

8. See Note 16 for Chapter 5.

9. From Table S2 in the online supplement to Antonio Dell'Anno and Roberto Danovaro, "Extracellular DNA plays a key role in deep-sea ecosystem functioning," *Science*, 309 (2005), p. 2179.

10. See Note 1 for Chapter 4.

11. See Note 8 for Chapter 7.

12. Based on Marion E. Dunshee, "A study of factors affecting the amount and kind of food eaten by nursery school children," *Child Development*, 2 (1931), pp. 163–183. This article gives the means, standard deviations, and correlation for 37 children, from which the data in Exercise 24.41 are simulated.

13. See Note 20 for Chapter 7.

14. From a plot in Dominique de Quervain et al., "The neural basis of altruistic punishment," *Science*, 305 (2004), pp. 1254–1258. I have simplified the description of the study shamelessly, though it still sounds a bit complicated.

Chapter 25 Notes

1. See Note 6 for Chapter 2.

2. See Note 9 for Chapter 22.

3. Elisabeth Wells-Parker et al., "An exploratory study of the relationship between road rage and crash experience in a representative sample of US drivers," *Accident Analysis and Prevention*, 34 (2002), pp. 271–278.

4. See Note 7 for Chapter 2.

5. Modified from M. C. Wilson and R. E. Shade, "Relative attractiveness of various luminescent colors to the cereal leaf beetle and the meadow spittlebug," *Journal of Economic Entomology*, 60 (1967), pp. 578–580.

6. See Note 14 for Chapter 2.

7. David B. Wooten, "One-of-a-kind in a full house: some consequences of ethnic and gender distinctiveness," *Journal of Consumer Psychology*, 4 (1995), 205–224.

8. John M. Jakicic et al., "Effects of intermittent exercise and use of home exercise equipment on adherence, weight loss, and fitness in overweight women," *Journal of the American Medical Association*, 282 (1999), pp. 1554–1560.

9. John P. Thomas, "Influences on mathematics learning and attitudes among African American high school students," *Journal of Negro Education*, 69 (2000), pp. 165–183.

10. See Note 18 for Chapter 18.

11. Annie C. St-Pierre et al., "Insulin resistance syndrome, body mass index and the risk of ischemic heart disease," *Canadian Medical Association Journal*, 172 (2005), pp. 1301–1305.

12. R. J. Safran et al., "Dynamic paternity allocation as a function of male plumage color in barn swallows," *Science*, 209 (2005), pp. 2210–2212.

13. Data from the online supplement to André Kessler and Ian T. Baldwin, "Defensive function of herbivore-induced plant volatile emissions in nature," *Science*, 291 (2001), pp. 2141–2144.

14. The data and the full story can be found in the Data and Story Library at lib.stat.cmu.edu. The original study is by Faith Loven, "A study of interlist

equivalency of the CID W-22 word list presented in quiet and in noise," MS thesis, University of Iowa, 1981.

15. Data provided by Matthew Moore.

16. See Note 13 for Chapter 22.

17. See Note 3 for Chapter 14.

18. See Note 1 for Chapter 19.

19. See Note 3 for Chapter 11.

20. Mark Kroll, Peter Wright, and Pochera Theerathorn, "Whose interests do hired managers pursue? An examination of select mutual and stock life insurers," *Journal of Business Research*, 26 (1993), pp. 133–148.

Tables

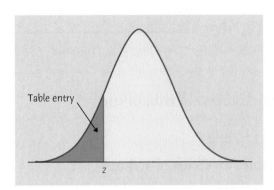

Table entry for z is the area under the standard Normal curve to the left of z.

TABLE A			Standard Normal probabilities							
z	.00	.01	.02	.03	.04	.05	.06	.07	.08	.09
−3.4	.0003	.0003	.0003	.0003	.0003	.0003	.0003	.0003	.0003	.0002
−3.3	.0005	.0005	.0005	.0004	.0004	.0004	.0004	.0004	.0004	.0003
−3.2	.0007	.0007	.0006	.0006	.0006	.0006	.0006	.0005	.0005	.0005
−3.1	.0010	.0009	.0009	.0009	.0008	.0008	.0008	.0008	.0007	.0007
−3.0	.0013	.0013	.0013	.0012	.0012	.0011	.0011	.0011	.0010	.0010
−2.9	.0019	.0018	.0018	.0017	.0016	.0016	.0015	.0015	.0014	.0014
−2.8	.0026	.0025	.0024	.0023	.0023	.0022	.0021	.0021	.0020	.0019
−2.7	.0035	.0034	.0033	.0032	.0031	.0030	.0029	.0028	.0027	.0026
−2.6	.0047	.0045	.0044	.0043	.0041	.0040	.0039	.0038	.0037	.0036
−2.5	.0062	.0060	.0059	.0057	.0055	.0054	.0052	.0051	.0049	.0048
−2.4	.0082	.0080	.0078	.0075	.0073	.0071	.0069	.0068	.0066	.0064
−2.3	.0107	.0104	.0102	.0099	.0096	.0094	.0091	.0089	.0087	.0084
−2.2	.0139	.0136	.0132	.0129	.0125	.0122	.0119	.0116	.0113	.0110
−2.1	.0179	.0174	.0170	.0166	.0162	.0158	.0154	.0150	.0146	.0143
−2.0	.0228	.0222	.0217	.0212	.0207	.0202	.0197	.0192	.0188	.0183
−1.9	.0287	.0281	.0274	.0268	.0262	.0256	.0250	.0244	.0239	.0233
−1.8	.0359	.0351	.0344	.0336	.0329	.0322	.0314	.0307	.0301	.0294
−1.7	.0446	.0436	.0427	.0418	.0409	.0401	.0392	.0384	.0375	.0367
−1.6	.0548	.0537	.0526	.0516	.0505	.0495	.0485	.0475	.0465	.0455
−1.5	.0668	.0655	.0643	.0630	.0618	.0606	.0594	.0582	.0571	.0559
−1.4	.0808	.0793	.0778	.0764	.0749	.0735	.0721	.0708	.0694	.0681
−1.3	.0968	.0951	.0934	.0918	.0901	.0885	.0869	.0853	.0838	.0823
−1.2	.1151	.1131	.1112	.1093	.1075	.1056	.1038	.1020	.1003	.0985
−1.1	.1357	.1335	.1314	.1292	.1271	.1251	.1230	.1210	.1190	.1170
−1.0	.1587	.1562	.1539	.1515	.1492	.1469	.1446	.1423	.1401	.1379
−0.9	.1841	.1814	.1788	.1762	.1736	.1711	.1685	.1660	.1635	.1611
−0.8	.2119	.2090	.2061	.2033	.2005	.1977	.1949	.1922	.1894	.1867
−0.7	.2420	.2389	.2358	.2327	.2296	.2266	.2236	.2206	.2177	.2148
−0.6	.2743	.2709	.2676	.2643	.2611	.2578	.2546	.2514	.2483	.2451
−0.5	.3085	.3050	.3015	.2981	.2946	.2912	.2877	.2843	.2810	.2776
−0.4	.3446	.3409	.3372	.3336	.3300	.3264	.3228	.3192	.3156	.3121
−0.3	.3821	.3783	.3745	.3707	.3669	.3632	.3594	.3557	.3520	.3483
−0.2	.4207	.4168	.4129	.4090	.4052	.4013	.3974	.3936	.3897	.3859
−0.1	.4602	.4562	.4522	.4483	.4443	.4404	.4364	.4325	.4286	.4247
−0.0	.5000	.4960	.4920	.4880	.4840	.4801	.4761	.4721	.4681	.4641

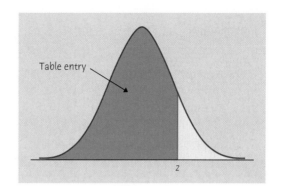

Table entry for z is the area under the standard Normal curve to the left of z.

TABLE A	Standard Normal probabilities (*continued*)								
z	.00	.01	.02	.03	.04	.05	.06	.07	.08	.09
0.0	.5000	.5040	.5080	.5120	.5160	.5199	.5239	.5279	.5319	.5359
0.1	.5398	.5438	.5478	.5517	.5557	.5596	.5636	.5675	.5714	.5753
0.2	.5793	.5832	.5871	.5910	.5948	.5987	.6026	.6064	.6103	.6141
0.3	.6179	.6217	.6255	.6293	.6331	.6368	.6406	.6443	.6480	.6517
0.4	.6554	.6591	.6628	.6664	.6700	.6736	.6772	.6808	.6844	.6879
0.5	.6915	.6950	.6985	.7019	.7054	.7088	.7123	.7157	.7190	.7224
0.6	.7257	.7291	.7324	.7357	.7389	.7422	.7454	.7486	.7517	.7549
0.7	.7580	.7611	.7642	.7673	.7704	.7734	.7764	.7794	.7823	.7852
0.8	.7881	.7910	.7939	.7967	.7995	.8023	.8051	.8078	.8106	.8133
0.9	.8159	.8186	.8212	.8238	.8264	.8289	.8315	.8340	.8365	.8389
1.0	.8413	.8438	.8461	.8485	.8508	.8531	.8554	.8577	.8599	.8621
1.1	.8643	.8665	.8686	.8708	.8729	.8749	.8770	.8790	.8810	.8830
1.2	.8849	.8869	.8888	.8907	.8925	.8944	.8962	.8980	.8997	.9015
1.3	.9032	.9049	.9066	.9082	.9099	.9115	.9131	.9147	.9162	.9177
1.4	.9192	.9207	.9222	.9236	.9251	.9265	.9279	.9292	.9306	.9319
1.5	.9332	.9345	.9357	.9370	.9382	.9394	.9406	.9418	.9429	.9441
1.6	.9452	.9463	.9474	.9484	.9495	.9505	.9515	.9525	.9535	.9545
1.7	.9554	.9564	.9573	.9582	.9591	.9599	.9608	.9616	.9625	.9633
1.8	.9641	.9649	.9656	.9664	.9671	.9678	.9686	.9693	.9699	.9706
1.9	.9713	.9719	.9726	.9732	.9738	.9744	.9750	.9756	.9761	.9767
2.0	.9772	.9778	.9783	.9788	.9793	.9798	.9803	.9808	.9812	.9817
2.1	.9821	.9826	.9830	.9834	.9838	.9842	.9846	.9850	.9854	.9857
2.2	.9861	.9864	.9868	.9871	.9875	.9878	.9881	.9884	.9887	.9890
2.3	.9893	.9896	.9898	.9901	.9904	.9906	.9909	.9911	.9913	.9916
2.4	.9918	.9920	.9922	.9925	.9927	.9929	.9931	.9932	.9934	.9936
2.5	.9938	.9940	.9941	.9943	.9945	.9946	.9948	.9949	.9951	.9952
2.6	.9953	.9955	.9956	.9957	.9959	.9960	.9961	.9962	.9963	.9964
2.7	.9965	.9966	.9967	.9968	.9969	.9970	.9971	.9972	.9973	.9974
2.8	.9974	.9975	.9976	.9977	.9977	.9978	.9979	.9979	.9980	.9981
2.9	.9981	.9982	.9982	.9983	.9984	.9984	.9985	.9985	.9986	.9986
3.0	.9987	.9987	.9987	.9988	.9988	.9989	.9989	.9989	.9990	.9990
3.1	.9990	.9991	.9991	.9991	.9992	.9992	.9992	.9992	.9993	.9993
3.2	.9993	.9993	.9994	.9994	.9994	.9994	.9994	.9995	.9995	.9995
3.3	.9995	.9995	.9995	.9996	.9996	.9996	.9996	.9996	.9996	.9997
3.4	.9997	.9997	.9997	.9997	.9997	.9997	.9997	.9997	.9997	.9998

TABLE B   Random digits

Line

101	19223	95034	05756	28713	96409	12531	42544	82853
102	73676	47150	99400	01927	27754	42648	82425	36290
103	45467	71709	77558	00095	32863	29485	82226	90056
104	52711	38889	93074	60227	40011	85848	48767	52573
105	95592	94007	69971	91481	60779	53791	17297	59335
106	68417	35013	15529	72765	85089	57067	50211	47487
107	82739	57890	20807	47511	81676	55300	94383	14893
108	60940	72024	17868	24943	61790	90656	87964	18883
109	36009	19365	15412	39638	85453	46816	83485	41979
110	38448	48789	18338	24697	39364	42006	76688	08708
111	81486	69487	60513	09297	00412	71238	27649	39950
112	59636	88804	04634	71197	19352	73089	84898	45785
113	62568	70206	40325	03699	71080	22553	11486	11776
114	45149	32992	75730	66280	03819	56202	02938	70915
115	61041	77684	94322	24709	73698	14526	31893	32592
116	14459	26056	31424	80371	65103	62253	50490	61181
117	38167	98532	62183	70632	23417	26185	41448	75532
118	73190	32533	04470	29669	84407	90785	65956	86382
119	95857	07118	87664	92099	58806	66979	98624	84826
120	35476	55972	39421	65850	04266	35435	43742	11937
121	71487	09984	29077	14863	61683	47052	62224	51025
122	13873	81598	95052	90908	73592	75186	87136	95761
123	54580	81507	27102	56027	55892	33063	41842	81868
124	71035	09001	43367	49497	72719	96758	27611	91596
125	96746	12149	37823	71868	18442	35119	62103	39244
126	96927	19931	36809	74192	77567	88741	48409	41903
127	43909	99477	25330	64359	40085	16925	85117	36071
128	15689	14227	06565	14374	13352	49367	81982	87209
129	36759	58984	68288	22913	18638	54303	00795	08727
130	69051	64817	87174	09517	84534	06489	87201	97245
131	05007	16632	81194	14873	04197	85576	45195	96565
132	68732	55259	84292	08796	43165	93739	31685	97150
133	45740	41807	65561	33302	07051	93623	18132	09547
134	27816	78416	18329	21337	35213	37741	04312	68508
135	66925	55658	39100	78458	11206	19876	87151	31260
136	08421	44753	77377	28744	75592	08563	79140	92454
137	53645	66812	61421	47836	12609	15373	98481	14592
138	66831	68908	40772	21558	47781	33586	79177	06928
139	55588	99404	70708	41098	43563	56934	48394	51719
140	12975	13258	13048	45144	72321	81940	00360	02428
141	96767	35964	23822	96012	94591	65194	50842	53372
142	72829	50232	97892	63408	77919	44575	24870	04178
143	88565	42628	17797	49376	61762	16953	88604	12724
144	62964	88145	83083	69453	46109	59505	69680	00900
145	19687	12633	57857	95806	09931	02150	43163	58636
146	37609	59057	66967	83401	60705	02384	90597	93600
147	54973	86278	88737	74351	47500	84552	19909	67181
148	00694	05977	19664	65441	20903	62371	22725	53340
149	71546	05233	53946	68743	72460	27601	45403	88692
150	07511	88915	41267	16853	84569	79367	32337	03316

Table entry for C is the critical value t^* required for confidence level C. To approximate one- and two-sided P-values, compare the value of the t statistic with the critical values of t^* that match the P-values given at the bottom of the table.

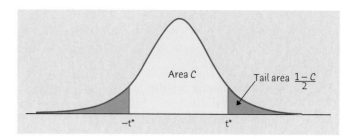

Area C

Tail area $\frac{1-C}{2}$

$-t^*$ t^*

TABLE C t distribution critical values

Degrees of freedom	Confidence level C											
	50%	60%	70%	80%	90%	95%	96%	98%	99%	99.5%	99.8%	99.9%
1	1.000	1.376	1.963	3.078	6.314	12.71	15.89	31.82	63.66	127.3	318.3	636.6
2	0.816	1.061	1.386	1.886	2.920	4.303	4.849	6.965	9.925	14.09	22.33	31.60
3	0.765	0.978	1.250	1.638	2.353	3.182	3.482	4.541	5.841	7.453	10.21	12.92
4	0.741	0.941	1.190	1.533	2.132	2.776	2.999	3.747	4.604	5.598	7.173	8.610
5	0.727	0.920	1.156	1.476	2.015	2.571	2.757	3.365	4.032	4.773	5.893	6.869
6	0.718	0.906	1.134	1.440	1.943	2.447	2.612	3.143	3.707	4.317	5.208	5.959
7	0.711	0.896	1.119	1.415	1.895	2.365	2.517	2.998	3.499	4.029	4.785	5.408
8	0.706	0.889	1.108	1.397	1.860	2.306	2.449	2.896	3.355	3.833	4.501	5.041
9	0.703	0.883	1.100	1.383	1.833	2.262	2.398	2.821	3.250	3.690	4.297	4.781
10	0.700	0.879	1.093	1.372	1.812	2.228	2.359	2.764	3.169	3.581	4.144	4.587
11	0.697	0.876	1.088	1.363	1.796	2.201	2.328	2.718	3.106	3.497	4.025	4.437
12	0.695	0.873	1.083	1.356	1.782	2.179	2.303	2.681	3.055	3.428	3.930	4.318
13	0.694	0.870	1.079	1.350	1.771	2.160	2.282	2.650	3.012	3.372	3.852	4.221
14	0.692	0.868	1.076	1.345	1.761	2.145	2.264	2.624	2.977	3.326	3.787	4.140
15	0.691	0.866	1.074	1.341	1.753	2.131	2.249	2.602	2.947	3.286	3.733	4.073
16	0.690	0.865	1.071	1.337	1.746	2.120	2.235	2.583	2.921	3.252	3.686	4.015
17	0.689	0.863	1.069	1.333	1.740	2.110	2.224	2.567	2.898	3.222	3.646	3.965
18	0.688	0.862	1.067	1.330	1.734	2.101	2.214	2.552	2.878	3.197	3.611	3.922
19	0.688	0.861	1.066	1.328	1.729	2.093	2.205	2.539	2.861	3.174	3.579	3.883
20	0.687	0.860	1.064	1.325	1.725	2.086	2.197	2.528	2.845	3.153	3.552	3.850
21	0.686	0.859	1.063	1.323	1.721	2.080	2.189	2.518	2.831	3.135	3.527	3.819
22	0.686	0.858	1.061	1.321	1.717	2.074	2.183	2.508	2.819	3.119	3.505	3.792
23	0.685	0.858	1.060	1.319	1.714	2.069	2.177	2.500	2.807	3.104	3.485	3.768
24	0.685	0.857	1.059	1.318	1.711	2.064	2.172	2.492	2.797	3.091	3.467	3.745
25	0.684	0.856	1.058	1.316	1.708	2.060	2.167	2.485	2.787	3.078	3.450	3.725
26	0.684	0.856	1.058	1.315	1.706	2.056	2.162	2.479	2.779	3.067	3.435	3.707
27	0.684	0.855	1.057	1.314	1.703	2.052	2.158	2.473	2.771	3.057	3.421	3.690
28	0.683	0.855	1.056	1.313	1.701	2.048	2.154	2.467	2.763	3.047	3.408	3.674
29	0.683	0.854	1.055	1.311	1.699	2.045	2.150	2.462	2.756	3.038	3.396	3.659
30	0.683	0.854	1.055	1.310	1.697	2.042	2.147	2.457	2.750	3.030	3.385	3.646
40	0.681	0.851	1.050	1.303	1.684	2.021	2.123	2.423	2.704	2.971	3.307	3.551
50	0.679	0.849	1.047	1.299	1.676	2.009	2.109	2.403	2.678	2.937	3.261	3.496
60	0.679	0.848	1.045	1.296	1.671	2.000	2.099	2.390	2.660	2.915	3.232	3.460
80	0.678	0.846	1.043	1.292	1.664	1.990	2.088	2.374	2.639	2.887	3.195	3.416
100	0.677	0.845	1.042	1.290	1.660	1.984	2.081	2.364	2.626	2.871	3.174	3.390
1000	0.675	0.842	1.037	1.282	1.646	1.962	2.056	2.330	2.581	2.813	3.098	3.300
z^*	0.674	0.841	1.036	1.282	1.645	1.960	2.054	2.326	2.576	2.807	3.091	3.291
One-sided P	.25	.20	.15	.10	.05	.025	.02	.01	.005	.0025	.001	.0005
Two-sided P	.50	.40	.30	.20	.10	.05	.04	.02	.01	.005	.002	.001

687

Table entry for p is the critical value F^* with probability p lying to its right.

TABLE D			F distribution critical values							
			Degrees of freedom in the numerator							
		p	1	2	3	4	5	6	7	8
Degrees of freedom in the denominator	1	.100	39.86	49.50	53.59	55.83	57.24	58.20	58.91	59.44
		.050	161.45	199.50	215.71	224.58	230.16	233.99	236.77	238.88
		.025	647.79	799.50	864.16	899.58	921.85	937.11	948.22	956.66
		.010	4052.2	4999.5	5403.4	5624.6	5763.6	5859	5928.4	5981.1
		.001	405284	500000	540379	562500	576405	585937	592873	598144
	2	.100	8.53	9.00	9.16	9.24	9.29	9.33	.35	9.37
		.050	18.51	19.00	19.16	19.25	19.30	19.33	19.35	19.37
		.025	38.51	39.00	39.17	39.25	39.30	39.33	39.36	39.37
		.010	98.50	99.00	99.17	99.25	99.30	99.33	99.36	99.37
		.001	998.50	999.00	999.17	999.25	999.30	999.33	999.36	999.37
	3	.100	5.54	5.46	5.39	5.34	5.31	5.28	5.27	5.25
		.050	10.13	9.55	9.28	9.12	9.01	8.94	8.89	8.85
		.025	17.44	16.04	15.44	15.10	14.88	14.73	14.62	14.54
		.010	34.12	30.82	29.46	28.71	28.24	27.91	27.67	27.49
		.001	167.03	148.50	141.11	137.10	134.58	132.85	131.58	130.62
	4	.100	4.54	4.32	4.19	4.11	4.05	4.01	3.98	3.95
		.050	7.71	6.94	6.59	6.39	6.26	6.16	6.09	6.04
		.025	12.22	10.65	9.98	9.60	9.36	9.20	9.07	8.98
		.010	21.20	18.00	16.69	15.98	15.52	15.21	14.98	14.80
		.001	74.14	61.25	56.18	53.44	51.71	50.53	49.66	49.00
	5	.100	4.06	3.78	3.62	3.52	3.45	3.40	3.37	3.34
		.050	6.61	5.79	5.41	5.19	5.05	4.95	4.88	4.82
		.025	10.01	8.43	7.76	7.39	7.15	6.98	6.85	6.76
		.010	16.26	13.27	12.06	11.39	10.97	10.67	10.46	10.29
		.001	47.18	37.12	33.20	31.09	29.75	28.83	28.16	27.65
	6	.100	3.78	3.46	3.29	3.18	3.11	3.05	3.01	2.98
		.050	5.99	5.14	4.76	4.53	4.39	4.28	4.21	4.15
		.025	8.81	7.26	6.60	6.23	5.99	5.82	5.70	5.60
		.010	13.75	10.92	9.78	9.15	8.75	8.47	8.26	8.10
		.001	35.51	27.00	23.70	21.92	20.80	20.03	19.46	19.03
	7	.100	3.59	3.26	3.07	2.96	2.88	2.83	2.78	2.75
		.050	5.59	4.74	4.35	4.12	3.97	3.87	3.79	3.73
		.025	8.07	6.54	5.89	5.52	5.29	5.12	4.99	4.90
		.010	12.25	9.55	8.45	7.85	7.46	7.19	6.99	6.84
		.001	29.25	21.69	18.77	17.20	16.21	15.52	15.02	14.63
	8	.100	3.46	3.11	2.92	2.81	2.73	2.67	2.62	2.59
		.050	5.32	4.46	4.07	3.84	3.69	3.58	3.50	3.44
		.025	7.57	6.06	5.42	5.05	4.82	4.65	4.53	4.43
		.010	11.26	8.65	7.59	7.01	6.63	6.37	6.18	6.03
		.001	25.41	18.49	15.83	14.39	13.48	12.86	12.40	12.05

Table entry for p is the critical value F^* with probability p lying to its right.

TABLE D		F distribution critical values (*continued*)							
		Degrees of freedom in the numerator							
	p	9	10	15	20	30	60	120	1000
1	.100	59.86	60.19	61.22	61.74	62.26	62.79	63.06	63.30
	.050	240.54	241.88	245.95	248.01	250.10	252.20	253.25	254.19
	.025	963.28	968.63	984.87	993.10	1001.4	1009.8	1014	1017.7
	.010	6022.5	6055.8	6157.3	6208.7	6260.6	6313	6339.4	6362.7
	.001	602284	605621	615764	620908	626099	631337	633972	636301
2	.100	9.38	9.39	9.42	9.44	9.46	9.47	9.48	9.49
	.050	19.38	19.40	19.43	19.45	19.46	19.48	19.49	19.49
	.025	39.39	39.40	39.43	39.45	39.46	39.48	39.49	39.50
	.010	99.39	99.40	99.43	99.45	99.47	99.48	99.49	99.50
	.001	999.39	999.40	999.43	999.45	999.47	999.48	999.49	999.50
3	.100	5.24	5.23	5.20	5.18	5.17	5.15	5.14	5.13
	.050	8.81	8.79	8.70	8.66	8.62	8.57	8.55	8.53
	.025	14.47	14.42	14.25	14.17	14.08	13.99	13.95	13.91
	.010	27.35	27.23	26.87	26.69	26.50	26.32	26.22	26.14
	.001	129.86	129.25	127.37	126.42	125.45	124.47	123.97	123.53
4	.100	3.94	3.92	3.87	3.84	3.82	3.79	3.78	3.76
	.050	6.00	5.96	5.86	5.80	5.75	5.69	5.66	5.63
	.025	8.90	8.84	8.66	8.56	8.46	8.36	8.31	8.26
	.010	14.66	14.55	14.20	14.02	13.84	13.65	13.56	13.47
	.001	48.47	48.05	46.76	46.10	45.43	44.75	44.40	44.09
5	.100	3.32	3.30	3.24	3.21	3.17	3.14	3.12	3.11
	.050	4.77	4.74	4.62	4.56	4.50	4.43	4.40	4.37
	.025	6.68	6.62	6.43	6.33	6.23	6.12	6.07	6.02
	.010	10.16	10.05	9.72	9.55	9.38	9.20	9.11	9.03
	.001	27.24	26.92	25.91	25.39	24.87	24.33	24.06	23.82
6	.100	2.96	2.94	2.87	2.84	2.80	2.76	2.74	2.72
	.050	4.10	4.06	3.94	3.87	3.81	3.74	3.70	3.67
	.025	5.52	5.46	5.27	5.17	5.07	4.96	4.90	4.86
	.010	7.98	7.87	7.56	7.40	7.23	7.06	6.97	6.89
	.001	18.69	18.41	17.56	17.12	16.67	16.21	15.98	15.77
7	.100	2.72	2.70	2.63	2.59	2.56	2.51	2.49	2.47
	.050	3.68	3.64	3.51	3.44	3.38	3.30	3.27	3.23
	.025	4.82	4.76	4.57	4.47	4.36	4.25	4.20	4.15
	.010	6.72	6.62	6.31	6.16	5.99	5.82	5.74	5.66
	.001	14.33	14.08	13.32	12.93	12.53	12.12	11.91	11.72
8	.100	2.56	2.54	2.46	2.42	2.38	2.34	2.32	2.30
	.050	3.39	3.35	3.22	3.15	3.08	3.01	2.97	2.93
	.025	4.36	4.30	4.10	4.00	3.89	3.78	3.73	3.68
	.010	5.91	5.81	5.52	5.36	5.20	5.03	4.95	4.87
	.001	11.77	11.54	10.84	10.48	10.11	9.73	9.53	9.36

Degrees of freedom in the denominator

TABLE D   F distribution critical values (continued)

	p	\multicolumn{8}{c}{Degrees of freedom in the numerator}
		1	2	3	4	5	6	7	8
9	.100	3.36	3.01	2.81	2.69	2.61	2.55	2.51	2.47
	.050	5.12	4.26	3.86	3.63	3.48	3.37	3.29	3.23
	.025	7.21	5.71	5.08	4.72	4.48	4.32	4.20	4.10
	.010	10.56	8.02	6.99	6.42	6.06	5.80	5.61	5.47
	.001	22.86	16.39	13.90	12.56	11.71	11.13	10.70	10.37
10	.100	3.29	2.92	2.73	2.61	2.52	2.46	2.41	2.38
	.050	4.96	4.10	3.71	3.48	3.33	3.22	3.14	3.07
	.025	6.94	5.46	4.83	4.47	4.24	4.07	3.95	3.85
	.010	10.04	7.56	6.55	5.99	5.64	5.39	5.20	5.06
	.001	21.04	14.91	12.55	11.28	10.48	9.93	9.52	9.20
12	.100	3.18	2.81	2.61	2.48	2.39	2.33	2.28	2.24
	.050	4.75	3.89	3.49	3.26	3.11	3.00	2.91	2.85
	.025	6.55	5.10	4.47	4.12	3.89	3.73	3.61	3.51
	.010	9.33	6.93	5.95	5.41	5.06	4.82	4.64	4.50
	.001	18.64	12.97	10.80	9.63	8.89	8.38	8.00	7.71
15	.100	3.07	2.70	2.49	2.36	2.27	2.21	2.16	2.12
	.050	4.54	3.68	3.29	3.06	2.90	2.79	2.71	2.64
	.025	6.20	4.77	4.15	3.80	3.58	3.41	3.29	3.20
	.010	8.68	6.36	5.42	4.89	4.56	4.32	4.14	4.00
	.001	16.59	11.34	9.34	8.25	7.57	7.09	6.74	6.47
20	.100	2.97	2.59	2.38	2.25	2.16	2.09	2.04	2.00
	.050	4.35	3.49	3.10	2.87	2.71	2.60	2.51	2.45
	.025	5.87	4.46	3.86	3.51	3.29	3.13	3.01	2.91
	.010	8.10	5.85	4.94	4.43	4.10	3.87	3.70	3.56
	.001	14.82	9.95	8.10	7.10	6.46	6.02	5.69	5.44
25	.100	2.92	2.53	2.32	2.18	2.09	2.02	1.97	1.93
	.050	4.24	3.39	2.99	2.76	2.60	2.49	2.40	2.34
	.025	5.69	4.29	3.69	3.35	3.13	2.97	2.85	2.75
	.010	7.77	5.57	4.68	4.18	3.85	3.63	3.46	3.32
	.001	13.88	9.22	7.45	6.49	5.89	5.46	5.15	4.91
50	.100	2.81	2.41	2.20	2.06	1.97	1.90	1.84	1.80
	.050	4.03	3.18	2.79	2.56	2.40	2.29	2.20	2.13
	.025	5.34	3.97	3.39	3.05	2.83	2.67	2.55	2.46
	.010	7.17	5.06	4.20	3.72	3.41	3.19	3.02	2.89
	.001	12.22	7.96	6.34	5.46	4.90	4.51	4.22	4.00
100	.100	2.76	2.36	2.14	2.00	1.91	1.83	1.78	1.73
	.050	3.94	3.09	2.70	2.46	2.31	2.19	2.10	2.03
	.025	5.18	3.83	3.25	2.92	2.70	2.54	2.42	2.32
	.010	6.90	4.82	3.98	3.51	3.21	2.99	2.82	2.69
	.001	11.50	7.41	5.86	5.02	4.48	4.11	3.83	3.61
200	.100	2.73	2.33	2.11	1.97	1.88	1.80	1.75	1.70
	.050	3.89	3.04	2.65	2.42	2.26	2.14	2.06	1.98
	.025	5.10	3.76	3.18	2.85	2.63	2.47	2.35	2.26
	.010	6.76	4.71	3.88	3.41	3.11	2.89	2.73	2.60
	.001	11.15	7.15	5.63	4.81	4.29	3.92	3.65	3.43
1000	.100	2.71	2.31	2.09	1.95	1.85	1.78	1.72	1.68
	.050	3.85	3.00	2.61	2.38	2.22	2.11	2.02	1.95
	.025	5.04	3.70	3.13	2.80	2.58	2.42	2.30	2.20
	.010	6.66	4.63	3.80	3.34	3.04	2.82	2.66	2.53
	.001	10.89	6.96	5.46	4.65	4.14	3.78	3.51	3.30

Degrees of freedom in the denominator

TABLE D F distribution critical values (continued)

Denominator df	p	Degrees of freedom in the numerator							
		9	10	15	20	30	60	120	1000
9	.100	2.44	2.42	2.34	2.30	2.25	2.21	2.18	2.16
	.050	3.18	3.14	3.01	2.94	2.86	2.79	2.75	2.71
	.025	4.03	3.96	3.77	3.67	3.56	3.45	3.39	3.34
	.010	5.35	5.26	4.96	4.81	4.65	4.48	4.40	4.32
	.001	10.11	9.89	9.24	8.90	8.55	8.19	8.00	7.84
10	.100	2.35	2.32	2.24	2.20	2.16	2.11	2.08	2.06
	.050	3.02	2.98	2.85	2.77	2.70	2.62	2.58	2.54
	.025	3.78	3.72	3.52	3.42	3.31	3.20	3.14	3.09
	.010	4.94	4.85	4.56	4.41	4.25	4.08	4.00	3.92
	.001	8.96	8.75	8.13	7.80	7.47	7.12	6.94	6.78
12	.100	2.21	2.19	2.10	2.06	2.01	1.96	1.93	1.91
	.050	2.80	2.75	2.62	2.54	2.47	2.38	2.34	2.30
	.025	3.44	3.37	3.18	3.07	2.96	2.85	2.79	2.73
	.010	4.39	4.30	4.01	3.86	3.70	3.54	3.45	3.37
	.001	7.48	7.29	6.71	6.40	6.09	5.76	5.59	5.44
15	.100	2.09	2.06	1.97	1.92	1.87	1.82	1.79	1.76
	.050	2.59	2.54	2.40	2.33	2.25	2.16	2.11	2.07
	.025	3.12	3.06	2.86	2.76	2.64	2.52	2.46	2.40
	.010	3.89	3.80	3.52	3.37	3.21	3.05	2.96	2.88
	.001	6.26	6.08	5.54	5.25	4.95	4.64	4.47	4.33
20	.100	1.96	1.94	1.84	1.79	1.74	1.68	1.64	1.61
	.050	2.39	2.35	2.20	2.12	2.04	1.95	1.90	1.85
	.025	2.84	2.77	2.57	2.46	2.35	2.22	2.16	2.09
	.010	3.46	3.37	3.09	2.94	2.78	2.61	2.52	2.43
	.001	5.24	5.08	4.56	4.29	4.00	3.70	3.54	3.40
25	.100	1.89	1.87	1.77	1.72	1.66	1.59	1.56	1.52
	.050	2.28	2.24	2.09	2.01	1.92	1.82	1.77	1.72
	.025	2.68	2.61	2.41	2.30	2.18	2.05	1.98	1.91
	.010	3.22	3.13	2.85	2.70	2.54	2.36	2.27	2.18
	.001	4.71	4.56	4.06	3.79	3.52	3.22	3.06	2.91
50	.100	1.76	1.73	1.63	1.57	1.50	1.42	1.38	1.33
	.050	2.07	2.03	1.87	1.78	1.69	1.58	1.51	1.45
	.025	2.38	2.32	2.11	1.99	1.87	1.72	1.64	1.56
	.010	2.78	2.70	2.42	2.27	2.10	1.91	1.80	1.70
	.001	3.82	3.67	3.20	2.95	2.68	2.38	2.21	2.05
100	.100	1.69	1.66	1.56	1.49	1.42	1.34	1.28	1.22
	.050	1.97	1.93	1.77	1.68	1.57	1.45	1.38	1.30
	.025	2.24	2.18	1.97	1.85	1.71	1.56	1.46	1.36
	.010	2.59	2.50	2.22	2.07	1.89	1.69	1.57	1.45
	.001	3.44	3.30	2.84	2.59	2.32	2.01	1.83	1.64
200	.100	1.66	1.63	1.52	1.46	1.38	1.29	1.23	1.16
	.050	1.93	1.88	1.72	1.62	1.52	1.39	1.30	1.21
	.025	2.18	2.11	1.90	1.78	1.64	1.47	1.37	1.25
	.010	2.50	2.41	2.13	1.97	1.79	1.58	1.45	1.30
	.001	3.26	3.12	2.67	2.42	2.15	1.83	1.64	1.43
1000	.100	1.64	1.61	1.49	1.43	1.35	1.25	1.18	1.08
	.050	1.89	1.84	1.68	1.58	1.47	1.33	1.24	1.11
	.025	2.13	2.06	1.85	1.72	1.58	1.41	1.29	1.13
	.010	2.43	2.34	2.06	1.90	1.72	1.50	1.35	1.16
	.001	3.13	2.99	2.54	2.30	2.02	1.69	1.49	1.22

Degrees of freedom in the denominator

Table entry for p is the critical value χ^* with probability p lying to its right.

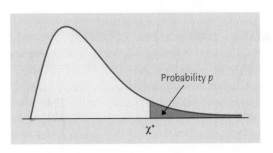

TABLE E   Chi-square distribution critical values

df	.25	.20	.15	.10	.05	.025	.02	.01	.005	.0025	.001	.0005
1	1.32	1.64	2.07	2.71	3.84	5.02	5.41	6.63	7.88	9.14	10.83	12.12
2	2.77	3.22	3.79	4.61	5.99	7.38	7.82	9.21	10.60	11.98	13.82	15.20
3	4.11	4.64	5.32	6.25	7.81	9.35	9.84	11.34	12.84	14.32	16.27	17.73
4	5.39	5.99	6.74	7.78	9.49	11.14	11.67	13.28	14.86	16.42	18.47	20.00
5	6.63	7.29	8.12	9.24	11.07	12.83	13.39	15.09	16.75	18.39	20.51	22.11
6	7.84	8.56	9.45	10.64	12.59	14.45	15.03	16.81	18.55	20.25	22.46	24.10
7	9.04	9.80	10.75	12.02	14.07	16.01	16.62	18.48	20.28	22.04	24.32	26.02
8	10.22	11.03	12.03	13.36	15.51	17.53	18.17	20.09	21.95	23.77	26.12	27.87
9	11.39	12.24	13.29	14.68	16.92	19.02	19.68	21.67	23.59	25.46	27.88	29.67
10	12.55	13.44	14.53	15.99	18.31	20.48	21.16	23.21	25.19	27.11	29.59	31.42
11	13.70	14.63	15.77	17.28	19.68	21.92	22.62	24.72	26.76	28.73	31.26	33.14
12	14.85	15.81	16.99	18.55	21.03	23.34	24.05	26.22	28.30	30.32	32.91	34.82
13	15.98	16.98	18.20	19.81	22.36	24.74	25.47	27.69	29.82	31.88	34.53	36.48
14	17.12	18.15	19.41	21.06	23.68	26.12	26.87	29.14	31.32	33.43	36.12	38.11
15	18.25	19.31	20.60	22.31	25.00	27.49	28.26	30.58	32.80	34.95	37.70	39.72
16	19.37	20.47	21.79	23.54	26.30	28.85	29.63	32.00	34.27	36.46	39.25	41.31
17	20.49	21.61	22.98	24.77	27.59	30.19	31.00	33.41	35.72	37.95	40.79	42.88
18	21.60	22.76	24.16	25.99	28.87	31.53	32.35	34.81	37.16	39.42	42.31	44.43
19	22.72	23.90	25.33	27.20	30.14	32.85	33.69	36.19	38.58	40.88	43.82	45.97
20	23.83	25.04	26.50	28.41	31.41	34.17	35.02	37.57	40.00	42.34	45.31	47.50
21	24.93	26.17	27.66	29.62	32.67	35.48	36.34	38.93	41.40	43.78	46.80	49.01
22	26.04	27.30	28.82	30.81	33.92	36.78	37.66	40.29	42.80	45.20	48.27	50.51
23	27.14	28.43	29.98	32.01	35.17	38.08	38.97	41.64	44.18	46.62	49.73	52.00
24	28.24	29.55	31.13	33.20	36.42	39.36	40.27	42.98	45.56	48.03	51.18	53.48
25	29.34	30.68	32.28	34.38	37.65	40.65	41.57	44.31	46.93	49.44	52.62	54.95
26	30.43	31.79	33.43	35.56	38.89	41.92	42.86	45.64	48.29	50.83	54.05	56.41
27	31.53	32.91	34.57	36.74	40.11	43.19	44.14	46.96	49.64	52.22	55.48	57.86
28	32.62	34.03	35.71	37.92	41.34	44.46	45.42	48.28	50.99	53.59	56.89	59.30
29	33.71	35.14	36.85	39.09	42.56	45.72	46.69	49.59	52.34	54.97	58.30	60.73
30	34.80	36.25	37.99	40.26	43.77	46.98	47.96	50.89	53.67	56.33	59.70	62.16
40	45.62	47.27	49.24	51.81	55.76	59.34	60.44	63.69	66.77	69.70	73.40	76.09
50	56.33	58.16	60.35	63.17	67.50	71.42	72.61	76.15	79.49	82.66	86.66	89.56
60	66.98	68.97	71.34	74.40	79.08	83.30	84.58	88.38	91.95	95.34	99.61	102.7
80	88.13	90.41	93.11	96.58	101.9	106.6	108.1	112.3	116.3	120.1	124.8	128.3
100	109.1	111.7	114.7	118.5	124.3	129.6	131.1	135.8	140.2	144.3	149.4	153.2

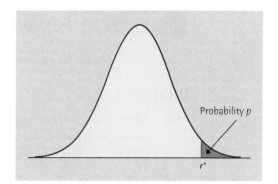

Table entry for p is the critical value r^* of the correlation coefficient r with probability p lying to its right.

Probability p

r^*

TABLE F			Critical values of the correlation r							
	Upper tail probability p									
n	.20	.10	.05	.025	.02	.01	.005	.0025	.001	.0005
3	0.8090	0.9511	0.9877	0.9969	0.9980	0.9995	0.9999	1.0000	1.0000	1.0000
4	0.6000	0.8000	0.9000	0.9500	0.9600	0.9800	0.9900	0.9950	0.9980	0.9990
5	0.4919	0.6870	0.8054	0.8783	0.8953	0.9343	0.9587	0.9740	0.9859	0.9911
6	0.4257	0.6084	0.7293	0.8114	0.8319	0.8822	0.9172	0.9417	0.9633	0.9741
7	0.3803	0.5509	0.6694	0.7545	0.7766	0.8329	0.8745	0.9056	0.9350	0.9509
8	0.3468	0.5067	0.6215	0.7067	0.7295	0.7887	0.8343	0.8697	0.9049	0.9249
9	0.3208	0.4716	0.5822	0.6664	0.6892	0.7498	0.7977	0.8359	0.8751	0.8983
10	0.2998	0.4428	0.5494	0.6319	0.6546	0.7155	0.7646	0.8046	0.8467	0.8721
11	0.2825	0.4187	0.5214	0.6021	0.6244	0.6851	0.7348	0.7759	0.8199	0.8470
12	0.2678	0.3981	0.4973	0.5760	0.5980	0.6581	0.7079	0.7496	0.7950	0.8233
13	0.2552	0.3802	0.4762	0.5529	0.5745	0.6339	0.6835	0.7255	0.7717	0.8010
14	0.2443	0.3646	0.4575	0.5324	0.5536	0.6120	0.6614	0.7034	0.7501	0.7800
15	0.2346	0.3507	0.4409	0.5140	0.5347	0.5923	0.6411	0.6831	0.7301	0.7604
16	0.2260	0.3383	0.4259	0.4973	0.5177	0.5742	0.6226	0.6643	0.7114	0.7419
17	0.2183	0.3271	0.4124	0.4821	0.5021	0.5577	0.6055	0.6470	0.6940	0.7247
18	0.2113	0.3170	0.4000	0.4683	0.4878	0.5425	0.5897	0.6308	0.6777	0.7084
19	0.2049	0.3077	0.3887	0.4555	0.4747	0.5285	0.5751	0.6158	0.6624	0.6932
20	0.1991	0.2992	0.3783	0.4438	0.4626	0.5155	0.5614	0.6018	0.6481	0.6788
21	0.1938	0.2914	0.3687	0.4329	0.4513	0.5034	0.5487	0.5886	0.6346	0.6652
22	0.1888	0.2841	0.3598	0.4227	0.4409	0.4921	0.5368	0.5763	0.6219	0.6524
23	0.1843	0.2774	0.3515	0.4132	0.4311	0.4815	0.5256	0.5647	0.6099	0.6402
24	0.1800	0.2711	0.3438	0.4044	0.4219	0.4716	0.5151	0.5537	0.5986	0.6287
25	0.1760	0.2653	0.3365	0.3961	0.4133	0.4622	0.5052	0.5434	0.5879	0.6178
26	0.1723	0.2598	0.3297	0.3882	0.4052	0.4534	0.4958	0.5336	0.5776	0.6074
27	0.1688	0.2546	0.3233	0.3809	0.3976	0.4451	0.4869	0.5243	0.5679	0.5974
28	0.1655	0.2497	0.3172	0.3739	0.3904	0.4372	0.4785	0.5154	0.5587	0.5880
29	0.1624	0.2451	0.3115	0.3673	0.3835	0.4297	0.4705	0.5070	0.5499	0.5790
30	0.1594	0.2407	0.3061	0.3610	0.3770	0.4226	0.4629	0.4990	0.5415	0.5703
40	0.1368	0.2070	0.2638	0.3120	0.3261	0.3665	0.4026	0.4353	0.4741	0.5007
50	0.1217	0.1843	0.2353	0.2787	0.2915	0.3281	0.3610	0.3909	0.4267	0.4514
60	0.1106	0.1678	0.2144	0.2542	0.2659	0.2997	0.3301	0.3578	0.3912	0.4143
80	0.0954	0.1448	0.1852	0.2199	0.2301	0.2597	0.2864	0.3109	0.3405	0.3611
100	0.0851	0.1292	0.1654	0.1966	0.2058	0.2324	0.2565	0.2786	0.3054	0.3242
1000	0.0266	0.0406	0.0520	0.0620	0.0650	0.0736	0.0814	0.0887	0.0976	0.1039

Answers to Selected Exercises

Chapter 1

1.1 (a) Vehicles. (b) Make/model, vehicle type, transmission type (all categorical); number of cylinders, city mpg, highway mpg (all quantitative).

1.3 (a) 10%. (b) A pie chart could be used.

1.5 The Arbitron data tell us neither the number of people who own MP3 players nor the number of those owners in that age group.

1.9 Skewed to the right, spread from 0% to 30%; midpoint lies in the 5%–10% class.

1.11 359 mg/dl is an outlier; the distribution is slightly right-skewed. Only four are in the desired range.

1.13 (a)   **1.14** (c)   **1.15** (c)   **1.16** (c)   **1.17** (b)

1.18 (b)   **1.19** (b)   **1.20** (c)   **1.21** (a)   **1.22** (c)

1.23 (a) Categorical. (b) Categorical. (c) Quantitative. (d) Categorical. (e) Quantitative.

1.25 About 7% are some other color. European cars are more often black, and rarely white, brown, red, or yellow.

1.27 Approximately 60% Mexican and 10% Puerto Rican.

1.31 (a) Slightly left-skewed. (b) Center: 0%–2%. (c) Lowest: −16% to −14%; highest: 12%–14%. (d) About 37%.

1.33 (a) Top five: Texas, Minnesota, Oklahoma, Missouri, and Illinois. Bottom five: Alaska, Puerto Rico, Rhode Island, Nevada, and Vermont. (b) The histogram is right-skewed, with nearly half in the "less than $10 million" category; spread from $0 to about $90 million. Texas, Minnesota, and Oklahoma might be outliers.

1.35 (a) Totals emissions would almost certainly be higher for very large countries. (b) Skewed to the right; the United States, Canada, and Australia appear to be outliers. For other countries, the distribution is spread from 0 to 11 metric tons per person.

1.37 (a) Most people will "round" their answers when asked to give an estimate like this. (b) The stemplots and midpoints (175 for women, 120 for men) suggest that women (claim to) study more than men.

1.39 (a) We cannot compare counts from groups of unequal sizes. (b) Marijuana usage and accident rates rise (and fall) together.

1.41 Both manufacturers have generally improved, apart from a slight jump in 2003. Toyota vehicles typically have fewer problems, but GM may be closing the gap.

1.43 (a) Prices appear to be highest in the summer and lowest in the winter. (b) Overall, prices rise gradually over the decade.

Chapter 2

2.1 30,841 pounds; only 6 pieces of wood had breaking strengths below the mean. The mean is made smaller by the left-skew of the distribution.

2.3 Median $216,200, mean $265,000.

2.5 **(a)** 23,040, 30,315, 31,975, 32,710, and 33,650 pounds. **(b)** The gaps between the minimum and Q_1 and between Q_1 and M are larger than the other two gaps.

2.7 No (barely).

2.9 **(a)** $\bar{x} = 5.4$ mg/dl. **(b)** $s \doteq 0.6419$ mg/dl.

2.11 **(a)** Not appropriate (outlier). **(b)** Appropriate. **(c)** Not appropriate (skewed).

2.13 (a) **2.14** (b) **2.15** (c) **2.16** (c) **2.17** (b)

2.18 (c) **2.19** (b) **2.20** (a) **2.21** (b) **2.22** (a)

2.23 Median $42,087, mean $53,581.

2.25 **(a)** $\bar{x} = 251.9$ and M = 236 doctors per 100,000 people. **(b)** Without DC: $\bar{x}^* = 243.26$ and M* = 234.5 doctors per 100,000 people.

2.27 The five-number summaries (in mm) are
bihai: Min = 46.34, Q_1 = 46.71, M = 47.12, Q_3 = 48.245, Max = 50.26;
red: Min = 37.40, Q_1 = 38.07, M = 39.16, Q_3 = 41.69, Max = 43.09;
yellow: Min = 34.57, Q_1 = 35.45, M = 36.11, Q_3 = 36.82, Max = 38.13.

2.29 M = 2, Q_1 = 1, and Q_3 = 4 servings.

2.31 **(a)** Symmetric distributions with no outliers. **(b)** Women: $\bar{x}$ changes from 165.2 to 158.4; s from 56.5 to 43.7 minutes. Men: $\bar{x}$ from 117.2 to 110.9; s from 74.2 to 66.9 minutes.

2.33 **(a)** RB: Min = 185, Q_1 = 199.5, M = 215.5, Q_3 = 221, Max = 235.
WR: Min = 154, Q_1 = 168, M = 183, Q_3 = 199, Max = 215.
OL: Min = 254, Q_1 = 283.5, M = 291, Q_3 = 317.5, Max = 337.
DL: Min = 230, Q_1 = 240, M = 264, Q_3 = 285.5, Max = 301.
LB: Min = 199, Q_1 = 214, M = 221, Q_3 = 233.5, Max = 237.
DB: Min = 177, Q_1 = 184, M = 188, Q_3 = 195, Max = 201.
(b) Offensive linemen are heaviest overall. Wide receivers and defensive backs are typically the lightest.
(c) There are no striking outliers.

2.35 For example: Saturday and Sunday are quite similar and considerably lower than other days.

2.37 Compressed: $\bar{x}$ = 2.9075, Min = 2.68, Q_1 = 2.795, M = 2.880, Q_3 = 2.99, Max = 3.18.
Intermediate: $\bar{x}$ = 3.3360, Min = 2.92, Q_1 = 3.130, M = 3.310, Q_3 = 3.45, Max = 4.26.
Loose: $\bar{x}$ = 4.2315, Min = 3.94, Q_1 = 4.015, M = 4.175, Q_3 = 4.32, Max = 4.91. Soil penetrability is greatest for loose soil and least for compressed soil.

2.39 The five-number summary is −34.54%, −5.4715%, 11.677%, 22.4145%, 34.167%. Returns have typically been positive, but with much variability and no clear pattern over time.

2.41 Answers will vary; 9 to 15 digits is typical.

2.45 (a) In units of metric tons per person: Min = 0, Q_1 = 0.75, M = 3.2, Q_3 = 7.8, Max = 19.9. The large gaps between M and Q_3 and between Q_3 and Max suggest the skew. (b) The IQR is 7.05; only the United States qualifies as an outlier by this rule.

2.47 $IQR = 27.886\%$; there are no outliers by this rule.

Chapter 3

3.3 Both are 0.5.

3.5 Place 64 at the center of the curve, then mark 61.3 and 66.7 at the change-of-curvature points.

3.7 (a) 218 to 314 days. (b) Shorter than 234 days.

3.9 Women: $z = 2.96$; men: $z = 0.96$.

3.11 (a) 0.2266. (b) 0.2260.

3.13 (a) $z \doteq -0.67$. (b) $z \doteq 0.25$.

3.15 (a) **3.16** (a) **3.17** (b) **3.18** (b) **3.19** (b)

3.20 (c) **3.21** (a) **3.22** (c) **3.23** (b) **3.24** (b)

3.25 The peak at 0 should be "tall and skinny." Near 1, the curve should be "short and fat."

3.27 (a) 50%. (b) 0.15%. (c) 16%.

3.29 (a) The stemplot looks Normal, although there are two low values. (b) $\bar{x} = 105.84$ and $s = 14.27$. The proportions are about 74.2% and 94.5%; a Normal distribution would have 68% and 95%.

3.31 (a) $z \doteq 0.84$. (b) $z \doteq 0.39$.

3.33 Jacob's score ($z = -1.02$) is higher than Emily's ($z = -1.70$).

3.35 About 1335.

3.37 15th percentile.

3.39 About 0.1%.

3.41 24.9 (round to 25) or above.

3.43 850, 974, 1078, and 1202.

3.45 About 2.9%.

3.47 Mean 250, standard deviation 175.8.

3.49 For a true Normal distribution, 89.8% of scores would be 27 or lower; the actual fraction was 0.8984—a good match.

3.51 (a) 0.6826; the 68–95–99.7 rule gives 0.68. (b) 0.9544 (compared with 0.95); 0.9974 (compared with 0.997).

3.53 A/B cutoff: mean plus 1.28 standard deviations; B/C cutoff: mean minus 1.28 standard deviations.

Chapter 4

4.1 (a) Explanatory: time spent studying; response: grade. (b) Explore the relationship. (c) Explanatory: time spent on extracurricular activities; response: GPA. (d) Explore the relationship.

4.3 For example, weight and gender.

4.5 Linear, negative, fairly weak; sparrowhawks are long-lived and territorial.

4.7 (b) Icicles seem to grow faster when the water runs more slowly.

4.9 No; units do not affect correlation.

4.11 These variables do not have a straight-line relationship; the association is neither positive nor negative.

4.12 (a)   **4.13** (a)   **4.14** (c)   **4.15** (a)   **4.16** (a)

4.17 (c)   **4.18** (b)   **4.19** (a)   **4.20** (b)   **4.21** (a)

4.23 (a) The response variable (estimated level) can take only the values 1, 2, 3, 4, 5. (b) The association is (weakly) positive. (c) The estimate is 4, which is an overestimate; that child had the lowest score on the test.

4.25 (a) Both show fairly steady improvement. Women have made more rapid progress, but their progress seems to have slowed, while men's records may be dropping more rapidly in recent years. (b) $r_{\text{men}} \doteq -0.9878$ and $r_{\text{women}} \doteq -0.9705$. (c) The data support the first claim but do not seem to support the second.

4.27 The scatterplot shows a strong positive linear association; correlation is appropriate. $r = 0.9953$.

4.29 The new points are generally slightly lower than the others, suggesting that gas usage has dropped slightly.

4.31 Correlation measures the strength of the association, not the slope of the line.

4.33 (b) $r \doteq 0.8770$ for both sets; units of measurement have no effect on the correlation.

4.35 (a) Gender is not quantitative. (b) r cannot exceed 1. (c) r has no units.

4.37 (a) $r = 1$ for a line. (c) Leave some space above your vertical stack. (d) The curve must be higher at the right than at the left.

4.39 Compute the survival rates (the percent of males returning). This is the response variable; a scatterplot of this variable against the number of breeding pairs shows a negative association, which supports the theory.

4.41 There is a negative association between 2002 return and 2003 return; that is, the worse a fund did in 2002, the better it did in 2003 (and vice versa). Only one fund return decreased from 2002 to 2003; every other fund increased its return by at least 8.3%.

Chapter 5

5.1 (a) On the average, reading score increases by 0.882 for each one-point increase in IQ. (b) Neither a reading score of -33.4 nor an IQ of 0 has any meaningful interpretation. (c) The predicted scores for $x = 90$ and $x = 130$ are about 46 and 81.3.

5.3 (a) The formula should be the same (apart from rounding differences). (b) $\bar{x} \doteq 324.75$, $s_x \doteq 257.66$, $\bar{y} \doteq 2.3875$, $s_y \doteq 1.1389$, $r \doteq -0.7786$.

5.5 (a) $\hat{y} = 132.45 + 0.402x$. The relationship appears to be curved rather than linear. (b) $r^2 = 0.0182$, so this line makes poor predictions. (c) When $x = \bar{x} = 18.82$ thousand plants/acre, $\hat{y} = \bar{y} = 140.02$ bushels/acre (except for rounding error).

5.7 (b) No; the pattern is curved, not linear. (c) The sum is -0.01.

5.9 (a) $\hat{y} = 1166.93 - 0.5868x$. (b) About 0.5868 million (586,800) per year; $r^2 \doteq 97.7\%$. (c) When $x = 2000$, $\hat{y} \doteq -6.65$.

5.11 For example, social status and ethnic background.

5.13 The patient's condition is a lurking variable.

5.14 (b) **5.15** (c) **5.16** (c) **5.17** (a) **5.18** (b)

5.19 (a) **5.20** (a) **5.21** (a) **5.22** (a) **5.23** (b)

5.25 (a) On the average, BOD rises (falls) by 1.507 mg/liter for every 1 mg/liter increase (decrease) in TOC. (b) -55.43 mg/liter; extrapolation.

5.27 $\hat{y} = 1.0892 + 0.1890x$; when $x = 20$ degree-days/day, $\hat{y} = 4.87$ hundred cubic feet. This prediction should be quite reliable.

5.29 (a) $\hat{y} = 157.7 - 2.993x$; when $x = 30$, about 68% of males will return. (b) 63.1%.

5.31 (a) $b = 0.16$, $a = 30.2$. (b) $\hat{y} = 78.2$. (c) Regression explains only $r^2 = 36\%$ of final-exam score variability.

5.33 (a) $r \doteq 0.9999$, so recalibration is not necessary. (b) $\hat{y} = 8.825x - 14.52$; when $x = 40$, $\hat{y} \doteq 338.5$ mg/l. (c) The relationship is strong, so the prediction should be very accurate.

5.35 (a) Ignoring the outlier, the plot shows a moderately strong negative linear relationship. (b) For all 12 points: $r = -0.3387$. Without the outlier: $r = -0.7866$. The outlier weakens the linear pattern.

5.37 For all 12 points: $\hat{y} = -492.6 - 33.79x$. Without the outlier: $\hat{y} = -1371.6 - 75.52x$. The line is pulled toward the outlier to reduce the very large vertical deviation of this point from the line.

5.39 (a) Any point that falls exactly on the regression line will not increase the sum of squared vertical distances. (b) Influential points are those whose x coordinates are outliers.

5.41 The scatterplot suggests a negative linear association, with correlation $r \doteq -0.9179$.

5.43 The 21 points in the scatterplot are divided into three clusters of seven points each.

5.45 **(a)** Residuals: 8.1, 12.1, −0.87, −9.9, 1.1, −3.9, −15.9, 6.1, 3.1. **(b)** $r = 0$.

5.47 People who are overweight are more likely to be on diets.

5.49 Lots of things change over time: students, teachers, technology, . . .

5.51 For example, suppose each worker's salary is his/her age (in thousands of dollars per year), and most workers are currently 30 to 50 years old. Over the next 10 years, all workers age, and their salaries increase. If each salary increases by between $4000 and $8000, then every worker will be making *more* money than he/she did 10 years before, but *less* money than a worker of that same age 10 years before.

5.53 About 4.1 points above the final-exam mean.

5.55 **(a)** What most people see as the "best line" is different from the line chosen by the least-squares process. **(b)** Most people tend to overestimate the slope.

Chapter 6

6.1 **(a)** 858 people. **(b)** 43 had arthritis. **(c)** 71 (8.3%) played elite soccer, 215 (25.1%) played non-elite soccer, and 572 (66.7%) did not play.

6.3 For example, $89/9321 \doteq 1.0\%$ of female college students are 15 to 17 years old.

6.5 14.1% of elite players have arthritis, compared to 4.2% of the other two groups.

6.7 **(a)** Alaska Airlines: 13.3%. America West: 10.9%. **(b)** For AA: 11.1%, 5.2%, 8.6%, 16.9%, and 14.2%. For AW: 14.4%, 7.9%, 14.5%, 28.7%, 23.3%. **(c)** AW has many Phoenix flights and few Seattle flights, while AA has many Seattle flights and few Phoenix flights.

6.9 (a) **6.10** (b) **6.11** (b) **6.12** (a) **6.13** (b)
6.14 (c) **6.15** (c) **6.16** (b) **6.17** (b) **6.18** (b)

6.19 Marital status: 4.1%, 93.9%, 1.5%, 0.5%. Job grade: 11.6%, 51.5%, 30.2%, 6.7%.

6.21 17.2%, 65.9%, 14.8%, 2.1%.

6.23 Age is the main lurking variable: married men are generally older.

6.25 **(a)** No-relapse percents are 58.3% (desipramine), 25.0% (lithium), and 16.7% (placebo). **(b)** Because random assignment was used, causation is indicated.

6.27 Women constitute a majority of associate's, bachelor's, and master's degrees but fall slightly below 50% for professional and doctor's degrees.

6.29 Percents hatching in each group: cold, 59.3%; neutral, 67.9%; hot, 72.1%. The cold temperature made hatching less likely.

6.31 (a) Males: 490 admitted, 210 not. Females: 280 admitted, 220 not. (b) Males: 70% admitted. Females: 56% admitted. (c) Business school: 80% of males, 90% of females. Law school: 10% of males, 33.3% of females. (d) Most male applicants apply to the business school, where admission is easier. A majority of women apply to the law school, which is more selective.

Chapter 7

7.1 For ideas, do a Web search for "college rankings" and read the online descriptions.

7.3 Income from theater showings has been relatively flat, while video and DVD sales have grown tremendously.

7.5 (a) The length changes from 1 to 3 centimeters over each 10-minute time interval. (b) $\hat{y} = -2.39 + 0.158x$. (c) After 1440 minutes, we predict a length of about 225 cm.

7.7 $\bar{x} \doteq 7.9235\%$ and $s \doteq 17.7559\%$; -45.34% to 61.19% is much wider than the actual span.

7.9 Stemplots or boxplots show little difference; the means (0.2426 mg for cicada, 0.2221 mg for control) and medians (0.2380 mg for cicada, 0.2410 mg for control) are also similar.

7.11 (a) The stemplot is roughly symmetric. (b) $\bar{x} = 0.2426$ and $s = 0.0476$ for all plants; without the extremes, $\bar{x} = 0.2433$ and $s = 0.0396$.

7.13 The IQR is 0.059; the smallest mass is an outlier by this rule.

7.15 Other brands account for 36.4% of the market.

7.17 (a) Slightly right-skewed; one observation is somewhat low, but not really an outlier. (b) $\bar{x} = 563.1$ and $M = 560$ km^3 of water. (c) $s = 136.5$ km^3 of water; the five-number summary is Min $= 290$, $Q_1 = 445$, $M = 560$, $Q_3 = 670$, Max $= 900$ km^3 of water.

7.19 The distribution seems to be fairly Normal apart from a high outlier. The five-number summary is Min $= 13°$, $Q_1 = 20°$, $M = 25°$, $Q_3 = 30°$, Max $= 50°$, while $\bar{x} = 25.42°$ and $s = 7.47°$.

7.21 (a) MA angle is explanatory. (b) A moderate-to-weak positive linear association, with one clear outlier. (c) MA angle can be used to give (very rough) estimates of HAV angle, but the spread is wide enough that they would not be too reliable.

7.23 (a) Centimeters. (b) Centimeters. (c) Centimeters. (d) No units.

7.25 Compute and compare the percents of each group giving each rating; for example, 5.9% of black parents rated schools as excellent.

7.27 (a) About 3.5%. (b) About 69.4 to 80.6 ksi.

7.29 (a) $\hat{y} = 133.2 - 6.31x$; the weight of the soap decreases by about 6.31 grams each day. (b) About 108 grams.

7.31 (a) Fidelity Technology Fund. (b) No.

7.33 It is now more common for these stocks to rise and fall together.

7.35 Because they feel more confident after taking the course, or because they have taken the test before.

7.37 A scatterplot shows a moderate positive association ($r \doteq 0.6821$), which supports the idea that the proportion of perch killed rises with the number of perch present.

7.39 The distribution is roughly Normal. $\bar{x} = 15.48$; $s = 5.989$; Min $= 1$, $Q_1 = 11$, $M = 16$, $Q_3 = 20$, Max $= 31$ days. The median date is May 5.

7.41 The five-number summaries are
Min $= 7$, $Q_1 = 12$, $M = 19$, $Q_3 = 22$, Max $= 26$;
Min $= 1$, $Q_1 = 11$, $M = 15.5$, $Q_3 = 19.75$, Max $= 27$;
Min $= 9$, $Q_1 = 13.5$, $M = 16.5$, $Q_3 = 19$, Max $= 31$;
Min $= 1$, $Q_1 = 9$, $M = 11$, $Q_3 = 18$, Max $= 25$.
There is no clearly discernible pattern in the boxes, but the minimum values suggest a cyclic pattern.

7.43 (a) Lean monkeys: $\bar{x} = 8.6833$ kg. Obese monkeys: $\bar{x} = 10.5167$ kg. (b) Lean monkeys: $\hat{y} = 0.541 + 0.0826x$. Obese monkeys: $\hat{y} = 0.371 + 0.0852x$. Energy increases at about the same rate for both types of monkeys, but obese monkeys have a lower intercept, meaning that they expend less energy overall.

7.45 (a) Weeds per meter is explanatory; corn yield is the response. (b) Yield decreases when there are more weeds.

Chapter 8

8.1 This is an observational study. Explanatory variable: cell phone usage. Response variable: presence/absence of brain cancer.

8.3 For example, less parental guidance or presence, less social interaction with peers.

8.5 Population: all U.S. households. Sample: the households from which responses are received.

8.7 It is a convenience sample.

8.9 Number from 01 to 33 and choose 16, 32, 18.

8.11 (a) 0001 through 1410. (b) 0769, 1315, 0094, 0720, and 0906.

8.13 Label midsize accounts from 001 to 500, and small accounts from 0001 to 4400. Midsize: 417, 494, 322, 247, and 097. Small: 3698, 1452, 2605, 2480, and 3716.

8.15 The first wording pulls respondents toward a tax cut.

8.17 (a)   **8.18** (c)   **8.19** (b)   **8.20** (a)   **8.21** (c)

8.22 (b)   **8.23** (a)   **8.24** (c)   **8.25** (a)   **8.26** (b)

8.27 An observational study; the explanatory variable is alcohol consumption, and the response variable is whether or not a subject dies.

8.29 (a) The doctor (not the researcher) chooses the treatment. (b) Type of surgery and the age, sex, and condition of the patient.

8.31 (a) Population: adult residents of the United States. Sample size: 1002. (b) If the order has any effect on how people respond, rotating the order cancels it out.

8.33   Those who feel most strongly are more likely to respond; this result is too high.

8.35   From line 117 we choose 38, 16, 32, 18, 37, 06, 23, 19, 03, 25.

8.37   89.1%.

8.39   Each student has a 10% chance of being interviewed, but each sample must contain exactly 3 older and 2 younger students.

8.41   (a) False. (b) True. (c) False.

8.43   With Table B, choose parcels 19, 27, 26, 17; then 09, 55, 32, 22; then 13, 07, 02, 27; then 40, 01, 18, 25.

8.45   (a) Households without telephones or with unlisted numbers. Such households would likely be made up of poor individuals, those who choose not to have phones, and those who do not wish to have their phone number published. (b) Those with unlisted numbers.

8.47   (a) Dialing a randomly chosen phone number can conceivably contact any person who has a telephone. (b) "Phone-answerers" and "non-phone-answerers" might have different characteristics; a good survey should fairly represent both groups.

8.49   (a) Population: Ontario residents. Sample: the 61,239 people interviewed. (b) Such a large sample should represent both men and women fairly well.

Chapter 9

9.1   Subjects: students. Factor: rate structure. Treatments: one flat rate and peak/off-peak rates. Response variables: amount and time of use.

9.3   Individuals: students. Factors: activity intervention (yes or no) and nutrition intervention (yes or no). Treatments: the four combinations of factor levels. Response variables: physical activity and lunchtime fat consumption.

9.5   (a) Randomly assign 115 students to each group. (b) Table B gives subjects 170, 005, 227, 118, and 007.

9.7   Randomly assign 15 trees to each group.

9.9   The first design is an observational study, and the second is an experiment. Other factors may make one more likely to exercise and less (or more) likely to have a heart attack.

9.11   Consult the definitions and explanations in the text.

9.13   For each person, flip a coin to decide which hand he or she should use first. Record the difference in hand strength for each person.

9.15   For each block (pair of lecture sections), randomly assign one section to be taught using standard methods and one to be taught with multimedia. Then (at the end of the term) compare final-exam scores and students' attitudes.

9.16   (a)   **9.17**   (b)   **9.18**   (b)   **9.19**   (a)   **9.20**   (c)

9.21   (a)   **9.22**   (b)   **9.23**   (a)   **9.24**   (b)

9.25   Treatments were not assigned.

9.27   Randomly assign 100 subjects to each group.

9.29   Use a completely randomized design. From Table B, we assign 20, 11, 38, 31, 07, 24, 17, 09, 06; 36, 15, 23, 34, 16, 19, 18, 33, 39; 08, 30, 27, 12, 04, 35; 02, 32, 25, 14, 29, 03, 22, 26, 10; the rest drink vodka and lemonade.

9.31   Randomly assign 6 schools to each treatment. Table B gives 07, 19, 14, 17, 13, 15 (Group 1), then 08, 21, 20, 11, 24, 09 (Group 2).

9.33   **(a)** Three factors (roller type, dyeing cycle time, and temperature), each with two levels, for a total of eight treatments. The experiment requires 24 fabric specimens. **(b)** Note that because there are eight treatments, this diagram is quite large.

9.35   **(a)** Randomly assign three circles to get extra carbon dioxide; the others are a control group. **(b)** Place pairs of circles close together, and randomly choose one of each pair for treatment.

9.37   **(a)** A block design.

9.39   Divide the men and women into three groups (each) of equal size—three groups with 60 men each, and three more with 40 women each.

9.41   The effects of factors other than the nonphysical treatment have been eliminated or accounted for, so that the differences in improvement observed between the subjects can be attributed to the differences in treatments.

9.43   All the women are assigned to one treatment and all the men to the other. If women and men respond differently to the treatment, the experiment will be strongly biased.

9.45   **(a)** Explanatory variable: beta-carotene/vitamin(s) taken each day (or not). Response variable: whether or not colon cancer develops. **(b)** Assign 216 subjects to each treatment. **(c)** and **(d)** See the definitions in this chapter. **(e)** Perhaps the benefit of fruits and vegetables is the fiber those foods contain. Also, persons who eat lots of fruits and vegetables may have healthier diets overall.

9.47   **(a)** In an observational study, we observe subjects who have chosen to take supplements and compare them with others who do not take supplements. In an experiment, we assign some subjects to take supplements and others to take a placebo. **(b)** Treatments are assigned at random, and a control group is used as a basis for comparison to observe the effects of the treatment. **(c)** Subjects who choose to take supplements are more likely to make healthy lifestyle choices. When random assignment is used, some of those subjects will take the supplement, and some will take the placebo.

Commentary: Data Ethics

1   Opinions may vary. (a) seems to qualify as minimal risk, while (c) seems to be excessive.

3   It is good to plainly state the *purpose* of the research, but refrain from stating the research *thesis*.

7   This offers anonymity, because names are never revealed.

Chapter 10

10.1   Out of many hands in which you hold a pair, the fraction in which you could make four of a kind would be about 88/1000.

10.3   **(a)** There are 4 zeros among the first 50, for a proportion of 0.08.

10.5   **(a)** $S = $ {all numbers between 0 and 24}. **(b)** $S = \{0, 0.01, 0.02, 0.03, \ldots\}$. **(c)** $S = \{A, B, C, D, F\}$. **(d)** $S = \{yes, no\}$.

10.7   Count how many ways each intelligence level can occur; the probabilities are counts/16.

10.9   **(a)** 0.11. **(b)** 0.41.

10.11   **(a)** 0.155. **(b)** 0.609. **(c)** 0.660.

10.13   **(a)** 0.4. **(b)** 0.4. **(c)** 0.2.

10.15   **(a)** $\{X \geq 10\}$. **(b)** Either 0.025 (68–95–99.7 rule) or 0.0228 (Table A).

10.17 $P(Y > 25) = 0.1977$.

10.19   (a)   **10.20**   (b)   **10.21**   (b)   **10.22**   (b)   **10.23**   (c)

10.24   (a)   **10.25**   (b)   **10.26**   (c)   **10.27**   (a)   **10.28**   (c)

10.29   Divide the count of heads by 50 to get your estimate.

10.31   **(a)** Legitimate. **(b)** Not legitimate: the total is more than 1. **(c)** Legitimate.

10.33   0.253, 0.747.

10.35   Results will vary.

10.37   **(a)** 0.4592. **(b)** 0.5408.

10.39   **(a)** 0.16. **(b)** 0.65.

10.41   Each color has probability 1/5.

10.43   **(a)** Discrete. **(b)** $P(X \geq 1) = 0.9$. **(c)** "No more than two nonword errors." $P(X \leq 2) = 0.6$; $P(X < 2) = 0.3$.

10.45   **(a)** Using initials: {(A, D), (A, M), (A, S), (A, R), (D, M), (D, S), (D, R), (M, S), (M, R), (S, R)} . **(b)** 0.1. **(c)** 0.4. **(d)** 0.3.

10.47   Y can be 1, 2, 3, . . . , 12, each with probability 1/12.

10.49   **(a)** 0.9652. **(b)** $P(Z \geq 8.42)$, which is basically 0.

10.51   **(a)** $P(Y > 300) = 0.5$. **(b)** $P(Y > 370) = 0.025$.

10.53   0.8164.

10.55   **(a)** Most answers will be between 35% and 65%.

Chapter 11

11.1   Both are statistics.

11.3   Parameter, statistic.

11.5 If 1 of the 12 homes were lost, it would cost more than the collected premiums. For many policies, the average claim should be close to $250.

11.7 **(a)** $\overline{x}$ is not systematically higher than or lower than μ. **(b)** With large samples, $\overline{x}$ is more likely to be close to μ.

11.9 **(a)** $P(X > 300) = 0.5$, $P(X > 335) = 0.16$. **(b)** Mean 300, standard deviation 17.5. **(c)** $P(\overline{x} > 300) = 0.5$ and $P(\overline{x} > 335) = 0.025$.

11.11 **(a)** 0.5 and 0.099 moths. **(b)** About 0.16.

11.13 We can be about 99.4% certain that average losses will not exceed $275 per policy.

11.15 **(a)** Center: 11.5. Control limits: 11.2 and 11.8. **(b)** Sets A and C each have two out-of-control points. **(c)** Set B is in control. Set A had the sudden shift (at about the 11th or 12th sample). The mean drifted gradually for Set C.

11.17 (c)   **11.18** (b)   **11.19** (b)   **11.20** (a)   **11.21** (c)

11.22 (a)   **11.23** (c)   **11.24** (a)

11.25 65 inches is a statistic; 64 inches is a parameter.

11.27 On the average, Joe loses 40 cents each time he plays.

11.31 Mean 6 strikes/km^2, standard deviation 0.7589 strikes/km^2.

11.33 **(a)** 1/6 inch. **(b)** $n = 283$.

11.35 **(a)** Nearly 1. **(b)** Nearly 0.

11.37 **(a)** About 0.0228. **(b)** Nearly 0.

11.39 About 0.2233 g/mi.

11.41 **(a)** Approximately $N(2.2, 0.1941)$. **(b)** 0.1515. **(c)** 0.0764.

11.43 **(a)** 19, 22, 39, 50, 34; $\hat{p} = 0.6$. **(b)** Two samples give $\hat{p} = 0.4$, four give 0.6, three give 0.8, and one gives 1. **(d)** Because an SRS is unbiased, 0.6 should be in the center.

11.45 Center: 4.22. Control limits: 4.05 and 4.39.

11.47 3.84 to 4.60.

11.49 **(a)** 99.8%. **(b)** 95.7%.

Chapter 12

12.1 About 0.38 (0.3773).

12.3 With a few assumptions, we find that this probability is about 0.5953.

12.5 **(a)** 30%. **(b)** 40%.

12.7 0.25.

12.9 0.3375.

12.11 3.64%.

12.13 75%.

12.15 30% are nonword errors.

12.17 (b)   **12.18** (b)   **12.19** (c)   **12.20** (a)   **12.21** (b)

12.22 (c)   **12.23** (c)   **12.24** (b)   **12.25** (c)   **12.26** (b)

12.27 0.1001.

12.29 (a) About 0.33. (b) About 0.66.

12.31 The two events (being 75 or older and being a woman) are probably not independent.

12.33 (a) 0.3. (b) 0.3. (c) Yes.

12.35 $P(D) = 0.4$.

12.37 (a) 0.294. (b) 0.2993.

12.39 (a) 1/3. (b) 1/2.

12.41 (a) 0.5756. (b) 0.4699. (c) No.

12.45 0.1.

12.47 (a) 5/36. (b) 25/216. (c) $(5/6)^3(1/6)$; $(5/6)^4(1/6)$; $(5/6)^k(1/6)$.

12.49 0.445.

12.51 About 34% (0.3371).

12.53 The unemployment rates are 0.0852, 0.0523, 0.0425, and 0.0272. If education and being employed were independent, the rates would be the same.

12.55 (a) $P(C|E) = 0.3287$. (b) $P(E|C) = 0.7578$.

12.57 (a) Either B or O. (b) $P(B) = 0.75$, $P(O) = 0.25$.

12.59 (a) 0.25. (b) 0.015625. (c) 0.140625.

Chapter 13

13.1 Yes.

13.3 No; p does not remain fixed.

13.5 (a) Caught: binomial, $n = 10$, $p = 0.7$. Missed: binomial, $n = 10$, $p = 0.3$. (b) 0.2668; 0.6172.

13.7 0.5294.

13.9 (a) 7 errors caught, 3 missed. (b) 1.4491 errors. (c) With $p = 0.9$, 0.9487 errors; with $p = 0.99$, 0.3146 errors. σ decreases toward 0 as p approaches 1.

13.11 $\mu \doteq 59.044$ home runs; $P(H \geq 70) \doteq P(Z \geq 1.52) = 0.0643$.

13.13 (b)   **13.14** (b)   **13.15** (c)   **13.16** (b)   **13.17** (c)

13.18 (b)   **13.19** (c)   **13.20** (a)   **13.21** (b)

13.23 (a) p varies from one attempt to another. (b) The binomial distribution is appropriate.

13.25 (a) $n = 20$ and $p = 0.25$. (b) 5 correct guesses. (c) $P(X = 5) \doteq 0.2023$.

13.27 Let N be the number of households with 3 or more cars. Then N has a binomial distribution with $n = 12$ and $p = 0.2$. (a) $P(N = 0) \doteq 0.0687$; $P(N \geq 1) \doteq 0.9313$. (b) $\mu = 2.4$ and $\sigma \doteq 1.3856$ households. (c) 0.4417.

13.29 (a) 3075 dropouts. (b) $P(X \geq 3500) \doteq P(Z > 8.18) \doteq 0$.

13.31 (a) $\mu = 148.8$ and $\sigma \doteq 11.4170$ Hispanics. (b) 125 to 172. (c) At least 1613 adults.

13.33 (a) 0.3115. (b) $\mu = 60$ red-blossomed plants. (c) 0.9951.

13.35 0.0901; this is some evidence against the coin being fair, but it is not overwhelming.

Chapter 14

14.1 (a) 1.8974. (b) $m \doteq 3.8$. (c) Both intervals should be 7.6 units wide. (d) 95%.

14.3 (a) Most answers: between 5 and 10 hits. (b) Most answers: between 76% and 84% hits in 1000 tries.

14.5 We are 95% confident that the concentration of active ingredient in this batch is between 0.8327 and 0.8481 g/l.

14.7 (a) 18.9 to 25.1 points. (b) 15.8 to 28.2 points. (c) 20.45 to 23.55 points. (d) 6.2, 3.1, and 1.55, respectively. Margin of error decreases with larger samples.

14.9 $n = 2401$.

14.11 (c)   **14.12** (c)   **14.13** (b)   **14.14** (a)   **14.15** (c)

14.16 (c)   **14.17** (a)   **14.18** (a)   **14.19** (b)   **14.20** (c)

14.21 5.91 ± 0.167, or 5.743 to 6.077.

14.23 Lower confidence requires a smaller margin of error.

14.25 (b) -4.526% to -2.648%.

14.27 (a) We assume that the 10 students can be considered to be an SRS of the population of students, and that odor thresholds are Normally distributed. The latter condition is supported by a stemplot. (b) 26.06 to 34.74 μg/l.

14.29 (a) The distribution is slightly skewed to the right. (b) 223.973 to 224.031 mm.

14.31 (a) 50 degrees. (b) 22.7 to 26.8 degrees.

14.33 (a) 10.0021 to 10.0025 g. (b) Take $n = 22$.

14.35 Other surveys should be close to the truth—not necessarily close to the results of this survey.

14.37 The sample size for women was more than twice as large as that for men.

14.39 For 92.5% confidence, the critical value is 1.780.

Chapter 15

15.1 (a) $N(12 \text{ g/dl}, 0.2263 \text{ g/dl})$. (b) 11.3 lies far from the middle of the curve and is therefore unlikely if in fact $\mu = 12$. 11.8 is close to the middle, so it would not be too surprising.

15.3 $H_0: \mu = 12$; $H_a: \mu < 12$.

15.5 $H_0: \mu = 51$; $H_a: \mu < 51$.

15.7 Hypotheses should be stated in terms of μ, not $\overline{x}$.

15.9 -3.09 and -0.88.

15.13 0.0010 and 0.1894.

15.15 Not significant at either level.

15.17 (a) Such results would rarely occur if vitamin C were ineffective. (b) Such results would occur less than 1% of the time if vitamin C were ineffective.

15.19 $\overline{x} = 13.1087$ points, $z \doteq 1.78$, $P \doteq 0.0375$; this is fairly strong evidence that the mean change is positive.

15.21 $z > 2.576$.

15.23 (a) $z \doteq -2.20$. (b) Significant at the 5% level. (c) Not significant at the 1% level. (d) z is between 2.054 and 2.326, so P is between 0.02 and 0.04.

15.25 (a) No. (b) Yes.

15.26 (a)   **15.27** (b)   **15.28** (c)   **15.29** (b)   **15.30** (b)

15.31 (c)   **15.32** (a)   **15.33** (a)   **15.34** (b)   **15.35** (a)

15.37 $H_0: \mu = 100$; $H_a: \mu \neq 100$; $z = 2.17$, $P = 0.0300$.

15.39 $H_0: \mu = 0\%$; $H_a: \mu < 0\%$; $z = -9.84$, so $P \doteq 0$.

15.41 The interval gives an estimated range for the true mean μ and also tells us that the result is not significant in a two-sided test at the 10% level, because 5.19 is in the interval.

15.43 (a) The alternative hypothesis should be formulated without looking at the data. Before looking at the data, we had no reason to expect that women would rate a movie more highly. (b) $P = 0.0358$.

15.45 μ is the mean difference between the two groups; $H_0: \mu = 0$; $H_a: \mu < 0$.

15.47 The differences observed would occur less than 1% of the time if pig skulls had no special meaning.

15.49 The differences in richness and total stem densities between the two areas were so small that they could easily occur by chance if population means were identical.

15.51 Something that occurs "less than once in 100 repetitions" also occurs "less than 5 times in 100 repetitions," but not vice versa.

15.53 It is essentially correct.

Chapter 16

16.1 (a) Yes. (b) No: the numbers are based on voluntary response rather than an SRS.

16.3 (a) Not included. (b) Not included. (c) Included.

16.5 (a) $z = 1.61$ is not significant. (b) $z = 1.67$ is significant.

16.7 (a) $z \doteq -0.89$, $P = 0.1867$. (b) $z \doteq -1.55$, $P = 0.0606$. (c) $z \doteq -2.53$, $P = 0.0057$.

16.9 (a) The differences observed might occur by chance even if SES had no effect. (b) This tells us that the test was not insignificant merely because of a small sample size.

16.11 (a) $n = 35$. (b) $n = 14$.

16.13 (a) Increase the sample size. (b) The power will increase. (c) The power will increase.

16.15 (a) H_0: Patient is healthy; H_a: Patient is ill. Type I error: sending a healthy patient to the doctor. Type II error: clearing a patient who is ill. (These hypotheses, and error types, could be switched.)

16.17 (a) Reject H_0 when $z < -1.645$. (b) Reject H_0 when $\bar{x} < 4.7877$. (c) The power is $P(Z < 0.68) = 0.7517$.

16.19 (c)   **16.20** (a)   **16.21** (b)   **16.22** (c)   **16.23** (a)

16.24 (a)   **16.25** (a)   **16.26** (b)   **16.27** (a)   **16.28** (b)

16.29 Were the 148 respondents chosen at random from the population? What was the rate of nonresponse?

16.31 (a) This is not an SRS from the population of all women. (b) It may be reasonable to view this sample as an SRS of women who shop at large suburban malls.

16.33 For example, poorly worded questions, a poorly chosen sample, nonresponse.

16.35 A significance test answers only question (b).

16.37 You have information about all states, not just a sample.

16.39 (a) Depending on the time of day or the day of the week, certain types of shoppers would or would not be present. (b) The distribution is strongly right-skewed, violating the assumption of Normality.

16.41 (a) 0.05. (b) We expect about 3 or 4 significant tests by chance.

16.43 Because of the large sample size, this significant difference may not indicate a strong preference.

16.45 (a) The observed difference would occur in less than 1% of all samples if the two populations actually have the same proportion remaining on welfare. (b) The method used is correct 95% of the time. (c) No: treatments were not randomly assigned.

16.47   A low-power test will often accept H_0 when it is false simply because it is difficult to distinguish between H_0 and nearby alternatives.

16.49   0.86.

16.51   **(a)** Power is $1 - P(-5.35 \le Z \le -1.43) \doteq 0.9236$. **(b)** Power is 0.9236. More than 90% of the time, this test will detect a difference of 6. **(c)** The power would be higher; greater differences are easier to detect.

Chapter 17

17.1   This is an experiment, because treatments are assigned. Explanatory variable: price history (steady or fluctuating). Response variable: price the subject expects to pay.

17.3   **(a)** Label from 0001 to 3478. **(b)** 2940, 0769, 1481, 2975, 1315. **(c)** The response variable is how much money the students earn in the summer.

17.5   **(a)** The control group should have 24 trees with no beehives. **(b)** Table B gives 53, 64, 56, and 68. **(c)** The response variable is elephant damage.

17.7   Both are statistics.

17.9   It is likely to weaken the association, because we expect that marijuana usage will be underreported to a greater degree than accidents caused.

17.11 $H_0: \mu = 188$; $H_a: \mu < 188$; $z \doteq -1.46$, $P = 0.0721$.

17.13 $z = -2.92$ and $P = 0.0018$; small differences can be significant with large sample sizes.

17.15 $H_0: \mu = 100$ ng/g; $H_a: \mu > 100$ ng/g; $z \doteq 14.54$, $P \doteq 0$.

17.17   84.8 to 90.4.

17.19   **(a)** The treatment was not assigned. **(b)** Socioeconomic and hereditary factors may also affect IQ.

17.21   **(a)** 0.19. **(b)** 0.287.

17.23   **(a)** All probabilities are between 0 and 1, and they add to 1. **(b)** 0.94. **(c)** 0.86. **(d)** Either $X \ge 4$ or $X > 3$; 0.06.

17.25   0.0125.

17.27   **(a)** Nearly all should be in the range 92 to 452. **(b)** $\bar{x}$ will nearly always fall in the range 254 to 290.

17.29 $z = -7.78$, $P \doteq 0$.

17.31   The interval is 1238.52 to 1243.14 ft^2.

17.33   **(a)** For example: Did subject get a job? Did subject keep the job? For the design, randomly assign about one-third of the group to each treatment, and observe the chosen response variables after a suitable amount of time. **(b)** Label from 00001 through 10065 and choose 06565, 00795, and 08727.

17.35 (a) A response at least as large at that observed would be seen almost half the time (just by chance) even if there were no effect in the entire population of rats. (b) The differences observed were so small that they would often happen just by chance.

17.37 The increase in fires over time would occur less than 1% of the time by chance. This straight-line relationship explains 61% of the variation in the number of fires.

17.39 Placebos can provide genuine pain relief. (Believing that one will experience relief can lead to actual relief.)

17.41 (a) Increase. (b) Decrease. (c) Decrease. (d) Decrease.

17.43 (a) Factors: storage method (fresh, room temperature for one month, refrigerated for one month) and preparation method (cooked immediately or after one hour). This makes six treatments (storage-preparation combinations). Response variables: tasters' color and flavor ratings. (b) Randomly allocate n potatoes to each of the 6 groups, then compare ratings. (c) For each taster, randomly choose the order in which the fries are tasted.

17.45 $P(A) = P(B) = \ldots = P(F) = 0.12$ and $P(1) = P(2) = \ldots = P(8) = 0.035$.

17.47 We cannot reject H_0, because $150,000 falls in the 99% confidence interval; H_a is two-sided, and $\alpha = 0.01$.

17.49 Type I: we conclude that mean IQ is less than 100 when it really is 100 (or more). Type II: we conclude that the mean IQ is 100 (or more) when it is truly less than 100.

17.51 0.1622.

17.53 (a) Binomial with $n = 1555$ and $p = 0.2$. (b) $P(X \le 300) \doteq P(Z \le -0.7) = 0.2420$.

17.55 Two consecutive years: 0.25. Four consecutive years: 0.0625.

17.57 $P(X \le 1090) \doteq P(Z \le 2.25) \doteq 0.9878$.

17.59 0.036.

17.61 About 22.8%.

17.63 $P(C|A) = 0.10 = 10\%$.

17.73 (a) The two extra patients can be randomly assigned to two of the three groups. (b) No one involved in administering the treatments or assessing their effectiveness knew which subjects were in which group. (c) The pain scores in Group A were so much lower than the scores in Group C that such a difference would not often happen by chance. However, the difference between A and B could be due to chance.

Chapter 18

18.1 4.8925 minutes.

18.3 (a) 2.015. (b) 2.518.

18.5 (a) 2.262. (b) 2.861. (c) 1.440.

18.7 The distribution is slightly, but not unreasonably, left-skewed, with no outliers. The interval is 55.71% to 63.47%.

18.9 (a) 24. (b) t is between 1.059 and 1.318, so $0.20 < P < 0.30$. (c) $t = 1.12$ is not significant at either level.

18.11 (a) μ is the mean difference in healing rates. $H_0: \mu = 0$, and H_a is either $\mu < 0$ or $\mu > 0$, depending on the order of subtraction. (b) The stemplot is roughly Normal. (c) $t = 2.02$, df $= 13$, $P = 0.032$.

18.13 (a) The outlier is the only significant departure from Normality. (b) $t = 2.076$, df $= 11$, $P = 0.031$ (all newts); $t = 1.788$, df $= 10$, $P = 0.052$ (without the outlier).

18.15 (b)   **18.16** (c)   **18.17** (a)   **18.18** (a)   **18.19** (c)

18.20 (a)   **18.21** (c)   **18.22** (a)   **18.23** (b)   **18.24** (c)

18.25 Student group: $t = 0.749$, for which Table C gives $0.4 < P < 0.5$. Nonstudent group: $t = 3.277$, for which Table C gives $0.005 < P < 0.01$.

18.27 (a) $\bar{x} = 15.59$ ft and $s = 2.550$ ft. (b) 14.81 to 16.37 ft. We reject the claim that $\mu = 20$ ft. (c) What population are we examining? Full-grown sharks? Male sharks? Can this be considered an SRS?

18.29 8.07 to 11.69 days (using Table C) or 8.10 to 11.66 days (using software).

18.31 The distribution is right-skewed, but t procedures are robust for large samples.

18.33 18.69 to 70.19 μg.

18.35 (a) Weather conditions that change from day to day can affect spore counts. (b) Take the differences, kill room count minus processing count. The interval is 843.2 to 2805.8 CFUs/m^3. (c) The data are counts, which are at best only approximately Normal, and we have only a small sample.

18.37 (a) A subject's responses to the two treatments would not be independent. (b) Yes ($t = -4.41$, $P = 0.0069$).

18.39 The data contain two extreme high outliers, 5973 and 8015. These may distort the t statistic.

18.41 The distribution is slightly skewed but has no apparent outliers, so t procedures are acceptable. To test $H_0: \mu = 224$ mm; $H_a: \mu \neq 224$ mm, we find $t \doteq 0.13$, df $= 15$, $P = 0.9$.

18.43 (a) For each subject, randomly select which knob should be used first. (b) μ is the mean of (right-hand-thread time minus left-hand-thread time); $H_0: \mu = 0$ sec; $H_a: \mu < 0$ sec. $t = -2.90$, df $= 24$, $P = 0.0039$; right-hand-thread times are less.

18.45 -21.2 to -5.5 sec. $\bar{x}_{RH}/\bar{x}_{LH} = 88.7\%$.

Chapter 19

19.1 Matched pairs.

19.3 Single sample.

19.5 (a) Oregon: $n = 6$, $\bar{x} = 26.9$, $s = 3.82$. California: $n = 7$, $\bar{x} = 11.9$, $s = 7.09$. (b) Use conservative df $= 5$.

19.7 (a) Compressed shows no particular cause for concern. Intermediate shows the skewness and outlier described in the text. (b) $H_0: \mu_C = \mu_I$; $H_a: \mu_C < \mu_I$; $t = -6.013$, $P < 0.001$.

19.9 -0.5126 to -0.2471 (df $= 18$) or -0.5092 to -0.2506 (df $= 28.6$).

19.11 (a) Breast-feeding women and other women. (b) $H_0: \mu_1 = \mu_2$; $H_a: \mu_1 < \mu_2$; $t = 8.50$, $P < 0.001$.

19.13 $\bar{x}_1 = 17.6\%$, $\bar{x}_2 = 9.49983\%$, $s_1 \doteq 6.3401\%$, and $s_2 \doteq 1.9501\%$.

19.15 $t = 2.99$, $P = 0.0246$; significant at 5% level.

19.17 (a) 3.68. (b) Not significant at either level.

19.19 $H_0: \sigma_I = \sigma_C$; $H_a: \sigma_I \neq \sigma_C$; $F \doteq 2.98$, $P = 0.0229$.

19.21 $H_0: \sigma_1 = \sigma_2$; $H_a: \sigma_1 \neq \sigma_2$; $F \doteq 10.57$, $P = 0.0217$.

19.22 (a)   **19.23** (c)   **19.24** (b)   **19.25** (a)   **19.26** (b)

19.27 (c)   **19.28** (a)   **19.29** (b)

19.31 (b) $H_0: \mu_G = \mu_B$; $H_a: \mu_G \neq \mu_B$; $t \doteq 1.64$, $P = 0.1057$.

19.33 -1.24 to 11.48 (df $= 30$) or -1.12 to 11.35 (df $= 56.9$).

19.35 851.0 to 3008.0 CFUs (df $= 3$) or 869.7 to 2989.3 CFUs (df $= 3.136$).

19.37 $t = -3.74$; $0.01 < P < 0.02$.

19.39 4.30 to 49.70 g (df $= 8$) or 5.77 to 48.23 g (df $= 17.08$); significant at 10%.

19.41 We test $H_0: \mu_1 = \mu_2$ versus $H_a: \mu_1 > \mu_2$ for both analyses. For Analysis 1, $t = 6.849$, df $= 4$ or 16.51. For Analysis 2, $t = 7.066$, df $= 9$ or 14.84. In both cases, P is very small.

19.43 (a) $H_0: \mu_1 = \mu_2$; $H_a: \mu_1 > \mu_2$; $t \doteq 2.646$; either df $= 426$ or 534.45 gives $P < 0.005$. (b) 0.06 to 15.94 points (df $= 100$) or 0.184 to 15.816 points (df $= 534.45$). (c) A 16-point gain on the SAT is unlikely to make a practical difference.

19.45 $H_0: \mu_1 = \mu_2$; $H_a: \mu_1 > \mu_2$; $t \doteq 1.914$; $0.025 < P < 0.05$. The confidence interval is 0.03 to 6.27 points (df $= 7$) or 0.25 to 6.05 points (df $= 13.92$).

19.47 $H_0: \mu_1 = \mu_2$; $H_a: \mu_1 \neq \mu_2$; $t \doteq 3.331$; $0.02 < P < 0.04$ (df $= 4$) or 0.0181 (df $= 5.476$).

19.49 0.7 and 8 pounds (df $= 4$) or 1.1 and 7.6 pounds (df $= 5.476$).

19.51 (a) A 95% confidence interval for μ_w is 3.84 to 4.71 drinks. (b) A 95% confidence interval for μ_m is 5.78 to 7.26 drinks. (c) To test $H_0: \mu_w = \mu_m$ versus $H_a: \mu_w \neq \mu_m$, we find $t \doteq -5.193$, $P < 0.001$. A 95% confidence interval for $\mu_m - \mu_w$ tells us that, on the average, sophomore men who drink claim an additional 1.4 to 3.1 drinks per day.

Chapter 20

20.1 (a) p is the proportion of the population (all college students) who say they pray at least once in a while. (b) $\hat{p} = 0.8425$.

20.3 (a) Mean 0.5, standard deviation 0.0041. (b) 0.9854.

20.5 0.4714, 0.7924, and 0.9886; larger sample sizes give more accurate estimates.

20.7 There were only 5 or 6 "successes" in the sample.

20.9 (a) $n = 1009$, the sample proportion is $\hat{p} = 0.70$, and the count (rounded) is 706. (b) Of the large number of samples conducted by Harris's method, 95% capture the true population proportion within the stated margin of error. (c) The interval is 0.7 ± 0.028, which has a margin of error of (roughly) $\pm 3\%$.

20.11 (a) The number of "successes" is only 9. (b) 0.1078 ± 0.0505, or 0.0573 to 0.1584.

20.13 (a) $\hat{p} \doteq 0.8185$; the margin of error is 0.0460. (b) With $p^* = \hat{p}$, we need $n = 635$.

20.15 $\hat{p} = 0.415$, $z \doteq -2.40$, $P = 0.0164$ (from Table A) or 0.0162 (software).

20.17 (a) $np_0 = n(1 - p_0) = 5$. (b) $n(1 - p_0) = 2$.

20.18 (b)   **20.19** (c)   **20.20** (c)   **20.21** (b)   **20.22** (c)

20.23 (a)   **20.24** (a)   **20.25** (a)   **20.26** (c)   **20.27** (a)

20.29 (a) 0.7479 to 0.9162. (b) We need to know how they were chosen. (All from the same school? Public or private? Etc.)

20.31 $\hat{p} \doteq 0.5812$ (or $\tilde{p} \doteq 0.5785$). With either large-sample or plus four methods, the interval is about 0.49 to 0.67.

20.33 $z = 1.76$, $P = 0.0392$ (from Table A) or 0.0395 (software).

20.35 (a) The failure count (5) is too small. (b) 0.6020 to 0.8795.

20.37 (a) Large-sample: $\hat{p} = 0.1486$, and the interval is 0.0913 to 0.2060. Plus four: $\tilde{p} = 0.1579$, and the interval is 0.0999 to 0.2159. (b) $n = 304$. (c) Nonresponse is one problem. These findings may not apply to businesses that are very different from those in the sample.

20.39 (a) 0.0588, 0.0784, 0.0898, 0.0960, 0.0980, 0.0960, 0.0898, 0.0784, 0.0588. (b) 0.0263, 0.0351, 0.0402, 0.0429, 0.0438, 0.0429, 0.0402, 0.0351, 0.0263. The new margins of error are less than half their former size.

20.41 To test $H_0: p = 1/3$ versus $H_a: p > 1/3$, we have $\hat{p} \doteq 0.3786$, $z \doteq 2.72$, $P = 0.0033$.

20.43 The interval is 0.5320 to 0.7180 (large sample) or 0.5288 to 0.7119 (plus four). To test $H_0: p = 0.5$ versus $H_a: p > 0.5$, we find $z \doteq 2.55$, $P = 0.0054$.

Chapter 21

21.1 0.2916 to 0.3691.

21.3 0.1306 to 0.3470.

21.5 $H_0: p_1 = p_2; H_a: p_1 > p_2; z \doteq 0.98, P = 0.1635$.

21.7 (b)   **21.8** (a)   **21.9** (c)   **21.10** (b)   **21.11** (b)

21.12 (a)   **21.13** (b)   **21.14** (b)

21.15 **(a)** One count is 0. **(b)** The plus four interval for $p_1 - p_2$ is 0.3978 to 0.8736. **(c)** Because 0 is not in the interval, we have very strong evidence that altered mice are more susceptible to tumors.

21.17 $H_0: p_1 = p_2; H_a: p_1 > p_2; z \doteq 2.96, P = 0.0015$.

21.19 $H_0: p_1 = p_2; H_a: p_1 \neq p_2; z \doteq 3.39, P = 0.0006$.

21.21 0.0631 to 0.2179 (plus four: 0.0614 to 0.2158).

21.23 The two samples are not independent, because the same 23 facilities were used for both.

21.25 $H_0: p_1 = p_2; H_a: p_1 < p_2; z \doteq -2.25, P = 0.0122$.

21.27 **(a)** An observational study, because no treatment was imposed. **(b)** $H_0: p_1 = p_2; H_a: p_1 > p_2; z \doteq 5.02, P$ is very small.

21.29 Use the plus four interval, because one count is only 7: –0.0399 to 0.3685.

21.31 $H_0: p_1 = p_2; H_a: p_1 < p_2; z \doteq -2.32, P = 0.0102$. A 95% confidence interval for $p_1 - p_2$ is –0.3474 to –0.0334 (plus four: –0.3401 to –0.0285).

21.33 The actual study used an experimental design; this exercise describes an observational study.

Chapter 22

22.1 **(a)** Two-sample z for proportions. **(b)** Two-sample t for means.

22.3 No: we have information about all players, not just a sample.

22.5 **(a)** Two-sample z for proportions. **(b)** Two-sample t for means. **(c)** Two-sample z for proportions.

22.7 Randomly allocate the given numbers of taxpayers to each of the three treatment groups, then compare how many open an IRA from each group.

22.9 $H_0: p_1 = p_2; H_a: p_1 < p_2; z \doteq -8.70, P$ is very small.

22.11 –$333.62 to $681.62 (df = 40) or –$328.19 to $676.19 (df = 61.37).

22.13 0.4422 to 0.4976 (plus four: 0.4423 to 0.4976).

22.15 315.24 to 318.76 points (using either df = 100 or 1013).

22.17 0.2544 to 0.3400 (plus four: 0.2556 to 0.3410).

22.19 H_0: $\mu_f = \mu_m$; H_a: $\mu_f > \mu_m$; $t \doteq 2.21$; $0.01 < P < 0.02$ (df = 100) or $P = 0.0143$ (df = 186.02).

22.21 $\hat{p}_{1998} = 85.3\%$. $\hat{p}_{2001} = 76.9\%$. H_0: $p_{1998} = p_{2001}$; H_a: $p_{1998} > p_{2001}$; $z \doteq 5.23$, P is very small.

22.23 0.6315 to 0.6485. (If we assume that $0.64 = 7794/12{,}178$, we can find a plus four interval: 0.6314 to 0.6485.)

22.25 H_0: $p = 0.5$; H_a: $p \neq 0.5$; $z \doteq 1.90$, $P = 0.0578$ (0.0574 with Table A).

22.27 H_0: $\mu_1 = \mu_2$; H_a: $\mu_1 > \mu_2$; $t \doteq 10.4$, $P < 0.0001$ (df = 19 or 32.39).

22.29 H_0: $\mu_1 = \mu_2$; H_a: $\mu_1 < \mu_2$; $t \doteq -3.50$, $P < 0.0005$ (df = 100 or 216.4).

22.31 H_0: $p_1 = p_2$; H_a: $p_1 \neq p_2$; $z \doteq 6.79$, P is very small.

22.33 –14.57 to 52.57 mg/dl (df = 22) or –13.64 to 51.64 mg/dl (df = 43.3).

22.35 We assume two SRSs from Normal populations. It is unlikely we have random samples from either population, especially among pets.

22.37 H_0: $\mu = 0.604$ inch; H_a: $\mu \neq 0.604$ inch; $t \doteq -1.403$; $0.10 < P < 0.20$ (df = 39).

22.39 H_0: $\mu_1 = \mu_2$; H_a: $\mu_1 \neq \mu_2$; $t \doteq 46.16$, P is very small (df = 7 or 10.87).

22.41 H_0: $\mu_1 = \mu_2$; H_a: $\mu_1 \neq \mu_2$; $t \doteq -0.727$; $0.40 < P < 0.50$ (df = 28) or $P = 0.47$ (df = 46.19).

22.43 (a) The diabetic potentials appear to be larger. (b) H_0: $\mu_D = \mu_N$; H_a: $\mu_D \neq \mu_N$; $t \doteq 3.077$; $0.005 < P < 0.01$ (df = 17) or $P = 0.0039$ (df = 36.60). (c) $t \doteq 3.841$; $0.001 < P < 0.002$ (df = 16) or $P = 0.0005$ (df = 37.15).

22.45 14.22 to 16.75 days, or May 3 through May 6.

22.47 (a) Standard error of the mean $= s/\sqrt{n}$. (b) Two-sample t-tests. (c) The observed differences between the two groups were so large that they would rarely occur if the two groups were not different. Smaller P is stronger evidence.

22.49 H_0: $\sigma_0 = \sigma_1$; H_a: $\sigma_0 \neq \sigma_1$; $F \doteq 1.54$, df = 48 and 239. With the $F(30, 200)$ distribution (Table D), $0.05 < P < 0.10$. With software, $P = 0.0393$.

22.51 (a) $t^* \doteq 2.423$. (b) Reject H_0 if $t \geq t^*$, that is, when $\overline{x} \geq 37$. (c) The power against $\mu = 100$ is $P(Z \geq -4.12) > 0.9998$. A sample of size 50 should be quite adequate.

Chapter 23

23.1 (a) 29.9%, 28.9%, 21.9%, 19.3%. (b) 26.6%, 30.9%, 19.4%, 23.0%; 39.8%, 21.1%, 27.1%, 12.0%. (c) There is no substantial difference between the first two groups, but university-educated men seem to be more likely to be nonsmokers or moderate smokers.

23.3 The z- and P-values are $z = 0.66$, $P = 0.5092$; $z = -1.84$, $P = 0.0658$; $z = -2.32$, $P = 0.0204$.

23.5 **(a)** 42.31, 36.22, 30.14, 24.34. The sum might differ slightly from 133 due to rounding. **(b)** The heavy-smoker count is less than expected, but the moderate-smoker count is higher.

23.7 **(b)** $X^2 = 13.305$, $P = 0.038$. **(c)** University-educated men contribute three of the four largest terms.

23.9 All expected cell counts are well over 5.

23.11 **(a)** The biggest difference is that a higher percent of women chose administration, while greater proportions of men chose other fields, especially finance. **(b)** Yes: only one (12.5%) count is less than 5. **(c)** $X^2 = 10.827$, $P = 0.013$. We have fairly strong evidence that gender and choice of major are related. **(d)** The two "administration" cells contribute the most: many more women (and fewer men) chose this major than we would expect if there were no relationship between gender and choice of major. **(e)** 46.5%.

23.13 **(a)** $(3 - 1)(4 - 1) = 6$. **(b)** $12.59 < X^2 < 14.45$, so $0.025 < P < 0.05$.

23.15 H_0: $p_1 = p_2 = p_3 = \frac{1}{3}$; H_a: not all three are equally likely; $X^2 = 16.11$, df $= 2$, $P < 0.0005$.

23.17 **(a)** 24.2%, 41.8%, 22.0%, 12.1%. Fewer A's, more D/F's. **(b)** 29.12, 37.31, 18.20, 6.37. **(c)** H_0: $p_1 = 0.32$, $p_2 = 0.41$, $p_3 = 0.20$, $p_4 = 0.07$; H_a: at least one of these probabilities is different. All expected counts are more than 5. $X^2 = 5.297$, df $= 3$, $P = 0.1513$.

23.19 (b) **23.20** (a) **23.21** (a) **23.22** (c) **23.23** (a)

23.24 (a) **23.25** (b) **23.26** (a) **23.27** (c) **23.28** (b)

23.29 **(a)** -0.1877 to -0.1077 (plus four: -0.1874 to -0.1076). **(b)** H_0: $p_r = p_s = p_u$; H_a: some proportion is different; $X^2 = 52.5$, df $= 2$, $P < 0.0005$.

23.31 **(a)** 0.6011 to 0.6834 (plus four: 0.6005 to 0.6827). **(b)** $\hat{p}_b \doteq 55.8\%$, $\hat{p}_w \doteq 65.4\%$, and $\hat{p}_o \doteq 67.3\%$. To test H_0: $p_b = p_w = p_o$ versus H_a: some proportion is different, we find $X^2 \doteq 4.319$, df $= 2$, $0.10 < P < 0.15$.

23.33 **(a)** Black: 273 belted, 96 not. Hispanic: 372 belted, 168 not. White: 193 belted, 64 not. **(b)** $X^2 = 4.513$, df $= 2$, $0.10 < P < 0.15$.

23.35 **(a)** $\hat{p}_b \doteq 0.6553$, $\hat{p}_g \doteq 0.5614$, $z \doteq 1.66$, $P \doteq 0.0970$. **(b)** $X^2 = 2.754$, df $= 1$, $0.05 < P < 0.10$.

23.37 **(a)** "Less than high school" had the highest support; "some college" was lowest. "Less than high school" contributes the most to X^2. Support is highest with the least and the most educated, and lowest in the middle. **(b)** df $= (2 - 1)(5 - 1) = 4$. $X^2 = 8.525$ is larger than 4, the mean under H_0; $P = 0.074$ tells us the evidence is not significant at $\alpha = 0.05$.

23.39 American students are more interested in saving time (25% of Americans, 14% of Asians) and ease (24% of Americans, 16% of Asians), while Asian students place much more emphasis on low price (American: 15%; Asian: 49%). To test H_0: there is no difference between American and Asian students versus H_a: at least one American/Asian proportion is different, we find $X^2 = 25.737$, df $= 5$, $P < 0.0005$.

23.41 $X^2 = 22.426$, df $= 8$, $P = 0.004$. Blacks are less likely, and Hispanics more likely, to consider schools excellent, while Hispanics and whites differ in percent considering schools good (whites are higher) and percent who "don't know" (Hispanics are higher).

23.43   The percents in each group who prefer the new detergent are 54%, 52%, 62%, and 58%. The differences are small; the "hard water, warm wash" group is most likely to prefer the new product. For testing H_0: no relationship between laundry habits and preference versus H_a: at least one proportion is different, we have $X^2 = 2.058$, df $= 3$, $P = 0.560$.

23.45   The counts of Democrats in each age group are 231, 265, 328, 361. The counts for Republicans are 185, 182, 272, and 319. The percents leaning Democrat are 55.5%, 59.3%, 54.7%, and 53.1%; support for the Democrats is highest in the 31 to 40 age group and drops for older groups.

Chapter 24

24.1   (a) The plot shows a positive linear association; $r = 0.955$; $\hat{y} = -0.9764 + 0.05429x$. (b) β is the rate at which deforestation changes with increases in the price of coffee. The estimates are the slope $b = 0.05429$ and intercept $a = -0.9764$ in the regression equation. (c) Residuals: –0.1080, 0.3949, –0.2651, –0.1894, 0.1677. The squares of the residuals add up to 0.3019, so $s = \sqrt{0.3019/3} = 0.3172$.

24.3   (a) $r^2 = 11.2\%$. (b) $\hat{y} = -2057 + 1.97x$, $s = 104.0$ km^3 of water.

24.5 $t \doteq 2.79$, df $= 62$, $P = 0.007$.

24.7   With $r = 0.9552$, Table F with $n = 5$ says that $0.005 < P < 0.01$.

24.9   With df $= 3$, the 95% confidence interval is 0.0543 ± 0.0309.

24.11   0.79 to 3.14 km^3/year; this interval does not contain 0.

24.13   (a) $\hat{y} = -2.3948 + 0.158483(200) = 29.3018$ cm. (b) We want the 95% confidence interval (CI): 28.393 to 30.211 cm.

24.15   (a) A child who is, say, above average in height at one age is likely to be tall at other ages, so that repeated measurements on the same child cannot be considered independent. (b) and (c) The residuals are first positive, then negative, then positive again. (d) There is slight right-skewness, but no clear deviations from Normality.

24.16   (b)   **24.17**   (c)   **24.18**   (b)   **24.19**   (a)   **24.20**   (b)

24.21   (b)   **24.22**   (a)   **24.23**   (a)   **24.24**   (b)

24.25   (a) For every additional kilogram of nitrogen per hectare, the species richness measure decreases by 0.408 on the average. (b) The straight-line relationship with nitrogen accounts for 55% of the observed variation in species richness. (c) H_0: $\beta = 0$; H_a: $\beta \neq 0$ (or $\beta < 0$). There is very strong evidence that β is negative, so species richness does decrease as nitrogen deposited increases.

24.27   (a) $\hat{y} = 0.1205 + 0.0086x$. The slope is positive. (b) 0.1886.

24.29   (a) Excel's interval is 0.0033 to 0.0138; this agrees (except for roundoff error) with $0.0086 \pm (2.145)(0.0025)$. (b) The 90% confidence interval is 0.0042 to 0.0130.

24.31 $0.6643 < r < 0.7114$, so $0.001 < P < 0.0025$. Excel's P-value is for a two-sided test.

24.33   The distribution is skewed to the right, but the sample is large, so t procedures should be safe. $\bar{x} = 0.2781$ and $s = 0.1803$, and the 95% confidence interval for μ is 0.2449 to 0.3113 g/m^2.

24.35   The scatterplot shows a positive association; the equation is $\hat{y} = 0.1523 + 8.1676x$, with $r^2 = 0.606$. The slope is significantly different from 0 ($t = 13.25$, $P < 0.001$).

24.37   **(a)** There is considerably greater scatter for larger values of the explanatory variable. **(b)** The distribution of residuals looks reasonably Normal.

24.39   **(a)** The residuals show a random scatter about the line, with roughly equal vertical spread across their range. This is what we expect when the conditions for regression inference hold. **(c)** The plot of residuals against the month of the sale shows steadily rising residuals (predicted prices are too high for early sales and too low for later sales). This is what we expect if selling prices are rising and appraised values aren't updated quickly enough to keep up.

24.41   **(a)** $\hat{y} = 560.65 - 3.0771x$. **(b)** The distribution of residuals has a slightly irregular appearance but is not markedly non-Normal. The scatterplot does not suggest that the standard deviation changes. **(c)** −4.8625 to −1.2917 calories per minute.

24.43   386 to 489 calories.

24.45   **(a)** $\bar{x} \doteq 0.00174$, $s \doteq 1.0137$. "Standardized" typically means $\bar{x} \doteq 0$ and $s \doteq 1$. **(b)** A stemplot is not strikingly non-Normal (for such a small sample). About 95% of the observations should be between −2 and 2, so −1.99 is quite reasonable. **(c)** The scatterplot gives no cause for concern.

24.47   −0.0398 to 0.0144; it does contain 0.

Chapter 25

25.1   **(a)** Randomly allocate 36 flies to each of four groups, which receive varying dosages of caffeine; observe length of rest periods. **(b)** H_0: All groups have the same mean rest period; H_a: At least one group has a different mean rest period. We conclude that caffeine reduces the length of the rest period.

25.3   **(a)** The stemplots show no extreme outliers or strong skewness (given the small sample sizes). **(b)** The means suggest that logging reduces the number of trees per plot, and that recovery is slow. **(c)** $F = 11.43$, $P = 0.000205$; H_0: $\mu_1 = \mu_2 = \mu_3$; H_a: not all means are the same.

25.5   **(a)** When the three means are similar, F is very small, and P is near 1. **(b)** By moving any mean, F increases and P decreases.

25.7   **(a)** The ratio of standard deviations is about 1.16. **(b)** The ratio of standard deviations is about 1.20.

25.9   **(a)** Compressed soil has the lowest penetrability ($\bar{x}_c = 2.9075$), intermediate is next ($\bar{x}_i = 3.3360$), and loose is highest ($\bar{x}_l = 4.2315$). **(b)** The standard deviations do not satisfy the rule of thumb. There are two outliers in the loose data, and one in the intermediate data; use of ANOVA would be risky. **(c)** Without the outliers, the rule of thumb is satisfied; ANOVA would be safe.

25.11 **(a)** df $= 2$ and 93; $P < 0.001$. **(b)** df $= 2$ and 87; $0.05 < P < 0.10$.

25.13 **(a)** Yes: the ratio of standard deviations is 1.24. **(b)** $\bar{x} \doteq 9.92$, and MSG $\doteq 10.0$. **(c)** MSE $\doteq 21.9$. **(d)** $F \doteq 0.46$. With df 2 and 112 (use 2 and 100 in the table), we find $P > 0.100$.

25.15 (c)   **25.16** (b)   **25.17** (c)   **25.18** (b)   **25.19** (b)

25.20 (a)   **25.21** (a)   **25.22** (b)   **25.23** (a)

25.25 Populations: morning people, evening people, neither. Response variable: difference in memorization scores. $I = 3, n_1 = 16, n_2 = 30, n_3 = 54, N = 100$; df $= 2$ and 97.

25.27 Populations: normal-weight men, overweight men, obese men. Response variable: triglyceride level. $I = 3, n_1 = 719, n_2 = 885, n_3 = 220, N = 1824$; df $= 2$ and 1821.

25.29 **(a)** Yes; the mean control emission rate is half the smallest of the others. **(b)** H_0: all groups have the same mean emission rate; H_a: at least one group has a different mean emission rate. **(c)** Are the data Normally distributed? Were these random samples? **(d)** $s = \text{SEM} \times \sqrt{8}$. The rule-of-thumb ratio is 1.4755.

25.31 **(a)** Means: 10.65, 10.425, 5.60, 5.45 cm; standard deviations: 2.053, 1.486, 1.244, 1.771 cm. The means and the stemplots suggest that the presence of too many nematodes reduces growth. ANOVA seems safe. **(b)** H_0: $\mu_1 = \cdots = \mu_4$; H_a: not all means are the same. We test whether nematodes affect mean plant growth. **(c)** $F = 12.08$, df $= 3$ and 12, $P = 0.001$. The first two levels are similar, as are the last two. Somewhere between 1000 and 5000 nematodes, the tomato plants are hurt by the worms.

25.33 **(a)** Randomly assign 8 pieces of cloth to each treatment, then compare lightness scores. **(b)** Method C is lightest and Method B is darkest. The differences in mean lightness are small but highly significant ($F = 22.77$, $P < 0.001$).

25.35 The means are 123.8, 123.6, and 134.4 lb; they do not consistently decrease. The standard deviations are 4.6043, 6.5422, and 9.5289 lb. $9.5289/4.6043 \doteq 2.07$; ANOVA is risky. If we do ANOVA anyway, $F = 3.70$ (df $= 2$ and 12) and $P = 0.056$; the differences are not significant.

25.37 The means are 134.8, 134.2, and 143.2 degrees, and the standard deviations are 1.92, 10.16, and 2.28 degrees (for Permafresh 55, Permafresh 48, and Hylite LF). Hylite LF, which had the lowest breaking strength, has the highest wrinkle resistance. ANOVA gives $F = 3.39$ and $P = 0.068$, but this cannot be trusted because there is evidence that the standard deviations are different.

25.39 $\bar{x} \doteq 21.585$, MSG $\doteq 745.5$, MSE $\doteq 460.2$, df $= 3$ and 28, $F \doteq 1.62$—not significant.

25.41 **(a)** A chi-square test. **(b)** ANOVA. **(c)** ANOVA.

Data Table Index

Table entry for C is the critical value t^* required for confidence level C. To approximate one- and two-sided P-values, compare the value of the t statistic with the critical values of t^* that match the P-values given at the bottom of the table.

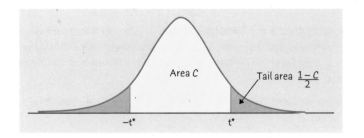

Area C

Tail area $\frac{1-C}{2}$

$-t^*$ t^*

TABLE C   t distribution critical values

Degrees of freedom	Confidence level C											
	50%	60%	70%	80%	90%	95%	96%	98%	99%	99.5%	99.8%	99.9%
1	1.000	1.376	1.963	3.078	6.314	12.71	15.89	31.82	63.66	127.3	318.3	636.6
2	0.816	1.061	1.386	1.886	2.920	4.303	4.849	6.965	9.925	14.09	22.33	31.60
3	0.765	0.978	1.250	1.638	2.353	3.182	3.482	4.541	5.841	7.453	10.21	12.92
4	0.741	0.941	1.190	1.533	2.132	2.776	2.999	3.747	4.604	5.598	7.173	8.610
5	0.727	0.920	1.156	1.476	2.015	2.571	2.757	3.365	4.032	4.773	5.893	6.869
6	0.718	0.906	1.134	1.440	1.943	2.447	2.612	3.143	3.707	4.317	5.208	5.959
7	0.711	0.896	1.119	1.415	1.895	2.365	2.517	2.998	3.499	4.029	4.785	5.408
8	0.706	0.889	1.108	1.397	1.860	2.306	2.449	2.896	3.355	3.833	4.501	5.041
9	0.703	0.883	1.100	1.383	1.833	2.262	2.398	2.821	3.250	3.690	4.297	4.781
10	0.700	0.879	1.093	1.372	1.812	2.228	2.359	2.764	3.169	3.581	4.144	4.587
11	0.697	0.876	1.088	1.363	1.796	2.201	2.328	2.718	3.106	3.497	4.025	4.437
12	0.695	0.873	1.083	1.356	1.782	2.179	2.303	2.681	3.055	3.428	3.930	4.318
13	0.694	0.870	1.079	1.350	1.771	2.160	2.282	2.650	3.012	3.372	3.852	4.221
14	0.692	0.868	1.076	1.345	1.761	2.145	2.264	2.624	2.977	3.326	3.787	4.140
15	0.691	0.866	1.074	1.341	1.753	2.131	2.249	2.602	2.947	3.286	3.733	4.073
16	0.690	0.865	1.071	1.337	1.746	2.120	2.235	2.583	2.921	3.252	3.686	4.015
17	0.689	0.863	1.069	1.333	1.740	2.110	2.224	2.567	2.898	3.222	3.646	3.965
18	0.688	0.862	1.067	1.330	1.734	2.101	2.214	2.552	2.878	3.197	3.611	3.922
19	0.688	0.861	1.066	1.328	1.729	2.093	2.205	2.539	2.861	3.174	3.579	3.883
20	0.687	0.860	1.064	1.325	1.725	2.086	2.197	2.528	2.845	3.153	3.552	3.850
21	0.686	0.859	1.063	1.323	1.721	2.080	2.189	2.518	2.831	3.135	3.527	3.819
22	0.686	0.858	1.061	1.321	1.717	2.074	2.183	2.508	2.819	3.119	3.505	3.792
23	0.685	0.858	1.060	1.319	1.714	2.069	2.177	2.500	2.807	3.104	3.485	3.768
24	0.685	0.857	1.059	1.318	1.711	2.064	2.172	2.492	2.797	3.091	3.467	3.745
25	0.684	0.856	1.058	1.316	1.708	2.060	2.167	2.485	2.787	3.078	3.450	3.725
26	0.684	0.856	1.058	1.315	1.706	2.056	2.162	2.479	2.779	3.067	3.435	3.707
27	0.684	0.855	1.057	1.314	1.703	2.052	2.158	2.473	2.771	3.057	3.421	3.690
28	0.683	0.855	1.056	1.313	1.701	2.048	2.154	2.467	2.763	3.047	3.408	3.674
29	0.683	0.854	1.055	1.311	1.699	2.045	2.150	2.462	2.756	3.038	3.396	3.659
30	0.683	0.854	1.055	1.310	1.697	2.042	2.147	2.457	2.750	3.030	3.385	3.646
40	0.681	0.851	1.050	1.303	1.684	2.021	2.123	2.423	2.704	2.971	3.307	3.551
50	0.679	0.849	1.047	1.299	1.676	2.009	2.109	2.403	2.678	2.937	3.261	3.496
60	0.679	0.848	1.045	1.296	1.671	2.000	2.099	2.390	2.660	2.915	3.232	3.460
80	0.678	0.846	1.043	1.292	1.664	1.990	2.088	2.374	2.639	2.887	3.195	3.416
100	0.677	0.845	1.042	1.290	1.660	1.984	2.081	2.364	2.626	2.871	3.174	3.390
1000	0.675	0.842	1.037	1.282	1.646	1.962	2.056	2.330	2.581	2.813	3.098	3.300
z^*	0.674	0.841	1.036	1.282	1.645	1.960	2.054	2.326	2.576	2.807	3.091	3.291
One-sided P	.25	.20	.15	.10	.05	.025	.02	.01	.005	.0025	.001	.0005
Two-sided P	.50	.40	.30	.20	.10	.05	.04	.02	.01	.005	.002	.001